To Senator +

With respect on
your service to the government, the
Church, and the University.

Monte S. Nyman
April 2004

I, Nephi, Wrote this Record

A Teaching Commentary on
The First Book of Nephi
and
The Second Book of Nephi

Volume 1

by

Monte S. Nyman

Distributed by:

Granite Publishing and Distribution, LLC
868 North 1430 West
Orem, Utah 84057
(801) 229-9023 • Toll Free (800) 574-5779
Fax (801) 229-1924

Cover Art "Lehi's Landing" painted by Clark Kelley Price
Used by permission of James Moser
Copyright © Clark Kelley Price

Page Layout & Design by Myrna Varga, The Office Connection, Inc.
Cover Design by Steve Gray

Library of Congress Control Number: 2003113593
ISBN: 1-932280-29-4

Printed in the United States of America

10 9 8 7 6 5 4 3 2 1

Contents

Introduction

The Book or Mormon is the most electrifying book of our time and the reader must go directly to the book itself to understand this statement. Just as with other great books, an experienced teacher can call attention to certain background information and cross references that will enable the student to understand the book better. When Philip asked the man of Ethiopia "Understandest thou what thou readest?" the man replied, "How can I, except some man should guide me?" (Acts 8:30, 31). As a teacher, I have studied and taught the Book of Mormon for over forty years. This work represents the materials and concepts I have collected and developed during these years. It is intended that this commentary will be a guide to your study of the Book of Mormon, recognizing that the notes and observations are only supplementary to the record itself.

The Book of Mormon is unique because it was written hundreds of years ago but is addressed to and for a people hundreds of years in the future. For example, Nephi wrote what are called the small plates, about 570 B.C. (see 2 Nephi 5:28). He addressed them to the people who would be living after A.D. 1830, some 2,400 years in the future. Moroni wrote about A.D. 400 and addressed it to the same audience some 1,400 years later. As we discover the uniqueness of the Book of Mormon, and follow its teachings by studying and restudying it, we come to a deeper appreciation of the book. We should also come to realize that the perfecting of the Saints may be greatly enhanced by our reading the Book of Mormon and applying its teachings to our lives. The Book of Mormon, after all, was written for us.

Mormon abridged the many other records of the Nephites sometime before A.D. 385, yet he addressed his work to a people who would live at least 1445 years later. Moroni made his last recordings in A.D. 421, some 1400 years before the Book of Mormon was translated in 1830. As the years roll on, the time between the authors and the reading audience lengthens, but the message is still as remarkably pertinent today as when it was first written.

There were four major people who abridged the Book of Mormon. They were all qualified to address the future because they had seen it. Nephi, the first major writer, was shown a vision of the nations and kingdoms of the Gentiles (see 1 Nephi 13–14). His vision included seeing the discovery of the Americas by a man moved upon by the Spirit of God; we know this man as Columbus.

Nephi also saw the remainder of the future of the earth's nations until the end of the world. He did not write all of what he was shown because he was forbidden. He was told (about 592 B.C.) that the Apostle John, of the meridian of time, had been designated to describe this future period of time (this is a clear confirmation of foreordination). Nevertheless, Nephi was fully aware of the situations and conditions of the day in which the Book of Mormon would come forth.

Evidence of the knowledge of these things is shown in Nephi's later writings as he described the pride and false theories that would be and are prevalent among the many churches of the last days, the secret combinations that would be and are in operation, and the priestcrafts that would and still stifle the people from approaching their God to obtain salvation in his kingdom (see 2 Nephi 26:19–33). Nephi also gave many other prophecies of the latter-day Gentiles that will not be discussed or even listed here (see 2 Nephi 28–29).

Jacob, the second major writer, was not as explicit in noting that his writings were intended for the latter days as was Nephi, however, he did confirm that he had seen the future. He spoke of having seen the return of the Jews to Jerusalem and of the Gentiles in the latter days (see 2 Nephi 6:9–13). In the book that carries his name, he addressed his beloved brethren of the latter days, a further indication that he had seen the day when the Book of Mormon would come forth (see Jacob 4:10–13, 17–18; 6:1, 5).

Mormon, the major abridger, did not speak of a specific vision of the latter days, but his writings certainly imply it. He spoke to all of the latter-day groups of Israel: the Lamanites, the Jews, the rest of the tribes of Israel, to the Gentiles, and to all the ends of the earth (see Mormon 3:19–22 and Mormon 5:8–15). His warnings and admonitions to the reader indicate he knew of the future, and that knowledge could only have come to him through vision or revelation (see Mormon 8:22–24).

It is only logical that Mormon would have been shown the day in which the Book of Mormon would come forth since he was the major contributor to the work. All the other three major contributors had been shown that time period in vision.

Moroni, son of Mormon, and the final writer and abridger, was the last major writer of the plates that were designated to come forth at the beginning of the dispensation of the fulness of times. He makes a direct, forthright statement that he had seen the day when the book would come forth, and this lends strong support to the idea that the others had had similar experiences. He declared:

> Behold, the Lord hath shown unto me great and marvelous things concerning that which must shortly come, at that day when these things shall come forth among you.
>
> Behold, I speak unto you as if ye were present, and yet ye are not. But behold, Jesus Christ hath shown you unto me, and I know your doing. [Mormon 8:34–35]

In further support that he had seen the latter days, he gave detailed descriptions of the day when the Book of Mormon would come forth. He described the Saints as being the victims of secret organizations, the conditions and acts of nature in foreign lands, and the moral status of the people (see Mormon 8:26–33). He further described the pride and pollutions among the people and their love of money (Mormon 8:36–37). Moroni could only have known such definite characteristics and instructions by vision or revelation, and the specific exactness of his wording supports the claim that he had seen it.

Since each of these major writers had seen the days when the Book of Mormon would come forth, they were qualified to address the readers—the people of our day—personally and specifically. Each writer seemed to have had a personal interest in both his own time and in our time. He periodically stopped what he was writing or abridging to give valuable insights and admonitions. These insights and admonitions are clearly comments to the latter-day readers.

For example, Nephi used the phrase "I will show unto you" (1 Nephi 1:20) as he prepared the reader for what he was about to record. When he wanted to stop and draw a conclusion or make sure his reader understood he had written about, he would introduce it with "thus we see" (1 Nephi 16:29).

Jacob and Mormon followed a pattern similar to Nephi's using the same introductory or concluding phrases. Moroni used a slight variation as he addressed various groups of people: the polluters, the hypocrites, and the false teachers (see Mormon 8:38–41); those who did not believe in Christ (see Mormon 9:1–6); those who denied revelation (see Mormon 9:7–14); and those who imagined God could not perform miracles (see Mormon 8:15–20). Moroni then admonished them collectively concerning the work of the Lord and the coming forth of the Book of Mormon in their day (see Mormon 9:21–37).

As Moroni abridged the book of Ether, he regularly stopped to address the reader with "And, now, we can behold," or "O, ye Gentiles" (Ether 2:9, 11). He also spoke directly to the latter-day translator (see Ether 5). In his concluding book that bears his name, Moroni wrote for the benefit of "my brethren, the Lamanites, in some future day" (Moroni 1:4; 10:1).

The above admonitions by the four major writers are some of the major precepts in the oft-quoted statement made by the Prophet Joseph

Smith in 1841: "I told the brethren that the Book of Mormon was the most correct of any book on earth, and the keystone of our religion, and a man would get nearer to God by abiding by its precepts, than by any other book" (*TPJS*, 194; quoted in Book of Mormon *Introduction*).

The Book of Mormon is the most correct of any book on earth because of the doctrine or the gospel that it teaches. The angel Moroni told Joseph Smith "that the fullness of the everlasting gospel was contained in the [record]." The Lord confirmed the angel's statement several times in modern revelation (see D&C 14:10; 20:9; 27:5; 35:17; 39:11; 42:12). Thus, it is a primary source of the doctrine of The Church of Jesus Christ of Latter-day Saints. The Prophet Isaiah foretold of the coming forth of the Book of Mormon (see Isaiah 29 and 2 Nephi 27). In the concluding statement of these chapters, he said: "They also that erred in spirit shall come to understanding, and they that murmured shall learn doctrine" (Isaiah 29:24; 2 Nephi 27:35). In a revelation concerning the translation of the Book of Mormon, the Lord said that in it "are all things written concerning the foundation of my church, my gospel and my rock" (D&C 18:4). On the day that the church was organized, the Lord specified many of the doctrines that the Book of Mormon teaches (see D&C 20:17–36). The doctrines taught in the chapters of the Book of Mormon covered in each chapter of this book will be summarized in the end of that chapter. There will undoubtedly be some doctrines overlooked, but the majority of them will be included.

The Book of Mormon is the keystone of our religion because it is a second witness of Jesus Christ, and it proves "to the world that the holy scriptures [Bible] are true, and that God does inspire men [give them revelation] and call them to his holy work [the priesthood] in this age and generation, as well as in generations of old" (D&C 20:11). The Prophet Joseph Smith said: "Take away the Book of Mormon and the revelations, and where is our religion? We have none; for without Zion, and a place of deliverance, we must fall" (*TPJS*, 71). Jesus Christ is spoken of prominently in all but six of the two hundred and thirty-nine chapters of the Book of Mormon, and these six chapters are historical, setting the stage for a testimony of his work. A summary of the sacred preaching, great revelations, and prophesying is also given in the end of each chapter.

Following a conference of the Church in June 1831, the Lord gave a revelation to the Elders of the Church covering missionary work. In the revelation, they were instructed to journey . . . "preaching the word by the way, saying none other things than *that which the prophets and apostles have written*, and that which is taught them by the Comforter through the prayer of faith." (D&C 52:9; italics added) The Lord repeated basically the same message again in the thirty-sixth verse.

The statements by some of the General Authorities of The Church of Jesus Christ of Latter-day Saints quoted in this work, or added at the end of the chapters, were made with the above admonition of the Lord in mind. They have been of great value to me in reading and teaching the Book of Mormon over the past some fifty years, and it is hoped will also be of great value to others as they study the Book of Mormon. A few statements pertaining to the entire book are quoted below as a conclusion to this introduction.

The Prophet Joseph Smith:

> The Book of Mormon is a record of the forefathers of our western tribes of Indians; having been found through the ministration of a holy angel, and translated into our own language by the gift and power of God, after having been hid up in the earth for the last fourteen hundred years, containing the word of God unto them. [History of the Church 2:52]

President Heber J. Grant:

> The Book of Mormon is the great, the grand, the most wonderful missionary that we have. (Conference Report, April 1937; *Improvement Era* 39:660)

Elder Melvin J. Ballard:

The Book of Mormon has converted more people than all the other literature combined that the Church has produced. Our enemies have regarded it the strongest evidence that we offer that we have a divine mission.

More efforts have been contributed to the destruction of the Book of Mormon than all the other efforts against the work, and yet at the end of a hundred years this book stands firm and unshaken, and the evidence of its divinity are increasing. [*Sermons and Missionary Services of Melvin J. Ballard, Bryant S. Hinckley*, 1949, 191]

President Joseph Fielding Smith:

I started to read the Book of Mormon before I was old enough to be a deacon, and I have been reading it ever since, and I know that it is true. Every member of the Church ought to know that it is true, and we ought to be prepared with an answer to all of these critics who condemn it . . .

It seems to me that any member of this Church would never be satisfied until he or she has read the Book of Mormon time and time again, and thoroughly considered it so that he or she could bear witness that it is in very deed a record with the inspiration of the Almighty upon it, and that its history is true. . . .

I want to address myself to the men holding the priesthood, particularly, and to their wives and to all other members of the Church. No member of this Church can stand approved in the presence of *God who has not seriously and carefully read the Book of Mormon.* [*Improvement Era*, June 1961, 925–26]

President Ezra Taft Benson:

In our day the Lord has inspired his servant to reemphasize the Book of Mormon to get the Church out from under condemnation— the scourge and judgment.

Every Latter-day Saint should make the study of this book a lifetime pursuit. Otherwise he is placing his soul in jeopardy and neglecting that which could give spiritual and intellectual unity to his whole life. There is a difference between a convert who is built on the rock of Christ through the Book of Mormon and stays hold of that iron rod, and one who is not (*A Witness And A Warning*, 1988, Introduction and pp.7–8).

The entire book is highly recommended. It contains the many great sermons on the Book of Mormon given while he was president of the Church and a member of the Council of the Twelve. Several excerpts will be quoted in other parts of these volumes on the Book of Mormon.

Elder Spencer W. Kimball.

A Book of Vital Messages, Conference Report, April 1963, also published in *Faith Precedes the Miracle*, chapter 32, 1972. Too long to be included here (9 pages), it has an intriguing message to all people of all walks of life. It is also highly recommended.

The above quotations and those that will be cited throughout this work will be selective in that only the heart of the sermon or article will be quoted. The references are given so that the reader may read more if they care to look them up. There will be some duplication of quotations and other materials in the chapters that follow. Some of the quotes are applicable to more than one part of the Book of Mormon. For convenience they will be quoted again so that the reader does not have to turn back to a previous lesson.

Chapter One

Lehi's Call to Warn Jerusalem

Title Page; 1 Nephi 1

*H*istorical Setting: Nephi's writings cover the period from approximately 600 B.C. to 546 B.C. His father Lehi left Jerusalem 600 years before the birth of Christ. He was called to warn Jerusalem in the first year of the reign of Zedekiah, king of Judah. How long Lehi prophesied before he left Jerusalem is not stated in the record. The information below will consider the date of Lehi's call to be 600 B.C.

Although Nephi's record covers at least 55 years (see Jacob 1:1), he did not write this record until "thirty years had passed away from the time we left Jerusalem" (2 Nephi 5:28). When he turned the records over to his younger brother Jacob, he admonished him to "not touch, save it were lightly, concerning the history of this people . . ." (Jacob 1:2). Nephi had certainly followed his own advice as he wrote First and Second Nephi. This is verified by an analysis of his writings.

Synopsis of History • Lehi's call

Year	Reference	Verse	Pages
600 B.C.	1 Nephi 1:1–7:22	163	13

Lehi is called to warn Jerusalem of its impending destruction. They reject him and the Lord warns him to leave. His sons return to Jerusalem for the plates of brass and later for the family of Ishmael.

It is assumed that all of these events took about one year. While these 7 chapters are basically historical, nearly half of them (71 verses, or 6 of the 13 pages) are of a spiritual nature—words spoken through the inspiration of the Lord. Every event is evidence of the Lord delivering his people as Nephi said he would, to show "the tender mercies of the Lord are over all those whom he hath chosen, because of their faith, to make them mighty even unto the power of deliverance"(1 Nephi 1:20).

The scripture quoted above (1 Nephi 1:20) is the first precept to appear in the regular text of the Book of Mormon. Nephi addresses the future readers of the book, and tells them what they should learn from the following chapters (2–5, 7). The first chapter sets the stage for the book's beginning, and the title page is a precept for the entire book. We will analyze the title page under the *Notes and Commentary* that will follow. Before doing so, a teaching outline of the super-scription and the entire first chapter provides a framework for a deeper study of the messages within the text.

OUTLINE • 1 NEPHI 1

Superscription: An account of Lehi, his wife Sariah, and his four sons.

- a. Beginning at the eldest: Laman, Lemuel, Sam, Nephi.
- b. The Lord warns Lehi to leave the land because the Jews seek to destroy his life when he prophesies to them of their iniquity.
- c. They journey three days into the wilderness.
- d. Nephi returns to Jerusalem with his brothers to get the record of the Jews (the brass plates).
- e. They suffer. They take the daughters of Ishmael to wife.
- f. They travel in the wilderness suffering afflictions.
- g. They come to the large waters. They call the place Bountiful. Nephi's brothers rebel, but he confounds them and builds a ship.

    h. They cross the large waters to the promised land.

    i.   The account was written by Nephi.

➤ 1:1–3   Nephi makes a record of his proceedings having been born of goodly parents and taught in the learning of his father.

    a. He has seen many afflictions but was highly favored of the Lord and knew of the goodness and mysteries of God (v. 1).

    b. His record was made in the language of his father, which consists of the learning of the Jews and the language of the Egyptians (v. 2).

    c. He knows the record is true; he makes it with his own hand and according to his knowledge (v. 3).

➤ 1:4–15   In the first year of Zedekiah, king of Judah, many prophets came to Jerusalem calling the people to repent or the great city Jerusalem would be destroyed.

    a. As Lehi went forth he prayed with all his heart in behalf of his people (v. 5).

    b. A pillar of fire came and dwelt upon a rock, and he saw and heard much that caused him to quake and tremble exceedingly (v. 6).

    c. He returned to his own house in Jerusalem and cast himself upon his bed, being overcome with the Spirit and the things he had seen (v. 7).

    d. Being overcome with the Spirit, he was carried away in a vision and he saw the heavens open (vv. 8–11).

        1. He thought he saw God sitting upon his throne surrounded with angels singing and praising God.

        2. He saw one descending out of heaven whose luster was above that of the noon-day sun.

        3. Twelve others followed him whose brightness exceeded the stars.

        4. They came to earth and went forth. The first came to Lehi and gave him a book and told him to read it.

     e. As Lehi read he was filled with the Spirit of the Lord (vv. 12–15).

       1. He saw that Jerusalem would be destroyed, many inhabitants would perish by the sword, and many carried captive into Babylon.

       2. When he had read and seen many great and marvelous things he praised the Lord.

       3. His soul did rejoice and his whole heart was filled because of what he had seen.

➤ 1:16–17   Nephi does not make a full account of his father's writings, only an abridgment.

     a. Lehi had written many things that he saw in visions and in dreams and had prophesied (v. 16).

     b. Nephi makes an account of his proceedings in his days (v. 17).

     c. He makes his record upon plates that he made with his own hands (v. 17).

➤ 1:18–20   Lehi begins to prophesy concerning the destruction of Jerusalem and to prophesy concerning the things he had seen and heard.

     a. The Jews mocked him because he testified of their wickedness and abominations (v. 19).

     b. He testified of the things he had read in the book manifesting the coming of the Messiah and the redemption of the world (v. 19).

     c. The Jews were angry with him, as they were with the prophets whom they had cast out and stoned and slain, and they sought his life (v. 20).

➤ 1:20   Nephi will show the reader that the tender mercies of the Lord are over all those he has chosen, because of their faith, to make them mighty unto the power of deliverance.

NOTES AND COMMENTARY

Introduction: The title page is a good place to begin a study of the Book of Mormon. It tells the reader what is in the book, to whom it is written, why it was written, how it was to come forth, and some advice to the reader.

Title Page • Written By Mormon and Moroni

The title page was written by Mormon and Moroni as they completed their abridgment and commentary upon the [large] plates of Nephi,[1] Mormon around A.D. 400 and Moroni around A.D. 421. The Prophet Joseph Smith verified the textual validity of the title page being upon the plates as he was completing the translation, securing the copyright, and making agreement with Egbert B. Grandin to print the first edition of the Book of Mormon. He explained,

> I wish to mention here, that the title-page of the Book of Mormon is a literal translation, taken from the very last leaf, on the left hand side of the collection or book of plates, which contained the record which has been translated, the language of the whole running the same as all Hebrew writing in general; (That is from left to right) and that said title-page is not by any means a modern composition, either of mine or of any other man who has lived or does live in this generation. Therefore, in order to correct an error, which generally exists concerning it, I give below that part of the title-page of the English version of the Book of Mormon, which is a genuine and literal translation of the title-page of the original Book of Mormon, as recorded on the plates. [HC, 1:71; see also *TPJS*, 7]

The third edition of the Book of Mormon (1840), printed under the direction of the Prophet Joseph, added the name Moroni at the bottom

---

[1] For an analysis of the title page in the various editions of the Book of Mormon see Daniel H. Ludlow, The title page, chap. 2, in *1 Nephi, The Doctrinal Foundation*, ed. Monte S. Nyman and Charles D. Tate, Jr, Religious Study Center, Brigham Young University, Provo, Utah 1988.

right hand side of the title page. The name Moroni was also printed there in the fourth edition (1852).

The title page has twelve statements, if the heading above the two paragraphs in the present edition are included. It is not printed here as a unit, but the twelve statements contain everything that is written on the page. These statements are separated by a dash instead of a period except for the heading and the beginning of the first and the second paragraphs.

The first, second, and ninth statements tell us what the Book of Mormon is.

1. THE BOOK OF MORMON, Another Testament of JESUS CHRIST,[2] an account written by the hand of Mormon, upon plates taken from the plates of Nephi.

2. Wherefore, it is an abridgment of the record of the people of Nephi, and also of the Lamanites.

9. An abridgment taken from the Book of Ether also, which is a record of the people of Jared, who were scattered at the time the Lord confounded the language of the people, when they were building a tower to get to heaven.

The third statement tells us to whom the record is written.

3. Written to the Lamanites, who are a remnant of the house of Israel; and also to Jew and Gentile.

The fourth, fifth, tenth, and eleventh statements tell us why the Book of Mormon was written.

4. Written by way of commandment, and also by the spirit of prophecy and of revelation [directed and inspired of God-scripture] (see D&C 68:2–4; 2 Peter 1:21).

5. Written and sealed up, and hid up unto the Lord, that they might not be destroyed.

---

[2] The sub-title, "Another Testament of Jesus Christ" was added by the First Presidency and the Twelve in 1982 (see Elder Boyd K. Packer, Conference Report, Oct. 1982, 75).

10. Which is to show unto the remnant of the House of Israel what great things the Lord hath done for their fathers; and that they may know the covenants of the Lord, that they are not cast off forever.

11. And also to the convincing of the Jew and Gentile That JESUS is the CHRIST, the ETERNAL GOD [note the capitalization of every letter], manifesting himself unto all nations [by the power of the Holy Ghost] (see 2 Nephi 26:13).

The sixth through the eighth statements tell us how the Book of Mormon was to come forth.

6. To come forth by the gift and power of God unto the interpretation thereof.

7. Sealed by the hand of Moroni, and hid up unto the Lord, to come forth in due time by way of the Gentiles.

8. The interpretation thereof by the gift of God.

Finally, the twelfth statement is a warning to the reader.

12. And now, if there are faults they are the mistakes of men; wherefore condemn not the things of God, that ye may be found spotless at the judgment-seat of Christ.

Translated by Joseph Smith, Jun.

In a letter to Mr. John Wentworth, editor and proprietor of the *Chicago Democrat*, the Prophet Joseph Smith confirmed many of the things written on the title page as quoted above.

> I was also informed concerning the aboriginal inhabitants of this country and shown who they were, and from whence they came; a brief sketch of their origin, progress, civilization, laws, governments, of their righteousness and iniquity, and the blessings of God being finally withdrawn from them as a people, was made known to me; I was also told where were deposited some plates on which were engraven an abridgement of the records of the ancient Prophets that had existed on this continent. The angel appeared to me three times the same night and unfolded the same things. After having received many visits from the angels of God unfolding the majesty and glory of the events that should transpire in the last days, on the morning of

the 22nd of September, A.D. 1827, the angel of the Lord delivered the records into my hands.

These records were engraven on plates which had the appearance of gold, each plate was six inches wide and eight inches long, and not quite so thick as common tin. They were filled with engravings, in Egyptian characters, and bound together in a volume as the leaves of a book, with three rings running through the whole. The volume was something near six inches in thickness, a part of which was sealed. The characters on the unsealed part were small, and beautifully engraved. The whole book exhibited many marks of antiquity in its construction, and much skill in the art of engraving. With the records was found a curious instrument, which the ancients called "Urim and Thummim," which consisted of two transparent stones set in the rim of a bow fastened to a breastplate. Through the medium of the Urim and Thummim I translated the record by the gift and power of God. [*HC*, 4:537]

The first edition of the Book of Mormon title page read, "Joseph Smith, Junior, Author and Proprietor." The Encyclopedia of Mormonism explains: "Some have suggested that Joseph Smith admitted that he was the author of the Book of Mormon because the title page of the first edition lists him as 'Author and Proprietor.' This language, however, comes from the federal copyright statutes and legal forms used in 1829 (1 Stat 125 [1790], amended 2 stat. 171 [1802])."[3]

The preface in the first edition of the Book of Mormon, the part of which is quoted below under 1 Nephi 1:16–17, further qualifies Joseph as the translator, not the author.

THE FIRST BOOK OF NEPHI
• His Reign and Ministry

> *An account of Lehi and his wife Sariah, and his four sons, being called, (beginning at the eldest) Laman, Lemuel, Sam, and Nephi. The Lord warns Lehi to depart out of the land of Jerusalem, because he prophesieth unto the people concerning their iniquity and they seek*

---

[3] D. Brent Anderson and Diane E. Wirth, "Book of Mormon Authorship," ed. Daniel H. Ludlow, MacMillan Publishing Company, New York [1992], 1:166.

to destroy his life. He taketh three days' journey into the wilderness with his family. Nephi taketh his brethren and their sufferings. They take the daughters of Ishmael to wife. They take their families and depart into the wilderness. Their sufferings and afflictions in the wilderness. The course of their travels. They come to the large waters. Nephi's brethren rebel against him. He confoundeth them, and buildeth a ship. They call the name of the place Bountiful. They cross the large waters into the promised land, and so forth. This is according to the account of Nephi; or in other words, I, Nephi, wrote this record.

"THE FIRST BOOK OF NEPHI," "His Reign and Ministry," and the above italicized paragraph are part of the original text that introduced the writing of Nephi on the small plates of the Book of Mormon. This superscription was written on the metal plates by Nephi and was translated by Joseph Smith. This is demonstrated by the last statement of the paragraph: "I Nephi wrote this record." The superscription is a brief historical overview of the entire book of First Nephi.

It was a common practice in Hebrew literature to include such a preface as part of the opening paragraph of a work. Superscriptions were commonly used in the Bible, but after many translations they are now used as the introductory verses of the first chapter or subsequent sections of the book. (i.e. Isaiah 1:1; Jeremiah 1:1–3; Ezekiel 1:1–3). This large superscription, which is one of several that appear throughout the Book of Mormon, is quite different from the chapter headings. These headings were not written on the plates by the original writer, but were added by a latter-day apostle to help the reader anticipant the subject matter of each chapter.[4]

The Bible begins with positive statements concerning the guiding hand behind the entire program of the creation and habitation of this world: "In the beginning God created the heaven and the earth" (Genesis 1:1). The Book of Mormon also begins with a positive

---

[4] The chapter headings have been modified as new editions of the Book of Mormon have been published. The modifications were always the work of one or more apostles of that time period.

statement showing that the Lord is guiding Lehi and his family in their endeavors: "The Lord warns Lehi to depart out of the land of Jerusalem. . . ."

1 Nephi 1:1–3 • A Record of My Proceedings

1 I, Nephi, having been born of goodly parents, therefore I was taught somewhat in all the learning of my father; and having seen many afflictions in the course of my days, nevertheless, having been highly favored of the Lord in all my days; yea, having had a great knowledge of the goodness and the mysteries of God, therefore I make a record of my proceedings in my days.

2 Yea, I make a record in the language of my father, which consists of the learning of the Jews and the language of the Egyptians.

3 And I know that the record which I make is true; and I make it with mine own hand; and I make it according to my knowledge.

The very first verse of the Book of Mormon points to its being a book of Hebrew origin. In keeping with traditional Hebrew custom, Lehi, as the family patriarch, was responsible for educating his sons. This education included lessons on the law, writings, prophets, and practices of Jewish religion and culture. Although some of this responsibility belonged to the mother, the head of the family was the one held accountable. Jacob, the brother of Nephi, carried on the same tradition in teaching his son, Enos (see Enos 1:1).

Approximately thirty years after his departure from Jerusalem (see 2 Nephi 5:28–31), Nephi began this record by giving honor and recognition to his parents. This fulfilled the ancient Hebrew commandment, "honour thy father and mother" (Deuteronomy 5:16).

Thirty years after leaving Jerusalem, Nephi simply notes that those years of travel were filled with afflictions. The experiences of journeying in the wilderness, making the ocean voyage, and colonizing the new world will be discussed later. Even though his life was filled with affliction, Nephi recognized God's blessings. His life had been preserved, he had seen visions, and he had become a ruler over the righteous branch of his father's family.

Before Nephi began to make a record upon these [small] gold plates, he was given a great knowledge of the goodness and the mysteries of God (v. 1). He was given visions about Jesus Christ, John the Baptist, John the Revelator, Jerusalem, the future of his own people, and of the nations and kingdoms of the Gentiles down to the end of the world (see 1 Nephi 11–14). He also witnessed the personal appearance of Jesus Christ. As he began to record some of the writings of the great prophet Isaiah, he testified that "I have seen him" (2 Nephi 11:3). Nephi also received revelations for the construction of a ship (see 1 Nephi 17:7–10; 18:1–3) and power to calm the seas (see 1 Nephi 18:21, 29).

The record he is making was done to fulfill a commandment of the Lord to "Make other plates; and thou shalt engraven many things upon them which are good in [the Lord's] sight, for the profit of thy people" (2 Nephi 5:30). Nephi had previously been commanded to make another record (see 1 Nephi 19:1–2). The first record of Nephi is generally called the large plates of Nephi, and the record he is now writing is referred to as the small plates.

Nephi's writing follows the thought pattern of the Hebrews but is written in reformed Egyptian (v. 2). Moroni, a later writer, tells us why they wrote in this manner: "if our plates had been sufficiently large we should have written in Hebrew" (Mormon 9:33). Moroni also writes, "we have written this record . . . in . . . the reformed Egyptian, being handed down and altered by us" (Mormon 9:32). Note that Moroni uses the plural "we" in his explanation, thus indicating that at least his father and he used reformed Egyptian and implying that such was the case from Nephi down. Moroni also indicates that further alterations have been made in this manner of writing even in his own day.

Nephi bears testimony to the truthfulness of his record according to the knowledge that he has received (v. 3). Joseph Smith confirms Nephi's testimony as to the truth of the Book of Mormon by referring to it as ". . . the most correct of any book on earth" (HC 4:461; Book of Mormon Introduction), and the Lord himself bears testimony that it is a true record. In a revelation through Joseph Smith to Oliver Cowdery, the major scribe for Joseph as he translated the record, the Lord said "that the words or the work which thou hast been writing are true" (D&C 6:17). In a revelation to the three special witnesses of the Book of Mormon and other sacred Nephite items, the Lord said:

> 5 And ye shall testify that you have seen them, even as my servant Joseph Smith, Jun., has seen them; for it is by my power that he has seen them, and it is because he had faith.
>
> 6 And he has translated the book, even that part which I have commanded him, and as your Lord and your God liveth it is true. [D&C 17:5–6]

1 Nephi 1:4–6 • The First Year of the Reign of Zedekiah

> 4 For it came to pass in the commencement of the first year of the reign of Zedekiah, king of Judah, (my father, Lehi, having dwelt at Jerusalem in all his days); and in that same year there came many prophets, prophesying unto the people that they must repent, or the great city Jerusalem must be destroyed.
>
> 5 Wherefore it came to pass that my father, Lehi, as he went forth prayed unto the Lord, yea, even with all his heart, in behalf of his people.
>
> 6 And it came to pass as he prayed unto the Lord, there came a pillar of fire and dwelt upon a rock before him; and he saw and heard much; and because of the things which he saw and heard he did quake and tremble exceedingly.

King "Zedekiah was twenty and one years old" when Nebuchad-nezzar appointed him puppet king over Judah (2 Kings 25:17–18). Traditionally, the beginning of his reign is recorded as 597 B.C., however, the Book of Mormon indicates an earlier date in that several times the advent of the Savior's coming to earth is prophesied as being 600 years from the time Lehi and his family left Jerusalem (see 1 Nephi 10:4; 19:8; 2 Nephi 25:19; 3 Nephi 1:1). Nephi states that the events he is about to narrate (1 Nephi 1:4–20) began in the commencement of the first year of Zedekiah's reign (v. 4). What period of time Lehi spent in Jerusalem after the first year of Zedekiah's reign is not mentioned, but, since Nephi does not mention another year, it is generally assumed that he went into the wilderness that same year. Nonetheless, the Book of Mormon is evidence that Zedekiah's reign began at least by the year 600 B.C.

Lehi "dwelt at Jerusalem in all his days" (v. 4). "At Jerusalem" suggests the area of Jerusalem but not necessarily the city specifically. A careful reading further on in the text reveals that his permanent residence was outside the city. When the four sons of Lehi failed in their first attempt to obtain the plates of brass held by Laban, they left Jerusalem to "go down to the land of our father's inheritance" (1 Nephi 3:16). It would thus seem that Lehi had a temporary place of residence he used when he was in the city, but his permanent residence was in the land of his inheritance where he kept his wealth.

What type of an individual was Lehi prior to being warned of the Lord? Was he a prophet of God, a contemporary of Jeremiah, as many have supposed? Perhaps he was, but another possibility is that he was one of many "brethren of the [Jewish] Church" (1 Nephi 4:26) who heard the message of the "many prophets" (v. 4). The city of Jerusalem was destroyed because the people would not hearken unto the message of the prophets. Jeremiah was even told that the city of Jerusalem would be pardoned if he could find a man, "that executeth judgment and seeketh the truth" (Jeremiah 5:1). Was not Lehi such a man?

Lehi might be pictured as a church member who was touched by the message of the prophets and responded to the message by praying unto the Lord as he went about his everyday activities. Others may have been touched, as Lehi was, however, just as in our own day, not all followed through on their promptings. Lehi did and, in response to his inquiry, joined the prophets in warning the inhabitants of Jerusalem. Thus the Lord could still hold out the conditions of pardon, mentioned above, to the city of Jerusalem.

The Bible verifies that there were many prophets sent by the Lord to Jerusalem in the beginning of Zedekiah's reign.

14 Moreover all the chief of the priests, and the people, transgressed very much after all the abominations of the heathen; and polluted the house of the LORD which he had hallowed in Jerusalem.

15 And the LORD God of their fathers sent to them by his messengers, rising up betimes, and sending; because he had compassion on his people, and on his dwelling place:

16 But they mocked the messengers of God, and despised his words, and misused his prophets, until the wrath of the LORD arose against his people, till *there was* no remedy. [2 Chronicles 36:14–16]

Jeremiah was one of these, "But neither [Zedekiah], nor his servants, nor the people of the land, did hearken unto the words of the Lord, which he spake by the prophet Jeremiah" (Jeremiah 37:1–2). The prophets Habakkuk and Zephaniah are also traditionally dated at this time period, and there may have been others.

Since Lehi was a prophet during the time of Jeremiah, some have thought that a record of his ministry should be in the Old Testament. Why there is no mention of it is not known. It is probable that 1 Nephi 1 is an account of his being called as a prophet, and that he did not remain in Jerusalem long afterwards. Even though we have no biblical record of Father Lehi, he did keep a record (see v. 16). The name "Lehi" is biblical, appearing in Judges 15:14, where it is the name of a place rather than a man.

One of the demanding characteristics of a true prophet is his concern for his fellowman, even when they are ripening for destruction. The Savior taught that "whosoever will be great among you, shall be your minister" (Mark 10:43). Lehi shows his greatness by pouring out his heart to God in behalf of his people, but the text does not clarify what he means by "his [Lehi's] people." Is Lehi their ecclesiastical steward (such as a bishop or stake president today), or is the relationship simply one of concern for his fellow-citizens of Jerusalem? Whatever that actual relationship, Lehi's prayer was offered with deep concern and doubtless was inspired by one or more of the many prophets that were warning of the destruction of Jerusalem.

Christ has manifest himself and his power in various signs. He "came down in the pillar of the cloud, and stood in the door of the tabernacle and called [to] Aaron and Miriam" (Numbers 12:5). He manifested his presence to Israel "by daytime in a pillar of a cloud, and in a pillar of fire by night" (Numbers 14:14). The pillar of fire before Lehi was probably the same as his appearance to Moses in "a flame of fire out of the midst of a bush" (Exodus 3:2). Both appearances are representative of the glory attending either Christ in his premortal state or one of his angelic messengers. The Prophet Joseph Smith taught:

> Spirits can only be revealed in flaming fire or glory. Angels have advanced further, their light and glory being tabernacled; and hence they appear in bodily shape. The spirits of just men are made ministering servants to those who are sealed unto life eternal, and it is through them that the sealing power comes down. [*TPJS*, 325]

Although there is no record of what Lehi saw and heard, it should be noted that he was given information as well as shown a vision. The message made him quake and tremble exceedingly. This could have been caused by the recognition of his own unworthiness (as in the case of Isaiah [see Isaiah 6:5]), or what he saw and heard concerning Jerusalem and its destruction.

1 Nephi 1:7–11 • Lehi Is Carried Away In a Vision

7 And it came to pass that he returned to his own house at Jerusalem; and he cast himself upon his bed, being overcome with the Spirit and the things which he had seen.

8 And being thus overcome with the Spirit, he was carried away in a vision, even that he saw the heavens open, and he thought he saw God sitting upon his throne, surrounded with numberless concourses of angels in the attitude of singing and praising their God.

9 And it came to pass that he saw One descending out of the midst of heaven, and he beheld that his luster was above that of the sun at noon-day.

10 And he also saw twelve others following him, and their brightness did exceed that of the stars in the firmament.

11 And they came down and went forth upon the face of the earth; and the first came and stood before my father, and gave unto him a book, and bade him that he should read.

Lehi's spiritual experience apparently left him in a weakened condition (v. 7). This is similar to the prophet Joseph Smith's spiritual experience in the Sacred Grove when he conversed with the Father and the Son. Joseph described his condition thus: "I had no strength; but soon recovering in some degree, I went home. And as I leaned up to the fireplace, mother inquired what the matter was" (JS—H 1:20). After "Moses was caught up into an exceedingly high mountain, And he saw God face to face and he talked with him, and the glory of God was upon him. . . . it was for the space of many hours before Moses did again receive his natural strength like unto man" (Moses 1:1, 10). Lehi's weakened condition supports his being called as a prophet on this occasion.

The later spiritual experiences of Joseph Smith, Moses, and Lehi (see 1 Nephi 2:1; 5:17; 8:1) do not leave them in a weakened condition. In fact, Joseph's later experiences become strengthening ones to him.

> On a subsequent visit to Hiram [Ohio] I arrived at Father Johnson's just as Joseph and Sidney were coming out of the vision alluded to in the book of Doctrine and Covenants, in which mention is made of the three glories. Joseph wore black clothes but at this time seemed to be dressed in an element of glorious white, and his face shown as if it were transparent; but I did not see the same glory attending Sidney. Joseph appeared as strong as a lion but Sidney seemed as weak as water. Joseph, noticing his condition smiled and said: "Brother Sidney is not as used to it as I am."[5]

Being overcome with the Spirit (the Holy Ghost) can also refer to one's being filled with the Spirit to the extent that he is no longer aware of physical things. In such a condition one is prepared to see and understand things of a spiritual nature. Being in this condition,

---

[5] N. B. Lundwall, comp., *The Vision, The Testimony of Philo Dibble*, Bookcraft Publishing Co., Salt Lake City, Utah, 11.

Lehi was then prepared for a further vision.

Although it is not recorded what Lehi saw and heard in the first vision, he was given another vision immediately after the original one (v. 8), possibly in support of the first one. Joseph Smith was visited three times by the angel Moroni, who repeated his original message each time and then related additional things to him (see JS—H 1:29–53).

Lehi's uncertainty of his seeing God (v. 8) is not a question of whether he saw but who he saw. His conclusion was that it must have been God and strongly suggests that he had not seen him before, again supporting that these several visions were his calling to be a prophet.

The personage he saw was sitting on his throne and surrounded with angels (v. 8). As an earthly throne represents temporal power, so God's heavenly throne represents the power and authority by which he rules and governs throughout the universe. This description is similar to the descriptions of other visions. John, on the Isle of Patmos saw a vision and cried "Salvation to our God which sitteth upon the throne, and unto the Lamb. And all the angels stood round about the throne" (Revelation 7:9–12). Isaiah "saw also the Lord sitting upon a throne, high and lifted up, and his train filled the temple. Above it stood the seraphim [angelic beings]" (Isaiah 6:1–4). These men were apparently so awed by their visions that they were unable to describe them except in symbolic terms. Lehi's awe is not stated until later (vv. 14–15), and even then his actual words are not recorded. Instead, Nephi, in making an abridgment of his fathers record (v. 16), gives a paraphrase that may account for the simplicity of the description compared to that of John and Isaiah.

The one descending out of heaven (v. 9) certainly refers to the spirit of Jesus Christ, and shows that the pre-mortal Christ was an eminent being from whom the light of truth radiated. The twelve following him undoubtedly represent the twelve apostles of Christ who were chosen in pre-mortal life, their ministry not being limited to their mortal life on earth but including work in other dispensations (see 1 Nephi 12:9; D&C 29:12; Mormon 3:18).

The book given to Lehi to read was like unto John the Revelator and Ezekiel, but they were told to eat the book (see Revelation 10; Ezekiel 2:8–10). The prophet Joseph Smith explained that the book eaten by John "was a mission, and an ordinance, for him to gather the tribes of Israel" (D&C 77:14). Ezekiel saw "written therein lamentations, and mourning, and woe" concerning the children of Israel [Judah]" (Ezekiel 2:10). As Lehi was filled with the Spirit of the Lord, he also saw and heard of the abominations of Jerusalem and its coming destruction (vv. 12–13).

1 Nephi 1:12–15 • My Father Read Many Things Concerning Jerusalem

12 And it came to pass that as he read, he was filled with the Spirit of the Lord.

13 And he read, saying: Wo, wo, unto Jerusalem, for I have seen thine abominations! Yea, and many things did my father read concerning Jerusalem—that it should be destroyed, and the inhabitants thereof; many should perish by the sword, and many should be carried away captive into Babylon.

14 And it came to pass that when my father had read and seen many great and marvelous things, he did exclaim many things unto the Lord; such as: Great and marvelous are thy works, O Lord God Almighty! Thy throne is high in the heavens, and thy power, and goodness, and mercy are over all the inhabitants of the earth; and, because thou art merciful, thou wilt not suffer those who come unto thee that they shall perish!

15 And after this manner was the language of my father in the praising of his God; for his soul did rejoice, and his whole heart was filled, because of the things which he had seen, yea, which the Lord had shown unto him.

That Lehi saw more things as he read is implied (v. 14), but regardless the future destruction of Jerusalem and the carrying of the Jews into captivity in Babylon were made known unto him (v. 13).

In spite of the sadness he must have felt over the coming demise of his people, he apparently recognized the justice of God in their downfall. He praised him for his mercy and goodness (vv. 13–14). The entire experience brought rejoicing to his soul, "and his whole heart was filled" (v. 15).

Lehi had come to a knowledge of, and had experiences with, all three members of the Godhead. He saw God sitting upon his throne (v. 8), had personal interaction with Jesus Christ (v. 11), and was filled with the Holy Ghost or Spirit of the Lord[6] (v. 12). Certainly, he was able to see God and Christ because of his being "quickened by the Spirit of God" (D&C 67:11). Lehi is now a special witness of the Lord Jesus Christ.

1 Nephi 1:16–17 • An Abridgment of the Record of My Father

16 And now I, Nephi, do not make a full account of the things which my father hath written, for he hath written many things which he saw in visions and in dreams; and he also hath written many things which he prophesied and spake unto his children, of which I shall not make a full account.

17 But I shall make an account of my proceedings in my days. Behold, I make an abridgment of the record of my father, upon plates which I have made with mine own hands; wherefore, after I have abridged the record of my father then will I make an account of mine own life.

As stated previously, Lehi kept a record of his ministry. It includes accounts of other visions and dreams. In the Preface of the first edition of the Book of Mormon, the Prophet Joseph wrote: "I would inform you that I translated, by the gift and power of God, and caused to be written, one hundred and sixteen pages, the which I took from the Book

---

[6] The Spirit of the Lord and the Holy Ghost are used interchangeably throughout Nephi's record. See the comments under 1 Nephi 11:11. The above reference seems to refer to the Holy Ghost whose mission is to teach (see John 14:26), as well as being a separate entity from the two members of the Godhead previously mentioned.

of Lehi, which was an account abridged from the plates of Lehi, by the hand of Mormon; which said account, some person or persons have stolen and kept from me, notwithstanding my utmost exertions to recover it again."[7] In the smaller plates, Nephi gave only a brief account of his father's record. Nephi used his father's record through the first eight chapters of these plates. He comments upon the two sets of plates in chapter nine, and begins to record his own proceedings in chapter ten (see 1 Nephi 9:1, 10:1). However, he still refers to his father's teachings as he proceeds with his own account.

1 Nephi 1:18–20 • Lehi Begins to Prophesy

18 Therefore, I would that ye should know, that after the Lord had shown so many marvelous things unto my father, Lehi, yea, concerning the destruction of Jerusalem, behold he went forth among the people, and began to prophesy and to declare unto them concerning the things which he had both seen and heard.

19 And it came to pass that the Jews did mock him because of the things which he testified of them; for he truly testified of their wickedness and their abominations; and he testified that the things which he saw and heard, and also the things which he read in the book, manifested plainly of the coming of a Messiah, and also the redemption of the world.

20 And when the Jews heard these things they were angry with him; yea, even as with the prophets of old, whom they had cast out, and stoned, and slain; and they also sought his life, that they might take it away. But behold, I, Nephi, will show unto you that the tender mercies of the Lord are over all those whom he hath chosen, because of their faith, to make them mighty even unto the power of deliverance.

Lehi now begins his active ministry as a special witness of the Lord. Although his prior callings or stewardships are not recorded, and not denying that he had previous callings, his visions had prepared him to be a special type of witness to the inhabitants of the land of Jerusa-

---

[7] See also Elder Erastus Snow in *Journal of Discourses*, 23:184.

lem (compare D&C 107:23). As a special witness of the Messiah, Lehi prophesies to his people. He becomes another witness along with the many prophets who had previously come to warn Jerusalem. As stated earlier, the length of time of his ministry to the Jews is not given, in context however, it seems to be short.

Nephi concludes his account of his Father's ministry in Jerusalem with the declaration that the Jews mocked and sought to take the life of his father even as they had the prophets of old (vv. 19–20). It is typical of a wicked generation to reject the warnings of the prophets concerning the Messiah and his justice, and to even seek their lives. While many incidents of the Old Testament could be cited to verify this fact, it was summarized by the Savior in the Beatitudes, "for so persecuted they the prophets who were before you" (Matthew 5:12; 3 Nephi 12:12).

The phrase, "I, Nephi, will show unto you," introduces to the reader the intent for which Nephi will select what he did in this small abridgment. The phrase is an example of what Joseph Smith calls a precept to bring you nearer to God as discussed in the "Introduction" preceding this chapter. This precept applies to chapter two through five and seven of 1 Nephi.

The Lord had prepared Lehi for his mission and now, as Nephi commences to show how that mission was accomplished, Nephi prepares the reader to look for the ways the Lord delivered Lehi and his associates from their difficult problems and circumstances. However, Nephi is not content to just tell the reader about Lehi, he wants the reader to know that the same is typical of every person whom the Lord chooses for his work. Of course a calling is dependent upon one's faith. By contrast, Laman and Lemuel serve as examples to the reader of the consequences that come to those who do not live by faith.

Nephi could personally testify of the tender mercies of the Lord being over those he has chosen (v. 20). This verse presents the basic message of the Book of Mormon that the reader should keep in mind as he studies the book further. Too often this vital message is overlooked while less significant facts and observations are emphasized. The Book of Mormon stands as a witness of Jesus Christ in a very active sense. It testifies that he will actively guide and influence the lives of those whom he has chosen—those who turn to him with all their hearts.

SACRED WRITING

Revelation Which is Great:

1 Nephi 1:6–14	Lehi sees God, Christ, the twelve Apostles, and much concerning Jerusalem.

Doctrines Learned:

1 Nephi 1:4	Prophets always warn before destruction.
1 Nephi 1:6	Heavenly beings may appear in flaming fire.
1 Nephi 1:7	The initial vision into heaven leaves a person weak.
1 Nephi 1:8	Angels surround the throne of God, praising him.
1 Nephi 1:9	Christ ministered in Old Testament times.
1 Nephi 1:10	Twelve ministers functioned with Christ in Old Testament times.
1 Nephi 1:12–14	Reading scripture may enable one to envision much more.
1 Nephi 1:19	Old Testament Prophets testified of the Messiah.
1 Nephi 1:20	The Lord promises deliverance according to our faith.

General Authorities Statements

Elder Marion D. Hanks • 1 Nephi 1:1

Suppose you were going to teach a lesson or give a talk to a group of young Latter-day Saints on the theme of the very first words in the Book of Mormon: "I, Nephi, having been born of goodly parents . . ." (1 Nephi 1:1). This wouldn't be very difficult, would it? After all, there could scarcely be a more universally accepted fact—it is a marvelous advantage to be born to good parents and into a home where the child is wanted and will be loved and trained and taught and given good examples.

But suppose you were well acquainted with the group you were to teach and knew that among them were at least several young people to whom this lesson, taught in the usual way, would be a heartbreak and a cause of uneasiness and embarrassment? Here is John whose parents have provided an example of a very unexemplary home, who have separated or divorced after bitterness and disloyalty and tragic constant controversy. John is fighting his way to a good life, anxious and determined to make something of himself and to prepare for a happy home of his own. There sits Phyllis whose folks have chosen a course directly opposite from that which they once followed and which she wants to live. Across the room is Robert who loves his dad but is confused because Dad thinks hunting and fishing and ball games, and maybe tobacco and alcohol, are more important than his priesthood opportunities.

How will you teach your lesson with these youngsters in the group?

You will want to face the facts of your situation squarely as you begin, acknowledging that while each of us understands that the enjoyment of a desirable heritage is a great blessing, many parents and homes are not what they ought to be. Frequently and commendably, devoted, courageous young people exert a favorable influence on parents and homes, but it is often true that there is discouragingly little can be done to change parents by sons or daughters who themselves are resolutely trying to improve upon their heritage.

What can and should be taught is that though we may not be in a position to do much about improving our parents, *there is everything we can do about deciding what kind of parents our own children will have!* From the great scriptural affirmation "I, Nephi, having been born of goodly parents . . ." we can teach with effective emphasis and sincerity, "I, John, desiring earnestly one day to become a goodly parent . . ."

Someone has said, "It is desirable to be well descended, but the glory belongs to our ancestors."

To *become* a goodly parent is a challenge and objective fit for the strongest and most determined young person, and the achieving of this goal lies squarely on the shoulders of the individual. One can become what he sincerely desires and wills to be.

There is, of course, much more that must be considered and said while one teaches such a lesson. There is the responsibility of children to parents, of parents to their children, and of prospective parents to their future children, to explore and ponder.

To Moses on the mount (Exodus 20:12) the Lord gave an eternally applicable commandment: "Honour thy father and thy mother . . ." In Proverbs 6:20 it is written: "My son, keep thy father's commandment, and forsake not the law of thy mother." Many young persons have the confusing and difficult problem of learning to differentiate between the honor due their parents because they are their parents and have blessed them with the chance to live, and the wrong choices those parents have made and the bad example they have set. No child is bound to follow a parent into degradation or dereliction or untruth, but every child is commanded of God to honor his father and mother. Would not any parent be honored to have his child improve upon his own example and contribution? . . .

The young have in them *now* the seeds of the future. Under normal circumstances and expectations there will one day be those who call them "father" or "mother" and who will be greatly influenced by the kind of mother of father they are. As prospective parents they need to learn the wondrous importance of good heritage, but they can be taught this from the scriptures in a way that will be stimulating and inspiring and that will give them the challenge and incentive to become "goodly parents." [*Improvement Era*, Feb. 1961, 97 & 113]

Elder Spencer W. Kimball • 1 Nephi 1:1

Though two of the brothers ignored those [Lehi's] teachings, using their own free agency, yet Nephi and others of his brothers were strongly fortified and all their lives could draw heavily on the reservoir built and filled by worthy parents. [CR, Oct. 1969, 29]

Elder Harold B. Lee • 1 Nephi 1:14

It was on the day or so following conference that President Stephen L. Richards, who was then chairman of the Church radio and publicity committee, approached me and said, "Brother Lee, next Sunday is Easter, and we have decided to ask you to give the Sunday night radio talk, the Easter talk, on the resurrection of the Lord." And then he added, "you understand now, of course, that as a member of the Council of the Twelve, you are to be one of the special witness of the life and mission of the Savior and of that great event." The most overwhelming of all the things that have happened to me was to begin to realize what a call into the Council of the Twelve meant.

During the days which followed, I locked myself in one of the rooms over in the Church Office building, and there I read the story of the life of the Savior. As I read the events of his life, and particularly the events leading up to and of the crucifixion, and then of the resurrection, I discovered that something was happening to me. I was not just reading a story; it seemed actually as though I was living the events; and I was reading them with a reality the like of which I had never before experienced. And when, on the Sunday night following, after I had delivered my brief talk and then declared, simply, "As one of the humblest among you, I, too, know that these things are true, that Jesus died and was resurrected for the sins of the world." I was speaking from a full heart, because I had come to know that week, with a certainty which I never before had known. [CR, April 1952, 126–27]

Spencer W. Kimball • 1 Nephi 1:14

I find that all I need to do to increase my love for my Maker and the gospel and the Church and my brethren is to read the scriptures. I have spent many hours in the scriptures during the last few days. I prescribe that for people who are in trouble. I cannot see how anyone can read the scriptures and not develop a testimony of their divinity and of the divinity of the work of the Lord, who is the spokesman in the scriptures.

I find that when I get casual in my relationships with divinity and when it seems that no divine ear is listening and no divine voice is speaking, that I am far, far away. If I immerse myself in the scriptures the distance narrows and the spirituality returns. I find myself loving more intensely those whom I must love with all my heart and mind and strength, and loving them more, I find it easier to abide their counsel. [*The Teachings of Spencer W. Kimball*, (1982), 135]

Challenges to Eternal Life:

(Select one and endeavor to improve your life).

1. Do you honor your parents today? The greatest way to honor your parents, even though they may have passed to the next world, is by living

the gospel of Jesus Christ. Resolve to live the gospel (1 Nephi 1:1).

2. Make a commitment to be, or prepare yourself to be, a "goodly parent" (1 Nephi 1:1).

3. Make a commitment to consistently study the scriptures, and, as you study, to be sensitive to the feelings and impressions of the Spirit (1 Nephi 1:12–14).

4. Select a challenge of your own from the principles and doctrines found in this reading and apply it to your life.

Chapter Two

From Jerusalem to the Valley of Lemuel

1 Nephi 2–5

*H*istorical Setting: These chapters tell us of Lehi and his family's journey into the wilderness, and of the great importance of obtaining the plates of brass. The dates of the incidents described are assumed to be in the first year of the record (see synopsis of History-chapter one).

Precept of this Reading • 1 Nephi 1:20

> I, Nephi, will show unto you that the tender mercies of the Lord are over all those whom he hath chosen, because of their faith, to make them mighty even unto the power of deliverance. [1 Nephi 1:20]

Nephi tells us what he wants us to learn from the following incidents. As a preparation for a deeper study, an outline of the four chapters included in this section follows.

OUTLINE • 1 NEPHI 2–5

➤ 2:1–2   The Lord commanded Lehi in a dream to take his family and depart into the wilderness.

        a.   Lehi was blessed because of the things he did (v. 1).

    b. Because he did what the Lord commanded him they sought his life (v. 1).

➤ 2:3–5   Lehi was obedient to the Lord and departed into the wilderness.

    a. He left his house, the land of his inheritance, gold, silver, and precious things. He took nothing but his family and provisions (v. 4).

    b. He came near the shores of the Red Sea and traveled in the borders nearer the shore of the Red Sea (v. 5).

    c. He traveled with his wife, Sariah, and four sons: Laman, Lemuel, Sam and Nephi (v. 5).

➤ 2:6–15   After three days into the wilderness (from the borders near the Red Sea), Lehi pitched his tent in a valley by the side of a river of water.

    a. He built an altar of stones, made an offering unto the Lord, and gave thanks (v. 7).

    b. He called the river Laman (v. 8).

       1. It emptied into the Red Sea.

       2. The valley was in the borders, near the mouth (of the Red Sea).

    c. Seeing the river emptied into the Red Sea, he told Laman that he wished he would be like this river, continually running into the fountain of all righteousness (v. 9).

    d. He told Lemuel that he wished he would be like the valley, firm and steadfast in keeping the commandment of the Lord (v. 10).

    e. Laman and Lemuel were stiffnecked and murmured against their father (vv. 11–13).

       1. He was a visionary man and had led them out of Jerusalem, leaving everything behind.

       2. He had done this because of the foolish imaginations of his heart.

    3.   They knew not the dealings of that God who had created them.

    4.   They did not believe that great city, Jerusalem, could be destroyed.

    5.   They were like unto the Jews at Jerusalem who had sought Lehi's life.

  f. Lehi spoke to them with power being filled with the Spirit until their frames shook (v. 14).

    1.   He did confound them that they dared not utter against him.

    2.   They did as he commanded them.

➤ 2:16–18   Nephi cried unto the Lord and was visited by him.

  a. Nephi was exceedingly young but large of stature (v. 16).

  b. Nephi had great desires to know the mysteries of God (v. 16).

  c. The Lord softened Nephi's heart, and he believed all the words spoken by his father (v. 16).

  d. Sam believed Nephi's words that the Lord manifested to him by the Holy Spirit (v. 17).

  e. Laman and Lemuel would not hearken to Nephi's words (v. 18).

  f. Nephi cried unto the Lord for them (v. 18).

➤ 2:19–24   The Lord said Nephi was blessed for his faith in diligently seeking him.

  a. Inasmuch as Nephi keeps the commandments, he shall prosper and be led to a land of promise (v. 20).

    1.   A land prepared by the Lord for them.

    2.   A land which is choice above all other lands.

  b. Inasmuch as Nephi's brethren rebel against Nephi they shall be cut off from the presence of the Lord (v. 21).

  c. Inasmuch as Nephi keeps the commandments, he shall be a ruler and a teacher over his brethren (v. 22).

     d.   In the day Nephi's brethren rebel against the Lord they will be cursed and have no power over Nephi's seed except they rebel also (v. 23).

     e.   Those who rebel will be a scourge to Nephi's seed to stir them up to remembrance (v. 24).

➤ 3:1–8   Nephi returned to his fathers tent and was told that the Lord had commanded his father to send him and his brethren to Jerusalem.

     a.   Laban has a record of the Jews and the genealogy of Lehi's forefathers engraven upon plates of brass (v. 3).

     b.   Lehi's sons are to go to the house of Laban and seek to bring back the records (vv. 4–6).

         1.   The older brothers say it is a hard thing that Lehi requires of them.

         2.   Lehi says it not him but the Lord who requires it.

         3.   Nephi is told to go and he would be favored of the Lord because he had not murmured.

     c.   Nephi said he would go for the Lord gives no commandment save he provides a means for them to accomplish it (v. 7).

     d.   Lehi was exceedingly glad for he knew Nephi had been blessed of the Lord (v. 8).

➤ 3:9–21   Nephi and his brethren returned to the land of Jerusalem.

     a.   The brothers cast lots, Laman was selected to go to Laban's house (vv. 10–13).

         1.   He desired the plates of brass from Laban.

         2.   Laban was angry and thrust him from his house accusing him of being a robber. He said he would slay Laman.

     b.   Laman returned and tells his brothers what Laban had done (v. 14).

         1.   They were exceedingly sorrowful

         2.   His brothers were about to return to their father in the wilderness.

     c. Nephi persuaded his brothers to be faithful in keeping the commandments of the Lord (vv. 15–16).

        1. Nephi said they would not go until they had done what the Lord commanded.

        2. He proposed they go to the land of their father's inheritance and get the gold and silver, and all manner of riches his father had left behind.

        3. His father had left them because he had been commanded.

     d. Lehi knew that Jerusalem must be destroyed because of wickedness (vv. 17–18).

        1. They had rejected the words of the prophets.

        2. Lehi had been commanded to leave or he would perish also.

     e. It was wisdom in God that they obtain these records (vv. 19–20).

        1. To preserve the language of their fathers for their children.

        2. To preserve the words of the prophets spoken by the spirit and power of God.

➤ 3:22–31   The sons of Lehi go to the land of their inheritance and get the gold and silver and precious things and return to the house of Laban.

     a. They offered to give him all their precious things for the brass plates (vv. 24–27).

        1. Laban saw their property, he lusted for it, thrust them out and sent his servants to slay them.

        2. Lehi's sons fled and left their property behind in Laban's hands.

        3. They hid themselves in the cavity of a rock.

     b. Laman and Lemuel were angry with Nephi and their father, and spake many hard words, and smote their younger brothers with a rod (v. 28).

     c. An angel of the Lord appeared and asked why they smote Nephi? (vv. 29–30).

1.   The Lord has chosen Nephi to be a ruler over them because of their iniquities.

    2.   They shall go back to Jerusalem again and the Lord will deliver Laban into their hands, and the angel departed.

  d. Laman and Lemuel again murmured and asked how it is possible for the Lord to deliver Laban? (v. 31).

    1.   He is a mighty man and can command fifty.

    2.   Even he can slay fifty, why not us?

➤ 4:1–5   Nephi spoke to his brethren urging them to go with him again to Jerusalem and keep the commandments of God (to obtain the plates).

  a. The Lord is mightier than all the earth, Laban and his fifty, or even his tens of thousands (v. 1).

  b. Nephi says let us be strong like Moses (vv. 2–3).

    1.   He spake and divided the waters of the Red Sea, our fathers came through on dry ground and the armies of Pharaoh were drowned.

    2.   His brethren know this is true, an angel has spoken to them. The Lord is able to deliver them and destroy Laban even as the Egyptians.

  c. The brethren murmured but followed him up to the walls of Jerusalem (vv. 4–5).

    1.   Nephi had them hide themselves without the walls.

    2.   Nephi crept into the city towards the house of Laban.

➤ 4:6–18   Nephi is led by the Spirit not knowing what he should do.

  a. Near Laban's house he found a man fallen and drunken with wine (vv. 7–9).

    1.   He found the man was Laban.

    2.   He withdrew Laban's sword. The hilt was of pure gold and of exceedingly fine workmanship, and the blade of precious steel.

  b. Nephi was constrained by the Spirit to kill Laban, but

he said in his heart never have I shed the blood of man, and shrunk from killing him (vv. 10–11).

1. The Spirit said the Lord had delivered him into his hands.
2. Nephi knew Laban had sought to take his own life.
3. He would not hearken to the commandments of God, and had taken away their property.

c. The Spirit again said to slay him (vv. 12–13).

1. The Lord slays the wicked to bring forth his righteous purposes (vv. 12–13).
2. It is better for one man to perish than a nation dwindle and perish in unbelief.

d. Nephi remembered the Lord's words, inasmuch as thy seed keep the commandments they shall prosper in the land (vv. 14–17).

1. They could not keep the law of Moses save they had the law.
2. The law was engraven on the plates of brass.
3. Nephi knew the Lord had delivered Laban into his hands that he might obtain the records.

e. Nephi obeyed the Lord and smote off Laban's head with his own sword (v. 18).

➤ 4:19–38   Nephi put on the garments of Laban, the armor about his loins, and went into the treasury of Laban.

a. He, in the voice of Laban, commanded the servant of Laban, who had the keys to the treasury, to go with him into the treasury (v. 20).

b. He supposed Nephi was his master, seeing the garment and sword (vv. 21–24).

1. He spake concerning the elders of the Jews knowing Laban had been among them.
2. Nephi spake unto him as if he were Laban.
3. Nephi told him that he (Nephi) was to carry the

    plates of brass to his elder brethren outside the walls.

c.   Nephi bade the servant to follow him, and the servant supposing Nephi was Laban and spoke of the brethren of the church, did follow Nephi (vv. 25–28).

    1.   He spake many times to Nephi concerning the brethren of the church.

    2.   When Nephi's brothers saw him they fled supposing he was Laban.

d.   Nephi called to his brothers and they ceased to flee (vv. 29–31).

    1.   The servant of Laban began to tremble and was about to flee.

    2.   Nephi, being large in stature and receiving strength from the Lord, seized him.

e.   Nephi told the servant that if he would hearken to his words, as the Lord lives and as Nephi lives, he would spare his life (vv. 32–34).

    1.   With an oath, Nephi said he need not fear, and was a free man if he would go with them.

    2.   He told him the Lord had commanded them to do this, and he would have place among them.

f.   Zoram, the servant, took courage at the words of Nephi and made an oath that he would go and would tarry with them from that time forth (vv. 35–37).

    1.   The brothers were desirous that he go with them so that the Jews would not know they had left lest they follow and destroy them.

    2.   Their fears did cease concerning Zoram after he had made an oath.

g.   The brothers take Zoram and the plates, and journey to their fathers tent (v. 38).

➤ 5:1–6   When Lehi's sons return, he is full of joy and Sariah, his wife, is exceedingly glad for she had truly mourned for them.

    a.   Sariah supposed they had perished in the wilderness, and complained that Lehi was a visionary man (vv. 2–3).

    b.   Lehi admitted he was a visionary man for had he not seen a vision they would have perished in Jerusalem (v. 4).

    c.   He had obtained a land of promise and knew the Lord would deliver his sons out of Laban's hands and bring them back (vv. 5–6).

➤ 5:7–9   When the sons returned, their joy was full, and Sariah was comforted.

    a.   She now knew the Lord had commanded her husband to flee into the wilderness, and had delivered her sons from Laban (v. 8).

    b.   They rejoiced exceedingly and offered sacrifice and burnt offering in thanks to God (v. 9).

➤ 5:10–15   Lehi searched the plates of brass from the beginning.

    a.   They contained the five books of Moses, an account of the creation of the world, and of Adam and Eve their first parents (v. 11).

    b.   They had a record of the Jews from the beginning to the reign of Zedekiah, king of Judah (v. 12).

    c.   Also the prophecies of the holy prophets down to Zedekiah, and many prophecies of Jeremiah (v. 13).

    d.   Lehi found the genealogy of his fathers (vv. 14–15).

        1.   He was a descendant of Joseph, who was sold into Egypt, and was preserved by the Lord to keep Jacob and his household from perishing.

        2.   Jacob's household was delivered from captivity in Egypt by the same God.

    e.   Laban was also a descendant of Joseph, and he and his fathers had kept the records (v. 16).

➤ 5:17–22   Lehi saw these things, was filled with the Spirit and prophesied.

       a.   The plates of brass would go forth to all nations, kindreds, tongues, and people who were of his seed (v. 18).

       b.   The plates of brass would never perish and not be dimmed by time (vv. 19–22).

           1.   Lehi and Nephi searched the records, and found them desirable and of great worth in preserving the commandments of the Lord for their children.

           2.   It was wisdom to carry the plates with them into the wilderness.

NOTES AND COMMENTARY

Introduction: There are fifteen events that Nephi uses "to show that the tender mercies of the Lord are over all those whom he has chosen, because of their faith, to make them mighty even unto the power of deliverance" (1 Nephi 1:20). However, the element of faith may not be fully understood by the reader. This is not a unique problem. Faith has been described as the most talked about and yet the least understood principle of the gospel. This description is probably given because there are at least three different principles of faith and people often do not differentiate between them. The Prophet Joseph Smith defined the different principles of faith in the *Lectures On Faith*.[1] He identified the first as the principle of action: "faith is the assurance which men have of the existence of things which they have not seen, and the principle of action in all intelligence beings" (*L on F*, 1:9).

The second principle of faith is one of power. The Prophet declared: "But faith is not only the principle of action but of power also, in all intelligent beings, whether in heaven or on earth." He said further, "it

---

[1] There are those who question Joseph Smith as the author of *Lectures On Faith*. This work will not discuss the issue but will treat them as though they were written by the Prophet.

is the principle by which Jehovah works and through which he exercises power over all temporal as well as eternal things" (*L on F*, 1:13, 16).

The third principle of faith was defined by Joseph Smith as faith unto life and salvation. He said that three things were necessary for any rational and intelligent being to obtain this third principle of faith:

"First, the idea that he [God] actually exists.

"Secondly, a correct idea of his character, perfections, and attributes.

"Thirdly, an actual knowledge that the course of life which he pursues is according to his will" (*L on F*, 3:2–5).

The third principle of faith is almost an extension of the first principle, the moving cause of action. However, the difference in the two is significant. The first is the cause of people doing things, while the third is a definite knowledge that what they are doing is the expressed mind and will of the Lord regardless of their own reasoning or prior understanding. To attain this principle of faith, we must follow the principle of sacrifice.

> Let us here observe that a religion that does not require the sacrifice of all things never has power sufficient to produce the faith necessary unto life and salvation. For from the first existence of man, the faith necessary unto the enjoyment of life and salvation never could be obtained without the sacrifice of all earthly things. It is through this sacrifice, and this only, that God has ordained that men should enjoy eternal life. And it is through the medium of the sacrifice of all earthly things that men do actually know that they are doing the things that are well pleasing in the sight of God. When a man has offered in sacrifice all that he has for the truth's sake, not even withholding his life, and believing before God that he has been called to make this sacrifice because he seeks to do His will, he does know, most assuredly, that God does and will accept his sacrifice and offering and that he has not and will not seek His face in vain. Under these circumstances, then, he can obtain the faith necessary for him to lay hold on eternal life. [*L on F*, 6:7]

This section will focus on four chapters of First Nephi (2–5). We will identify the principle of faith and the attributes that produce such faith. As you read this section I hope your faith will further develop and increase.

1 Nephi 2:1–4 • The Lord Speaks to Lehi in a Dream

1 For behold, it came to pass that the Lord spake unto my father, yea, even in a dream, and said unto him: Blessed art thou Lehi, because of the things which thou hast done; and because thou hast been faithful and declared unto this people the things which I commanded thee, behold, they seek to take away thy life.

2 And it came to pass that the Lord commanded my father, even in a dream, that he should take his family and depart into the wilderness.

3 And it came to pass that he was obedient unto the word of the Lord, wherefore he did as the Lord commanded him.

4 And it came to pass that he departed into the wilderness. And he left his house, and the land of his inheritance, and his gold, and his silver, and his precious things, and took nothing with him, save it were his family, and provisions, and tents, and departed into the wilderness.

Lehi's call to take his family and leave Jerusalem, departing into the wilderness (v. 2), is an example of faith unto life and salvation. He was not told his destination or the extent of his journey. He received this call because of his previous faith unto action. His call was based upon the principle of sacrifice. He left his house, the land of his inheritance, his gold, his silver, and his precious things. He took nothing with him, save it were his family, provisions, and tents (v. 4). We are not told the method of travel they used, but we assume it was the traditional camels and perhaps donkeys.

When we depart this earthly life, we will not take our earthly possessions. We will only be able to take our family, and unless we inherit the celestial kingdom we will not even be able to take our family. Accordingly, President David O. McKay has said: "No other success can compensate for failure in the home,"[2] and President Harold B. Lee has said: "the greatest of the Lord's work you brethren will ever do as fathers will be within the walls of your own home" (CR, April 1973, 130).

Dreams have been used frequently by the Lord to give instruction and warning. The Book of Mormon uses dreams and visions interchangeably. Lehi later says "I have dreamed a dream; or in other words, I have seen a vision" (1 Nephi 8:2). Joseph Smith changed the word "dream" to "vision" in several places in his translation of the Bible (i.e. Matthew 2:19, 22). "The angel of the Lord appeared to Joseph [the husband of Mary] saying. Arise and take the young child and his mother and flee to Egypt." "An angel of the Lord appeared in a vision to Joseph in Egypt" and told him to return to the land of Israel after "Herod was dead" (JST, Matthew 3:13, 19). Lehi's dream is only one of several dreams mentioned in 1 Nephi (see 1:16; 3:1; 8:2). Apparently dreams were a frequent source of revelation.

The Lord commanding Lehi to take his family and depart (v. 2) seems to refer to the same dream cited in verse one. As mentioned in chapter one, Lehi's residence appears to have been outside the city of Jerusalem but still encompassed in the larger area called Jerusalem. The wilderness that Lehi departed into was waste or desert land, not jungle or forest. Lehi was not told the extent of his journey, or the trials he would encounter. He was simply sent. How similar this is to each individual's sojourn through the "wilderness" of this earth. Upon arrival, none of us know the length of time of our sojourn nor do we know the trials that we will encounter. We must all proceed with faith.

Every person, every generation, must pass the test of obedience before eternal rewards are given. Lehi was commanded to leave his wealth and earthly possessions and flee. The Mormon pioneers were commanded to leave their homes and all but the provisions they could carry and cross the plains. There was no promised land (the Americas)

---

[2] *Family Home Evening Manual* [1965–66], p. iii.

for Lehi until he passed the test of obedience. There was no promised land for the pioneers until they passed the test of obedience. Zion (Independence, Missouri) will not be redeemed until enough Saints have "learned to be obedient to the things which [the Lord] required at their hands" (D&C 105:3).

1 Nephi 2:5–7 • To the Red Sea and Three Days Into the Wilderness

> 5 And he came down by the borders near the shore of the Red Sea; and he traveled in the wilderness in the borders which are nearer the Red Sea; and he did travel in the wilderness with his family, which consisted of my mother, Sariah, and my elder brothers, who were Laman, Lemuel, and Sam.
>
> 6 And it came to pass that when he had traveled three days in the wilderness, he pitched his tent in a valley by the side of a river of water.
>
> 7 And it came to pass that he built an altar of stones, and made an offering unto the Lord, and gave thanks unto the Lord our God.

The nearest point of the Red Sea to Jerusalem is over two hundred miles. It is not stated how many days the family spent getting to the Red Sea, but it must have been around two weeks plus the three days. Although they would be hurrying, they would also have been careful not to attract attention.

The expressions "river of water" (v. 6) and "altar of stones" (v. 7) are called Hebrew idioms. In the Middle East there are rivers of sand or valleys and dry river beds called wadi's that have water in them only in the spring of the year. If Joseph Smith had been writing the book himself he would have said "river" and "stone altar," the vernacular of his day. Other Hebrew idioms will be identified as they appear in the text.

The altar of stones was undoubtedly a mound of uncut stones in accordance with the instructions given to Moses.

> 25 And if thou wilt make me an altar of stone, thou shalt not build

it of hewn stone: for if thou lift up thy tool upon it, thou hast polluted it. [Exodus 20:25; see also Deuteronomy 27:5–6; Joshua 8:31]

Therefore, the altar was not man-made but an edifice to God constructed of items that God had made.

Later, when the sons return with the plates of brass, they all rejoice and make an offering (1 Nephi 5:9). Except for Nephi and possibly Sam the family did not share in thankfulness unto the Lord at this time. This premise will be supported in the subsequent events.

1 Nephi 2:8–15 • The River Laman and the Valley of Lemuel

8 And it came to pass that he called the name of the river, Laman, and it emptied into the Red Sea; and the valley was in the borders near the mouth thereof.

9 And when my father saw that the waters of the river emptied into the fountain of the Red Sea, he spake unto Laman, saying: O that thou mightest be like unto this river, continually running into the fountain of all righteousness!

10 And he also spake unto Lemuel: O that thou mightest be like unto this valley, firm and steadfast, and immovable in keeping the commandments of the Lord!

11 Now this he spake because of the stiffneckedness of Laman and Lemuel; for behold they did murmur in many things against their father, because he was a visionary man, and had led them out of the land of Jerusalem, to leave the land of their inheritance, and their gold, and their silver, and their precious things, to perish in the wilderness. And this they said he had done because of the foolish imaginations of his heart.

12 And thus Laman and Lemuel, being the eldest, did murmur against their father. And they did murmur because they knew not the dealings of that God who had created them.

13 Neither did they believe that Jerusalem, that great city, could be destroyed according to the words of the prophets. And they were like unto the Jews who were at Jerusalem, who sought to take away the life of my father.

14 And it came to pass that my father did speak unto them in the valley of Lemuel, with power, being filled with the Spirit, until their frames did shake before him. And he did confound them, that they durst not utter against him; wherefore, they did as he commanded them.

15 And my father dwelt in a tent.

Lehi's naming of the river and the valley after his sons is also consistent with the background and language of the Middle East, but that is not the reason that the naming of them is included in the abridgment. Lehi hoped that the names would have an effect upon his wayward sons' lives; continuously righteous, symbolic of the river, and firm and steadfast and immovable in keeping the commandments, symbolic of the valley (v. 10). This is the first mention of the character of Laman and Lemuel. Although they too were born of goodly parents (1:1), they murmured against their father, desired the material things of the world, and knew not the dealings of God (vv. 10–11). President David O. McKay compared the members of the Church who murmur with Laman and Lemuel:

> In the Church we sometimes find two groups of people: the builders and the murmurers. Let each ask himself: in which class should I be placed?
>
> We are called upon to perform duties. When the priesthood leadership introduces new programs, many of the members will say, "Yes, we will do it. Let us perform in these new programs." But sometimes we hear a murmurer, a faultfinder, who will say, "No, we cannot do that." Misjudging motives, some soon find themselves with Laman, and Lemuel instead of with Nephi, whose actions expressed willingness to follow the voice of God. . . . Murmuring against Priesthood and auxiliary leadership is one of the most poisonous things that can be introduced into the home of a Latter-day Saint. [3]

Laman and Lemuel's rejection of the prophecy of the future destruction of Jerusalem is a rejection of revelation from living

---

[3] *Improvement Era*, March 1969, 3.

prophets. They were the product of their wicked Jewish environment (v. 13). They chose to follow their natural desires for worldly possessions rather than the prophets and the Spirit (see Mosiah 3:16–19). This is one of the tests to which mankind is subjected. The pressure of society, or peer groups, is often in conflict with parents, and the Church and its leaders. Each individual must make a choice of which to follow. Nephi and Sam, from the same family, made the right choice.

The Lord came to the aid of Lehi by granting him the power to keep his rebellious sons in line (v. 14). This is an example of faith as a principle of power. It was not oratorical or physical power that compelled Laman and Lemuel to be obedient, but the Spirit of God that caused their frames to shake. There are at least two reasons for the Lord's assistance. First, Lehi's great concern for the spiritual welfare and salvation of his sons; secondly, the mission the Lord had for Lehi and his sons. Of course the agency of man was honored, but the witness was so strong that they were left without excuse.[4]

"And my father dwelt in a tent" is one of the shortest verses in the Book of Mormon. Hugh Nibley states that to an Arab this sentence says everything.[5] The tent is the center of life for an Arab, and for the next eight years it will also be the center for Lehi and his party.

1 Nephi 2:16–18 • I Nephi
Being Exceedingly Young

16 And it came to pass that I, Nephi, being exceedingly young, nevertheless being large in stature, and also having great desires to know of the mysteries of God, wherefore, I did cry unto the Lord; and behold he did visit me, and did soften my heart that I did believe all the words which had been spoken by my father; wherefore, I did not rebel against him like unto my brothers.

17 And I spake unto Sam, making known unto him the things

---

[4] See Elder Spencer W. Kimball under *General Authority Quotes* 1 Nephi 1:1.

[5] For a more complete discussion see *Lehi in the Desert and the World of the Jaredites* [1952], 57–59.

which the Lord had manifested unto me by his Holy Spirit. And it came to pass that he believed in my words.

18 But, behold, Laman and Lemuel would not hearken unto my words; and being grieved because of the hardness of their hearts I cried unto the Lord for them.

The Lord often calls people in their youth for great missions. The Lord called Samuel when he was a child (see 1 Samuel 3:4–14). Mormon was "visited of the Lord" when only "fifteen years of age" (Mormon 1:15). John the Baptist "was ordained by an angel of God at the time he was eight days old," and his father Zacharias prophesied that he would "go before the face of the Lord to prepare the way" (D&C 84:28; Luke 1:76 [57–80]). Of course, Joseph Smith was only fourteen years of age when he "saw two Personages, whose brightness and glory defy all description. . . . One of them calling [him] by name and said, pointing to the other—*This is My Beloved Son. Hear Him!"* (JS—H 1:7, 17).

Nephi's cry unto the Lord (v. 16) is an example of faith as a principle of action. It was rewarded by a visit of the Lord (v. 19). Lehi's family probably followed him out of loyalty to a kind and loving father, a good provider. However, Nephi was not content to follow blindly. He desired his own witness. The Lord has said:

13 To some it is given by the Holy Ghost to know that Jesus Christ is the Son of God, and that he was crucified for the sins of the world.

14 To others it is given to believe on their words, that they also might have eternal life if they continue faithful. [D&C 46:13–14]

Those who desire to know that Jesus is the Christ are undoubtedly those to whom it is given to know. But all must eventually come to this knowledge if they attain eternal life. President Heber C. Kimball testified: "The time will come when no man nor woman will be able to endure on borrowed light. Each will have to be guided by the light within himself. If you do not have it how can you stand?"[6] A person may believe on another's word while he seeks to find his own witness. President Harold B. Lee stated: "To you who may not have that testimony, may I ask you to hold to my testimony until you have developed one for yourself. But work on it, study, and pray until you too can know with a certainty that these things are true."[7]

Nephi is a good example of what President Lee taught. He had cried unto the Lord, and the Lord softened his heart that he did believe (v. 16).

Sam's belief is another example of faith as a principle of action (v. 17). He believed the words of Nephi and continued to exercise faith. President Howard W. Hunter noted:

> Many who read the story of the great prophet Nephi almost completely miss another valiant son of Lehi whose name was Sam. Nephi is one of the most famous figures in the entire Book of Mormon. But Sam? Sam's name is mentioned only ten times in the scriptures. . . .
>
> Sam's role was basically one of supporting and assisting his more acclaimed younger brother, and he ultimately received all the blessings promised to Nephi and his posterity. Nothing promised to Nephi was withheld from the faithful Sam, yet we know very little of the details of his service and contribution. He was almost an unknown in life, but he is obviously a triumphant leader and victor in the annals of eternity.[8]

Laman and Lemuel would not hearken to Nephi's words (v. 18). Although they had had a great manifestation of the power of the Spirit, unlike Nephi, they hardened their hearts instead of softening them. They were like the Pharaoh of Egypt, as described by Brigham Young and Willard Richard: "the Lord manifested Himself in so many glorious and mighty ways, that Pharaoh could not resist the truth without becoming harder" (*History of the Church*, 4:264).

---

[6] Orson F. Whitney, *The Life of Heber C. Kimball* [1945], 450.

[7] *The Teachings of Harold B. Lee*, ed. Clyde J, Williams [1996], 640.

[8] *BYU Speeches of the Year* [1990–91], 3.

1 Nephi 2:19–24 • The Lord Spake to Nephi

19 And it came to pass that the Lord spake unto me, saying: Blessed art thou, Nephi, because of thy faith, for thou hast sought me diligently, with lowliness of heart.

20 And inasmuch as ye shall keep my commandments, ye shall prosper, and shall be led to a land of promise; yea, even a land which I have prepared for you; yea, a land which is choice above all other lands.

21 And inasmuch as thy brethren shall rebel against thee, they shall be cut off from the presence of the Lord.

22 And inasmuch as thou shalt keep my commandments, thou shalt be made a ruler and a teacher over thy brethren.

23 For behold, in that day that they shall rebel against me, I will curse them even with a sore curse, and they shall have no power over thy seed except they shall rebel against me also.

24 And if it so be that they rebel against me, they shall be a scourge unto thy seed, to stir them up in the ways of remembrance.

Nephi is a second example of the principle of faith unto life and salvation. The Lord visited him and assured him that they were all being led to a land of promise, and that Nephi was to play a leadership role in this great endeavor (vv. 19–22). Thus he knew that he was pursuing the right course or the will of the Lord.

The promise to Nephi is the first of many references to the land of promise, a land choice above all other lands, not only to Nephi and his people, but to all who inhabit it. It is a blessed land for all upon the same conditions of righteousness. To the brother of Jared, the Lord said,

10 For behold, this is a land which is choice above all other lands; wherefore he that doth possess it shall serve God or shall be swept off; for it is the everlasting decree of God. And it is not until the fulness of iniquity among the children of the land, that they are swept off.

11 And this cometh unto you, O ye Gentiles, that ye may know

the decrees of God—that ye may repent, and not continue in your iniquities until the fulness come, that ye may not bring down the fulness of the wrath of God upon you as the inhabitants of the land have hitherto done.

12 Behold, this is a choice land, and whatsoever nation shall possess it shall be free from bondage, and from captivity, and from all other nations under heaven, if they will but serve the God of the land, who is Jesus Christ, who hath been manifested by the things which we have written. [Ether 2:10–12]

Thus, the promise is still in effect today. While there is a tendency for some to think that this promise is only to those who live in the United States, the Prophet Joseph Smith said: "The whole of America is Zion itself from north to south, and is described by the Prophets, who declare that it is the Zion where the mountain of the Lord should be, and that it should be in the center of the land" (*TPJS*, 362).

Other promises made to those who live in the Americas include:

1. The land was promised to a remnant of Joseph, who was sold into Egypt (see 2 Nephi 3:5; 3 Nephi 15:12–13).
2. The land is the everlasting inheritance of Lehi's seed, and all others that the Lord would lead here (see 2 Nephi 1:5–7).
3. God would establish the principles of freedom for all other lands through the Constitution of the United States (see 3 Nephi 21:4; D&C 98:5–10; 101:77–80).
4. The New Jerusalem will be built in the center of the land (3 Nephi 20:22; Ether 13:4, 6–10; D&C 57:3; 84:1–5).

Nephi was given a personal blessing regarding the choice land. He would be led to the land and "inasmuch as thou shalt keep my commandments, thou shalt be made a ruler and a teacher over thy brethren" (vv. 20, 22). This promise may be read as conditional or unconditional. The writer believes it to be unconditional, the Lord knew he would keep the commandments, and thus made the promise. Therefore it is labeled as faith unto life and salvation.

The Lord also knew Laman and Lemuel would rebel against Nephi

(v. 21). They were cut off from the Lord about thirty years later (2 Nephi 5:1–8). For years they had cut themselves off from personal revelation because of sin and transgression, but after thirty years, they cut themselves off from Nephi, the Lord's prophet. They continued to cut themselves off spiritually and temporally because of their rebellion against God. Their separation, their curse, and their being a scourge to Nephi's seed will be discussed later (see discussion under 2 Nephi 5).

1 Nephi 3:1–8 • The Lord Commanded— Return to Jerusalem

1 And it came to pass that I, Nephi, returned from speaking with the Lord, to the tent of my father.

2 And it came to pass that he spake unto me, saying: Behold I have dreamed a dream, in the which the Lord hath commanded me that thou and thy brethren shall return to Jerusalem.

3 For behold, Laban hath the record of the Jews and also a genealogy of my forefathers, and they are engraven upon plates of brass.

4 Wherefore, the Lord hath commanded me that thou and thy brothers should go unto the house of Laban, and seek the records, and bring them down hither into the wilderness.

5 And now, behold thy brothers murmur, saying it is a hard thing which I have required of them; but behold I have not required it of them, but it is a commandment of the Lord.

6 Therefore go, my son, and thou shalt be favored of the Lord, because thou hast not murmured.

7 And it came to pass that I, Nephi, said unto my father: I will go and do the things which the Lord hath commanded, for I know that the Lord giveth no commandments unto the children of men, save he shall prepare a way for them that they may accomplish the thing which he commandeth them.

8 And it came to pass that when my father had heard these words he was exceedingly glad, for he knew that I had been blessed of the Lord.

The Lord again gave Lehi a commandment in a dream (v. 2). Laban had been the custodian of the brass plates, the record of the Jews. There is now proof that the ancients in both hemispheres used metal tablets to record their history.[9]

The importance of these records is shown when King Benjamin taught his sons that "were it not for these plates . . . we must have suffered in ignorance . . . not knowing the mysteries of God" (Mosiah 1:3). A contrast may be seen with the Mulekites who "had brought no records with them; and they denied the being of their creator" (Omni 1:17). Judged by human rationale, what the Lord commanded was a hard thing. Lehi's family had just traveled over two hundred difficult miles from Jerusalem to their present encampment. Laman and Lemuel must have wondered why the Lord didn't tell them to obtain the plates before they left. They had little enthusiasm for making the long dangerous journey back to Jerusalem. Their murmuring showed they doubted that God had actually commanded their father to do this.

Lehi had confidence in Nephi because he had not murmured as Laman and Lemuel had (v. 6). He reminded Nephi that it was the Lord, not him, who had commanded the return to Jerusalem (v. 5). People often think a commandment is not really of God when it is given by a servant of the Lord. We should remember the Lord's admonition; "Whether by my voice or by the voice of my servants, it is the same" (D&C 1:38).

Nephi's response to go and do as the Lord had commanded is one of the most famous Book of Mormon quotations. It is another example of faith as a principle of action. While Nephi has been praised for his attitude, and rightfully so, it should not be overlooked that he had seen this same kind of faith expressed in his father's actions (vv. 5–6). He had learned obedience by the precept and example of his father. Many

---

[9] See Curtis H. Wright, "Metallic Documents of Antiquity" BYU Studies, 10:4, Summer 1970, 457–477, and or Paul R. Chessman, "Ancient Writings on Metal Plates," Horizon Publishers, Bountiful, Utah, 1985.

leaders and members of the Church have adopted Nephi's example. President Heber J. Grant said:

> I read the Book of Mormon as a young man and fell in love with Nephi more than any other character in profane or sacred history that I ever read, except the Savior of the world. No other individual has made such a strong impression upon me as Nephi. He has been one of the guiding stars of my life.[10]

All scripture indicates that when a people go with their might to accomplish what God has commanded, success follows. Lehi would obviously rejoice in Nephi's willingness to obey any and all commandments of God (v. 8). Nephi had just returned from speaking with the Lord when Lehi presented to him the commandment to return for the record. However, Lehi did not know of the Lord's visit to Nephi at the time. He apparently recognized that Nephi's faith had now developed to where he would assist him in the work of the Lord. Lehi would no longer be left alone in urging others to obey the Lord. There is an interesting parallel in the life of the young Prophet Joseph Smith.

> When they returned to the house it was between three and four o'clock P.M. Mrs. Whitmer, Mr. Smith and myself were sitting in a bedroom at the same time. On coming in, Joseph threw himself down beside me, and exclaimed, "Father, mother, you do not know how happy I am: the Lord has now caused the plates to be shown to three more besides myself. They have seen an angel, who has testified to them, and they will have to bear witness to the truth of what I have said, for now they know for themselves, that I do not go about to deceive people, and I feel as if I was relieved of a burden which was almost too heavy for me to bear, and it rejoices my soul, that I am not any longer to be entirely alone in the world.[11]

1 Nephi 3:9–13 • Laman Goes Into the House of Laban

9 And I, Nephi, and my brethren took our journey in the wilder-

---

[10] *Improvement Era*, Sept. 1941, 525.

[11] Lucy Smith, *History of Joseph Smith* [1958], 152.

ness, with our tents, to go up to the land of Jerusalem.

10 And it came to pass that when we had gone up to the land of Jerusalem, I and my brethren did consult one with another.

11 And we cast lots—who of us should go in unto the house of Laban. And it came to pass that the lot fell upon Laman; and Laman went in unto the house of Laban, and he talked with him as he sat in his house.

12 And he desired of Laban the records which were engraven upon the plates of brass, which contained the genealogy of my father.

13 And behold, it came to pass that Laban was angry, and thrust him out from his presence; and he would not that he should have the records. Wherefore, he said unto him: Behold thou art a robber, and I will slay thee.

Lehi's sons taking their tents with them suggests that their journey was to be lengthy (v. 9). As the eldest son, Laman would be expected to be the spokesman, but the sons resorted to casting lots (v. 11). Although casting of lots was an ancient custom (see Joshua 18:6, 10; Acts 1:26), the way it was done is unclear. When the lot fell on Laman it gave the right to act to whom it rightfully belonged.

While there is no proof that Lehi was entitled to the records, they did contain his genealogy. The charge that Laman was a robber (v. 13) was without validity since he openly made his request. However, this accusation provided an excuse for Laban to legally slay Laman.

1 Nephi 3:14–21 • Be Faithful
In Keeping the Commandments

14 But Laman fled out of his presence, and told the things which Laban had done, unto us. And we began to be exceedingly sorrowful, and my brethren were about to return unto my father in the wilderness.

15 But behold I said unto them that: As the Lord liveth, and as we live, we will not go down unto our father in the wilderness until we have accomplished the thing which the Lord hath commanded us.

16 Wherefore, let us be faithful in keeping the commandments of the Lord; therefore let us go down to the land of our father's

inheritance, for behold he left gold and silver, and all manner of riches. And all this he hath done because of the commandments of the Lord.

17 For he knew that Jerusalem must be destroyed, because of the wickedness of the people.

18 For behold, they have rejected the words of the prophets. Wherefore, if my father should dwell in the land after he hath been commanded to flee out of the land, behold, he would also perish. Wherefore, it must needs be that he flee out of the land.

19 And behold, it is wisdom in God that we should obtain these records, that we may preserve unto our children the language of our fathers;

20 And also that we may preserve unto them the words which have been spoken by the mouth of all the holy prophets, which have been delivered unto them by the Spirit and power of God, since the world began, even down unto this present time.

21 And it came to pass that after this manner of language did I persuade my brethren, that they might be faithful in keeping the commandments of God.

Having made one good effort, everyone but Nephi was ready to give up the assigned task. Nephi was forced to assert his leadership over his older brothers. He took a serious oath, "as the Lord liveth," to complete their assignment before they return to their father (v. 15). The significance of this oath is shown by the Lord's use of it to affirm to the three witnesses of the Book of Mormon that "[Joseph Smith] has translated the book, even that part which I have commanded him, and as your Lord and your God liveth it is true" (D&C 17:6).[12]

In addition to the oath he had taken, Nephi comes up with an alternate plan, to purchase the plates with his father's riches (v. 16). Perhaps this was one reason why the Lord had commanded Lehi to leave his riches behind. In his foreknowledge, the Lord was leaving Laban without excuse. Nephi then reasons with his brothers to further

---

[12] For further discussion of the seriousness of the oriental oath, see Hugh Nibley's *An Approach to the Book of Mormon*, 109–11.

convince them of why their father had been commanded to flee out of the land (vv. 17–18). They had heard these reasons before, but it set the stage for the real purpose of their return, to get the plates. Nephi gives two purposes for the plates; to preserve for their children the language of their fathers, and to preserve the prophecies of all the holy prophets since the world began (vv. 19–20). His arguments were persuasive.

1 Nephi 3:22–27 • They Went Up Again to the House of Laban

22 And it came to pass that we went down to the land of our inheritance, and we did gather together our gold, and our silver, and our precious things.

23 And after we had gathered these things together, we went up again unto the house of Laban.

24 And it came to pass that we went in unto Laban, and desired him that he would give unto us the records which were engraven upon the plates of brass, for which we would give unto him our gold, and our silver, and all our precious things.

25 And it came to pass that when Laban saw our property, and that it was exceedingly great, he did lust after it, insomuch that he thrust us out, and sent his servants to slay us, that he might obtain our property.

26 And it came to pass that we did flee before the servants of Laban, and we were obliged to leave behind our property, and it fell into the hands of Laban.

27 And it came to pass that we fled into the wilderness, and the servants of Laban did not overtake us, and we hid ourselves in the cavity of a rock.

Laban's reaction to the offer to purchase the records not only left him without excuse, but also showed his depraved character. He was willing to rob and murder to satiate his greed (v. 25). Truly, he was ripe for destruction.

In fleeing from Laban, the brothers head for the wilderness—

probably the area between Jerusalem and the Dead Sea. The area is saturated with caves where they could hide (v. 27). In our day, the famous Dead Sea Scrolls were found in that area.

1 Nephi 3:28–31 • Laman Was Angry With Me and Also With My Father

28 And it came to pass that Laman was angry with me, and also with my father; and also was Lemuel, for he hearkened unto the words of Laman. Wherefore Laman and Lemuel did speak many hard words unto us, their younger brothers, and they did smite us even with a rod.

29 And it came to pass as they smote us with a rod, behold, an angel of the Lord came and stood before them, and he spake unto them, saying: Why do ye smite your younger brother with a rod? Know ye not that the Lord hath chosen him to be a ruler over you, and this because of your iniquities? Behold ye shall go up to Jerusalem again, and the Lord will deliver Laban into your hands.

30 And after the angel had spoken unto us, he departed.

31 And after the angel had departed, Laman and Lemuel again began to murmur, saying: How is it possible that the Lord will deliver Laban into our hands? Behold, he is a mighty man, and he can command fifty, yea, even he can slay fifty; then why not us?

Things had gone wrong. To relieve their frustrations, Laman and Lemuel became angry. An angel appeared to rebuke them for smiting their brothers with a rod. This is another example of faith as a principle of power. While the text makes no specific mention of faith at this time, Nephi had continually expressed his own faith and urged his brothers to be faithful. When a person has done all that he can, his faith is rewarded.

Part of an angel's ministry "is to call men unto repentance, and to fulfil and do the work of the covenants of the Father" (Moroni 7:31). The angel appearing to Laman and Lemuel fit both of these purposes. The angel also informs them that they forfeited their right to family leadership because of iniquities (v. 29). Under the law of primogeniture the eldest son was heir to governmental authority in the family. The matter of family leadership remained a point of contention for the Lamanites in spite of the angel's message (see Mosiah 10:15).

Laman and Lemuel now had a spiritual witness of the mission they were on. To one with faith it seems incredible that Laman and Lemuel could still doubt, but they immediately began to rationalize. They were more impressed with the power of men, Laban and his fifty, than they were with the assurance from an angel that their mission would be a success.

1 Nephi 4:1–4 • Wherefore Can Ye Doubt

1 And it came to pass that I spake unto my brethren, saying: Let us go up again unto Jerusalem, and let us be faithful in keeping the commandments of the Lord; for behold he is mightier than all the earth, then why not mightier than Laban and his fifty, yea, or even than his tens of thousands?

2 Therefore let us go up; let us be strong like unto Moses; for he truly spake unto the waters of the Red Sea and they divided hither and thither, and our fathers came through, out of captivity, on dry ground, and the armies of Pharaoh did follow and were drowned in the waters of the Red Sea.

3 Now behold ye know that this is true; and ye also know that an angel hath spoken unto you; wherefore can ye doubt? Let us go up; the Lord is able to deliver us, even as our fathers, and to destroy Laban, even as the Egyptians.

4 Now when I had spoken these words, they were yet wroth, and did still continue to murmur; nevertheless they did follow me up until we came without the walls of Jerusalem.

Nephi cites two examples of faith as a principle of power. The first was Moses parting of the Red Sea (v. 2), and the second was their visitation by an angel (v. 3). He tried to assure them that the Lord would provide a way for them to obtain the records. Although Moses had lived hundreds of years earlier, Nephi knew of him apparently from his parent's teachings or his own reading. This illustrates another way to develop faith, from the reading of the scriptures. They show us the Lord's dealings with others. In a revelation to the Prophet Joseph

Smith, the Lord said that one of the main purposes of the Book of Mormon was to prove "to the world that the Holy Scriptures are true" (D&C 20:11). The Book of Mormon is a second witness to the authenticity that Moses parted the Red Sea by the power of God (see Exodus 14:21–22). Nephi's reference to the Red Sea's parting is the first of five times it is referred to in the Book of Mormon (see 1 Nephi 17:26–27; Mosiah 7:19; Alma 36:28; Helaman 8:11). The Doctrine and Covenants adds a third witness (D&C 8:3). "In the mouth of two or three witnesses every word may be established" (Matthew 18:16; Deuteronomy 19:15). These witnesses are particularly significant in light of the tendency today to explain these events away as natural occurrences or myths. The acceptance of miracles coming by the power of God can also increase our faith and "make [us] mighty unto the power of deliverance" (1 Nephi 1:20).

There is a difference between compliance and obedience. Laman and Lemuel followed Nephi, but they were complying and murmuring as they did so (v. 4). However, as promised, Nephi was now directing the activities.

1 Nephi 4:5–9 • I Was Led By the Spirit Not Knowing Beforehand

5 And it was by night; and I caused that they should hide themselves without the walls. And after they had hid themselves, I, Nephi, crept into the city and went forth towards the house of Laban.

6 And I was led by the Spirit, not knowing beforehand the things which I should do.

7 Nevertheless I went forth, and as I came near unto the house of Laban I beheld a man, and he had fallen to the earth before me, for he was drunken with wine.

8 And when I came to him I found that it was Laban.

9 And I beheld his sword, and I drew it forth from the sheath thereof; and the hilt thereof was of pure gold, and the workmanship thereof was exceedingly fine, and I saw that the blade thereof was of the most precious steel.

Being led by the Spirit, an example of faith as a principle of action, the promise of the angel was fulfilled. The Lord delivered Laban into Nephi's hands. All the promises of the Lord will be fulfilled if we walk by the Spirit.

Laban's sword was greatly admired by Nephi, who seemed most impressed with the blade of precious steel (v. 9). This sword was to become one of the sacred artifacts of the Nephite nation, and it is still preserved under the care of the Lord. The three witnesses were promised to "have a view of the plates, and also of the breastplate, the sword of Laban, the Urim and Thummim" and the Liahona (D&C 17:1). On 7 September 1878, Orson Pratt and Joseph F. Smith interviewed David Whitmer, one of the three witnesses. He told them: "Joseph, Oliver and myself were together when I saw them (the plates). We not only saw the plates of the Book of Mormon, but also the brass plates, the plates of the Book of Ether . . . and also the sword of Laban, the directors . . . and the interpreters."[13] Nephi took the sword with him when his people separated from the people of Laman (see 2 Nephi 5:14), and it was handed down with the records from generation to generation (see Mosiah 1:16).

1 Nephi 4:10–18 • Never Have I Shed the Blood of Man

10 And it came to pass that I was constrained by the Spirit that I should kill Laban; but I said in my heart: Never at any time have I shed the blood of man. And I shrunk and would that I might not slay him.

11 And the Spirit said unto me again: Behold the Lord hath delivered him into thy hands. Yea, and I also knew that he had sought to take away mine own life; yea, and he would not hearken unto the commandments of the Lord; and he also had taken away our property.

12 And it came to pass that the Spirit said unto me again: Slay him, for the Lord hath delivered him into thy hands;

---

[13] Andrew Jenson, *Historical Record*, 208.

13 Behold the Lord slayeth the wicked to bring forth his righteous purposes. It is better that one man should perish than that a nation should dwindle and perish in unbelief.

14 And now, when I, Nephi, had heard these words, I remembered the words of the Lord which he spake unto me in the wilderness, saying that: Inasmuch as thy seed shall keep my commandments, they shall prosper in the land of promise.

15 Yea, and I also thought that they could not keep the commandments of the Lord according to the law of Moses, save they should have the law.

16 And I also knew that the law was engraven upon the plates of brass.

17 And again, I knew that the Lord had delivered Laban into my hands for this cause—that I might obtain the records according to his commandments.

18 Therefore I did obey the voice of the Spirit, and took Laban by the hair of the head, and I smote off his head with his own sword.

Nephi's reluctance to slay Laban (v. 10) was not disobedience, but a reservation to do what was abhorrent to his nature. The Lord used Nephi's slaying of Laban to teach the law of righteous retaliation to the Saints in the early days of the latter-day Church.

23 Now, I speak unto you concerning your families—if men will smite you, or your families, once, and ye bear it patiently and revile not against them, neither seek revenge, ye shall be rewarded;

24 But if ye bear it not patiently, it shall be accounted unto you as being meted out as a just measure unto you.

25 And again, if your enemy shall smite you the second time, and you revile not against your enemy, and bear it patiently, your reward shall be an hundred fold.

26 And again, if he shall smite you the third time, and ye bear it patiently, your reward shall be doubled unto you four-fold;

27 And these three testimonies shall stand against your enemy if he repent not, and shall not be blotted out.

28 And now, verily I say unto you, if that enemy shall escape my

vengeance, that he be not brought into judgment before me, then ye shall see to it that ye warn him in my name, that he come no more upon you, neither upon your family, even your children's children unto the third and fourth generation.

29 And then, if he shall come upon you or your children, or your children's children unto the third and fourth generation, I have delivered thine enemy into thine hands;

30 And then if thou wilt spare him, thou shalt be rewarded for thy righteousness; and also thy children and thy children's children unto the third and fourth generation.

31 Nevertheless, thine enemy is in thine hands; and if thou rewardest him according to his works thou art justified; if he has sought thy life, and thy life is endangered by him, thine enemy is in thine hands and thou art justified.

32 Behold, this is the law I gave unto my servant Nephi, and thy fathers, Joseph, and Jacob, and Isaac, and Abraham, and all mine ancient prophets and apostles. [D&C 98:23–32]

Three times Laban had reviled against Lehi's sons. First, when Laman went to seek the records for his father, Laban was angry, thrust him out and threatened to slay him (3:13). Second, when they returned and offered to purchase the records, Laban again threatened them and robbed them of their riches (3:25). Third, Laban was not content to take their riches, but sent his servants to slay them (3:26). All three of these offenses are brought to Nephi's mind as he deliberates the Spirit's commandment to slay Laban. The Lord had delivered Laban into his hands (v. 11), the law of the Lord was revealed.

The second time the Spirit tells Nephi to slay Laban, he adds another reason, one usually quoted in defense of Nephi; "it is better that one man should perish than that a nation dwindle and perish in unbelief" (v. 13). This reasoning should not be used alone. The law of the Lord was given twice by the Spirit; "the Lord hath delivered him into thy hands" (vv. 11–12, compare D&C 98:29, 31 above). The Lord had revealed this law to all his "ancient prophets and apostles" (D&C 98:32) to bring about his righteous purposes. The Prophet

"Samuel hewed Agag in pieces before the Lord" (1 Samuel 15:33). The Prophet "Elijah brought [the prophets of Baal] down to the brook Kishon, and slew them there" (1 Kings 18:40). Moses was commanded to "take all the heads of the people [who had joined unto Baal-peor] and hang them up before the Lord" (Numbers 25:1–5). Nevertheless, whatever the Lord's reasons may be, mortal man cannot assume the responsibility to kill for the same reasons.

The Prophet Joseph added a further dimension applicable to the Laban situation:

> That which is wrong under one circumstance, may be, and often is, right under another.
>
> God said, "Thou shalt not kill"; at another time He said, "Thou shalt utterly destroy." This is the principle on which the government of heaven is conducted—by revelation adapted to the circumstances in which the children of the kingdom are placed. Whatever God requires is right, no matter what it is, although we may not see the reason thereof till long after the events transpire. [*TPJS*, 256]

Some may deduce from this statement that truth is relative, but such reasoning is faulty. God understands the eternal and long-range effects of every situation and will always reveal the absolute truth. If the variables are the same, the same directions will be given. However, man is not able to comprehend the variables is as God. When we keep the commandments we comprehend God's reasoning better. Knowledge as a principle of faith unto life and salvation is verified in Nephi's slaying of Laban: "when a man is willing to sacrifice he will know" that the course he is pursuing is the will of the Lord (*Lectures on Faith*, 1:12, 15).

1 Nephi 4:19–29 • I Commanded Him In the Voice of Laban

19 And after I had smitten off his head with his own sword, I took the garments of Laban and put them upon mine own body; yea, even every whit; and I did gird on his armor about my loins.

20 And after I had done this, I went forth unto the treasury of Laban. And as I went forth towards the treasury of Laban, behold, I saw the servant of Laban who had the keys of the treasury. And I commanded him in the voice of Laban, that he should go with me into the treasury.

21 And he supposed me to be his master, Laban, for he beheld the garments and also the sword girded about my loins.

22 And he spake unto me concerning the elders of the Jews, he knowing that his master, Laban, had been out by night among them.

23 And I spake unto him as if it had been Laban.

24 And I also spake unto him that I should carry the engravings, which were upon the plates of brass, to my elder brethren, who were without the walls.

25 And I also bade him that he should follow me.

26 And he, supposing that I spake of the brethren of the church, and that I was truly that Laban whom I had slain, wherefore he did follow me.

27 And he spake unto me many times concerning the elders of the Jews, as I went forth unto my brethren, who were without the walls.

28 And it came to pass that when Laman saw me he was exceedingly frightened, and also Lemuel and Sam. And they fled from before my presence; for they supposed it was Laban, and that he had slain me and had sought to take away their lives also.

29 And it came to pass that I called after them, and they did hear me; wherefore they did cease to flee from my presence.

Armor in this period of time was is sometimes referred to as a coat of mail (1 Samuel 17:5, 38). This was made out of brass for the leaders and leather for the common soldier. This outfit consisted of a breastplate for front and back, and a harness to protect the lower part.[14]

Nephi's going into the treasury is another example of faith as a principle of action. For a young man, an outsider, to enter such a prestigious place was more than presumptuous it was extremely dangerous. Only on the basis of faith would he dare to proceed.

One of the best examples of faith as a principle of power is Nephi's encounter with Zoram, the servant of Laban. Nephi was so convincing in speaking in the voice of Laban that the servant obediently followed him (vv. 20–25). He also conversed freely with Nephi as he carried the plates of brass outside the walls of Jerusalem (v. 27). The time involved and the distance covered could have been quite extensive. Therefore, this was no temporary misidentification, but illustrates how completely convinced the servant was that Nephi was Laban. Furthermore, it is logical that Zoram knew Laban's voice well. It was not until Nephi spoke in his own voice to his frightened brothers, who had also mistaken Nephi for Laban, that the servant realized that Nephi was not Laban (vv. 29–30).

Apparently Nephi's large stature was similar to that of Laban, and in the nighttime darkness the probable great difference in age could not be recognized. What was the secret to Nephi's voice change? Was it not a gift of the Spirit, a form of the gift of tongues, a power poured out on him because of his faith? It was God's will that Nephi obtain the plates of brass, therefore he could bless Nephi, because of his faith, with the ability to sound like Laban.

The Christian world supposes that the church did not exist until the time of the New Testament. The reference to the brethren of the church (v. 26) is evidence that the church did exist at the time of the Old Testament. The New Testament likewise affirms the existence of the Old Testament church. Stephen, the first martyr after Jesus was resurrected, testified that "[Moses] was in the church in the wilderness with the angel which spake to him in the mount Sina, and with our

---

[14] Hastings, *Dictionary of the Bible*, 55.

fathers: who received the living oracles to give unto us" (Acts 7:38). The living oracles are the infallible authority or the keys to minister in the ordinances of the gospel. In our day, Joseph Smith was told:

> 3 Verily I say unto you, the keys of this kingdom shall never be taken from you, while thou art in the world, neither in the world to come;
>
> 4 Nevertheless, through you shall the oracles be given to another, yea, even unto the church. [D&C 90:3–4]

Stephen was apparently referring to a similar occurrence with Moses being given the keys and passing on the oracles to future generations of the church in Old Testament times.

1 Nephi 4:30–38 • Having received Much Strength Of the Lord

> 30 And it came to pass that when the servant of Laban beheld my brethren he began to tremble, and was about to flee from before me and return to the city of Jerusalem.
>
> 31 And now I, Nephi, being a man large in stature, and also having received much strength of the Lord, therefore I did seize upon the servant of Laban, and held him, that he should not flee.
>
> 32 And it came to pass that I spake with him, that if he would hearken unto my words, as the Lord liveth, and as I live, even so that if he would hearken unto our words, we would spare his life.
>
> 33 And I spake unto him, even with an oath, that he need not fear; that he should be a free man like unto us if he would go down in the wilderness with us.
>
> 34 And I also spake unto him, saying: Surely the Lord hath commanded us to do this thing; and shall we not be diligent in keeping the commandments of the Lord? Therefore, if thou wilt go down into the wilderness to my father thou shalt have place with us.
>
> 35 And it came to pass that Zoram did take courage at the words which I spake. Now Zoram was the name of the servant; and he promised that he would go down into the wilderness unto our father. Yea, and he also made an oath unto us that he would tarry with us from that time forth.

36 Now we were desirous that he should tarry with us for this cause, that the Jews might not know concerning our flight into the wilderness, lest they should pursue us and destroy us.

37 And it came to pass that when Zoram had made an oath unto us, our fears did cease concerning him.

38 And it came to pass that we took the plates of brass and the servant of Laban, and departed into the wilderness, and journeyed unto the tent of our father.

Faith as a principle of power is exemplified here. Although large in stature, Nephi received much strength of the Lord (v. 31). Zoram was apparently a righteous man, the situation had not yet been conducive for Nephi to persuade him to come with them, as was obviously the Lord's will. It seems it was necessary to get him outside the walls of the city in order to prevent a scene that would attract the attention of others.

Zoram exercised faith as a principle of action when he promised to go down into the wilderness with them. Once more the binding power of the oath in the ancient world was shown. In addition to the sparing of Zoram's life, Nephi assured him "as the lord liveth" that he would be a free man like unto us" (vv. 32–33). Thus he would no longer be a servant as he had been in the house of Laban. He would have equal status with Nephi and his family. Nephi also informed him that they were doing what the Lord had commanded them to do (v. 34). That Nephi could talk to him in this manner and Zoram responding as he did is another evidence of his being a righteous man. Zoram's willingness to make an oath in return also showed his integrity. Regarding the oath, Dr. Hugh Nibley has written:

> When he (Zoram) saw the brethren and heard Nephi's real voice he got the shock of his life and in a panic made a break for the city. In such a situation there was only one thing Nephi could possibly have done, both to spare Zoram and to avoid giving alarm—and no westerner could have guessed what it was. Nephi, a powerful fellow, held the terrified Zoram in a vice-like grip long enough to swear a solemn oath in his ear, "as the Lord liveth, and as I live" (1 Nephi 4:32), that he would not harm him if he would listen. Zoram immedi-

ately relaxed, and Nephi swore another oath to him that he would be
a free man if he would join the party: 'Therefore, if thou wilt go down
into the wilderness to my father thou shalt have place with us.' [1
Nephi 4:34]

The oath of power: What astonishes the western reader is the
miraculous effect of Nephi's oath on Zoram, who upon hearing a few
conventional words promptly becomes tractable, while as for the
brothers, as soon as Zoram "made an oath unto us that he would tarry
with us from that time forth . . . our fears did cease concerning him."
(1 Nephi 4:35, 37).

The reaction of both parties makes sense when one realizes that
the oath is the one thing that is most sacred and inviolable among the
desert people and their descendants: "Hardly will an Arab break his
oath, even if his life is in jeopardy," for "there is nothing stronger,
and nothing more sacred than the oath among the nomads," and even
the city Arabs, if it be exacted under special conditions. "The taking
of an oath is a holy thing with the Bedouins," says one authority, "Wo
to him who swears falsely; his social standing will be damaged and
his reputation ruined. No one will receive his testimony, and he must
also pay a money fine."

But not every oath will do. To be most binding and solemn an oath
should be by the *life* of something, even if it be but a blade of grass.
The only oath more awful than that "by my life" or (less commonly)
"by the life of my head," is the *wa hayat Allah* "by the life of God,"
or "as the Lord liveth," the exact Arabic equivalent of the ancient
Hebrew *hai Elohim*. . . .

So we see that the only way that Nephi could possibly have
pacified the struggling Zoram in an instant was to utter the one oath
that no man would dream of breaking, the most solemn of all the oaths
to the Semite: "as the Lord liveth, and as I live!" [1 Nephi 4:32] [15]

It was important to take Zoram along because the sons did not want
to be pursued by the Jews (v. 36), but apparently the Lord had other
reasons that were not evident to Nephi. The family of Ishmael, who
were soon to join them, had one more daughter than Lehi had sons,

---

[15] *An Approach to the Book of Mormon* [1957], 109–111.

and Zoram, being a righteous man, would fit well into the Lord's program by marrying the eldest daughter (see 1 Nephi 16:7).

1 Nephi 5:1–9 • My Mother Sariah Had Complained Against My Father

1 And it came to pass that after we had come down into the wilderness unto our father, behold, he was filled with joy, and also my mother, Sariah, was exceedingly glad, for she truly had mourned because of us.

2 For she had supposed that we had perished in the wilderness; and she also had complained against my father, telling him that he was a visionary man; saying: Behold thou hast led us forth from the land of our inheritance, and my sons are no more, and we perish in the wilderness.

3 And after this manner of language had my mother complained against my father.

4 And it had come to pass that my father spake unto her, saying: I know that I am a visionary man; for if I had not seen the things of God in a vision I should not have known the goodness of God, but had tarried at Jerusalem, and had perished with my brethren.

5 But behold, I have obtained a land of promise, in the which things I do rejoice; yea, and I know that the Lord will deliver my sons out of the hands of Laban, and bring them down again unto us in the wilderness.

6 And after this manner of language did my father, Lehi, comfort my mother, Sariah, concerning us, while we journeyed in the wilderness up to the land of Jerusalem, to obtain the record of the Jews.

7 And when we had returned to the tent of my father, behold their joy was full, and my mother was comforted.

8 And she spake, saying: Now I know of a surety that the Lord hath commanded my husband to flee into the wilderness; yea, and I also know of a surety that the Lord hath protected my sons, and delivered them out of the hands of Laban, and given them power whereby they could accomplish the thing which the Lord hath commanded them. And after this manner of language did she speak.

9 And it came to pass that they did rejoice exceedingly, and did

offer sacrifice and burnt offerings unto the Lord; and they gave thanks unto the God of Israel.

Sariah had been an obedient wife even though she had not yet received a spiritual witness of her husband's mission. She had exercised her faith as a principle of action. With the feared loss of her sons, added to the adverse living conditions, she complained against her husband (v. 2). Sariah should not be judged too harshly for her reaction, most would sympathize with her under these conditions. She had passed one of her great tests when she left Jerusalem with her husband. It is reasonable to suppose that as God had foreordained Lehi for his great calling, this noble woman was also foreordained to stand at his side.

The elder sons had previously called their father a visionary man (2:11), now Sariah does the same. Lehi comforted her by bearing testimony that he had indeed seen visions, and he knew that the Lord would deliver his sons out of the hands of Laban (v. 5). Lehi knew that the course he was pursuing was the will of the Lord, and Sariah now received that same assurance. She had faith unto salvation (v. 8). In the spirit of worship and thanksgiving she joins Lehi to "offer sacrifice and burnt offerings" (v. 9). Before only Lehi had made the offering. (2:7). This was again another example of Sariah exercising faith as a principle of action.

1 Nephi 5:10–19 • Lehi Did Search the Records From the Beginning

10 And after they had given thanks unto the God of Israel, my father, Lehi, took the records which were engraven upon the plates of brass, and he did search them from the beginning.

11 And he beheld that they did contain the five books of Moses, which gave an account of the creation of the world, and also of Adam and Eve, who were our first parents;

12 And also a record of the Jews from the beginning, even down to the commencement of the reign of Zedekiah, king of Judah;

13 And also the prophecies of the holy prophets, from the begin-

ning, even down to the commencement of the reign of Zedekiah; and also many prophecies which have been spoken by the mouth of Jeremiah.

14 And it came to pass that my father, Lehi, also found upon the plates of brass a genealogy of his fathers; wherefore he knew that he was a descendant of Joseph; yea, even that Joseph who was the son of Jacob, who was sold into Egypt, and who was preserved by the hand of the Lord, that he might preserve his father, Jacob, and all his household from perishing with famine.

15 And they were also led out of captivity and out of the land of Egypt, by that same God who had preserved them.

16 And thus my father, Lehi, did discover the genealogy of his fathers. And Laban also was a descendant of Joseph, wherefore he and his fathers had kept the records.

17 And now when my father saw all these things, he was filled with the Spirit, and began to prophesy concerning his seed—

18 That these plates of brass should go forth unto all nations, kindreds, tongues, and people who were of his seed.

19 Wherefore, he said that these plates of brass should never perish; neither should they be dimmed any more by time. And he prophesied many things concerning his seed.

Lehi searched the newly acquired records (v. 10). The definition of *search* in this instance is to explore deeply. It is one thing to know that a record is true, but only through searching that record can one find the contents of truth. The contents of the plates were important and are summarized below:

1. The five books of Moses (v. 11) are the first five books of the Old Testament referred to today as the Pentateuch or "The Law." It was originally canonized separately and was regarded as the most authentic of Hebrew scriptures. Its designation as the books of Moses adds credence to the traditional Mosaic authorship that is refuted by many modern scholars. Other passages in the Book of Mormon also support Mosaic authorship (see 2 Nephi 3:17; 3 Nephi 15:4–5; also see Moses 1:40).

2. The record of the Jews down to Zedekiah, king of Judah, about 600 B.C. (v. 12), would include the historical books of Joshua, Judges, Samuel, and Kings to the time of Zedekiah or Lehi. There may have been other books. These books are known as the Former Prophets in the Hebrew publication. The arrangement of the Hebrew Bible is different than the King James Version and other versions.

3. The prophecies of the holy prophets including many of Jeremiah's prophecies (v. 13). In the Hebrew Bible these are known as the Later Prophets (Isaiah, Jeremiah, Ezekiel) and the Twelve Minor Prophets (Hosea through Malachi). Obviously many of these had not been written at the time of Lehi (Ezekiel, and several of the Twelve Prophets), but there were many other prophet's writings included in the brass plates that have been lost (Zenos, Zenoch, Neum, and others. See 1 Nephi 19:10). The Jews continued to keep records after the plates of brass were taken. Evidence of this can be found in the records included in many of today's Bibles.

4. A genealogy of Lehi's fathers (vv. 14–16) was not a separate section, or at least in today's Bibles they are interspersed throughout the other books. Knowing he was a descendant of Joseph, who was sold into Egypt, (v. 14) was undoubtedly a strengthening factor for Lehi as he faced his impending mission. The Lord had used Joseph to accomplish his purposes, and Lehi in turn gained confidence that the Lord was using him to preserve a remnant of the seed of Joseph. As we learn later in the Book of Mormon, Lehi read of the great covenants made to Joseph of a righteous branch being broken off from his seed and preserved (see 2 Nephi 3). As the latter day branch of Joseph, to whom that covenant was also made, we too should be strengthened by the knowledge of this covenant.

Laban most likely lost his assignment to keep the records because of his unworthiness. While there may have been duplicate records, there was probably only one permanent record, the plates of brass. Lehi being a direct descendant of Joseph was entitled to the record (v. 16). Lehi's prophecy that the plates of brass would yet go forth to the people of his seed (v. 18) implies that they will eventually be translated. Faith as a principle of power was exercised by Lehi and his ancestors. They believed the brass plates would be preserved by the power of the Lord (v. 19). Today we continue to exercise this faith as we look forward to the plates of brass being translated and going forth to the seed of Joseph.

1 Nephi 5:20–22 • They Were Desirable and of Great Worth Unto Us

20 And it came to pass that thus far I and my father had kept the commandments wherewith the Lord had commanded us.

21 And we had obtained the records which the Lord had commanded us, and searched them and found that they were desirable; yea, even of great worth unto us, insomuch that we could preserve the commandments of the Lord unto our children.

22 Wherefore, it was wisdom in the Lord that we should carry them with us, as we journeyed in the wilderness towards the land of promise.

As exciting as the future coming forth of these plates is, Nephi reminds us of their value at that time, "to preserve the commandments of the Lord unto our children" (v. 21). As with Nephi, the Lord has promised the restoration of many other records to us in the not too distant future, but more important is the purpose of the ones he has already restored. These were given "to try [our] faith, and if it shall so be that they shall believe these things then shall the greater things be made manifest unto [us]" (3 Nephi 26:9).

THREE PRINCIPLES OF FAITH SUMMARY

Faith As a Principle of Action:

1 Nephi 2:16	Nephi cries unto the Lord to know of the mysteries of God.
1 Nephi 2:17	Sam believes in Nephi's words (and follows Nephi).
1 Nephi 3:7	Nephi agrees to return to Jerusalem to get the plates.
1 Nephi 3:15–21	Nephi persuades his brothers to keep trying to get the plates.
1 Nephi 5:1–6	Sariah has followed Lehi who now comforts her about her sons.
1 Nephi 5:7–9	Sariah joins Lehi in offering sacrifice.

Faith As a Principle of Power:

1 Nephi 2:14	Lehi speaks with power to confound Laman and Lemuel.
1 Nephi 3:24	An angel appears to Laman and Lemuel after they smite Nephi and Sam.
1 Nephi 4:2	Moses spoke and divided the Red Sea.
1 Nephi 4:19–26	Nephi speaks with Zoram in the voice of Laban.
1 Nephi 4:31	Nephi receives strength from the Lord and seizes Zoram.
1 Nephi 5:17–19	Lehi is filled with the Spirit and prophesies.

Faith Unto Salvation—Know the Course
You pursue Is the Will of the Lord:

1 Nephi 2:1–4	Lehi takes his family and departs into the wilderness.
1 Nephi 2:19–24	The Lord speaks to Nephi and promises to lead him to a promised land.
1 Nephi 4:5–18	Nephi is commanded to slay Laban and he does.
1 Nephi 5:8	Sariah knew of a surety the Lord had commanded her husband and protected her sons.

SACRED WRITING

Preaching which is Sacred:

1 Nephi 3:15–20; 4:1–3	Nephi to his brothers regarding obtaining the plates.
1 Nephi 5:4–5	Lehi to Sariah concerning his being a visionary man.

Great revelations:

1 Nephi 2:1–2	Lehi commanded to leave Jerusalem.
1 Nephi 3:2–4	Lehi commanded to send his sons for the plates of brass.
1 Nephi 4:10–17	The Spirit directs Nephi to slay Laban.

Prophesying:

1 Nephi 2:19–24	The Lord foretells the future of Nephi.
1 Nephi 3:29	An angel said Laban will be delivered into their hands.
1 Nephi 5:17–19	Lehi prophecies that the plates of brass will go to all the seed of Joseph and will never perish or be dimmed.

Doctrines Learned:

1 Nephi 2:1–2	Revelation can be given in dreams.
1 Nephi 2:20	The Americas are a choice land of promise above all other lands.
1 Nephi 3:7	The Lord prepares a way to accomplish his purposes.
1 Nephi 3:19–20	Records of God preserve the language and words of prophets.
1 Nephi 3:29	Angels appear to call men to repentance.
1 Nephi 4:11	After three transgressions borne patiently the Lord intervenes.
1 Nephi 4:13	The Lord may slay the wicked to bring about his purposes.

| 1 Nephi 4:26 | The Church of Christ existed in the Old Testament times. |
| 1 Nephi 5:14–15 | The Lord preserved Joseph in Egypt and Israel in the wilderness. |

General Authority Quotes

President David O McKay • 1 Nephi 2:20

Finally, let us be true to our country and to our country's ideals. Nearly three thousand years ago an ancient prophet said that this is a land choice above all other lands (see 1 Nephi 2:20), and it is; and the Constitution of the United States, as given to us by our fathers, is the real government under which individuals may exercise free agency and individual initiative.

Let us oppose any subversive influence that would deprive us of our individual freedom or make this government a dictator instead of a servant to the people. [CR, Oct. 1965, 146]

Elder Marion G. Romney • 1 Nephi 3:7

I am persuaded, my brothers and sisters, that it is irrational to hope to escape the lusts of the world without substituting for them as the subjects of our thoughts the things of the Spirit, and I know that the things of the Spirit are taught with mighty power in the Book of Mormon. I believe with all my heart, for example, that if our young people could come out of our homes thoroughly acquainted with the life of Nephi, imbued with the spirit of his courage and love of truth, they would choose the right when a choice is placed before them.

How marvelous it would be if, when they must make a decision, there would flash into their minds, from long and intimate association with them, the words of Nephi: (Quotes 1 Nephi 3:7). [CR, April 1960]

Challenges to Eternal Life:

1. Pray for the Lord to soften your heart that you may believe and understand his word (1 Nephi 2:16)
2. Commit yourselves to keep the written commandments of God that you may prosper in the land where you live (1 Nephi 2:20).

3. Adopt the philosophy of Nephi to go and do the things that the Lord has commanded through his servants (1 Nephi 3:7).

4. Select a challenge of your own from the principles and doctrine you found in your reading.

Chapter Three

Lehi's Vision

1 Nephi 6–9

Historical Synopsis: The sons of Lehi had just returned to the valley of Lemuel with the plates of brass they had obtained from Laban. After searching the plates, Lehi prophesied concerning his seed. In these chapters, Nephi comments on his father's findings, further instructions for his sons to return to return to Jerusalem to bring back the family of Ishmael, a dream his father had, and the two records he was commanded to keep.

Precept of Chapter Three:

> And I said unto them that it was the word of God; and whoso would hearken unto the word of God, and would hold fast unto it, they would never perish; neither could the temptations and the fiery darts of the adversary overpower them unto blindness, to lead them away to destruction. [1 Nephi 15:24]

The Nephites were a record keeping people. The record we read in 1 Nephi was written thirty years after Lehi and his family left Jerusalem. Nephi abridged his father's record and then wrote his own shorter but more significant account. His record has become known as "the small plates of Nephi." The two records for which Nephi was responsible are mentioned in both chapter six and nine of First Nephi. A teaching outline of the four chapters covered herein is given to prepare for a deeper study.

OUTLINE • 1 NEPHI 6–8

➤ 6:1–6   Nephi does not give his genealogy, just declares they are descendants of Joseph.

a. The genealogy is given in the record kept by his father (vv. 1–3).

1. His father's full account cannot be written on these plates.

2. He desires to write the things of God.

b. Nephi intends to persuade men to come to the God of Abraham, Isaac, and Jacob (vv. 4–6).

1. He does not write the things pleasing to the world, but things pleasing to God.

2. His seed are commanded not to occupy the plates with things of no worth to the children of men.

➤ 7:1–5   The Lord commanded Lehi to send his sons to Jerusalem for Ishmael and his family.

a. His sons were to take wives to raise up seed unto the Lord in the land of promise (v. 1).

b. They visit Ishmael, the Lord softens his heart, and they journey into the wilderness (vv. 4–5).

➤ 7:6–15   As they journey, Laman, Lemuel, two daughters of Ishmael, two sons of Ishmael and their families, rebel against Nephi, Sam, Ishmael, his wife, and his three other daughters.

a. They desire to return to Jerusalem. Nephi speaks to Laman and Lemuel (vv. 7–12).

1. Why are they so hard in their hearts, and blind in their minds that their younger brother has to speak to them and set an example for them?

2. Why have they not hearkened to the Lord, forgotten seeing an angel, and the great things done for them in obtaining the plates from Laban?

3. Why have they forgotten that the Lord is able to do

all things according to his will, if they exercise faith in him.

   b. If faithful, we will obtain the land of promise, and know Jerusalem is destroyed (vv. 13–14).

      1. The Spirit of the Lord soon ceaseth to strive with the Jews in Jerusalem.

      2. The Jews rejected the prophets, and Jeremiah was cast into prison.

   c. The Spirit says if the brothers return to Jerusalem they will perish (v. 15).

➤ 7:16–22   Nephi's brothers bind him with cords, and seek to take his life.

   a. He prays for strength to burst his bands, is loosed and stands before his brothers (vv. 17–18).

   b. The brothers are angry, but one of Ishmael's daughters, her mother, and one son of Ishmael plead with them, and they soften their hearts (v. 19).

   c. The brothers plead with Nephi for forgiveness, and he frankly forgave them (vv. 20–21).

   d. Nephi exhorts them to ask God for forgiveness, and they do (v. 21).

   e. They go to the tent of their father, give thanks, and offer burnt offerings to the Lord (v. 22).

➤ 8:1–20   Lehi's people had gathered seeds of all kinds of grain and fruit.

   a. While Lehi tarried in the wilderness, he had a dream (vv. 2–4).

      1. He saw that Nephi and Sam and many of their seed would be saved.

      2. He feared for Laman and Lemuel because of what he saw.

   b. A man in a white robe bade Lehi to follow him into a dark and dreary waste (vv. 5–10).

       1.   After many hours in darkness, he prayed for mercy.

       2.   He beheld a large and spacious field, and a tree whose fruit was to make one happy.

   c.   Lehi partook of the fruit; it was most sweet above all he had ever tasted (vv. 11–12).

       1.   It was white above all he had ever seen, and filled his soul with exceedingly great joy.

       2.   He was desirous that his family partake, it was desirable above all fruit.

   d.   Lehi looked for his family and saw a river that ran by the tree (vv. 13–18).

       1.   At the head, he saw his wife Sariah, Sam, and Nephi.

       2.   He beckoned them to come and partake of the fruit, and they did.

       3.   He saw that Laman and Lemuel would not come and partake of the fruit.

   e.   Lehi saw a rod of iron along the bank of the river that led to the tree (vv. 19–20).

       1.   A strait and narrow path by the iron rod led to the tree.

       2.   It also led by the head of the fountain to a large and spacious field, as if it had been a world.

➢ 8:21–33   Lehi saw numberless people, many pressing forward to obtain the path to the tree.

   a.   Some started on the path, a mist of darkness arose, they lost their way and were lost (vv. 22–23).

   b.   Others took hold of the rod, clung to it through the darkness, and tasted the fruit (vv. 24–28).

       1.   After they partook, they cast their eyes about as if ashamed.

       2.   Lehi looked and saw a great and spacious building as if in mid-air, above the earth.

       3.   It was filled with people, old and young, male and

female, in fine dress, pointing and mocking those who partook of the fruit.

4. Those who partook were ashamed because of the scoffing. They fell away into forbidden paths.

c. Nephi did not write all his fathers words, but he saw multitudes continually hold to the rod, come to the tree, fall down and partake of the fruit (vv. 29–30).

d. Lehi saw multitudes who felt their way toward the great and spacious building (vv. 31–34).

1. Many were drowned in the depths of the fountain.

2. Many were wandering in strange roads.

3. A great multitude entered into the strange building.

4. They pointed their finger of scorn at those who partook of the fruit.

5. As many as heeded the finger of scorn fell away.

➤ 8:35–38　Laman and Lemuel did not partake, Lehi feared they would be cast off from the presence of the Lord.

a. He exhorts them with all the feelings of a tender parent to hearken to his words (v. 37).

b. After preaching and prophesying, he bade them to keep the commandments of God (v. 38).

➤ 9:1–4　Lehi saw these things, and a great many that cannot be written, as they dwelt in a tent in the valley of Lemuel.

a. The full account of the history is on the other plates, also called the plates of Nephi (v. 2).

b. These plates are written for the special purpose of engraving the ministry of the people (v. 3).

c. The other plates record the reign of the kings, the wars and contentions (v. 4).

➤ 9:5–6　These plates are made for a wise purpose in the Lord, which Nephi does not know.

a. The Lord knows all things from the beginning, and prepares a way to accomplish all his works (v. 6).

b.   The Lord has all power unto the fulfilling of all his
     words (v. 6).

NOTES AND COMMENTARY

Introduction: The majority of the members of The Church of Jesus
Christ of Latter-day Saints are descendants of Joseph who was sold
into Egypt (see Genesis 37), either by lineage or by adoption. A
complete answer to why this is the case and its significance will not
be discussed in this chapter, but the background information will be
established for further study. The Book of Mormon periodically adds
parts of the answer and these will be discussed as they appear in the
book.

1 Nephi 6:1–3 • Lehi and His People are Descendants of Joseph

1 And now I, Nephi, do not give the genealogy of my fathers in
this part of my record; neither at any time shall I give it after upon
these plates which I am writing; for it is given in the record which
has been kept by my father; wherefore, I do not write it in this work.

2 For it sufficeth me to say that we are descendants of Joseph.

3 And it mattereth not to me that I am particular to give a full
account of all the things of my father, for they cannot be written upon
these plates, for I desire the room that I may write of the things of God.

Evidence of Nephi's being a descendant of Joseph is in his father's
record where many other things of his father are recorded (v. 1). Lehi
later told his son Joseph, "great were the covenants of the Lord which
he made to Joseph" (2 Nephi 3:4). After recording one of the prophecies that Lehi quoted to his son Joseph, Nephi told us why Joseph's
prophesies were great; "he truly prophesied concerning all his seed.
And the prophecies which he wrote, there are not many greater. And
he prophesied concerning us, and our future generations; and they are
written upon the plates of brass" (2 Nephi 4:2). Since many members
of The Church of Jesus Christ of Latter-day Saints are part of the future
generations descended from Joseph, they are surely in the prophecies

of Joseph. Such prophecies may be read when those plates "go forth unto all nations, kindreds, tongues, and people who were of his seed" as Lehi prophesied they would (1 Nephi 5:18–19).

However, the fulfillment of one of the basic prophecies about Joseph's seed is recorded in 1 Nephi 7 and is discussed below.

1 Nephi 6:4–6 • The Things Pleasing to God Written by Nephi

> 4 For the fulness of mine intent is that I may persuade men to come unto the God of Abraham, and the God of Isaac, and the God of Jacob, and be saved.
>
> 5 Wherefore, the things which are pleasing unto the world I do not write, but the things which are pleasing unto God and unto those who are not of the world.
>
> 6 Wherefore, I shall give commandment unto my seed, that they shall not occupy these plates with things which are not of worth unto the children of men.

In writing the things of God, Nephi's ultimate desire was to bring his reader to the God of Abraham, Isaac, and Jacob and be saved. The God Nephi speaks of is Christ (see 1 Nephi 19:10). The things of worth written by Nephi are the things that will bring salvation. Those who do not like what Nephi has written are labeling themselves as being of the world. Nephi gives even a harsher castigation as he concludes his writing: "no man will be angry at the words which I have written save he shall be of the spirit of the devil" (2 Nephi 33:5). Jacob was commanded by Nephi to follow the same guidelines as he became the keeper of the records. He was to engraven upon the plates "as much as it were possible, for Christ's sake, and for the sake of the people" (Jacob 1:4).

1 Nephi 7:1–5 • The Sons Return Again to the Land of Jerusalem

> 1 And now I would that ye might know, that after my father, Lehi, had made an end of prophesying concerning his seed, it came to pass

that the Lord spake unto him again, saying that it was not meet for him, Lehi, that he should take his family into the wilderness alone; but that his sons should take daughters to wife, that they might raise up seed unto the Lord in the land of promise.

2 And it came to pass that the Lord commanded him that I, Nephi, and my brethren, should again return unto the land of Jerusalem, and bring down Ishmael and his family into the wilderness.

3 And it came to pass that I, Nephi, did again, with my brethren, go forth into the wilderness to go up to Jerusalem.

4 And it came to pass that we went up unto the house of Ishmael, and we did gain favor in the sight of Ishmael, insomuch that we did speak unto him the words of the Lord.

5 And it came to pass that the Lord did soften the heart of Ishmael, and also his household, insomuch that they took their journey with us down into the wilderness to the tent of our father.

The Lord's commandment for Lehi's sons to return to Jerusalem a second time was to eventually fulfill a blessing given by his father Jacob, who was the father of the twelve tribes of Israel. The blessing given to Joseph was:

22 Joseph *is* a fruitful bough, *even* a fruitful bough by a well; *whose* branches run over the wall:

23 The archers have sorely grieved him, and shot *at him*, and hated him:

24 But his bow abode in strength, and the arms of his hands were made strong by the hands of the mighty *God* of Jacob; (from thence *is* the shepherd, the stone of Israel:)

25 *Even* by the God of thy father, who shall help thee; and by the Almighty, who shall bless thee with blessings of heaven above, blessings of the deep that lieth under, blessings of the breasts, and of the womb:

26 The blessings of thy father have prevailed above the blessings of my progenitors unto the utmost bound of the everlasting hills: they shall be on the head of Joseph, and on the crown of the head of him that was separate from his brethren. [Genesis 49:22–26]

Joseph had two sons, Manasseh and Ephraim. Lehi "was a descendant of Manasseh" (Alma 10:3), and Ishmael was a descendant of Ephraim. The lineage of Ishmael comes from the Book of Lehi, according to Elder Erastus Snow, an earlier member of the Quorum of the Twelve.

> Whoever has read the Book of Mormon carefully will have learned that the remnants of the house of Joseph dwelt upon the American continent; and that Lehi learned by searching the records of his fathers that were written upon the plates of brass, that he was of the lineage of Manasseh. The Prophet Joseph informed us that the record of Lehi, was contained on the 116 pages that were first translated and subsequently stolen, and of which an abridgement is given us in the first Book of Nephi, which is the record of Nephi individually, he himself being of the lineage of Manasseh; but that Ishmael was of the lineage of Ephraim, and that his sons married into Lehi's family, and Lehi's sons married Ishmael's daughters, thus fulfilling the words of Jacob upon Ephraim and Manasseh in the 48th chapter of Genesis which says: "And let my name be on them, and the name of my fathers Abraham and Isaac; and let them grow into a multitude in the midst of the land." Thus these descendants of Manasseh and Ephraim grew together upon this American continent, with a sprinkling from the house of Judah, from Mulek descended, who left Jerusalem eleven years after Lehi, and founded the colony afterwards known as Zarahemla and found by Mosiah—thus making a combination, an intermixture of Ephraim and Manasseh with the remnants of Judah, and for aught we know, the remnants of some other tribes that might have accompanied Mulek. And such have grown up on the American continent. [*Journal of Discourses*, 23:184–185][1]

The Lord was involved in getting the two families together. He softened the heart of Ishmael so he would go into the wilderness (v. 5). Both branches of Joseph, Manasseh, and Ephraim, were brought to the utmost bound of the everlasting hills, the Americas, and became

---

[1] *Journal of Discourses*, 1:184–85. The source of Elder Snow's remarks was apparently the Preface to the First Edition of The Book of Mormon quoted in the end of this section of Notes and Commentary.

very fruitful in posterity. Of course there are many more of the posterity of Joseph that went with the ten tribes into Assyria and the North. The Lord said: "I will sift [scatter] the house of Israel among all nations, like as corn is sifted in a sieve" (Amos 9:8–9), and today they are and have been gathered out of many of those nations.

1 Nephi 7:6–7 • Some Rebel Against Nephi as They Journey in the Wilderness

6 And it came to pass that as we journeyed in the wilderness, behold Laman and Lemuel, and two of the daughters of Ishmael, and the two sons of Ishmael and their families, did rebel against us; yea, against me, Nephi, and Sam, and their father, Ishmael, and his wife, and his three other daughters.

7 And it came to pass in the which rebellion, they were desirous to return unto the land of Jerusalem.

There were at least fifteen adult people in the group returning to the valley of Lemuel. Ishmael and his family consisted of five daughters and two sons, for a total of nine. Lehi's four sons, and at least two daughters, were there from Lehi's family, for a total of six. The five daughters of Ishmael later marry Lehi's four sons and Zoram, the servant of Laban (1 Nephi 16:7). It is assumed all five daughters of Ishmael were adults. Two of Lehi's daughters had previously married Ishmael's two sons, according to Elder Erastus Snow's remarks above.[2] Eight of the adults staged the rebellion. Apparently, Zoram remained with Lehi and Sariah in the valley of Lemuel, probably for his own safety. Counting these three, upon the groups return, Lehi's party would total eighteen adults.

1 Nephi 7:8–15 • Nephi Reasons with His Rebellious Brothers

---

[2] Nephi later refers to his sisters going with him into the wilderness after the death of Lehi (see 2 Nephi 5:6). These sisters may have been born after they left Jerusalem, during the eight years in the wilderness before arriving at the sea they called Irreantum (see 1 Nephi 17:1–6). They did have two sons during this time (see 1 Nephi 18:7).

8 And now I, Nephi, being grieved for the hardness of their hearts, therefore I spake unto them, saying, yea, even unto Laman and unto Lemuel: Behold ye are mine elder brethren, and how is it that ye are so hard in your hearts, and so blind in your minds, that ye have need that I, your younger brother, should speak unto you, yea, and set an example for you?

9 How is it that ye have not hearkened unto the word of the Lord?

10 How is it that ye have forgotten that ye have seen an angel of the Lord?

11 Yea, and how is it that ye have forgotten what great things the Lord hath done for us, in delivering us out of the hands of Laban, and also that we should obtain the record?

12 Yea, and how is it that ye have forgotten that the Lord is able to do all things according to his will, for the children of men, if it so be that they exercise faith in him? Wherefore, let us be faithful to him.

13 And if it so be that we are faithful to him, we shall obtain the land of promise; and ye shall know at some future period that the word of the Lord shall be fulfilled concerning the destruction of Jerusalem; for all things which the Lord hath spoken concerning the destruction of Jerusalem must be fulfilled.

14 For behold, the Spirit of the Lord ceaseth soon to strive with them; for behold, they have rejected the prophets, and Jeremiah have they cast into prison. And they have sought to take away the life of my father, insomuch that they have driven him out of the land.

15 Now behold, I say unto you that if ye will return unto Jerusalem ye shall also perish with them. And now, if ye have choice, go up to the land, and remember the words which I speak unto you, that if ye go ye will also perish; for thus the Spirit of the Lord constraineth me that I should speak.

Nephi is the recorded spokesman in refuting the argumentative brothers. He reminds his two older brothers that it is not his role as the younger brother to censor them, but since they are insensitive to the Lord's will, the Spirit had compelled him to speak. He reminds them of the miraculous experiences that should have convinced them. These incidences confirm once more that spectacular experiences like seeing angels does not necessarily produce faith. However, faith in the Lord's word will lead them to the promised land. His promise of their knowing that Jerusalem was destroyed was later fulfilled when Lehi testified to his sons that he had "seen a vision, in which [he] knew that Jerusalem [was] destroyed." The vision was undoubtedly given because of Nephi's faith as well as Lehi's (2 Nephi 1:4).

"In the commencement of the first year of the reign of Zedekiah, king of Judah . . . their came many prophets" into Jerusalem calling them to repentance (1 Nephi 1:4). Their coming is verified in biblical history.[3] However, the same biblical texts imply that Jeremiah was not imprisoned until just prior to the invasion of Jerusalem by Nebuchadnezzar, king of Babylon, when Zedekiah turned to the Pharaoh of Egypt for help[4] (see Jeremiah 37–38; 2 Chronicles 36; 2 Kings 25). If Jeremiah was not imprisoned until after Lehi left Jerusalem, how did Nephi know he was cast into prison? Perhaps Jeremiah was imprisoned at other times, a likely probability; perhaps Lehi had been shown in vision, as he was later shown the destruction of Jerusalem mentioned above; or perhaps the Spirit had testified to Nephi. We will have to wait until we are given access to the fuller record of Nephi and the plates of brass to know the answer to this question.

---

[3] Moreover all the chief of the priests, and the people, transgressed very much after all the abominations of the heathen; and polluted the house of the LORD which he had hallowed in Jerusalem.

And the LORD God of their fathers sent to them by his messengers, rising up betimes, and sending; because he had compassion on his people, and on his dwelling place:

But they mocked the messengers of God, and despised his words, and misused his prophets, until the wrath of the LORD arose against his people, till *there was* no remedy (2 Chronicles 36:14–16).

[4] Josephus records that Zedekiah served the king of Babylon for eight years before he "revolted to the Egyptians" causing Nebuchadnezzar to come upon Jerusalem in a two year siege and destroy Jerusalem (Book X, chapter VII: 3–4, 218–19). Whiston, William, A.M. Translator *Josephus Complete Works*, Kregel Publications, Grand Rapids, Michigan Seventh Printing, 1970.

1 Nephi 7:16–18 • Nephi Bursts the Bands by His Faith

16 And it came to pass that when I, Nephi, had spoken these words unto my brethren, they were angry with me. And it came to pass that they did lay their hands upon me, for behold, they were exceedingly wroth, and they did bind me with cords, for they sought to take away my life, that they might leave me in the wilderness to be devoured by wild beasts.

17 But it came to pass that I prayed unto the Lord, saying: O Lord, according to my faith which is in thee, wilt thou deliver me from the hands of my brethren; yea, even give me strength that I may burst these bands with which I am bound.

18 And it came to pass that when I had said these words, behold, the bands were loosed from off my hands and feet, and I stood before my brethren, and I spake unto them again.

Nephi's breaking of the bands with which his brothers had bound him is another example of faith as a principle of power. They intended to leave him "in the wilderness to be devoured by wild beasts" (v. 16). Nephi prayed for strength "according to [his] faith." The natural man would ask the Lord to break the bands, or send an angel or someone to loose him. Nephi, the spiritual giant that he was, sought the power through his faith. What a great example this younger brother was to his siblings and to us.

1 Nephi 7:19–22 • Nephi Frankly Forgives His Brothers

19 And it came to pass that they were angry with me again, and sought to lay hands upon me; but behold, one of the daughters of Ishmael, yea, and also her mother, and one of the sons of Ishmael, did plead with my brethren, insomuch that they did soften their hearts; and they did cease striving to take away my life.

20 And it came to pass that they were sorrowful, because of their wickedness, insomuch that they did bow down before me, and did plead with me that I would forgive them of the thing that they had done against me.

21 And it came to pass that I did frankly forgive them all that they had done, and I did exhort them that they would pray unto the Lord their God for forgiveness. And it came to pass that they did so. And after they had done praying unto the Lord we did again travel on our journey towards the tent of our father.

22 And it came to pass that we did come down unto the tent of our father. And after I and my brethren and all the house of Ishmael had come down unto the tent of my father, they did give thanks unto the Lord their God; and they did offer sacrifice and burnt offerings unto him.

After speaking again to his brothers, others of the group, including one daughter,[5] and one son of Ishmael who had been rebellious, came to Nephi's aid verbally (v. 19). Their efforts softened his angry brothers' hearts to the extent that they begged Nephi's forgiveness (v. 20). The character of Nephi is illustrated by his response, "I did frankly forgive them."

This is another great example given us by Nephi, and later taught by the Savior: "forgive us our debts as we forgive our debtors" (3 Nephi 14:11). Was Nephi's admonition to pray for forgiveness a catalyst? It seems so; they not only prayed for forgiveness, but again acknowledged the Lord God and sacrificed unto him as they came to their father's tent (v. 22).

1 Nephi 8:1–2 • Lehi has a Dream or a Vision

1 And it came to pass that we had gathered together all manner of seeds of every kind, both of grain of every kind, and also of the seeds of fruit of every kind.

2 And it came to pass that while my father tarried in the wilderness

---

[5] There were five single daughters of Ishmael, and four sons of Lehi, plus Zoram, the servant of Laban who had joined them. Their purpose in returning to Jerusalem to get Ishmael's family was to get wives to raise up seed unto the Lord (vv. 1–2). Had one of Ishmael's daughters and her mother counted the eligible bachelors, and realized there would be one short if Nephi's life was taken? This seems to be more a probability than a possibility.

he spake unto us, saying: Behold, I have dreamed a dream; or, in other words, I have seen a vision.

Lehi equates his dream with having a vision. Joseph Smith made the same comparison in his work on the New Testament, changing the word dream to vision (see Matthew 1:20, 24; 2:13, 19; JST, Matthew 2:3, 7; 3:12, 19). However, it should be remembered that not all dreams are visions, nor do all visions come in dreams. Dreams are only one mode of receiving revelation. Lehi "was carried away in a vision" as he lay upon his bed in midday (1 Nephi 1:7–8). Nephi later speaks of "things which my father saw in visions and in dreams," the two being mentioned together strongly suggests that some visions were not dreams. It seems that visions that come in dreams must leave an indelible impression upon the mind, not because of its being bizarre or weird, but because of there being a significant message. It should also be remembered that sometimes the message is not discernable until the time of fulfillment.[6]

1 Nephi 8:3–4 • Rejoice in the Lord for Nephi and Sam, Fear for Laman and Lemuel

3 And behold, because of the thing which I have seen, I have reason to rejoice in the Lord because of Nephi and also of Sam; for I have reason to suppose that they, and also many of their seed, will be saved.

4 But behold, Laman and Lemuel, I fear exceedingly because of you; for behold, methought I saw in my dream, a dark and dreary wilderness.

Lehi's mixed reaction represents two great extremes. Rejoicing over Nephi and Sam (v. 3) reminds us of what John the Beloved wrote: "I have no greater joy than to hear that my children walk in truth" (3 John 1:4). In contrast, "the heavens wept" over Lucifer's fall (D&C

---

[6] See Bruce R. McConkie, *Mormon Doctrine*, 2nd ed. [1966], 823–24, for many biblical and modern-day examples of visions and the principles that govern their being received.

76:26–27). How painful it must be to see your own children in jeopardy of their salvation, as represented by Laman and Lemuel being in "a dark and dreary wilderness" (v. 4).

1 Nephi 8:5–10 • A Large and Spacious Field, a Tree Whose Fruit was Desirable

5 And it came to pass that I saw a man, and he was dressed in a white robe; and he came and stood before me.

6 And it came to pass that he spake unto me, and bade me follow him.

7 And it came to pass that as I followed him I beheld myself that I was in a dark and dreary waste.

8 And after I had traveled for the space of many hours in darkness, I began to pray unto the Lord that he would have mercy on me, according to the multitude of his tender mercies.

9 And it came to pass after I had prayed unto the Lord I beheld a large and spacious field.

10 And it came to pass that I beheld a tree, whose fruit was desirable to make one happy.

Lehi's vision was figurative; each object he saw was an image or representation of something else. To understand the vision, the imagery must be identified. The imagery is given piecemeal throughout the next several chapters. Each symbol will be identified as it is mentioned in the text. The chart at the end of the chapter (Figure 3, p. 117) summarizes the imagery. The man in the white robe is never identified nor mentioned after verses five and six. He is obviously angelic. The dark and dreary waste is not identified either, but Lehi beheld Laman and Lemuel in it. He was also in that waste before he prayed. The context suggests it is where the light of truth or understanding is not found. The darkness was dispersed after Lehi sought the mercy of the Lord. Elder Marion D. Hanks has observed:

Only then did [Lehi] taste the inspiration, the soul-filling joy of the love of God. It is likely that all who have effectively served the Lord have had to travel "for the space of many hours in darkness."

The story of Joseph Smith is perhaps best known. As he knelt in prayer, seeking light and knowledge, he was "seized upon by some power" which overcame him. "Thick darkness" gathered around him, and it seemed to him for a time as if he were "doomed to sudden destruction." But He fought and prayed, and after a time the darkness was dispelled, the light shone, and the magnificent visitation followed.[7]

Lehi first sees a large and spacious field. He later sees a path that led "unto a large and spacious field, as if it had been a world" (v. 20). He does not say it is the same field, but it appears to be the same field in both scenes of the vision. The angel asked Nephi "the meaning of the tree of life which thy Father saw?" He said "it is the love of God, which sheddeth itself abroad in the hearts of the children of men; wherefore, it is the most desirable above all things." The angel added: "Yea, and the most joyous to the soul" (1 Nephi 11:21–23). Nephi then beheld that it was the tree of life and "was a representation of the love of God" (1 Nephi 11:25). The fruit of the tree that Lehi said "was desirable to make one happy" (v. 10) was later described by Nephi to his brothers as the "most precious and most desirable above all other fruits; yea, and it is the greatest of all the gifts of God" (1 Nephi 15:36). With this imagery background, the continuing account of Lehi's vision should be more easily understood and appreciated.

1 Nephi 8:11–18 • The Fruit of the Tree, Most Sweet Above All Ever Tasted

11 And it came to pass that I did go forth and partake of the fruit thereof; and I beheld that it was most sweet, above all that I ever before tasted. Yea, and I beheld that the fruit thereof was white, to exceed all the whiteness that I had ever seen.

12 And as I partook of the fruit thereof it filled my soul with exceedingly great joy; wherefore, I began to be desirous that my family should partake of it also; for I knew that it was desirable above all other fruit.

---

[7] *Improvement Era*, May 1961, 321.

13 And as I cast my eyes round about, that perhaps I might discover my family also, I beheld a river of water; and it ran along, and it was near the tree of which I was partaking the fruit.

14 And I looked to behold from whence it came; and I saw the head thereof a little way off; and at the head thereof I beheld your mother Sariah, and Sam, and Nephi; and they stood as if they knew not whither they should go.

15 And it came to pass that I beckoned unto them; and I also did say unto them with a loud voice that they should come unto me, and partake of the fruit, which was desirable above all other fruit.

16 And it came to pass that they did come unto me and partake of the fruit also.

17 And it came to pass that I was desirous that Laman and Lemuel should come and partake of the fruit also; wherefore, I cast mine eyes towards the head of the river, that perhaps I might see them.

18 And it came to pass that I saw them, but they would not come unto me and partake of the fruit.

Lehi's partaking of the fruit and his soul being filled with great joy (v. 12) confirms what was said above about the imagery. His desire for his family to partake was discussed above (vv. 3–4). Being shown which members of his family would partake was possibly so that Lehi would do all in his power to get Laman and Lemuel to partake. Therefore if they did not partake, they were left without excuse. Of course Lehi was desirous for all of his family to partake of the fruit, but the Lord allows everyone to exercise their agency and make their own choices. The river of water that ran near the tree was later explained to Nephi by an angel as a "fountain of filthy water . . . and the depths thereof are the depths of hell" (1 Nephi 12:16). Nephi later told his brothers that his father's mind was so "swallowed up in other things that he beheld not the filthiness of the water" (1 Nephi 15:27). The things that occupied his mind were probably concerning how to persuade Laman and Lemuel to partake.

1 Nephi 8:19–20 • A Rod of Iron that Led to the Tree

> 19 And I beheld a rod of iron, and it extended along the bank of the river, and led to the tree by which I stood.

> 20 And I also beheld a strait and narrow path, which came along by the rod of iron, even to the tree by which I stood; and it also led by the head of the fountain, unto a large and spacious field, as if it had been a world.

More imagery is introduced. Later, Nephi beheld that the rod of iron "was the word of God, which led to the fountain of living waters, or to the tree of life" (1 Nephi 15:25). The fountain of living waters, or the tree of life, must not be confused with the river of water which is also called a fountain (1 Nephi 15:32). Nephi's explanation to his brothers of the iron rod being the word of God (1 Nephi 15:24) is the proposed precept of chapter three and will be commented on later. The book of Revelation uses the same symbolism. John speaks of the faithful ruling over the nations with "a rod of iron" (Revelation 2:26–27).

The Joseph Smith Translation interprets John's promise in the eternal context, having "power over many kingdoms," and "shall rule them with the word of God," confirming Nephi's definition of the "rod of iron" (see the JST text in the LDS Bible appendix p. 812).

The strait and narrow path is not defined, but is the path to the tree of life as will be shown in further analysis of the vision.

There are four classes of people described in the following fourteen verses and are first summarized.

The Four Classes of People

THE ROD OF IRON	END RESULTS	APPLICATION	REFERENCES
Commence in the path but do not take hold.	Mist of darkness (temptations of the devil), lose their way.	Seek other pleasures, world's goods, carnal.	1 Ne. 8:21–23 Matt. 13: 4, 19.

THE ROD OF IRON	END RESULTS	APPLICATION	REFERENCES
Caught the end of the rod, cling thru the mist.	Partake of the fruit, are ashamed, fall in forbidden paths.	Cling to a few scriptures, yield to social pressures. No depths.	1 Ne. 8:24–28 Matt. 13:5–6, 20–21.
Hold the rod, holding fast continually.	Fall down, partake of the fruit.	Hunger and thirst after righteousness, bear fruit, 100, 60, 30.	1 Ne. 8:30 Matt. 13:8, 23.
Feel toward the great & spacious building, many drowned, wander in strange roads.	Many enter the building, finger of scorn at those who partake the fruit.	No interest, do not want to understand, choke the word.	1 Ne. 8:31–33 Matt. 13:7, 22.

Earth → **the path to eternal life** → Heaven   1 Nephi 5:24

Figure 1. The Four Classes of People

1 Nephi 8:21–23 • Commence in the Path, a Mist of Darkness Arises

21 And I saw numberless concourses of people, many of whom were pressing forward, that they might obtain the path which led unto the tree by which I stood.

22 And it came to pass that they did come forth, and commence in the path which led to the tree.

23 And it came to pass that there arose a mist of darkness; yea, even an exceedingly great mist of darkness, insomuch that they who had commenced in the path did lose their way, that they wandered off and were lost.

This is the first of four major classes of people described in Lehi's vision. Note the similarities between the groups described in the vision and the groups described by the Savior, in the Parable of the Sower in the New Testament (Matthew 13:1–23 quoted below). Both sources depict the course of men and their reaction to the word of God or the gospel. They also give the formula for overcoming the pitfalls and reaching the highest goal—eternal life.

> And when he sowed, some *seeds* fell by the way side, and the fowls came and devoured them up (Matthew 13:4)

Jesus interpreted this parable for us.

> 19 When any one heareth the word of the kingdom, and under-standeth *it* not, then cometh the wicked *one,* and catcheth away that which was sown in his heart. This is he which received seed by the way side. [Matthew 13:19]

The seeds that fell by the wayside are symbolically the same as the people who do not take hold iron rod. The fowls that eat the seeds are symbolically the same as the mist of darkness, both being the temptations of the devil.

1 Nephi 8:24–28 • Partake of the Fruit and Are Ashamed

> 24 And it came to pass that I beheld others pressing forward, and they came forth and caught hold of the end of the rod of iron; and they did press forward through the mist of darkness, clinging to the rod of iron, even until they did come forth and partake of the fruit of the tree.
>
> 25 And after they had partaken of the fruit of the tree they did cast their eyes about as if they were ashamed.
>
> 26 And I also cast my eyes round about, and beheld, on the other side of the river of water, a great and spacious building; and it stood as it were in the air, high above the earth.
>
> 27 And it was filled with people, both old and young, both male and female; and their manner of dress was exceedingly fine; and they were in the attitude of mocking and pointing their fingers towards those who had come at and were partaking of the fruit.
>
> 28 And after they had tasted of the fruit they were ashamed, because of those that were scoffing at them; and they fell away into forbidden paths and were lost.

The second group entered the path (were baptized), took hold of the rod (knew and understood some of the scriptures or the gospel), and clung to it through the mist of darkness (the temptations of the devil). To cling suggests that they did not have a real firm hold. They knew some basic principles, but did not continue to build upon their knowledge. They relied on their previous experiences and basic knowledge. After partaking of the fruit, suggesting they had had the Spirit bear witness to them of their basic truths, they were ashamed when the people in the great and spacious building mocked them.

The man in a white robe (angel) also identified the great and spacious building for Nephi. He called it "the world and the wisdom thereof." Nephi then saw and bore record that it was "the pride of the world" (1 Nephi 11:35–36). Still later the angel said it "was the vain imaginations and the pride of the children of men" (1 Nephi 12:18). We will call it the pride and wisdom of the world. Because of the mocking and scoffing of those in the building, the people on the path "fell away into forbidden paths and were lost" (v. 28). Forbidden suggests the breaking of God's commandments. King Benjamin defines sin as "having transgressed the laws of God contrary to [their] own knowledge" (Mosiah 2:34). These people had tasted the fruit and knew what was right. The text says they "were lost" (v. 28). Their eternal fate seems to fit the description of the telestial glory: they "received not the gospel, neither the testimony of Jesus, neither the prophets, neither the everlasting covenant" (D&C 76:101).

The second group, described above, equates with the seeds in the Parable of the Sower that fell on stony ground.

> 5 Some fell upon stony places, where they had not much earth: and forthwith they sprung up, because they had no deepness of earth:
>
> 6 And when the sun was up, they were scorched; and because they had no root, they withered away. [Matthew 13:5–6]

Jesus interpreted these to be those who were ashamed of the pride and wisdom of the world.

> 20 But he that received the seed into stony places, the same is he that heareth the word, and anon with joy receiveth it;

> 21 Yet hath he not root in himself, but dureth for a while: for when tribulation or persecution ariseth because of the word, by and by he is offended. [Matthew 13:20–21]

Perhaps they were returned missionaries, or former priesthood and women's organization leaders who, upon being released, no longer studied, or served, or listened to the counsel of their Church leaders. They rely on what they previously memorized, or learned in former classes. They probably do not remember clearly, and are losing "even that which they have" (2 Nephi 28:30). As they continued their schooling or joined the working world they became ashamed of the word of God because they allowed the beliefs of their new environment to hold precedence over their involvement with the Church Educational System or their own personal study program. They relied on reasoning alone, and did not correlate it with revelation.

1 Nephi 8:29–30 • Continually Holding Fast to the Rod

> 29 And now I, Nephi, do not speak all the words of my father.
>
> 30 But, to be short in writing, behold, he saw other multitudes pressing forward; and they came and caught hold of the end of the rod of iron; and they did press their way forward, continually holding fast to the rod of iron, until they came forth and fell down and partook of the fruit of the tree.

The third group has a firm grasp on the word of God. They continually study, listen to their church leaders, meditate, and increase their knowledge and understanding of the gospel. Therefore they can differentiate between the truth, and the "doctrines of devils, or the commandments of men" (D&C 46:7). Although it is not stated in the text, it is implied that they endure to the end. This group equates with the seed that fell on good ground in the Parable of the Sower.

> 8 But other fell into good ground, and brought forth fruit, some an hundredfold, some sixtyfold, some thirtyfold.
>
> 9 Who hath ears to hear, let him hear. [Matthew 13:8–9]

The concept that some brought forth a hundredfold, some sixtyfold, some thirtyfold is not in Lehi's vision. This concept may suggest the three groups represent the "three heavens or degrees" in the celestial glory (D&C 131:1). Jesus' interpretation ties it to the word of God.

> 23 But he that received seed into the good ground is he that heareth the word, and understandeth *it;* which also beareth fruit, and bringeth forth, some an hundredfold, some sixty, some thirty. [Matthew 13:23]

Note that one must understand as well as hear the word. Also, his answer implies a difference between the bearing of fruit and the bringing forth of fruit. To bear fruit may mean to increase one's own spiritual stature, and to bring forth fruit may mean to be instrumental in helping others to grow in spiritual stature.

Another aspect of bearing and bringing forth fruit may be the doctrine taught by the Prophet Joseph Smith in May of 1843, near the end of his mortal life. To attain the highest degree of the celestial glory, "a man must enter into this order of the priesthood [meaning the new and everlasting covenant of marriage]; And if he does not, he cannot obtain it . . . he cannot have an increase" (D&C 131:1–4). Preceding this revelation the Prophet Joseph taught: "those who are married by the power and authority of the priesthood in this life, and continue without committing the sin against the Holy Ghost, will continue to have children in the celestial glory" (*TPJS*, 301). Jesus may be alluding to this doctrine in the parable, but Lehi was not shown the doctrine of eternal increase at this time because he and his people were not yet prepared to receive it.

1 Nephi 8:31–34 • Those Who Enter into the Strange Building

> 31 And he also saw other multitudes feeling their way towards that great and spacious building.

> 32 And it came to pass that many were drowned in the depths of the fountain; and many were lost from his view, wandering in strange roads.

> 33 And great was the multitude that did enter into that strange building. And after they did enter into that building they did point the finger of scorn at me and those that were partaking of the fruit also; but we heeded them not.
>
> 34 These are the words of my father: For as many as heeded them, had fallen away.

There seems to be several different objectives and destinies represented in the multitudes seen by Lehi in the fourth group. Those feeling their way toward the great and spacious building were probably seeking the wisdom and learning of the world (v. 31). Those drowned in the depths of the fountain were probably those whose action on earth had already determined going to the depths of hell. Those wandering on strange roads (v. 32) were probably different than those who fell into the forbidden paths of the second group. These people did not fall into the depths of hell, but they followed paths that do not lead to eternal life in the celestial kingdom. They may have been seeking salvation through the various philosophies of men. Perhaps they were even "honorable men of the earth, who were blinded by the craftiness of men" (D&C 76:75). The ones who enter the spacious building and point their finger at those who partake of the fruit had been lifted up in pride, and "suppose that [they] are better than [their brethren]" (Jacob 2:13). None of these people ever entered the path (were not baptized by authority), nor had a connection with the rod of iron or the word of God. These multitudes equate with the seeds that fell among thorns in the Parable of the Sower. "And some fell among thorns; and the thorns sprung up, and choked them:" (Matthew 13:7).

The Savior's interpretation was:

> 22 He also that received seed among the thorns is he that heareth the word; and the care of this world, and the deceitfulness of riches, choke the word, and he becometh unfruitful. [Matthew 13:22]

His interpretation fits perfectly the symbolism of the great and spacious building, the pride and wisdom of the world. The Book of Mormon repeatedly associates pride with the obtaining of riches (i.e. Jacob 2:13;

Alma 4:6; 3 Nephi 6:10). It also equates it with learning (see 3 Nephi 6:12). To choke a seed, the sources of growth are cut off: water, soil ingredients, and sunlight. To choke the word of God, the living water of Christ (see John 4:13–14), the bread of life [Christ] (see John 6:35), the light of Christ (see John 9:5), and the Holy Ghost (see John 7:37–39) the sources of spiritual growth are cut off.

The real message portrayed in the vision is the importance of the word of God in leading "to the fountain of living water, or to the tree of eternal life" (1 Nephi 11:25). The four groups of people could also be classified by their studying and listening habits. The first group entered the path (were baptized) and wanted to follow it, but did not make the time to grasp the iron rod (read the scriptures). They spent their time making money, watching TV, and seeking worldly pleasures.

The second group entered the path (were baptized) grasped onto the end of the rod (knew a few scriptures), and clung to it until the world tore away the limited knowledge they had previously grasped. Their beliefs held no depth. They did not return to the rod, but wandered off on the paths of the world.

The fourth group wanted someone else to interpret the scriptures for them. They use the excuse of not understanding, and in their confusion they follow the path that appeals to their carnal or sensual nature. These are they who will not partake. Laman and Lemuel, although possibly baptized, furnish prime examples. "They would neither come unto Lehi nor partake of the fruit" (1 Nephi 8:17–18). They asked Nephi for an interpretation "concerning the things which my father had spoken unto them" (1 Nephi 15:2).

The third group is the only one to receive the greatest of all the gifts of God, eternal life. This group caught hold of the iron rod (read and accepted the word), pressed forward (lived by the teachings of the word of God), continually held fast to the rod (established a habit of studying, pondering and applying), and fell down at the tree and partook of the fruit (were not puffed up with their knowledge, but recognized the condescension of God in their behalf). Nephi's answer to his rebellious brothers shows the eternal effect of holding to the rod:

> 23 What meaneth the rod of iron which our father saw, that led to the tree?
>
> 24 And I said unto them that it was the word of God; and whoso would hearken unto the word of God, and would hold fast unto it, they would never perish; neither could the temptations and the fiery darts of the adversary overpower them unto blindness, to lead them away to destruction. [1 Nephi 15:23–24]

1 Nephi 8:35–38 • Lehi Exhorts Laman and Lemuel As a Tender Parent

> 35 And Laman and Lemuel partook not of the fruit, said my father.
>
> 36 And it came to pass after my father had spoken all the words of his dream or vision, which were many, he said unto us, because of these things which he saw in a vision, he exceedingly feared for Laman and Lemuel; yea, he feared lest they should be cast off from the presence of the Lord.
>
> 37 And he did exhort them then with all the feeling of a tender parent, that they would hearken to his words, that perhaps the Lord would be merciful to them, and not cast them off; yea, my father did preach unto them.
>
> 38 And after he had preached unto them, and also prophesied unto them of many things, he bade them to keep the commandments of the Lord; and he did cease speaking unto them.

Eternal life "is the greatest of all the gifts of God" (D&C 14:7). Those who have tasted of this gift, even though they have not fully eaten, are desirous for their loved ones to partake. This is not only true for Lehi, but also for other parents, bishops, friends, and teachers. Hopefully the people who have righteous leaders concerned for them will understand this concept and appreciate the hopes and prayers spent on their behalf.

1 Nephi 9:1–4 • An Account of the Ministry of My People

1 And all these things did my father see, and hear, and speak, as he dwelt in a tent, in the valley of Lemuel, and also a great many more things, which cannot be written upon these plates.

2 And now, as I have spoken concerning these plates, behold they are not the plates upon which I make a full account of the history of my people; for the plates upon which I make a full account of my people I have given the name of Nephi; wherefore, they are called the plates of Nephi, after mine own name; and these plates also are called the plates of Nephi.

3 Nevertheless, I have received a commandment of the Lord that I should make these plates, for the special purpose that there should be an account engraven of the ministry of my people.

4 Upon the other plates should be engraven an account of the reign of the kings, and the wars and contentions of my people; wherefore these plates are for the more part of the ministry; and the other plates are for the more part of the reign of the kings and the wars and contentions of my people.

Again Nephi reiterates the contents of the two sets of plates that he was commanded to keep. The accompanying chart illustrates the various sets of plates mentioned in the Book of Mormon. Through the years there have been many such charts made and published. This one is simple and intended only as a brief illustration to help new readers (see Figure 2, next page).

1 Nephi 9:5–6 • The Lord Knoweth All Things From the Beginning

5 Wherefore, the Lord hath commanded me to make these plates for a wise purpose in him, which purpose I know not.

6 But the Lord knoweth all things from the beginning; wherefore, he prepareth a way to accomplish all his works among the children of men; for behold, he hath all power unto the fulfilling of all his words. And thus it is. Amen.

Nephi acknowledges that the foreknowledge of God has dictated the keeping of the two records. He did not know the wise purpose of the Lord, but hindsight confirms that the Lord knew that the first 116 pages of Joseph Smith's translations would be lost. He commanded

SMALL PLATES OF NEPHI
First Nephi through Words of Mormon

1 Nephi 5:11–14	Mormon 2:18; 5:9	2 Nephi 27:7
Plates of Brass	**Book of Mormon**	**Sealed Portion**
1. 5 Books of Moses	Book of Mosiah	Revelation from the beginning to the end of the world
2. Record of Jews to Zedekiah	Book of Alma	Ether 3:25 – All the inhabitants of the earth that had been or would be.
3. Prophets to Jeremiah	Book of Helaman	
	Book of Third Nephi	
4. Genealogy	Book of Fourth Nephi	
	24 Gold Plates found by Limhi	
	Book of Ether (abridged by Moroni) Book of Moroni (added)	

Figure 2. Plates of Nephi

Nephi to keep two records, and inspired Mormon to include the small plates as he made an abridgment of Nephi's large plates (see Words of Mormon 1:3–4). The Prophet Joseph tells it in his own words in the preface of the first edition of the Book of Mormon, published in 1830.

To the Reader—

As many false reports have been circulated respecting the following work, and also many unlawful measures taken by evil designing persons to destroy me, and also the work, I would inform you that I translated, by the gift and power of God, and caused to be written, one hundred and sixteen pages, the which I took from the Book of Lehi, which was an account abridged from the plates of Lehi, by the hand of Mormon; which said account, some person or persons have stolen and kept from me, not withstanding my utmost exertions to recover it again—and being commanded of the Lord that I should not translate the same over again, for Satan had put it into their hearts to tempt the Lord their God, by altering the words, that they did read contrary from that which I translated and caused to be written; and if I should bring forth the same words again, or, in other words, if I should translate the same over again, they would publish that which they had stolen, and Satan would stir up the hearts of this generation, that they might not receive this work: but behold, the Lord said unto me, I will not suffer that Satan shall accomplish his evil design in this thing: therefore thou shalt translate from the plates of Nephi, until ye come to that which ye have translated, which ye have retained; and behold ye shall publish it as the record of Nephi; and thus I will confound those who have altered my words. I will not suffer that they shall destroy my work; yea, I will show them that my wisdom is greater than the cunning of the Devil. Wherefore, to be obedient unto the commandments of God, I have, through his grace and mercy, accomplished that which he hath commanded me respecting this thing. I would also inform you that the plates of which hath been spoken, were found in the township of Manchester, Ontario county, New York.

—The Author

Note: The basis of Joseph's Preface is from the Doctrine and Covenants sections three and ten.

SACRED WRITING

Preaching Which Is Sacred:

1 Nephi 7:8–15	Nephi to his brothers regarding their second return to Jerusalem to get the family of Ishmael.

Great Revelations:

1 Nephi 7:1–2	The Lord speaks to Lehi and commands him to send his sons to Jerusalem and bring Ishmael and his family into the wilderness. Lehi's sons were to take Ishmael's daughters to wife and raise up seed unto the Lord in the land of promise.
1 Nephi 8:2–33	Lehi's vision of the tree of life, the people's reaction to the word of God.

Doctrines Learned:

1 Nephi 6:2	The people of Lehi were descendants of Joseph.
1 Nephi 6:4	The God of Abraham, Isaac, and Jacob [Jesus Christ] is the source of salvation (see 1 Nephi 19:10 for the identification of Christ as that God).
1 Nephi 6:5	The Book of Mormon contains things pleasing to God, not the world
1 Nephi 9:5	The Lord knows all things from the beginning.
1 Nephi 9:6	The Lord prepares a way to accomplish his works, and has power to bring it to pass.

General Authority Quotes

The Prophet Joseph Smith • 1 Nephi 6 and 9

I was also informed concerning the aboriginal inhabitants of this country and shown who they were, and from whence they came; a brief sketch of their origin, progress, civilization, laws, governments, of their righteousness and iniquity, and the blessings of God being finally withdrawn from them as a people, was made known to me . . . After having received many visits from the angels of God unfolding the majesty and glory of the events that should transpire in the last days, on the morning of the 22nd of September, A.D. 1827, the angel of the Lord delivered the records into my hands.

These records were engraven on plates which had the appearance of gold, each plate was six inches wide and eight inches long, and not quite so thick as common tin. they were filled with engravings, in Egyptian characters, and bound together in a volume as the leaves of a book, with three rings running through the whole. The volume was something near six inches in thickness, a part of which was sealed. The characters on the unsealed part were small, and beautifully engraved. The whole book exhibited many marks of antiquity in its construction, and much skill in the art of engraving. With the records was found a curious instrument, which the ancients called "Urim and Thummim," which consisted of two transparent stones set in the rim of a bow fastened to a breast plate. Through the medium of the Urim and Thummim I translated the record by the gift and power of God. [*HC*, 4:537]

President Joseph Fielding Smith • 1 Nephi 6:2

There is the fact revealed through the Prophet Joseph Smith, who was of the lineage of Joseph through the loins of Ephraim, that the majority of the people who have been first to receive the gospel and priesthood of the latter-day dispensation, are descendants of some of the house of Ephraim scattered among the nations. . . .

It is clearly shown from these [patriarchal] blessings and the interpretations given to the scriptures that the brethren from the beginning of the Church in these last days believed and taught *that lineage is a matter of blood relationship*. However, if a person should join the Church, and he is a pure Gentile, the prophet has said the old blood would be purged out and he would be grafted into the house of Israel. In such a case the individual could be properly assigned to one of the tribes, probably to Ephraim. [*Doctrines of Salvation*, 3:247–49]

President Harold B. Lee • 1 Nephi 8

As an answer to those who may be wandering aimlessly, searching for something to satisfy their need and to end their state of confusion and emptiness, I would like to introduce a few thoughts by relating a remarkable vision which came to an ancient prophet by the name of Lehi—600 years before Christ. To the faithful members of the Church this will be an oft-related incident recorded in the Book of Mormon. To those not of our faith this may, if they will ponder seriously, be very significant in the light of many trends in our modern society. . . .

As with many other ancient prophets in biblical history, dreams or visions of this nature were effective means by which the Lord communicated with his people through prophet-leaders. . . .

The scorners, so the Lord revealed, represented the so-called wisdom of the world, and the building itself in which they were gathered was the "pride of the world." [see 1 Nephi 11:12]

If there is any one thing most needed in this time of tumult and frustration, when men and women and youth and young adults are desperately seeking for answers to the problems which afflict mankind, it is an "iron rod" as a safe guide along the straight path on the way to eternal life, amidst the strange and devious roadways that would eventually lead to destruction and to the ruin of all that is "virtuous, lovely, or of good report" . . . .

There are many who profess to be religious and speak of themselves as Christians, and, according to one such, "as accepting the scriptures only as sources of inspiration and moral truth," and then ask in their smugness: "Do the revelations of God give us a handrail to the kingdom of God, as the Lord's messenger told Lehi, or merely a compass?"

Unfortunately, some are among us who claim to be Church members but are somewhat like the scoffers in Lehi's vision—standing aloof and seemingly inclined to hold in derision the faithful who choose to accept Church authorities as God's special witnesses of the gospel and his agents in directing the affairs of the Church. . . .

Wouldn't it be wonderful if, when there are questions which are unanswered because the Lord hasn't seen fit to reveal the answers as yet, all such could say, as Abraham Lincoln is alleged to have said, "I accept all I read in the Bible that I can understand, and accept the rest on faith". . . .

Wouldn't it be a great thing if all who are well schooled in secular learning could hold fast to the "iron rod," or the word of God, which could lead them, through faith, to an understanding, rather than to have them stray away into strange paths of man-made theories and be plunged into the murky waters of disbelief and apostasy? [Conference Report, April 1971, 89–91]

Elder Marion D. Hanks • 1 Nephi 8:10–12

How many thousands of times has a father, mother, brother, sister, son or daughter tasted the sweetness of the fruit and at once been moved with the burning desire that " my family should partake of it also"? How many neighbors and true friends? How many missionaries? How many converts? In the early days of the Church the convert of one day became the missionary of the next, and under the stimulation of the same spirit that moved them in those days, the story is the same today. Converts season in the Church a little time and often depart to share with others of God's children, their brothers and sisters, the joy that filled their souls. The receiving and sharing go on, the kingdom rolls forth, the Spirit increases in the earth, the purposes of God for his children are being accomplished. ["Alone in the Moonlight!" *Improvement Era*, April 1961, 239]

Challenges to Eternal Life:

1. Consider some advice you were given by a parent, teacher, or someone that you thought was old fashioned. Was it desirable to make you happy? (1 Nephi 8:12, 37). You may still be able to follow that advice. Write, phone, or tell the person who gave you that advice, thank them and tell them you have been or are going to follow it.

2. Set up a daily or consistent study schedule, and pray for a deeper understanding of the gospel as you do so.

3. In light of the four classes of people represented in Lehi's vision (1 Nephi 8:21–34), make a resolution to continually hold "fast to the iron rod" (v. 30).

4. Choose a challenge or modern message from this reading and apply it to your life.

THE IMAGERY OF LEHI'S VISION

The Image	1 Nephi	The Symbol	1 Nephi Interp.
Man in White Robe	8:5	None	
Dark & Dreary Wilderness or Waste	8:4	None	
Large & Spacious Field	8:9	The World	8:20
Tree (Of Life)	8:10	Love of God	11:21–23, 25
Fruit of the Tree	8:10–11	Greatest Gift of God (Eternal Life)	15:36; 14:7
River of Filthy Water	8:13	Depths of Hell	12:16; 15:27
Rod of Iron	8:19	The Word of God	11:25; 15:24
Strait & Narrow Path	8:20	(To Eternal Life)	2 Nephi 31:17–18
Mist of Darkness	8:23	Temptations of Devil	12:17
Great & Spacious	8:26	Pride & Wisdom of	11:35–36; 12:18
Or Strange Building	8:33	The World	
Forbidden Paths	8:23	(Break Commandments)	12:17 (Mos. 2:34)
Strange Roads	8:32	(Seek Other Ways of Salvation)	D&C 76:75

*Items in parenthesis indicate interpretations from scriptures not directly connected to the vision.

Figure 3. The Imagery of Lehi's Vision

Chapter Four

The Mysteries of God

1 Nephi 10–12

*H*istorical Setting: When Lehi left Jerusalem, "he came down by the borders near the shore of the Red Sea" and "when he had traveled three days journey into the wilderness, he pitched his tent in a valley by the side of a river of water. . . . He called the name of the river, Laman, and it emptied into the Red Sea; and the valley [which he named Lemuel] was in the borders near the mouth thereof" (1 Nephi 2:5–8). The length of time they had spent here is not given, but was considerable since Lehi's sons had made two return trips to Jerusalem; the first to get the plates of brass, and the second to get the family of Ishmael. The things spoken of in these three chapters "were done as [Nephi's] father dwelt in a tent, in the valley of Lemuel" (1 Nephi 10:16), after their return trips to Jerusalem.

Precept of chapter four • 1 Nephi 10:19

19 For he that diligently seeketh shall find; and the mysteries of God shall be unfolded unto them, by the power of the Holy Ghost, as well in these times as in times of old, and as well in times of old as in times to come; wherefore, the course of the Lord is one eternal round.

What is the difference between a mystery and a mystery of God? A mystery is something that the Lord has not revealed unto the children of men. A mystery of God is something that the Lord only reveals to those who are faithful and qualified to receive it. We are admonished to not delve into the mysteries, but we are commanded to diligently seek to understand the mysteries of God. 1 Nephi 8–14 records many mysteries of God that were revealed to Lehi and Nephi. It also contains the formula for how Lehi and Nephi obtained the mysteries of God. Many of these events are, today, historical facts or prophecy fulfilled, but they were originally mysteries of God. An outline of chapters ten through twelve follows in preparation for a deeper study.

OUTLINE • 1 NEPHI 10–12

➤ 10:1   Nephi gives an account of his reign and ministry, but to proceed he must speak of his father and his brethren.

➤ 10:2–11   Lehi speaks concerning the future of the Jews.

    a. After Jerusalem is destroyed and many carried captive to Babylon, they will be brought out of captivity and possess again the land of their inheritance (v. 3).

    b. Six hundred years after Lehi left Jerusalem the Messiah would be raised up among the Jews (vv. 4–6).

        1. Many prophets had testified of the Redeemer of the world.

        2. All men were lost and fallen and ever would be unless they relied on this Redeemer.

    c. A prophet would prepare the way of the Lord (vv. 7–10).

        1. He would baptize with water beyond Jordan and baptize the Messiah.

        2. And bear record of the lamb of God, who would take away the sins of the world.

    d. The gospel would be preached among the Jews, who would dwindle in unbelief (v. 11).

        1. After the Messiah was slain, he would rise from the dead.

        2. He would manifest himself to the Gentiles by the Holy Ghost.

➤ 10:12–14   Lehi spake of the future of the Gentiles and of the house of Israel.

    a. He compared Israel to an olive tree whose branches were broken off and scattered upon all the face of the earth (vv. 12–13).

    b. They would be gathered after the Gentiles had received the fulness of the gospel (v. 14).

        1. The natural branches, or remnants of Israel, would be grafted in.

        2. They would come to the knowledge of the true Messiah, their Redeemer.

➤ 10:15–16   Lehi prophesied many things not written in this book.

    a. Many expedient things were written in Nephi's other book (v. 15).

    b. These things were done as Lehi dwelt in a tent in the valley of Lemuel (v. 16).

➤ 10:17–22   Nephi was desirous to see, hear, and know of the things Lehi saw by the power of the Holy Ghost.

    a. The power of the Holy Ghost comes by faith on the Son of God (vv. 17–19).

        1. It is the gift of God to all those who diligently seek him.

        2. It is the same in times of old as in times to come.

        3. The Holy Ghost is the same yesterday, today, and forever.

        4. The course of the Lord is one eternal round.

    b. Remember all thy doings shall be brought into judgment (vv. 20–21).

        1. If ye seek wickedness, ye are found unclean before the judgment bar.

        2. No unclean thing can dwell with God, but will be cast off.

    c.   The Holy Ghost gave Nephi authority to speak these things, and deny them not (v. 22).

➤ 11:1–12   Nephi is caught away in the Spirit of the Lord and sees the tree his father saw.

    a.   Nephi is blessed because he believes the words of his father and in the Son of the most high God (vv. 4–6).

    b.   Nephi shall be given a sign after he has beheld the tree his father saw (v. 7).

        1.   He shall behold a man descending out of heaven.

        2.   He shall bear record that it is the Son of God.

    c.   The tree exceeded all beauty, the whiteness of driven snow and is precious above all (vv. 8–9).

    d.   Nephi desires to know the interpretation of the tree (vv. 10–12).

        1.   The Spirit was in the form of a man, but it was the Spirit of the Lord.

        2.   The Spirit told him to look and then disappeared.

➤ 11:13–23   Nephi sees Jerusalem, and other cities. He also sees a virgin in the city of Nazareth.

    a.   The heavens open, an angel descends and asks Nephi what he saw? (vv. 14–18).

        1.   He saw a virgin most beautiful and fair above all other virgins.

        2.   The angel asked if he knows the condescension of God.

        3.   Nephi knows God loves his children, but Nephi does not know all things.

        4.   The angel said the virgin is the mother of the Son of God after the flesh.

    b.   Nephi beheld the virgin carried away in the Spirit, and after a time sees her bearing a child in her arms (vv. 19–23).

        1.   The angel identified the child as the Son of the Eternal Father

2. He asked if Nephi knows the meaning of the tree?

3. Nephi says it is the love of God in men's hearts and is desirable above all things.

4. The angel says; yea, and most joyous to the soul.

➤ 11:24–31 Nephi is told to look again and he saw the Son of God going among the children of men, many fell down and worshipped him.

    a. Nephi beheld the rod of iron leads to the tree. It is the word of God (v. 25).

        1. The fountain of living waters represents the love of God

        2. The tree of life also represented the love of God.

    b. The angel invited Nephi to behold the condescension of God (vv. 26–29).

        1. The prophet who is to prepare the way before Him shall baptize the Lamb of God.

        2. The Holy Ghost came down in the form of a dove and abode upon him.

        3. The Lamb of God ministered unto the multitude in power and great glory.

        4. Twelve others followed him and were carried away in the Spirit.

    c. Nephi looks again, he saw angels descend and minister to the people (vv. 30–31).

        1. He saw the sick and afflicted were healed by the power of the Lamb of God.

        2. The devils and the unclean spirits were cast out.

➤ 11:32–36 The angel told Nephi to see the Son of God judged by the world.

    a. He was lifted upon the cross and slain for the sins of the world (v. 33).

    b. After, the multitudes gathered to fight the apostles of the Lamb (vv. 34–35).

      1. The multitudes of the earth gathered into a large and spacious building like Lehi had seen.

      2. The angel identified the spacious building as the world and the wisdom thereof.

      3. The house of Israel gathered to fight against the twelve apostles of the Lamb.

  c. The great and spacious building fell, and the fall was exceedingly great (v. 36).

      1. Nephi saw that it was the pride of the world.

      2. The angel said that all nations, kindreds, tongues, and people that shall fight against the twelve apostles of the Lamb shall be destroyed.

➤ 12:1–5   The angel told Nephi to behold his seed and the seed of his brothers.

  a. He beheld the land of promise and multitudes of people (vv. 1–3).

      1. Multitudes gathered to battle against one another.

      2. There were wars and rumors of wars, and great slaughters with the sword.

      3. Many generations passed away with wars and contentions.

      4. There were many cities, even that he did not number them.

  b. Nephi saw a mist of darkness on the face of the land of promise (vv. 4–5).

      1. There were lightnings, thunderings, earthquakes, and tumultuous noises.

      2. The earth and rocks were rent, mountains tumbled, and the plains were broken up.

      3. Cities were sunk, burned, and tumbled to the earth because of quaking.

      4. The vapor of darkness passed, and multitudes had survived the terrible judgments.

➤ 12:6–12   Nephi saw the heavens open and the Lamb of God descend out of heaven unto the multitude.

     a.   The Holy Ghost fell on twelve who were ordained to minister to Nephi's seed (vv. 7–8).

     b.   The twelve apostles of the Lamb shall judge the twelve tribes of Israel (vv. 9–10).

         1.   The twelve ministers of Nephi's seed shall be judged of them.

         2.   The twelve ministers of Nephi's seed shall judge his seed.

         3.   Because of faith in the Lamb of God, their garments are made white in his blood.

     c.   Nephi saw three generations pass away in righteousness (vv. 11–12).

         1.   Their garments were made white in his blood because of their faith in the Lamb of God.

         2.   Many of the fourth generation passed away in righteousness.

➤ 12:13–22   Nephi saw multitudes of his seed gather to battle against the seed of his brethren.

     a.   The angel identified the fountain of filthy water as the depths of hell (vv. 16–18).

         1.   The mists of darkness represent the temptations of the devil that lead people away.

         2.   The large and spacious building represents the vain imaginations and pride of men.

         3.   A great and terrible gulf divides them, which is the justice of God and the Messiah.

     b.   The seed of Nephi's brethren contend with his seed because of pride and the temptations of the devil (vv. 19–21).

         1.   The seed of his brethren overcome the seed of Nephi.

2. The seed of Nephi's brethren go forth in multitudes upon the face of the land.

3. The multitudes have wars and rumors of wars for many generations.

c. The angel said the multitudes shall dwindle in unbelief (vv. 22–23).

1. Nephi beheld that they became a dark, loathsome, and filthy people.

2. They were full of idleness and all manner of abominations.

NOTES AND COMMENTARY

Introduction: What is different about The Church of Jesus Christ of Latter-day Saints and the other Christian churches? On November 29, 1839 the President of the United States asked the Prophet Joseph Smith this question. Joseph is reported to have answered: "We differ in the mode of baptism and the gift of the Holy Ghost by the laying of hands. We consider that all other considerations were contained in the gift of the Holy Ghost" (*History of the Church*, 4:42). Does the bestowal of this gift guarantee one will be different? No, "A man may receive the Holy Ghost, and it may descend upon him and not tarry with" (D&C 130:23). However, obtaining the "power of the Holy Ghost" is what will make an individual and the Church collectively different. This reading gives valuable insights into obtaining the power of the Holy Ghost.

1 Nephi 10:1 • Nephi's Account of His Reign and Ministry

1 And now I, Nephi, proceed to give an account upon these plates of my proceedings, and my reign and ministry; wherefore, to proceed with mine account, I must speak somewhat of the things of my father, and also of my brethren.

Although Nephi had concluded the abridgment of his father's record, he still relies upon the experiences of the family for this account. Since "thirty years had passed away" when he received the commandment to "Make other plates (the small plates of Nephi)" (2 Nephi 5:28–33), his reference to "my proceedings, and my reign and ministry" would include his personal experiences, his political activities as their leader, and his church leadership. Since the second record was to emphasize the "things of God" (1 Nephi 6:3), the things he included would be of a spiritual nature.

1 Nephi 10:2–6 • Lehi Speaks Concerning the Future of the Jews

2 For behold, it came to pass after my father had made an end of speaking the words of his dream, and also of exhorting them to all diligence, he spake unto them concerning the Jews—

3 That after they should be destroyed, even that great city Jerusalem, and many be carried away captive into Babylon, according to the own due time of the Lord, they should return again, yea, even be brought back out of captivity; and after they should be brought back out of captivity they should possess again the land of their inheritance.

4 Yea, even six hundred years from the time that my father left Jerusalem, a prophet would the Lord God raise up among the Jews—even a Messiah, or, in other words, a Savior of the world.

5 And he also spake concerning the prophets, how great a number had testified of these things, concerning this Messiah, of whom he had spoken, or this Redeemer of the world.

6 Wherefore, all mankind were in a lost and in a fallen state, and ever would be save they should rely on this Redeemer.

Many of the Jews were carried captive into Babylon at the time of the conquest of the Southern Kingdom of Judah in about 589 B.C.[1] There were two waves of Jewish captives taken to Babylon before Jerusalem was destroyed, the first in the third year of Jehoiakim (Daniel 1:1). He reigned for eleven years as king of Judah, the third year would be 609 B.C., Book of Mormon dating, or 606 B.C. traditional dating. The second wave was at the end of Jehoiachin's short three month reign, "and ten thousand captives" were taken. Zedekiah was then made the puppet king of Judah (2 Kings 24:5–17), about 600 B.C. A casual reading may conclude that the Jews were to be taken captive after "that great city Jerusalem" was destroyed, but a more careful reading shows that Lehi was speaking in general terms of the destruction and the captivity as a background for his prophecy that in "the own due time of the Lord [the Jews] would return again" (v. 3).[2]

The great number of prophets who had testified of the Messiah being raised up was probably an enumeration drawn by Lehi from his reading the plates of brass. Jacob, his son, later records: "all the holy prophets which were before us" had a hope of his glory, and none "have written or prophesied save they have spoken concerning this

---

[1] 589 B.C. is according to Book of Mormon dating. 1 Nephi 10:4 states that Lehi left 600 years before the Messiah was born. Although we do not know how long Lehi prophesied to the Jews before he left Jerusalem, it is assumed he left in the first year of Zedekiah, the year of the beginning of the Book of Mormon record (1 Nephi 1:4). There is a discrepancy of three years between the traditional date of Zedekiah's reign as the king of Judah and the Book of Mormon date. The traditional date of Zedekiah's beginning to reign is 597 B.C., which places the destruction of Jerusalem at 586 B.C. instead of 589 B.C. If Lehi prophesied for more than a year it would widen the discrepancy.

[2] Jeremiah records that 832 persons were taken in the 18th year of Nebuchadnezzar, and five years later 745 persons were taken into Babylon (Jeremiah 52: 29–30). One escaped and joined Ezekiel's people in the twelfth year of their captivity "saying the City [Jerusalem] is smitten" Ezekiel 33:21). The 18th year would be just before Jerusalem's destruction. Nebuchadnezzar reigned for about seven years or more while Jehoiakim was king, three months while Jehoiachin was, and eleven years of Zedekiah's reign. Nebuchadnezzar came against Judah in the ninth year of Zedekiah's reign. After a year and a half siege, the city fell and Zedekiah was captured, had his eyes put out, and was carried into Babylon. In the nineteenth year of Nebuchadnezzar, he burned the city (2 Kings 24:1–25:12).

Christ" (Jacob 4:4; 7:11). While still in the valley of Lemuel, where they are now, Nephi learned "that there are many plain and precious things taken away from [the record of the Jews]" by the "great and abominable church," (1 Nephi 13:26–28), and the devil "was the founder of it" (1 Nephi 13:6). Thus the devil was primarily responsible for those losses. A knowledge of the coming of the Messiah would be on the top of his list for deletion. While there are many prophecies still remaining in the Bible,[3] many of them were lost as will be shown later in this work. Lehi is the only prophet who gave an exact time of the savior's birth, six hundred years from the time of his leaving Jerusalem (v. 4). At least there are no prophecies to that effect in our present Bible.

The doctrine of all mankind being "in a lost and fallen state," and therefore in need of a redeemer, is taught throughout the Book of Mormon.[4] The Pearl of Great Price is another testimony to the doctrine of fallen man being known and taught from the day of Adam (see Moses 6:48–62). Of course the doctrine is in the Bible, but has many variant interpretations in the Christian world. The Book of Mormon and the Pearl of Great Price are two witnesses to the correct interpretation.

1 Nephi 10:7–11 • A Prophet to Prepare the Way of the Lord

7 And he spake also concerning a prophet who should come before the Messiah, to prepare the way of the Lord—

8 Yea, even he should go forth and cry in the wilderness: Prepare ye the way of the Lord, and make his paths straight; for there standeth

---

[3] Some of the prophets whose prophecies still remain are: Moses, Deuteronomy 18:15 (see also Acts 3:22–23); Balaam, Numbers 24:15–19; Joshua 5:15–19; Isaiah 7:14; 9:6–7; Jeremiah 23:5–6; Ezekiel 1:26–28; Daniel 10:4–9; Hosea 11:1 (see Matthew 2:15); and Micah 5:1–2. For confirmation of Jacobs declaration of all the prophets knowing of the Messiah see 3 Nephi 20:24; and Moses 6:57–63.

[4] See 2 Nephi 2:4–6; 9:5–6; Mosiah 16:3–6; Alma 12:22; Helaman 14:16; Mormon 9:12–13; and Ether 3:2.

one among you whom ye know not; and he is mightier than I, whose shoe's latchet I am not worthy to unloose. And much spake my father concerning this thing.

9 And my father said he should baptize in Bethabara, beyond Jordan; and he also said he should baptize with water; even that he should baptize the Messiah with water.

10 And after he had baptized the Messiah with water, he should behold and bear record that he had baptized the Lamb of God, who should take away the sins of the world.

11 And it came to pass after my father had spoken these words he spake unto my brethren concerning the gospel which should be preached among the Jews, and also concerning the dwindling of the Jews in unbelief. And after they had slain the Messiah, who should come, and after he had been slain he should rise from the dead, and should make himself manifest, by the Holy Ghost, unto the Gentiles.

The prophet who was to prepare the way before the Messiah was also a doctrine taught in the plates of brass. Isaiah is the obvious source of Lehi's teachings since he uses almost the verbatim language of the present text of Isaiah.[5] However the text quoted by Lehi is much more complete, and it contains the words spoken by John the Baptist at the time of Jesus' baptism (v. 8).[6] This suggests that some plain and precious parts of the text of Isaiah have been lost.

After quoting what Lehi said, Nephi adds some of the other things Lehi taught, where John would baptize, and that he would bear record of having baptized the Lamb of God (vv. 9–10). Bethabara, the place where he would baptize, is confirmed in the Gospel of John: "These things were done in Bethabara beyond Jordan, where John was baptizing" (John 1:28). The other synoptic Gospels give only a general

---

[5] The voice of him that crieth in the wilderness, Prepare ye the way of the LORD, make straight in the desert a highway for our God (Isaiah 40:3).

[6] I indeed baptize you with water unto repentance: but he that cometh after me is mightier than I, whose shoes I am not worthy to bear: he shall baptize you with the Holy Ghost, and *with* fire: (Matthew 3:11; see also Mark 1:7–8; Luke 3:16; and John 1:26–27).

description, i.e. "all the country about Jordan" (Luke 3:3; see also Matthew 3:1 and Mark 1:4–5), which has led to much speculation among scholars.[7] While the location of Bethabara is not known, it does give us a specific area to search out.

The Book of Mormon states that "after he had baptized the Messiah with water, he should behold and bear record that he had baptized the Lamb of God" (v. 10). The Gospel of John states: "The next day John seeth Jesus coming unto him, and saith, Behold the Lamb of God, which taketh away the sin of the world" (John 1:29). Thus the Book of Mormon bears record of the Gospel of John, and the Gospel of John bears record of the Book of Mormon. As Mormon later testified, "if ye believe [the Bible] ye will believe the [Book of Mormon] also" (Mormon 7:9).

The dwindling of the Jews in unbelief [the apostasy], the slaying of the Messiah, and his rising from the dead (v. 11) are historically accurate. The Book of Mormon is again a second witness to these events having been prophesied (see 1 Nephi 19:10, quoted later under 1 Nephi 11:26–29). The Messiah being manifest to the Gentiles by the Holy Ghost (v. 11) is not a personal appearance. As Jesus taught the Nephites when he appeared to them after his resurrection, "the Gentiles should not at any time hear my voice—that I should not manifest myself unto them save it were by the Holy Ghost" (3 Nephi 15:23).

---

[7] Almost all other translations say Bethany instead of Bethabara. They also footnote that it is not the Bethany on the east side of the Mount of Olives, over the hill from Jerusalem, but was probably in the Transjordan or east side of the Jordan River. Bethabara is thought by some to be the crossing point of the Jordan River by the children of Israel under Joshua when they entered the promised land. The Prophet Joseph once stated: "the world will prove Joseph Smith a true prophet by circumstantial evidence" (*TPJS*, 267). The evidence of Bethabara will fall in this category.

[8] Biblical references to sustain his manifestation not being a personal visit are: "Go not by way of the Gentiles. . . . But go rather to the lost sheep of the house of Israel" (Matthew 10:5–6); and "I am not sent but unto the lost sheep of the house of Israel (Matt.15:21–28).

1 Nephi 10:12–16 • Lehi Compares the Gentiles and the House of Israel to an Olive Tree

12 Yea, even my father spake much concerning the Gentiles, and also concerning the house of Israel, that they should be compared like unto an olive-tree, whose branches should be broken off and should be scattered upon all the face of the earth.

13 Wherefore, he said it must needs be that we should be led with one accord into the land of promise, unto the fulfilling of the word of the Lord, that we should be scattered upon all the face of the earth.

14 And after the house of Israel should be scattered they should be gathered together again; or, in fine, after the Gentiles had received the fulness of the Gospel, the natural branches of the olive-tree, or the remnants of the house of Israel, should be grafted in, or come to the knowledge of the true Messiah, their Lord and their Redeemer.

15 And after this manner of language did my father prophesy and speak unto my brethren, and also many more things which I do not write in this book; for I have written as many of them as were expedient for me in mine other book.

16 And all these things, of which I have spoken, were done as my father dwelt in a tent, in the valley of Lemuel.

Lehi's comparison of the house of Israel to an olive tree is evidence that the Prophet Zenos' allegory of the tame and wild olive trees was originally on the plates of brass. Lehi would have had a lot of time to study the plates while his sons made their second return to Jerusalem to get the family of Ishmael (1 Nephi 7). Nephi alludes to Lehi's coming to the knowledge he spoke of above "while dwelling in a tent in the valley of Lemuel" (v. 16). As Jacob, brother of Nephi, recorded the allegory upon the small plates of Nephi he asked: "Behold, my brethren, do ye not remember the words of the prophet Zenos, which he spake unto the house of Israel," (Jacob 5:1). This questions also verifies that the brass plates were available for them to read. However, Jacob 4 addresses "our beloved brethren and our children" as he explains the difficulty of engraving upon the plates. Apparently he was concerned, that the allegory would be among the plain and precious things lost from the record of the Jews, so he did "labor diligently to engraven" them upon the plates of Nephi for future generations (Jacob 4:1–3).

Paul also alludes to the allegory of the olive tree in his writings to the Romans (11:11–27). While some may not agree that Paul was basing his message to the Romans on the allegory, his reference to the Gentiles, the context of his message, and the conclusions he draws are the same as found in the allegory, and the same as drawn by Lehi and illustrated below.

Lehi • 1 Nephi 10	Zenos • Jacob 5	Paul • Romans 11
Broken off and scattered upon all the face of the earth (v. 12).	Nethermost part of my vineyard . . . preserve unto myself the natural branches (v. 13).	Through their fall salvation is come to Gentiles (v. 11).
Land of promise (v. 13).	The last planted in a good spot of ground (v. 25).	Out of Sion [Zion] (v. 26).
After receiving the fullness of the gospel (v. 14).	The end soon cometh, brought forth much fruit, none is good (v. 34).	Blindness until the fullness of Gentiles come in (v. 25).
Come to knowledge of the Messiah (v. 14).	The Lord of the vineyard labored with them . . . preserved unto himself the natural fruit (v. 74).	All Israel saved . . . [by] the Deliverer (v. 26–27).

Figure 4. Allegory of the Olive Tree

While the Spirit may have given all three prophets the same prophecy, it is more probable that Lehi and Paul were relying on Zenos. Both Lehi and Paul help us to interpret the allegory. The branches of Israel will be scattered, they will be gathered after the Gentiles have received the fulness of the gospel (v. 14), and they will all come to the knowledge of the true Messiah.

1 Nephi 10:17–19 • The Power of the Holy Ghost—the Gift of God

17 And it came to pass after I, Nephi, having heard all the words of my father, concerning the things which he saw in a vision, and also the things which he spake by the power of the Holy Ghost, which power he received by faith on the Son of God—and the Son of God was the Messiah who should come—I, Nephi, was desirous also that I might see, and hear, and know of these things, by the power of the Holy Ghost, which is the gift of God unto all those who diligently seek him, as well in times of old as in the time that he should manifest himself unto the children of men.

18 For he is the same yesterday, today, and forever; and the way is prepared for all men from the foundation of the world, if it so be that they repent and come unto him.

19 For he that diligently seeketh shall find; and the mysteries of God shall be unfolded unto them, by the power of the Holy Ghost, as well in these times as in times of old, and as well in times of old as in times to come; wherefore, the course of the Lord is one eternal round.

Nephi bears testimony that Lehi received the power of the Holy Ghost "by faith on the Son of God." Nephi "was desirous also that [he] might see, and hear, and know of these things by the power of the Holy Ghost, which is the gift of God unto all those who diligently seek him" (v. 17). While it may seem presumptuous of Nephi to want to know of the things his father had seen, such desires are not offensive to the Lord. The Prophet Joseph taught: "God hath not revealed anything to Joseph, but what he will make known unto the Twelve, and even the least Saint may know all things as fast as he is able to bear them" (*TPJS*, 149). By diligently seeking, Nephi was living righteously, and thus received a knowledge of the mysteries. As Nephi sat pondering over the things he had heard from his father, he was caught away in the Spirit of the Lord into an exceeding high mountain and was taught by the Spirit. To ponder is to study or weigh spiritually in one's mind. Thus, the formula for obtaining the power of the Holy Ghost, in order to learn the mysteries of God, is to exercise faith and ask God (pray), to diligently seek after God by living worthily to receive revelation (knock), and to ponder in your heart and mind (study) the possible meanings of the experience or scripture. "Ask, and it shall be given unto you; seek, and ye shall find; knock, and it shall be opened unto you" (3 Nephi 14:7; Matthew 7:7).

Nephi further testifies that God is unchanging; and therefore the power of the Holy Ghost has always been, and will always be, the source by which the mysteries of the kingdom can be unfolded (vv. 18–19). Of course these mysteries are not the ones from which we are admonished to refrain, but those God has reserved for the faithful to have revealed to them. "It is given unto many to know the mysteries of God . . . and he that will not harden his heart, to him is given the greater portion of the word, until it is given unto him to know the mysteries of God until he know them in full" (Alma 12:9–10; see also 26:21–22).

1 Nephi 10:20–22 • The Holy Ghost Gave Nephi Authority to Speak These Things

20 Therefore remember, O man, for all thy doings thou shalt be brought into judgment.

21 Wherefore, if ye have sought to do wickedly in the days of your probation, then ye are found unclean before the judgment-seat of God; and no unclean thing can dwell with God; wherefore, ye must be cast off forever.

22 And the Holy Ghost giveth authority that I should speak these things, and deny them not.

The context of the warning given by Nephi seems to be saying that without the power of the Holy Ghost, and a knowledge of the mysteries of God, the natural man is prone to do wickedly and be found unclean at "the judgment-seat of God" (vv. 20–21). If this was not his intent, it is still a true concept. King Benjamin certainly taught this doctrine:

19 For the natural man is an enemy to God, and has been from the fall of Adam, and will be, forever and ever, unless he yields to the enticings of the Holy Spirit, and putteth off the natural man and

becometh a saint through the atonement of Christ the Lord, and becometh as a child, submissive, meek, humble, patient, full of love, willing to submit to all things which the Lord seeth fit to inflict upon him, even as a child doth submit to his father. [Mosiah 3:19]

Nephi had many mysteries unfolded to him and the Holy Ghost gave him authority to record them for our benefit (v. 22). A knowledge of the mysteries revealed to him are certainly needed in the world today and will help us from being cast off.

1 Nephi 11:1–7 • Nephi is Caught Away by the Spirit into an Exceedingly High Mountain

1 For it came to pass after I had desired to know the things that my father had seen, and believing that the Lord was able to make them known unto me, as I sat pondering in mine heart I was caught away in the Spirit of the Lord, yea, into an exceedingly high mountain, which I never had before seen, and upon which I never had before set my foot.

2 And the Spirit said unto me: Behold, what desirest thou?

3 And I said: I desire to behold the things which my father saw.

4 And the Spirit said unto me: Believest thou that thy father saw the tree of which he hath spoken?

5 And I said: Yea, thou knowest that I believe all the words of my father.

6 And when I had spoken these words, the Spirit cried with a loud voice, saying: Hosanna to the Lord, the most high God; for he is God over all the earth, yea, even above all. And blessed art thou, Nephi, because thou believest in the Son of the most high God; wherefore, thou shalt behold the things which thou hast desired.

7 And behold this thing shall be given unto thee for a sign, that after thou hast beheld the tree which bore the fruit which thy father tasted, thou shalt also behold a man descending out of heaven, and him shall ye witness; and after ye have witnessed him ye shall bear record that it is the Son of God.

Nephi met the conditions given him by the angel for him to see what his father had seen. He believed what his father said about having faith on the son of God and the power of the Holy Ghost, and he kept the commandments. His desire to know was accompanied by prayer, and as he sat pondering or studying those thing in his mind he was carried away in the Spirit of the Lord (v. 1). The mountain was unknown to Nephi. Suffice it to say that the Lord often uses mountains to reveal his mysteries when there are no temples. Enoch was told to climb Mount Simeon and while there he "beheld the heavens opened, and (Enoch) was clothed upon with glory" (Moses 7:2–3). "Moses was caught up into an exceedingly high mountain, And he saw God face to face, and he talked with him" (Moses 1:1–2).[9] Jesus took "Peter, James, and John his brother, and bringeth them up into an high mountain apart" and was shown great things (Matthew 17:1–9) "of which account the fulness (we) have not yet received" (D&C 63:21). There were probably many more similar occasions throughout the history of the world.

The sign given to Nephi (v. 7) will be discussed when it is fulfilled (12:6).

1 Nephi 11:8–12 • Nephi Speaks to the Spirit of the Lord as One Man Speaketh to Another

8 And it came to pass that the Spirit said unto me: Look! And I looked and beheld a tree; and it was like unto the tree which my father had seen; and the beauty thereof was far beyond, yea, exceeding of all beauty; and the whiteness thereof did exceed the whiteness of the driven snow.

9 And it came to pass after I had seen the tree, I said unto the Spirit: I behold thou hast shown unto me the tree which is precious above all.

10 And he said unto me: What desirest thou?

---

[9] The account in Moses is more complete than the account found in Exodus. "And the LORD came down upon mount Sinai, on the top of the mount: and the LORD called Moses *up* to the top of the mount; and Moses went up" (Exodus 19:20). Moses also went up several other times (see Exodus 19:3, 8; 20:21; 24:9–10; 32:31;34:4).

11 And I said unto him: To know the interpretation thereof—for I spake unto him as a man speaketh; for I beheld that he was in the form of a man; yet nevertheless, I knew that it was the Spirit of the Lord; and he spake unto me as a man speaketh with another.

12 And it came to pass that he said unto me: Look! And I looked as if to look upon him, and I saw him not; for he had gone from before my presence.

The desire of Nephi to see the tree was granted. What followed is a good example of how revelation comes to mankind. "For behold, thus saith the Lord God: I will give unto the children of men line upon line, precept upon precept, here a little and there a little; and blessed are those who hearken unto my precepts, and lend an ear unto my counsel, for they shall learn wisdom; for unto him that receiveth I will give more" (2 Nephi 28:30). Nephi was given more revelation as the Book of Mormon chapters that follow illustrate.

Who the Spirit was that accompanied Nephi is considered a mystery, something that the Lord has not seen necessary to reveal. Some people become more concerned over who he is than learning from the message that he delivered. Hopefully, without detracting from that message, and with the desire that the mission and power of the Holy Ghost may be further exemplified, the comments of Dr. Sidney B. Sperry are included.

> Two schools of thought prevail among students of the Book of Mormon, and each gives a plausible answer to the problem. One of them holds that the Spirit beheld by Nephi was none other than the pre-existent Christ. Those who adhere to this point of view direct our attention to a precedent which they think should have great weight in convincing one of the correctness of their position. This precedent was the open appearance of our pre-existent Lord of the brother of Jared (Ether 3:13–16). The other school of thought believes that the Spirit of the Lord who talked with Nephi was the Holy Ghost in person.
>
> The resolving of the problem raised here is of great importance, theologically speaking, for if it can be shown that the Spirit that talked to Nephi was the Holy Ghost in person, we may regard 1 Nephi

11:1–11 as the one classical passage in all scripture which testifies of the Holy Ghost as a male personage with whom man may speak face to face. . . .

From 1 Nephi 10:17 we learn that Nephi was so highly impressed with the vision of his father Lehi that he was desirous also to "see, and hear, and know of these things, *by the power of the Holy Ghost.*" (Italics mine.) Notice that Nephi wanted to know by the power of the Holy Ghost. He continues with a discussion about the Holy Ghost (1 Nephi 10:17–21) and ends by saying, "And the Holy Ghost giveth authority that I should speak these things, and deny them not." (1 Nephi 10:22)[10]

Since the entire context is dealing with the Holy Ghost it seems evident that this personage is the Holy Ghost, however, the final answer will come when the Lord is ready to reveal it.

By analyzing the mysteries of God that were revealed to Nephi it will become evident that it is important to share them with the troubled world. Further, it should be more evident of our individual need to obtain the power of the Holy Ghost in our individual lives.

1 Nephi 11:13–23 • Nephi Sees a Virgin in Nazareth Who is the Mother of the Son of God

13 And it came to pass that I looked and beheld the great city of Jerusalem, and also other cities. And I beheld the city of Nazareth; and in the city of Nazareth I beheld a virgin, and she was exceedingly fair and white.

14 And it came to pass that I saw the heavens open; and an angel came down and stood before me; and he said unto me: Nephi, what beholdest thou?

15 And I said unto him: A virgin, most beautiful and fair above all other virgins.

16 And he said unto me: Knowest thou the condescension of God?

17 And I said unto him: I know that he loveth his children; nevertheless, I do not know the meaning of all things.

---

[10] *Answers to Book of Mormon Questions* [1967], 27–30.

18 And he said unto me: Behold, the virgin whom thou seest is the mother of the Son of God, after the manner of the flesh.

19 And it came to pass that I beheld that she was carried away in the Spirit; and after she had been carried away in the Spirit for the space of a time the angel spake unto me, saying: Look!

20 And I looked and beheld the virgin again, bearing a child in her arms.

21 And the angel said unto me: Behold the Lamb of God, yea, even the Son of the Eternal Father! Knowest thou the meaning of the tree which thy father saw?

22 And I answered him, saying: Yea, it is the love of God, which sheddeth itself abroad in the hearts of the children of men; wherefore, it is the most desirable above all things.

23 And he spake unto me, saying: Yea, and the most joyous to the soul.

Nephi's vision of Jerusalem and the other cities may have been to set the scene for what was to come. He names only Jerusalem and Nazareth. He may have done that because he wasn't aware of the other names. Although he lived outside of Jerusalem (v. 13), he had been there to obtain the plates of brass. As discussed earlier, Dr. Hugh B. Nibley's analysis of Lehi being a trader and wide traveler suggests the possibility of Nephi having gone to Nazareth with his father. Another possibility is Nephi's seeing some identification of the city in the vision.

After seeing the cities, there is a change of messengers. In the place of the Spirit he sees an angel descend from the heavens (v. 14). Once more the messenger is not identified. The angel follows a question and answer process similar to the Spirit.

Nephi twice describes the beauty and fairness of the virgin (vv. 13, 15). This is a unique contribution of the Book of Mormon, the New Testament gives no physical description of her. The next question asked by the angel, "Knowest thou the condescension of God?," is centered on the beautiful virgin, but judging from his answer, Nephi does not quite seem to make the connection (v. 15). The angel's identification of her as "the mother of the Son of God, after the manner of the flesh" (v. 18)[11] is followed by Nephi seeing her carried away in the Spirit for a space of time and then he sees her "bearing a child in her arms" (v. 20). The angel now identifies the father of the child: "the Lamb of God, yea, even the Son of the Eternal Father" (v. 21). Thus the question of the condescension of God is answered.

To condescend is to leave a higher plane for a lower or lesser plane. Our Father in Heaven, commonly known as Elohim, was to be the literal father of Jesus Christ, the Lamb of God. He had left his exalted plane of glory to father a child with a mortal woman, Mary, the beautiful virgin "after the manner of the flesh." Thus the explanation given in the New Testament is clarified. The account in Matthew quotes an angel telling Joseph, espoused to Mary, "that which is conceived in her is of the Holy Ghost" (Matthew 1:20). The Luke account has an angel appearing to Mary and telling her, "The Holy Ghost shall come upon thee, and the power of the Highest shall overshadow thee: therefore also that holy thing that shall be born of thee shall be called the Son of God" (Luke 1:35). The New Testament accounts are the equivalent of Nephi seeing the virgin (Mary) carried away in the Spirit, enabling her to conceive the Son of the Eternal Father, or as Alma later prophesies, "she being a virgin, a precious and chosen vessel, who shall be overshadowed and conceive by the power of the Holy Ghost" (Alma 7:10). The manner or method in which she conceived is not told us nor is it necessary to know. Elder Melvin J. Ballard made the following statement:

> Mary told the story most beautifully when she said that an angel
> of the Lord came to her and told her that she had found favor in the

---

[11] The first edition of the text stated: "behold, the virgin whom thou seest is *the mother of God*" but Joseph Smith changed the second edition to read the "*mother of the Son of God.*" The Nephites understood that Christ was the God or the administrator of the Old Testament. Later Nephi proclaimed "there is a God, and he is Christ" (2 Nephi 11:7). Nephi also calls him "the God of Abraham, and of Isaac, and the God of Jacob" (1 Nephi 19:10).

sight of God, and had come to be worthy of the fulfillment of the promises heretofore made, to become the virgin mother of the Redeemer of the world. She afterwards, referring to the event, said: God hath done wonderful things unto me." "And the Holy Ghost came upon her," is the story, "and she came into the presence of the highest." No man or woman can live in mortality and survive the presence of the Highest except by the sustaining power of the Holy Ghost. So it came upon her to prepare her for admittance into the divine presence, and the power of the Highest, who is the Father, was present, and overshadowed her, and the holy Child that was born of her was called the Son of God.

Men who deny this, or who think that it degrades our Father, have no true conception of the sacredness of the most marvelous power with which God has empowered mortal men—the power of creation. Even though that power be abused and may become a mere harp of pleasure to the wicked, nevertheless it is the most sacred and holy and divine function with which God has endowed man. Made holy, it is retained by the Father of us all, and in his exercise of that great and marvelous creative power and function, he did not debase himself, degrade himself, nor debauch his daughter. Thus Christ became the literal Son of a divine Father, and no one else was worthy to be his father.[12]

A parenthetical comment on the above is appropriate. "The mother of the Son of God, after the manner of the flesh" implies that there is a mother after the manner of the spirit as well. Christ was "in the beginning with the Father, and [was] the Firstborn" of the spirits of our Father in Heaven (D&C 93:21). The Bible teaches the same doctrine.[13] A favorite Latter-day Saint hymn, written by Eliza R. Snow, approaches the subject of Heavenly Mother: "In the heavens are parents single? No, the thought makes reason stare! Truth is reason; truth

---

[12] Bryant S. Hinckley, *Sermons and Missionary Services of Melvin Joseph Ballard*, 1949, 167.

[13] Who hath delivered us from the power of darkness, and hath translated *us* into the kingdom of his dear Son: In whom we have redemption through his blood, *even* the forgiveness of sins: Who is the image of the invisible God, the firstborn of every creature (Colossians 1:13–15).

eternal tells me I've a mother there."[14] While she is sometimes credited with (or accused of) teaching this truth as a personal belief, the Book of Mormon, is the original latter-day source of this doctrine.

The angel now comes back to Nephi's original desire, to know the interpretation of the tree. He asks if Nephi now knows the meaning of the tree? (v. 21). Nephi's answer, "Yea, it is the love of God" (v. 22), may seem like the same answer that he gave to the question about the condescension of God, but it is not. His first answer acknowledged the love of God for his children, but he was unsure of his answer (v. 17). The second answer was positive, recognizing the universal love of God for all men. It was being spread abroad, extending his love to all the inhabitants of this earth. The angel confirmed his answer, and its being 'joyous to the soul"(vv. 21–22). Nephi's vision of the coming birth of the Son of God seems to have brought him to the same conclusion as John the Beloved apostle: "For God so loved the world, that he gave his only begotten Son, that whosoever believeth in him should not perish, but have everlasting life" (John 3:16). Lehi saw that the tree produced fruit that was "desirable to make one happy" (1 Nephi 8:10). Nephi later described the fruit as the "most desirable above all other fruits; yea, and it is the greatest of all the gifts of God" (1 Nephi 15:36).

In a revelation to David Whitmer, June 1829, the Lord defined eternal life as "the greatest of all the gifts of God" (D&C 14:7). Thus the tree symbolized eternal life. Nephi's vision of Jerusalem and the other cities had helped him understand the condescension of God. Being the son of the mortal Mary and the immortal Eternal Father would give the Son mortality, the "power to lay it down (his life), and have power (immortality) to take it (up) again" (John 10:18). From his eternal nature, he was able to suffer "even more than man can suffer" (Mosiah 3:7), and thus "make his soul an offering for sin" (Isaiah 53:10; Mosiah 14:10) in the Garden of Gethsemane. Wherefore,

---

[14] "O My Father," *Hymns of the Church of Jesus Christ of Latter-day Saints* [1985], 292.

by his mercy he "redeemed them (mankind), and satisfied the demands of justice" (Mosiah 15:9). Through the power of the Holy Ghost Nephi had been shown the effect of the coming Atonement of Jesus Christ.

1 Nephi 11:24–25 • The Rod of Iron, the Fountain of Living Waters, and the Tree of Life

24 And after he had said these words, he said unto me: Look! And I looked, and I beheld the Son of God going forth among the children of men; and I saw many fall down at his feet and worship him.

25 And it came to pass that I beheld that the rod of iron, which my father had seen, was the word of God, which led to the fountain of living waters, or to the tree of life; which waters are a representation of the love of God; and I also beheld that the tree of life was a representation of the love of God.

Having understood the miraculous birth of Jesus Christ, Nephi is next shown his mortal ministry, "the Son of God going forth among the children of men" (v. 24). Again the central figure is the tree of life, but the iron rod or the word of God is what leads to the living waters, or the tree of life. These both represent the love of God (v. 25). Keep in mind Nephi's definition of the tree of life: "it is the love of God, which sheddeth itself abroad in the hearts of the children of men" (v. 22). As used in Christ's mortal ministry, "sheddeth" means to give off or disperse the word of God to all who will receive it. The word of God leads to the tree of life which produces the fruit. One obtains eternal life through eating the fruit. God's love, therefore, is available to those who will firmly grasp the rod of iron, come to the tree, and eat the fruit.

1 Nephi 11:26–29 • Behold (Again) the Condescension of God

26 And the angel said unto me again: Look and behold the condescension of God!

27 And I looked and beheld the Redeemer of the world, of whom my father had spoken; and I also beheld the prophet who should

prepare the way before him. And the Lamb of God went forth and was baptized of him; and after he was baptized, I beheld the heavens open, and the Holy Ghost come down out of heaven and abide upon him in the form of a dove.

28 And I beheld that he went forth ministering unto the people, in power and great glory; and the multitudes were gathered together to hear him; and I beheld that they cast him out from among them.

29 And I also beheld twelve others following him. And it came to pass that they were carried away in the Spirit from before my face, and I saw them not.

Nephi is again invited to "behold the condescension of God" (v. 26). He had just seen the condescension of Elohim to be the father of his Only Begotten Son in the flesh. He is now invited to see the condescension of the great Jehovah. Jehovah was "the God of [their] fathers, who were led out of Egypt, out of bondage, and also were preserved in the wilderness by him, yea, the God of Abraham, and of Isaac, and the God of Jacob [who] yieldeth himself, according to the words of the angel,[15] as a man, into the hands of wicked men, to be lifted up, according to the words of Zenock, and to be crucified, according to the words of Neum" (1 Nephi 19:10). In other words, Jehovah was the Old Testament name of Jesus Christ, the God who ministered to the people of the earth in his spirit body before he was born.

The Apostle Paul also testified that Christ was the Old Testament God.

1 Moreover, brethren, I would not that ye should be ignorant, how that all our fathers were under the cloud, and all passed through the sea;

2 And were all baptized unto Moses in the cloud and in the sea;

3 And did all eat the same spiritual meat;

---

[15] Nephi's reference to "the words of the angel" shows that everything he was told during his visions was not recorded. He seems to have reflected back on his vision as he is writing about Jesus Christ.

4 And did all drink the same spiritual drink: for they drank of that spiritual Rock that followed them: and that Rock was Christ. [1 Corinthians 10:1–4]

Thus Nephi was shown that God (Jesus Christ) would condescend from Godhood to come down among the children of men, and take upon him flesh and blood.

Nephi saw the baptism of the Lamb of God by John the Baptist (v. 27), of which the New Testament Gospels had testified as discussed under 1 Nephi 10:7–10. Jesus' ministry among the multitudes in power and great glory (v. 28) is not enlarged upon by Nephi, but what he said is a confirmation of the New Testament accounts. The twelve others following him (v. 29) was the pattern for the New Testament and the present dispensation.

13 And he goeth up into a mountain, and calleth *unto him* whom he would: and they came unto him.

14 And he ordained twelve, that they should be with him, and that he might send them forth to preach,

15 And to have power to heal sicknesses, and to cast out devils. [Mark 3:13–15]

The Prophet Joseph Smith was also instructed by the Lord to call twelve apostles to assist in the work of the restoration of the gospel in this latter day.

26 And now, behold, there are others who are called to declare my gospel, both unto Gentile and unto Jew;

27 Yea, even twelve; and the Twelve shall be my disciples, and they shall take upon them my name; and the Twelve are they who shall desire to take upon them my name with full purpose of heart.

28 And if they desire to take upon them my name with full purpose of heart, they are called to go into all the world to preach my gospel unto every creature.

29 And they are they who are ordained of me to baptize in my name, according to that which is written;

30 And you have that which is written before you; wherefore, you

must perform it according to the words which are written. [D&C 18:26–30)

The Twelve latter-day apostles were called and organized on February 14, 1835 (see *HC*, 2:186–189). There have been Twelve special witnesses of the Savior serving from that day to the present time.

1 Nephi 11:30–31 • The Lamb of God Ministers Among the Children of Men

30 And it came to pass that the angel spake unto me again, saying: Look! And I looked, and I beheld the heavens open again, and I saw angels descending upon the children of men; and they did minister unto them.

31 And he spake unto me again, saying: Look! And I looked, and I beheld the Lamb of God going forth among the children of men. And I beheld multitudes of people who were sick, and who were afflicted with all manner of diseases, and with devils and unclean spirits; and the angel spake and showed all these things unto me. And they were healed by the power of the Lamb of God; and the devils and the unclean spirits were cast out.

The ministering of angels (plural) upon the children of men (v. 30) is also a general statement. The New Testament records several specific visits of angels to Jesus and the Lord's chosen vessels around the time of his birth. "The angel of the Lord appeared unto [Joseph, Mary's husband] in a dream" (Matthew 1:20). "There appeared unto [Zacharias, father of John the Baptist] an angel of the Lord," and "the angel came in unto [Mary]" and told her she was "highly favoured" among women (Luke 1:11, 28). "The angel of the Lord came upon [the shepherds]" when Jesus was born (Luke 2:9–12). Prior to Jesus' making the atonement "there appeared an angel unto him, strengthening him" (Luke 22:43), but there are no accounts of them ministering to the people. However it is assumed that they ministered at the blessing of little children, the miraculous feeding of multitudes, and many other occasions. This assumption is based on verse thirty quoted above, and on what happened among the Nephites when Christ appeared (see

3 Nephi 17 & 19). In the Bible either the angels ministered unseen, as they often do, or their ministering was recorded and has been lost through the "plain and precious things taken away from the book" (1 Nephi 13:28).

Nephi also observed the healing power of the Lamb of God (v. 31). Note the two types of healing: the *physically sick,* those with all manner of diseases, and the *spiritually sick,* those having devils and unclean spirits cast out. Both such healings by the power of God are questioned today by the sophisticated intellectual world, but God's power is superior to that of man.

1 Nephi 11:32–36 • The Lamb of God Slain For the Sins of the World

32 And it came to pass that the angel spake unto me again, saying: Look! And I looked and beheld the Lamb of God, that he was taken by the people; yea, the Son of the everlasting God was judged of the world; and I saw and bear record.

33 And I, Nephi, saw that he was lifted up upon the cross and slain for the sins of the world.

34 And after he was slain I saw the multitudes of the earth, that they were gathered together to fight against the apostles of the Lamb; for thus were the twelve called by the angel of the Lord.

35 And the multitude of the earth was gathered together; and I beheld that they were in a large and spacious building, like unto the building which my father saw. And the angel of the Lord spake unto me again, saying: Behold the world and the wisdom thereof; yea, behold the house of Israel hath gathered together to fight against the twelve apostles of the Lamb.

36 And it came to pass that I saw and bear record, that the great and spacious building was the pride of the world; and it fell, and the fall thereof was exceedingly great. And the angel of the Lord spake unto me again, saying: Thus shall be the destruction of all nations, kindreds, tongues, and people, that shall fight against the twelve apostles of the Lamb.

Although Nephi saw the Savior lifted up upon the cross, the visions he was shown were intended to demonstrate what would happen after he was slain. Lehi had already taught Nephi of the crucifixion and resurrection of the Messiah (1 Nephi 10:11–12). Nephi does add that "the Son of the everlasting God was judged of the world,"[16] meaning that he was sentenced to death by worldly standards and not by the standards of God. He does not speak of the illegality or unfairness of the trials, although it is implied. Being slain for the sins of the world is again a general statement for the overall mission of the Savior. His suffering in Gethsemane was "the bitter cup which the Father hath given me[17] . . . taking upon me the sins of the world" (3 Nephi 11:11), but Nephi does not go into detail. The first lesson the angel wanted Nephi to understand was that after the death of Jesus the multitudes would combine to fight against the apostles of the Lamb, those who had been chosen to carry on his work. He was using "fight against" symbolically not literally, although many of the apostles were also later killed. The symbolism is verified by the angel. Nephi was shown the great and spacious building that his father had seen. It was identified as "the world and the wisdom thereof" who had "gathered to fight the twelve apostles of the Lamb" (v. 35). Jesus did not minister to the world, but was sent only "unto the lost sheep of the house of Israel" (Matthew 15:24), and it was the house of Israel who had rejected the teachings of Jesus and his Apostles.

Nephi saw the fall of the great and spacious building, or the pride of the world, and then was taught the third lesson by the angel: "Thus shall be the destruction of all nations, kindreds, tongues, and people, that shall fight against the twelve apostles of the Lamb" (v. 36). This principle is and will always be true.

---

[16] The first edition of the Book of Mormon states "the everlasting God was judged" instead of "the Son of the everlasting God." Joseph Smith apparently added "the Son of" to avoid confusion, but the doctrine is not changed as the Nephites understood that "There is a God, and he is Christ, and he cometh in the fulness of his own time" (2 Nephi 11:7). See also the discussion above on the condescension of Jehovah.

[17] Jesus referred to this cup as he prayed in Gethsemane "O my Father, if it be possible, let this cup pass from me: nevertheless not as I will, but as thou wilt" (Matthew 26:39).

1 Nephi 12:1–5 • Nephi Beholds His
Seed and the Seed of His Brethren

1 And it came to pass that the angel said unto me: Look, and behold thy seed, and also the seed of thy brethren. And I looked and beheld the land of promise; and I beheld multitudes of people, yea, even as it were in number as many as the sand of the sea.

2 And it came to pass that I beheld multitudes gathered together to battle, one against the other; and I beheld wars, and rumors of wars, and great slaughters with the sword among my people.

3 And it came to pass that I beheld many generations pass away, after the manner of wars and contentions in the land; and I beheld many cities, yea, even that I did not number them.

4 And it came to pass that I saw a mist of darkness on the face of the land of promise; and I saw lightnings, and I heard thunderings, and earthquakes, and all manner of tumultuous noises; and I saw the earth and the rocks, that they rent; and I saw mountains tumbling into pieces; and I saw the plains of the earth, that they were broken up; and I saw many cities that they were sunk; and I saw many that they were burned with fire; and I saw many that did tumble to the earth, because of the quaking thereof.

5 And it came to pass after I saw these things, I saw the vapor of darkness, that it passed from off the face of the earth; and behold, I saw multitudes who had not fallen because of the great and terrible judgments of the Lord.

The scene changes, Nephi is shown his seed and the seed of his brethren in the land of promise (the Americas), where they were destined to go. There are actually three scenes, each one covering a different time period, that are shown to Nephi in this chapter. The first scene covers the period from after their arrival in the promised land, through their multiplying exceedingly, until the visit of the Savior in A.D. 34 (vv. 1–10). Many generations represent several hundreds of years. Forty years after leaving Jerusalem they "had already had wars and contentions with [their] brethren" (2 Nephi 5:34). Wars continued periodically throughout the next nearly six hundred years. Nephi's brief summary is appropriate for the time period.

Nephi saw the terrible three-hour storm in the beginning of A.D. 34, followed by three days of darkness (3 Nephi 8:4). The mist of darkness was literal, not the symbolic temptations of the devil in Lehi's dream as later interpreted by the angel (v. 17). However, the darkness over the land just prior to the Savior's visit was brought about by the people previously having yielded to Satan's temptations. Those who survived "the great and terrible destructions of the Lord" were the more righteous. Nephi then gives us a brief but great overview of the Savior's visit.

1 Nephi 12:6–10 • The Lamb of God Descends Among the Righteous Nephites

6 And I saw the heavens open, and the Lamb of God descending out of heaven; and he came down and showed himself unto them.

7 And I also saw and bear record that the Holy Ghost fell upon twelve others; and they were ordained of God, and chosen.

8 And the angel spake unto me, saying: Behold the twelve disciples of the Lamb, who are chosen to minister unto thy seed.

9 And he said unto me: Thou rememberest the twelve apostles of the Lamb? Behold they are they who shall judge the twelve tribes of Israel; wherefore, the twelve ministers of thy seed shall be judged of them; for ye are of the house of Israel.

10 And these twelve ministers whom thou beholdest shall judge thy seed. And, behold, they are righteous forever; for because of their faith in the Lamb of God their garments are made white in his blood.

The sign given to Nephi by the Spirit [Holy Ghost], before the angel becomes his messenger or guide, to "behold a man descending out of heaven" (11:7), is now given (v. 6). Nephi bears record that it is "the Lamb of God." The Spirit had said he would "bear record that it is the Son of God" (11:7).

Nephi bears record that the Holy Ghost fell upon twelve disciples who were chosen and ordained to minister to Nephi's seed (vv. 7–8). Although they are called disciples, probably to distinguish between them and the Jerusalem twelve, they were ordained apostles. The

Prophet Joseph taught: "The book of Mormon tells us that our Savior made His appearance upon this continent after His resurrection; that he planted the gospel here in all its fulness, and richness, and power, and blessing; that they had Apostles, Prophets, Pastors, Teachers, and Evangelists; the same order, the same priesthood the same ordinances, gifts, powers, and blessings that were enjoyed on the eastern continent" (*HC,* 4:538). Moroni also calls them apostles. Quoting the words of Christ to the twelve Nephite disciples; he said, "ye shall give the Holy Ghost; and in my name shall ye give it, for thus do mine apostles" (Moroni 2:2). However, Nephi is shown a distinction between the two apostolic bodies of priesthood. The Jerusalem Twelve will judge (stand as special witnesses) all the house of Israel, and thus they will be judges of the Nephite Twelve; while the Nephite Twelve will only judge the seed of Nephi and his brethren (vv. 9–10). Mormon later enlarges upon the roles of these two priesthood quorums as judges (Mormon 3:17–22).[18] Nephi also observes that the Nephite Twelve "are righteous forever; for because of their faith in the Lamb of God their garments are made white in his blood" (v. 10). This is Nephi's way of saying that their calling and election would be made sure, or they would receive the more sure word of prophecy, or the Second Comforter.[19] In other words, their salvation was assured.

1 Nephi 12:11–12 • Nephi Beholds Three Generations Pass Away in Righteousness

11 And the angel said unto me: Look! And I looked, and beheld three generations pass away in righteousness; and their garments were

---

[18] For further analysis of the Twelve being judges, see Monte S. Nyman, "The Judgment Seat of Christ," chap. 16, 199–213, published in, *The Book of Mormon, Fourth Nephi through Moroni, from Zion to Destruction,* ed. Monte S. Nyman and Charles D. Tate, Religious Study Center, Brigham Young University, 1995.

[19] Joseph Smith said: This doctrine ought (in its proper place) to be taught, for God hath not revealed anything to Joseph, but what he will make known to the Twelve, and even the least Saint may know all things as fast as he is able to bear them (*TPJS,* 149). For a deeper understanding of this doctrine, see *TPJS,* 149–151; 298. See also D&C 131 5–6.

white even like unto the Lamb of God. And the angel said unto me: These are made white in the blood of the Lamb, because of their faith in him.

12 And I, Nephi, also saw many of the fourth generation who passed away in righteousness.

In the second scene, Nephi is now invited to look upon the three generations and part of the fourth following the ministry of Christ among the Nephites. These would also attain eternal life. For some reason there is little said about these generations in the abridgment of the Nephite records. Mormon's abridgment of A.D. 34 to A.D. 320 is a mere four pages in our present Book of Mormon. A generation was considered to be one hundred years. Mormon records "that two hundred years had passed away; and the second generation had all passed away save it were a few" (4 Nephi 1:22). Samuel the Lamanite prophesied that "four hundred years pass not away save the sword of justice falleth upon this people" (Helaman 13:5; see also vv. 6–10). There is a seeming contradiction between what Mormon recorded and what Nephi saw. However, the following should be considered.

Nephi beheld three generations pass away in righteousness (v. 11). As quoted above, Mormon says "two hundred years had passed away; and the second generation had all passed away save it were a few" (4 Nephi 1:22). He then describes the gradual downfall that started in the two hundred and first year, and gradually became worse until "both the people of Nephi and Lamanites had become exceedingly wicked . . . and there were none that were righteous save it were the disciples of Jesus" (4 Nephi 1:45–46). These "disciples" must be the faithful members of the church, not the Twelve. As the pattern of the Nephite society and other societies shows, it is the rising generation that make up the core of those turning to wickedness.[20] During the third genera-

---

[20] Now it came to pass that there were many of the rising generation that could not understand the words of king Benjamin, being little children at the time he spake unto his people; and they did not believe the tradition of their fathers (Mosiah 26:1; see also 1 Nephi 1:29–30).

tion (A.D. 200–300), "there was a great division among the people. . . . there arose a people who were called the Nephites, and they were true believers in Christ" (4 Nephi 1:35–36). Therefore the seed of Nephi and his righteous brothers remained faithful for the third generation. The fourth generation became more and more wicked, but there were still disciples of Jesus into the fourth generation (4 Nephi 1:46 quoted above). The two groups; Nephi's seed and the seed of his brethren continues in the rest of Nephi's vision as will be seen. There is no contradiction between what Nephi saw and what Mormon recorded.

A comment on Mormon's brevity seems appropriate. Many of the blessings given to the Nephites during their Zion society (great period of righteousness), only briefly mentioned in 4 Nephi, were the greater ones that would not be understood by the world, or those first investigating the Church. These blessings include such doctrines as eternal marriage, the law of consecration, and calling and election made sure. Mormon was probably told not to teach about these blessings in his writings. They were left for the Prophet Joseph Smith to teach. Many of them are recorded in the Doctrine and Covenants. President Ezra Taft Benson taught about the importance of using both sets of scriptures. "God bless us all to use all of the scriptures, but in particular the instrument He designed to bring us to Christ—the Book of Mormon, the keystone of our religion—along with its companion volume, the capstone, the Doctrine and Covenants, the instrument to bring us to Christ's kingdom, The Church of Jesus Christ of Latter-day Saints."[21]

1 Nephi 12:13–18 • The People of Nephi's Seed Gather Against the Seed of His Brothers

---

[21] Conference Report, April 1987, 104–108; also published in, *a Witness and a Warning*, chap. 5, The Book of Mormon and the Doctrine and Covenants. It is recommended that the entire chapter be read. The Prophet Joseph labeled the Book of Mormon "the keystone of our religion," but Pres. Benson coined the phrase "the capstone."

13 And it came to pass that I saw the multitudes of the earth gathered together.

14 And the angel said unto me: Behold thy seed, and also the seed of thy brethren.

15 And it came to pass that I looked and beheld the people of my seed gathered together in multitudes against the seed of my brethren; and they were gathered together to battle.

16 And the angel spake unto me, saying: Behold the fountain of filthy water which thy father saw; yea, even the river of which he spake; and the depths thereof are the depths of hell.

17 And the mists of darkness are the temptations of the devil, which blindeth the eyes, and hardeneth the hearts of the children of men, and leadeth them away into broad roads, that they perish and are lost.

18 And the large and spacious building, which thy father saw, is vain imaginations and the pride of the children of men. And a great and a terrible gulf divideth them; yea, even the word of the justice of the Eternal God, and the Messiah who is the Lamb of God, of whom the Holy Ghost beareth record, from the beginning of the world until this time, and from this time henceforth and forever.

The third scene shown to Nephi by the angel is the time period of the destruction of his brethren in the fourth generation (of one hundred years) following Christ's ministry, and the many generations that followed. The angel's clarifications of the vision given to father Lehi were discussed previously and so will not be repeated here, but are certainly pertinent to what happened to Nephi's people. This is implied in the last of verse eighteen, and the following verses.

1 Nephi 12:19–23 • The Seed of Nephi's Brothers Overpower the Seed of Nephi

19 And while the angel spake these words, I beheld and saw that the seed of my brethren did contend against my seed, according to the word of the angel; and because of the pride of my seed, and the temptations of the devil, I beheld that the seed of my brethren did overpower the people of my seed.

20 And it came to pass that I beheld, and saw the people of the seed of my brethren that they had overcome my seed; and they went forth in multitudes upon the face of the land.

21 And I saw them gathered together in multitudes; and I saw wars and rumors of wars among them; and in wars and rumors of wars I saw many generations pass away.

22 And the angel said unto me: Behold these shall dwindle in unbelief.

23 And it came to pass that I beheld, after they had dwindled in unbelief they became a dark, and loathsome, and a filthy people, full of idleness and all manner of abominations.

Nephi lists two causes of the fall of his brethren: pride, and the temptations of the devil (v. 19). Mormon 1–6 discusses these two issues, but they will not be discussed at this time.

After seeing many generations pass away following the overcoming of his seed (v. 20), the angel tells Nephi that "these shall dwindle in unbelief" (v. 22). To dwindle is to gradually decline. History has proven the angel's declaration. Nephi then observed that "after they had dwindled in unbelief they became a dark, and loathsome, and a filthy people, full of idleness and all manner of abominations" (v. 23). Mormon later uses basically the same descriptions as Nephi, but adds "beyond the description of that which ever hath been among us . . . because of their unbelief and idolatry" (Mormon 5:15). One of the purposes of the Book of Mormon is to correct the Lamanites' unbelief and abominations and help them become "a pure and delightsome people" (2 Nephi 30:4–6). The restoration of those people is well underway. More about their restoration will be discussed in Chapter Twenty of this work.

SACRED WRITING

Preaching Which Is Sacred:

1 Nephi 10:2–14   Lehi concerning the Messiah, the prophet to prepare the way, and the olive tree.

Great Revelation:

1 Nephi 11	Nephi's vision of Jerusalem, other cities, and the city of Nazareth.
1 Nephi 12	Nephi's vision of the land of promise .

Prophesying:

1 Nephi 10:17–22	Nephi concerning the power of the Holy Ghost.

Doctrines Learned:

1 Nephi 10:6	All mankind are in a lost and fallen state, and will be until they rely on their Redeemer.
1 Nephi 10:11	Jesus manifested himself to the Gentiles by the Holy Ghost, not a personal appearance as to the house of Israel.
1 Nephi 10:17	The power of the Holy Ghost comes through faith on the Son of God, and by diligently seeking him.
1 Nephi 10:18	The Holy Ghost is the same yesterday, today, and tomorrow.
1 Nephi 10:19	The mysteries of God are unfolded by the power of the Holy Ghost.
1 Nephi 11:18	Mary is the mother of the Son of God after the manner of the flesh, therefore he has a mother of his spirit.
1 Nephi 11:19	The Lamb of God is the son of the Eternal Father.
1 Nephi 12:9	The twelve apostles chosen in the Holy Land will judge the twelve tribes of Israel.
1 Nephi 12:10	The twelve apostles chosen in America will judge the people of Lehi.
1 Nephi 12:19	Pride and the temptations of the devil caused the downfall of the Nephites

General Authority Quotes

The Prophet Joseph Smith • 1 Nephi 10–14

The great Jehovah contemplated the whole of the events connected with the earth, pertaining to the plan of salvation, before it rolled into existence, or ever "the morning stars sang together" for joy; the past, the present, and the future were and are, with Him, one eternal "now;" He knew of the fall of Adam, the iniquities of the antediluvians, of the depth of iniquity that would be connected with the human family, their weakness and strength, their power and glory, apostasies, their crimes, their righteousness and iniquity; He comprehended the fall of man, and his redemption; He knew the plan of salvation and pointed it out; He was acquainted with the situation of all nations and with their destiny; He ordered all things according to the council of His own will; He knows the situation of both the living and the dead, and has made ample provision for their redemption, according to their several circumstances, and the laws of the kingdom of God, whether in this world, or the world to come. [*TPJS*, 220]

By a little reflection it will be seen that the idea of the existence of these attributes in the Deity is necessary to enable any rational being to exercise faith in him; for without the idea of the existence of these attributes in the Deity men could not exercise faith in him for life and salvation; seeing that without the knowledge of all things, God would not be able to save any portion of his creatures; for it is by reason of the knowledge which he has of all things, from the beginning to the end, that enables him to give the understanding to his creatures by which they are partakers of eternal life; and if it were not for the idea existing in the minds of men that God had all knowledge it would be impossible for them to exercise faith in him. [*Lectures on Faith*, 4:11]

The Prophet Joseph Smith • 1 Nephi 10:17–19

Search the scriptures—search the revelations which we publish, and ask your Heavenly Father, in the name of His Son Jesus Christ, to manifest the truth unto you, and if you do it with an eye single to His glory nothing doubting, He will answer you by the power of His Holy Spirit. You will then know for yourself and not for another. You will not then be dependent on man for the knowledge of God; nor will there any room for speculation. [*TPJS*, 11–12]

President Joseph F. Smith • 1 Nephi 10–14

I believe that our Savior is the ever-living example to all flesh in all these things. He no doubt possessed a foreknowledge of all the vicissitudes through which he would have to pass in the world tabernacle. . . .

If Christ knew beforehand, so did we. But in coming here, we forgot all, that our agency might be free indeed, to choose good or evil, that we might merit the reward of our own choice and conduct. [*Gospel Doctrine*, Eleventh Edition, 1959, 13–14]

Challenges to Eternal Life:

1. Seek the power of the Holy Ghost to clarify a principle or doctrine that is a mystery to you (1 Nephi 10:19).
2. 1 Nephi 11 will teach you of the divinity of Jesus Christ. Once you have obtained this testimony, bear it to others.
3. The world and the wisdom thereof is often in opposition to the words of the Twelve Apostles. Seek and follow the counsel of modern Church leaders (1 Nephi 12:35)
4. The Nephites fell because of pride and the temptations of the devil. Guard against these problems in your own life through prayer and living the gospel.
5. Choose another challenge or modern message from this reading and apply it to your life.

Chapter Five

Nephi's Vision of the Gentile Nations

1 Nephi 13–14

*H*istorical Setting: Nephi's visions of the Gentile nations were given on the same mountain and on the same occasion while they were camped in the valley of Lemuel. Chapter 13 is a vision of those nations at the time following Christ's mortal ministry. Chapter 14 is a vision of those nations in the latter-days. It is important to keep the two periods separate.

Precept of Chapter Five:

> But the Lord knoweth all things from the beginning; wherefore he prepareth a way to accomplish all his works among the children of men; for behold, he hath all power unto the fulfilling of all his words. [1 Nephi 9:6]

The visions of the Gentile nations is of particular interest to our day because it deals with us, our immediate ancestors, and our posterity. They also point out one of the basic principles of eternity, the agency of man. "Satan rebelled against [God], and sought to destroy the agency of man, which I, the Lord God, had given him" (Moses 4:3). He continues to try to overthrow the plan of salvation. The Lord in his foreknowledge has prepared means whereby he can accomplish his works in spite of the efforts of the devil. These chapters point to the

Lord's endeavors to guide the Gentile nations and the devil's attempts to mislead them unto destruction. Mankind must choose whom to follow. A teaching outline follows to prepare the reader for a deeper study.

OUTLINE • 1 NEPHI 13–14

➤ 13:1–3   The angel shows Nephi many nations and kingdoms of the Gentiles.

➤ 13:4–9   Nephi sees a great and abominable church among them, most abominable above all other churches.

      a. It slayeth the saints of God, tortureth them, and binds them with a yoke of iron (v. 5).

      b. The devil is the founder of that church (v. 6).

      c. The desires of the devil's church are precious metals, fine clothes, and harlots (vv. 7–8).

      d. For the praise of the world, they destroy the saints of God and bring them to captivity (v. 9).

➤ 13:10–13   Many waters separate the Gentiles from the seed of Nephi's brethren.

      a. The wrath of God is upon the seed of Nephi's brethren (v. 11).

      b. The Spirit of God leads a man across the many waters to the promised land (v. 12).

      c. The Spirit leads other Gentiles out of captivity upon the many waters (v. 13).

➤ 13:14–19   Multitudes of Gentiles on the promised land scatter the seed of Nephi's brethren.

      a. The Spirit causes the Gentiles to prosper, and obtain the land for an inheritance (vv. 15–19).

          1. They are white, and beautiful, like Nephi's people before they were slain.

          2. They humble themselves before the Lord, and his power was upon them.

      b. Their mother Gentiles were gathered on the waters and on the land to battle the Gentiles (vv. 17–19).

         1. God's power is with the Gentiles, and his wrath is on those gathered against them.

         2. The Gentiles are delivered by the power of God from the other nations.

> 13:20–33   The Gentiles prosper on the land, and a book was carried among them.

      a. It came from a Jew and is a record of the Jews, and contains the covenants the Lord made to the house of Israel and many prophecies of the prophets (vv. 22–23).

         1. It is a record like the plates of brass save not so many.

         2. The record is of great worth unto the Gentiles.

      b. When the book came from the Jew, it contained the fullness of the gospel of the Lord, of whom the twelve apostles bear record (vv. 24–25).

         1. They bear record according to the truth which is in the Lamb of God.

         2. It goes from the Jews in purity to the Gentiles.

      c. After it goes from the twelve apostles, the great and abominable church takes away many plain and precious parts from the gospel and also many covenants (v. 26).

      d. The plain and precious parts are taken away to pervert the right ways of the Lord, blind the eyes, and harden the hearts of men (vv. 27–29).

      e. After the book loses plain and precious parts, it goes to all Gentile nations (v. 29).

         1. It goes even across the waters with the Gentiles who went out of captivity.

         2. Because of the losses, a great many stumble, and Satan has great power over them.

      f. God will not allow the Gentiles to utterly destroy the seed of Nephi and his brethren (vv. 30–33).

       1. He will not allow the Gentiles to remain in their state of blindness.

       2. He will be merciful unto the Gentiles, and visit the remnant of Israel in judgment.

➤ 13:34–37   After the seed of Lehi are smitten by the Gentiles, and the Gentiles stumble, the Lord will bring forth much of his plain and precious gospel.

    a. The Lamb shall manifest plain and precious things to Nephi and his seed (vv. 35–36).

       1. After the Nephites are destroyed, these things shall come forth to the Gentiles by the gift and power of the Lamb.

       2. The gospel of the Lamb, and his rock and salvation shall be written in them.

    b. Those who seek to bring forth Zion shall have the gift and power of the Holy Ghost (v. 37).

    c. If they endure to the end, they shall be saved in the everlasting kingdom of God (v. 37).

➤ 13:38–42   The book of the Jew shall come from the Gentiles unto Lehi's seed.

    a. Other books shall come from the Gentiles unto Lehi's seed unto the convincing of the Gentiles, Lehi's seed, and the Jews that the records of the prophets and the twelve apostles are true (vv. 39–40).

       1. The other books shall establish the truth of the twelve apostles record.

       2. They shall make known the plain and precious parts that were lost.

       3. All nations, kindreds, tongues, and people shall know that the Lamb of God is the Son of the Eternal Father, and the Savior of the world.

       4. All men must come unto him according to the words established by the Lamb or they cannot be saved.

b. The words of the Lamb shall be known in the record of Nephi, and in the twelve apostles of the Lamb and shall be one, for there is one God and one shepherd (v. 41).

c. The time comes for the Lamb to be manifest to all nations, both Jew and Gentile (v. 42).

    1. He will manifest himself to the Jews and then the Gentiles, and then to the Gentiles and then the Jews.

    2. The last shall be first and the first shall be last.

➤ 14:1–4   If the Gentiles hearken to the Lamb, they will be blessed on the land forever.

a. He will manifest himself in word, in power, and in deed, and take away their stumbling blocks (vv. 1–2).

    1. If they harden not their hearts, they will be numbered among the house of Israel.

    2. They will no more be taken in captivity; and the house of Israel will no more be confounded.

b. The great pit dug by the great and abominable church for the destruction of men, shall be filled with those that dug it (vv. 3–4).

    1. The soul will not be utterly destroyed, but cast into hell that has no end.

    2. This will be according to the captivity of the devil and the justice of God.

➤ 14:5–7   The angel said that if the Gentiles repent it shall be well with them because of the covenants of the Lord to the house of Israel.

a. Wo unto the Gentiles if they harden their hearts against the Lamb of God (v. 6).

b. The Lamb shall work a great and marvelous work that shall be everlasting (v. 7).

    1. It will convince them unto peace and life eternal.

    2. The hard of heart and blind of mind will be brought to captivity and destroyed both temporally and spiritually.

➤ 14:8–12   The angel asks if Nephi remembers the covenants made to the house of Israel?

 a.   Nephi sees the great and abominable church, the mother of abominations, founded by the devil (vv. 9–10).

   1.   There are two churches only, the church of the Lamb of God and that of the devil.

   2.   Whosoever belongs not to one belongs to the other.

 b.   The abominable church sits up on many waters, having dominion over all the earth (v. 11).

 c.   The church of the Lamb of God were few in numbers because of the whore who sat upon the waters (v. 13).

   1.   The saints of God were upon all the face of the earth.

   2.   Their dominion was small because of the wickedness of the great whore.

➤ 14:13–17   The mother of abominations gathers many from among all nations of the Gentiles to fight the Lamb.

 a.   The power of God is upon the saints and they are armed with righteousness and great glory (v. 14).

 b.   God's wrath was poured upon the great and abominable church (vv. 15–17).

   1.   Wars and rumors of war are among all the nations which belong to the abominable church.

   2.   In that day, the Father will commence fulfilling His covenants with Israel.

➤ 14:18–27   Nephi sees a man in a white robe who is one of the apostles of the Lamb.

 a.   He shall see and write the remainder of these things to the end of the world (vv. 21–23).

   1.   His writings are just and true, and are written in the book coming from the Jew.

   2.   When written they were plain and precious and easy to understand.

       b. Nephi saw many things written by the apostle, and shall see the remainder (vv. 24–26).

          1. He shall not write the things shown hereafter; the apostle was ordained to write them.

          2. Others have seen these things and written them.

          3. They are sealed up in purity to come forth in the due time of the Lord.

       c. Nephi hears and bears record that the apostle's name is John (v. 27).

➤ 14:28–30   Nephi was forbidden to write but a small part of the things he saw.

       a. He saw the things his father saw, and an angel made them known to him (v. 29),

       b. He saw them while carried away in the Spirit, and the things written are true (v. 30).

NOTES AND COMMENTARY

Introduction: Almost every reader of the Book of Mormon asks, as he reads these chapters of the Book of Mormon (13–14), "What is the great and abominable church that the angel describes for Nephi? The Church has made no official identity of this church, and the questions that should be asked are: "What does it do?" and "Where does it operate?" Other important questions are: "Why did God allow the loss of plain and precious parts from His scriptures?" and "How does God compensate His children for the wrong doings of such evil men?" We will answer these questions as we analyze these chapters, but the reader must remember to keep an open mind as to the identity of the abominable church.

1 Nephi 13:1–3 • The Nations and Kingdoms of the Gentiles

1 And it came to pass that the angel spake unto me, saying: Look! And I looked and beheld many nations and kingdoms.

2 And the angel said unto me: What beholdest thou? And I said:

I behold many nations and kingdoms.

3 And he said unto me: These are the nations and kingdoms of the Gentiles. [1 Nephi 13:1–3]

One of the first questions to be answered is: "Who are the Gentiles?" Jesus answered this question when he visited the Nephites after his resurrection. He defined them as those who believe "in me, in and of the Holy Ghost, which witnesses unto them of me and of the Father" (3 Nephi 16:6). Lehi had taught his sons that after the Messiah "should rise from the dead, (he) should make himself manifest, by the Holy Ghost, unto the Gentiles" (1 Nephi 10:11). In Jerusalem, after his resurrection, he instructed the eleven apostles: "Go ye into all the world, and preach the gospel to every creature" (Mark 16:14–15). Prior to this time they had been instructed to "Go not into the way of the Gentiles, . . . But go rather to the lost sheep of the house of Israel" (Matthew 10:5–6). In the last year of his mortal ministry, Jesus taught the Pharisees a parable of the sheepfold at the Feast of Tabernacles in Jerusalem:

1 Verily, verily, I say unto you, He that entereth not by the door into the sheepfold, but climbeth up some other way, the same is a thief and a robber.

2 But he that entereth in by the door is the shepherd of the sheep.

3 To him the porter openeth; and the sheep hear his voice: and he calleth his own sheep by name, and leadeth them out.

4 And when he putteth forth his own sheep, he goeth before them, and the sheep follow him: for they know his voice.

5 And a stranger will they not follow, but will flee from him: for they know not the voice of strangers.

In interpreting his own parable, Jesus said: (John 10:14–16).

14 I am the good shepherd, and know my *sheep,* and am known of mine.

15 As the Father knoweth me, even so know I the Father: and I lay down my life for the sheep.

16 And other sheep I have, which are not of this fold: them also I must bring, and they shall hear my voice; and there shall be one fold, *and* one shepherd.

John records that the Pharisees "understand not what things they were" in the parable (John 10:6).

Jesus told the Nephites that those in Jerusalem "because of stiff-neckedness and unbelief they understood not my word" (3 Nephi 15:18). He then explained:

21 And verily I say unto you, that ye are they of whom I said: Other sheep I have which are not of this fold; them also I must bring, and they shall hear my voice; and there shall be one fold, and one shepherd.

22 And they understood me not, for they supposed it had been the Gentiles; for they understood not that the Gentiles should be converted through their preaching.

23 And they understood me not that I said they shall hear my voice; and they understood me not that the Gentiles should not at any time hear my voice—that I should not manifest myself unto them save it were by the Holy Ghost.

24 But behold, ye have both heard my voice, and seen me; and ye are my sheep, and ye are numbered among those whom the Father hath given me. [3 Nephi 15:21–24][1]

The apostles, after Christ's ascension into heaven, took the gospel

---

[1] Jesus did make one exception:

Then Jesus went thence, and departed into the coasts of Tyre and Sidon. And, behold, a woman of Canaan came out of the same coasts, and cried unto him, saying, Have mercy on me, O Lord, *thou* Son of David; my daughter is grievously vexed with a devil. But he answered her not a word. And his disciples came and besought him, saying, Send her away; for she crieth after us. But he answered and said, I am not sent but unto the lost sheep of the house of Israel. Then came she and worshipped him, saying, Lord, help me. But he answered and said, It is not meet to take the children's bread, and to cast *it* to dogs. And she said, Truth, Lord: yet the dogs eat of the crumbs which fall from their masters' table. Then Jesus answered and said unto her, O woman, great *is* thy faith: be it unto thee even as thou wilt. And her daughter was made whole from that very hour. [Matthew 15:21–24] through parts of Asia and into Europe, the homes of the Gentile nations. As the apostles taught the gospel to them, the Holy Ghost bore witness of Jesus Christ, and many were converted. However, the apostasy came, and many pagan beliefs were adopted into the Church. These beliefs led to the formation of many separate Christian denominations. Some of these forms of Christianity were adopted by the various nations as their state religions. Thus these Christian nations would be the "nations and kingdoms of the Gentiles" shown to Nephi (vv. 1–3).

1 Nephi 13:4–9 • The Great and Abominable Church Founded by the Devil

4 And it came to pass that I saw among the nations of the Gentiles the formation of a great church.

5 And the angel said unto me: Behold the formation of a church which is most abominable above all other churches, which slayeth the saints of God, yea, and tortureth them and bindeth them down, and yoketh them with a yoke of iron, and bringeth them down into captivity.

6 And it came to pass that I beheld this great and abominable church; and I saw the devil that he was the founder of it.

7 And I also saw gold, and silver, and silks, and scarlets, and fine-twined linen, and all manner of precious clothing; and I saw many harlots.

8 And the angel spake unto me, saying: Behold the gold, and the silver, and the silks, and the scarlets, and the fine-twined linen, and the precious clothing, and the harlots, are the desires of this great and abominable church.

9 And also for the praise of the world do they destroy the saints of God, and bring them down into captivity.

The church that Nephi observes is singular, and is defined as "most abominable above all other churches" (v. 5). It is the angel, not Nephi, who makes this statement, and also gives the reason for making the statement; "which (the abominable church) slayeth the saints of God," tortures them and binds them "with a yoke of iron, and bringeth them down into captivity" (v. 5). The angel's statement answers the question of "what the abominable church goes?" As the church gradually apostatized, it incorporated the Greek culture, called the hellenization of Christianity.[2] The Roman government eventually made Christianity their state religion, thus bringing the Saints into captivity by the iron kingdom of Rome. Thus the political leaders directed the church rather than divinely appointed leaders who would have received revelation from God. Of course, as Nephi saw, the devil was the source of the apostasy and the political captivity (v. 6). Nephi was also told by the angel that the desires of the great and abominable church were gold, silver, all manner of precious clothing, and harlots (v. 8). Such desires again describe the apostasy. The angel said the reason for destroying the saints of God, and bringing others into captivity, was to get "the praise of the world" (v. 9). Nephi later describes priestcraft in similar terms: to "get the gain and praise of the world" (2 Nephi 26:29). Priest-craft is Satan's counterpart of the priesthood of God. Rather than seeking the desires of the world, the priesthood holder's eye should be "single to the glory of God" (D&C 82:19). If this is not his goal, he too could be guilty of priestcraft.

Two more questions are now pertinent. The first, why would God allow an apostasy, his saints to be slain and tortured, and brought into captivity? The answer is, "the agency of man." President David O. McKay stated: "Next to the bestowal of life itself, the right to direct our lives is God's greatest gift to mankind" (Conference Report, October 1965, 8). The second question is: "What does God do to compensate for man's wrong choices that encroach upon God's gifts to future generations? The things shown and told to Nephi answers this question.

---

[2] See Stephen E. Robinson, *Early Christianity and 1 Nephi 13–14*, chap. 12, published in, Monte S. Nyman, and Charles D. Tate Jr., editors, *The Book of Mormon, First Nephi the Doctrinal Foundation*, Religious Study Center, BYU, 1988.

1 Nephi 13:10–13 • The Spirit of God
leads a man to the Promised Land

10 And it came to pass that I looked and beheld many waters; and they divided the Gentiles from the seed of my brethren.

11 And it came to pass that the angel said unto me: Behold the wrath of God is upon the seed of thy brethren.

12 And I looked and beheld a man among the Gentiles, who was separated from the seed of my brethren by the many waters; and I beheld the Spirit of God, that it came down and wrought upon the man; and he went forth upon the many waters, even unto the seed of my brethren, who were in the promised land.

13 And it came to pass that I beheld the Spirit of God, that it wrought upon other Gentiles; and they went forth out of captivity, upon the many waters.

The Gentiles being separated from the seed of Nephi's brethren shows that what Nephi had seen about the abominable church had taken place on the eastern continent. Again, we remind you not to draw a conclusion as yet about the identity of the great church. The wrath of God upon the seed of Nephi's brethren indicates a period of time after the fourth generation from the visit of Christ to the Nephites. It was previously described, by the angel: "Behold (Nephi's seed) shall dwindle in unbelief" (1 Nephi 12:22).

The first specific thing noted by Nephi is that God was responsible for leading the Gentiles out of captivity from all other nations (vv. 12–13). The Book of Mormon has identified one person who is directly involved in this event—the discovery of the New World. Columbus is accredited with this discovery. What evidence is there of this identification? While today many people are attempting to discredit the accomplishments of Columbus, various scholars have furnished further evidence supporting Columbus.[3]

From my first youth onward, I was a seaman and have so continued

---

[3] See Arnold K. Garr, *Christopher Columbus, a Latter-day Saint Perspective* [1992].

until this day. The Lord was well disposed to my desire and He bestowed upon me courage and understanding; knowledge of seafaring. He gave me in abundance, and of geometry and astronomy likewise. Further, He gave me joy and cunning in drawing maps and thereon cities, mountains, rivers, islands, and harbors, each one in its place. I have seen and truly I have studied all books and cosmographies, histories and chronologies for which our Lord with provident hand unlocked my mind, sent me upon the seas and gave me fire for the deed. Those who heard of my enterprise called it foolish, mocked me and laughed, but who can doubt but that the Holy Ghost inspired me.[4]

The Book of Mormon comes to the aid of these scholars in defending Columbus, and confirms that God did direct the history of the latter-days in the establishment of a great nation among the Gentiles (vv. 12–19). The Spirit of God also wrought upon other Gentiles (the pilgrims) (v. 13). The Lord had preserved a land, a choice land above all other lands, for these people. As Lehi was led to prophesy by the Spirit: "this land shall be kept as yet from the knowledge of other nations; for behold, many nations would overrun the land, that there be no place for an inheritance" (2 Nephi 1:8). Also he was led to prophesy, as Nephi's vision serves as an example, "there should none come into this land save they shall be brought by the hand of the Lord" (2 Nephi 1:6).

1 Nephi 13:14–19 • The Gentiles Prosper and Obtain the Promised Land For Their Inheritance

14 And it came to pass that I beheld many multitudes of the Gentiles upon the land of promise; and I beheld the wrath of God, that it was upon the seed of my brethren; and they were scattered before the Gentiles and were smitten.

15 And I beheld the Spirit of the Lord, that it was upon the Gentiles, and they did prosper and obtain the land for their inheritance; and I beheld that they were white, and exceedingly fair and beautiful, like unto my people before they were slain.

---

[4] Jacob Wasserman, *Columbus, the Don Quixote of the Seas* [1930], 19–20.

16 And it came to pass that I, Nephi, beheld that the Gentiles who had gone forth out of captivity did humble themselves before the Lord; and the power of the Lord was with them.

17 And I beheld that their mother Gentiles were gathered together upon the waters, and upon the land also, to battle against them.

18 And I beheld that the power of God was with them, and also that the wrath of God was upon all those that were gathered together against them to battle.

19 And I, Nephi, beheld that the Gentiles that had gone out of captivity were delivered by the power of God out of the hands of all other nations.

As the inhabitants of the land increased (multitudes), the Lord in his wrath, allowed Nephi's brother's seed to be scattered before the Gentiles (v. 14). Because of their unbelief they had become a "loathsome, and a filthy people, full of idleness and all manner of abominations" (1 Nephi 12:23). The Gentile immigrants had the Spirit and power of God with them, and prospered both physically and spiritually (vv. 12:15–16).

Nephi next observed that God was involved in the American Revolutionary War. His power was with the Gentiles whom he had led to the choice land, and they were delivered by him from the mother nation Great Britain. His wrath was poured out on those fighting on the opposing side (vv. 17–18). This suggests that as with the Lamanites, the Spirit withdrew from them, and they "depended upon their own strength" rather than the Lord's (Mosiah 10:11). Their being "delivered by the power of God out of the hands of all other nations" (v. 19) seems a general statement about the Civil War and other future wars:

3 For behold, the Southern States shall be divided against the Northern States, and the Southern States will call on other nations, even the nation of Great Britain, as it is called, and they shall also call upon other nations, in order to defend themselves against other nations; and then war shall be poured out upon all nations. [D&C 87:3]

It is also an example of the law of war, revealed to the Lord's ancients, and to the Prophet Joseph in August 1833.

33 And again, this is the law that I gave unto mine ancients, that they should not go out unto battle against any nation, kindred, tongue, or people, save I, the Lord, commanded them.

34 And if any nation, tongue, or people should proclaim war against them, they should first lift a standard of peace unto that people, nation, or tongue;

35 And if that people did not accept the offering of peace, neither the second nor the third time, they should bring these testimonies before the Lord;

36 Then I, the Lord, would give unto them a commandment, and justify them in going out to battle against that nation, tongue, or people.

37 And I, the Lord, would fight their battles, and their children's battles, and their children's children's, until they had avenged themselves on all their enemies, to the third and fourth generation.

38 Behold, this is an ensample unto all people, saith the Lord your God, for justification before me. [D&C 98:33–38]

1 Nephi 13:20–23 • A Record of the Jews Containing the Covenants of the Lord and Prophecies

20 And it came to pass that I, Nephi, beheld that they did prosper in the land; and I beheld a book, and it was carried forth among them.

21 And the angel said unto me: Knowest thou the meaning of the book?

22 And I said unto him: I know not.

23 And he said: Behold it proceedeth out of the mouth of a Jew. And I, Nephi, beheld it; and he said unto me: The book that thou beholdest is a record of the Jews, which contains the covenants of the Lord, which he hath made unto the house of Israel; and it also containeth many of the prophecies of the holy prophets; and it is a record like unto the engravings which are upon the plates of brass, save there are not so many; nevertheless, they contain the covenants of the Lord, which he hath made unto the house of Israel; wherefore, they are of great worth unto the Gentiles.

The book that was seen by Nephi being carried by the Gentiles in the promised land was, of course, the Bible. The meaning of the book explained by the angel is significant in light of the verses that follow. That it proceeded out of the mouth of a Jew, and is the record of the Jews seems to identify the role of Jesus in the Bible. As "the God of Israel, and the God of the whole earth" (3 Nephi 11:14), out of his mouth, a Jew, proceeded what was recorded in that book (v. 23). It was he who made the covenants with Adam, Enoch, Noah, Abraham, Isaac, Jacob, Joseph, and Moses; or with the house of Israel and those who preceded them. It was he who gave revelation to the patriarchs, prophets, and apostles, and inspired them to write the future happenings to the covenant people. It was his Spirit, voice, and will that spoke to Isaiah, Jeremiah, and all of the prophets until Malachi.

However, that book was not as large as the plates of brass which "did contain the five books of Moses, . . . a record of the Jews from the beginning, even down to the commencement of the reign of Zedekiah, king of Judah (the historical books); and also the prophecies of the holy prophets . . . and many prophecies which have been spoken by the mouth of Jeremiah." And they also contained "a genealogy of (Lehi's) fathers" (1 Nephi 5:11–14). Many of the writings that were in the Bible carried by the Pilgrims were written after Lehi left Jerusalem. These include part of Jeremiah (implied above), Ezekiel, Daniel, Zephaniah, Habakkuk, Haggai, Zechariah, Malachi, Ezra, Nehemiah and part of the historical books of Kings and Chronicles following Zedekiah (600 B.C.). A tabulation of the number of pages in the King James Version of these later written books shows at least a hundred and sixty pages of material, plus the four hundred pages of the New Testament that were not in the plates of brass, and yet the plates of brass were larger. Therefore, at least six hundred pages of materials have been lost from the present day Bible that Nephi is told about by the angel of the Lord.

Nevertheless, the covenants of the Lord to the house of Israel were retained, and these were of great worth to the gentiles.

1 Nephi 13:24–29 • The Bible Went Forth in Purity but Plain and Precious Things Were Lost

24 And the angel of the Lord said unto me: Thou hast beheld that the book proceeded forth from the mouth of a Jew; and when it proceeded forth from the mouth of a Jew it contained the fulness of the gospel of the Lord, of whom the twelve apostles bear record; and they bear record according to the truth which is in the Lamb of God.

25 Wherefore, these things go forth from the Jews in purity unto the Gentiles, according to the truth which is in God.

26 And after they go forth by the hand of the twelve apostles of the Lamb, from the Jews unto the Gentiles, thou seest the formation of that great and abominable church, which is most abominable above all other churches; for behold, they have taken away from the gospel of the Lamb many parts which are plain and most precious; and also many covenants of the Lord have they taken away.

27 And all this have they done that they might pervert the right ways of the Lord, that they might blind the eyes and harden the hearts of the children of men.

28 Wherefore, thou seest that after the book hath gone forth through the hands of the great and abominable church, that there are many plain and precious things taken away from the book, which is the book of the Lamb of God.

29 And after these plain and precious things were taken away it goeth forth unto all the nations of the Gentiles; and after it goeth forth unto all the nations of the Gentiles, yea, even across the many waters which thou hast seen with the Gentiles which have gone forth out of captivity, thou seest—because of the many plain and precious things which have been taken out of the book, which were plain unto the understanding of the children of men, according to the plainness which is in the Lamb of God—because of these things which are taken away out of the gospel of the Lamb, an exceedingly great many do stumble, yea, insomuch that Satan hath great power over them. [1 Nephi 13:24–29]

When the book "proceeded forth from the mouth of a Jew, it contained the fulness of the gospel of Lord, of whom the twelve apostles bear record . . . according to the truth and which is in the Lamb of God." This describes the New Testament gospels. Jesus Christ is the "Spirit of truth . . . even of all truth" (D&C 93:26). Therefore, the New Testament contained the pure, and the fulness of the gospel of the Lord (vv. 24–25). The gospels are traditionally dated as having been written between A.D. 65 and 95. However, "after they go forth by the hand of the twelve apostles, from the Jews unto the Gentiles," the great and abominable church took away many plain and precious parts (v. 26). From this statement we learn that the gospels were written before they were taken to the Gentiles. The apostles were commanded by Jesus after he was resurrection to take the gospel to all nations (the Gentiles), but they were to "tarry ye in the city of Jerusalem until ye be endued [endowed] with power from on high" (Luke 24:49). The endowment of power came fifty days after the Passover, or after the crucifixion.

> 1 And when the day of Pentecost was fully come, they were all with one accord in one place.
>
> 2 And suddenly there came a sound from heaven as of a rushing mighty wind, and it filled all the house where they were sitting.
>
> 3 And there appeared unto them cloven tongues like as of fire, and it sat upon each of them.
>
> 4 And they were all filled with the Holy Ghost, and began to speak with other tongues, as the Spirit gave them utterance. [Acts 2:1–4]

Peter was later given the revelation to take the gospel to the Gentiles. An angel appeared to Cornelieus, a Gentile, and told him to send men to Joppa to see Peter. In the meantime, Peter had a vision of meats that were unclean according to the law of Moses. He was commanded to eat them because God had cleansed them. After the men sent by Cornelieus came to Joppa and found Peter, he willingly returned with them to Caesarea (see Acts 10:1–33). After meeting Cornelieus, Peter interpreted his vision to mean that the gospel was now to go to the Gentiles.

> 34 Then Peter opened *his* mouth, and said, Of a truth I perceive that God is no respecter of persons:

> 35 But in every nation he that feareth him, and worketh right-
> eousness, is accepted with him. [Acts 10:34–35]

This revelation to Peter came as early as A.D. 35, but no later than A.D. 43. Paul's first missionary journey to the Gentiles traditionally took place in the mid A.D. 40's. Therefore the account of the twelve apostles bearing record of Christ (the gospels) were written before the traditional dates mentioned above.

Plain and precious parts were taken from the gospel of the Lamb (New Testament), and also many covenants (Old Testament) (v. 26). The Prophet Joseph Smith observed: "From sundry revelations which had been received, it was apparent that many important points touching the salvation of men, had been taken from the Bible, or lost before it was compiled" (*TPJS*, 9–10). These revelations would include but not be limited to, "the fullness of John's record is hereafter to be revealed" (D&C 93:6), the things that "were all written in the book of Enoch, and are to be testified of in due time" (D&C 107:57). The Book of Moses and the Book of Abraham, already restored in the Pearl of Great Price, give further support to the loss of plain and precious things. A few other examples will illustrate the errors or deletions in the texts. A comparison of the Sermon on the Mount (Matthew 5–7), and the same sermon given to the Nephites (3 Nephi 12:1–15), or a comparison of the discourse of the signs of his coming (Matthew 24) with the JST, Matthew 24 in the Pearl of Great Price and D&C 45 each show some of the losses in the New Testament. The covenants lost from the Old Testament are verified in the Book of Mormon where Lehi quotes some of the great covenants made to Joseph (2 Nephi 3). Also a more complete account of the covenant made to Abraham is found in the Book of Abraham 2:8–11 than is found in Genesis 12:2–3.

The reason the devil's church took away these truths was to "pervert the ways of the Lord," and to "blind the eyes and harden the hearts of the children of men" (v. 27). Perverting the ways of the Lord can be seen as a continuation of the war in heaven between "Michael and his angels" and "the dragon and his angels" (Revelation 12:7). The losses to the text were part of the blinding of the eyes and the hardening of the hearts of men (v. 27). When the book went through the hands of the great and abominable church of the devil it lost its original purity (v. 28). This was the apostasy in the early centuries A.D. It was not the Catholic Church.

The Catholic Church actually preserved the many truths that remained in the book. Despite keeping the lay people in ignorance the Catholic Church housed and preserved copies of the manuscripts. The monks tediously copied the manuscripts. Copying the texts, of course, left room for other omissions or copying errors. The Prophet Joseph declared: "I believe the Bible as it read when it came forth from the pen of the original writers. Ignorant translators, careless transcribers, or designing and corrupt priests have committed many errors" (*TPJS*, 327). Thus, there were the errors of man that crept in, plus the work of the devil, that created the need for the eighth Article of Faith: "We believe the Bible to be the word of God as far as it is translated correctly." "Wherefore an exceeding great many do stumble [over the loss of plain and precious things from the Bible], yea, insomuch that Satan hath great power over them" (v. 29). However, to paraphrase Nephi, A Bible! A Bible! What thank they the Catholics for the Bible that they preserved for the Gentiles (cp. 2 Nephi 29:3–4).

1 Nephi 13:30–33 • The Gentiles Will Not Utterly Be Destroyed

30 Nevertheless, thou beholdest that the Gentiles who have gone forth out of captivity, and have been lifted up by the power of God above all other nations, upon the face of the land which is choice above all other lands, which is the land that the Lord God hath covenanted with thy father that his seed should have for the land of their inheritance; wherefore, thou seest that the Lord God will not suffer that the Gentiles will utterly destroy the mixture of thy seed, which are among thy brethren.

31 Neither will he suffer that the Gentiles shall destroy the seed of thy brethren.

32 Neither will the Lord God suffer that the Gentiles shall forever remain in that awful state of blindness, which thou beholdest they are

in, because of the plain and most precious parts of the gospel of the
Lamb which have been kept back by that abominable church, whose
formation thou hast seen.

33 Wherefore saith the Lamb of God: I will be merciful unto the
Gentiles, unto the visiting of the remnant of the house of Israel in great
judgment. [1 Nephi 13:30–33]

The Lord promised that the seed of Nephi and his brothers would
not be utterly destroyed. This promise has been fulfilled. The Lord
named all of the various groups of people who are part of the living
remnant of the Lamanites: "the Nephites, and the Jacobites, and the
Josephites, and the Zoramites, . . . the Lamanites, and the Lemuelites,
and the Ishmaelites' (D&C 3:16–17). All of Lehi's sons are named
except Sam whose "seed (was) numbered with (Nephi's) seed"
(2 Nephi 4:11). Their promised blessings will be discussed later.
However, there was to be a great judgment that did come upon them.
The angel explained this as being "merciful to the Gentiles" (v. 33).
The Gentiles were promised not to be left "in that awful state of
blindness, . . . because of the plain and most precious parts of the
gospel" being taken away (v. 32). Mormon further explained how this
mercy would be brought to pass.

19 And behold, the Lord hath reserved their blessings, which they
might have received in the land, for the Gentiles who shall possess
the land.

20 But behold, it shall come to pass that they shall be driven and
scattered by the Gentiles; and after they have been driven and scattered
by the Gentiles, behold, then will the Lord remember the covenant
which he made unto Abraham and unto all the house of Israel.

21 And also the Lord will remember the prayers of the righteous,
which have been put up unto him for them. [Mormon 5:19–21]

The Gentiles in the Americas have and will be offered all the blessings
that were offered to the people of Lehi. Namely the blessings promised
in the covenant made to Abraham. The great judgment upon the
Lamanites was their being driven and scattered by the Gentiles.

1 Nephi 13:34–37 • Much of the Lord's Gospel to Come to the Gentiles

34 And it came to pass that the angel of the Lord spake unto me, saying: Behold, saith the Lamb of God, after I have visited the remnant of the house of Israel—and this remnant of whom I speak is the seed of thy father—wherefore, after I have visited them in judgment, and smitten them by the hand of the Gentiles, and after the Gentiles do stumble exceedingly, because of the most plain and precious parts of the gospel of the Lamb which have been kept back by that abominable church, which is the mother of harlots, saith the Lamb—I will be merciful unto the Gentiles in that day, insomuch that I will bring forth unto them, in mine own power, much of my gospel, which shall be plain and precious, saith the Lamb.

35 For, behold, saith the Lamb: I will manifest myself unto thy seed, that they shall write many things which I shall minister unto them, which shall be plain and precious; and after thy seed shall be destroyed, and dwindle in unbelief, and also the seed of thy brethren, behold, these things shall be hid up, to come forth unto the Gentiles, by the gift and power of the Lamb.

36 And in them shall be written my gospel, saith the Lamb, and my rock and my salvation.

37 And blessed are they who shall seek to bring forth my Zion at that day, for they shall have the gift and the power of the Holy Ghost; and if they endure unto the end they shall be lifted up at the last day, and shall be saved in the everlasting kingdom of the Lamb; and whoso shall publish peace, yea, tidings of great joy, how beautiful upon the mountains shall they be.

The angel identifies the remnant of Israel who will be visited in judgment as the seed of Nehi's father. This was implied above. Another blessing to come to the Gentiles is the coming forth of the Book of Mormon. It was hid up and meant to come forth "by the gift and power of the Lamb" (v. 35). This was accomplished through the angel Moroni and is described in Joseph Smith's History. Those who read the Book of Mormon with real intent will understand why the Doctrine and

Covenants calls it "a marvelous work and a wonder" (see D&C 4:1; 6:1–2; 11:1–2; 12:1–2; 14:1–2).

It did come under the direction of the Lord. It does contain [Christ's] gospel, [Christ's] rock, and [Christ's] salvation (v. 36). The ultimate purpose of the Book of Mormon is to establish Zion and to bring about salvation in the everlasting kingdom of the Lamb. These blessings shall come through the gift and power of the Holy Ghost (v. 37). Isaiah's words will thus be fulfilled: "How beautiful upon the mountains [of Zion] are the feet of him that bringeth good tidings, that publisheth peace [the word of God]; that bringeth good tidings of good, that publisheth salvation; that saith unto Zion, Thy God reigneth! (Isaiah 52:7).

1 Nephi 13:38–42 • The Records of the Prophets and the Twelve Apostles of the Lamb are True

38 And it came to pass that I beheld the remnant of the seed of my brethren, and also the book of the Lamb of God, which had proceeded forth from the mouth of the Jew, that it came forth from the Gentiles unto the remnant of the seed of my brethren.

39 And after it had come forth unto them I beheld other books, which came forth by the power of the Lamb, from the Gentiles unto them, unto the convincing of the Gentiles and the remnant of the seed of my brethren, and also the Jews who were scattered upon all the face of the earth, that the records of the prophets and of the twelve apostles of the Lamb are true.

40 And the angel spake unto me, saying: These last records, which thou hast seen among the Gentiles, shall establish the truth of the first, which are of the twelve apostles of the Lamb, and shall make known the plain and precious things which have been taken away from them; and shall make known to all kindreds, tongues, and people, that the Lamb of God is the Son of the Eternal Father, and the Savior of the world; and that all men must come unto him, or they cannot be saved.

41 And they must come according to the words which shall be established by the mouth of the Lamb; and the words of the Lamb shall be made known in the records of thy seed, as well as in the records of the twelve apostles of the Lamb; wherefore they both shall

be established in one; for there is one God and one Shepherd over all the earth.

42 And the time cometh that he shall manifest himself unto all nations, both unto the Jews and also unto the Gentiles; and after he has manifested himself unto the Jews and also unto the Gentiles, then he shall manifest himself unto the Gentiles and also unto the Jews, and the last shall be first, and the first shall be last.

The Lord in his foreknowledge provided a way to counteract the work of the devil in taking away the plain and precious things. He brought forth other scriptures, The Book of Mormon, The Doctrine and Covenants, The Pearl Great Price, and The Joseph Smith Translation to compensate for the precious things that were lost from the Bible (vv. 24–29).

Before these records came forth, Nephi saw that the seed of his brethren would receive the record of the Jews (the Bible) from the Gentiles (v. 38). There were four purposes of the Lord in bringing forth these other records. The first reason is to establish the truth of the records of the prophets (the Old Testament) and those of the twelve apostles of the Lamb (New Testament). Second, to make known the plain and precious parts that had been lost from the Old and New Testaments. Third, to "make known to all kindreds, tongues, and people that the Lamb of God is the Son of the Eternal Father, and the Savior of the world." The fourth reason is to make known that "all man must come unto (Christ) or they cannot be saved." (vv. 39–40).

Although the Bible had suffered from the hands of the great and abominable church, it still contained the words needed to prepare the people for the restoration. The false conclusions that had been drawn from the Bible can now be clarified by reading the other records God had preserved. The work in the field of biblical criticism, in questioning the authorship of the various books of the Bible, is refuted by Nephi's record as he describes the purposes for which the other records came forth. The angel of the Lord repeatedly cites the apostles and the prophets that are traditionally accepted as the true authors of the Bible (vv. 23; 39–41). The two records were to be established as one, for there is one God and one shepherd (v. 41).

Nephi gives another witness to the basic message of the Bible, that Jesus is the Christ and the Savior of all mankind (1 Nephi 13:40–41). Thus, although the devil has, through the agency of man, caused many to stumble, the Book of Mormon comes forth to allow mankind to regain his footing. The Lamb of God, who is the son of the Eternal Father, the Savior of the world, and the Good Shepherd, shall come after the days of Nephi to manifest himself to all nations (v. 42). However, there is an order and a time period between his manifestations. He will (in the meridian of time) manifest himself to the Jews (including all the house of Israel), and then to the Gentiles (by the power of the Holy Ghost). After this (in the fullness of times), he will manifest himself to the Gentiles first, and then to the Jews (including all the house of Israel). The first shall be last and the last shall be first (v. 42). He taught the same concept to the Jews in their record, "And, behold, there are last which shall be first, and there are first which shall be last" (Luke 13:30).

The purpose of the restoration was also verified to Joseph Smith: "That through your administration they may receive the word, and through their administration the word may go forth unto ends of the earth, unto the Gentiles first, and then, behold, and lo, they shall turn unto the Jews" (D&C 90:9).

1 Nephi 14:1–4 • The Gentiles Shall Be Numbered Among the House of Israel

1 And it shall come to pass, that if the Gentiles shall hearken unto the Lamb of God in that day that he shall manifest himself unto them in word, and also in power, in very deed, unto the taking away of their stumbling blocks—

2 And harden not their hearts against the Lamb of God, they shall be numbered among the seed of thy father; yea, they shall be numbered among the house of Israel; and they shall be a blessed people upon the promised land forever; they shall be no more brought down into captivity; and the house of Israel shall no more be confounded.

3 And that great pit, which hath been digged for them by that great and abominable church, which was founded by the devil and his children, that he might lead away the souls of men down to hell—yea, that great pit which hath been digged for the destruction of men shall be filled by those who digged it, unto their utter destruction, saith the Lamb of God; not the destruction of the soul, save it be the casting of it into that hell which hath no end.

4 For behold, this is according to the captivity of the devil, and also according to the justice of God, upon all those who will work wickedness and abomination before him.

The fourteenth chapter changes time periods. It is speaking of the last days when the Lamb of God is manifest to the Gentiles in word (other volumes of scripture) and also in power (the Spirit poured out),[5] in very deed (translated by revelation, a marvelous work), unto taking away the stumbling blocks (understanding the Bible) (v. 1). The cultural Gentiles (those gathered from among the Gentiles) shall be numbered with the house of Israel (grafted back into the mother tree), and be a blessed (Zion) people upon the promised land forever (permanently established as a church and kingdom in peace, working toward eternal life) (v. 2).

The "great pit which hath been digged for the destruction of men shall be filled by those who digged it" (v. 3), illustrates the principal taught by Christ: "For with what judgment ye judge, ye shall be judged; and with what measure ye mete, it shall be a measured to you again" (Matthew 7:2; 3 Nephi 14:2). Or as Moroni said, "do not judge wrong-

---

[5] When the angel Moroni appeared to Joseph Smith, in September 1823, "He also quoted the second chapter of Joel, from the twenty-eighth verse to the last. He also said that this was not yet fulfilled, but was soon to be. And he further stated that the fulness of the Gentiles was soon to come in (JS—H 1:41). The verses he quoted from Joel are the basis of the above interpretation: "And it shall come to pass afterward, *that* I will pour out my spirit upon all flesh; and your sons and your daughters shall prophesy, your old men shall dream dreams, your young men shall see visions:

And also upon the servants and upon the handmaids in those days will I pour out my spirit" (2:28–29).

fully; for with that same judgment which ye judge ye shall also be judged" (Moroni 7:18).

The devil seeks to destroy man. Since "he [the devil] had fallen from heaven, and had become miserable forever, he sought also the misery of all mankind" (2 Nephi 2:18). Those who become captive to him (both temporally and spiritually) have their souls cast into hell, but not destroyed physically, according to the justice of God (vv. 3–4).

1 Nephi 14:5–7 • A Marvelous Work Which Shall Be Everlasting

5 And it came to pass that the angel spake unto me, Nephi, saying: Thou hast beheld that if the Gentiles repent it shall be well with them; and thou also knowest concerning the covenants of the Lord unto the house of Israel; and thou also hast heard that whoso repenteth not must perish.

6 Therefore, wo be unto the Gentiles if it so be that they harden their hearts against the Lamb of God.

7 For the time cometh, saith the Lamb of God, that I will work a great and a marvelous work among the children of men; a work which shall be everlasting, either on the one hand or on the other— either to the convincing of them unto peace and life eternal, or unto the deliverance of them to the hardness of their hearts and the blindness of their minds unto their being brought down into captivity, and also into destruction, both temporally and spiritually, according to the captivity of the devil, of which I have spoken.

Much of the interpretation given for verses one through four above is taken from the three verses just quoted. The judgment upon the righteous and the wicked being everlasting was not commented on (v. 7). This statement seems to refute the idea of progression from one kingdom of glory to another after the final judgment. Being destroyed temporarily (v. 7), but the soul not being destroyed (v. 3), suggests a permanent or "endless state. . . , which is after the resurrection of the dead" (Alma 12:24). If resurrected to a telestial body, it would never become a terrestrial or celestial body. Being destroyed spiritually is defined in the Book of Mormon as to "die as to things pertaining unto righteousness" (Alma 12:16), or to be "cut off from the presence of the Lord" (Alma 42:9). In other words they will not go to celestial kingdom. Although there are other statements that seems to refute this idea we will not comment further at this time.

1 Nephi 14:8–10 • There are Two Churches Only, the Lamb's and the Devil's

> 8 And it came to pass that when the angel had spoken these words, he said unto me: Rememberest thou the covenants of the Father unto the house of Israel? I said unto him, Yea.
>
> 9 And it came to pass that he said unto me: Look, and behold that great and abominable church, which is the mother of abominations, whose founder is the devil.
>
> 10 And he said unto me: Behold there are save two churches only; the one is the church of the Lamb of God, and the other is the church of the devil; wherefore, whoso belongeth not to the church of the Lamb of God belongeth to that great church, which is the mother of abominations; and she is the whore of all the earth.

The Church and the Book of Mormon have been criticized for the statement about there being two churches only (v. 10). The Lord confirmed there is only one true church in the latter days when he called the newly restored Church "the only true and living church upon the face of the whole earth, with which I, the Lord, am welled pleased" (D&C 1:30). Note again that this was said by the angel of the Lord, not Nephi. Furthermore, the concept is not unique to the Book of Mormon. Jesus taught the same concept when accused of casting out devils by the power of Beelzebub (Satan).

> 24 But when the Pharisees heard *it,* they said, This *fellow* doth not cast out devils, but by Beelzebub the prince of the devils.
>
> 25 And Jesus knew their thoughts, and said unto them, Every kingdom divided against itself is brought to desolation; and every city or house divided against itself shall not stand:

26 And if Satan cast out Satan, he is divided against himself; how shall then his kingdom stand?

27 And if I by Beelzebub cast out devils, by whom do your children cast *them* out? therefore they shall be your judges.

28 But if I cast out devils by the Spirit of God, then the kingdom of God is come unto you.

29 Or else how can one enter into a strong man's house, and spoil his goods, except he first bind the strong man? and then he will spoil his house.

30 He that is not with me is against me; and he that gathereth not with me scattereth abroad. [Matthew 12:24–30]

The angel spoke in the context of the covenants of the Father unto the house of Israel. There is only one church, the Church of the Lamb, that can give these covenants (1 Nephi 14:10). To receive the covenants and to break them brings destruction, not eternal life. The great and abominable church is again active in the latter days endeavoring to bring about the destruction of those who have made covenants (see Figure 6, page 199).

Who or what is the great and abominable church? The great and abominable church has been the subject of much controversy over the years. Two facts are evident about this church. Its foundation was among the Gentiles in the Eastern Hemisphere (1 Nephi 13:4–10), and it was responsible for the loss of many parts of the gospel and many covenants (1 Nephi 13:26).

When it comes to identifying the great and abominable church let us consider this question. Should we be labeling various organizations or should we use the Holy Ghost to discern all evil regardless of the situation or organization? The answer should be evident.

Another question, is it possible to be a member of The Church of Jesus Christ of Latter-day Saints and also to be a member of the great and abominable church? Jacob gave us the answer to this question: "Wherefore, he that fighteth against Zion, both Jew and Gentile, both bond and free, both male and female, shall perish; for they are they who are the whore of all the earth; for they who are not for me are against me, saith our God" (2 Nephi 10:16).

Another question, does a person who is associated with an evil organization automatically fight against God? No, however, such are still under bondage of sin. "And the whole world lieth in sin, and groaneth under darkness and under the bondage of sin. And by this you may know they are under the bondage of sin, because they come not unto me. For whoso cometh not unto me is under the bondage of sin" (D&C 84:49–51). Christ invites all to "repent and come unto me and be baptized in my name" (3 Nephi 21:6; see also 12:1–3; 27:20).

The Lord has also given us another answer to the question of belonging to other organizations. "For there are many yet on the earth among all sects, parties, and denominations, who are blinded by the subtle craftiness of men, whereby they lie in wait to deceive, and who are only kept from the truth because they know not where to find it" (D&C 123:12).

One more consideration, there is a difference between the church of the devil and the kingdom of the devil. The church of the devil is a part of the kingdom of the devil, but the kingdom of the devil is much broader than the church. The kingdom is involved in many aspects of life; business, education, politics, and others (see Figure 5). Nephi gave a description of the Kingdom of the devil:

> 23 For the time speedily shall come that all churches which are built up to get gain, and all those who are built up to get power over the flesh, and those who are built up to become popular in the eyes of the world, and those who seek the lusts of the flesh and the things of the world, and to do all manner of iniquity; yea, in fine, all those who belong to the kingdom of the devil are they who need fear, and tremble, and quake; they are those who must be brought low in the dust; they are those who must be consumed as stubble; and this is according to the words of the prophet. [1 Nephi 22:23]

He also gave a description of the one church of God.

> 25 And he gathereth his children from the four quarters of the earth; and he numbereth his sheep, and they know him; and there shall

be one fold and one shepherd; and he shall feed his sheep, and in him they shall find pasture. [1 Nephi 22:25]

This description is also in keeping with the admonition of Alma.

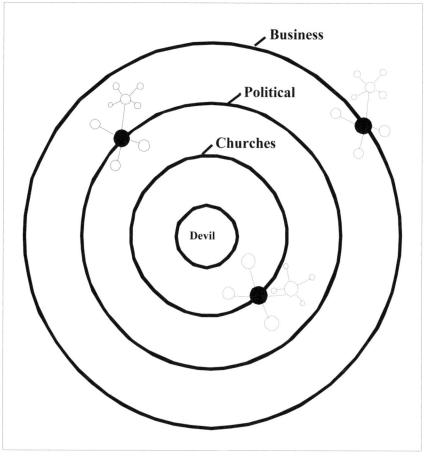

Figure 5. The Kingdom of the Devil

37 O ye workers of iniquity; ye that are puffed up in the vain things of the world, ye that have professed to have known the ways of righteousness nevertheless have gone astray, as sheep having no shepherd, notwithstanding a shepherd hath called after you and is still

calling after you, but ye will not hearken unto his voice!

38 Behold, I say unto you, that the good shepherd doth call you; yea, and in his own name he doth call you, which is the name of Christ; and if ye will not hearken unto the voice of the good shepherd, to the name by which ye are called, behold, ye are not the sheep of the good shepherd.

39 And now if ye are not the sheep of the good shepherd, of what fold are ye? Behold, I say unto you, that the devil is your shepherd, and ye are of his fold; and now, who can deny this? Behold, I say unto you, whosoever denieth this is a liar and a child of the devil.

40 For I say unto you that whatsoever is good cometh from God, and whatsoever is evil cometh from the devil. [Alma 5:37–40]

Having discussed and hopefully answered the questions about the two churches, we will discuss their status in the latter days.

1 Nephi 14:11–17 • The Two Churches Are Over All the Earth

11 And it came to pass that I looked and beheld the whore of all the earth, and she sat upon many waters; and she had dominion over all the earth, among all nations, kindreds, tongues, and people.

12 And it came to pass that I beheld the church of the Lamb of God, and its numbers were few, because of the wickedness and abominations of the whore who sat upon many waters; nevertheless, I beheld that the church of the Lamb, who were the saints of God, were also upon all the face of the earth; and their dominions upon the face of the earth were small, because of the wickedness of the great whore whom I saw.

13 And it came to pass that I beheld that the great mother of abominations did gather together multitudes upon the face of all the earth, among all the nations of the Gentiles, to fight against the Lamb of God.

14 And it came to pass that I, Nephi, beheld the power of the Lamb of God, that it descended upon the saints of the church of the Lamb, and upon the covenant people of the Lord, who were scattered upon all the face of the earth; and they were armed with righteousness and with the power of God in great glory.

15 And it came to pass that I beheld that the wrath of God was poured out upon that great and abominable church, insomuch that there were wars and rumors of wars among all the nations and kindreds of the earth.

16 And as there began to be wars and rumors of wars among all the nations which belonged to the mother of abominations, the angel spake unto me, saying: Behold, the wrath of God is upon the mother of harlots; and behold, thou seest all these things—

17 And when the day cometh that the wrath of God is poured out upon the mother of harlots, which is the great and abominable church of all the earth, whose founder is the devil, then, at that day, the work of the Father shall commence, in preparing the way for the fulfilling of his covenants, which he hath made to his people who are of the house of Israel.

Nephi, in describing the future of these two churches, gives good reason for staying with the Church of the Lamb of God. Both churches will be worldwide, but the church of the Lamb of God will be small because of the wickedness of the whore of all the earth (vv. 11–12). John the Revelator also saw the mother of abominations, who gathered multitudes from among all nations of the Gentiles (v. 13).

15 And he saith unto me, The waters which thou sawest, where the whore sitteth, are peoples, and multitudes, and nations, and tongues. [Revelation 17:15]

Nephi sees the small church armed with righteousness and the power of God in contrast to the wrath of God poured out upon the great and abominable church that was among all nations (vv. 14–16).

The Lord has led his people away from destruction many times. Moses was led out of Egypt, Lehi was led out of Jerusalem, and the saints were led to the West. The time that Nephi is seeing is past the fleeing stage; the Lord will now defend his Church with his power because of the Saints righteousness. He will establish Zion in fulfillment of his covenant (v. 17). Nephi earlier saw the day of those "who shall seek to bring forth my Zion" as the day of the coming forth of the Book of Mormon records (1 Nephi 13:35–37).

In 1831, the Saints gathered into "the land of promise, and the place for the city of Zion" (D&C 57:1–2), but three years later were told they "should wait a little season for the redemption of Zion" (D&C 105:9). Nephi was apparently seeing the time when Zion would be established (v. 17). He was shown the entire future of the Church in the latter days.

The dependence of the church of the Lamb of God upon God was emphasized by President J. E. Reuben Clark.

> The scriptures state that in the last days there will be two churches. John the Revelator spoke of the great church with worldly power that had under its dominion and leadership the kings of the earth—he spoke of it as Babylon, the mother of Harlots. Nephi's spoke of it as the great and abominable church. I am not going to say what that church is, though I have a very definite and clear idea. But I want to say that those scriptures also tell us that the other church is a weak church, a church to whose assistance God has come in order to preserve it. We certainly are not the great church, for no kings are tied to the chariot wheels of our church. We are the other church.[6]

1 Nephi 14:18–27 • John, One of the Apostles of the Lamb

18 And it came to pass that the angel spake unto me, saying: Look!

19 And I looked and beheld a man, and he was dressed in a white robe.

20 And the angel said unto me: Behold one of the twelve apostles of the Lamb.

21 Behold, he shall see and write the remainder of these things; yea, and also many things which have been.

22 And he shall also write concerning the end of the world.

23 Wherefore, the things which he shall write are just and true; and behold they are written in the book which thou beheld proceeding out of the mouth of the Jew; and at the time they proceeded out of the mouth of the Jew, or, at the time the book proceeded out of the mouth of the Jew, the things which were written were plain and pure,

---

[6] CR, April 1949, 162.

and most precious and easy to the understanding of all men.

24 And behold, the things which this apostle of the Lamb shall write are many things which thou hast seen; and behold, the remainder shalt thou see.

25 But the things which thou shalt see hereafter thou shalt not write; for the Lord God hath ordained the apostle of the Lamb of God that he should write them.

26 And also others who have been, to them hath he shown all things, and they have written them; and they are sealed up to come forth in their purity, according to the truth which is in the Lamb, in the own due time of the Lord, unto the house of Israel.

27 And I, Nephi, heard and bear record, that the name of the apostle of the Lamb was John, according to the word of the angel.

While Nephi saw the remainder of the world's history, it was left to John the apostle of Jesus, to write it (vv. 19–27). This undoubtedly referred to the Book of Revelation in the New Testament, and affirms the authorship of this book which is questioned by the Christian world. Originally, the things written by John were plain and pure, and easy to be understood (v. 23). Therefore, it was easier to understand than it is today.

The angel's comment concerning others who have been shown all things (v. 26) would include Enoch (Moses 7:4, 23–24, 67), the brother of Jared (Ether 3:24–26), Moses (Moses 1:8), and others. The seeing of the future requires a brief comment:

Let it not be said that divine omniscience is of itself a determining cause whereby events are inevitably brought to pass. A mortal father, who knows the weaknesses and frailties of his son, may by reason of that knowledge sorrowfully predict the calamities and sufferings awaiting his wayward boy. He may foresee in that son's future a forfeiture of blessings that could have been won, loss of positions, self-respect, and reputation and honor, even the dark shadows of a felon cell and the night of a drunkard grave may appear in the saddening visions of that fond father's soul; yet, convinced by experience of the impossibility of bringing about that son's reform, he foresees the dread developments of the future, and he finds but sorrow and anguish in his knowledge. Can it be said that the father's foreknowledge is the cause of the son's sinful life?[7]

Elder S. Dilworth Young made this interesting analysis that describes how God has guided and will guide the destinies of this world:

> We of the Church of Jesus Christ of Latter-day Saints have an assurance, borne of the Holy Ghost, that the Lord God planned this world and chartered its course from the beginning to the end. We testify that at the proper times men were born to carry out God's purposes. Some of these were moved by an inspiration they did not understand; others had the heavens opened and received direct revelation of the things they were to say and the action they were to take. Of the first, the making of the Constitution of the United States is an example, as was the inspiration which moved the Pilgrims of 1620 to these shores. Columbus himself testified that he was inspired to sail west. Of this second group, Moses, Isaiah, and Joseph Smith are other excellent examples.
>
> In each period of time these men met their destiny and solved their problems against the economy of the times and the customs of the people of the day. During the periods of history when they walked the stage and said their lines, events seemed to have shaped themselves in such a way that the performance of each was made possible by the intervention of divine guidance. A student of history may say that events shaped themselves in such a way that the right man rose up at the right time. With the knowledge revealed of God, which we possess, it is clear that events didn't just happen, hit or miss, but rather that the design of the Master is traceable upon the pattern of the struggle.[8]

In due time we will be given further verification of the Lord's foreknowledge. The records of those who were shown all things will be brought forth (v. 26).

---

[7] James E. Talmage, *Jesus the Christ*, 19th ed. [1951], 28.

[8] *Improvement Era*, Oct. 1962, 725–26.

1 Nephi 14:28–30 • Nephi Is Forbidden to Write More

28 And behold, I, Nephi, am forbidden that I should write the remainder of the things which I saw and heard; wherefore the things which I have written sufficeth me; and I have written but a small part of the things which I saw.

29 And I bear record that I saw the things which my father saw, and the angel of the Lord did make them known unto me.

30 And now I make an end of speaking concerning the things which I saw while I was carried away in the spirit; and if all the things which I saw are not written, the things which I have written are true. And thus it is. Amen.

Nephi's final words regarding his three visions of the Jews, the Nephites, and the Gentile Nations are important. Writing under the inspiration of the Spirit, he gave us all he was allowed to give, although it was a small part of what he saw (vv. 28, 30). He was shown what he had asked to see, "the things which my father saw" (1 Nephi 13:3, v. 29). He concludes with his testimony that what he had written was true (v. 30). The same Spirit can also give us that same testimony of Nephi's words.

SACRED WRITING

Revelations Which Are Great:

1 Nephi 13–14	Nephi's vision of the nations and kingdoms of the Gentiles.

Doctrines Learned:

1 Nephi 13:6	The devil is the founder of the great and abominable church.
1 Nephi 13:12–13	The Spirit led (Columbus) and the (Pilgrims) to the promised land (the Americas).

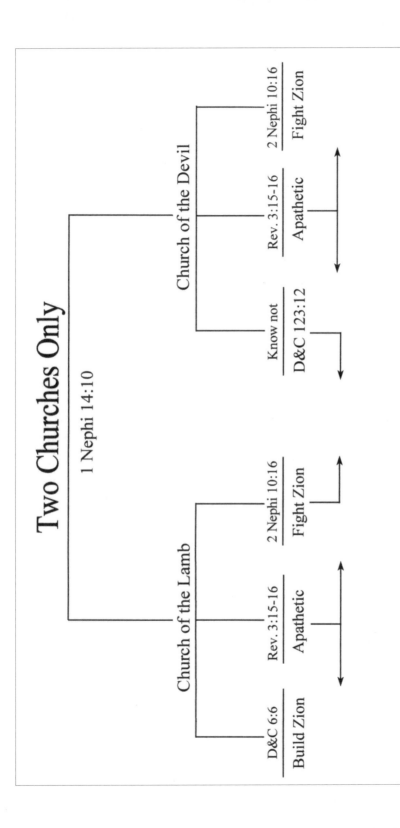

Figure 6. Two Churches Only

1 Nephi 13:24–26	Plain and precious parts were taken from the Bible after it went from the hands of the twelve apostles of the Lamb.
1 Nephi 13:39–40	The Book of Mormon and other books are to establish the truth of the Bible, and make known the precious parts that were lost.
1 Nephi 14:10	There are two churches only, the church of the Lamb of God and the church of the devil. Those who do not belong to the church of the Lamb belong to the other church.
1 Nephi 14:21–22; 27	John, an apostle of the Lamb (the Revelator), saw and wrote about the end of the world (book of Revelation).

General Authority Quotes

Elder Marion G. Romney • 1 Nephi 13

I like the Book of Mormon, and you will like it, because it is a great American book. It was written in America, by Americans, for Americans. It has peculiar application to America. It is not full of foreign ideologies uninspired interpretations of man. I believe that I am within the mark when I say that between the pages of that great book there is more ultimate truth about the overall history of America than there is in any other book, and I will go far as to say, more than in all the libraries of the world where there isn't a Book of Mormon.

In it the history of this great land of America is foretold. Up until 420 A.D. the coming to pass of the history as it was foretold was faithfully recorded by the historians who witnessed it. We who are acquainted with the Book of Mormon know that the history of America from 421 A.D. to the present time is clearly foretold therein—the long withholding of the knowledge of the land from the Gentiles, the coming of Columbus . . . the coming of the Pilgrim fathers, the establishment of this great nation, the ushering in of this great last dispensation. All these things are there foretold us clearly as anyone can write them now after they have transpired. The coming to pass of these great prophecies of the Book of Mormon is an evidence of its divinity which the world cannot destroy. [CR, April 1949, 38–39]

Elder B. H. Roberts • 1 Nephi 13:5

"The Church of the devil" here alluded to, I understand to mean not any particular church among men, or any one sect of religion, but something larger than that—something that includes within its boundaries all evil wherever it may be found; be as well as in schools of philosophy as in Christian sects, as well in systems of ethics as in systems of religion—something that includes the whole empire of Satan—what I shall call "the Kingdom of Evil." —The question was once submitted to me, "Is the Catholic Church the church referred to—the church of the devil?" "Well," said I, in answer, "I would not like to take that position, because it would leave me with a lot of churches on my hands that I might not then be able to classify." So far as the Catholic Church is concerned, I believe she has retained even more truth than the other divisions of so-called Christendom; and there is just as much virtue in the Roman Catholic Church as there is in Protestant Christendom; and I am sure there is more strength. I would not like, therefore, to designate the Catholic church as the church of the devil. Neither would I like to designate any one or all of the various divisions and subdivisions of Protestant Christendom combined as such church; nor the Greek Catholic Church; nor the Buddhist sects; nor the followers of Confucius; nor the followers of Mohammad; nor would I like to designate even the society's formed by deists and atheists as constituting the church of the devil. The Book of Mormon text ought to be read in connection with its context—with the chapter that precedes it and the remaining portions of the chapter in which the expression is found—then, I think, those who study it in that manner will be forced to the conclusion that the prophet here has in mind no particular church, no particular division of Christendom, but he has in mind, as just stated, the whole empire of Satan, and perhaps the thought of the passage would be more nearly expressed if we use the term "the Kingdom of Evil" as constituting the church of the devil. [*New Witnessess For God*, 3:264. 1951]

The Prophet Joseph Smith • 1 Nephi 13:26–29

I believe the Bible as it read when it came from the pen of the original writers. Ignorant translators, careless transcribers, or designing and corrupt priests have committed many errors. [*TPJS*, 327]

Peter penned the most sublime language of any of the apostles. [*TPJS*, 301]

Brigham Young • 1 Nephi 13:39–40

We take this book, the Bible, which I expect to see voted out of the so-called Christian world very soon, they are coming to it as fast as possible, I say we take this book for our guide, for our rule of action; we take it as the foundation of our faith. [*Discourses of Brigham Young*, selected and arranged by John A. Widtsoe, 1951, 125.]

Elder Mark E. Petersen • 1 Nephi 13:26–29

Does the Bible contain enough detail to instruct them fully regarding the original Christian Church and its doctrines, so that they really may accomplish this return?

On this latter point, the clerics say that the Bible is sufficient, for it contains all of God's word. And yet the Bible itself admits that it is an incomplete record and does not contain all of God's word. It mentions other books of scripture which are not within its covers and therefore are not available for study by anyone seeking the full truth of the gospel.

Moses spoke of the "Book of the Covenant" (Exodus 24:4), which we do not have. He also mentions the "Book of the Wars of Israel," which has never been found. [Exodus 24:7]

We might not miss reading about their wars, but it would be most helpful in a return to God if mankind had the book of the sacred covenants which the Almighty made with his people.

The "Book of Jasher," referred to by Joshua, is not in the Bible (Joshua 10:13; 2 Samuel 1:18). The same is true of the "Book of the Acts of Solomon," referred to in First Kings.

The books of Nathan and Gad, both of whom were prophets and seers, are missing (1 Chronicles 1:29; 2 Chronicles 9:29). As inspired men, their writings would be an enlightening guide on the way of truth.

Ahijah and Iddo were prophets and seers likewise (2 Chronicles 12:15; 13:22). Would their works not inspire modern people if they were available? But where are they? Can we say that our Bible is actually complete without them?

The "Book of Jehu" is mentioned in the Old Testament (2 Chronicles 20:34) is not included in it. Isaiah wrote a second book known as the "Acts of Uzziah," but where is it (2 Chronicles 26:22)? Will anyone say that Isaiah's writings are not inspirational? His second book might prove to be most invaluable if we had it.

"The Sayings of the Seers," another book of sacred writings, is referred to in the Bible (2 Chronicles 33:19). Where is it now? Would it not be good for today's Christians in their spiritual meanderings?

Paul wrote letters, in addition to those we have in the Bible, and speaks of them. He wrote a third letter to the Corinthians (1 Corinthians 5:9), and at least another one to the Ephesians (Ephesians 3:3). Where are they? He also wrote an Epistle to the Laodiceans, but it is not in our possession (Colossians 4:16). Is the Bible then complete? Does it contain all of God's word?

Jude wrote another Epistle in addition to the one in the New Testament (Jude 1:3). He also mentions a volume of scripture known as the "Prophecies of Enoch" to which he evidently had access, but which we do not have today. [Jude 1:14]

Then there is the matter of the Savior's teachings. He lived an intensive and full life during the three years of his public ministry. He preached to multitudes repeatedly. He conversed with individuals almost constantly, and gave many intimate instructions to the Twelve.

Can anyone say that his three years of instruction are contained in the Bible? May they be read in the few hours it takes to peruse what he said in the four Gospels? Can three years of the Savior's eloquent teachings be condensed into three hours of reading material? The Apostle John says twice in his Gospel that not a fraction of the Savior's ministry is recorded. [John 20:30–31; 21:25]

Much as we love it, sincerely as we believe it, can we in all truth say that the Bible is complete, that it contains all of God's word, or even the full text of the Savior's instructions?

Obviously the Lord gave other revelations anciently. He had prophets in addition to those usually mentioned in the Bible. They spoke for him. They gave enlightenment to ancient men, and they would give us light, too, if only we had their writings. [CR, April 1964, 18–19; references added]

Elder Howard W. Hunter • 1 Nephi 13:39–40

There is a great effort on the part of so-called modernists to change religious beliefs and teachings of the past to conform to modern thought and critical research. They de-emphasize the teachings of the Bible by modern critical methods and deny that scripture is inspired. The modernist teaches that Christ is not the Son of God. He denies the doctrine of the atoning sacrifice by which all men may be saved. He denies the fact of the resurrection of the Savior of the world and relegates him to the status of a teacher of ethics. Where, then, is hope? What has become of faith?

The Old Testament unfolds the story of the creation of the earth and man by God. Should we now disregard this account and modernize the creation according to the theories of the modernists? Can we say there was no Garden of Eden or an Adam and Eve? Because modernists now declare the story of the flood is unreasonable and impossible, should we disbelieve the account of Noah and the flood as related in the Old Testament? . . .

There are those who declare it is old-fashioned to believe in the Bible. Is it old-fashioned to believe in God, in Jesus Christ, the Son of the Living God? Is it old-fashioned to believe in his atoning sacrifice and the resurrection and the life? If it is, I declare myself to be old-fashioned and the Church is old-fashioned. [CR, Oct. 1970, 129–130]

Elder Marion G. Romney • 1 Nephi 13:39–40

Another reason I like the Book of Mormon and want you to read it is that it will sustain you against attacks being made by the modernists against that other great scripture, the Bible. The Book of Mormon is not only a new witness for God, it is also a witness to the truth of the Bible. . . . The Book of Mormon accepts the Bible unreservedly as the word of God. It accepts the five books of Moses as having been written by Moses. This the modernists deny. It accepts the great prophecies of Isaiah as the prophecies of the son of Amos. The resurrected Lord himself said, as recorded in the Book of Mormon, "Great are the words of Isaiah." And he advises us to read them. Further, this Book of Mormon, the doctrines in it will sustain you against many false doctrines that are current in the world today. [*Improvement Era,* June 1960, 435–36]

Challenges To Eternal Life:

1. Contrast or compare your desires with those of the great and abominable church (1 Nephi 13:7–9). Are your desires for precious clothing and the praise of the world greater than those for the plain and precious truths of the gospel? (1 Nephi 13:40).

2. Think of the gospel covenants you have made, and analyze your efforts to keep them (1 Nephi 14:5–7).

3. In light of your activities, are you building Zion or fighting against it? (1 Nephi 13:37; 2 Nephi 10:16).

4. Make a commitment to arm yourself with righteousness that the power of God may protect you from the efforts of the adversary (1 Nephi 14:14).

5. Choose a challenge from this reading and apply it to your life.

Chapter Six

Journeys in the Wilderness

1 Nephi 15:1–17:4

*H*istorical Setting: Nephi returns to the tent of his father in the valley of Lemuel after having received several visions of the future. He finds his brothers disputing over what their father had taught them. Nephi endeavors to help them understand. The length of time he spent trying to teach them is not given but was probably short. Chapter 15:1–16:8 covers the last events in the valley of Lemuel. Chapter 16:9–17:4 briefly covers the next eight years of their traveling in the wilderness until they reach the sea.

Precepts of Chapter Six:

The guilty taketh the truth to be hard, for it cutteth them to the very center. [1 Nephi 16:2]

And thus we see that by small means the Lord can bring about great things. [1 Nephi 16:29]

And thus we see that the commandments of God must be fulfilled. And if it so be that the children of men keep the commandments of God he doth nourish them, and strengthen them, and provide means whereby they can accomplish the thing which he has commanded them; wherefore, he did provide means for us while we did sojourn in the wilderness. [1 Nephi 17:3]

Some people seem to be more spiritually oriented than others. Is this an innate characteristic or is it acquired? If it is innate, does it come with us from the pre-mortal life, or do we develop it as we experience mortality? As it would be expressed in today's world, are we a product of our genetics or our environment? As we study the interchange between Nephi and his brothers and the events in the wilderness, we will gain some insights into some of these questions. Before doing so, we will review some of the events that preceded this interchange.

Laman and Lemuel were the two eldest sons of Lehi and Sariah. In the biblical world, Laman was the birthright holder, responsible for the patriarchal leadership of the family and successor to Lehi. As discussed earlier, father Lehi made great efforts to bring Laman and Lemuel to fulfill their foreordained role, an opportunity earned in the pre-mortal life. As mentioned before, he named the river and the valley after them hoping they would follow their likeness (1 Nephi 2:8–10). He had recognized the stiffneckedness of Laman and Lemuel because "they did murmur in many things against their father," and "they knew not the dealings of that God who created them" (1 Nephi 2:11–12). Furthermore, they were the product of the wicked Jewish environment. They "were like unto the Jews at Jerusalem" (1 Nephi 2:13). Their environment had influenced them more than their family, the church, and the prophets.[9] The Lord left Laman and Lemuel without excuse. He blessed Lehi with the power of the Spirit as he spoke to them, "until their frames did shake before him," confounding them and causing them to no more rebel against him. However, they only followed him in fearful compliance, not faithful obedience (1 Nephi 2:14). The Lord also gave Laman and Lemuel a second witness. Nephi taught them the things he had learned by the Holy Spirit, but unlike Sam, they would not hearken to his words; and Nephi "cried unto the lord for them" (1 Nephi 2:17–18). The Lord blessed Nephi, but recognized that Laman

---

[9] There are those who would blame Lehi and Sariah for failing to teach their sons, but there is no scriptural evidence to support this charge. Also, there was a church in the area at this time (see 1 Nephi 4:26). Although we do not know how strong it was, we do know that the more righteous were led into Babylon rather than be destroyed (1 Nephi 17:38; 2 Kings 24:10–16). Furthermore, there were many prophets warning them to repent (1 Nephi 1:4). Since Lehi responded to them, his family was certainly exposed to them.

and Lemuel would eventually "be cut off from [his] presence" and be cursed "even with a sore curse" (1 Nephi 2:21, 23). The Lord allowed them to use their agency.

Elder Neal A. Maxwell, in encouraging us to liken the scriptures unto ourselves, made this application:

> Illustratively, words which we should so "liken" occur twice with regard to Laman and Lemuel, mistakenly regarded by some as merely "stick figures." Consider, therefore, how the applications of these next words go far beyond those two: "And thus Laman and Lemuel . . . did murmur . . . because they knew not the dealings of that God who had created them." [1 Nephi 2:12; see also Mosiah 10:14]
>
> Failing to understand the "dealings" of the Lord with his children—meaning His relations with and treatment of His children—is very fundamental. Murmuring is but one of the symptoms, and not the only consequence either; in fact, brothers and sisters, this failure affects everything else!
>
> To misread something so crucial constitutes a failure to know God, who then ends up being wrongly seen as unreachable, uninvolved, uncaring, and unable—a disabled and diminished Deity, really, about whose seeming limitations, ironically, some then quickly complain. [Conference Report, Oct. 1999, 4–5]

When the sons of Lehi returned to Jerusalem to obtain the plates of brass from Laban, they drew lots as to who should go in to see Laban, and "the lot fell upon Laman" (1 Nephi 3:11). Although the exact manner of casting lots is not known, was the choice influenced by the Lord? Was he giving Laman another opportunity to assume his foreordained leadership role? Such a possibility should certainly be considered. Failing in his attempt, Nephi's brothers were about to return to their father (1 Nephi 3:14). Does this further show their character? Their skepticism was certainly a contrast to Nephi's faith. After a second failure, Laman and Lemuel were angry and "did smite [their younger brothers] even with a rod." An angel appeared, giving another great spiritual evidence to them; but once more, after the angel had departed, they "again began to murmur" (1 Nephi 3:28– 31). They also led the rebellion when returning from their second trip to Jerusalem. Nephi reminded them of their many spiritual witnesses, which only caused them to bind him and leave him "in the wilderness to be devoured by wild beasts." They were humbled "and did plead with [Nephi] that [he] would a forgive them" (1 Nephi 7:6–22). Their humility may have lasted somewhat longer than usual, but was still short lived. Lehi was shown that they would not partake of the fruit (of eternal life), bringing him great sorrow (see 1 Nephi 8:17–18, 36–38). The truth had been manifest. An outline of the reading in this chapter is given in preparation for a deeper study.

OUTLINE • 1 NEPHI 15, 16, 17:1-4

➤ 15:1–3   Nephi returns to his father's tent and finds his brothers disputing over the things spoken of by their father.

    a.   Lehi spake many great things hard to understand save they inquired of the Lord (v. 3).

    b.   The brothers were hard in their hearts, they did not look unto the Lord (v. 3).

➤ 15:4–5   Nephi was grieved because of the hardness of his brothers' hearts because of the things he had seen and knew must unavoidably come to pass.

    a.   Because of the great wickedness of men (v. 4).

    b.   Because he had seen the destruction of his people (v. 5).

➤ 15:6–20   Nephi receives strength and asks his brothers the cause of their disputations.

    a.   They cannot understand the words about the natural branches of the olive tree and the Gentiles (vv. 7–9

        1.   Nephi asks if they have inquired of the Lord?

        2.   They say no, for the Lord makes no such thing known to us.

    b.   Nephi asks why they do not keep the commandments of the Lord and would they rather perish (v. 10).

    c.   Nephi quotes the Lord about the principle of making these things known (v. 11).

    1. Do not harden your hearts but ask in faith.

    2. Believe ye shall receive and with diligence keep the commandments.

d. Nephi explains: The house of Israel was compared to an olive tree by the Spirit (vv. 12–18).

    1. Are we not broken off but are a branch of the house of Israel?

    2. The grafting in of the natural branches, through the fulness of the Gentiles, will be in the latter days, after our seed have dwindled in unbelief.

    3. Many generations after the Messiah is manifest in the body, the fullness of the gospel will come to the Gentiles, and from them to the remnant of our seed

e. The remnant of our seed shall know they are of the house of Israel, and are a covenant people (vv. 14–16).

    1. They shall come to the knowledge of their forefathers, and the gospel of their redeemer.

    2. They shall come to the knowledge of the points of his doctrine, and how to come unto him and be saved.

    3. They will praise their everlasting God, receive strength from the true vine, and come to the true fold of God.

    4. Being a natural branch, they will be remembered and grafted into the true olive tree.

f. The grafting will be after their remnant are scattered by the Gentiles (vv. 17–18).

    1. The grafting will come by way of the Gentiles, that the Lord may show his power unto the Gentiles, the very cause of his rejection by the Jews and the house of Israel.

    2. Lehi spoke of all the house of Israel, pointing to the covenant to Abraham blessing all the kindreds of the earth.

g. Nephi spake much concerning the restoration of the Jews in the latter days (vv. 19–20).

    1. He rehearses Isaiah, after they are restored they would not be confounded or scattered.

    2. His brothers are pacified and humble themselves before the Lord.

➤ 15:21–36   The brothers ask, so Nephi explains the meaning of their father's dream.

    a. The tree is a representation of the tree of life (vv. 21–23).

    b. The rod of iron represents the word of God, whoso holds fast will never perish (vv. 23–25).

       1. He exhorts them to hearken to the word of God.

       2. He exhorts them to keep the commandments of God in all things.

    c. The river of water is an awful gulf separating the wicked from the tree of life and also from the saints of God (vv. 26–30).

       1. Lehi did not notice the filthiness of the water, his mind being on other things.

       2. It represented that awful hell prepared for the wicked.

       3. Lehi saw that the justice of God divided the wicked from the righteous.

    d. The brothers ask if the wicked are tormented in the days of probation, or in the final state of the soul, or does it speak of temporal things? (vv. 31–36).

       1. Nephi says the torment speaks of both temporal and spiritual.

       2. They will be judged of the works done in the temporal body.

       3. If they die in wickedness, they will be cast off from spiritual things.

       4. If judged filthy, they cannot dwell in the kingdom of God.

       5. The kingdom of God is not filthy, but there is an awful hell prepared by the devil.

6. The final state is to dwell in the kingdom of God, or be cast out because of justice.

7. The wicked are rejected from the righteous and from the tree of life.

8. The fruit of the tree of life is the most precious and most desirable of all fruits, and the greatest of all the gifts of God.

➤ 16:1–6   Nephi's brothers accuse him of speaking hard things, more than they can bear.

     a. Nephi says he speaks hard things against the wicked, according to the truth (v. 2).

         1. He justified the righteous and testified of their being lifted up at the last day.

         2. The guilty take the truth to be hard, it cutteth to the very center.

     b. If his brothers were righteous and willing to hearken to the truth, they would not murmur (v. 3).

     c. Nephi exhorts them to keep the commandments of God (vv. 4–5).

         1. They humble themselves before the Lord.

         2. He had joy and hope that they would walk in the paths of righteousness.

     d. All these things were done as they dwelt in a tent in the valley of Lemuel (v. 6).

➤ 16:7–8   Lehi had fulfilled all the commandments the Lord had given him.

     a. Nephi, his brothers, and Zoram married the daughters of Ishmael (v. 7).

     b. Nephi had been blessed of the Lord exceedingly (v. 8).

➤ 16:9–11   Lehi is commanded of the Lord to take his journey into the wilderness.

     a. Lehi finds a round ball of curious workmanship made of fine brass at the tent door (v. 10).

        1.   Within the ball were two spindles.

        2.   One pointed the way they should go into the wilderness.

   b.   They gathered provisions and seed needed for the wilderness (v. 11).

➤ 16:12–27   Lehi and his people take their tents and cross the river Laman into the wilderness.

   a.   They travel four days south-southeast and pitch their tent in a place they call Shazer (v. 13).

        1.   They take bows and arrows and slay food for their families.

        2.   They return to Shazer.

   b.   They travel in the same direction, in the borders near the Red Sea (vv. 14–17).

        1.   They travel many days, slaying food by the way.

        2.   They follow the directions of the ball.

   c.   Nephi breaks his bow which was made of fine steel (vv. 18–21).

        1.   His brothers are angry because they can obtain no food.

        2.   Their families suffer much for the want of food.

        3.   Laman and Lemuel murmur, and his father began to murmur against the Lord.

        4.   The brothers bows had lost their spring, and they could not obtain food.

   d.   Nephi spake to his brothers, they harden their hearts and complain against the Lord (v. 22).

   e.   Nephi made a bow out of wood, and an arrow out of a stick, and also takes a sling and some stones (vv. 23–24).

        1.   He asks his father where he should go to obtain food.

        2.   Lehi is humbled by Nephi's words, and inquires of the Lord.

f. The voice of the Lord comes to Lehi and truly chastened him for murmuring (vv. 25–27).

      1. He is to look upon the things written on the ball.

      2. He and Nephi and his brothers fear and tremble over what is written.

➤ 16:28–29 Nephi beholds that the ball did work according to the faith and diligence given it.

    a. There was a new writing, plain to be read, and was changed from time to time (vv. 28–29).

    b. By small things the Lord can bring about great things (v. 29).

➤ 16:30–39 Nephi goes to the top of the mountain as directed by the ball.

    a. Nephi slays wild beasts to obtain food for their families (v. 31–32).

      1. The families joy is great.

      2. The families humble themselves and give thanks to the Lord.

    b. They travel many days in the same direction and pitch their tents (vv. 33–36).

      1. Ishmael dies in a place called Nahom.

      2. His daughters murmur against Lehi and Nephi, and want to return to Jerusalem.

    c. Laman says to Lemuel and Ishmaels sons: Let us slay our father and Nephi (vv. 37–38).

      1. Nephi has taken it upon himself to be our ruler and teacher.

      2. Nephi says the Lord has talked to him, and angels have ministered to him.

      3. We know Nephi lies and works things by his cunning arts to deceive us.

    d. The voice of the Lord chastened them, their anger ceased, they repented, and the Lord blessed them again with food (v. 39).

➤ 17:1–4   Lehi's people travel nearly eastward in the wilderness for the next eight years.

    a.   They suffer much affliction, and their women bear children (v. 1).

    b.   The blessings of the Lord were so great that they ceased murmuring (v. 2).

        1.   They lived on raw meat.

        2.   Their women gave plenty of suck for their children, and were strong like unto men.

    c.   The commandments of God must be kept (v. 3).

        1.   Those who keep them are nourished and strengthened, and means are provided.

        2.   The Lord did provide for them.

NOTES AND COMMENTARY

Introduction: "What is truth?" This question, asked by Pilate to Jesus (John 18:38), has been asked, and debated, by theologians and philosophers ever since the question was asked, and undoubtedly before. The answer was given by revelation to The Prophet Joseph Smith: "And truth is knowledge of things as they are, and as they were, and as they are to come" (D&C 93:24).

An analysis of the verses that follow the definition of truth show what the definition means. "Knowledge of things as they are" = mortal life. "He that keepeth his commandments receiveth truth and light, until he is glorified in truth and knoweth all things" (D&C 93:28; see also vv. 30–32, 39). "Knowledge of things as they were" = pre-mortal life. "Man was also in the beginning with God. Intelligence, or the light of truth, was not created or made, neither indeed can be" (D&C 93:29, see also vv. 36–38). "Knowledge of things as they are to come" = post-mortal life. "For man is spirit. The elements are eternal, and spirit and element, inseparably connected, receive a fulness of joy" (D&C 93:33 see also vv. 34–35).

In light of this revelation on truth, let us see what we can learn about Laman, Lemuel, Lehi, and Nephi.

1 Nephi 15:1–3 • Laman And Lemuel Disputing Over Their Father's Sayings

1 And it came to pass that after I, Nephi, had been carried away in the spirit, and seen all these things, I returned to the tent of my father.

2 And it came to pass that I beheld my brethren, and they were disputing one with another concerning the things which my father had spoken unto them.

3 For he truly spake many great things unto them, which were hard to be understood, save a man should inquire of the Lord; and they being hard in their hearts, therefore they did not look unto the Lord as they ought.

The key to understanding spiritual things is to "inquire of the Lord." Nephi recognizes that Laman and Lemuel had failed to look to the Lord because of the hardness of their hearts. Failure to understand the Book of Mormon, or other words coming from the Lord or his servants, is for the same reason today. Elder Marion D. Hanks commented on the words of Nephi cited above:

There is no way to understand spiritual truth except through the Spirit of God. Natural ability, brilliance of intellect, training, diligent search are all inadequate of themselves to give understanding of spiritual things if he who possess them is not led by the Spirit. ". . . to be learned is good if they hearken unto the counsels of God." [2 Nephi 9:29]

The Prophet Lehi tried with great patience to teach his sons Laman and Lemuel the principles of the gospel, but they would not learn. They were unable to understand because they would not humble themselves and call on the Lord; therefore, they could not receive a knowledge of truth through the Spirit. . . .

The only way to know spiritual truth is through the Spirit of God which may be enjoyed only by those who humble themselves and call upon him and hearken to his voice. Nothing is more clear in scripture or in life than this truth. The things of the Spirit are "hard to be understood, save a man should inquire of the Lord; . . ." in sincerity and humility. Through "study and also by faith," through reverent search and humble prayer, men can know with certain assurance the things of God.

For those who will not pay the price, the truths of the gospel will always be a "stumbling block," "foolishness," "hard to be understood." In their pride and stubbornness they fail to learn the most important truths of eternity. [*Improvement Era*, Aug. 1961, 587]

After quoting 1 Nephi 15:3, Elder Neal A. Maxwell commented:

This failure to believe in a revealing God was especially basic. Some moderns who wish to distance themselves from God try placing His pavilion firmly in the past. By believing in such a disabled God, people can do pretty much as they please. It is then not many steps further to saying there is no God, and therefore no law and no sin! [see 2 Nephi 2:13; see also Alma 30:28]

Like Laman and Lemuel, many today would consign God only to the past; He thereby ceases to be the constant God of yesterday, today, and tomorrow (see 2 Nephi 27:23). Actually, God has the past, present, and future ever before Him, constituting "an eternal now." [*Teachings of the Prophet Joseph Smith*, sel. Joseph Fielding Smith (1976), 220; see also D & C 130:7]

In short, Laman and Lemuel's own lack of character kept them from understanding the perfect character of God! No wonder the Prophet Joseph Smith said, "If men do not comprehend the character of God, they do not comprehend themselves" (*Teachings of the Prophet Joseph Smith*, 343). [CR, Oct. 1999, 5]

1 Nephi 15:4–11 • Nephi Questions His Brothers

4 And now I, Nephi, was grieved because of the hardness of their hearts, and also, because of the things which I had seen, and knew they must unavoidably come to pass because of the great wickedness of the children of men.

5 And it came to pass that I was overcome because of my afflictions, for I considered that mine afflictions were great above all, because of the destruction of my people, for I had beheld their fall.

6 And it came to pass that after I had received strength I spake unto my brethren, desiring to know of them the cause of their disputations.

7 And they said: Behold, we cannot understand the words which our father hath spoken concerning the natural branches of the olive-tree, and also concerning the Gentiles.

8 And I said unto them: Have ye inquired of the Lord?

9 And they said unto me: We have not; for the Lord maketh no such thing known unto us.

10 Behold, I said unto them: How is it that ye do not keep the commandments of the Lord? How is it that ye will perish, because of the hardness of your hearts?

11 Do ye not remember the things which the Lord hath said?—If ye will not harden your hearts, and ask me in faith, believing that ye shall receive, with diligence in keeping my commandments, surely these things shall be made known unto you.

Nephi's grief at this time was two fold: (1) he recognized the cause of his brothers' failure to understand; and (2) he knew his people in Jerusalem would be destroyed. After regaining the strength that had been taken from him as he had experienced his great vision, he attempted to help his brothers to understand and therefore escape similar judgments of God.

Nephi asked four questions of Laman and Lemuel as they confessed they could not understand their fathers words regarding the natural branches of the olive tree, and also concerning the Gentiles. First, had they inquired of the Lord, or had they prayed for understanding? The brothers admitted that they had not prayed. Nephi's next three questions are a follow-up to the first one. Second, why weren't they keeping the commandments?, third, why were they willing to perish because of the hardness of their hearts?, and fourth, do ye not remember the things which the Lord hath said? He then apparently quotes a scripture that shows prayer to be a commandment (v. 11). Nephi does not identify the reference of his scriptural quote, but it was probably from the plates of brass. Another possibility is that it was something that their father had told them. Regardless, Nephi, their younger brother, is chastising them. His constructive criticism is followed by some meaningful commentary on their father's instruction. Nephi was not merely pointing out their faults, but was trying to help soften their hardened hearts.

As readers of the Book of Mormon, we should learn from Nephi. We can learn how to understand spiritual things and also how to help people who are spiritually derelict. First, we, or they, must pray for understanding (v. 8). Secondly, we, or they, must be worthy to receive personal revelation through keeping the commandments. Thirdly, we, or they, must search the scriptures.

1 Nephi 15:12–20 • Nephi Expounds On His Father's Teachings and the Olive Tree

12 Behold, I say unto you, that the house of Israel was compared unto an olive-tree, by the Spirit of the Lord which was in our father; and behold are we not broken off from the house of Israel, and are we not a branch of the house of Israel?

13 And now, the thing which our father meaneth concerning the grafting in of the natural branches through the fulness of the Gentiles, is, that in the latter days, when our seed shall have dwindled in unbelief, yea, for the space of many years, and many generations after the Messiah shall be manifested in body unto the children of men, then shall the fulness of the gospel of the Messiah come unto the Gentiles, and from the Gentiles unto the remnant of our seed—

14 And at that day shall the remnant of our seed know that they are of the house of Israel, and that they are the covenant people of the Lord; and then shall they know and come to the knowledge of their forefathers, and also to the knowledge of the gospel of their Redeemer, which was ministered unto their fathers by him; wherefore, they shall come to the knowledge of their Redeemer and the very points of his doctrine, that they may know how to come unto him and be saved.

15 And then at that day will they not rejoice and give praise unto their everlasting God, their rock and their salvation? Yea, at that day, will they not receive the strength and nourishment from the true vine? Yea, will they not come unto the true fold of God?

16 Behold, I say unto you, Yea; they shall be remembered again

among the house of Israel; they shall be grafted in, being a natural branch of the olive-tree, into the true olive-tree.

17 And this is what our father meaneth; and he meaneth that it will not come to pass until after they are scattered by the Gentiles; and he meaneth that it shall come by way of the Gentiles, that the Lord may show his power unto the Gentiles, for the very cause that he shall be rejected of the Jews, or of the house of Israel.

18 Wherefore, our father hath not spoken of our seed alone, but also of all the house of Israel, pointing to the covenant which should be fulfilled in the latter days; which covenant the Lord made to our father Abraham, saying: In thy seed shall all the kindreds of the earth be blessed.

Although the allegory of the house of Israel given by Zenos and recorded on the plates of brass had not yet been written on the plates of Nephi, it seems that Lehi had been interpreting the allegory for his sons, or had been shown the same things Zenos saw. We do not have Lehi's words, but we do have Nephi's explanation of his father's words. His explanation will be valuable when the allegory that is recorded in Jacob chapter five is studied.

Nephi says "that the house of Israel was compared unto an olive tree by the Spirit of the Lord which was in our father" (v. 12). Zenos makes the same comparison: "I will liken thee, O house of Israel, like unto a tame olive tree" (Jacob 5:3). Nephi makes the comparison applicable to the people of Lehi by declaring that they had been broken off from the house of Israel and were a branch of the same (v. 12). He then explained what his father meant "concerning the grafting in of the natural branches through the fullness of the Gentiles" (v. 13). Zenos quotes the Lord of the vineyard: "I have grafted in the natural branches again into their mother tree" (Jacob 5:60). However, Nephi gives a specific time period for the grafting, "in the latter days." The latter days are after "our seed (of Lehi) shall have dwindled in unbelief, yea, for the space of many years, and many generations after the Messiah shall be manifested in body unto the children of men" (v. 13). "The fullness of the gospel of the Messiah" was to come unto the (cultural)

Gentiles,[10] and the Gentiles would then take it unto the remnant of Lehi's people (v. 13). Nephi's explanation helps one to understand that the allegory of Zenos, Jacob 5, is speaking essentially of the latter days, many generations after the meridian of time. Furthermore, an analysis of the allegory shows that Jacob 5:30–75 is about the latter days.

Nephi outlines four specific blessings that will come to the remnant of the people of Lehi in the latter days (vv. 14–15). First, they will "know that they are of the house of Israel, and that they are the covenant people of the Lord." This statement implies that the knowledge of their ancestors will be lost after they dwindle in unbelief. Second, they will "come to a knowledge of their forefathers," meaning the people who lived on the American continent from the time of Lehi, 600 B.C., to the time of the Nephite's destruction, A.D. 385. The Book of Mormon will be the source of this information. Third, they will come "to the knowledge of the gospel of their Redeemer which was ministered unto their fathers by him; wherefore, they shall come the knowledge of their Redeemer and the very points of his doctrine." This knowledge will enable them "to come unto him and be saved." Nephi had been promised that his seed would "write many things which [the Lord] shall minister unto them," and "shall be hid up, to come forth unto the Gentiles, by the gift and power of the Lamb. And in them shall be written my gospel, saith the Lamb, and my rock and my salvation" (1 Nephi 13:35–36). The Lord "covenanted with [Enos] that he would bring them forth unto the Lamanites in his own due time" (Enos 1:16). Mormon was commanded: "they are to be hid up unto the Lord that they may come forth in his own due time. . . . that the seed of this

---

[10] Amos, the Old Testament Prophet, prophesied that the Lord would "sift the house of Israel among all nations" (Amos 9:8). Thus "cultural Gentiles" are those who are of the blood of Israel, but were scattered among the Gentile nations of the earth, and are now gathered again to Israel. In the dedicatory prayer of the Kirtland Temple, which "was given to him by revelation" (section heading), Joseph Smith described the members of the Church as those "who are identified with the Gentiles" (D&C 109:60). For further support of this doctrine see Monte S. Nyman, "The Second Gathering of the Literal Seed," published in *Doctrines For Exaltation*, Chapter 14, Deseret Book Company, Salt Lake City, Utah 1989.

people may more fully believe his gospel, which shall go forth unto them from the Gentiles" (Mormon 5:12–13, 15).

The Lord fulfilled those promises through to Joseph Smith:

> This work (the Book of Mormon) does contain all those parts of my gospel which my holy prophets, yea, and also my disciples, desired in their prayers should come forth unto this people.
>
> And I said unto them, that it should be granted unto them according to their faith in their prayers;
>
> Yea, and this was their faith—that my gospel, which I gave unto them that they might preach in their days, might come unto their brethren the Lamanites, and also all that had become Lamanites because of their dissensions.
>
> Now, this is not all—their faith in their prayers was that this gospel should be made known also, if it were possible that other nations should possess this land;
>
> And thus they did leave a blessing upon this land in their prayers, that whosoever should believe in this gospel in this land might have eternal life;
>
> Yea, that it might be free unto all of whatsoever nation, kindred, tongue, or people they may be.
>
> And now, behold, according to their faith in their prayers will I bring this part of my gospel to the knowledge of my people. [D&C 10:46–52]

The Book of Mormon is indeed another testament of Jesus Christ and his gospel. His gospel is not given in general terms or concepts, but gives very specific points of his doctrine. The Book of Mormon is once more labeled as the source of the doctrine of the Church.

The fourth blessing specified by Nephi was they will "receive the strength and nourishment from the true vine." Jesus said, "I am the true vine" (John 15:1). The Lamanites today, when they join the Church, are "grafted in, being a natural branch of the olive-tree, into the true olive-tree" (1 Nephi 15:16). Strength and nourishment comes from His Spirit, His words, and His priesthood.

1 Nephi 15:19–20 • The Restoration
of the Jews in the Latter Days

19 And it came to pass that I, Nephi, spake much unto them concerning these things; yea, I spake unto them concerning the restoration of the Jews in the latter days.

20 And I did rehearse unto them the words of Isaiah, who spake concerning the restoration of the Jews, or of the house of Israel; and after they were restored they should no more be confounded, neither should they be scattered again. And it came to pass that I did speak many words unto my brethren, that they were pacified and did humble themselves before the Lord.

Lehi and his seed are not the only branch to be grafted into the olive tree. All of the branches of the house of Israel will be grafted in. The allegory of Zenos speaks of three natural branches: "the first and the second and also the last" (Jacob 5:39). Nephi spoke to his brothers of one of the two other natural branches, "the restoration of the Jews in the latter days" (v. 19). He only recorded their general destiny, but also gave the source of his comments, "the words of Isaiah."[11] The other branch, the lost tribes, will be identified and both of these branches will be discussed more fully when the Book of Mormon text refers to them. The covenant made to Abraham will be fulfilled in the latter days through the grafting in of the natural branches and in the offering of the blessings of the gospel to all nations as Abraham was promised (v. 18). Mormon gave a second witness to the fulfillment of Abraham's covenant being in the latter days:

And behold, the Lord hath reserved their blessings, which they might have received in the land, for the Gentiles who shall possess the land.

But behold, it shall come to pass that they shall be driven and scattered by the Gentiles; and after they have been driven and scattered

---

[11] For an analysis of Isaiah's prophecies concerning the Jews, see Monte S. Nyman, *Isaiah: Prophecies of the Restoration*, chap. 8, "Isaiah's Many Prophecies of Latter-day Judah," [1998], 129–142.

by the Gentiles, behold, then will the Lord remember the covenant which he made unto Abraham and unto all the house of Israel.

And also the Lord will remember the prayers of the righteous, which have been put up unto him for them. [Mormon 5:19–21]

Nephi's interpretive comments caused his brothers to ask further questions.

1 Nephi 15:21–30 • Nephi Interprets His Father's Dream for His Brothers

21 And it came to pass that they did speak unto me again, saying: What meaneth this thing which our father saw in a dream? What meaneth the tree which he saw?

22 And I said unto them: It was a representation of the tree of life.

23 And they said unto me: What meaneth the rod of iron which our father saw, that led to the tree?

24 And I said unto them that it was the word of God; and whoso would hearken unto the word of God, and would hold fast unto it, they would never perish; neither could the temptations and the fiery darts of the adversary overpower them unto blindness, to lead them away to destruction.

25 Wherefore, I, Nephi, did exhort them to give heed unto the word of the Lord; yea, I did exhort them with all the energies of my soul, and with all the faculty which I possessed, that they would give heed to the word of God and remember to keep his commandments always in all things.

26 And they said unto me: What meaneth the river of water which our father saw?

27 And I said unto them that the water which my father saw was filthiness; and so much was his mind swallowed up in other things that he beheld not the filthiness of the water.

28 And I said unto them that it was an awful gulf, which separated the wicked from the tree of life, and also from the saints of God.

29 And I said unto them that it was a representation of that awful hell, which the angel said unto me was prepared for the wicked.

30 And I said unto them that our father also saw that the justice of God did also divide the wicked from the righteous; and the brightness thereof was like unto the brightness of a flaming fire, which ascendeth up unto God forever and ever, and hath no end.

The imagery given in the above verses were discussed in the interpretation of the dream or vision given to Lehi in 1 Nephi 8. A few additional observations will be made here. What we should learn from Lehi's dream (vv. 24–24) was the precept for the previous discussion in chapter three). Nephi, having seen the same vision, observed some things that his father had not: the filthiness of the water and its interpretation (vv. 27–29). Nephi then recounts what his father saw (v. 30).

1 Nephi 15:31–36 • A Representation of Things Both Temporal and Spiritual

31 And they said unto me: Doth this thing mean the torment of the body in the days of probation, or doth it mean the final state of the soul after the death of the temporal body, or doth it speak of the things which are temporal?

32 And it came to pass that I said unto them that it was a representation of things both temporal and spiritual; for the day should come that they must be judged of their works, yea, even the works which were done by the temporal body in their days of probation.

33 Wherefore, if they should die in their wickedness they must be cast off also, as to the things which are spiritual, which are pertaining to righteousness; wherefore, they must be brought to stand before God, to be judged of their works; and if their works have been filthiness they must needs be filthy; and if they be filthy it must needs be that they cannot dwell in the kingdom of God; if so, the kingdom of God must be filthy also.

34 But behold, I say unto you, the kingdom of God is not filthy, and there cannot any unclean thing enter into the kingdom of God; wherefore there must needs be a place of filthiness prepared for that which is filthy.

35 And there is a place prepared, yea, even that awful hell of which I have spoken, and the devil is the preparator of it; wherefore the final

state of the souls of men is to dwell in the kingdom of God, or to be cast out because of that justice of which I have spoken.

36 Wherefore, the wicked are rejected from the righteous, and also from that tree of life, whose fruit is most precious and most desirable above all other fruits; yea, and it is the greatest of all the gifts of God. And thus I spake unto my brethren. Amen.

The first question asked by Laman and Lemuel, does "it speak of the things which are temporal?" (v. 31), is typical for them and typical of questions still being asked today about scriptures and other spiritual experiences. Nephi's answer was appropriate for them and is still appropriate for us today, "It was (or is) a representation of things both temporal and spiritual" (v. 32). Furthermore, his warning regarding the filthy not being able to dwell in the kingdom of God because no unclean thing can enter into the kingdom of God, and "the final state of the souls of men" is to dwell in the kingdom of God or be cast out (vv. 33–35) is not only still appropriate, but also much needed in our society today. His final message, also a part of the previous discussion, is worth repeating. The fruit of the tree of life "is most precious and most desirable above all other fruits" (v. 36). Eternal life "is the greatest of all the gifts of God" (D&C 14:7).

Nephi's commentary proves most helpful to understand the allegory of the house of Israel (Jacob 5), the vision of the tree of life shown to his father (1 Nephi 8), and the importance of our obtaining the fruit of the tree or eternal life (v. 36).

1 Nephi 16:1–6 • The Guilty Taketh the Truth to Be Hard

1 And now it came to pass that after I, Nephi, had made an end of speaking to my brethren, behold they said unto me: Thou hast declared unto us hard things, more than we are able to bear.

2 And it came to pass that I said unto them that I knew that I had spoken hard things against the wicked, according to the truth; and the righteous have I justified, and testified that they should be lifted up at the last day; wherefore, the guilty taketh the truth to be hard, for

it cutteth them to the very center.

3 And now my brethren, if ye were righteous and were willing to hearken to the truth, and give heed unto it, that ye might walk uprightly before God, then ye would not murmur because of the truth, and say: Thou speakest hard things against us.

4 And it came to pass that I, Nephi, did exhort my brethren, with all diligence, to keep the commandments of the Lord.

5 And it came to pass that they did humble themselves before the Lord; insomuch that I had joy and great hopes of them, that they would walk in the paths of righteousness.

6 Now, all these things were said and done as my father dwelt in a tent in the valley which he called Lemuel.

Hard things, or hard doctrines, are those things that prick our conscience because we know we are not living according to these truths. Nephi acknowledged that he had taught "hard things against the wicked, according to the truth," but the righteous were justified and would "be lifted up at the last day." He then coined this salient truth, "the guilty taketh the truth to be hard" (v. 2). In modern revelation the Lord warns us to "give heed unto my word, which is quick and powerful, sharper than a two-edged sword" (D&C 6:2). A two-edged sword cuts whatever it contacts either way it is swung. The word of God or the truth has the same effect. We cannot avoid being affected by it either positively by our taking heed, or negatively by rejecting it. Jesus taught this same doctrine as he attended the Feast of Tabernacles in the last year of his mortal life. He had "walked in Galilee: for he would not walk in Jewry, because the Jews sought to kill him" (John 7:1–2).

14 Now about the midst of the feast Jesus went up into the temple, and taught.

15 And the Jews marvelled, saying, How knoweth this man letters, having never learned?

16 Jesus answered them, and said, My doctrine is not mine, but his that sent me.

17 If any man will do his will, he shall know of the doctrine,

whether it be of God, or *whether* I speak of myself.

18 He that speaketh of himself seeketh his own glory: but he that seeketh his glory that sent him, the same is true, and no unright-eousness is in him. [John 7:14–18]

Nephi told his brothers the same thing Jesus told the Jews at the feast; "if ye were righteous and were willing to hearken to the truth, and give heed unto it, that ye might walk uprightly before God, then ye would not murmur because of the truth, and say: Thou speakest hard things against us" (1 Nephi 16:3). We too should follow Nephi's exhortation to his brothers "to keep the commandments of the Lord" (v. 4). As will be seen, the brothers humility and repentance was short lived.

1 Nephi 16:7–8 • Marriages Fulfill All the Commandments of the Lord to Lehi

7 And it came to pass that I, Nephi, took one of the daughters of Ishmael to wife; and also, my brethren took of the daughters of Ishmael to wife; and also Zoram took the eldest daughter of Ishmael to wife.

8 And thus my father had fulfilled all the commandments of the Lord which had been given unto him. And also, I, Nephi, had been blessed of the Lord exceedingly.

After the marriages of the sons and daughters who had come out of Jerusalem (v. 7), Lehi had kept all the commandments given him by the Lord (v. 8). They had remained in the valley of Lemuel until these commandments were kept (v. 6). In Lehi's dream of the tree of life, he "beheld a tree, whose fruit was desirable to make one happy" (1 Nephi 8:10). Everyone wants to be happy, but each seeks it in his or her own way. True and eternal happiness comes only in the Lord's way, by keeping his commandments. The Prophet Joseph taught: "Happiness is the object and design of our existence; and will be the end thereof, if we pursue the path that leads to it; and this path is virtue, uprightness, faithfulness, holiness, and keeping all the commandments of God" (*TPJS*, 255–56). Keeping all the commandments is a lifetime endeavor. After the Passover meal, just prior to his crucifixion, Jesus taught his apostles:

> If ye love me, keep my commandments.
>
> And I will pray the Father, and he shall give you another Comforter, that he may abide with you for ever;
>
> *Even* the Spirit of truth; whom the world cannot receive, because it seeth him not, neither knoweth him: but ye know him; for he dwelleth with you, and shall be in you. [John 14:15–17]

1 Nephi 16:9 • Lehi Commanded to Journey into the Wilderness

> And it came to pass that the voice of the Lord spake unto my father by night, and commanded him that on the morrow he should take his journey into the wilderness. [1 Nephi 16:9]

The teaching of the Prophet Joseph, partially quoted above, is appropriate here. "But we cannot keep all the commandments without first knowing them, and we cannot expect to know all, or more than we now know unless we comply with or keep those we have already received" (*TPJS*, 256). Lehi followed the revelation not knowing what awaited them, but with faith he was doing the Lord's will. Joseph's comments are again cited: "This is the principle on which the government of heaven is conducted—by revelation adapted to the circumstances in which the children of the kingdom are placed. Whatever God requires is right, no matter what it is. Although we may not see the reason thereof till long after the events transpire. If we seek first the kingdom of God, all good things will be added" (*TPJS*, 256). As they journey into the wilderness, obedience to the principles of happiness is continually tested.

1 Nephi 16:10–11 • A Round Ball of Curious Workmanship

> 10 And it came to pass that as my father arose in the morning, and went forth to the tent door, to his great astonishment he beheld upon

the ground a round ball of curious workmanship; and it was of fine brass. And within the ball were two spindles; and the one pointed the way whither we should go into the wilderness.

11 And it came to pass that we did gather together whatsoever things we should carry into the wilderness, and all the remainder of our provisions which the Lord had given unto us; and we did take seed of every kind that we might carry into the wilderness.

Having kept all the commandments, the Lord gave them some help to travel in the wilderness. The "round ball of curious workmanship" (v. 10) was a divine instrument to receive "revelation adapted to the circumstances" they would meet in the wilderness (*TPJS*, 256). More will be said about this instrument under 1 Nephi 16:28–29.

1 Nephi 16:12–16 • Travel South-Southeast in the Wilderness Near the Red Sea

12 And it came to pass that we did take our tents and depart into the wilderness, across the river Laman.

13 And it came to pass that we traveled for the space of four days, nearly a south-southeast direction, and we did pitch our tents again; and we did call the name of the place Shazer.

14 And it came to pass that we did take our bows and our arrows, and go forth into the wilderness to slay food for our families; and after we had slain food for our families we did return again to our families in the wilderness, to the place of Shazer. And we did go forth again in the wilderness, following the same direction, keeping in the most fertile parts of the wilderness, which were in the borders near the Red Sea.

15 And it came to pass that we did travel for the space of many days, slaying food by the way, with our bows and our arrows and our stones and our slings.

16 And we did follow the directions of the ball, which led us in the more fertile parts of the wilderness. [1 Nephi 16:12–16]

These five verses telling of many days traveling in the wilderness are very general. Comments on their travels will be included later.

Hugh Nibley connects the name "Shazer" (v. 13) with Palestinian words to mean "a weak but reliable water supply—or a clump of trees." Lehi's people could hardly have picked a better name for their first suitable stopping place."[12] Hugh Nibley's connection fits the text, a place to camp long enough to obtain food. However, the main point of these verses is that they were led by revelation through a region that was unknown to them.

1 Nephi 16:17–25 • I Did Break My Bow Which Was Made of Fine Steel

17 And after we had traveled for the space of many days, we did pitch our tents for the space of a time, that we might again rest ourselves and obtain food for our families.

18 And it came to pass that as I, Nephi, went forth to slay food, behold, I did break my bow, which was made of fine steel; and after I did break my bow, behold, my brethren were angry with me because of the loss of my bow, for we did obtain no food.

19 And it came to pass that we did return without food to our families, and being much fatigued, because of their journeying, they did suffer much for the want of food.

20 And it came to pass that Laman and Lemuel and the sons of Ishmael did begin to murmur exceedingly, because of their sufferings and afflictions in the wilderness; and also my father began to murmur against the Lord his God; yea, and they were all exceedingly sorrowful, even that they did murmur against the Lord.

21 Now it came to pass that I, Nephi, having been afflicted with my brethren because of the loss of my bow, and their bows having lost their springs, it began to be exceedingly difficult, yea, insomuch that we could obtain no food.

22 And it came to pass that I, Nephi, did speak much unto my brethren, because they had hardened their hearts again, even unto complaining against the Lord their God.

23 And it came to pass that I, Nephi, did make out of wood a bow,

---

[12] *Lehi in the Desert and the World of the Jaredites* [1952], 90.

and out of a straight stick, an arrow; wherefore, I did arm myself with a bow and an arrow, with a sling and with stones. And I said unto my father: Whither shall I go to obtain food?

24 And it came to pass that he did inquire of the Lord, for they had humbled themselves because of my words; for I did say many things unto them in the energy of my soul.

25 And it came to pass that the voice of the Lord came unto my father; and he was truly chastened because of his murmuring against the Lord, insomuch that he was brought down into the depths of sorrow.

As Joseph taught, in order to obtain happiness we must keep all the commandments. When we fail to keep the commandments, the Spirit withdraws, and we become unhappy. Without food it is natural for man to murmur and complain as did Laman, Lemuel, and the sons of Ishmael. Their hunger must have been great and must have been for an extended period of time because even father Lehi "began to murmur against the Lord" (v. 20). But here the great character of Nephi is illustrated. He not only tries to appease his brothers, but he does something to alleviate their difficult situation. He improvises a wooden bow and arrow, and then asks his father "whither shall I go to obtain food" (v. 23). Nephi was honoring his father in spite of his father's temporary loss of faith. This act is even more significant in light of the promise the Lord had given him that he would "be made a ruler and a teacher over thy brethren" (1 Nephi 2:22). Most people would probably have seen this as an opportunity to take over, and justify his doing so because of the previous promise. However, Nephi was determined to keep all the commandments of the Lord. Honoring his father certainly bolstered his father's faith as well. This is the only time the record tells of Lehi faltering, and the example of his youngest son must have been a great inspiration to him.

Elder Marion D. Hanks confirms and adds to the above observations:

I see a lesson of life here that I do not think Joseph Smith could possibly have contrived. It has too much meaning. He did not have the experience. He had not lived long enough. This is so simple a thing that I doubt many would pause to note it. It is the lesson of the day Nephi broke his bow when they were in the wilderness, This bow was a symbol of food. He was keeping them alive, being a great hunter. And when that bow broke they were in trouble. Laman and Lemuel complained, of course. They were habituated to, they were looking for trouble. But for the first and only time the book tells us about, that I know of, even wonderful old father Lehi complained. He to whom God had revealed his will, this Lehi, when it came to facing starvation, even he complained. Then what happened? This situation is sometime present in almost every business, every college, every governmental unit in the land, in many homes, in churches, where there is a crown prince and heir apparent, the boy who is ready to step up. Lehi was the prophet, but he was old. Nephi had already been designated to succeed. He had seen angels and had talked with the spirit of the Lord. He had had marvelous experiences. The time was here, now, for him to take over-his dad was wavering. The old man had lost it.

What to do? Nephi says he made a bow and an arrow out of some available wood, got a sling and stones and, "I said unto my Father, 'Whither shall I go to obtain food?'" It is a simple thing, isn't it? This is what Goethe meant when he said, "If you treat an individual as he is, he will stay as he is. But if you treat him as if he were what he could be and ought to be, he will become what he ought to be." This means that Nephi went to his father and said, "Dad, the Lord has blessed you. You are his servant. I need to know where to go to get food. Dad, you ask him, will you?" Oh, he could have gone to his own knees. He could have taken over.

I count this one of the really significant lessons of life in the book, and, I repeat, the pages are full of them. A son who had strength enough, and humility enough, and manliness enough to go to his wavering superior and say, "You ask God, will you?" because somehow he knew this is how you make men strong, that wise confidence in men builds them. Lehi asked God and God told him, and Lehi's leadership was restored. [Elder Marion D. Hanks, May 4, 1960, BYU Speeches of the Year, 6]

Some have challenged the use of steel (v. 18) at this period of time. However, the knowledge of steel, and its use in bows has been verified. Dr. Hugh Nibley has written:

Through the years critics of the Book of Mormon have constantly called attention to the mention of steel in that book as a gross anachronism. But now we are being reminded that one cannot be dogmatic in dating the appearance of steel since there is more than one kind of steel with "a whole series of variants in the combination of iron and steel components" in ancient times; and when a particularly fine combination was hit upon it would be kept secret in "individual workshops" and "passed on from father to son for many generations." Hence it is not too surprising to learn that "even in early European times" there is evidence of the production of steel "of very high quality" and extreme hardness. Further east steel is attested even earlier.[13]

Earlier Dr. Nibley wrote:

A steel bow was not necessarily a solid piece of metal, anymore than the Canaanites' "chariots of iron" (Joshua 17:16–18; Judges 1:19, 4:3) were solid iron, or than various implements mentioned in the Old Testament. . . . It was in all probability a steel-ribbed bow, since it broke at about the same time that the wooden bows of his brothers "lost their spring." Only composite bows were used in Palestine, that is, bows of more than one piece, and a steel backed bow would be called a steel bow just as an iron-trimmed chariot was called a "chariot of iron."[14]

1 Nephi 16:26–32 • A New Writing upon the Ball which Was Plain to Be Read

26 And it came to pass that the voice of the Lord said unto him: Look upon the ball, and behold the things which are written.

27 And it came to pass that when my father beheld the things which were written upon the ball, he did fear and tremble exceedingly, and also my brethren and the sons of Ishmael and our wives.

28 And it came to pass that I, Nephi, beheld the pointers which were in the ball, that they did work according to the faith and diligence and heed which we did give unto them.

---

[13] *Since Cumorah* [1967], 254.

[14] *Lehi in the Desert and the World of the Jaredites* [1952], 66–67.

29 And there was also written upon them a new writing, which was plain to be read, which did give us understanding concerning the ways of the Lord; and it was written and changed from time to time, according to the faith and diligence which we gave unto it. And thus we see that by small means the Lord can bring about great things.

30 And it came to pass that I, Nephi, did go forth up into the top of the mountain, according to the directions which were given upon the ball.

31 And it came to pass that I did slay wild beasts, insomuch that I did obtain food for our families.

32 And it came to pass that I did return to our tents, bearing the beasts which I had slain; and now when they beheld that I had obtained food, how great was their joy! And it came to pass that they did humble themselves before the Lord, and did give thanks unto him.

Although the round ball found by Nephi is not named here, it is later called the "Liahona" (Alma 37–38). It was, as stated earlier, an instrument through which revelation was received. The revelations were written and were "plain to be read" (v. 29). This strongly implies the revelations were in sentences. The writings were not given until faith and diligence were exercised by the receiver. The messages were changed on the same basis. It seems the Prophet Joseph followed the same process in using the "urim and thummim" in translating the Book of Mormon. In a revelation concerning Martin Harris, "Joseph was told, God had given thee sight and power to translate," (D&C 3:12). Oliver Cowdery was given the opportunity to translate and was told:

8 But, behold, I say unto you, that you must study it out in your mind; then you must ask me if it be right, and if it is right I will cause that your bosom shall burn within you; therefore, you shall feel that it is right.

9 But if it be not right you shall have no such feelings, but you shall have a stupor of thought that shall cause you to forget the thing which is wrong; therefore, you cannot write that which is sacred save it be given you from me.

It was a sight process that required faith and diligence just as did

the Liahona. The expression, "thus we see" introduces the precept that Nephi wants us to learn from their travels in the wilderness thus far: "that by small means the Lord can bring about great things" (v. 29). In light of the miraculous nature of the round ball, the "small means" must refer to being small from the world's point of view, not the Lord's. To believe revelation is given through such an instrument is diametrically opposed to the world's concept of reasoning and rationalization. On the other extreme, the devil has his counterfeits through such means as crystal ball reading, palm reading, astrology, and the like. Nephi's small means were not limited to the Liahona. The Lord has given us several small means to bless our lives. While a comparison was made to the "urim and thummim," the use of it was limited to the prophet or his close associates. Our guidance will come from a few minutes each day reading the Book of Mormon or other scriptures; attending the temple a few hours each week or so, as our time and geographic location permits; receiving and periodically reading our patriarchal blessings for guidance in our decisions; enrolling in seminary, institute, or university religion classes; and the many other small means the Lord has provided in this dispensation. The Liahona worked for Lehi, and brought direction and great joy to the entire traveling group (vv. 16, 30–32). The small means the Lord has provided for us in this dispensation will also bring direction to our lives and great joy and happiness.

1 Nephi 16:33–39 • Ishmael Dies and is Buried in Nahom

33 And it came to pass that we did again take our journey, traveling nearly the same course as in the beginning; and after we had traveled for the space of many days we did pitch our tents again, that we might tarry for the space of a time.

34 And it came to pass that Ishmael died, and was buried in the place which was called Nahom.

35 And it came to pass that the daughters of Ishmael did mourn exceedingly, because of the loss of their father, and because of their afflictions in the wilderness; and they did murmur against my father,

because he had brought them out of the land of Jerusalem, saying: Our father is dead; yea, and we have wandered much in the wilderness, and we have suffered much affliction, hunger, thirst, and fatigue; and after all these sufferings we must perish in the wilderness with hunger.

36 And thus they did murmur against my father, and also against me; and they were desirous to return again to Jerusalem.

37 And Laman said unto Lemuel and also unto the sons of Ishmael: Behold, let us slay our father, and also our brother Nephi, who has taken it upon him to be our ruler and our teacher, who are his elder brethren.

38 Now, he says that the Lord has talked with him, and also that angels have ministered unto him. But behold, we know that he lies unto us; and he tells us these things, and he worketh many things by his cunning arts, that he may deceive our eyes, thinking, perhaps, that he may lead us away into some strange wilderness; and after he has led us away, he has thought to make himself a king and a ruler over us, that he may do with us according to his will and pleasure. And after this manner did my brother Laman stir up their hearts to anger.

39 And it came to pass that the Lord was with us, yea, even the voice of the Lord came and did speak many words unto them, and did chasten them exceedingly; and after they were chastened by the voice of the Lord they did turn away their anger, and did repent of their sins, insomuch that the Lord did bless us again with food, that we did not perish.

The expedition moved on only to encounter another discouraging experience, the death of Ishmael (v. 34). It is not clear whether "Nahom" was named by the group, or was already named such. There is no mention of their finding other people or other places that were already named. Nibley comments:

Note that this is not "a place which *we* called Nahom," but *the* place which *was* so called, a desert burial ground . . . though Bedouins sometimes bury the dead where they die, many carry the remains great distances to bury them. The Arabic root NHM has the basic meaning of "to sigh or moan," . . . At this place, we are told, "the daughters of Ishmael did mourn exceedingly," and are reminded that among the desert

Arabs mourning rites are a monopoly of the women.[15]

The devil seems to attack us or tempt us when we are weakened by sadness, failure, or disappointment. Such seems the cause at the death of Ishmael. It is also an indication that the commandments of God were not being kept. The Prophet Joseph taught: "the devil has no power only as we permit him. The moment we revolt at anything which comes from God, the devil takes power" (*TPJS*, 181).

Laman once again leads the revolt. His proposal to "slay our father, and also our brother Nephi" (v. 37) discloses his character. He accuses Nephi of lying to the group concerning the Lord talking to him and angels appearing (v. 38). It is obvious that Laman is the one who is lying, an angel had appeared to Laman and Lemuel and confirmed "that the Lord hath chosen (Nephi) to be a ruler over you" (1 Nephi 3:29). Through these accusations, Laman did "stir up their hearts to anger" (v. 38). One of Satan's tools is to "stir them up to anger against that which is good" (2 Nephi 28:20). Again the Lord came to the aid of his faithful and "did chasten them exceedingly" (v. 39).

Elder Neal A. Maxwell made this observation:

> Early on, Laman rejected the role he should have played and, instead, wanted to be "top dog in the manger," resenting all the while Nephi's spiritual leadership. Lemuel was not only Laman's dutiful satellite, but he was also his enabler by allowing himself to be "stirred up" by Laman (see 1 Nephi 16:37–38). If, instead, Laman had been fully isolated, certain outcomes could have been very different. We have enablers in our society too. They allow themselves to be stirred up against that which is good. They are not entitled to a free pass any more than Lemuel. Like him, their comparative visibility is low, but their hypocrisy is high. [CR, Oct. 1999, 5]

1 Nephi 17:1–4 • Eight Years in the Wilderness

> 1 And it came to pass that we did again take our journey in the wilderness; and we did travel nearly eastward from that time forth. And we did travel and wade through much affliction in the wilderness;

---

[15] *Lehi in the Desert and the World of the Jaredites*, 90–91. The Bedouins are a nomadic people, and thus have no local burial grounds. The author has seen a Bedouin burial ground still in use near the ancient "tel of Beersheva."

and our women did bear children in the wilderness.

2 And so great were the blessings of the Lord upon us, that while we did live upon raw meat in the wilderness, our women did give plenty of suck for their children, and were strong, yea, even like unto the men; and they began to bear their journeyings without murmurings.

4 And we did sojourn for the space of many years, yea, even eight years in the wilderness.

These verses summarize their total time in the wilderness, eight years. They enumerate both their afflictions and their blessings as they head nearly eastward from then on. Nephi also gives us another precept, or what he wants us to learn from the past eight years in the wilderness.

3 And thus we see that the commandments of God must be fulfilled. And if it so be that the children of men keep the commandments of God he doth nourish them, and strengthen them, and provide means whereby they can accomplish the thing which he has commanded them; wherefore, he did provide means for us while we did sojourn in the wilderness.

While the commandments of God must be kept, it must be remembered that we have our agency and do not personally have to keep the commandments. If we do not keep the commandments the Lord has given us, he will get someone else to fulfill the things we were commanded to do. Even the Prophet Joseph was so warned: "Behold, thou art Joseph, and thou wast chosen to do the work of the Lord, but because of transgression, if thou art not aware thou wilt fall" (D&C 3:9).

The Lord brought Lehi's people through the wilderness in spite of the opposition of many. When Laman failed to live up to his foreordained leadership role, the Lord had Nephi "waiting in the wings" so to speak. Our foreordained mission in this life is also based upon our keeping the commandments here and now.

SACRED WRITING

Preaching Which is Sacred:

1 Nephi 15:10–16:3   Nephi to Laman and Lemuel on their father's visions and teachings.

Revelation Which is Great:

1 Nephi 16:10, 16, 25–30   The directions given through the round ball of curious workmanship.

Doctrines Learned:

1 Nephi 16:28–29   The Lord sometimes gives revelation through sacred instruments.

General Authority Quotes

Elder Delbert L. Stapley • 1 Nephi 15:8

Nephi, another great American prophet, records that he was led by the Spirit of God in the things that he did. Explaining to the understanding of his brothers on one occasion about the teachings of their father which they did not comprehend, he asked them this enlightening question:

"Have ye inquired of the Lord?" [1 Nephi 15]

Here is an important key. It takes faith to inquire of the Lord, and faith requires righteousness of lives to secure an answer from God. [CR, April 1965, 24]

Elder Spencer W. Kimball • 1 Nephi 15:33–34

In an interview with a young man in Mesa, Arizona, I found him only a little sorry he had committed adultery but not sure he wanted to cleanse himself. After long deliberations in which I seemed to make little headway against his rebellious spirit I finally said, "Goodbye, Bill, but I warn you, don't break a speed limit, be careful what you eat, take no chances on your life. Be careful in traffic for you must not die before this matter is cleared up. Don't you dare die." I quoted this scripture—1 Nephi 15:33–34.

A slow death has its advantages over the sudden demise. The cancer victim who is head of a family, for instance, should use his time to be an adviser to those who survive him. The period of inactivity after a patient learns there is no hope for this life can be a period of great productivity. How much more true this is of one who has been involved in deliberate sin! He must not die until he has made his peace with God. He must be careful and not have an accident. [145–46] . . . To the prophets the term unclean in this context (1 Nephi 15:34; 10:21) means what it means to God. To man the word may be relative in meaning—one minute speck of dirt does not make a white shirt or dress unclean, for example. But to God who is perfection, cleanliness means moral and personal cleanliness. Less than that is, in one degree or another, uncleanliness and hence cannot dwell with God. [*Miracle of Forgiveness*, 1969, 19]

Challenges to Eternal Life:

1. As you read the Book of Mormon, or any of the scriptures, inquire of the Lord for understanding (1 Nephi 15:7–8).
2. When some teaching seems difficult, re-examine it against the truth, or the word of God (1 Nephi 16:2).
3. Evaluate your happiness in light of your keeping the commandments of God (1 Nephi 17:3).
4. Choose a challenge or message from this reading and apply it to your life.

Chapter Seven

From Bountiful to the Promised Land

1 Nephi 17:5–55; 18

Historical Setting: The events in this reading take place in the land they called Bountiful, on the seashore of the waters they called Irreantum, meaning many waters. Here they built a ship to sail to the promised land. 1 Nephi 18:5–22 tells of their sailing upon the waters to the promised land. 1 Nephi 18:23 tells of their arrival at the promised land. The date of their arrival, given on the bottom right hand corner of the page, "Probably about 589 B.C." is an estimation of the following events: Their travels from Jerusalem to the valley of Lemuel; their camping in that valley while the sons made two return trips to Jerusalem; their eight years of sojourning in the wilderness; their building of a ship in the land they called Bountiful; and their sailing upon the waters to reach the promised land. The estimate of about eleven years seems a fair evaluation of the time period. 1 Nephi 18:23–25 tells of their going forth upon the land and settling themselves. No time period is given for their being upon the water or their going forth upon the land and getting settled. Their direction of travel, or the distance of travel after they land is also not given.

Precepts of Chapter Seven:

> [God] loveth those who will have him to be their God. [1 Nephi 17:40]

> If God had commanded me to do all things I could do them. . . .
> If the Lord has such great power, and has wrought so many miracles
> among the children of men, how is it that he cannot instruct me, . . .
> [1 Nephi 17:50–51]

As we continue in the saga of Nephi, God's dealings with his children—both the house of Israel in the east and the Nephites in the west—are evident. Since God is everlasting and unchanging he deals with mankind in the same manner today. An outline of this chapter will illustrate this concept and prepare the reader for a deeper study.

OUTLINE • 1 NEPHI 17:4–55; 18

➤ 17:5–14   Lehi's people come to the land they called Bountiful because there the Lord had provided much fruit and wild honey.

      a.   They call the sea by which they pitched their tents Irreantum, meaning many waters. They rejoice exceedingly (vv. 5–6).

      b.   After many days, the Lord commands Nephi to go to the mountain (vv. 7–10).

           1.   Nephi is commanded to build a ship, as he will be shown, to carry them across the waters.

           2.   He asks the Lord where to find ore to make tools with which to build.

           3.   The Lord tells him where to find ore.

      c.   Nephi makes a bellows, and smites two stones together to make fire (vv. 11–13).

           1.   The Lord had not allowed them to have much fire in the wilderness.

           2.   He had made their meat sweet unto them.

           3.   The Lord would be their light in the wilderness, if they kept the commandments.

    d. After they arrive in the promised land, they will know the Lord delivered them (v. 14).

➤ 17:15–22 Nephi endeavors to keep the commandments of the Lord.

    a. He makes tools of the ore moltened out of the rock (v. 16).

    b. His brothers murmur against Nephi because he thinks he can build a ship (vv. 17–18).

      1. They complain and will not labor to help him.

      2. They do not believe he was instructed of the Lord.

    c. Nephi is sorrowful; the brothers say they knew he could not build a ship (vv. 19–22).

      1. He is led by foolish imaginations.

      2. He has led us in the wilderness these many years, and it would have been better had we died before coming out of Jerusalem.

      3. They could have enjoyed their possessions in the land of their inheritance.

      4. The people in Jerusalem were righteous, they kept the law of Moses, and our father has misjudged them.

➤ 17:23–32 Nephi answers his brothers objections with questions about Moses.

    a. Do you believe the house of Israel would have been led out of Egypt if they had not hearkened to the word of the Lord? (vv. 23–25).

      1. The Lord commanded Moses to lead them out of Egypt.

      2. Israel was laden with tasks grievous to be borne.

    b. You know that the Lord commanded Moses to do a great work (vv. 26–30).

      1. He divided the waters of the Red Sea.

      2. The armies of Pharaoh were drowned in the Red Sea.

      3. Israel was fed with manna in the wilderness.

    4.   Moses smote the rock and water came out to quench their thirst.

    5.   The Lord led them by day and gave light to them by night.

  c. The Lord did all things for Israel, yet they reviled against Moses and God (v. 30).

  d. After crossing the Jordan, Israel drove the people of the land out (v. 32).

➤ 17:33–47   Nephi teaches his brethren about God.

  a. The Lord esteems all flesh as one, the righteous are favored of God (vv. 33–35).

    1.   Those driven out of the land were not righteous.

    2.   Our fathers would not have been more choice had those driven out been righteous.

    3.   Those driven out were ripe in iniquity, and God's wrath was upon them.

    4.   The Lord cursed the land to them and blessed it to Israel.

  b. The Lord created the earth that it might be inhabited and created his children to inhabit it (vv. 36–38).

    1.   He raises up a righteous nation and destroys the nations of the wicked.

    2.   He leads the righteous into precious lands, destroys the wicked, and curses the land unto them for their sake.

  c. The Lord rules high in the heavens, it is his throne, and the earth is his footstool (vv. 39–42).

    1.   He loves those who will have him to be their God.

    2.   He covenanted with Abraham, Isaac, and Jacob; and brought them out of Egypt.

    3.   He straightened them in the wilderness because of their iniquity.

    4.   He sent fiery serpents among them and prepared a way to heal them that was simple and easy.

>> 5. They reviled against Moses and God; nevertheless, He led them to the promised land.

> d. After all these blessings from the Lord, the Jews are nearly ripe in iniquity this day and are about to be destroyed (v. 43).

> e. The Lord led my father out of Jerusalem, and the Jews are about to be destroyed (vv. 44–47).

>> 1. Ye sought his life and are also murderers in your hearts.

>> 2. Ye are swift to do iniquity but slow to remember the Lord.

>> 3. Ye have seen an angel, and he has spoken to you.

>> 4. Ye have heard his voice from time to time and heard the still small voice.

>> 5. Ye were past feeling and could not feel his words.

>> 6. Ye know that by the power of his word he can cause changes in the earth.

>> 7. Nephi fears his brothers are to be cast off forever.

>> 8. Nephi is full of the Spirit, insomuch that his frame has no strength.

➤ 17:48–51   Nephi's brothers are angry and are desirous to throw him into the sea.

> a. Nephi commands that they not touch him; he is full of the power of God, and God will smite them (v. 48).

> b. He tells them to murmur no more and to not withhold their labor, for God has commanded him to build a ship (vv. 49–51).

>> 1. If God commanded him to do all things, he could do them.

>> 2. If God has such great power to make miracles, why can't he command me to build a ship?

➤ 17:52–55   His brothers dared not touch him for many days so powerful was the Spirit of God within him.

> a. As commanded by the Lord, Nephi stretches forth his

hand, and the Lord shocks them that they may know He is the Lord their God (vv. 53–54).

  b. The brothers acknowledge the Lord is with Nephi, and his power has shaken them (v. 55).

  c. They fall down to worship Nephi, but he tells them to worship the Lord and to honor their father and mother (v. 55).

➤ 18:1–4 Nephi's brothers worship the Lord, and help Nephi work timbers of curious workmanship.

  a. The Lord showed Nephi from time to time how to work the timbers (vv. 1–2).

   1. They were not worked after the manner of men.

   2. The ship was built as shown to Nephi by the Lord.

  b. Nephi went unto the mount oft, and the Lord showed him great things (v. 3).

  c. His brothers acknowledge the workmanship, and again they humble themselves before the Lord (v. 4).

➤ 18:5–7 The Lord's voice tells Lehi to go down into the ship.

  a. Lehi prepares provisions of fruit, meats, and honey in abundance as commanded by the Lord (v. 5).

  b. They all go into the ship according to age with their wives and children (v. 6).

  c. Lehi begat two sons while in the wilderness, Jacob and Joseph (v. 7).

➤ 18:8–11 Lehi's people put forth into the sea, and they are driven by the wind toward the promised land.

  a. After many days, Nephi's brothers, Ishmael's sons and their wives begin to make merry, with much rudeness, and forget what power had brought them there (v. 9).

  b. Nephi fears the Lord's anger will swallow them up in the sea (v. 10).

   1. Nephi speaks to them with much soberness.

   2. They are angry and say their younger brother will
      not rule over them.

c. Laman and Lemuel bind Nephi, and treat him with
   much harshness (v. 11).

➤ 18:11–20   The Lord allowed these things that he might show his power,
             and fulfill his word concerning the wicked.

a. The compass prepared of the Lord did cease to work,
   and they knew not where to steer the ship (vv. 12–13).

b. A great storm arose, and they were driven back for three
   days (v. 13).

   1. They feared they would be drowned in the sea.

   2. They would not loosen Nephi.

c. On the fourth day they are driven back; the tempest is
   exceedingly sore (vv. 14–16).

   1. Nephi's brothers recognize that the judgments of
      God are upon them.

   2. They loosen Nephi's bands, and his wrists and
      ankles are greatly swollen.

   3. Nephi praises the Lord all day long and does not
      murmur.

d. Lehi said many things to Laman, Lemuel, and the sons
   of Ishmael (vv. 17–19).

   1. They threatened anyone who speaks for Nephi.

   2. Nephi's parents suffered much and being stricken
      in years are brought to their sickbeds.

   3. Their grief and sorrow over the iniquity of Laman
      and Lemuel brought them near to death.

   4. Jacob and Joseph, being young, needed nourishment
      and were grieved because of the affliction of their
      mother.

   5. Nephi's wife with her tears and prayers along with
      her children's did not soften their hearts.

e. Only the power of God threatening destruction could
   soften their hearts (v. 20).

➤ 18:21–22   Nephi takes the compass, and it works.

    a.   Nephi prays unto the Lord, and the winds cease (v. 21).

    b.   Nephi guides the ship to the promised land (v. 22).

➤ 18:23–25   Lehi and his people arrive at the promised land.

    a.   They till the earth and plant seeds that grow in abundance (v. 24).

    b.   They travel in the wilderness, and find many animals (v. 25).

        1.   The cow and the ox, the horse and the ass, and the goat and the wild goat.

        2.   All manner of wild animals for the use of man.

    c.   They find all manner of ore: gold, silver, and copper (v. 25).

NOTES AND COMMENTARY

Introduction: One of the popular concepts in the Christian world today, and among some of the members of the Church, is the "unconditional love" of God and Christ. However, the scriptural concept of God's love is somewhat different than what is implied by the meaning of unconditional love. "Perfect love casteth out fear" (1 John 4:18), and is therefore not dependent upon the influence or approval of any of mankind. Neither is it indiscriminately showered upon all who ask for it. As taught in these chapters of 1 Nephi, the actions of Nephi, Lehi, and Sam; versus the actions of Laman and Lemuel, illustrates that although God loves all his children, and is no respecter of persons; his love is only promised to those who meet his conditions. God is a just God who acts according to eternal law. His laws were "irrevocably decreed in heaven before the foundation of this world, . . . all blessings are predicated . . ." upon obedience to his law (D&C 130:20–21). The Lord is "bound when ye do what [he says], but when ye do not what [he says], ye have no promise" (D&C 82:10). "Justice (the law) exerciseth all his demands, and mercy (the Atonement) claimeth all which is her own . . . mercy can(not) rob justice" (Alma 42:24–25).

These Book of Mormon chapters teach these principles, and give many examples of God's perfect love.

1 Nephi 17:5–7 • The Land Bountiful— Nephi Goes to the Mountain

> 5 And we did come to the land which we called Bountiful, because of its much fruit and also wild honey; and all these things were prepared of the Lord that we might not perish. And we beheld the sea, which we called Irreantum, which, being interpreted, is many waters.
>
> 6 And it came to pass that we did pitch our tents by the seashore; and notwithstanding we had suffered many afflictions and much difficulty, yea, even so much that we cannot write them all, we were exceedingly rejoiced when we came to the seashore; and we called the place Bountiful, because of its much fruit.
>
> 7 And it came to pass that after I, Nephi, had been in the land of Bountiful for the space of many days, the voice of the Lord came unto me, saying: Arise, and get thee into the mountain. And it came to pass that I arose and went up into the mountain, and cried unto the Lord. [1 Nephi 17:5–7]

In contrast to their eight years in the wilderness, the people "exceedingly rejoiced" when they reached the beautiful land they called Bountiful (vv. 5–6). Therefore, they were not prepared for the revelation that came to Nephi when the Lord called him to go up into the mountain. The mountain is not named, but was probably a prominent one close to Bountiful. Although the Lord could have spoken to Nephi in Bountiful, the Lord probably called him into the mountain to have him isolated from the less faithful members of the group. As before, the Lord was using the mountain as his temple.

1 Nephi 17:8–15 • Nephi Commanded to Build a Ship

> 8 And it came to pass that the Lord spake unto me, saying: Thou shalt construct a ship, after the manner which I shall show thee, that I may carry thy people across these waters.
>
> 9 And I said: Lord, whither shall I go that I may find ore to molten,

that I may make tools to construct the ship after the manner which thou hast shown unto me?

10 And it came to pass that the Lord told me whither I should go to find ore, that I might make tools.

11 And it came to pass that I, Nephi, did make a bellows wherewith to blow the fire, of the skins of beasts; and after I had made a bellows, that I might have wherewith to blow the fire, I did smite two stones together that I might make fire.

12 For the Lord had not hitherto suffered that we should make much fire, as we journeyed in the wilderness; for he said: I will make thy food become sweet, that ye cook it not;

13 And I will also be your light in the wilderness; and I will prepare the way before you, if it so be that ye shall keep my commandments; wherefore, inasmuch as ye shall keep my commandments ye shall be led towards the promised land; and ye shall know that it is by me that ye are led.

14 Yea, and the Lord said also that: After ye have arrived in the promised land, ye shall know that I, the Lord, am God; and that I, the Lord, did deliver you from destruction; yea, that I did bring you out of the land of Jerusalem.

15 Wherefore, I, Nephi, did strive to keep the commandments of the Lord, and I did exhort my brethren to faithfulness and diligence.

The commandment to "construct a ship" is the first mention in the text of the land of promise being "across these waters" (v. 8). The faith of Nephi is shown in his immediate response of where to "find ore to molten, that I may make tools to construct the ship" (v. 9). He again illustrates what he said to his father regarding the sons first return to Jerusalem; "I know that the Lord giveth no commandments unto the children of men, save he shall prepare a way for them that they may accomplish the thing which he commandeth them" 1 Nephi 3:7).

Nephi's mention of fire apparently reminded him of other blessings the Lord had provided for them in the wilderness. He had sweetened their meat so they would not need to cook it (v. 12). This was probably so that the fire would not attract marauding nomadic tribes in the area.

The Lord had also promised to be their "light in the wilderness" (v. 13). Nephi does not enlarge upon how the Lord did this, but it reminds us of the Lord leading the children of Israel in the wilderness. He "went before them by day in a pillar of a cloud, to lead them the way; and by night in a pillar of fire" (Exodus 13:21). However he led them, they certainly knew the Lord was with them.

1 Nephi 17:16–22 • Nephi's Brothers Murmur Against His Building a Ship

16 And it came to pass that I did make tools of the ore which I did molten out of the rock.

17 And when my brethren saw that I was about to build a ship, they began to murmur against me, saying: Our brother is a fool, for he thinketh that he can build a ship; yea, and he also thinketh that he can cross these great waters.

18 And thus my brethren did complain against me, and were desirous that they might not labor, for they did not believe that I could build a ship; neither would they believe that I was instructed of the Lord.

19 And now it came to pass that I, Nephi, was exceedingly sorrowful because of the hardness of their hearts; and now when they saw that I began to be sorrowful they were glad in their hearts, insomuch that they did rejoice over me, saying: We knew that ye could not construct a ship, for we knew that ye were lacking in judgment; wherefore, thou canst not accomplish so great a work.

20 And thou art like unto our father, led away by the foolish imaginations of his heart; yea, he hath led us out of the land of Jerusalem, and we have wandered in the wilderness for these many years; and our women have toiled, being big with child; and they have borne children in the wilderness and suffered all things, save it were death; and it would have been better that they had died before they came out of Jerusalem than to have suffered these afflictions.

21 Behold, these many years we have suffered in the wilderness, which time we might have enjoyed our possessions and the land of our inheritance; yea, and we might have been happy.

22 And we know that the people who were in the land of Jerusalem

were a righteous people; for they kept the statutes and judgments of the Lord, and all his commandments, according to the law of Moses; wherefore, we know that they are a righteous people; and our father hath judged them, and hath led us away because we would hearken unto his words; yea, and our brother is like unto him. And after this manner of language did my brethren murmur and complain against us.

Laman and Lemuel's amazement at Nephi's contemplating the building of a ship (vv. 17–18), is further evidence of their party not knowing they would have to cross the waters to get to the promised land. Their objections, other than about Nephi's inability to build a ship, were basically the same ones they had previously repented of or acknowledged to be inaccurate since leaving Jerusalem.

1 Nephi 17:23 • Nephi Cites Israel Being Led Out of Egypt

23 And it came to pass that I, Nephi, spake unto them, saying: Do ye believe that our fathers, who were the children of Israel, would have been led away out of the hands of the Egyptians if they had not hearkened unto the words of the Lord? [1 Nephi 17:23]

Nephi's response to his brother's objections constitute a major purpose of the Book of Mormon and the other books that he was shown that would come forth among the Gentile—to "establish the truth of the first (Bible)" (1 Nephi 13: 39–40), or to prove "to the world that the holy scriptures are true" (D&C 20:11). He reviews the miraculous events of the Lord leading the children of Israel out of the hands of the Egyptians (v. 23). His review, taken from the plates of brass, serves as a second witness to the following biblical events that are often watered down or explained away in today's sophisticated world.

Moses led Israel out of Egypt

7 And the Lord said, I have surely seen the affliction of my people which *are* in Egypt, and have heard their cry by reason of their taskmasters; for I know their sorrows;

8 And I am come down to deliver them out of the hand of the

Egyptians, and to bring them up out of that land unto a good land and a large, unto a land flowing with milk and honey; unto the place of the Canaanites, and the Hittites, and the Amorites, and the Perizzites, and the Hivites, and the Jebusites. [Exodus 3:7–8]

1 Nephi 17:24–25 • Nephi Bore Testimony to Laman and Lemuel

24 Yea, do ye suppose that they would have been led out of bondage, if the Lord had not commanded Moses that he should lead them out of bondage?

25 Now ye know that the children of Israel were in bondage; and ye know that they were laden with tasks, which were grievous to be borne; wherefore, ye know that it must needs be a good thing for them, that they should be brought out of bondage. [1 Nephi 17:24–25]

Nephi later speaks of "the God of our fathers, who were led out of Egypt, out of bondage, and also were preserved in the wilderness by him" and then identifies God as Jesus Christ (1 Nephi 19:10). Alma tells his son Helaman: "I will praise [God] forever, for he has brought our fathers out of Egypt" (Alma 36:28).

Moses Divides the Red Sea

21 And Moses stretched out his hand over the sea; and the LORD caused the sea to go *back* by a strong east wind all that night, and made the sea dry *land*, and the waters were divided.

22 And the children of Israel went into the midst of the sea upon the dry *ground*: and the waters *were* a wall unto them on their right hand, and on their left.

23 And the Egyptians pursued, and went in after them to the midst of the sea, *even* all Pharaoh's horses, his chariots, and his horsemen.

27 And Moses stretched forth his hand over the sea, and the sea returned to his strength when the morning appeared; and the Egyptians fled against it; and the LORD overthrew the Egyptians in the midst of the sea.

28 And the waters returned, and covered the chariots, and the horsemen, *and* all the host of Pharaoh that came into the sea after them; there remained not so much as one of them.

29 But the children of Israel walked upon dry *land* in the midst of the sea; and the waters *were* a wall unto them on their right hand, and on their left. [Exodus 14:21–23; 27–29]

1 Nephi 17:26–27 • Nephi Testified to Laman and Lemuel of the Red Sea

26 Now ye know that Moses was commanded of the Lord to do that great work; and ye know that by his word the waters of the Red Sea were divided hither and thither, and they passed through on dry ground.

27 But ye know that the Egyptians were drowned in the Red Sea, who were the armies of Pharaoh.

There are four other references in the Book of Mormon testifying that Moses divided the Red Sea. In responding to his brother's objection to returning to the house of Laban to obtain the plates of brass, Nephi argued:

1 And it came to pass that I spake unto my brethren, saying: Let us go up again unto Jerusalem, and let us be faithful in keeping the commandments of the Lord; for behold he is mightier than all the earth, then why not mightier than Laban and his fifty, yea, or even than his tens of thousands?

2 Therefore let us go up; let us be strong like unto Moses; for he truly spake unto the waters of the Red Sea and they divided hither and thither, and our fathers came through, out of captivity, on dry ground, and the armies of Pharaoh did follow and were drowned in the waters of the Red Sea. [1 Nephi 4:1–2]

King Limhi testified to his people that God "caused that [Israel] should walk through the Red Sea on dry ground" (Mosiah 7:19). Alma told his son Helaman that "[God] has swallowed up the Egyptians in the Red Sea" (Alma 36:28); and Nephi, son of Helaman, asks his brethren: "have ye not read that God gave power unto one man, even Moses, to smite upon the waters of the Red Sea, and they parted hither and thither, insomuch that the Israelites, who were our fathers, came through upon dry ground, and the waters closed upon the armies of the Egyptians and swallowed them up?" (Helaman 8:11). The Doctrine and Covenants adds this witness:

> 2 Yea, behold, I will tell you in your mind and in your heart, by the Holy Ghost, which shall come upon you and which shall dwell in your heart.
>
> 3 Now, behold, this is the spirit of revelation; behold, this is the spirit by which Moses brought the children of Israel through the Red Sea on dry ground. [D&C 8:2–3]

In writing to the Corinthians, Paul testified: "Moreover, brethren, I would not that ye should be ignorant, how that all our fathers were under the cloud, and all passed through the sea; And were all baptized unto Moses in the cloud and in the sea" (1 Corinthians 10:1–2). Writing to the Hebrews, he used the miracle as an example of faith: "By faith they passed through the Red sea as by dry *land:* which the Egyptians assaying to do were drowned" (Hebrews 11:29).

The thinking of many Bible scholars is that it was the Reed Sea, not the Red Sea, and the natural movement of the tide going out when the Israelites crossed, and the tide coming back in that drowned the Egyptians.[1] As we have just read, the Book of Mormon refutes this theory.

Israel Was Fed Manna in the Wilderness

> 14 And when the dew that lay was gone up, behold, upon the face of the wilderness *there lay* a small round thing, *as* small as the hoar frost on the ground.
>
> 15 And when the children of Israel saw *it,* they said one to another, It *is* manna: for they wist not what it *was.* And Moses said unto them, This *is* the bread which the LORD hath given you to eat.
>
> 16 This *is* the thing which the LORD hath commanded, Gather of it every man according to his eating, an omer for every man, *according*

---

[1] Many Bible commentaries give this explanation and the ones that will follow i.e. *The Interpreters Bible,* vol. 1:834–35; 958–59; 1080–82. Most any other commentary that is available will probably give the same explanation.

to the number of your persons; take ye every man for *them* which *are* in his tents.

17 And the children of Israel did so, and gathered, some more, some less. [Exodus 16:14–17]

1 Nephi 17:28 • Nephi Testified of the Manna to his Brothers:

28 And ye also know that they were fed with manna in the wilderness.

King Limhi later testified to his people that God "fed [Israel] with Manna that they might not perish in the wilderness" (Mosiah 7:19). In the New Testament, the Savior himself verified, to the unbelieving Jews, the miracle of manna, and its relationship to him.

30 They said therefore unto him, What sign shewest thou then, that we may see, and believe thee? what dost thou work?

31 Our fathers did eat manna in the desert; as it is written, He gave them bread from heaven to eat.

32 Then Jesus said unto them, Verily, verily, I say unto you, Moses gave you not that bread from heaven; but my Father giveth you the true bread from heaven.

33 For the bread of God is he which cometh down from heaven, and giveth life unto the world.

34 Then said they unto him, Lord, evermore give us this bread.

35 And Jesus said unto them, I am the bread of life: he that cometh to me shall never hunger; and he that believeth on me shall never thirst. [John 6:30–35]

Paul says "they did all eat the same spiritual meat" (1 Corinthians 10:3), undoubtedly referring to the manna. He also says that "the golden pot that had manna" was a memorial kept in the ark of the covenant (Hebrews 9:4).

A prevalent theory explaining away this miracle is that there is a bush in the desert, with which Moses was familiar, that naturally secrets a honey-like substance that was eaten by the desert travelers, and the children of Israel attributed it to be coming from God (see footnote 1). This theory does not explain how the excess that was "left of it till morning, . . . bred worms, and stank" except on the day before the Sabbath when it "did not stink, neither was there any worm therein" (Exodus 16:19– 24).

Water Came from the Rock Smitten by Moses

2 Wherefore the people did chide with Moses, and said, Give us water that we may drink. And Moses said unto them, Why chide ye with me? wherefore do ye tempt the LORD?

3 And the people thirsted there for water; and the people murmured against Moses, and said, Wherefore *is* this *that* thou hast brought us up out of Egypt, to kill us and our children and our cattle with thirst?

4 And Moses cried unto the LORD, saying, What shall I do unto this people? they be almost ready to stone me.

5 And the LORD said unto Moses, Go on before the people, and take with thee of the elders of Israel; and thy rod, wherewith thou smotest the river, take in thine hand, and go.

6 Behold, I will stand before thee there upon the rock in Horeb; and thou shalt smite the rock, and there shall come water out of it, that the people may drink. And Moses did so in the sight of the elders of Israel. [Exodus 17:2–6]

1 Nephi 17:29 • Nephi Testified to Laman and Lemuel of Moses Smiting the Rock

29 Yea, and ye also know that Moses, by his word according to the power of God which was in him, smote the rock, and there came forth water, that the children of Israel might quench their thirst. [1 Nephi 17:29]

Nephi later wrote that God "also gave [Moses] power that he should smite the rock and the water should come forth" (2 Nephi 25:20).

The typical explanation for this miracle is that Moses was familiar with this area, and knew that winter debris had clogged the exit of water from somewhere near the rock, and also knew that a good blow upon the rock would dislodge the debris and start the water flowing again. However, the people attributed this to the power of God (see footnote 1).

The Lord Led Israel Through the Wilderness

21 And the LORD went before them by day in a pillar of a cloud, to lead them the way; and by night in a pillar of fire, to give them light; to go by day and night:

22 He took not away the pillar of the cloud by day, nor the pillar of fire by night, *from* before the people. [Exodus 13:21–22]

1 Nephi 17:30–31 • Nephi's Testifies that the Lord Led Israel

30 And notwithstanding they being led, the Lord their God, their Redeemer, going before them, leading them by day and giving light unto them by night, and doing all things for them which were expedient for man to receive, they hardened their hearts and blinded their minds, and reviled against Moses and against the true and living God.

31 And it came to pass that according to his word he did destroy them; and according to his word he did lead them; and according to his word he did do all things for them; and there was not any thing done save it were by his word. [1 Nephi 17:30–31]

Paul verified the incident with a spiritual interpretation:

4 And did all drink the same spiritual drink: for they drank of that spiritual Rock that followed them: and that Rock was Christ. [1 Corinthians 10:4]

One attempt to explain away the light that the Israelites saw leading them is the glorious sunsets that are seen in the deserts in that area. It is claimed that this was a natural phenomenon interpreted by Israel to be a manifestation from God (see footnote 1).

The Inhabitants of the Land (of Canaan) Driven out

23 So Joshua took the whole land, according to all that the LORD said unto Moses; and Joshua gave it for an inheritance unto Israel

according to their divisions by their tribes. And the land rested from war. [Joshua 11:23]

1 Nephi 17:23 • Nephi Bore Testimony that They Were Scattered and Destroyed

32 And after they had crossed the river Jordan he did make them mighty unto the driving out of the children of the land, yea, unto the scattering them to destruction.

Thus there are many witnesses to the miracles attending the children of Israel as they were led out of Israel. The Book of Mormon is a major witness.

1 Nephi 17:33–40 • God Loves Those Who Will Have Him to be Their God

33 And now, do ye suppose that the children of this land, who were in the land of promise, who were driven out by our fathers, do ye suppose that they were righteous? Behold, I say unto you, Nay.

34 Do ye suppose that our fathers would have been more choice than they if they had been righteous? I say unto you, Nay.

35 Behold, the Lord esteemeth all flesh in one; he that is righteous is favored of God. But behold, this people had rejected every word of God, and they were ripe in iniquity; and the fulness of the wrath of God was upon them; and the Lord did curse the land against them, and bless it unto our fathers; yea, he did curse it against them unto their destruction, and he did bless it unto our fathers unto their obtaining power over it.

36 Behold, the Lord hath created the earth that it should be inhabited; and he hath created his children that they should possess it.

37 And he raiseth up a righteous nation, and destroyeth the nations of the wicked.

38 And he leadeth away the righteous into precious lands, and the wicked he destroyeth, and curseth the land unto them for their sakes.

39 He ruleth high in the heavens, for it is his throne, and this earth is his footstool.

40 And he loveth those who will have him to be their God. Behold, he loved our fathers, and he covenanted with them, yea, even Abraham, Isaac, and Jacob; and he remembered the covenants which he had made; wherefore, he did bring them out of the land of Egypt.

Nephi's conclusions following his review of the miracles of the exodus are thought provoking and doctrinally profound. Happiness in the final sense depends upon righteousness. Although "the Lord esteemeth all flesh in one, he that is righteous is favored of God" (v. 35). Righteousness is the precondition for receiving favored blessings. As a second witness to another biblical principle, Nephi taught that the inhabitants of Canaan were cursed and destroyed because they "had rejected every word of God, and they were ripe in iniquity" (v. 35). The Lord told Abraham that his seed would not return to the land given him until the fourth generation "for the iniquity on the Amorites was not yet full," showing that they would be destroyed when they were ripe in iniquity (Genesis 15:13–16). Wickedness is the condition that brings the wrath of God.

The earth was created to be inhabited, and God's children were to inhabit it (v. 36). Those who are righteous will be raised up into a blessed nation, but the wicked nations will be destroyed (v. 37). This concept is not only why the Lord destroyed the people of Canaan, but also why the Lord flooded the earth.

28 The earth was corrupt before God, and it was filled with violence.

29 And God looked upon the earth, and, behold, it was corrupt, for all flesh had corrupted its way upon the earth.

30 And God said unto Noah: The end of all flesh is come before me, for the earth is filled with violence, and behold I will destroy all flesh from off the earth. [Moses 8:28–30; Genesis 6:11–13]

The wickedness of a nation also explains why the Nephites and the Jaredites were destroyed. Before the Lord destroys a nation ripened in iniquity, he leads the righteous into precious lands (v. 38). But "never hath any of them been destroyed save it were foretold them by the prophets of the Lord" (2 Nephi 25:9). The more righteous of the northern ten tribes of Israel were led into the north before they were destroyed by Assyria in about 722 B.C.

> 22 For the children of Israel walked in all the sins of Jeroboam which he did; they departed not from them;
>
> 23 Until the Lord removed Israel out of his sight, as he had said by all his servants the prophets. So was Israel carried away out of their own land to Assyria unto this day. [2 Kings 17:22–23]

Thousands of Jews were carried into Babylon before Jerusalem was destroyed by King Nebuchadnezzar in 589 B.C. (Book of Mormon dating).

> 11 And Nebuchadnezzar king of Babylon came against the city, and his servants did besiege it.
>
> 12 And Jehoiachin the king of Judah went out to the king of Babylon, he, and his mother, and his servants, and his princes, and his officers: and the king of Babylon took him in the eighth year of his reign.
>
> 13 And he carried out thence all the treasures of the house of the Lord, and the treasures of the king's house, and cut in pieces all the vessels of gold which Solomon king of Israel had made in the temple of the Lord, as the Lord had said.
>
> 14 And he carried away all Jerusalem, and all the princes, and all the mighty men of valour, *even* ten thousand captives, and all the craftsmen and smiths: none remained, save the poorest sort of the people of the land. [2 Kings 24:11–14]

The Book of Mormon demonstrates the concept of leading out the righteous before a nation is destroyed. Lehi and his people had been led out of Jerusalem in "the first year of the reign of Zedekiah" (1 Nephi 1:4), just before Jehoiachin and his people were taken into Babylon.

After the death of Lehi, "it came to pass that not many days after his death, Laman and Lemuel and the sons of Ishmael were angry with me because of the admonitions of the Lord. For I, Nephi, was constrained to speak unto them, according to his word; for I had spoken many things unto them, and also my father" (2 Nephi 4:13–14). They had been warned by the prophets.

> 5 And it came to pass that the Lord did warn me, that I, Nephi, should depart from them and flee into the wilderness, and all those who would go with me.
>
> 6 Wherefore, it came to pass that I, Nephi, did take my family, and also Zoram and his family, and Sam, mine elder brother and his family, and Jacob and Joseph, my younger brethren, and also my sisters, and all those who would go with me. *And all those who would go with me were those who believed in the warnings and the revelations of God; wherefore, they did hearken unto my words.* [2 Nephi 5:5–6; italics added]

King Mosiah was also warned to leave the land of Zarahemla; "he being warned of the Lord that he should flee out of the land of Nephi, *and as many as would hearken unto the voice of the Lord* should also depart out of the land with him, into the wilderness" (Omni 1:12; italics added). "Leading away the righteous into precious lands" (v. 37) is an eternal principle.

The Lord "ruleth high in the heavens" is more than a location statement. It depicts his supreme view and thus knowledge of all that goes on upon the earth. "His throne" (v. 40) tells us that it his place to govern the earth. His governing power is shown in the Book of Abraham:

> 7 For I am the Lord thy God; I dwell in heaven; the earth is my footstool; I stretch my hand over the sea, and it obeys my voice; I cause the wind and the fire to be my chariot; I say to the mountains— Depart hence—and behold, they are taken away by a whirlwind, in an instant, suddenly. [Abraham 2:7]

The "earth is his footstool" (v. 40) is another way of saying that he created or built it. That it was created for "his children" (v. 36) is again stated in the Book of Moses: "they were created and became living souls in the land upon the footstool of God" (Moses 6:9). Later in the same chapter these same concepts are emphasized. "The heavens he made; the earth is his footstool; and the foundation thereof is his. Behold, he laid it, an host of men hath he brought in upon the face thereof" (Moses 6:44). In Isaiah the Lord says: "The heaven is my throne, and the earth is my footstool," in questioning why a house has not been built for "the place of my rest" (Isaiah 66:1). The Book of Lamentations states that the Lord "remembers not his footstool in the day of his anger" (Lamentations 2:1), or he refuses to bless them when they reject his word (1 Nephi 17:35). A footstool is used to stand upon, and the Lord reveals that: "I have made the earth rich, and behold it is my footstool, wherefore, again I will stand upon it" (D&C 38:17).

The Lord "loveth those who will have him to be their God" (v. 40). This places a condition upon his love. As stated in the introduction, God loves all his children, but his love is only received by those who meet the conditions he has set. There are several supporting references to conditional love in the Book of Mormon and the Doctrine and Covenants. Samuel the Lamanite said that God had hated the Lamanites "because their deeds have been evil continually, and this because of the iniquity of the traditions of their fathers." However, he still held out salvation "unto them through the preaching of the Nephites" (Helaman 15:4). Neither they nor their fathers would "have him to be their God" (v. 40), but those who accepted the plan of salvation would have him as such. The choice to follow God always belongs to the person. "The voice of the Lord came unto [Mormon], saying: Vengeance is mine, and I will repay; and because this people repented not after I had delivered them, behold, they shall be cut off from the face of the earth" (Mormon 3:14–15). The Book of Mormon people who are described above fit the condition given to the modern-day saints:

> 11 Verily I say unto you, it is my will that you should build a house. If you keep my commandments you shall have power to build it.
>
> 12 If you keep not my commandments, the love of the Father shall not continue with you, therefore you shall walk in darkness. [D&C 95:11–12]

The love of the Father did not continue with the wicked Nephites, and they walked in darkness.

As quoted in the introduction: "I, the Lord, am bound when ye do what I say; but when ye do not what I say, ye have no promise" (D&C 82:10). Another condition was given in modern revelation: "blessed is my servant Hyrum Smith; for I, the Lord, love him because of the integrity of his heart, and because he loveth that which is right before me, saith the Lord" (D&C 124:15). God's love is perfect and is based on a balance of justice and mercy.

> 22 But there is a law given, and a punishment affixed, and a repentance granted; which repentance, mercy claimeth; otherwise, justice claimeth the creature and executeth the law, and the law inflicteth the punishment; if not so, the works of justice would be destroyed, and God would cease to be God.
>
> 23 But God ceaseth not to be God, and mercy claimeth the penitent, and mercy cometh because of the atonement; and the atonement bringeth to pass the resurrection of the dead; and the resurrection of the dead bringeth back men into the presence of God; and thus they are restored into his presence, to be judged according to their works, according to the law and justice.
>
> 24 For behold, justice exerciseth all his demands, and also mercy claimeth all which is her own; and thus, none but the truly penitent are saved.
>
> 25 What, do ye suppose that mercy can rob justice? I say unto you, Nay; not one whit. If so, God would cease to be God.
>
> 26 And thus God bringeth about his great and eternal purposes, which were prepared from the foundation of the world. And thus cometh about the salvation and the redemption of men, and also their destruction and misery. [Alma 42:22–26]

Nephi reminds his brothers of the covenants of God made with Abraham, Isaac, and Jacob as a token of his love for them (v. 40). That same covenant is renewed in our day through the Prophet Joseph Smith because of God's love for his children.

> 58 And as I said unto Abraham concerning the kindreds of the

earth, even so I say unto my servant Joseph: In thee and in thy seed shall the kindred of the earth be blessed. [D&C 124:58]

As members of the Church, we should understand and appreciate this covenant.

Moses Lifted up a Brazen Serpent in the Wilderness

5 And the people spake against God, and against Moses, Wherefore have ye brought us up out of Egypt to die in the wilderness? for *there is* no bread, neither *is there any* water; and our soul loatheth this light bread.

6 And the LORD sent fiery serpents among the people, and they bit the people; and much people of Israel died.

7 Therefore the people came to Moses, and said, We have sinned, for we have spoken against the LORD, and against thee; pray unto the LORD, that he take away the serpents from us. And Moses prayed for the people.

8 And the LORD said unto Moses, Make thee a fiery serpent, and set it upon a pole: and it shall come to pass, that every one that is bitten, when he looketh upon it, shall live.

9 And Moses made a serpent of brass, and put it upon a pole, and it came to pass, that if a serpent had bitten any man, when he beheld the serpent of brass, he lived. [Numbers 21:5–9]

1 Nephi 17:41–42 • Nephi Verifies and Explains the Serpent Being Lifted Up

41 And he did straiten them in the wilderness with his rod; for they hardened their hearts, even as ye have; and the Lord straitened them because of their iniquity. He sent fiery flying serpents among them; and after they were bitten he prepared a way that they might be healed; and the labor which they had to perform was to look; and because of the simpleness of the way, or the easiness of it, there were many who perished.

42 And they did harden their hearts from time to time, and they did revile against Moses, and also against God; nevertheless, ye know that they were led forth by his matchless power into the land of promise.

There are other references in the Book of Mormon verifying the brazen serpent. Later Nephi states that the Lord God "gave unto Moses power that he should heal the nations after they had been bitten by the poisonous serpents, if they would cast there eyes unto the serpent which he did raise up before them" (2 Nephi 25:20). Alma also testified of Moses and the serpent:

> 19 Behold, he was spoken of by Moses; yea, and behold a type was raised up in the wilderness, that whosoever would look upon it might live. And many did look and live.

> 20 But few understood the meaning of those things, and this because of the hardness of their hearts. But there were many who were so hardened that they would not look, therefore they perished. Now the reason they would not look is because they did not believe that it would heal them. [Alma 33:19–20]

Nephi, son of Helaman, tells us that Moses had "spoken concerning the Messiah":

> 14 Yea, did he not bear record that the Son of God should come? And as he lifted up the brazen serpent in the wilderness, even so shall he be lifted up who should come.

> 15 And as many as should look upon that serpent should live, even so as many as should look upon the Son of God with faith, having a contrite spirit, might live, even unto that life which is eternal. [Helaman 8:13–15]

In the New Testament, Jesus himself taught the symbolism of the serpent being lifted up: "And as Moses lifted up the serpent in the wilderness, even so must the Son of man be lifted up: That whosoever believeth in him should not perish, but have eternal life" (John 3:14–15). There is another symbol that should be considered. Just as the serpent looked like a serpent, it was made of brass, and Jesus looked like a man, but was really the Son of God. He had the power to give eternal life to those who believed just as the healing power was given to the Israelites who would look upon the brazen serpent with faith on the Son of God.

Nephi says the people who refused to look were not healed "because of the simpleness of the way, or the easiness of it" (v. 40). We face a similar challenge today. We live in a world of sophisticated medical discoveries that can heal many things. God has given us these sources of healing just as he had given the "excellent qualities of the many plants and roots which God had prepared to remove the cause of diseases" among the Nephites (Alma 46:40). He has also given us promises of healing by faith.

> 43 And whosoever among you are sick, and have not faith to be healed, but believe, shall be nourished with all tenderness, with herbs and mild food, and that not by the hand of an enemy.
>
> 44 And the elders of the church, two or more, shall be called, and shall pray for and lay their hands upon them in my name; and if they die they shall die unto me, and if they live they shall live unto me. [D&C 42:43–44]

Do some feel this is too simple a way in light of modern technology? The New Testament taught those people the same procedure for blessing the sick.

> 14 Is any sick among you? let him call for the elders of the church; and let them pray over him, anointing him with oil in the name of the Lord:
>
> 15 And the prayer of faith shall save the sick, and the Lord shall raise him up; and if he have committed sins, they shall be forgiven him. [James 5:14–15]

Laying hands on the sick is probably an eternal procedure also, one based on doing the will of the Father. "If they die they shall die unto me, and if they live they shall live unto me" (D&C 42:44). When we place our lives in the hands of God the outcome doesn't really matter.

1 Nephi 17:43–47 • Jerusalem Is About to Be Destroyed

> 43 And now, after all these things, the time has come that they have become wicked, yea, nearly unto ripeness; and I know not but they

are at this day about to be destroyed; for I know that the day must surely come that they must be destroyed, save a few only, who shall be led away into captivity.

44 Wherefore, the Lord commanded my father that he should depart into the wilderness; and the Jews also sought to take away his life; yea, and ye also have sought to take away his life; wherefore, ye are murderers in your hearts and ye are like unto them.

45 Ye are swift to do iniquity but slow to remember the Lord your God. Ye have seen an angel, and he spake unto you; yea, ye have heard his voice from time to time; and he hath spoken unto you in a still small voice, but ye were past feeling, that ye could not feel his words; wherefore, he has spoken unto you like unto the voice of thunder, which did cause the earth to shake as if it were to divide asunder.

46 And ye also know that by the power of his almighty word he can cause the earth that it shall pass away; yea, and ye know that by his word he can cause the rough places to be made smooth, and smooth places shall be broken up. O, then, why is it, that ye can be so hard in your hearts?

47 Behold, my soul is rent with anguish because of you, and my heart is pained; I fear lest ye shall be cast off forever. Behold, I am full of the Spirit of God, insomuch that my frame has no strength.

Nephi again confirms the impending destruction of Jerusalem, and the leading of a few more righteous out of the land into captivity (vv. 43). At least a partial fulfillment of this prophecy that Nephi may be quoting came after the downfall of Jerusalem.

21 And it came to pass in the twelfth year of our captivity, in the tenth *month*, in the fifth *day* of the month, *that* one that had escaped out of Jerusalem came unto me, saying, The city is smitten. [Ezekiel 33:21]

Ezekiel had been carried away with thousands of others about eleven years before Jerusalem was destroyed. The people carried into captivity were not yet ripe in iniquity and were not destroyed, but they were not righteous enough to be led to a land of freedom. Lehi and his people were righteous enough to be given a choice land of promise. Jeremiah was told by the Lord:

> 1 Run ye to and fro through the streets of Jerusalem, and see now, and know, and seek in the broad places thereof, if ye can find a man, if there be *any* that executeth judgment, that seeketh the truth; and I will pardon it.
>
> 2 And though they say, The LORD liveth; surely they swear falsely. [Jeremiah 5:1–2]

Jerusalem becoming ripe in iniquity is certainly indicated by the Lord's offer to Jeremiah. Although Lehi may not have left the area before the above decree was given, he did not live in Jerusalem or "in the broad places thereof." Before his sons made their second attempt to obtain the plates of brass from Laban; they "went *down* to the land of our inheritance, and we did gather together our gold, and our silver, and our precious things. And after we had gathered these things together, we went *up* again unto the house of Laban" (1 Nephi 3:22–23; italics added).

The wickedness of Laman and Lemuel (vv. 44–45) raises the question of why they were brought out to a land of promise? Nephi describes them as "like unto the Jews" at the time of their leaving (1 Nephi 2:13), and they certainly dit not change. They had "heard his voice from time to time," both the "still small voice," and in power "like unto the voice of thunder" (vv. 45–46), but they were beyond the feeling of the Spirit. Nephi had spoken under the inspiration of the Spirit of God to the extent that he feared they would be cast off forever (v. 47). They had probably been brought out because of the righteousness of their parents and to be given a further chance to repent.

1 Nephi 17:48–52 • Nephi Filled With the Power of God

> 48 And now it came to pass that when I had spoken these words they were angry with me, and were desirous to throw me into the depths of the sea; and as they came forth to lay their hands upon me I spake unto them, saying: In the name of the Almighty God, I

command you that ye touch me not, for I am filled with the power of God, even unto the consuming of my flesh; and whoso shall lay his hands upon me shall wither even as a dried reed; and he shall be as naught before the power of God, for God shall smite him.

49 And it came to pass that I, Nephi, said unto them that they should murmur no more against their father; neither should they withhold their labor from me, for God had commanded me that I should build a ship.

50 And I said unto them: If God had commanded me to do all things I could do them. If he should command me that I should say unto this water, be thou earth, it should be earth; and if I should say it, it would be done.

51 And now, if the Lord has such great power, and has wrought so many miracles among the children of men, how is it that he cannot instruct me, that I should build a ship?

52 And it came to pass that I, Nephi, said many things unto my brethren, insomuch that they were confounded and could not contend against me; neither durst they lay their hands upon me nor touch me with their fingers, even for the space of many days. Now they durst not do this lest they should wither before me, so powerful was the Spirit of God; and thus it had wrought upon them.

Laman and Lemuel responded as usual, in anger, but once more the Lord demonstrated that he was with Nephi. They were "confounded and could not contend against [Nephi]." Nephi commanding them to no more murmur against their father and not "withhold their labor" in the building of a ship indicates Nephi's continual love for his father and his desire to honor him (v. 49).

There is a great lesson to be learned from Nephi's declaration that he could do whatever God commanded him to do (v. 50). Nephi believed he could do what the Lord commanded because Moses had been able to do what the Lord commanded of him. In turn, we should believe that if Moses and Nephi were both able to do what the Lord commanded, we can also do as the Lord commands of us. This is a major precept of this chapter.

The Spirit was so powerful that the brothers were in fear for several days (v. 52). Only the power of God could have had such a lasting effect, but God gave them one more witness of his power.

1 Nephi 17:53–55 • Nephi Stretches His Hand—the Lord Shocks the Brothers

> 53 And it came to pass that the Lord said unto me: Stretch forth thine hand again unto thy brethren, and they shall not wither before thee, but I will shock them, saith the Lord, and this will I do, that they may know that I am the Lord their God.
>
> 54 And it came to pass that I stretched forth my hand unto my brethren, and they did not wither before me; but the Lord did shake them, even according to the word which he had spoken.
>
> 55 And now, they said: We know of a surety that the Lord is with thee, for we know that it is the power of the Lord that has shaken us. And they fell down before me, and were about to worship me, but I would not suffer them, saying: I am thy brother, yea, even thy younger brother; wherefore, worship the Lord thy God, and honor thy father and thy mother, that thy days may be long in the land which the Lord thy God shall give thee.

Lehi had previously spoken to Laman and Lemuel with such power of the Spirit that "their frames did shake before him," and they were confounded (1 Nephi 2:14). The shock coming from Nephi's hand brought a result that had not been obtained before. They acknowledged the Lord and his power was with Nephi (v. 55). Before they had submitted to Lehi, Nephi, and even an angel of the Lord (1 Nephi 3:29), out of fear; they knew the Lord was with them. Before, when they saw the power of God in Nephi, they "did plead with (him) that he would forgive them" (1 Nephi 7:20). Now, they "were about to worship [him]." On both occasions he turns their attention to the Lord to seek his forgiveness and to worship him (v. 55). This time, Nephi adds an admonition to "honor thy father and mother, that thy days may be long in the land" (v. 55). Nephi is quoting the 5th of the Ten Commandments (Exodus 20:12). Tying his admonition to his previous warnings, those who honor their parents will not become "ripe in iniquity," nor be destroyed as a nation (vv. 35–38). Laman and Lemuel were left without excuse for their future actions.

1 Nephi 18:1–4 • Nephi Builds a Ship By Revelation

1 And it came to pass that they did worship the Lord, and did go forth with me; and we did work timbers of curious workmanship. And the Lord did show me from time to time after what manner I should work the timbers of the ship.

2 Now I, Nephi, did not work the timbers after the manner which was learned by men, neither did I build the ship after the manner of men; but I did build it after the manner which the Lord had shown unto me; wherefore, it was not after the manner of men.

3 And I, Nephi, did go into the mount oft, and I did pray oft unto the Lord; wherefore the Lord showed unto me great things.

4 And it came to pass that after I had finished the ship, according to the word of the Lord, my brethren beheld that it was good, and that the workmanship thereof was exceedingly fine; wherefore, they did humble themselves again before the Lord. [1 Nephi 18:1–4]

Nephi had no knowledge of ship building. He emphasized that the construction was not after the manner of men, but as the Lord revealed it to him. Certainly the Lord knew the extent of the journey, and how to build a ship to endure the rigorous trip. He had previously instructed Noah to build an ark "three hundred cubits" in length, "the breadth of it fifty cubits, and the height of it thirty cubits," that could house Noah and his family, and male and female of all the animals and fowls of the earth. The ark sailed for over "an hundred and fifty days" (Genesis 6:15–7:24). The Jaredites built barges "according to the instructions of the Lord" that were "three hundred and forty four days upon the water. And they did land upon the shore of the promised land" (Ether 2:16; 6:11–12). These were not small boats, but ships, and "the workmanship thereof was exceedingly fine" (v. 4).

1 Nephi 18:5–8 • The Ship Is Loaded and Put Forth to Sea

5 And it came to pass that the voice of the Lord came unto my father, that we should arise and go down into the ship.

6 And it came to pass that on the morrow, after we had prepared all things, much fruits and meat from the wilderness, and honey in abundance, and provisions according to that which the Lord had commanded us, we did go down into the ship, with all our loading and our seeds, and whatsoever thing we had brought with us, every one according to his age; wherefore, we did all go down into the ship, with our wives and our children.

7 And now, my father had begat two sons in the wilderness; the elder was called Jacob and the younger Joseph.

8 And it came to pass after we had all gone down into the ship, and had taken with us our provisions and things which had been commanded us, we did put forth into the sea and were driven forth before the wind towards the promised land.

The loading of the ship, "every one according to his age" (v. 6), was according to the patriarchal order of the Hebrew culture.[2] This is the first mention of Lehi's two young sons, Jacob and Joseph, born during the eight years in the wilderness.

1 Nephi 18:9–14 • A Fierce Storm at Sea

9 And after we had been driven forth before the wind for the space of many days, behold, my brethren and the sons of Ishmael and also their wives began to make themselves merry, insomuch that they began to dance, and to sing, and to speak with much rudeness, yea, even that they did forget by what power they had been brought thither; yea, they were lifted up unto exceeding rudeness.

10 And I, Nephi, began to fear exceedingly lest the Lord should be angry with us, and smite us because of our iniquity, that we should be swallowed up in the depths of the sea; wherefore, I, Nephi, began

---

[2] Eldin Ricks, *Book of Mormon Commentary* [1953], 1:217.

to speak to them with much soberness; but behold they were angry with me, saying: We will not that our younger brother shall be a ruler over us.

11 And it came to pass that Laman and Lemuel did take me and bind me with cords, and they did treat me with much harshness; nevertheless, the Lord did suffer it that he might show forth his power, unto the fulfilling of his word which he had spoken concerning the wicked.

12 And it came to pass that after they had bound me insomuch that I could not move, the compass, which had been prepared of the Lord, did cease to work.

13 Wherefore, they knew not whither they should steer the ship, insomuch that there arose a great storm, yea, a great and terrible tempest, and we were driven back upon the waters for the space of three days; and they began to be frightened exceedingly lest they should be drowned in the sea; nevertheless they did not loose me.

14 And on the fourth day, which we had been driven back, the tempest began to be exceedingly sore.

The memories of Laman and Lemuel were short and they again led certain members of the family to revolt against Nephi and their father (vv. 8–9). Elder Neal A. Maxwell commented on their rude behavior on the ship: "Their periodic violence indicated their resentments weren't merely abstract, intellectual differences" (CR, Oct. 1999, 6–7). Nephi quickly recognizes why the compass failed to work and why the great storm had arisen (vv. 12–13). However, the rebellious brothers did not recognize the Lord's hand in these dilemmas.

1 Nephi 18:15–20 • The Brothers Again Recognize the Power of God

15 And it came to pass that we were about to be swallowed up in the depths of the sea. And after we had been driven back upon the waters for the space of four days, my brethren began to see that the judgments of God were upon them, and that they must perish save that they should repent of their iniquities; wherefore, they came unto me, and loosed the bands which were upon my wrists, and behold they had swollen exceedingly; and also mine ankles were much swollen,

and great was the soreness thereof.

16 Nevertheless, I did look unto my God, and I did praise him all the day long; and I did not murmur against the Lord because of mine afflictions.

17 Now my father, Lehi, had said many things unto them, and also unto the sons of Ishmael; but, behold, they did breathe out much threatenings against anyone that should speak for me; and my parents being stricken in years, and having suffered much grief because of their children, they were brought down, yea, even upon their sick-beds.

18 Because of their grief and much sorrow, and the iniquity of my brethren, they were brought near even to be carried out of this time to meet their God; yea, their grey hairs were about to be brought down to lie low in the dust; yea, even they were near to be cast with sorrow into a watery grave.

19 And Jacob and Joseph also, being young, having need of much nourishment, were grieved because of the afflictions of their mother; and also my wife with her tears and prayers, and also my children, did not soften the hearts of my brethren that they would loose me.

20 And there was nothing save it were the power of God, which threatened them with destruction, could soften their hearts; wherefore, when they saw that they were about to be swallowed up in the depths of the sea they repented of the thing which they had done, insomuch that they loosed me.

The two brothers finally recognized that the judgments of God were upon them, and loosened the bands of Nephi (v. 15). The character of Nephi once more shines forth as he praises the Lord in spite of the physical afflictions brought upon him by his brothers. The rebellious sons again do not honor their parents, nor do the sufferings of the children and women soften their hearts (vv. 17–19). Only the fear of destruction by the power of God brought them to repentance, and as will be shown later, their sorrow was not "godly sorrow [that] worketh repentance to salvation" as defined by Paul (2 Corinthians 7:10).

1 Nephi 18:21–23 • Nephi Guides
Them to the Promised Land

21 And it came to pass after they had loosed me, behold, I took the compass, and it did work whither I desired it. And it came to pass that I prayed unto the Lord; and after I had prayed the winds did cease, and the storm did cease, and there was a great calm.

22 And it came to pass that I, Nephi, did guide the ship, that we sailed again towards the promised land.

23 And it came to pass that after we had sailed for the space of many days we did arrive at the promised land; and we went forth upon the land, and did pitch our tents; and we did call it the promised land.

Nephi again becomes the Lord's servant, and brings the ship to the promised land (vv. 21–23). Their travels of the last ten or eleven years may be charted from the Book of Mormon as follows. Lehi traveled from Jerusalem to the borders of the Red Sea, went three days into the wilderness into a valley they named Lemuel, with a river that emptied into the Red Sea (1 Nephi 2:4–8). From the valley of Lemuel, they traveled in a "south-southeast direction" many days following "the directions of the ball" to a place called Nahom (1 Nephi 16:13–17, 33–34). From Nahom, they "did travel nearly eastward from that time forth" until they "did come to the land which they called Bountiful" (1 Nephi 17:1, 5). From Bountiful they "were driven forth before the wind towards the promised land" (1 Nephi 18:8, 22–23).

Another account of Lehi's travels comes to us from Fredrick G. Williams, a counselor in the First Presidency to the Prophet Joseph Smith. At the dedication of the Kirtland Temple, in 1836, "President Fredrick G. Williams arose and testified that while President Rigdon (the other counselor in the First Presidency) was making his first prayer, an angel entered the window and took his seat between Father Smith and himself and remained there during the prayer.

President David Whitmer also saw angels in the house" (*HC,* 2:427).

Elder Heber C. Kimball also bore testimony that "an angel appeared and sat near Joseph Smith Sen., and Fredrick G. Williams," and gave more detail which will not be given here.[3] Following the quoting of the above references, the biography of Fredrick G. William's life states:

> Fredrick had in his pocket a piece of paper which he carried to take notes on. On this he wrote in pencil: "John the beloved"—then a space followed and a few lines written in another language. A large space followed and then at the bottom of the page he wrote the following revelation: "The course that Lehi traveled from the city of Jerusalem to the place that he and his family took ship: They traveled nearly south, southeast direction until they came to the nineteenth degree of north latitude. Then nearly east to the Sea of Arabia; then south, southeast direction and landed on the continent of South America in Chile, thirty degrees south latitude."

> Returning home he transcribed the revelation in ink on another sheet of paper. Rebecca kept these papers with his other notes until her death. Their son, Ezra, loaned them to the Church Historian's Office in Salt Lake City in the 1860's where they have lain these many years, known only to historians, to be brought to light and published for the first time.[4]

In 1952 Hugh Nibley, a great Book of Mormon scholar, observed:

> After traveling a vast distance in a south-southeast direction (16:14, 33), the party struck off almost due eastward through the worst desert of all, where they "did wade through much affliction," to emerge in a state of almost complete exhaustion into a totally unexpected paradise by the sea. There is such a paradise in the Qara Mountains on the southern coast of Arabia. To reach it by moving "nearly eastward" (17:1) from the Red Sea coast, one would have to turn east

---

[3] Orson F. Whitney, *The Life of Heber C. Kimball,* 3rd ed. [1967], 91.

[4] Nancy Clement Williams, *After 100 Years,* Zion's Printing and Publishing Company, Independence, Missouri [1951], 101–102. In a footnote, the author states: The original, written in pencil was shown by a historian in the early 1930's, and was the only one she had seen until February 29, 1949, when she was shown the film and the letter from which it was taken—and received with others a wonderful manifestation that it was indeed a revelation given to Fredrick G. Williams for him and his family. The original, written in pencil, cannot be found at this writing.

on the nineteenth parallel. In the *Improvement Era* for September 1951 the present writer published a map in which his main concern was to make Lehi reach the sea in the forested sector of the Hadhramaut, and no other consideration dictated his sketching of the map. He foolishly overlooked the fact that Dr. John A. Widtsoe had published in the *Era* some months previously what purports to be, and probably is, a genuine "Revelation to Joseph the Seer," in which it is stated that Lehi's party "traveled nearly a south, south-east direction until they came to the nineteenth degree of north latitude; then nearly east to the sea of Arabia. . . ." By an interesting coincidence, the route shown in the author's map turned east exactly at the nineteenth parallel. This correlation of data from two totally different sources is a strong indication that both are correct.[5]

In 1842, the Prophet Joseph Smith, after reading of John L. Stephens exploration to Central America, commented:

> When we read in the Book of Mormon . . . that Lehi went down by the Red Sea to the great Southern Ocean, and crossed over to this land, and landed a little south of the Isthmus of Darien, and improved the country according to the word of the Lord, as a branch of the house of Israel, and then read such a goodly traditionary account as the one below we cannot help but think the Lord has a hand in bringing to pass his strange act, and proving the Book of Mormon true in the eyes of all people. [*TPJS*, 267]

Some see a contradiction between Joseph Smith's and Fredrick G. William's statements on the landing places. However, the statements can be correlated. The term "a little south" should be considered in the general context of the entire statement of the Prophet's statement. Fredrick G. William's statement gives a more specific landing. "A little south" on a map may be a lot farther than a reference to "a little south" when giving directions from a street corner to an individual. On a map, Chile is a little south of the Isthmus of Darien. It is also a little south from Central America where the John L. Stephens' expedition was and then being read about by the Prophet Joseph. While the place Lehi

---

[5] Hugh Nibley, *Lehi in the Desert and the World of the Jaredites* [1952], 124–125.

landed is not of extreme importance, the above information should not be treated lightly.

1 Nephi 18:24–25 • What Was Found in the Land of Promise

24 And it came to pass that we did begin to till the earth, and we began to plant seeds; yea, we did put all our seeds into the earth, which we had brought from the land of Jerusalem. And it came to pass that they did grow exceedingly; wherefore, we were blessed in abundance.

25 And it came to pass that we did find upon the land of promise, as we journeyed in the wilderness, that there were beasts in the forests of every kind, both the cow and the ox, and the ass and the horse, and the goat and the wild goat, and all manner of wild animals, which were for the use of men. And we did find all manner of ore, both of gold, and of silver, and of copper.

Note that Lehi's party "went forth upon the land" after they landed (v. 23 above). They also journeyed in the wilderness "upon the promised land" (v. 25). How far they went, or for how long, is not stated in either case, but having spoken of their eight years in the wilderness in similar general terms, it could have been extensive. The finding of gold, silver, and copper may be a clue to their early travels. Where are all three of these metals found in the same area? Perhaps they were found in separate areas, but this would extend the distances of their travel. We are not reading a geography book, and must be cautious in drawing conclusions.

SACRED WRITING

Preaching Which Is Sacred:

1 Nephi 17:23–51   Nephi to Laman and Lemuel concerning his ability to build a ship.

Great Revelations:

1 Nephi 17:7–10; 12–14; 18:21–22   The Lord instructs Nephi on building the ship.

Doctrines Learned:

1 Nephi 17:23–32, 40–43	The Book of Mormon proves (bears witness) that the miracles of the Bible are true.
1 Nephi 17:35	The Lord esteems all flesh as one, but the righteous are favored of God.
1 Nephi 17:35	The Lord curses a land unto destruction when the inhabitants are ripe in iniquity.
1 Nephi 17:36	The Lord created the earth to be inhabited, and his children to possess it.
1 Nephi 17:37	The Lord raises up a righteous nation, and destroys the nations of the wicked.
1 Nephi 17:38	The Lord leads the righteous into precious lands, and destroys and curses the land of the wicked for their sakes.
1 Nephi 17:39	The Lord ruleth high in the heavens, it is his throne, and the earth is his footstool.
1 Nephi 17:40	The Lord loves those who will have him to be their God
1 Nephi 17:40	The Lord covenanted with Abraham, Isaac, and Jacob because of he loved them.
1 Nephi 17:50	If the Lord commands man, he can do all things.

General Authority Quotes

Elder Marion G Romney • 1 Nephi 17:50

Here is an example of faith and courage which, if we can emulate, will do much to help us through our doubting and discouragement, for we serve the same God that Nephi served, and He will sustain us even as he sustained Nephi if we will serve him even as Nephi served him. [CR, April 1949, 40]

President Heber J. Grant • 1 Nephi 18:15–16

We find here a man of faith; a man who submits to affliction without murmuring. In all his history we find that he followed the commandments of the Lord. The Lord said to him in the beginning that if he followed His commandments he should be prospered in the land, and he was prospered.

I wish to bear my testimony to the Latter-day Saints that all of us who will obey the commandments of God will be prospered in the land. Sacrifice doth bring forth the blessings of heaven. [CR, Oct. 1899, 19]

Challenges to Eternal Life:

1. Do not pass the principles of the gospel off as simple or easy, but follow them meticulously, and you will be blessed (1 Nephi 17:41).

2. Make a commitment to have God as your God, and keep the covenants he has made with us (1 Nephi 17:40).

3. Remember that if God commanded Nephi or Moses to do something and provided a way for them to do it, he will provide a way for me to do what he has commanded me.

4. Select a message from this reading, and apply it to your life.

Chapter Eight

More Fully Persuade to Believe in the Redeemer

1 Nephi 19–20

*H*istorical Setting: Nephi pauses in the abridgment of his "first plates" onto these (smaller) plates to tell us again that he was keeping two sets of plates (1 Nephi 19:1–4). His promise to tell us more later "of my making these [smaller] plates" (v. 5) has reference to thirty years after they left Jerusalem when he was commanded to make the second set of plates (see 2 Nephi 5:28–32). This chapter discusses this historical event. While stopped from abridging his father's record, he bears testimony of Christ by quoting from the prophecies on the plates of brass (v. 21). He quotes the prophet Isaiah at length (1 Nephi 20; Isaiah 48).

Precepts of this Reading:

7 For the things which some men esteem to be of great worth, both to the body and soul, others set at naught and trample under their feet. Yea, even the very God of Israel do men trample under their feet; I say, trample under their feet but I would speak in other words—they set him at naught, and hearken not to the voice of his counsels. [1 Nephi 19:7]

18 And I, Nephi, have written these things unto my people, that perhaps I might persuade them that they would remember the Lord their Redeemer.

19 Wherefore, I speak unto all the house of Israel, if it so be that they should obtain these things. [1 Nephi 19:18–19]

... but that I might more fully persuade them to believe in the Lord their Redeemer I did read unto them that which was written by the prophet Isaiah; for I did liken all scriptures unto us, that it might be for our profit and learning. [1 Nephi 19:23]

Mormons are often accused of not being "Christians." Such accusations are totally without foundation. One who has read the Book of Mormon with an open mind will find it speaks of Christ in all but six of the two hundred and thirty-nine chapters contained in the book (Mosiah 19, 22; Alma 51–52; Helaman 1–2). These six chapters describe apostasy and war, and then quickly return to Christ as the solution to overcoming these problems. Jesus Christ was known by various names in both the Old and New Testament, and he is the central figure throughout the Book of Mormon. This chapter will illustrate the Nephite's belief in the true Christ as the God of both the Old and the New Testaments. It also shows the position of The Church of Jesus Christ of Latter-day Saints regarding Christ. An outline of the reading follows as a preparation for a deeper study.

OUTLINE • 1 NEPHI 19–20

➤ 19:1–7   The Lord commands Nephi to make plates of ore and engraven upon them the record of his people.

   a. He engraves the record of his father, their journeyings in the wilderness, the prophecies of his father, and many of his own prophecies (v. 1).

   b. Nephi was later commanded to make this record, a more particular account. The genealogy of his fathers is on the first set of plates (v. 2).

   c. The second set of plates was to contain the more plain and precious parts of the ministry and prophecies (v. 3).

      1. The things written should be kept for the instruction of those who possessed the land.

2. It was also for other wise purposes known to the Lord.

  d. An account of the wars and contentions, and destruction of Nephi's people is on the other plates (v. 4).

  e. The first set of plates was to be handed down from one generation to another, and from one prophet to another (v. 4).

  f. An account of his making these plates shall be given later in order to keep the more sacred things for the people (v. 5).

  g. Nephi writes only things he considered sacred upon any of the plates (vv. 6–7).

      1. If he errs, those of old also erred.

      2. He does not excuse himself because of other men, but because of the weakness of the flesh.

      3. What some esteem of great worth, others set at naught and trample under their feet.

      4. Men trample the very God of Israel under their feet, or set him at naught and hearken not to his counsel.

➤ 19:8–10   Nephi writes that the very God of Israel will come, according to the words of an angel, six hundred years after Nephi's father left Jerusalem

  a. The world will judge him as a thing of naught, scourge and smite him, spit upon him, and he suffereth it because of his long suffering and loving kindness for the children of men (v. 9).

  b. The God of Abraham, Isaac, and Jacob, according to the words of an angel, yieldeth himself to the hands of wicked men (v. 10).

      1. He will be lifted up according to the words of Zenock.

      2. He will be crucified according to the words of Neum.

      3. He will be buried in the sepulchre according to the words of Zenos

➤ 19:10–17   Nephi writes more of the prophecies of Zenos.

    a.   Three days of darkness at Christ's death will be a sign to those on the Isles of the sea, especially those of the house of Israel (v. 10).

    b.   The Lord God will visit his people, some with his voice because of their righteousness, and others with thundering, lightnings, tempest, fire, darkness, the opening of the earth, and mountains carried up (v. 11).

    c.   Because of the groanings of the earth, many of the kings of the Isles of the sea shall be wrought upon by the Spirit of God to exclaim: "The God of Nature suffers" (v. 12).

    d.   Those at Jerusalem shall be scourged by all people because they crucify the God of Israel, rejecting signs and wonders and glory of the God of Israel (vv. 13–15).

        1.   They shall wander in the flesh and perish, and become a hiss and a byword, and be hated among all nations.

        2.   When they no more turn their hearts against the Holy One of Israel, he will remember the covenants he made to their fathers.

    e.   He will remember the isles of the sea, and all the house of Israel will he gather from the four quarters of the earth, and all the earth shall see the salvation of the Lord (vv. 16–17).

➤ 19:18–22   Nephi writes these things to persuade his people to remember the Lord their Redeemer.

    a.   He speaks to all the house of Israel, if they obtain this record (v. 19).

    b.   The Spirit wearies him because of those at Jerusalem, had Nephi not been shown concerning them, he would have perished also (v. 20).

    c.   The Lord did show unto the prophets of old all things concerning the Jews, and did show many concerning the Nephites. They are written upon the plates of brass (v. 21).

    d.   He taught his brethren from the plates of brass, that they might know the doings of the Lord in other lands, among people of old (v. 22).

19:23–24   Nephi read many things unto his brethren that were written in the books of Moses and that he might more fully persuade them to believe in their Redeemer, he read what was written by the prophet Isaiah.

    a.   He likens all scripture unto them for their profit and learning (v. 23).

    b.   He invites them to hear the words of Isaiah that were written to all the house of Israel (v. 24).

    c.   He invites them, a branch who had been broken off, to liken Isaiah's words to themselves that they may also have hope (v. 24).

20:1–2   (Isaiah 48:1–2) The baptized members of Judah have apostatized.

    a.   They swear by the name of the Lord but not in truth or righteousness (v. 1).

    b.   They claim to be of the holy city but do not rely on the Lord (v. 2).

20:3–8   (Isaiah 48:3–8) The Lord foretold Judah's destiny even from the beginning.

    a.   They were shown the things which would happen before they happened (v. 3).

    b.   They were shown these things because they were obstinate and stubborn (v. 4).

    c.   They were shown these things so they could not give credit to their idols (v. 5).

    d.   They saw prophecy fulfilled and were told of the future, and yet would not hear; this the Lord also knew (vv. 6–8).

➤ 20:9–11   (Isaiah 48:9–11) The Lord will defer his anger and will not cut Judah off.

    a.   They will be sent through the furnace of affliction (v. 10).

    b.   The Lord will not allow his name to be polluted (v. 11).

➤ 20:12–17   (Isaiah 48:12–17) Jacob and Israel are invited to hearken unto God, who is the first and the last.

    a.   He created the heavens and the earth, and they obey him (v. 13).

    b.   He will fulfill his word on the Gentiles (v. 14).

    c.   Israel will declare God's word, and Israel will prosper (v. 15).

    d.   The Lord has spoken of this from the beginning (vv. 16–17).

➤ 20:18–22   (Isaiah 48:18–22) If Israel had obeyed the commandments, they would not have been destroyed.

    a.   The Lord has delivered his people before (vv. 20–21).

    b.   There is no peace for the wicked (v. 22).

NOTES AND COMMENTARY

Introduction: Nephi was commanded to write "the more plain and precious parts" of "the ministry and prophecies" upon these plates (1 Nephi 19:3). Why did he include Isaiah? Isaiah contained precious prophecies, but they certainly were not plain. Nephi himself later acknowledged that Isaiah was "hard for many of my people to understand" (2 Nephi 25:1). Nephi answers this question just prior to recording the first of Isaiah's prophecies (1 Nephi 20–21). He desired to "more fully persuade them to believe in the Lord their Redeemer" (1 Nephi 19:23). He had earlier attempted to persuade them by quoting the words of an angel (19:8–10), quoting other prophesies from the plates of brass (19:10–18), and had given his own testimony (19:19–21). We will consider them in the order they were given by Nephi.

1 Nephi 19:1–5 • A Second Set of Plates

1 And it came to pass that the Lord commanded me, wherefore I did make plates of ore that I might engraven upon them the record of my people. And upon the plates which I made I did engraven the record of my father, and also our journeyings in the wilderness, and the prophecies of my father; and also many of mine own prophecies have I engraven upon them.

2 And I knew not at the time when I made them that I should be commanded of the Lord to make these plates; wherefore, the record of my father, and the genealogy of his fathers, and the more part of all our proceedings in the wilderness are engraven upon those first plates of which I have spoken; wherefore, the things which transpired before I made these plates are, of a truth, more particularly made mention upon the first plates.

3 And after I had made these plates by way of commandment, I, Nephi, received a commandment that the ministry and the prophecies, the more plain and precious parts of them, should be written upon these plates; and that the things which were written should be kept for the instruction of my people, who should possess the land, and also for other wise purposes, which purposes are known unto the Lord.

4 Wherefore, I, Nephi, did make a record upon the other plates, which gives an account, or which gives a greater account of the wars and contentions and destructions of my people. And this have I done, and commanded my people what they should do after I was gone; and that these plates should be handed down from one generation to another, or from one prophet to another, until further commandments of the Lord.

5 And an account of my making these plates shall be given hereafter; and then, behold, I proceed according to that which I have spoken; and this I do that the more sacred things may be kept for the knowledge of my people.

These verses are the second reference Nephi made of the two sets of plates (the first is 1 Nephi 9), and the third mention of the small plates (1 Nephi 6 speaks of only the small plates). Nephi was commanded to make the first set of plates (v. 1), which Church literature usually refers to as the large plates. The commandment was probably given after they landed in the promised land because it was the first time they had access to ore from which they could make plates. Lehi had kept a record and Nephi had made "an abridgment of the record of my father" (1 Nephi 1:16–17). The type of materials Lehi wrote upon is not stated. Making a record on plates of ore would certainly be more permanent. Nephi was commanded to keep the second set of plates many years later and they will be discussed under 2 Nephi 5. Nephi stresses the sacredness of them. The purpose of the second set of plates is to preserve knowledge for his people (v. 6). This knowledge is for future generations.

1 Nephi 19:6–7 • Sacred Things Upon These Plates

6 Nevertheless, I do not write anything upon plates save it be that I think it be sacred. And now, if I do err, even did they err of old; not that I would excuse myself because of other men, but because of the weakness which is in me, according to the flesh, I would excuse myself.

7 For the things which some men esteem to be of great worth, both to the body and soul, others set at naught and trample under their feet. Yea, even the very God of Israel do men trample under their feet; I say, trample under their feet but I would speak in other words—they set him at naught, and hearken not to the voice of his counsels.

Nephi knows the importance and the sacredness of making a record for future generations. He acknowledges his weakness as a mortal man in keeping the record, but is not making excuses. He senses that he will be criticized by some no matter what he records. He laments the insensitivity of mortal man to sacred things, specifically when they trample the words of counsel from the very God of Israel. This is a sobering metaphor. To trample the God of Israel under our feet or setting at naught his words has been a problem in every age of the world. To set at naught his words is to ignore them either by failure to listen or refusal to read them. To not hearken is to be aware of what they teach, but to not do as they say. The Lord condemned the early Church in a similar manner.

54 And your minds in times past have been darkened because of unbelief, and because you have treated lightly the things you have received—

55 Which vanity and unbelief have brought the whole church under condemnation.

56 And this condemnation resteth upon the children of Zion, even all.

57 And they shall remain under this condemnation until they repent and remember the new covenant, even the Book of Mormon and the former commandments which I have given them, not only to say, but to do according to that which I have written—

58 That they may bring forth fruit meet for their Father's kingdom; otherwise there remaineth a scourge and judgment to be poured out upon the children of Zion.

59 For shall the children of the kingdom pollute my holy land? Verily, I say unto you, Nay. [D&C 84:54–59]

The condemnation was reiterated in the 1980's through President Ezra Taft Benson. "In section 84 of the Doctrine and Covenants, the Lord declares that the whole Church and all the children of Zion are under condemnation because of the way we have treated the Book of Mormon. (vv. 54–58). This condemnation has not been lifted, nor will it be until we repent. . . . In our day the Lord has inspired His servant to reemphasize the Book of Mormon to get the Church out from under condemnation—the scourge and judgment."[1] We must learn the word of God and hearken to it. Whether it comes directly from him or from his servants it is still the word of God.

1 Nephi 19:8–10 • Nephi Quotes an Angel and the Prophets Concerning Christ

8 And behold he cometh, according to the words of the angel, in six hundred years from the time my father left Jerusalem.

9 And the world, because of their iniquity, shall judge him to be

---

[1] Ezra Taft Benson, *A Witness and a Warning* [1988], pp. vll–vlll.

a thing of naught; wherefore they scourge him, and he suffereth it; and they smite him, and he suffereth it. Yea, they spit upon him, and he suffereth it, because of his loving kindness and his long-suffering towards the children of men.

10 And the God of our fathers, who were led out of Egypt, out of bondage, and also were preserved in the wilderness by him, yea, the God of Abraham, and of Isaac, and the God of Jacob, yieldeth himself, according to the words of the angel, as a man, into the hands of wicked men, to be lifted up, according to the words of Zenock, and to be crucified, according to the words of Neum, and to be buried in a sepulchre, according to the words of Zenos, which he spake concerning the three days of darkness, which should be a sign given of his death unto those who should inhabit the isles of the sea, more especially given unto those who are of the house of Israel.

Nephi's lament sets the stage for his testimony of the very God of Israel, Jesus Christ. Nephi was told by an angel that the date of his coming to earth as a mortal being would be six hundred years from the time Lehi left Jerusalem (v. 8). Quoting from the same source, Nephi foretells the world's general judgment, or reception, of Christ (vv. 9–10).[2] The New Testament verifies the world's reaction. Nephi then quotes several prophecies from the plates of brass. These prophecies tell what will happen to Christ when he comes to earth.

Nephi's designation of Christ as "the God of our fathers, who were led out of Egypt," and "the God of Abraham, and of Isaac, and of Jacob" shows that Christ was the God who ministered to Israel in Old Testament times. Paul bore a similar testimony:

1 Moreover, brethren, I would not that ye should be ignorant, how

---

[2] The angel to whom Nephi refers, may have been the one who guided him through a series of visions after he had been shown Jerusalem, Nazareth, and other cities (1 Nephi 11:14–14:27). Another possibility is that he is referring to an angel who told his father Lehi of this six hundred year time period, although no visit of an angel is associated with it (1 Nephi 10:4). However, after the series of visions were given to Nephi, he bore "record that I saw the things which my father saw, and the angel of the Lord did make them known unto me" (1 Nephi 14:29). There could also have been an angel appear on another occasion of which we have no record.

that all our fathers were under the cloud, and all passed through the sea;

2 And were all baptized unto Moses in the cloud and in the sea;

3 And did all eat the same spiritual meat;

4 And did all drink the same spiritual drink: for they drank of that spiritual Rock that followed them: *and that Rock was Christ.* [1 Corinthians 10:1–4; italics added]

The prophecies from the plates of brass, now missing from the Old Testament as part of "the many plain and precious things which have been taken out of the book" (1 Nephi 13:29) are from three sources. The prophet Zenock foretold of Christ being "lifted up" by wicked men; another prophet, Neum, prophesied of his being "crucified;" and a third prophet, Zenos, spoke concerning "three days of darkness" as "a sign given of his death" to those in "the isles of the sea, more especially given unto those who are of the house of Israel." Nephi continues to quote the prophet Zenos for the following seven verses, although he only identifies him in two verses (12, 16) and calls him "the prophet" in the other five verses.

1 Nephi 19:11–17 • Zenos' Testimony of Christ

11 For thus spake the prophet: The Lord God surely shall visit all the house of Israel at that day, some with his voice, because of their righteousness, unto their great joy and salvation, and others with the thunderings and the lightnings of his power, by tempest, by fire, and by smoke, and vapor of darkness, and by the opening of the earth, and by mountains which shall be carried up.

12 And all these things must surely come, saith the prophet Zenos. And the rocks of the earth must rend; and because of the groanings of the earth, many of the kings of the isles of the sea shall be wrought upon by the Spirit of God, to exclaim: The God of nature suffers.

13 And as for those who are at Jerusalem, saith the prophet, they shall be scourged by all people, because they crucify the God of Israel, and turn their hearts aside, rejecting signs and wonders, and the power and glory of the God of Israel.

14 And because they turn their hearts aside, saith the prophet, and

have despised the Holy One of Israel, they shall wander in the flesh, and perish, and become a hiss and a byword, and be hated among all nations.

15 Nevertheless, when that day cometh, saith the prophet, that they no more turn aside their hearts against the Holy One of Israel, then will he remember the covenants which he made to their fathers.

16 Yea, then will he remember the isles of the sea; yea, and all the people who are of the house of Israel, will I gather in, saith the Lord, according to the words of the prophet Zenos, from the four quarters of the earth.

17 Yea, and all the earth shall see the salvation of the Lord, saith the prophet; every nation, kindred, tongue, and people shall be blessed.

We know little about the prophet Zenos except that he and Zenock, who Nephi also quoted above, were slain because they testified of Christ. "They stoned [Zenock] to death" (Alma 33:17) and "Zenos did testify boldly; for the which he was slain (Helaman 8:19). "They testified particularly concerning [the Nephites], who are the remnant of their seed" . . . and "are not we a remnant of the seed of Joseph" (3 Nephi 10:16–17). Other Nephite prophets quoted them extensively (see Jacob 5; Alma 33:3–17; 34:7; Helaman 15:11). Assuming that Helaman 8:19–20 is a chronological listing of prophets who have testified of Christ, we could place Zenos and Zenock somewhere between the time of Abraham (about 2000 B.C.) and Isaiah (about 740 B.C.).[3]

19 And now I would that ye should know, that even since the days of Abraham there have been many prophets that have testified these things; yea, behold, the prophet Zenos did testify boldly; for the which he was slain.

20 And behold, also Zenock, and also Ezias, and also Isaiah, and Jeremiah, (Jeremiah being that same prophet who testified of the destruction of Jerusalem) and now we know that Jerusalem was destroyed according to the words of Jeremiah. [Helaman 8:19–20]

---

[3] For possible identities of Zenos and other missing prophets see Hugh W. Nibley, *Since Cumorah* [1967], 311–27.

Elder Bruce R. McConkie has suggested that Zenos was second only to Isaiah among the prophets: "I do not think I overstate the matter when I say that next to Isaiah himself—who is the prototype, pattern, and model for all the prophets—there was not a greater prophet in all Israel than Zenos. And our knowledge of his inspired writings is limited to the quotations and paraphrasing summaries found in the Book of Mormon."[4]

Zenos prophesied that the Lord God (Christ) would visit all the house of Israel at the time of his death, some with his voice and some with destruction (v. 11). The Bible says that "the veil of the temple was rent in twain from the top to the bottom; and the earth did quake, and the rocks rent" (Matthew 27:51), but it does not tell us of any of the people being destroyed. Based on Zenos' prophecy there may have been some destroyed. The Book of Mormon records the fulfillment of Zenos' prophecy among the Nephites. "There arose a great storm, such an one as never had been known in all the land;" cities were burned, sunk into the sea, the earth carried upon them, "and the inhabitants thereof were slain, and the places left desolate." After three days, "there was a voice heard among all the inhabitants of the earth" (3 Nephi 8:5– 9:1). There were certainly similar things that happened among the ten tribes. We will learn more of these things when "the Nephites and the Jews shall have the words (records) of the lost tribes of Israel" (2 Nephi 29:13). As Mormon abridged the account in Third Nephi, he acknowledged that "it was the more righteous part of the people who were saved . . . all these deaths and destructions" were "unto the fulfilling of the prophecies . . . Yea, the prophet Zenos did testify of these things, and also Zenock" that were "written upon the plates of brass" (3 Nephi 10:12–17).

What the kings of the Isles of the sea were moved to say by the Spirit of God must be accepted as truth. Therefore, the designation of

---

[4] Bruce R. McConkie, The Doctrinal Restoration, chap. 1 in *The Joseph Translation*. ed. Monte S. Nyman and Robert L. Millet, Religious Study Center, Brigham Young University, Provo, Utah [1985], 17.

Christ as "the God of nature" (v. 12) is another important title for him. He is the God who controls the earth and its happenings. As he spoke to the more righteous Nephites, he proclaimed: "Behold, that great city of Zarahemla have I burned with fire, and the inhabitants thereof" (3 Nephi 9:3). He went on to take the responsibility for the other catastrophic events that had just taken place (see 3 Nephi 9:4–10). He caused these destructions "because of their wickedness and abominations" (3 Nephi 9:12). All of these teachings to the Nephites verify that he is the God of nature. The prophet Amos in the Bible gives us a second witness:

> 6 And I also have given you cleanness of teeth in all your cities, and want of bread in all your places: yet have ye not returned unto me, saith the LORD.
>
> 7 And also I have withholden the rain from you, when *there were* yet three months to the harvest: and I caused it to rain upon one city, and caused it not to rain upon another city: one piece was rained upon, and the piece whereupon it rained not withered.
>
> 8 So two *or* three cities wandered unto one city, to drink water; but they were not satisfied: yet have ye not returned unto me, saith the LORD.
>
> 9 I have smitten you with blasting and mildew: when your gardens and your vineyards and your fig trees and your olive trees increased, the palmerworm devoured *them*: yet have ye not returned unto me, saith the LORD.
>
> 10 I have sent among you the pestilence after the manner of Egypt: your young men have I slain with the sword, and have taken away your horses; and I have made the stink of your camps to come up unto your nostrils: yet have ye not returned unto me, saith the LORD.
>
> 11 I have overthrown *some* of you, as God overthrew Sodom and Gomorrah, and ye were as a firebrand plucked out of the burning: yet have ye not returned unto me, saith the LORD.
>
> 12 Therefore thus will I do unto thee, O Israel: *and* because I will do this unto thee, prepare to meet thy God, O Israel.
>
> 13 For, lo, he that formeth the mountains, and createth the wind, and declareth unto man what *is* his thought, that maketh the morning

darkness, and treadeth upon the high places of the earth, The LORD, The God of hosts, *is* his name. [Amos 4:6–13]

The Doctrine and Covenants gives a third witness:

25 How oft have I called upon you by the mouth of my servants, and by the ministering of angels, and by mine own voice, and by the voice of thunderings, and by the voice of lightnings, and by the voice of tempests, and by the voice of earthquakes, and great hailstorms, and by the voice of famines and pestilences of every kind, and by the great sound of a trump, and by the voice of judgment, and by the voice of mercy all the day long, and by the voice of glory and honor and the riches of eternal life, and would have saved you with an everlasting salvation, but ye would not! [D&C 43:25]

The Book of Mormon later testifies that the earth obeys the commands of the everlasting God, or the God of nature:

8 For behold, the dust of the earth moveth hither and thither, to the dividing asunder, at the command of our great and everlasting God.

9 Yea, behold at his voice do the hills and the mountains tremble and quake.

10 And by the power of his voice they are broken up, and become smooth, yea, even like unto a valley.

11 Yea, by the power of his voice doth the whole earth shake;

12 Yea, by the power of his voice, do the foundations rock, even to the very center.

13 Yea, and if he say unto the earth—Move—it is moved.

14 Yea, if he say unto the earth—Thou shalt go back, that it lengthen out the day for many hours—it is done;

15 And thus, according to his word the earth goeth back, and it appeareth unto man that the sun standeth still; yea, and behold, this is so; for surely it is the earth that moveth and not the sun.

16 And behold, also, if he say unto the waters of the great deep—Be thou dried up—it is done.

17 Behold, if he say unto this mountain—Be thou raised up, and

come over and fall upon that city, that it be buried up—behold it is
done. [Helaman 12:8–17]

Zenos continued to prophesy concerning the people of Jerusalem
who would crucify their God (vv. 13–14). He foretold of their wander-
ings (the diaspora), of their becoming a hiss and a by-word, and of
being hated of all nations (anti-semitism). It must be remembered that
these actions against the Jews were the result of the agency of men,
and were not necessarily the will of God. God, knowing they would
happen, and, ironically often in the name of religion, foretold them
but did not cause them. Those who brought it about will certainly be
accountable for their atrocious deeds. Mormon, as he abridged the
records of the Nephites, warned the reader:

> 8 Yea, and ye need not any longer hiss, nor spurn, nor make game
> of the Jews, nor any of the remnant of the house of Israel; for behold,
> the Lord remembereth his covenant unto them, and he will do unto
> them according to that which he hath sworn.
>
> 9 Therefore ye need not suppose that ye can turn the right hand
> of the Lord unto the left, that he may not execute judgment unto the
> fulfilling of the covenant which he hath made unto the house of Israel.
> [3 Nephi 29:8–9]

Nephi concludes his quoting of the prophecy of Zenos with the
prophet's promise that the covenants made to the fathers of the house
of Israel will be fulfilled (v. 15). The extensiveness of the scattering
of the house of Israel is shown by the promise to gather them from the
four quarters of the earth (v. 16). Another Old Testament prophet had
prophesied that they would be sifted "among all nations" (Amos 9:9).
The reference to the "isles of the sea" is of the Americas. Jacob, the
younger brother of Nephi, later commented that "we are upon the isles
of the sea. But great are the promises of the Lord unto them who are
upon the isles of the sea" (2 Nephi 10:20–21). The Americas are "the
land of [the remnant of Joseph's] inheritance; and the Father hath given
it unto [them]" (3 Nephi 15:12–13). As quoted above, Zenos was a
descendant of Joseph (of Egypt, 3 Nephi 10:16). Through the gathering
of Israel in the latter days, "all the earth shall see the salvation of the

Lord . . . every nation, kindred, tongue, and people shall be blessed" (v. 17). Of course those blessings will come from "another angel (Moroni) [flying] in the midst of heaven, having the everlasting gospel (the Book of Mormon) to preach unto them that dwell on the earth, and to every nation, and kindred, and tongue, and people" (Revelation 14:6).

1 Nephi 19:18–21 • The Prophets of Old Told of the Jews and the Nephites

18 And I, Nephi, have written these things unto my people, that perhaps I might persuade them that they would remember the Lord their Redeemer.

19 Wherefore, I speak unto all the house of Israel, if it so be that they should obtain these things.

20 For behold, I have workings in the spirit, which doth weary me even that all my joints are weak, for those who are at Jerusalem; for had not the Lord been merciful, to show unto me concerning them, even as he had prophets of old, I should have perished also.

21 And he surely did show unto the prophets of old all things concerning them; and also he did show unto many concerning us; wherefore, it must needs be that we know concerning them for they are written upon the plates of brass. [1 Nephi 19:18–21]

Nephi's overall purpose was to convince his own people to "remember the Lord their Redeemer" (v. 18), but he spoke to all the house of Israel because he knew by the Spirit that his writings would go to all of them. He had been shown the inhabitants of Jerusalem the same as had been seen by the prophets of old (vv. 19–20). However, not all of the prophets had been shown the Nephites (v. 21). Isaiah was one of the prophets who had been shown the future destiny of both the Jews and the people of Lehi. Wherefore, Nephi recorded one of his prophecies of the Jews (Isaiah 48; 1 Nephi 20); and one of his prophecies concerning the people of Lehi (Isaiah 49; 1 Nephi 21). His prophecies were written on the plates of brass, the source used by Nephi.

The Bible confirms, but the references are too numerous to be included here, that the prophets of old were shown many revelations concerning the Jews. Some of the many prophets, besides Isaiah, who prophesied extensively of the Nephites,[5] and who were shown the people of Lehi, would include Jacob the father of the house of Israel (Genesis 49:22–26); Moses (Deuteronomy 33:13–17); Ezekiel (37:15–28; 17:22–23); and King David (Psalm 85:10–11).[6] As discussed above, Zenos's prophecies of the remnant of Joseph were once on the plates of brass.

1 Nephi 19:22–24 • Isaiah to More Fully Convince Them of Their Redeemer

22 Now it came to pass that I, Nephi, did teach my brethren these things; and it came to pass that I did read many things to them, which were engraven upon the plates of brass, that they might know concerning the doings of the Lord in other lands, among people of old.

23 And I did read many things unto them which were written in the books of Moses; but that I might more fully persuade them to believe in the Lord their Redeemer I did read unto them that which was written by the prophet Isaiah; for I did liken all scriptures unto us, that it might be for our profit and learning.

24 Wherefore I spake unto them, saying: Hear ye the words of the prophet, ye who are a remnant of the house of Israel, a branch who have been broken off; hear ye the words of the prophet, which were written unto all the house of Israel, and liken them unto yourselves,

---

[5] Isaiah 29 is an extensive treatise of the destruction of the Nephite people, and the coming forth of the Book of Mormon. This chapter will be analyzed in chapter 19 of this work. There are many other prophecies of Isaiah regarding the people of Nephi, but will not be included here because it is not the purpose of this book to give a thorough analysis of Isaiah's writings, except those quoted in the Book of Mormon which will be discussed in subsequent chapters of this work.

[6] The Psalms were the hymns of Israel, and the words were often paraphrased from the prophets writings. The 85th Psalm may have been based on a prophecy of Enoch found in the book of Moses (7:62), a part of the work of Joseph Smith in his translation of the Bible, and is now included in the Pearl of Great Price.

that ye may have hope as well as your brethren from whom ye have been broken off; for after this manner has the prophet written. [1 Nephi 19:22–24]

Nephi's reading of many things "concerning the doings of the Lord in other lands, among people of old" (v. 22) would include the books of Moses (v. 23). The plates of brass "did contain the five books of Moses, which gave an account of the creation of the world, and also of Adam and Eve, who were our first parents" (1 Nephi 5:11). These books, in our present Bible, are Genesis, Exodus, Leviticus, Numbers, and Deuteronomy. However, Nephi recognized Isaiah as the more significant source to convince his people of the Lord their Redeemer (v. 23).

To liken Isaiah's writings unto themselves for their "profit and learning" (v. 23) should not be interpreted to mean that Nephi merely applied them to his people. That Nephi's prophecies are dual in nature and pertinent to all branches of Israel, is evident from Nephi's statement that follows: "hear ye the words of the prophet, which were written to all the house of Israel" (v. 24). Jacob later affirmed: "which Isaiah spake concerning all the house of Israel; wherefore, they may be likened unto you, for ye are of the house of Israel." Jesus also used the same passages of Isaiah (52:8–10) to teach about the future of the Lamanites (3 Nephi 16:18–20) and of the Jews (3 Nephi 20:32–35). Furthermore, it should be observed that Isaiah 48 specifically addresses the people who "come forth out of the waters of Judah" (1 Nephi 20:1) and that Isaiah 49 specifically addresses the house of Israel "that are scattered abroad" in the "isles" (1 Nephi 21:1). Nephi calls his people "a remnant of the house of Israel, a branch who have been broken off" (v. 24). We will analyze the message of Isaiah to Judah in this chapter, and the message to the people of Lehi in the following chapter.

Every verse of Isaiah 48 taken from the plates of brass is different than those from the King James Bible, except verse eighteen, which only differs in punctuation. However, the punctuation in the Book of

Mormon was provided by translators and printers.[7] The Book of Mormon text was taken from the plates of brass, which is an older source than the source from which the KJV text was translated (prior to 600 B.C.). Thus the Book of Mormon has retained a textual purity that the Bible has not. Twelve of these retentions are significant. They help explain Isaiah's original message. A comparison of the two texts highlights the retentions in the Book of Mormon.

1 Nephi 20:1–2 • Judah In a State of Apostasy

1 *Hearken* and hear this, O house of Jacob, who are called by the name of Israel, and are come forth out of the waters of Judah, or *out of the waters of baptism,* who swear by the name of the Lord, and make mention of the God of Israel, *yet they swear* not in truth nor in righteousness.

2 *Nevertheless,* they call themselves of the holy city, but they do not stay themselves upon the God of Israel, who is the Lord of Hosts; yea, the Lord of Hosts is his name. [1 Nephi 20:1–2]

1 Hear ye this, O house of Jacob, which are called by the name of Israel, and are come forth out of the waters of Judah, which swear by the name of the LORD, and make mention of the God of Israel, but not in truth, nor in righteousness.

2 For they call themselves of the holy city, and stay themselves upon the God of Israel; The LORD of hosts is his name. [Isaiah 48:1–2]

The first two verses of this chapter show that Isaiah is describing a period of time when Judah, the southern nation of the divided kingdom of Israel, was in a state of apostasy. This was probably in Isaiah's day. The phrase "out of the waters of Judah" refers to those of Judah who are baptized into the Church. The Prophet Joseph Smith added the phrase "or out of the waters of baptism" to the text in the

---

[7] Oliver Cowdery, the scribe who wrote as Joseph translated, made a copy of the original manuscript. John H. Gilbert, the typesetter who worked for E. B. Grandin, who was contracted to print the first edition of the Book of Mormon, wrote concerning the printers copy of the manuscript: "Every chapter . . . was one solid paragraph, without a punctuation mark, from beginning to end. . . . I punctuated it to make it read as I supposed the Author intended, and but very little punctuation was altered in proof reading." John H. Gilbert, "Memorandum" September 8, 1892, Palmyra, New York; reprinted in Wilford C. Woodruff, *Joseph Smith Begins His Work.* Other editions of the Book of Mormon have made some few punctuation changes.

third edition of the Book of Mormon (1840). This clarifies the meaning of the term "waters of Judah." Their false swearing, hypocritical actions, and failure to trust in the Lord depicts their apostasy. The Book of Mormon retains the words "but they do not" (v. 2) which helps us see the apostate condition of Judah. It also retains the phrase "who is the Lord of Hosts" to further identify or describe the God of Israel, but this does not add meaning to the text.

1 Nephi 20:3–8 • Why the Lord Foretells the Future

3 *Behold*, I have declared the former things from the beginning; and they went forth out of my mouth, and I showed them. I did *show* them suddenly.

4 *And I did it* because I knew that thou art obstinate, and thy neck is an iron sinew, and thy brow brass;

5 *And* I have even from the beginning declared to thee; before it came to pass I showed *them* thee; and *I showed them for* fear lest thou shouldst say—Mine idol hath done them, and my graven image, and my molten image hath commanded them.

6 Thou hast *seen and* heard all this; and will ye not declare *them? And that* I have showed thee new things from this time, even hidden things, and thou didst not know them.

7 They are created now, and not from the beginning, even before the day when thou heardest them not *they were declared unto thee*, lest thou shouldst say—Behold I knew them.

8 Yea, *and* thou heardest not; yea, thou knewest not; yea, from that time thine ear was not opened; for I knew that thou wouldst deal very treacherously, and wast called a transgressor from the womb. [1 Nephi 20:3–8]

3 I have declared the former things from the beginning; and they went forth out of my mouth, and I shewed them; I did *them* suddenly, and they came to pass.

4 Because I knew that thou *art* obstinate, and thy neck *is* an iron sinew, and thy brow brass;

5 I have even from the beginning declared *it* to thee; before it came to pass I shewed *it* thee: lest thou shouldest say, Mine idol hath done them, and my graven image, and my molten image, hath commanded them.

6 Thou hast heard, see all this; and will not ye declare *it?* I have shewed thee new things from this time, even hidden things, and thou didst not know them.

7 They are created now, and not from the beginning; even before the day when thou heardest them not; lest thou shouldest say, Behold, I knew them.

8 Yea, thou heardest not; yea, thou knewest not; yea, from that time *that* thine ear was not opened: for I knew that thou wouldest deal very treacherously, and wast called a transgressor from the womb. [Isaiah 48:3–8]

Through his prophets the Lord foretold the apostasy of Judah. The prophets foretold the things that would happen, even from the beginning. Jeremiah was another prophet besides Isaiah to warn the Jews. He warned of the coming of Nebuchadnezzar, the king of Babylon.

> 11 And this whole land shall be a desolation, *and* an astonishment; and these nations shall serve the king of Babylon seventy years.
>
> 12 And it shall come to pass, when seventy years are accomplished, *that* I will punish the king of Babylon, and that nation, saith the LORD, for their iniquity, and the land of the Chaldeans, and will make it perpetual desolations. [Jeremiah 25:11–12]

Because the people of Judah had been warned many times, they were responsible for their obstinate and stubborn actions.

It is important to know why the Lord shows the future to his prophets. The principle of foreknowledge is difficult to understand, but several prophets who have been shown the future have affirmed its importance. Nephi was shown the future until the beginning of the last days. Then he was told that an apostle of the Lamb of God would write "many things which thou hast seen; and behold the remainder shalt thou see." The apostle's name was John. He was also told that others "hath (God) shown all things" (1 Nephi 14:24–27). The Lord had also "showed unto the brother of Jared all the inhabitants of the earth which had been, and also all that would be" (Ether 3:25). "Enoch saw the day of the coming of the Son of Man, even in the flesh" (Moses 7:47), and that he would come "in the last days, to dwell on the earth in righteousness for the space of a thousand years" (Moses 7:65). The Lord told Abraham and Isaiah that "he knew the end from the beginning" (Abraham 2:6; Isaiah 46:10). Although the text doesn't say they saw all things, they were shown great and marvelous things, which may have included to the end of times.

The Lord shows the future so that false gods will not be worshipped or given credit for the Lord's doings (v. 5). The people of Judah had been shown and told of future events, but they had rejected this knowledge. The Lord knew they would reject it. He told them anyway so they would be accountable for their sins. An understanding of foreknowledge and why it is shared with the prophets is a unique and an important contribution that comes from Isaiah's writing.

1 Nephi 20:9–11 • Judah To Be Refined in the Furnace of Affliction

9 *Nevertheless,* for my name's sake will I defer mine anger, and for my praise will I refrain *from* thee, that I cut thee not off.

10 *For,* behold, I have refined thee, I have chosen thee in the furnace of affliction.

11 For mine own sake, *yea,* for mine own sake will I do *this,* for *I will not suffer* my name to be polluted, and I will not give my glory unto another. [1 Nephi 20:9–11]

9 For my name's sake will I defer mine anger, and for my praise will I refrain for thee, that I cut thee not off.

10 Behold, I have refined thee, **but not with silver**; I have chosen thee in the furnace of affliction.

11 For mine own sake, *even* for mine own sake, will I do *it*: for how should *my name* be polluted? and I will not give my glory unto another. [Isaiah 48:9–11]

Christ was to be born through the lineage of Judah. For this reason he will be patient with their transgressions. The doctrine of his lineage being determined in the pre-mortal life supports Paul's teachings regarding all people.

26 And hath made of one blood all nations of men for to dwell on all the face of the earth, and hath determined the times before appointed, and the bounds of their habitation; [Acts 17:26]

Moses taught the same doctrine concerning the house of Israel:

7 Remember the days of old, consider the years of many generations: ask thy father, and he will shew thee; thy elders, and they will tell thee.

8 When the most High divided to the nations their inheritance, when he separated the sons of Adam, he set the bounds of the people according to the number of the children of Israel.

9 For the LORD's portion *is* his people; Jacob *is* the lot of his inheritance. [Deuteronomy 32:7–9]

The Book of Mormon wording "I will refrain from thee" instead of "for thee" (v. 9) shows that the Lord will withdraw from Judah rather than intercede for her. This retention fits the context of the apostasy in the previous verses. The Lord used this apostate period to refine Judah. Symbolic of the refining of metals, the Lord would refine her by allowing her to be sent through the furnace of affliction (v. 10). A study of the history of the Jewish people reflects many periods of afflictions: the Babylonian captivity, 607–538; the Roman conquest, A.D. 70; the Crusades; the Inquisition; and the anti-semitic persecutions. Although the Book of Mormon does not include the KJV phrase "but not with silver" (v. 10), the Anchor Bible translates the phrase "I have tested you like silver." This fits the symbolism used to describe the refining of the house of Judah.

The Book of Mormon text shows why the Lord suffered or allowed Judah's afflictions. It reads: "I will not *suffer* my name to be polluted" in place of "how shall my name be polluted?" (v. 11; italics added). This reading is much more logical.

1 Nephi 20:12–14 • The Lord Will Do His Pleasure on Babylon

12 Hearken unto me, O Jacob, and Israel my called, *for* I am he; I am the first, *and* I am *also* the last.

13 Mine hand *hath also* laid the foundation of the earth, and my right hand hath spanned the heavens. I call unto them and they stand up together.

14 All ye, assemble yourselves, and hear; *who* among them hath declared these things *unto them?* The Lord hath loved him; *yea, and he will fulfil his word which he hath declared by them; and* he will do his pleasure on Babylon, and his arm shall *come up*on the Chaldeans. [1 Nephi 20:12–14]

12 Hearken unto me, O Jacob and Israel, my called; I *am* he; I *am* the first, I also *am* the last.

13 Mine hand also hath laid the foundation of the earth, and my right hand hath spanned the heavens: *when* I call unto them, they stand up together.

14 All ye, assemble yourselves, and hear; which among them hath declared these *things?* The LORD hath loved him: he will do his pleasure on Babylon, and his arm *shall be on* the Chaldeans. [Isaiah 48:12–14]

I am the first and the last (v. 12) identifies Jesus Christ. In the beginning of the New Testament book of Revelation he says "I am the first and the last" (Revelation 1:17), and in it's ending (see Revelation

22:13). Thus he is the God of the Old Testament and the New Testament. Isaiah states further that he is the creator of the earth and the heavens (v. 13). Paul said "that by him were all things created, that are in heaven, and that are in earth" (Colossians 1:16). Again the Old Testament and the New Testament bear the same testimony of him. The heavens and the earth obey him (v. 13); therefore, he has the power to bring about his purposes with Judah and Israel.

One of the challenges of understanding Isaiah is identifying the pronouns in the text. The following identities should help. "All ye (Judah) assemble (gather) yourselves, and hear (the word of God); who (the prophets) among [Judah] hath declared these things unto [Judah]? The Lord hath loved [Judah]; yea, and [the Lord] will fulfill his word which he hath declared by [the prophets]; and he will do his pleasure (desired outcome) on Babylon (who captured Judah), and [the Lord's] arm (power) shall come upon the Chaldeans (the portion of Babylon in the south and east, the learned class) (v. 14). The interpretive brackets are based upon "the judgments of God, which came to pass among the Jews" that helped Nephi understand Isaiah (2 Nephi 25:6). Some bible scholars interpret the "him" to be Cyrus who allowed the Jews to return from Babylon, but in the author's opinion the Book of Mormon text supports the broader interpretation.

1 Nephi 20:15–17 • The Restoration of the Jews

15 *Also, saith the Lord*; I *the Lord, yea,* I have spoken; yea, I have called him *to declare,* I have brought him, and he shall make his way prosperous.

16 Come ye near unto me; I have not spoken in secret; from the beginning, from the time that it was *declared have I spoken*; and the Lord God, and his Spirit, hath sent me.

17 And thus saith the Lord, thy Redeemer, the Holy One of Israel; *I have sent him*, the Lord thy God who teacheth thee to profit, *who*

15 I, **even** I, have spoken; yea, I have called him: I have brought him, and he shall make his way prosperous.

16 Come ye near unto me, **hear ye this**; I have not spoken in secret from the beginning; from the time that it was, **there** *am* I: and **now** the Lord GOD, and his Spirit, hath sent me.

17 Thus saith the LORD, thy Redeemer, the Holy One of Israel; I *am* the LORD thy God which teacheth thee to profit, which leadeth

leadeth thee by the way thou shouldst go, *hath done it.* [1 Nephi 20:15–17]

thee by the way *that* thou shouldest go. [Isaiah 48:15–17]

Nephi had previously spoken unto his rebellious brothers "concerning the restoration of the Jews in the latter days. . . . And I did rehearse unto them the words of Isaiah" (1 Nephi 15:19–20). The 14th verse as interpreted above spoke of the gathering of the Jews after being taken into Babylon. These verses speak of the restoration of the Jews in the latter days, of whom Nephi spoke earlier.

There are many other chapters and verses in Isaiah that speak of the restoration of the Jews. Some of the more extensive ones are chapters eighteen, twenty-six, and fifty-two. The one whom the Lord "called him to declare" (v. 15) is, in my opinion, Joseph Smith and modern Israel. The gospel has been restored among modern Israel and they have been gathered to take the gospel to the rest of Israel. This interpretation comes from the next chapter of Isaiah (49) where those in the isles of the sea are gathered to be "my servant, O Israel, in whom [the Lord] will be glorified" (1 Nephi 21:1–3). This interpretation will be further verified in the following chapter of this work. The Lord has declared his plan to gather Judah "from the beginning" and, as will be shown in the following chapter, Israel was foreordained to be the gatherer. The Book of Mormon retention "have sent him" (v. 17) shows that all of the verses are speaking of Israel as the servant called by the Lord. The other retention "hath done it" verifies that it is the Lord's work.

1 Nephi 20:18–22 • There Is No Peace unto the Wicked

18 O that thou hadst hearkened to my commandments—then had thy peace been as a river, and thy righteousness as the waves of the sea.

19 Thy seed also had been as the sand; the offspring of thy bowels like the gravel thereof; his name should not have been cut off nor destroyed from before me.

18 O that thou hadst hearkened to my commandments! then had thy peace been as a river, and thy righteousness as the waves of the sea:

19 Thy seed also had been as the sand, **and** the offspring of thy bowels like the gravel thereof; his name should not have been cut off nor destroyed from before me.

20 Go ye forth of Babylon, flee ye from the Chaldeans, with a voice of singing declare ye, tell this, utter to the end of the earth; say ye: The Lord hath redeemed his servant Jacob.

21 And they thirsted not; he led them through the deserts; he caused the waters to flow out of the rock for them; he clave the rock also and the waters gushed out.

22 *And notwithstanding he hath done all this, and greater also,* there is no peace, saith the Lord, unto the wicked. [1 Nephi 20:18–22]

20 Go ye forth of Babylon, flee ye from the Chaldeans, with a voice of singing declare ye, tell this, utter **it even** to the end of the earth; say ye, The Lord hath redeemed his servant Jacob.

21 And they thirsted not **when** he led them through the deserts: he caused the waters to flow out of the rock for them: he clave the rock also, and the waters gushed out.

22 *There is* no peace, saith the Lord, unto the wicked. [Isaiah 48:18–22]

As stated above, there is only one verse in 1 Nephi 20 that does not have any words retained or deleted from the King James text (v. 18). There is one punctuation difference. In the King James text, the exclamation point was changed to a hyphen in later editions of the Book of Mormon text. Since the whole verse is one complete thought, the hyphen is more correct. The thought is that if Judah had not apostatized, but had hearkened to the commandments of the Lord, they would not have been destroyed as a nation. The surviving people would not have been scattered. Instead of going through the furnace of affliction they would have experienced three great blessings, the first being peace and righteousness (v. 18).

The second blessing was their seed would have been as numberless "as the sand" (v. 19). The Lord promised Abraham that he would "multiply thy seed as the stars of the heaven, and as the sand which is upon sea shore" (Genesis 22:17). This blessing was reiterated to Jacob, the father of the twelve tribes, giving him the promise of "thy seed shall be as the dust of the earth" (Genesis 28:14). How many more millions of posterity would Judah have had were it not for the inquisition, the crusades, and the holocaust? We have no answer to this question, but the number would have been enormous. The second phrase: "the offspring of thy bowels like the gravel thereof" is a Hebrew parallelism, the second stanza repeating the same message as the first only in different wording. The only textual change in the verse is the "and" that is deleted following the first phrase. This is not a significant difference.

The third blessing was "his (Jehovah's) name should not have been cut off" (v. 19). The name is not spoken today among the Jewish people because they hold it too sacred to vocalize. They substitute the word "Adonai," a title of respect. It is like the name of the Melchizedek Priesthood in the Church today.

> 2 Why the first is called the Melchizedek Priesthood is because Melchizedek was such a great high priest.
>
> 3 Before his day it was called *the Holy Priesthood, after the Order of the Son of God.*
>
> 4 But out of respect or reverence to the name of the Supreme Being, to avoid the too frequent repetition of his name, they, the church, in ancient days, called that priesthood after Melchizedek, or the Melchizedek Priesthood. [D&C 107:2–4]

The name "Jehovah" is used in the Book of Mormon, the Doctrine and Covenants, and the Pearl of Great Price, but it is used sparingly.

The invitation to come out of Babylon and flee from the Chaldeans (v. 20) may have a dual meaning. The Jews were invited by Cyrus in 538 B.C. to come out of Babylon following the seventy year captivity that had been prophesied by Jeremiah:

> 1 Now in the first year of Cyrus king of Persia, that the word of the LORD by the mouth of Jeremiah might be fulfilled, the LORD stirred up the spirit of Cyrus king of Persia, that he made a proclamation throughout all his kingdom, and *put it* also in writing, saying,
>
> 2 Thus saith Cyrus king of Persia, The LORD God of heaven hath given me all the kingdoms of the earth; and he hath charged me to build him an house at Jerusalem, which *is* in Judah.
>
> 3 Who *is there* among you of all his people? his God be with him, and let him go up to Jerusalem, which *is* in Judah, and build the house of the LORD God of Israel, (he *is* the God,) which *is* in Jerusalem.
>
> 4 And whosoever remaineth in any place where he sojourneth, let the men of his place help him with silver, and with gold, and with

goods, and with beasts, beside the freewill offering for the house of God that *is* in Jerusalem. [Ezra 1:1–4]

They are again invited to come out of spiritual Babylon for "the restoration of the Jews in the later days" (1 Nephi 15:19).

13 And let them who be of Judah flee unto Jerusalem, unto the mountains of the Lord's house.

14 Go ye out from among the nations, even from Babylon, from the midst of wickedness, which is spiritual Babylon. [D&C 133:13–14]

The mountain of the Lord's house is the temple, which must be built before the Lord's Second Coming. "Judah must return, Jerusalem must be rebuilt, and the temple . . . all this must be done before the Son of Man will make his appearance" (*TPJS*, 286). Another evidence of this being the latter-day gathering is the declaration "to the end of the earth; say ye: The Lord hath redeemed his servant Jacob" (v. 20). As mentioned above, and will be verified in the following chapter, the servant is Israel, the restored Church of Jesus Christ of Latter-day Saints. The only change in the text of this verse is the deletion of "it *even*" (v. 20) from the KJV. The italicized word *even* acknowledges that the translators placed the word there to make it read better, or that it was their educated guess. The pronoun "it" is unnecessary to establish what is being uttered.

The restoration context is also the reason for a deletion in the next verse (21). The italicized word "when," that follows the first phrase (KJV), is not in the First Nephi text. The natural reflection is the Israelites being led out of Egypt, which is probably the reason for the King James translators adding it, but Isaiah seems to be using it as symbolism for great miracles also attending the saints in the restoration movement, such as the miracles accompanying the pioneers in crossing the plains. Perhaps it is a dual prophecy as well.

The first line and almost all of the second line of the last verse is also retained in the First Nephi text. It emphasizes the miracles that had been done by the Lord. Its loss from the original text was probably an error committed by a "careless transcriber" as categorized by Joseph Smith (see *TPJS*, 327). The ending "there is no peace, saith the Lord, unto the wicked" is almost identical to the ending of Isaiah chapter fifty-seven. It is often paraphrased among Christian people as "there's no rest for the wicked." A similar phrase is used by Alma "wickedness never was happiness" (Alma 41:10). The principle is a fit ending for Isaiah's description of the apostate condition of Judah.

SACRED WRITING

Preaching Which is Sacred:

1 Nephi 19:18–24	Nephi speaks to his people, and to all the house of Israel, of the prophets writings on the plates of brass concerning those at Jerusalem, and of Lehi's people. He teaches from the prophets in general, the Book of Moses, but more importantly from Isaiah.

Great Revelations:

1 Nephi 20	Nephi quotes Isaiah 48 concerning the future of the Jews.

Prophesying:

1 Nephi 19:8–17	Nephi quotes an angel and many prophets on what will happen to the Messiah.

Doctrines Learned:

1 Nephi 19:10	Jesus Christ was the God of Abraham, Isaac, Jacob, and Moses.
1 Nephi 19:10	The sign of Jesus' death given to the Nephites was three days of darkness.
1 Nephi 19:12	Jehovah is the God of nature
1 Nephi 19:15–16	All the house of Israel will be gathered in the latter days.
1 Nephi 21	All the ancient prophets knew the destiny of the Jews, and many knew concerning the people of Lehi.

1 Nephi 20:1	The Jews practiced baptism in Old Testament times.
1 Nephi 20:5	God foretells the future to men so they will not give credit to idols or other false gods

General Authority Quotes

President Joseph Fielding Smith • 1 Nephi 19:10

All revelation since the fall has come through Jesus Christ, who is the Jehovah of the Old Testament. In all of the scriptures, where God is mentioned and where he has appeared, it is Jehovah who talked with Abraham, with Noah, Enoch, Moses and all the prophets. He is the God of Israel, the Holy One of Israel; the one who led that nation out of Egyptian bondage, and who gave and fulfilled the law of Moses. The Father has never dealt with man directly and personally since the fall, and he has never appeared except to introduce and bear record of the Son. Thus the _Inspired Version_ records that "no man hath seen God at any time, except he hath borne record of the Son. [Bruce R. McConkie, compiler _Doctrines of Salvation_ 1:27, 1954]

Elder James E. Talmage • 1 Nephi 19:10

We claim scriptural authority for the assertion that Jesus Christ was and is God the Creator, the God who revealed Himself to Adam, Enoch, and all the antediluvial prophets down to Noah; the God of Abraham, Isaac, and Jacob; the God of Israel as a united people, and the God of Ephraim and Judah after the dispersion of the Hebrew nation; the God who made Himself to the prophets from Moses to Malachi; the God of the Old Testament record; and the God of the Nephites. We affirm that Jesus Christ was and is Jehovah, the Eternal One. [_Jesus The Christ_, eleventh edition 1951]

Elder David O. McKay • 1 Nephi 19:13–18

Twenty-three hundred years ago the prophet looking down through the vista of time saw this day. He saw Israel scattered among all nations. He saw them become a hiss and a by-word, but added, "nevertheless, when the day cometh when that they no more turn aside their hearts against the Holy One of Israel"—note he does not say when they accept them as their Redeemer, nor necessarily declare to the world that he was the Messiah to come to their people—the prophet words it most significantly; viz., "when they no more turn aside their hearts against the Redeemer, then in that day will he remember the covenants that he made to their fathers."

Brethren, isn't it a significant thing that today there is a change in the hearts of the descendants of Israel in regards to the Holy One of Israel? [CR, Oct. 1918, 45]

Challenges to Eternal Life:

1. In light of 1 Nephi 19:7, we have had a true knowledge of Jesus Christ restored to us. Make a commitment to not trample him under your feet but to hearken to his counsel given in the Book of Mormon and other sources of truth.

2. To whom do we give credit for knowing the future? Read again your patriarchal blessing and thank God for the guidelines and opportunities that are conditionally yours (1 Nephi 20:3–7).

3. Since there is no peace for the wicked, strive to live a righteous life that you might have peace in your soul (1 Nephi 20:22).

4. Choose a challenge or message of your own from this reading, and apply it to your life.

Chapter Nine

Thou Art My Servant, O Israel

Nephi 21–22

*H*istorical Setting: Nephi recorded Isaiah 49 from the plates of brass as evidence that the Lord did show many of his prophets of old concerning the people of Lehi (1 Nephi 19:21). See the historical setting of Chapter Eight.

Precepts of this Reading:

> By the Spirit are all things made known to the prophets, which shall come upon the children of men according to the flesh [1 Nephi 22:2]

> Ye should consider that the things written upon the plates of brass are true; and they testify that a man must be obedient to the commandments of God. [1 Nephi 22:30]

This prophecy of Isaiah extended to Nephi's people in the latter days. As recognized by President Wilford: "The 49th chapter of Isaiah is having its fulfillment."[1]

Therefore, 1 Nephi 21 is one of the most important chapters in the whole Book of Mormon because it clearly foretells the mission of the Latter-day Saints, and the destiny of the land of America in connection with the house of Israel. It is of such importance that it ought to be

---

[1] Quoted in Joseph Fielding Smith, *The Signs of the Times* [1970], 112.

studied diligently by every member of the Church. There are many significant retentions in the First Nephi text of Isaiah 49 that help us understand Isaiah's words more clearly and fully. Nephi interprets the chapter for us in 1 Nephi 22, but often readers do not recognize that it is an interpretation of the previous chapter. The New Testament, the Doctrine and Covenants, and modern Church leaders also add significantly to our understanding. An outline of the two chapters is included to facilitate a deeper study.

OUTLINE • 1 NEPHI 21–22

➤ 21:1–4   (Isaiah 49:1–4) Israel is the Lord's servant in whom he will be glorified.

    a.   The children of Israel were scattered upon the isles of the sea (v. 1).

    b.   They were foreordained to their work (v. 1).

    c.   Their message will be cutting because it is the word of God (v. 2).

    d.   The Lord has hidden them in his hand (v. 2).

    e.   He has polished Israel and hid them in his hand (v. 2).

    f.   Israel is the Lord's servant in whom he will be glorified (v. 3).

    g.   Israel feels their former work has been in vain (v. 4).

➤ 21:5–12   (Isaiah 49:5–12) Israel's foreordained mission is to gather Jacob again in the strength of God.

    a.   They are to raise up the tribes of Jacob (v. 6).

    b.   They are to restore the preserved of Israel (v. 6).

    c.   They are also to be a light unto the Gentiles (v. 6).

    d.   Kings will see, and princes will worship (v. 7).

    e.   The Lord will establish his servant Israel as a covenant people in the isles of the sea; then they will "inherit the desolate heritages" (v. 8).

    f.   The prisoners will be led by the Lord, and the way will be opened for them (vv. 9–11). The house of Israel will gather from all lands (v. 12).

➤ 21:13–17 (Isaiah 49:13–17) The Lord will show that he has not forgotten his promises to Zion [the Americas].

   a. Heaven and earth will rejoice when he establishes his people in the east (Jerusalem), and in the mountains (Americas) (v. 13).

   b. The Lord's promises are never forgotten (v. 15).

   c. He has engraven them upon the palms of his hands (v. 16).

   d. Joseph's children shall prosper over the Gentiles (v. 17).

➤ 21:18–23 (Isaiah 49:18–23) Many will gather to Zion, who will be adorned as a bride.

   a. People will come from far away and build up Zion's desolate places (v. 19).

   b. Many will come seeking freedom or fewer restrictions (vv. 20–21).

   c. The Lord will lift up his standard to the Gentiles (v. 22).

   d. The Gentile kings and queens will nurse Israel's children (vv. 22–23).

   e. The Gentiles will bow down to Israel (v. 23).

➤ 21:24–26 (Isaiah 49:25–26) Israel will be delivered from the Gentiles.

   a. The Lord will contend with those who fight against Israel (v. 25).

   b. The wicked will fight among themselves (v. 26).

   c. All flesh will know that the Lord is the Redeemer (v. 26).

➤ 22:1–5 Nephi explains the meaning of the things he had read, whether they were spiritual, or according to the flesh.

   a. He said they were manifest to the prophet by the Spirit (v. 2).

   b. They were both temporal and spiritual (v. 3).

c.   The house of Israel, sooner or later, will be scattered upon all the face of the earth, and also among all nations (v. 3).

    d.   Many tribes are already lost, and scattered upon the isles of the sea (v. 4).

    e.   These prophecies are concerning the lost tribes and those who shall yet be scattered among all nations and hated of all men (v. 5).

➤ 22:6–9   Those of Israel who are scattered will be nursed temporally by the Gentiles, according to the covenants of the Lord.

    a.   This means us, and all others who are of the house of Israel (v. 6).

    b.   The time comes when the Lord God will raise up a mighty nation among the Gentiles upon this land (v. 7).

    c.   After Lehi's seed is scattered, God will do a marvelous work among the Gentile that will be of great worth to our seed (vv. 8–9).

        1.   It is likened to our being nourished by the Gentiles.

        2.   It will also be of great worth to the Gentiles.

        3.   The covenant of Abraham will also bless all the nations of the earth.

➤ 22:10–12   The Lord God will bear his arm to all nations in bringing about his covenants and gospel to the house of Israel.

    a.   He will bring them out of captivity to the lands of their inheritance (v. 12).

    b.   He will bring them out of obscurity and darkness (v. 12).

    c.   They shall know the Lord is their Savior and Redeemer, the Mighty One of Israel (v. 12).

➤ 22:13–14   The great and abominable church shall war among themselves.

    a.   Every nation that wars against the house of Israel shall fall (v. 14).

    b.   All that fight against Zion shall be destroyed (v. 14).

        c.   The great and abominable church shall fall (v. 14).

➤ 22:15–17   Nephi quotes the prophet concerning the day when Satan shall have no power over the hearts of men.

        a.   All the proud and wicked shall be destroyed (v. 15).

        b.   The fullness of the wrath of God shall be poured out that the wicked will not destroy the righteous (v. 16).

        c.   He will preserve the righteous by his power, and they need not fear (v. 17).

➤ 22:18–23   These prophesied judgments must come according to the flesh if they harden their hearts against the Holy One of Israel.

        a.   The righteous shall not perish; all who fight Zion will be cut off (v. 19).

        b.   The prophecy of Moses, shall be fulfilled (vv. 20–21).

           1.   A prophet will be raised up like unto Moses.

           2.   Those who will not hear him will be cut off.

           3.   The prophet is the Holy One of Israel.

        c.   The kingdom of the devil shall be brought low (vv. 22–23).

           1.   All churches that do iniquity shall fall.

           2.   All these shall be consumed.

➤ 22:24–28   The righteous shall be led up as calves in a stall, and the Holy one of Israel shall reign.

        a.   He gathers his children (sheep) from the four quarters of the earth, there will be one fold and one shepherd (v. 25).

        b.   Satan has no power because of the righteousness of the people, and will not be loosed for many years (v. 26).

        c.   All nations, kindreds, tongues, and people who repent will dwell safely in the Holy One of Israel (v. 28).

➤ 22:29–31   Nephi ends speaking for he dares not speak further.

   a.   The things that are written on the plates of brass are true (v. 30).

   b.   They testify that a man must be obedient to the commandments of God (v. 30).

   c.   Nephi and his father are not the only ones who have testified and taught (v. 31).

   d.   Be obedient to the commandments, endure to the end, and ye shall be saved (v. 31).

NOTES AND COMMENTARY

Introduction: Most Bible scholars interpret Isaiah 49 as a servant song unto Christ. While that may be a good application, the text of Isaiah does not support this thesis, nor does Nephi's interpretation given in the following chapter. We will follow Nephi's interpretation of what was given to Isaiah "by the voice of the Spirit" (1 Nephi 22:2).

1 Nephi 21:1–4 (Isaiah 49:1–4) • Israel Called to be the Lord's Servant

1 *And again: Hearken, O ye house of Israel, all ye that are broken off and are driven out because of the wickedness of the pastors of my people; yea, all ye that are broken off, that are scattered abroad, who are of my people, O house of Israel.* Listen, O isles, unto me, and hearken ye people from far; the Lord hath called me from the womb; from the bowels of my mother hath he made mention of my name.

1 Listen, O isles, unto me; and hearken, ye people, from far; The LORD hath called me from the womb; from the bowels of my mother hath he made mention of my name.

2 And he hath made my mouth like a sharp sword; in the shadow of his hand hath he hid me, and made me a polished shaft; in his quiver hath he hid me;

3 And said unto me: Thou art my servant, O Israel, in whom I will be glorified.

4 Then I said, I have labored in vain, I have spent my strength for

naught and in vain; surely my judgment is with the Lord, and my work with my God.

The loss of the first part of verse one from the King James Version and other manuscripts is the work of the great and abominable church foretold by Nephi as "many plain and precious things taken away from the book" (1 Nephi 13:28). The important designation of the subject of this chapter, the scattering of Israel, is thus lost. The first line of verse twelve "And then O house of Israel," and the last phrase of verse fifteen "O house of Israel," have also been removed from ancient manuscripts. These important designations of Israel as the subject of Isaiah's text seems to have been purposely removed.[2]

The Book of Mormon text retention designates those who are "broken off" or "scattered abroad" as the segment of the house of Israel who is invited to hearken. This retention clarifies what the Lord means by the KJV "Listen O Isles." Since Nephi's brothers could not understand Isaiah's words, Nephi explaining them provided us with an inspired interpretation of Isaiah.

> 1 And now it came to pass that after I, Nephi, had read these things which were engraven upon the plates of brass, my brethren came unto me and said unto me: What meaneth these things which ye have read? Behold, are they to be understood according to things which are spiritual, which shall come to pass according to the spirit and not the flesh?
>
> 2 And I, Nephi, said unto them: Behold they were manifest unto the prophet by the voice of the Spirit; for by the Spirit are all things made known unto the prophets, which shall come upon the children of men according to the flesh.
>
> 3 Wherefore, the things of which I have read are things pertaining

---

[2] For other examples of the "house of Israel" being removed from the Isaiah text, compare the Book of Mormon text of Isaiah 50:2, 4 (2 Nephi 7:2, 4) with the KJV text. The Prophet Joseph Smith declared "I believe the Bible as it came from the pens of the original scribes, but ignorant translators, careless transcribers, and wicked and designing priests have committed many errors" (*TPJS*, 327). The house of Israel deletions seem to definitely be the work of "wicked and designing priests."

to things both temporal and spiritual; for it appears that the house of Israel, sooner or later, will be scattered upon all the face of the earth, and also among all nations. [1 Nephi 22:1–3]

The spiritual and temporal meaning of Isaiah's words will be illustrated in Nephi's ensuing comments. As a prophet himself, Nephi has the Spirit to interpret what was given to Isaiah by that same Spirit. Nephi said: "the house of Israel, sooner or later, will be scattered upon all the face of the earth, and also among all nations" (1 Nephi 22:3). This statement clearly delineates two types of scattering; those who maintained their identity as a people, and others who were absorbed into the culture of the nation where they were scattered. Speaking of others who had or would be scattered, Nephi said

4 And behold, there are many who are already lost from the knowledge of those who are at Jerusalem. Yea, the more part of all the tribes have been led away; and they are scattered to and fro upon the isles of the sea; and whither they are none of us knoweth, save that we know that they have been led away.

5 And since they have been led away, these things have been prophesied concerning them, and also concerning all those who shall hereafter be scattered and be confounded, because of the Holy One of Israel; for against him will they harden their hearts; wherefore, they shall be scattered among all nations and shall be hated of all men. [1 Nephi 22:4–5]

Nephi implies that his people are upon one of the isles of the sea where Israel would be scattered, but his brother Jacob later makes it definite: "we have been driven out of the land of our inheritance; but we have been led to a better land, for the Lord has made the sea our path, and we are upon an isle of the sea. But great are the promises of the Lord unto them who are upon the isles of the sea; wherefore as it says isles, there must needs be more than this, and they are inhabited also by our brethren" (2 Nephi 10:20–21). According to Elder George Reynolds and Janne M. Sjodahl: "Sir Isaac Newton observes that to the Hebrews the continents of Asia and Africa were 'the earth,' because they had access to them by land, while the parts of the earth to which they sailed over the sea were the 'isles of the sea.'"[3]

The "me" whom "the Lord hath called . . . from the womb" (1 Nephi 22:1) is also identified as "my servant O Israel" (1 Nephi 21:3). Being called from the womb is an obvious reference to foreordination. "From the bowels of my mother hath he made mention of my name" (1 Nephi 21:1) is another good example of Hebrew synonymous parallelism, the repeating of the same thought in the second stanza or line. The wording of Isaiah is similar to the wording of the foreordination of Jeremiah: "Then the word of the LORD came unto me, saying, Before I formed thee in the belly I knew thee; and before thou camest forth out of the womb I sanctified thee, *and* I ordained thee a prophet unto the nations" (Jeremiah 1:4–5). The foreordained work of the Lord's servant will be shown in verse six.

"He hath made my mouth like a sharp sword" (1 Nephi 21:2) is a reference to the message the servant will bear, which is the word of God. In modern revelation, the Lord said: "Behold, I am God; give heed unto my word, which is quick and powerful, sharper than a two-edged sword, to the dividing asunder of both joints and marrow; therefore give heed unto my words" (D&C 6:2). This metaphor is used repeatedly in the Doctrine and Covenants (see D&C 11:2; 12:2; 14:2; 15:2; 16:2; 33:1). The sword symbolizes the cutting nature of the truth of the word of God. As Nephi wrote, "the guilty taketh the truth to be hard, for it cutteth to the very center" (1 Nephi 16:20). The book of Revelation describes one like the Son of Man, "and out of his mouth went a sharp two edged sword" (Revelation 1:16). Perhaps there is a connection to the modern phrase we hear occasionally, "the truth hurts."

The Lord is hiding me (Israel) "in the shadow of his hand" is clarified in modern revelation, where the Lord declares that the priesthood holders of this last dispensation are "through the lineage of your fathers—For ye are lawful heirs, according to the flesh, and

---

[3] *Commentary on the Book of Mormon* 1:214 Deseret Book Company, Salt Lake City, Utah 19.

have been hid from the world with Christ in God" (D&C 86:8–9). Thus priesthood holders are literal descendants of Abraham, Isaac, and Jacob to whom Abraham was promised: "that this right shall continue in thee, and in thy seed after thee (that is to say, the literal seed, or the seed of the body) shall all the families of the earth be blessed, even with the blessings of the Gospel, which are the blessings of salvation, even of life eternal" (Abraham 2:11). The Doctrine and Covenants also identifies the Church members as "the children of Israel, and of the seed of Abraham" (D&C 103:17). Returning to the idea of Israel being in the Lord's hand, the world did not know who or where Israel was, but the Lord knew and had concealed them in his protection until the appropriate time.

The "polished shaft" hidden in the Lord's quiver (1 Nephi 21:2) seems to be a direct reference to Joseph Smith. Joseph who was sold into Egypt testified: "A seer shall the Lord my God raise up, who shall be a choice seer unto the fruit of my loins" (2 Nephi 3:6). Jesus told the Nephites; "the life of my servant shall be in my hands" (3 Nephi 21:10). The rest of these two chapters just cited supports Joseph's being the seer and the servant spoken of, but this fact will not be discussed here. They are quoted here in support of Joseph's description of himself as being the polished shaft. He said:

> I am like a huge, rough stone rolling down from a high mountain; and the only polishing I get is when some corner gets rubbed off by coming in contact with something else, striking with accelerated force against religious bigotry, priestcraft, lawyer-craft, doctor craft, lying editors, suborned judges and jurors, and the authority of perjured executives, backed by mobs, blasphemers, licentious and corrupt men and women—all hell knocking off a corner here and a corner there. Thus I will become a smooth and polished shaft in the quiver of the Almighty, who will give me dominion over all and every one of them, when their refuge of lies shall fail, and their hiding place shall be destroyed, while these smooth-polished stones with which I come in contact become marred (*TPJS*, 304).

A few weeks later, June 11, 1843, the Prophet again equated himself with the rough stone: "I am a rough stone. The sound of the hammer and chisel was never heard on me until the Lord took me in hand. I desire the learning and wisdom of heaven alone" (*TPJS*, 307).

The shaft of the arrow is polished that it might fly truer and faster, and the shaft that is polished is generally reserved for one's most important shot. Therefore, the Lord saved his "polished shaft" for the latter-day work. Paul names and tells what will happen in that day: "That in the dispensation of the fulness of times, he might gather together in one all things in Christ, both which are in heaven, and which are on earth; even in him" (Ephesians 1:10). Joseph Smith was called by the Lord "that this generation shall have [the Lord's] word through you (Joseph)." A study of Joseph's life will show what a thorough job he did.

The servant through whom the Lord would be glorified is Israel (v. 3) as already recognized above. It has been repeatedly identified in other Isaiah references.

8 But thou, Israel, *art* my servant, Jacob whom I have chosen, the seed of Abraham my friend.

9 *Thou* whom I have taken from the ends of the earth, and called thee from the chief men thereof, and said unto thee, Thou *art* my servant; I have chosen thee, and not cast thee away. [Isaiah 41:8–9]

10 Ye *are* my witnesses, saith the LORD, and my servant whom I have chosen: that ye may know and believe me, and understand that I *am* he: before me there was no God formed, neither shall there be after me. [Isaiah 43:10]

1 Yet now hear, O Jacob my servant; and Israel, whom I have chosen:

2 Thus saith the LORD that made thee, and formed thee from the womb, *which* will help thee; Fear not, O Jacob, my servant; and thou, Jesurun, whom I have chosen.

21 Remember these, O Jacob and Israel; for thou *art* my servant: I have formed thee; thou *art* my servant: O Israel, thou shalt not be forgotten of me. [Isaiah 44:1–2, 21]

The Joseph Smith Translation further substantiates that Israel is the Lord's servant.

> 19 For I will send my servant unto you who are blind; yea, a messenger to open the eyes of the blind, and unstop the ears of the deaf;
>
> 20 And they shall be made perfect notwithstanding their blindness, if they will hearken unto the messenger, the Lord's servant. [JST, Isaiah 42:19–20]

The servant spoken of in the verses above is more accurately the tribe of Ephraim, because they hold the birthright for the twelve tribes.

> 1 Now the sons of Reuben the firstborn of Israel, (for he *was* the firstborn; but, forasmuch as he defiled his father's bed, his birthright was given unto the sons of Joseph the son of Israel: and the genealogy is not to be reckoned after the birthright.
>
> 2 For Judah prevailed above his brethren, and of him *came* the chief ruler; but the birthright *was* Joseph's:). [1 Chronicles 5:1–2]

Of Joseph's sons, the birthright was given to Ephraim through father Jacob who "set Ephraim before Manasseh" (Genesis 48:20). That this was the Lord's doing was verified to Jeremiah: "I am a father to Israel, and Ephraim is my firstborn" (Jeremiah 31:9). Joseph Smith is the leader of Ephraim, or the head of the dispensation of the fullness of times.

> 2 Therefore, thou art blessed from henceforth that bear the keys of the kingdom given unto you; which kingdom is coming forth for the last time.
>
> 3 Verily I say unto you, the keys of this kingdom shall never be taken from you, while thou art in the world, neither in the world to come;
>
> 4 Nevertheless, through you shall the oracles be given to another, yea, even unto the church. [D&C 90:2–4]

Joseph Smith is certainly the root of Jesse spoken of in Isaiah 11:10, a descendant "of Joseph, unto whom rightly belongs the priesthood, and the keys of the kingdom, for an ensign, and for the gathering of my people in the last days" (D&C 113:5–6).

The identification of the one who has "labored in vain" and "spent my strength for naught" (1 Nephi 21:4) has perplexed scholars for years. Most interpret it as Isaiah's reaction to his call, but this does not fit the context of the chapter. The statement apparently refers to the Ephraimites who had been scattered among the Gentiles and been absorbed into that culture. They are devout members of the various Christian churches, but their membership and ordinances in those churches have been of no avail as far as obtaining salvation in the celestial kingdom of God. As Paul taught the Thessalonians; the day of Christ "shall not come, except there come a falling away first [the apostasy]" (2 Thessalonians 2:2–3). The "Christian" churches had no authority. Those scattered Ephraimites must now turn their efforts to their foreordained work of God. They work under the restoration of God's authority, and they will be judged or held accountable for what they do with their responsibility.

1 Nephi 21:5–6 (Isaiah 49:5–6) • The Mission of the Lord's Servant Israel

5 And now, saith the Lord—that formed me from the womb **that I should be** his servant, to bring Jacob again to him—though Israel be not gathered, yet shall I be glorious in the eyes of the Lord, and my God shall be my strength.

6 And he said: It is a light thing that thou shouldst be my servant to raise up the tribes of Jacob, and to restore the preserved of Israel. I will also give thee for a light to the Gentiles, that thou mayest be my salvation unto the **ends** of the earth. [1 Nephi 21:5–6]

5 And now, saith the LORD that formed me from the womb **to be** his servant, to bring Jacob again to him, Though Israel be not gathered, yet shall I be glorious in the eyes of the LORD, and my God shall be my strength.

6 And he said, It is a light thing that thou shouldest be my servant to raise up the tribes of Jacob, and to restore the preserved of Israel: I will also give thee for a light to the Gentiles, that thou mayest be my salvation unto the **end** of the earth. [Isaiah 49:5–6]

The servant now states what the Lord had said in response to his expression of having labored in vain among the Christian Churches. The Lord reaffirms that Israel has been foreordained to be his servant in gathering together the scattered remnant of Israel who had culturally become Gentiles. The servant acknowledges that his work would be glorious in the eyes of the Lord, and that God would be his strength (v. 5).

The servant, through Isaiah, now quotes what the Lord had said to him (v. 6). The "light thing" is the glorious work of the Lord that the servant is to undertake. Scriptural light means edifying or truthful, not insignificant or lighthearted as in our society. Through the strength of the Lord, Ephraim will accomplish three things. The first will be "to raise up the tribes of Jacob." Originally there were twelve tribes, but now they are divided into three segments; "the Nephites and the Jews . . . and the lost tribes" (2 Nephi 29:13). Although each group remained intact after their dispersion, they were not producing fruit at the time of the Restoration. "The first and the second and the last had all become corrupt" (Jacob 5:39).

The second part of Ephraim's mission is "to restore the preserved of Israel" (v. 6), those who have the blood of Israel, but have been scattered "among all nations" as prophesied by Amos (9:8–9). This group has lost their identity and have become "identified with the Gentiles" (D&C 109:60).

The third part of Ephraim's mission is to be "a light to the Gentiles" (v. 6). At the same time Ephraim is gathering those having the blood of Israel from among the Gentiles, he will be giving the Gentiles an opportunity to be adopted into Israel. Thus, Nephi's interpretation will be fulfilled: "it shall also be of great worth unto the Gentiles . . . unto the making known of the covenants of the Father of heaven unto Abraham, saying: In thy seed shall all the kindreds of the earth be blessed" (1 Nephi 22:9).

Those who receive the "Gospel shall be called after [Abraham's] name, and shall be accounted [Abraham's] seed, and shall rise up and bless [Abraham], as their father" (Abraham 2:10). Modern revelation has called the priesthood holders of this dispensation to be "a light unto the Gentiles, and through this priesthood, a savior unto [God's] people

Israel" (D&C 86:11). Therefore, the servant Ephraim will "be [the Lord's] salvation unto the ends of the earth" (v. 6).

1 Nephi 21:7 (Isaiah 49:7) • Kings and Princes shall Worship Israel

7 Thus saith the Lord, the Redeemer of Israel, his Holy One, to him whom man despiseth, to him whom the nations abhorreth, to servant of rulers: Kings shall see and arise, princes also shall worship, because of the Lord that is faithful. [1 Nephi 21:7]

7 Thus saith the LORD, the Redeemer of Israel, **and** his Holy One, to him whom man despiseth, to him whom the nation abhorreth, to **a** servant of rulers, Kings shall see and arise, princes also shall worship, because of the LORD that is faithful, **and the Holy One of Israel, and he shall choose thee**. [Isaiah 49:7]

Isaiah further identifies and quotes the Lord to his covenant people in Israel who have been traditionally despised and abhorred by the Gentiles. Even the Gentile kings and princes are going to recognize the work of the servant Israel. The 1 Nephi text and the KJV are basically the same. The bold words in the KJV above are deleted in the First Nephi text, but only the last two bold phrases have any significance. However, the point of the two phrases was firmly established in the previous verses of the chapter. Someone apparently added these words to the original text since the words of Isaiah recorded on the plates of Nephi were written on the plates of brass before 600 B.C.

1 Nephi 21:8–12 (Isaiah 49:8–12) • In the Isles of the Sea shall the Covenant be Established

8 Thus saith the Lord: In an acceptable time have I heard thee, **O isles of the sea**, and in a day of salvation have I helped thee; and I will preserve thee, and give thee **my servant** for a covenant of the people, to establish the earth, to cause to inherit the desolate heritages;

8 Thus saith the LORD, In an acceptable time have I heard thee, and in a day of salvation have I helped thee: and I will preserve thee, and give thee for a covenant of the people, to establish the earth, to cause to inherit the desolate heritages;

9 That thou mayest say to the prisoners:

9 That thou mayest say to the prisoners,

Go forth; to them that **sit** in darkness: Show yourselves. They shall feed in the ways, and their pastures shall be in all high places.

10 They shall not hunger nor thirst, neither shall the heat nor **the** sun smite them; for he that hath mercy on them shall lead them, even by the springs of water shall he guide them.

11 And I will make all my mountains a way, and my highways shall be exalted.

12 **And then, O house of Israel**, behold, these shall come from far; and lo, these from the north and from the west; and these from the land of Sinim. [1 Nephi 21:8–12]

Go forth; to them that ***are*** in darkness, Shew yourselves. They shall feed in the ways, and their pastures *shall be* in all high places.

10 They shall not hunger nor thirst; neither shall the heat nor sun smite them: for he that hath mercy on them shall lead them, even by the springs of water shall he guide them.

11 And I will make all my mountains a way, and my highways shall be exalted.

12 Behold, these shall come from far: and, lo, these from the north and from the west; and these from the land of Sinim. [Isaiah 49:8–12]

The Lord says "my servant" (a book of Mormon retention) will establish scattered Israel in the "isles of the sea" (another Book of Mormon text retention) (v. 8). The expression "to establish the earth, to cause to inherit the desolate heritages" may have reference to the choice land, and promised blessings of the Nephites that were destroyed and negated because of their wickedness (v. 8).

Nephi gives the following interpretation of the verses quoted above (8–12):

10 And I would, my brethren, that ye should know that all the kindreds of the earth cannot be blessed unless he shall make bare his arm in the eyes of the nations.

11 Wherefore, the Lord God will proceed to make bare his arm in the eyes of all the nations, in bringing about his covenants and his gospel unto those who are of the house of Israel.

12 Wherefore, he will bring them again out of captivity, and they shall be gathered together to the lands of their inheritance; and they shall be brought out of obscurity and out of darkness; and they shall know that the Lord is their Savior and their Redeemer, the Mighty One of Israel. [1 Nephi 22:10–12]

The Lord will show his power, or "make bare his arm in the eyes of all nations" (1 Nephi 22:10) by "bringing about his covenants and his gospel" to those of the house of Israel. The children of Israel ("Prisoners" in 1 Nephi 21:9) will be brought out of the spiritual captivity of the Gentiles, and "be gathered together to the lands of their inheritance" (1 Nephi 22:12). They will "be brought out of obscurity" (not identified with Israel), "and out of darkness (taught the truth), and "come to know that the Lord is their Savior and their Redeemer, the Mighty One of Israel" (the true knowledge of God) (1 Nephi 22:12). The Lord will miraculously open the way for them to return to their lands (1 Nephi 21:9–11). The pioneer trek from Nauvoo, Illinois to the Rocky Mountains, was the major and most obvious example of the Lord opening the way. The way has been opened, and will be opened, in every land to one degree or another. The power of God will be both physical and spiritual in redeeming and delivering his people. The Book of Mormon retention of "And then O house of Israel" (1 Nephi 21:12) shows that the majority of the people of Israel will be gathered after the major trek to the west. The verses that follow further substantiate this thesis.

1 Nephi 21:13–17 (Isaiah 49:13–17)
• The Lord Has not Forgotten Israel

13 Sing, O heavens; and be joyful, O earth; **for the feet of those who are in the east shall be established**; and break forth into singing, O mountains; **for they shall be smitten no more**; for the Lord hath comforted his people, and will have mercy upon his afflicted.	13 Sing, O heavens; and be joyful, O earth; and break forth into singing, O mountains: for the LORD hath comforted his people, and will have mercy upon his afflicted.
14 But, *behold*, Zion hath said: The Lord hath forsaken me, and my Lord hath forgotten me—**but he will show that he hath not**.	14 But Zion said, The LORD hath forsaken me, and my Lord hath forgotten me.
15 **For** can a woman forget her sucking child, that she should not have compassion on the son of her womb? Yea, they may forget, yet will I not forget thee, **O house of Israel**.	15 Can a woman forget her sucking child, that she should not have compassion on the son of her womb? yea, they may forget, yet will I not forget thee.
16 Behold, I have graven thee upon the	16 Behold, I have graven thee upon the

palms of my hands; thy walls are continually before me.

palms of *my* hands; thy walls *are* continually before me.

17 Thy children shall make haste **against** thy destroyers; and they that made thee waste shall go forth of thee. [1 Nephi 21:13–17]

17 Thy children shall make haste; thy destroyers and they that made thee waste shall go forth of thee. [Isaiah 49:13–17]

The First Nephi text retains two whole clauses that have been lost from the KJV (v. 13). The first, "for the feet of those who are in the east shall be established" points to Jerusalem. The "mountains" would fit "this land (the Americas), unto the fulfilling of the covenant which I (Jesus Christ) made with your father Jacob; and it shall be the New Jerusalem" (3 Nephi 20:22). Therefore, the Lord is declaring that the two capitals of Israel's gathering shall be established. The second retention, "for they shall be smitten no more," promises permanent, peaceful cities of Zion and Jerusalem. The heavens and the earth will rejoice when this happens.

The mountains referring to the Zion of America is further substantiated by the subject of the next verse (14) shifting from the people to the land promised to them. The land speaks, bemoaning a seeming lack of evidence that the Lord has comforted his people, and shown mercy to the afflicted upon the land. The land feels as if the Lord has forsaken and forgotten it. The retention in First Nephi "but he will show that he hath not" (v. 14) declares not only the future happenings, but also forms a logical transition to his answer, bridging the gap that exists in the KJV.

A woman's love for her offspring is considered to be one of the strongest bonds that exist, but the Lord's love and promises are even stronger and are never forgotten. Zion (the Americas) is "the land of [Joseph's] inheritance; and the Father [in heaven] hath given it to [Joseph]" (3 Nephi 15:12–13). Jacob, the father of the twelve tribes, had blessed his son Joseph with the same promise: "Joseph *is* a fruitful bough, *even* a fruitful bough by a well; *whose* branches run over the wall: ... The blessings of thy father have prevailed above the blessings of my progenitors unto the utmost bound of the everlasting hills: they shall be on the head of Joseph, and on the crown of the head of him that was separate from his brethren." (Genesis 49:22, 26). Another witness of the Americas being Zion was given by the Prophet Joseph:

> You know there has been great discussion in relation to Zion— where it is, and where the gathering of the dispensation is and which I am going to tell you. The prophets have spoken and written upon it; but I will make a proclamation that will cover a broader ground. The whole of America is Zion itself from north to south, and is described by the Prophets, who declare that it is Zion where the mountain of the Lord should be, and that it should be in the center of the land. When Elders shall take up and examine the old prophecies in the Bible, they will see it. [*TPJS*, 362]

The land of Zion speaking (v. 14) is consistent with another scripture representing the earth speaking.

> 48 And it came to pass that Enoch looked upon the earth; and he heard a voice from the bowels thereof, saying: Wo, wo is me, the mother of men; I am pained, I am weary, because of the wickedness of my children. When shall I rest, and be cleansed from the filthiness which is gone forth out of me? When will my Creator sanctify me, that I may rest, and righteousness for a season abide upon my face? [Moses 7:48]

The earth is a living thing and will become the eternal abode of the celestial beings of this earth, and it "must needs be sanctified from all unrighteousness that it may be prepared for the celestial glory" (D&C 88:17–18). Therefore, Zion must also be sanctified and prepared to be the New Jerusalem. Apparently the earth looks forward to that time.

"O house of Israel," retained at the end of verse fifteen, is what is graven "upon the palms of (the Lord's) hands" (v. 16). The Jews used phylacteries to continually remind them of the commandments of God.

> 6 And these words, which I command thee this day, shall be in thine heart:
>
> 7 And thou shalt teach them diligently unto thy children, and shalt

talk of them when thou sittest in thine house, and when thou walkest by the way, and when thou liest down, and when thou risest up.

8 And thou shalt bind them for a sign upon thine hand, and they shall be as frontlets between thine eyes.

9 And thou shalt write them upon the posts of thy house, and on thy gates. [Deuteronomy 6:6–9]

Probably in the symbolism of these writings, the Lord was declaring that he was keeping the promises made to Zion. He would fulfill his promises in the manner and in the time he had said. Another deeper meaning would have reference to the covenant made by Christ to atone for the sins of the world, and to bring to pass the resurrection. This covenant would be sealed or completed by his being nailed to the cross. The nail prints in the palms of his hands would be a sign to the world, and especially to the Jews, that he had kept his promise.[4]

As an additional evidence that the Lord had not forgotten his promises to the house of Israel, he declared that Zion's walls were continually before him (v. 16). He had kept the Americas hidden from "the knowledge of other nations; for behold, many nations would overrun the land, and there would be no place for an inheritance" (2 Nephi 1:8).

---

[4] 23 And I will fasten him *as* a nail in a sure place; and he shall be for a glorious throne to his father's house. [Isaiah 22:23]

9 And it shall come to pass in that day, *that* I will seek to destroy all the nations that come against Jerusalem.

10 And I will pour upon the house of David, and upon the inhabitants of Jerusalem, the spirit of grace and of supplications: and they shall look upon me whom they have pierced, and they shall mourn for him, as one mourneth for *his* only *son*, and shall be in bitterness for him, as one that is in bitterness for *his* firstborn. [Zechariah 12:9–10]

6 And *one* shall say unto him, What *are* these wounds in thine hands? Then he shall answer, *Those* with which I was wounded *in* the house of my friends. [Zechariah 13:6]

51 And then shall the Jews look upon me and say: What are these wounds in thine hands and in thy feet?

52 Then shall they know that I am the Lord; for I will say unto them: These wounds are the wounds with which I was wounded in the house of my friends. I am he who was lifted up. I am Jesus that was crucified. I am the Son of God. [D&C 45:51–53]

The Lord makes one more prophecy about the children of Israel in the land of Zion; Joseph's children, to whom the land is given, will "make haste against thy destroyers" (v. 17). As prophesied by Mormon (Mormon 5:20), the Lamanites were "driven and scattered by the Gentiles" who possessed the land. Isaiah says the tables will be turned, and the Gentiles will be driven by the Lamanites. The second half of the verse is a Hebrew synonymous parallelism that repeats the same message. More detail on this is given later in the chapter.

1 Nephi 21:18–21 (Isaiah 49:18–21)
• Zion to be Adorned as a Bride

18 Lift up thine eyes round about and behold; all these gather themselves together, and **they shall** come to thee. *And* as I live, saith the Lord, thou shalt surely clothe thee with them all, as with an ornament, and bind them on **even** as a bride.

19 For thy waste and thy desolate places, and the land of thy destruction, shall even now be too narrow by reason of the inhabitants; and they that swallowed thee up shall be far away.

20 The children **whom** thou shalt have, after thou hast lost **the first**, shall again in thine ears say: The place is too strait for me; give place to me that I may dwell.

21 Then shalt thou say in thine heart: Who hath begotten me these, seeing I have lost my children, and am desolate, a captive, and removing to and fro? And who hath brought up these? Behold, I was left alone; these, where **have** they been?
[1 Nephi 21:18–21]

18 Lift up thine eyes round about, and behold: all these gather themselves together, *and* come to thee. *As* I live, saith the LORD, thou shalt surely clothe thee with them all, as with an ornament, and bind them *on thee*, as a bride *doeth*.

19 For thy waste and thy desolate places, and the land of thy destruction, shall even now be too narrow by reason of the inhabitants, and they that swallowed thee up shall be far away.

20 The children **which** thou shalt have, after thou hast lost the other, shall say again in thine ears, The place *is* too strait for me: give place to me that I may dwell.

21 Then shalt thou say in thine heart, Who hath begotten me these, seeing I have lost my children, and am desolate, a captive, and removing to and fro? and who hath brought up these? Behold, I was left alone; these, where **had** they *been*?
[Isaiah 49:18–21]

The Lord invites Zion to look into the future and behold the multitudes that will come and adorn the land as a bride (v. 18). The symbolism of a bride is that a young lady on her wedding day is traditionally very meticulous in her dress and grooming. America is going to be made beautiful by those who come in the future. The land has lain waste and desolate, but will be built up until man will reason that it is too small for the multitude that has come. Their reasoning is fallacious however, because "there shall none come into this land save they shall be brought by the hand of the Lord" (2 Nephi 1:6). These multitudes will come from afar seeking freedom because their former lands were "too strait"(restrictive) (v. 20). These multitudes will come after the time when the "first" of Joseph's children, the Nephites, shall have forfeited their blessings in this "land which is choice above all other lands" (1 Nephi 2:20).[5] The migrations to come are going to be so numerous that it will astonish the land of Zion, who was previously complaining that the Lord had forgotten her (v. 21).

1 Nephi 21:22–23 (Isaiah 49:22–23)
• Israel to be Nursed by the Gentiles

> 22 Thus saith the Lord God: Behold, I will lift up mine hand to the Gentiles, and set up my standard to the people; and they shall bring thy sons in their arms, and thy daughters shall be carried upon their shoulders.

> 23 And kings shall be thy nursing fathers, and their queens thy nursing mothers; they shall bow down to thee with their face towards the earth, and lick up the dust of thy feet; and thou shalt know that I am the Lord; for they shall not be ashamed that wait for me. [1 Nephi 21:22–23]

The KJV text is not quoted above because it is identical to the First Nephi text except for some of the punctuation, which does not affect the message. Nephi and Jacob interpreted these two verses for us. Nephi gave both a temporal and a spiritual interpretation. The temporal one is given first. As quoted before, many of the tribes of Israel had been and more would be "scattered among all nations" (1 Nephi 22:5).

---

[5] The KJV says "the other." The Book of Mormon text says "the first," another important retention.

6 Nevertheless, after they shall be nursed by the Gentiles, and the Lord has lifted up his hand upon the Gentiles and set them up for a standard, and their children have been carried in their arms, and their daughters have been carried upon their shoulders, behold these things of which are spoken are temporal; for thus are the covenants of the Lord with our fathers; and it meaneth us in the days to come, and also all our brethren who are of the house of Israel.

7 And it meaneth that the time cometh that after all the house of Israel have been scattered and confounded, that the Lord God will raise up a mighty nation among the Gentiles, yea, even upon the face of this land; and by them shall our seed be scattered. [1 Nephi 22:6–7]

The Lord setting "them up for a standard" suggests he is preparing them for a standard (v. 6). Jesus told the Nephites, when he visited them in person, "that it was wisdom in the Father that [the Gentiles] should be established in this land, and be set up as a free people by the power of the Father, that [the Book of Mormon] might come forth from [the Gentiles] unto a remnant of [the Nephites'] seed" (3 Nephi 21:4). Therefore, the Lord raised "up a mighty nation among the Gentiles, yea, even upon the face of this land" (1 Nephi 21:7) by establishing the United States of America. The U.S. Constitution helped prepare an environment for the restoration of the gospel. The Gentiles nursed the house of Israel who had been scattered among them and lost their identity, but the Lord was preparing these members of the house of Israel "who [were] identified with the Gentiles" (D&C 109:60) to bring forth the Book of Mormon. Although the Gentiles who set up the mighty nation scattered the seed of the Nephites (1 Nephi 22:7), they nursed them in the temporal sense by placing them on reservations and giving them government assistance.

For many years this assistance was meager and inadequate, but the last half of the twentieth century brought a more extensive fulfillment of prophecy, as reported by Elder Spencer W. Kimball:

In 1947 the cry was raised: "The Navajo's are freezing and starving." You remember I'm sure. Truckloads of clothing and food were fathered here in Utah and taken from our Church welfare storehouses for these distressed Indians. Simultaneously, the press took up the cry and warm hearted people of the nation, and particularly of the West, answered the call with bedding, food, clothing, and money. The echoes resounded from ocean to ocean, and a sleeping nation roused itself.

Pictures and stories of want and starvation were printed in newspapers and magazines; pressures were brought to bear upon officials; and the important prophecies began to be fulfilled, and the arms of the gentile nation which had scattered the Lamanites now opened to enfold them, and the shoulders which once were used to into reservations, now squared away to carry these deprived ones to their destiny. Even within the past two or three years, great strides have been made. Education, the common denominator and leveler, is coming to the red man. The clinic and hospital are available to him. Indian children are being born in hospitals, sanitation is being taught, and the sun is rising on the Indian world with the government, churches, and many agencies becoming "nursing parents" to them.

Yesterday tribal people resisted education: today they grasp it eagerly. Not long ago nearly all Indians were illiterate and unschooled; today many in 1956 nearly every Indian child in America may have some training. Yesterday Indian children were kidnapped from their parents and forced to school. Today parents beg for school, and children eagerly attend.[6]

There has been much more nursing of these people, the remnants of Joseph, in the past fifty years, but there is more to be done.

Nephi said the temporal nursing came because of "the covenants of the Lord with our fathers; and it meaneth us in days to come, and also all our brethren who are of the house of Israel" (1 Nephi 21:6). Jacob, "according to the words of the angel who spake it unto [him]," interpreted how these verses (1 Nephi 21:22–23) would be fulfilled among the Jews. After reading them, which he also said "Isaiah spake concerning all the house of Israel" (2 Nephi 6:5–7), he commented:

> 8 And now I, Jacob, would speak somewhat concerning these words. For behold, the Lord has shown me that those who were at

---

[6] Conference Report, Oct. 1956; or *The Improvement Era*, Dec.1956, 937 .

Jerusalem, from whence we came, have been slain and carried away captive.

9 Nevertheless, the Lord has shown unto me that they should return again. And he also has shown unto me that the Lord God, the Holy One of Israel, should manifest himself unto them in the flesh; and after he should manifest himself they should scourge him and crucify him, according to the words of the angel who spake it unto me.

10 And after they have hardened their hearts and stiffened their necks against the Holy One of Israel, behold, the judgments of the Holy One of Israel shall come upon them. And the day cometh that they shall be smitten and afflicted.

11 Wherefore, after they are driven to and fro, for thus saith the angel, many shall be afflicted in the flesh, and shall not be suffered to perish, because of the prayers of the faithful; they shall be scattered, and smitten, and hated; nevertheless, the Lord will be merciful unto them, that when they shall come to the knowledge of their Redeemer, they shall be gathered together again to the lands of their inheritance. [2 Nephi 6:8–11]

The prophecy of the Jews returning from their captivity (in Babylon); Christ being crucified, and their being smitten and afflicted again is now a matter of history (1 Nephi 22:8–10). Their being gathered again as they come to the knowledge of their Redeemer is now in the beginning stages, and will likewise be fulfilled. Jacob himself enlarges upon this prophecy by Isaiah of the Jews being gathered, but we will consider it more fully then, (2 Nephi 10:1–9; chapter twelve of this work).

The spiritual interpretation, given by Nephi, of Isaiah's prophecy: "I (the Lord) will lift up mine hand to the Gentiles, and set up my standard to the people" (1 Nephi 21:22), was partially mentioned before, but given in full here.

8 And after our seed is scattered the Lord God will proceed to do a marvelous work among the Gentiles, which shall be of great worth unto our seed; wherefore, it is likened unto their being nourished by the Gentiles and being carried in their arms and upon their shoulders.

9 And it shall also be of worth unto the Gentiles; and not only unto the Gentiles but unto all the house of Israel, unto the making known

of the covenants of the Father of heaven unto Abraham, saying: In thy seed shall all the kindreds of the earth be blessed. [2 Nephi 22:8–9]

Nephi interprets what Isaiah calls the Lord's "standard" as "a marvelous work among the Gentiles" (1 Nephi 22:8). Later, as quoted by Nephi, the Lord equates the marvelous work and the standard with the coming forth of the Book of Mormon.

> But behold, there shall be many—at that day when I shall proceed to do a marvelous work among them, that I may remember my covenants which I have made unto the children of men, that I may set my hand again the second time to recover my people, which are of the house of Israel;
>
> 2 And also, that I may remember the promises which I have made unto thee, Nephi, and also unto thy father, that I would remember your seed; and that the words of your seed should proceed forth out of my mouth unto your seed; and my words shall hiss forth unto the ends of the earth, for a standard unto my people, which are of the house of Israel. [2 Nephi 29:1–2]

Later, in a revelation to the Church through Joseph Smith, the Lord extends the definition:

> 9 And even so I have sent mine everlasting covenant into the world, to be a light to the world, and to be a standard for my people, and for the Gentiles to seek to it, and to be a messenger before my face to prepare the way before me. [D&C 45:9]

Wherefore, the everlasting covenant, or the restoration of the covenants of the gospel of Jesus Christ, and the coming forth of the Book of Mormon may be seen as the beginning of the spiritual fulfillment of the prophecy of Isaiah. These instruments of salvation must be extended to others of the house of Israel. In 1965 Elder Spencer W. Kimball gave this admonition:

> They are a chosen people with rich blood in their veins. They are casting off the fetters of superstition, fear, ignorance, and prejudice and are clothing themselves with knowledge, good works, and righteousness. And this Church is elated to have an important part in bringing about this transformation. . . .

Yesterday they were deprived, weakening, vanishing; today thousands are benefitting in the Indian seminaries, in regular seminaries and institutes as they become involved in the placement program and church work within the stakes and missions. Numerous are receiving secular as well as spiritual training in Mexico, South America, and Hawaii and the isles of the sea. Many are now in college and large numbers in full-time missions. Tens of thousands are now eligible for superior training and service through church organizations and in all the Americas and in the pacific. Lamanite-Nephite leaders are now standing forth to direct and inspire their people. The day of the Lamanite is come, and tomorrow will be even better. . . .

This day of the Lamanite brings opportunity. Millions farm the steep hillsides of Andean ranges and market their produce with llamas and horses and burros. They must have the emancipating gospel. Millions serve in menial labor, eke out bare subsistence from soil and toil. They must hear the compelling truths of the gospel. Millions are tied to reservations, deprived, untrained, and less than they could be. They must have the enlightening gospel. It will break their fetters, stir their ambition, increase their vision and open new worlds of opportunity to them. Their captivity will be at an end— captivity from misconceptions, illiteracy, superstitions fear. "The clouds of error disappear before the rays of truth divine (Parley P. Pratt, *Hymns* 269). . . .

The brighter day has dawned. The scattering has been accomplished; the gathering is in process. May the Lord bless us all as we become nursing fathers and mothers (see Isaiah 49:23 and 1 Nephi 21:23) unto our Lamanite brethren and hasten the fulfillment of the great promises made to them, I pray in the name of Jesus Christ, Amen.[7]

In the April 2001 General Conference, another program was introduced to bring further spiritual nourishment to the Lamanites. President Gordon B. Hinckley announced:

We have many missionaries, both young men and young women, who are called locally and who serve with honor in Mexico, Central America, South America, the Philippines, and other places. They have

---

[7] CR, Oct. 1965, 71–72.

very little money, but they make a contribution with what they have. . . . They work with faith and devotion. Then comes the day of their release. They return to their homes. Their hopes are high. But many of them have great difficulty finding employment because they have no skills. They sink right back into the pit of poverty from which they came. . . .

The Church is establishing a fund largely from the contributions of faithful Latter-day Saints who have and will contribute for this purpose. . . . We shall call it the Perpetual Education Fund . . . loans will be made to ambitious young men and women, for the most part returned missionaries, so that they borrow money to attend school. Then when they qualify for employment, it is anticipated that they will return that which they have borrowed together with a small amount of interest as an incentive to repay the loan. . . . It will work because it will follow priesthood lines and because it will function on a local basis. . . . Participation in the program will carry with it no stigma of any kind, but rather a sense of pride in what is happening. It will not be a welfare effort. Commendable as those efforts are, but rather an educational opportunity.[8]

Thousands will be nourished educationally and spiritually by this fund, and other programs will probably be instituted in the future to nurse the house of Israel.

1 Nephi 21:24–26 (Isaiah 49:24–26) • Shall the Prey be Taken from the Mighty?

24 **For** shall the prey be taken from the mighty, or the lawful captives delivered?

25 But thus saith the Lord, even the captives of the mighty shall be taken away, and the prey of the terrible shall be delivered; for I will contend with **him** that contendeth with thee, and I will save thy children.

26 And I will feed them that oppress thee with their own flesh; they shall be drunken with their own blood as with sweet wine; and

---

[8] CR, April 2001, *Ensign*, 51–52. For further details see the entire address of President Hinckley.

all flesh shall know that I, the Lord, am thy Savior and thy Redeemer, the Mighty One of Jacob.

Isaiah 49:24 is not quoted above because it is identical to First Nephi except the bold **For** at the beginning. "For" ties the question to the previous verse more firmly, where it is prophesied that the Gentiles would bow down to the house of Israel. Thus the "prey" is the House of Israel, which has been captive to the "mighty" (Gentiles). The question suggests that it may seem highly unlikely that Israel could overcome the mighty gentile nations who have been ruling the world for hundreds of years. However, the Lord, who is "mightier than all the earth" (1 Nephi 4:10), will be on Israel's side, as the Prophet Joseph made clear.

> 25 But thus saith the Lord; even the captives of the mighty shall be taken away, and the prey of the terrible shall be delivered; *for the mighty God shall deliver his covenant people. For thus saith the Lord*, I will contend with *them* that contend with thee, and I will save thy children. [JST, Isaiah 49:25).

The King James text is identical to the First Nephi text (v. 25) except the Nephi text says **him**, and the KJV says "them." However the Prophet Joseph did not change the JST to "them," one being singular and the other plural. Both pronouns fit, and does not affect the meaning; the Nephite text referring to the Gentiles as a singular unit, and the KJV and the JST referring to the nations as plural. The JST change is the way it was quoted by Jacob in 2 Nephi 6:17, except Jacob does not quote the last phrase "and I will save thy children." This suggests that Jacob was paraphrasing to assure his people that the "I" was referring to the mighty God who would deliver his covenant people. Again the message is not changed. God will fulfill the covenant he made to Israel through the Gentiles.

The only difference in the King James text (v. 26) is an "and" at the beginning of the second phrase, therefore it is not quoted above. Nephi interprets these verses for us:

> 13 And the blood of that great and abominable church, which is

the whore of all the earth, shall turn upon their own heads; for they shall war among themselves, and the sword of their own hands shall fall upon their own heads, and they shall be drunken with their own blood.

14 And every nation which shall war against thee, O house of Israel, shall be turned one against another, and they shall fall into the pit which they digged to ensnare the people of the Lord. And all that fight against Zion shall be destroyed, and that great whore, who hath perverted the right ways of the Lord, yea, that great and abominable church, shall tumble to the dust and great shall be the fall of it. [1 Nephi 22:13–14]

These waring factions within the great and abominable church will be part of Israel's deliverance. It will be as Jesus taught: Every kingdom divided against itself is brought to desolation; and every city or house divided against itself shall not stand (Matthew 12:25).

A second reason is that "the Lord, will fight [Israel's] battles" as promised (D&C 98:37). The Lord will establish Zion and protect her. The righteous will be protected, and those who pervert the ways of the Lord will fall.

1 Nephi 22:1–14 • Nephi's commentary on 1 Nephi 21

These fourteen verses are Nephi's interpretation of Isaiah's words, and have been quoted previously. A brief outline of their location follows:

1 Nephi 22:1–5	Commented on under 1 Nephi 21:1–3
1 Nephi 22:6–7	Commented on under 1 Nephi 21:22–23
1 Nephi 22:8–9	Commented on under 1 Nephi 21:5–6; and 21:22–23
1 Nephi 22:10–12	Commented on under 1 Nephi 21:8–12
1 Nephi 22:13–14	Commented on under 1 Nephi 21:26

1 Nephi 22:15–17 • Satan shall have No More Power over the Children of Men

15 For behold, saith the prophet, the time cometh speedily that Satan shall have no more power over the hearts of the children of men; for the day soon cometh that all the proud and they who do wickedly shall be as stubble; and the day cometh that they must be burned.

16 For the time soon cometh that the fulness of the wrath of God shall be poured out upon all the children of men; for he will not suffer that the wicked shall destroy the righteous.

17 Wherefore, he will preserve the righteous by his power, even if it so be that the fulness of his wrath must come, and the righteous be preserved, even unto the destruction of their enemies by fire. Wherefore, the righteous need not fear; for thus saith the prophet, they shall be saved, even if it so be as by fire. [1 Nephi 22:15–17]

Nephi is quoting "the prophet" which seems to be a continuation of his quoting Isaiah. However, the text does not specify who Nephi is quoting. Another possibility is that he is quoting Zenos. Nephi had earlier referred repeatedly to Zenos as "the prophet" (1 Nephi 19: 10–17). Elder Bruce R. McConkie called him:

Some unnamed Old Testament prophet, who obviously was Zenos, as the Book of Mormon testifies, spoke of the day when the wicked would be destroyed as stubble; when the righteous would be "led up as calves of the stall;" when Christ should "rise from the dead, with healing in his wings;" and when the Holy One of Israel would then reign on earth.

Malachi, who lived more than two hundred years after Nephi, uses these very expressions in his prophetic writings. Can we do other than conclude that both Nephi and Malachi had before them the writings of Zenos (or Isaiah)? [9]

The time period spoken of by "the Prophet" is definitely the Second

---

[9] As quoted in "The Doctrinal Restoration" chap. 1, p. 18; published in "The Joseph Smith Translation," ed. Monte S. Nyman and Robert L. Millet, Religious Study Center, Brigham Young University 1985.

Coming of Christ when the righteous will be preserved and the wicked destroyed. It is a continuation of Nephi's interpretation of Isaiah 49:26, the great and abominable church warring among themselves. Since it is either Zenos or Isaiah speaking, it was not included in Nephi's commentary on 1 Nephi 21:26.

1 Nephi 22:18–19 • The Righteous Shall Not Perish

18 Behold, my brethren, I say unto you, that these things must shortly come; yea, even blood, and fire, and vapor of smoke must come; and it must needs be upon the face of this earth; and it cometh unto men according to the flesh if it so be that they will harden their hearts against the Holy One of Israel.

19 For behold, the righteous shall not perish; for the time surely must come that all they who fight against Zion shall be cut off. [1 Nephi 22:18–19]

These are Nephi's own words given as a warning and an incentive to be righteous and escape the destruction of the wicked at the Second Coming. There are two specific warnings: do not harden your heart against the Holy One of Israel; and do not fight against Zion. Zion, as used here has reference to a people "of one heart and one mind, and [who] dwelt in righteousness" (Moses 7:18).

1 Nephi 22:20–23 • The Prophet Spoken of by Moses was the Holy One of Israel

20 And the Lord will surely prepare a way for his people, unto the fulfilling of the words of Moses, which he spake, saying: A prophet shall the Lord your God raise up unto you, like unto me; him shall ye hear in all things whatsoever he shall say unto you. And it shall come to pass that all those who will not hear that prophet shall be cut off from among the people.

21 And now I, Nephi, declare unto you, that this prophet of whom Moses spake was the Holy One of Israel; wherefore, he shall execute judgment in righteousness.

22 And the righteous need not fear, for they are those who shall not be confounded. But it is the kingdom of the devil, which shall be

built up among the children of men, which kingdom is established among them which are in the flesh—

23 For the time speedily shall come that all churches which are built up to get gain, and all those who are built up to get power over the flesh, and those who are built up to become popular in the eyes of the world, and those who seek the lusts of the flesh and the things of the world, and to do all manner of iniquity; yea, in fine, all those who belong to the kingdom of the devil are they who need fear, and tremble, and quake; they are those who must be brought low in the dust; they are those who must be consumed as stubble; and this is according to the words of the prophet.

The prophecy of Moses is from the book of Deuteronomy, which is worded slightly different than Nephi's, but is the same meaning.

18 I will raise them up a Prophet from among their brethren, like unto thee, and will put my words in his mouth; and he shall speak unto them all that I shall command him.

19 And it shall come to pass, *that* whosoever will not hearken unto my words which he shall speak in my name, I will require *it* of him. [Deuteronomy 18:18–19]

Nephi's identification of that prophet as "the Holy One of Israel" is the same as given by the Apostle Peter in the New Testament.

20 And he shall send Jesus Christ, which before was preached unto you:

21 Whom the heaven must receive until the times of restitution of all things, which God hath spoken by the mouth of all his holy prophets since the world began.

22 For Moses truly said unto the fathers, A prophet shall the Lord your God raise up unto you of your brethren, like unto me; him shall ye hear in all things whatsoever he shall say unto you.

23 And it shall come to pass, *that* every soul, which will not hear that prophet, shall be destroyed from among the people. [Acts 3:20–23]

Peter's words are also slightly different, but the same message. The differences are probably because of the translation from different languages. Both Peter and Nephi use the prophecy as a latter-day event, although the Deuteronomy text speaks of the prophet (Christ) being raised up. Wherefore, being raised up may have reference to the Lord's appearance. Jesus paraphrased this prophecy to the Nephites.

> 11 Therefore it shall come to pass that whosoever will not believe in my words, who am Jesus Christ, which the Father shall cause him to bring forth unto the Gentiles, and shall give unto him power that he shall bring them forth unto the Gentiles, (it shall be done even as Moses said) they shall be cut off from among my people who are of the covenant. [3 Nephi 21:11]

The Book of Mormon contains the words of Jesus that are to be brought to the Nephites. Those who reject it will be cut off. Therefore, the prophecy of Moses will not be fulfilled until the Book of Mormon has been sent "to every nation, and kindred, and tongue, and people" as John the Revelator testified (Revelation 14:6).

As a further clarification of the meaning of being cut off from God's people (gathered Israel), Nephi speaks of the fall of the kingdom of the devil. He enumerates those who are included in that kingdom (1 Nephi 22:22–23). All churches and their various characteristics means there are many churches, not just one. These many churches supports our earlier conclusion that the kingdom of the devil is not a single organization, but embraces all the organizations and teachings of evil that oppose the kingdom of God. This is similar to the admonition given to the Three Witnesses of the Book of Mormon "Contend against no church, save it be the church of the devil" (D&C 18:20).

1 Nephi 22:24–28 • The Righteous Led Up, the Holy One of Israel Reigns

> 24 And the time cometh speedily that the righteous must be led up as calves of the stall, and the Holy One of Israel must reign in dominion, and might, and power, and great glory.
>
> 25 And he gathereth his children from the four quarters of the earth; and he numbereth his sheep, and they know him; and there shall

be one fold and one shepherd; and he shall feed his sheep, and in him they shall find pasture.

26 And because of the righteousness of his people, Satan has no power; wherefore, he cannot be loosed for the space of many years; for he hath no power over the hearts of the people, for they dwell in righteousness, and the Holy One of Israel reigneth.

27 And now behold, I, Nephi, say unto you that all these things must come according to the flesh.

28 But, behold, all nations, kindreds, tongues, and people shall dwell safely in the Holy One of Israel if it so be that they will repent. [1 Nephi 22:24–28]

The righteous led up as calves of the stall (v. 24) once more reminds us of Malachi, but once more we must be reminded that Nephi and Malachi were quoting from an earlier prophet. The important things to learn from Nephi's admonitions are that Christ will reign, his children (Israel) will be gathered and protected as calves in a stall, and Satan will be bound.

The binding of Satan was also foretold by John the Revelator:

1 And I saw an angel come down from heaven, having the key of the bottomless pit and a great chain in his hand.

2 And he laid hold on the dragon, that old serpent, which is the Devil, and Satan, and bound him a thousand years,

3 And cast him into the bottomless pit, and shut him up, and set a seal upon him, that he should deceive the nations no more, till the thousand years should be fulfilled: and after that he must be loosed a little season. [Revelation 20:1–3]

It is also confirmed in the Doctrine and Covenants:

30 For the great Millennium, of which I have spoken by the mouth of my servants, shall come.

31 For Satan shall be bound, and when he is loosed again he shall only reign for a little season, and then cometh the end of the earth. [D&C 43:30–31]

Nephi's contribution to our understanding is that Satan's power is lost because of the righteousness of the people (1 Nephi 22:26). Whether his power is restricted by Christ because of the people's righteousness, or whether it is solely dependent upon the people is not stated, but his power is gone. The Book of Revelation suggests that Satan's power will be restricted by the setting "of a seal upon him" (Revelation 20:3). The Prophet Joseph taught, as quoted earlier: "Satan has no power over us only as we allow him, and the moment we break a commandment, the devil has power over us" (*TPJS*, 181). This teaching is that the power over Satan comes because of righteousness. Earlier Nephi had seen the saints of God "armed with righteousness and with the power of God in great glory" (1 Nephi 14:14). It is probably a combination of both righteousness and God's power. The important point is that "they dwell in righteousness, and the Holy One of Israel reigneth" (1 Nephi 22:26).

1 Nephi 22:29–31 • The Things Written on the Plates of Brass are True

29 And now I, Nephi, make an end; for I durst not speak further as yet concerning these things.

30 Wherefore, my brethren, I would that ye should consider that the things which have been written upon the plates of brass are true; and they testify that a man must be obedient to the commandments of God.

31 Wherefore, ye need not suppose that I and my father are the only ones that have testified, and also taught them. Wherefore, if ye shall be obedient to the commandments, and endure to the end, ye shall be saved at the last day. And thus it is. Amen. [1 Nephi 22:29–31]

The last several chapters written by Nephi were based on the prophecies of Isaiah, Zenos, and other prophets taken from the plates of brass. He bears testimony that these writings are true. Although he had many personal revelations, he still relied on the scriptures to teach his posterity and us that we might be obedient to the commandments of God, endure to the end, and "be saved at the last day" (1 Nephi 22:31). With Nephi we concur by saying "And thus it is. Amen"

SACRED WRITING

Preaching which is Sacred:

1 Nephi 22:2–31	Nephi explains Isaiah and possibly Zenos to his brothers.

Great Revelations:

1 Nephi 21	Nephi quotes Isaiah 49 to show that the prophets knew of the people of Lehi

Doctrines Learned:

1 Nephi 21:1–3	Israel was foreordained to be the Lord's servant in the latter days.
1 Nephi 21:13	There are two central gathering places for the house of Israel; (Jerusalem) in the east, and (Zion) in the mountains.
1 Nephi 21:22–23	The Gentiles are to nurse the house of Israel in the latter days.
1 Nephi 22:3	Isaiah's prophecies have a temporal and spiritual fulfillment.
1 Nephi 22:7	The Lord would establish a mighty nation among the Gentiles in the Americas.
1 Nephi 22:8–9	The Lord would do a marvelous work among the Gentiles that would be of great worth to Nephi's seed, to the gentiles, and to all nations in fulfilling the covenant made to Abraham.
1 Nephi 22:16–17	The righteous will be preserved by God's power when the fullness of God's wrath is poured out upon all men.
1 Nephi 22:20–21	The Holy One of Israel is the prophet spoken of by Moses who must be hearkened to or be cut off from his people.

1 Nephi 22:22–23	The kingdom of the devil must fall which includes all churches that do all manner of iniquity, and all who belong to his kingdom.
1 Nephi 22:25–26	The Lord will gather the righteous and reign over them in power and great glory, and Satan shall have no power over them.
1 Nephi 22:30	The things written upon the plates of brass are true.

General Authority Quotes

Elder Orson Pratt • 1 Nephi 21:22 (Isaiah 49:22)

This is a great latter-day work also for the gathering of the house of Israel—a work which shall commence among the Gentiles. In ancient days the Lord commenced his work among Israel. The kingdom of heaven was preached among the Jews, but they proved themselves unworthy, and says Paul, "Lo, we turn to the Gentiles," and the kingdom was taken from the Jews and given to a nation bringing forth the fruits thereof. The natural branches of Israel were broken off, and the branches of the wild olive tree—the Gentiles—were grafted in. But the Gentiles, since they were grafted in, 1800 years ago, have fallen after the same example of unbelief that the ancient Jews did, and they have lost the power and authority which they once possessed; and for many centuries they have had no apostles, no prophets, no angels from heaven, no power of godliness made manifest among them, and nothing but the teachings and precepts of uninspired men. But in the great latter-day work, the Lord begins where he left off—"the first shall be last, and the last shall be first." As the Jews, in ancient days were first, and the Gentiles last, so in the great latter-day work, the Gentiles will be first and Israel will be last. Hence the Prophet says, "Behold, thus saith the Lord God, I will lift up mine hand to the Gentiles, and they shall bring thy sons in their arms, and thy daughters upon their shoulders, and I will lift up my standard to the Gentiles." [*JD*, 16:85]

Elder Marion G. Romney • 1 Nephi 21:22 (Isaiah 49:22)

This Church is the standard which Isaiah said the Lord would set up for the people in the latter days. This Church was given to be a light to the world and to be a standard for God's people and for the Gentiles to seek to. This Church is the ensign on the mountain spoken of by the Old Testament prophets. It is the way, the truth, and the life. [CR April 1961, 119]

Elder Spencer W. Kimball • 1 Nephi 21:23

May I conclude with this experience of my friend and brother, Boyd K. Packer, as he returned from Peru. It was in a branch Sacrament meeting. The chapel was filled, the opening exercises finished, and the Sacrament in preparation. A little Lamanite ragamuffin entered from the street. His two shirts would scarcely make one, so ragged they were and torn and worn. It was unlikely that those shirts had ever been off that little body since they were donned. Calloused and chapped were the little feet which brought him in the open door, up the aisle, and to the Sacrament table. There was a dark and dirty testimony of deprivation, want, unsatisfied hungers—spiritual as well as physical. Almost unobserved he shyly came to the Sacrament table, and with a seeming spiritual hunger, leaned against the table and lovingly rubbed his unwashed face against the cool, smooth, white linen.

A woman on a front seat, seemingly outraged by the intrusion, caught his eye and with motion and frown sent the little ragamuffin scampering down the aisle out into this world, the street.

A little later, seemingly compelled by some inner urge, he overcame his timidity and came stealthily, cautiously down the aisle again, fearful, ready to escape if necessary, but impelled as though directed by inaudible voices with "a familiar spirit" and as though memories long faded were reviving, as though some intangible force were crowding him on to seek something for which he yearned but could not identify.

From his seat on the stand, Elder Packer caught his eye, beckoned to him, and stretched out big, welcoming arms. A moment's hesitation and the little ragamuffin was nestled comfortably on his lap, in his arms, the tousled head against a great warm heart—a heart sympathetic to waifs, and especially to little Lamanite ones. It seemed the little one had found a safe harbor from a stormy sea, so contented he was. The cruel, bewildering, frustrating world was outside. Peace, security, acceptance enveloped him.

Later Elder Packer sat in my office and, in tender terms and with a subdued voice, rehearsed this incident to me. As he sat forward on his chair, his eyes glistening, a noticeable emotion in his voice, he said, "As this little one relaxed in my arms, it seemed it was not a single little Lamanite I held. It was a nation, indeed a multitude of nations of deprived, hungering souls, wanting something deep and warm they could not explain—a humble people yearning to revive memories all but faded out—of ancestors standing wide-eyed, openmouthed, expectant and excited, looking up and seeing a holy, glorified Being descend from celestial areas, and hearing a voice say: "Behold, I am Jesus Christ, the Son of God. I created the heavens and the earth, and all things that in them are. . . . and in me hath the Father glorified his name. . . .

"I am the light and the life of the world. I am Alpha and Omega, the beginning and the end" (3 Nephi 9:15, 18).

This day of the Lamanite brings opportunity. Millions farm the steep hillsides of Andean ranges and market their produce with llamas and horses and burros. They must have the emancipating gospel. Millions serve in menial labor, eke out bare subsistence from soil and toil. They must hear the compelling truths of the gospel. Millions are tied to reservations, deprived, untrained, and less than they could be. They must have the enlightening gospel. It will break their fetters, stir their ambition, increase their vision, and open new worlds of opportunity to them. Their captivity will be at an end—captivity from misconceptions, illiteracy, superstition, fear. "The clouds of error disappear before the rays of truth divine (Parley P. Pratt, *Hymns,* 269).

And Nephi's vision is realized: ". . . I beheld that the church of the Lamb, who were the saints of God, were also upon all the face of the earth. . . ." (1 Nephi 14:12).

The brighter day has dawned. The scattering has been accomplished; the gathering is in process. May the Lord bless us all as we become nursing fathers and mothers (see Isaiah 49:23 and 1 Nephi 21:23) unto our Lamanite brethren and hasten the fulfillment of the great promises made to them, I pray in the name of Jesus Christ, Amen. [CR, Oct. 1965, 71–72]

Elder Ezra Taft Benson • 1 Nephi 22:16–17

Yes, it was here under a free government and a strong nation that protection was provided for his restored Church. Now God will nor permit his base of operations—America—to be destroyed. He has promised protection to this land if we will but serve the God of the land. He has also promised protection to the righteous even, if necessary, to send fire from heaven to destroy their enemies (Ether 2:12; 1 Nephi 22:17).

No, God's base of operation will not be destroyed. But it may be weakened and made less effective. One of the first rules of war strategy— and we are at war with the adversary and his agents—is to protect the base of operations. This we must do if we are to build up the kingdom throughout the world and safeguard our God-given freedom. [CR, April 1962, 104–05]

Joseph Smith, the Prophet • 1 Nephi 22:19

I explained concerning the coming of the Son of Man; also that it is a false idea that the Saints will escape all the judgments, whilst the wicked suffer; for all flesh is subject to suffer, and "the righteous shall hardly escape;" still many of the Saints will escape, for the just shall live by faith; yet many of the righteous shall fall a prey to disease, to pestilence, etc., by reason of the weakness of the flesh, and yet be saved in the Kingdom of God. So that it is an unhallowed principle to say that such and such have transgressed because they have been preyed upon by disease or death, for all flesh is subject to death; and the Savior has said, "Judge not, lest ye be judged." [*TPJS*, 162]

Challenges to Eternal Life:

1. As a member of the Lord's gathered people, make a commitment to be a servant in his hand to help the marvelous work go forward. [1 Nephi 22:8]

2. Make a commitment to bind Satan from having power over you by keeping the commandments of God. [1 Nephi 22:26]

3. Seek righteousness that you may be preserved from the enemies of destruction. [1 Nephi 22:17]

4. Choose a challenge or message from the reading and apply it to your life.

Chapter Ten

Lehi Blesses His Children

2 Nephi 1–2

*H*istorical setting: The events of the first four chapters of Second Nephi happened some time after their arrival in the promised land and 570 B.C. The dating given in the right hand corner of the bottom of the page [between 588 and 570 B.C.] are the estimated dates placed there in subsequent editions after the Book of Mormon was translated and first published. The latter date is determined from "thirty years had passed away from the time we left Jerusalem," and Nephi was commanded to "Make other plates" (2 Nephi 5:28–30). They left "six hundred years" before the Messiah was born, or 600 B.C. (1 Nephi 10:4). The first date, 588 B.C., is an estimated time of their arrival in the promised land (see *Historical Setting*, chapter seven). Therefore, Lehi's instructions to his children, 2 Nephi 1:1–4:11, were given just prior to his death (2 Nephi 4:12) in the eighteen year period following their arrival in the promised land.

Precept of these chapters:

28 And now, my sons, I would that ye should look to the great Mediator, and hearken unto his great commandments; and be faithful unto his words, and choose eternal life, according to the will of his Holy Spirit.

29 And not choose eternal death, according to the will of the flesh and the evil which is therein, which giveth the spirit of the devil power

to captivate, to bring you down to hell, that he may reign over you
in his own kingdom. [2 Nephi 2:28–29]

Every father in Israel has a right and a responsibility to bless his
children. Additional blessings are given in our dispensation, as well
as other dispensations, through the priesthood office of patriarch. The
blessings given by Lehi, recorded in these chapters, were probably a
combination of both since Lehi blesses both his sons and the sons of
Ishmael, their father having "died, and was buried in the place they
called Nahom" (1 Nephi 16:34). These chapters also record other
visions, prophecies, and teachings of Lehi. The large plates of Nephi
will tell us more of the church organization and leadership of Lehi at
this time. An outline of the two chapters discussed here, as an overview
in preparation for a deeper study, follows.

OUTLINE • 2 NEPHI 1–2

➤1:1–2　　　　Lehi teaches his sons how the Lord had done great things
　　　　　　　for them.

　　　　a.　He was merciful in bringing them out of Jerusalem
　　　　　　(v. 1).

　　　　b.　He was merciful in not destroying them for rebelling
　　　　　　upon the waters (v. 2).

➤1:3–11　　　Lehi spake concerning the land of promise they had ob-
　　　　　　　tained.

　　　　a.　He saw a vision, and knew that Jerusalem had been
　　　　　　destroyed, and they would have also perished had they
　　　　　　not left (v. 4).

　　　　b.　The Lord had covenanted the land, choice above all
　　　　　　other lands, to his seed forever, and to all those led here
　　　　　　by the Lord (v. 5).

　　　　c.　He prophesied that none will come to this land save by
　　　　　　the hand of the Lord (vv. 6–8).

　　　　　　1.　It shall be a land of liberty and not brought into

captivity except for iniquity, and then it will be cursed for their sakes.

    2. It is wisdom that the land be kept from a knowledge of other nations lest it be overrun.

  d. Lehi was promised prosperity if the commandments of God are kept, and there shall be none to molest them (vv. 8–11).

    1. If they dwindle in unbelief, and reject the Messiah, the judgments of God will come.

    2. He will bring other nations, and he will cause them to be scattered and smitten.

➤ 1:12–22   Lehi asks his sons to remember and to awaken from their sleep of hell.

  a. Awake and hear the words of a parent who will soon go the way of all the earth (v. 14).

  b. The Lord has redeemed his soul, Lehi has beheld his glory, and he is eternally encircled in his love (v. 15).

  c. Observe the statutes and judgments of the Lord, as I have always wanted (vv. 16–20).

    1. I have feared you would be cut off and destroyed forever.

    2. Or that ye be cursed for many generations, and be led and captured by the devil.

    3. May these things not come, but ye be a choice and favored people of the Lord.

    4. The Lord has said: Keep the commandments and prosper; do not and be cut off.

  d. Arise from the dust, and be men, determined in one mind, one heart, and be united in all things, that ye not into captivity and become cursed (vv. 21–22).

➤ 1:23–29   Awake, put on the armor of righteousness, shake off the chains that bind you, and arise from the dust.

  a. Rebel no more against your brother who has been an instrument in the hands of God. Were it not for him, we would have perished in the wilderness (v. 24).

     b.   You accuse him of seeking power and authority over you, but he has sought the glory of God and your own welfare (v. 25).

     c.   You murmur because he used sharpness, but it was the power of God which was in him (v. 26).

     d.   The Spirit of the Lord opened his mouth that he could not shut it (v. 27).

     e.   If you, my sons and the sons of Ishmael will hearken to Nephi ye shall not perish (vv. 28–29).

        1.   If ye hearken, I leave you my first blessing.

        2.   If you do not hearken, I will put it upon him.

➤ 1: 30–32   Lehi blesses Zoram, the servant of Laban and a true friend to Nephi.

     a.   Zoram's seed is blessed with Nephi's seed and will prosper except for iniquity (v. 31).

     b.   The Lord has consecrated the land for the security of Zoram's and Nephi's seed (v. 32).

➤ 2:1–4   Lehi speaks to Jacob, his first born in the wilderness.

     a.   Jacob suffered much affliction because of his brothers rudeness (v. 1).

     b.   The greatness of God will turn his afflictions to his gain (v. 2).

     c.   He shall dwell safely with Nephi and be in the service of God (v. 3).

     d.   He is redeemed; the Redeemer will bring salvation to men in the fullness of time (v. 3).

     e.   In his youth he beheld the Redeemer and is blessed (v. 4).

➤ 2:4–7   The way is prepared from the fall of man and salvation is free.

     a.   Men are instructed sufficiently to know good from evil (v. 5).

     b.   No man is justified by the law but are cut off temporally and also perish spiritually (v. 5).

   c.   Redemption cometh in and through the grace and truth of the Holy Messiah (v. 6).

   d.   The Messiah offereth himself a sacrifice for sin to answer the ends of the law unto all who have a broken heart and a contrite spirit (v. 7).

➤ 2:8–10   No flesh can dwell in the presence of God except through the merits, mercy, and grace of the Holy Messiah.

   a.   He lays down his life and taketh it up again by the power of the Spirit, the first resurrected (v. 8).

   b.   He shall make intercession for all men, and they who believe shall be saved (v. 9).

   c.   All men will be judged by God according to the truth and holiness that is in him (v. 10).

   d.   The law inflicts punishment in opposition to happiness. Both are affixed to the ends of the atonement (v. 10).

➤ 2:11–13   There must be opposition in all things to bring either righteousness or wickedness.

   a.   Without opposition there would be no purpose in the creation (v. 12).

   b.   The wisdom of God; his eternal purposes; and the power, mercy, and justice of God would be destroyed (v. 12).

   c.   If there is no law there is no sin, righteousness, happiness, punishment, misery, no creation, and nothing to act or be acted upon (v. 13).

➤ 2:14–18   There is a God who created all things to act and to be acted upon.

   a.   Our first parents, Adam and Eve, were given the forbidden fruit in opposition to the tree of life (v. 15).

   b.   Man could not act except he were enticed by one or the other (v. 16).

   c.   An angel of God fell from the presence of God and became the devil (v. 17).

d. The devil enticed Eve to partake of the forbidden fruit (v. 18).

➤ 2:19–23   Adam and Eve were driven out of the garden of Eden, to till the earth.

a. They brought forth the whole family of the earth (v. 20).

b. Their days were prolonged and were given a state of probation to repent (v. 21).

c. All men were lost because of the transgression of their parents (v. 21).

d. If Adam had not transgressed, they would have remained in the garden forever, and all things would have remained in the same state forever (v. 22).

e. There would have been no children, they would have remained in a state of innocence, having no joy and doing no good (v. 23).

➤ 2:24–27   All things were done in the wisdom of God who knoweth all things.

a. Adam fell that men might be; and men are that they might have joy (v. 25).

b. The Messiah comes in the fullness of time to redeem man from the fall (v. 26).

c. They have become free forever, knowing good from evil, to act for themselves and not to be acted upon, except by the punishment of the law at the last day (v. 26).

d. They are free to choose liberty and eternal life, or captivity and death (v. 27).

➤ 2:28–30   Lehi tells his sons to look to the great Mediator and choose eternal life.

a. Do not choose eternal death according to the evil of the flesh which gives the devil power to bring you to hell (v. 29).

b. These are Lehi's last days, and he has chosen the good part (v. 30).

c. His whole object is for the welfare of their souls (v. 30).

NOTES AND COMMENTARY

Introduction: The terms agency, freedom, free agency, and free will are often used interchangeably in our society and in the Church today. They have also been used differently in different time periods of the past. This is a common problem in society and the Church. For example, a reading of Church literature of former years shows a different usage than in our own day.[1] Because of this usage, some of the principles and doctrines of the Gospel are misunderstood. To avoid such misunderstanding, we will define the terms as used in this work.

Agency = The ability to choose. As used in the scriptures (emphasis added):

3 Wherefore, because that Satan rebelled against me, and sought to destroy the **agency** of man, which I, the Lord God, had given him, and also, that I should give unto him mine own power; by the power of mine Only Begotten, I caused that he should be cast down; [Moses 4:3]

32 The Lord said unto Enoch: Behold these thy brethren; they are the workmanship of mine own hands, and I gave unto them their knowledge, in the day I created them; and in the Garden of Eden, gave I unto man his **agency**; [Moses 7:32]

35 Behold, I gave unto him that he should be an **agent unto himself**; and I gave unto him commandment, but no temporal commandment gave I unto him, for my commandments are spiritual; they are not natural nor temporal, neither carnal nor sensual.

36 And it came to pass that Adam, being tempted of the devil— for, behold, the devil was before Adam, for he rebelled against me, saying, Give me thine honor, which is my power; and also a third part

---

[1] Elder Dallin H. Oaks addressed this problem in BYU's Third Annual Book of Mormon Symposium. This excellent address titled "Free Agency and Freedom," too long to be included here, was published in *The Book of Mormon: Second Nephi, The Doctrinal Structure*, ed. Monte S. Nyman and Charles D. Tate Jr. Religious Study Center, Brigham Young University 1989, 1–17.

of the hosts of heaven turned he away from me because of their **agency**; [D&C 29:35–36]

31 Behold, here is the **agency** of man, and here is the condemnation of man; because that which was from the beginning is plainly manifest unto them, and they receive not the light.

32 And every man whose spirit receiveth not the light is under condemnation. [D&C 93:31–32]

77 According to the laws and constitution of the people, which I have suffered to be established, and should be maintained for the rights and protection of all flesh, according to just and holy principles;

78 That every man may act in doctrine and principle pertaining to futurity, according to the moral *agency* which I have given unto him, that every man may be accountable for his own sins in the day of judgment. [D&C 101:77–78]

Free will = The desire to choose, precedes action. As used in the scriptures (emphasis added):

12 Wherefore, all things which are **good cometh of God**; and that which is evil cometh of the devil; for the devil is an enemy unto God, and fighteth against him continually, and inviteth and **enticeth to sin**, and to do that which is evil continually. [Moroni 7:12]

a. Desire to choose good.

10 Now I say unto you, if this be the **desire of your hearts**, what have you against being baptized in the name of the Lord, as a witness before him that ye have entered into a covenant with him, that ye will serve him and keep his commandments, that he may pour out his Spirit more abundantly upon you?

11 And now when the people had heard these words, they clapped their hands for joy, and exclaimed: This is the **desire of our hearts**. [Mosiah 18:10–11]

27 But behold, if ye will awake and arouse your faculties, even to an experiment upon my words, and exercise a particle of faith, yea, even if ye can no more than **desire to believe,** let this desire work in you, even until ye believe in a manner that ye can give place for a portion of my words. [Alma 32:27]

b. Desire to do evil:

15 Now behold, I say unto you that if ye will return unto Jerusalem ye shall also perish with them. And now, if ye have **choice [desire]**, go up to the land, and remember the words which I speak unto you, that if ye go ye will also perish; for thus the Spirit of the Lord constraineth me that I should speak. [1 Nephi 7:15]

12 Having gone **according to their own carnal wills and desires**; having never called upon the Lord while the arms of mercy were extended towards them; for the arms of mercy were extended towards them, and they would not; they being warned of their iniquities and yet they would not depart from them; and they were commanded to repent and yet they would not repent. [Mosiah 16:12]

Note: Physical force may prevent you from acting, but it cannot prevent your desire to act.

Free agency = The ability to make the right choice. As used in the scriptures (emphasis added).

5 And men are instructed sufficiently that they **know good from evil**. [2 Nephi 2:5]

32 And ye shall know the truth, and the **truth shall make you free**. [John 8:32]

27 And no man **receiveth a fulness unless he keepeth his commandments**.

28 He that keepeth his commandments receiveth truth and light, until he is **glorified in truth and knoweth all things**. [D&C 93:27–28]

36 The glory of God is **intelligence**, or, in other words, **light and truth**.

37 Light and truth forsake that evil one. [D&C 93:36–37]

Eternal progression comes as we make the correct choices. As we keep the commandments, we have the opportunity for priesthood ordinations, serving as missionaries and other service in the kingdom, temple endowment, and temple marriage. If we choose to be immoral, break the word of wisdom, or other commandments, we forfeit those blessings until we repent and qualify for the blessings.

> 20 There is a law, irrevocably decreed in heaven before the foundations of this world, upon which all blessings are predicated—

> 21 And when we obtain any blessing from God, it is by obedience to that law upon which it is predicated. [D&C 130:20–21]

Lehi's instructions to his sons, especially those given to Jacob are based upon the above explanations (2 Nephi 1).

Superscription • A brief overview of the Book of Second Nephi

> *An account of the death of Lehi. Nephi's brethren rebel against him. The Lord warns Nephi to depart into the wilderness. His journeyings in the wilderness, and so forth.*

The above italicized words above are taken from under the title "THE SECOND BOOK OF NEPHI." They were translated from the plates of Nephi (see the explanation under Superscription of "THE FIRST BOOK OF NEPHI"). The chapter headings under CHAPTER 1, and subsequent chapters, were placed there by men of this dispensation.

2 Nephi 1:1–3 • Lehi Testifies of the Mercy of the Lord

> 1 And now it came to pass that after I, Nephi, had made an end of teaching my brethren, our father, Lehi, also spake many things unto them, and rehearsed unto them, how great things the Lord had done for them in bringing them out of the land of Jerusalem.

> 2 And he spake unto them concerning their rebellions upon the waters, and the mercies of God in sparing their lives, that they were not swallowed up in the sea.

> 3 And he also spake unto them concerning the land of promise, which they had obtained—how merciful the Lord had been in warning us that we should flee out of the land of Jerusalem. [2 Nephi 1:1–3]

These verses are a brief summation of what Lehi taught his sons. A fuller account was in the Book of Lehi. An abridgment of the Book of Lehi was in the 116 lost pages. The central theme was the mercy the Lord extended to them when they fled out of Jerusalem.

2 Nephi 1:4–5 • Lehi's Vision of Jerusalem

> 4 For, behold, said he, I have seen a vision, in which I know that Jerusalem is destroyed; and had we remained in Jerusalem we should also have perished.
>
> 5 But, said he, notwithstanding our afflictions, we have obtained a land of promise, a land which is choice above all other lands; a land which the Lord God hath covenanted with me should be a land for the inheritance of my seed. Yea, the Lord hath covenanted this land unto me, and to my children forever, and also all those who should be led out of other countries by the hand of the Lord. [2 Nephi 1:4–5]

Lehi's vision of Jerusalem's destruction (v. 4) was a spiritual witness confirming what the Spirit of the Lord had told him earlier, "that it should be destroyed" (1 Nephi 1:13). It also justified why "he should take his family and depart into the wilderness" (1 Nephi 2:2). Several generations later the Nephites received a physical witness when they met "the people of Zarahemla (who) came out of Jerusalem at the time that Zedekiah, king of Judah, was carried away captive into Babylon" (Omni 1:15). Even hundreds of years later Nephi, the son of Helaman, uses this evidence against the wicked Nephites. "And now will you dispute that Jerusalem was destroyed? Will ye say that the sons of Zedekiah were not slain, all except it were Mulek? Yea, and do ye not behold that the seed of Zedekiah are with us, and they were driven out of the land of Jerusalem?" (Helaman 8:21). The Lord provides witnesses as they are needed, and the Spirit would verify that witness to them personally, giving them two witnesses. Thus the people were left without excuse.

Lehi also testified to his sons that where they had landed was a land "choice above all other lands" (v. 5). This is the first recording of Lehi calling it a promised land, although he certainly must have known and called it such earlier. It was recorded as the destiny given to Nephi by the Lord which he had "prepared for you; yea, a land which is choice above all other lands" (1 Nephi 2:20). This was made known to Nephi in the valley of Lemuel a short time after they departed from Jerusalem. He "did believe all the words which had been spoken by my father" (1 Nephi 2:16). It is probable that the Lord was confirming what Lehi had told Nephi. Furthermore, he had been told of the land many times by an angel in the visions shown to him because of his "desire to behold the things which my father saw" (1 Nephi 11:3; 13:12, 30; 14:2). Obtaining the promised land was recorded as their objective from the time of the Lord's appearance to Nephi. Nephi was commanded by the Lord to build a ship, and to be "led towards the promised land" (1 Nephi 17:13–14). Lehi now discloses that the Lord God had "covenanted with [him] should be a land for the inheritance . . . unto me, and to my children forever," and to all others "who should be led out of other countries by the hand of the Lord" (v. 5). There is no account of when this covenant was made with him, but the implication is that the vision of the destruction of Jerusalem and the covenant were made at the same time, and that it was after their arrival in the promised land. When the Savior visited the Nephites, he taught them that, as remnants of Joseph, "this is the land of your inheritance, and the Father hath given it unto you" (3 Nephi 15:12–13). Of course Lehi was from Manasseh, son of Joseph, and Ishmael was from Joseph's other son, Ephraim (see commentary on 1 Nephi 7:3). The Father's giving the land to Joseph's remnant may have been referring to the covenant made to Lehi.

1 Nephi 1:6–8 • The Prophecy of Lehi

6 Wherefore, I, Lehi, prophesy according to the workings of the Spirit which is in me, that there shall none come into this land save they shall be brought by the hand of the Lord.

7 Wherefore, this land is consecrated unto him whom he shall bring. And if it so be that they shall serve him according to the commandments which he hath given, it shall be a land of liberty unto them; wherefore, they shall never be brought down into captivity; if

so, it shall be because of iniquity; for if iniquity shall abound cursed shall be the land for their sakes, but unto the righteous it shall be blessed forever.

8 And behold, it is wisdom that this land should be kept as yet from the knowledge of other nations; for behold, many nations would overrun the land, that there would be no place for an inheritance. (1 Nephi 1:6–8)

The prophecy of Lehi can be broken into three parts: (1) None shall come to this land save they are brought by the hand of the Lord (v. 6); (2) it will be a land of liberty and never be brought into captivity except because of iniquity (v. 7); and (3) it is wisdom that the land be kept from a knowledge of other nations lest it be overrun, and there be no place for an inheritance. Lehi expounds upon these promises to his sons.

Does the first part of the prophecy, being brought to this land by the hand of the Lord, apply to all time periods or just from Lehi to Columbus? The prophecy makes no distinctions and must be considered as future from Lehi's time. Any exceptions to the prophecy would have been or will be announced by the Lord through his prophets. Those who question the time frame sometimes ask: were people who are criminals, or secret organizations, or others of questionable character and continue their works of darkness on this continent, brought here by the Lord? The purposes of the Lord are not always known or understood, but some possibilities are offered. Perhaps the Lord was giving these individuals an opportunity to repent and forsake their doings or associations. Laman and Lemuel "were like unto the Jews who were at Jerusalem" (1 Nephi 2:13), yet the Lord brought them and gave them many opportunities to repent. This presents another possibility, perhaps it was because of the desires of a family or faithful friends that unrighteous characters were included in a group that the Lord brought here. Again they were given an opportunity for a new environment and chance to change their ways. As the Lord said to the Prophet Isaiah: "For my thoughts *are* not your thoughts, neither *are* your ways my ways, saith the LORD" (Isaiah 55:8). Also, Jacob, brother of Nephi, wrote:

> 8 Behold, great and marvelous are the works of the Lord. How unsearchable are the depths of the mysteries of him; and it is impossible that man should find out all his ways. And no man knoweth of his ways save it be revealed unto him; wherefore, brethren, despise not the revelations of God. [Jacob 4:8]

Someday we will know the Lord's purposes, and then we will undoubtedly see Lehi's prophecy verified.

The second part of Lehi's prophecy: the inhabitants of this land will "never be brought down into captivity" except because of iniquity (v. 7) should be a great comfort, and also an incentive to Americans to shun iniquity as we fight the war on terrorism. We should also make every effort to live righteously, because even if "iniquity abounds" the righteous "shall be blessed forever" (v. 8).

The third part of Lehi's prophecy: a knowledge of this land kept from other nations, may have been fulfilled when the Spirit of God "came down and wrought upon the man (Columbus) and he went forth . . . unto . . . the promised land . . . and it wrought upon other Gentiles; and they went forth out of captivity" (1 Nephi 13:12–13). Since that time the Americas have been known to all the world. Some may argue that if the third part of the prophecy ended with Columbus, why not the first part, and even the second part also? In response, the promises made by Lehi to his sons indicate an extension of the first two parts, but not the third. Furthermore, the land remains a promised land for many reasons, but the main one because of "the covenant which [the Lord] made with your father Jacob; and it shall be a New Jerusalem" (3 Nephi 20:22). "Zion is the whole of America . . . where the mountain of the Lord should be" (*TPJS*, 362).

2 Nephi 1:9–12 • The Promises Made to Lehi

> 9 Wherefore, I, Lehi, have obtained a promise, that inasmuch as those whom the Lord God shall bring out of the land of Jerusalem shall keep his commandments, they shall prosper upon the face of this

land; and they shall be kept from all other nations, that they may possess this land unto themselves. And if it so be that they shall keep his commandments they shall be blessed upon the face of this land, and there shall be none to molest them, nor to take away the land of their inheritance; and they shall dwell safely forever.

10 But behold, when the time cometh that they shall dwindle in unbelief, after they have received so great blessings from the hand of the Lord—having a knowledge of the creation of the earth, and all men, knowing the great and marvelous works of the Lord from the creation of the world; having power given them to do all things by faith; having all the commandments from the beginning, and having been brought by his infinite goodness into this precious land of promise—behold, I say, if the day shall come that they will reject the Holy One of Israel, the true Messiah, their Redeemer and their God, behold, the judgments of him that is just shall rest upon them.

11 Yea, he will bring other nations unto them, and he will give unto them power, and he will take away from them the lands of their possessions, and he will cause them to be scattered and smitten.

12 Yea, as one generation passeth to another there shall be bloodsheds, and great visitations among them; wherefore, my sons, I would that ye would remember; yea, I would that ye would hearken unto my words. [2 Nephi 1:9–12]

The blessing of peace and prosperity forever was a conditional promise (v. 9). Since Jehovah knows "the end from the beginning" (Abraham 2:8), he knew they would not always keep his commandments, as indicated by "when the time cometh" (v. 10). The knowledge given to Lehi's people of the creation of the earth and of all men is not given in detail upon the plates of Nephi, but will come forth when the things "expedient that [we] should have first, to try [our] faith," are believed, then we have and know the greater things (3 Nephi 26:9). The plates of brass "gave an account of the creation of the earth, and also of Adam and Eve," and were to "go forth unto all nations, kindreds, tongues, and people who were of [Lehi's] seed" (1 Nephi 5:11, 18; see also Alma 37:3–5). The twenty-four plates, from which Moroni took his account of the Jaredites, also spoke "concerning the creation of the world, and also of Adam" (Ether 1:2–3). Modern revelation also promises more information on the creation when Christ comes: "Yea, verily I say unto you, in that day when the Lord shall come, he shall reveal all things—Things which have passed, and hidden things which no man knew, things of the earth, by which it was made, and the purpose and the end thereof" (D&C 101:32–33).

Although the Book of Mormon does not give details of the creation, it does testify of the creator. Lehi at this time testifies to his sons that "[God] hath created all things, both the heavens and the earth, and all things that in them are" (2 Nephi 2:14). An angel identified Jesus Christ to King Benjamin as "the Father of heaven and earth, the creator of all things from the beginning" (Mosiah 3:8).[2] When Jesus Christ spoke to the Nephites after their cities had been destroyed, he said: "I created the heavens and the earth, and all things that in them are" (3 Nephi 9:15). The Bible teaches of the same creator, although it is often overlooked. The Gospel of John records: "In the beginning was the Word, and the Word was with God, and the Word was God. The same was in the beginning with God. All things were made by him; and without him was not any thing made that was made. He was in the world, and the world was made by him, and the world knew him not. (John 1:1–3, 10). In Colossians we read of God's dear Son:

> 14 In whom we have redemption through his blood, *even* the forgiveness of sins:
>
> 15 Who is the image of the invisible God, the firstborn of every creature:
>
> 16 For by him were all things created, that are in heaven, and that are in earth, visible and invisible, whether *they be* thrones, or dominions, or principalities, or powers: all things were created by him, and for him. [Colossians 1:14–16]

Paul addresses the Hebrews regarding God speaking "unto us by his Son, whom he hath appointed heir of all things, *by whom also he made the worlds*" (Hebrews 1:2; italics added). Therefore, when Lehi

---

[2] The Book of Mormon repeatedly bears testimony of the creator, see Mosiah 15:1, 4; Alma 11:38–39; 22:9–11; Helaman 14:12; and Mormon 9:9–11.

foretells the judgments of God coming upon the Nephites when "they will reject the Holy One of Israel," it is in the context of their knowledge of the creation and Christ being their creator (v. 10 above). The Book of Mormon further testifies that the "earth was created by the power of [Christ's] word" (Jacob 4:9), or by the power of his voice" (Helaman 12:8–14). The Nephites were destroyed as a nation, scattered and smitten because of their rejecting the knowledge of the creation and the true Messiah, as Lehi prophesied. This evidence should also serve as a warning to us in our world of scientific emphasis.

2 Nephi 1:13–23 • Awake from the Sleep of Hell, Shake Off the Chains that Bind You

13 O that ye would awake; awake from a deep sleep, yea, even from the sleep of hell, and shake off the awful chains by which ye are bound, which are the chains which bind the children of men, that they are carried away captive down to the eternal gulf of misery and woe.

14 Awake! and arise from the dust, and hear the words of a trembling parent, whose limbs ye must soon lay down in the cold and silent grave, from whence no traveler can return; a few more days and I go the way of all the earth.

15 But behold, the Lord hath redeemed my soul from hell; I have beheld his glory, and I am encircled about eternally in the arms of his love.

16 And I desire that ye should remember to observe the statutes and the judgments of the Lord; behold, this hath been the anxiety of my soul from the beginning.

17 My heart hath been weighed down with sorrow from time to time, for I have feared, lest for the hardness of your hearts the Lord your God should come out in the fulness of his wrath upon you, that ye be cut off and destroyed forever;

18 Or, that a cursing should come upon you for the space of many generations; and ye are visited by sword, and by famine, and are hated, and are led according to the will and captivity of the devil.

19 O my sons, that these things might not come upon you, but that ye might be a choice and a favored people of the Lord. But behold, his will be done; for his ways are righteousness forever.

20 And he hath said that: Inasmuch as ye shall keep my commandments ye shall prosper in the land; but inasmuch as ye will not keep
my commandments ye shall be cut off from my presence.

21 And now that my soul might have joy in you, and that my heart
might leave this world with gladness because of you, that I might not
be brought down with grief and sorrow to the grave, arise from the
dust, my sons, and be men, and be determined in one mind and in one
heart, united in all things, that ye may not come down into captivity;

22 That ye may not be cursed with a sore cursing; and also, that
ye may not incur the displeasure of a just God upon you, unto the
destruction, yea, the eternal destruction of both soul and body.

23 Awake, my sons; put on the armor of righteousness. Shake off
the chains with which ye are bound, and come forth out of obscurity,
and arise from the dust. [2 Nephi 1:13–23]

Three times in these verses Lehi urges his sons to awake. Thus he
recognizes they have been asleep. He first urges them to "awake from
a deep sleep, yea, even from the sleep of hell" (v. 13). The sleep of
hell must have reference to their being destined to awake in hell, or
the spirit prison if they do not change their ways. The awful chains
that carry them "captive down to the eternal gulf of misery and woe"
is spoken of often in the Book of Mormon. Alma describes the chains
of hell to Zeezrom:

10 And therefore, he that will harden his heart, the same receiveth
the lesser portion of the word; and he that will not harden his heart,
to him is given the greater portion of the word, until it is given unto
him to know the mysteries of God until he know them in full.

11 And they that will harden their hearts, to them is given the lesser
portion of the word until they know nothing concerning his mysteries;
and then they are taken captive by the devil, and led by his will down
to destruction. Now this is what is meant by the chains of hell. [Alma
12:10–11]

Lehi next invites his sons to "Awake! And arise from the dust"
(v. 14). Being in the dust implies they are being held down, or are
walking where they are being soiled. They are living in dirt or sin. The

words of Lehi to "hear the words of a trembling parent, whose limbs ye must soon lay down in the cold and silent grave, from whence no traveler can return" (v. 14),[3] expresses his desire for his sons to learn from his experiences of a long life rather than to follow the well-traveled dusty road they are on, the way of the world.

The road Lehi had traveled had led to his soul being redeemed—"I have beheld his glory, and I am encircled about eternally in the arms of his love" (v. 14). In the words of Peter he had made his "calling and election sure" (2 Peter 1:10). The Prophet Joseph explained: "When the Lord has thoroughly proved him, and finds that the man is determined to serve him at all hazards, then the man will find his calling and his election made sure, then it will be his pleasure to receive the other comforter . . . he will have the personage of Jesus Christ to attend him, or appear unto him from time to time" (*TPJS*, 150–51). Lehi had apparently had this experience. The following instructions to his sons were to encourage them to follow the same course.

The statutes that the sons are admonished to observe (v. 16) are the written commandments that the Lord has revealed to them. The judgments of the Lord (v. 16) are the answers to decisions that they must make which will be given by the Spirit, or relying on personal revelation rather on their own reasoning. Of course we are to "study [our decisions] out in [our] minds; then [we] must ask if it be right" (D&C 9:8), but not rely on reasoning alone.

Lehi had been shown that Laman and Lemuel "would not come unto [him] and partake of the fruit" (1 Nephi 8:19), but he would not give up (vv. 17–19). He continued to exhort them "with all the feeling of a tender parent, that they would hearken to his words" (1 Nephi

---

[3] Some have accused Joseph Smith of authoring the Book of Mormon, and point to 2 Nephi 1:14 as evidence of his carelessly quoting or paraphrasing Shakespeare. Lehi was probably acquainted with Job from the plates of brass, but it is more probable that both Lehi and Shakespeare are paraphrasing or quoting from Job. The verses from Job are: "Seeing his days *are* determined, the number of his months *are* with thee, thou hast appointed his bounds that he cannot pass;" (14:5), and "When a few years are come, then I shall go the way *whence* I shall not return" (16:22).

8:37). He yielded to the will of the Lord (v. 19). "Faith in God unto life and salvation" comes through "an actual knowledge that the course of life which one is pursuing is according to His will" (*Lectures on Faith* 3:2–3). Lehi had followed this course, and his soul was redeemed (v. 15), but he had "this anxiety of [his] soul from the beginning" for his sons (v. 16).

Lehi again reminds his sons of the conditional promises of prospering in the land if they keep the Lord's commandments (v. 20). Nephi first recorded this promise when the Lord spoke to him in the valley of Lemuel (see 1 Nephi 2:19–21), but may have been told to Lehi before that. It is repeated throughout the Book of Mormon, and is "the everlasting decree of God" to whomever "doth possess [the land]" (Ether 2:10). Therefore, it is still applicable to us today. Furthermore, it is the promised land of Zion where will be fulfilled "the covenant which [Christ] made with your father Jacob; and it shall be a New Jerusalem" (3 Nephi 20:22). In fact, Lehi alludes to a Zion society when he invites his sons to "be men, and be determined in one mind and in one heart, united in all things" (v. 21). "The Lord called [Enoch's] people Zion, because they were of one heart and one mind, and dwelt in righteousness; and there was no poor among them" (Moses 7:18). To be of one heart and one mind is to be united in truth, or doctrine; and in understanding. "The Spirit speaketh the truth and lieth not" (Jacob 4:13). Those who seek to bring forth Zion "shall have the gift and the power of the Holy Ghost" (1 Nephi 13:37). The words of Christ (scriptures), which are given by the power of the Holy Ghost, "will tell you all things what ye should do," and "will show you all things what ye should do (revelation). Behold, this is the doctrine of Christ" (2 Nephi 32:3–6). King Benjamin urged his people to "open your ears that ye may hear, and your hearts that ye may understand, and your minds that the mysteries of God may be unfolded to your view" (Mosiah 2:9).

To be of one mind is to have "your eye be single to [Christ's] glory.... Therefore sanctify yourselves that your minds become single to God" (D&C 88:67–68). Thus, through these means, Lehi pleads with his sons to become "a choice and a favored people of the Lord" instead of coming "down into captivity," and incurring the "destruction of both soul and body" (2 Nephi 1:19, 21–22).

The third time that Lehi invited his sons to awake, he urged them to put on the armor of righteousness, and referred again to the two previous problems, to shake off the chains of hell and to arise from the dust, (v. 23). In the context of the armor, to come out of obscurity suggests that they take the offensive in the war against evil.

2 Nephi 1:24–27 • Lehi Defends His Faithful Son Nephi

24 Rebel no more against your brother, whose views have been glorious, and who hath kept the commandments from the time that we left Jerusalem; and who hath been an instrument in the hands of God, in bringing us forth into the land of promise; for were it not for him, we must have perished with hunger in the wilderness; nevertheless, ye sought to take away his life; yea, and he hath suffered much sorrow because of you.

25 And I exceedingly fear and tremble because of you, lest he shall suffer again; for behold, ye have accused him that he sought power and authority over you; but I know that he hath not sought for power nor authority over you, but he hath sought the glory of God, and your own eternal welfare.

26 And ye have murmured because he hath been plain unto you. Ye say that he hath used sharpness; ye say that he hath been angry with you; but behold, his sharpness was the sharpness of the power of the word of God, which was in him; and that which ye call anger was the truth, according to that which is in God, which he could not restrain, manifesting boldly concerning your iniquities.

27 And it must needs be that the power of God must be with him, even unto his commanding you that ye must obey. But behold, it was not he, but it was the Spirit of the Lord which was in him, which opened his mouth to utterance that he could not shut it.

Lehi's defense of Nephi to the brothers is direct and understandable, but note that he depicts his faithful son as a person of Zion. Nephi had been an instrument in the hand of God to bring the entire group to the promised land (v. 24). He sought only for the glory of God, and the eternal welfare of his people (v. 25). The sharpness he had used was the sharpness of the power of the word of God (v. 26). It was the power of the word of God, or the Spirit, that opened his mouth to command his people (v. 27). Nephi was truly of one heart and one mind, and had been foreordained to lead his people to the promised land.

2 Nephi 1:28–29 • Lehi's First Blessing

28 And now my son, Laman, and also Lemuel and Sam, and also my sons who are the sons of Ishmael, behold, if ye will hearken unto the voice of Nephi ye shall not perish. And if ye will hearken unto him I leave unto you a blessing, yea, even my first blessing.

29 But if ye will not hearken unto him I take away my first blessing, yea, even my blessing, and it shall rest upon him.

The Lord had told Nephi that he would "be made a ruler and a teacher over his brethren" because "thy brethren shall rebel against [the Lord]" (1 Nephi 2:22). Although he had been fulfilling this role since they had left the valley of Limhi, Lehi holds out hope and one more opportunity for his rebellious sons to obtain their blessings of birth. To Laman in particular, it was a chance to assume his leadership of the family, one merited in the pre-mortal life, in a new environment and situation. Lehi probably assumed that Laman would not rise to the occasion, but he apparently still felt it was possible.

2 Nephi 1:30–32 • Zoram the True Friend of Nephi

30 And now, Zoram, I speak unto you: Behold, thou art the servant of Laban; nevertheless, thou hast been brought out of the land of Jerusalem, and I know that thou art a true friend unto my son, Nephi, forever.

31 Wherefore, because thou hast been faithful thy seed shall be blessed with his seed, that they dwell in prosperity long upon the face of this land; and nothing, save it shall be iniquity among them, shall harm or disturb their prosperity upon the face of this land forever.

32 Wherefore, if ye shall keep the commandments of the Lord, the Lord hath consecrated this land for the security of thy seed with the seed of my son.

We do not know the ethnic background or bloodline of Zoram, the true friend of Nephi. Being a servant to Laban suggests he was not of the blood of Israel. Regardless, as patriarch of Joseph's branch of Israel, Lehi extends all the blessings of the Lord to this faithful man and to his seed. If he were not of the house of Israel, he was adopted into it. These blessings were to come through the family unit of Nephi (another suggestion that he was not of the blood of Israel), but were conditional upon their keeping the commandments of Lord.

2 Nephi 2 • The Blessing of Jacob, the First-born in the Wilderness

The entire chapter is addressed to Jacob, the first of two sons born to Lehi and Sariah in the wilderness. Lehi had spoken briefly and collectively to his sons Laman, Lemuel, Sam, and the sons of Ishmael, and had individually blessed Zoram, but it was also a brief blessing. Perhaps Laman, Lemuel, Sam and Nephi had been given longer blessings before they left Jerusalem, or even since they left. Jacob (and Joseph) may have been given an extensive blessing because of this being their first one or because of their youthfulness. Nevertheless, the blessing to Jacob is filled with great doctrinal concepts drawn from the prophets who had written or been written about on the plates of brass, and are applicable to all mankind in a doctrinal sense.

2 Nephi 2:1–4 • Jacob in his Youth

1 And now, Jacob, I speak unto you: Thou art my first-born in the days of my tribulation in the wilderness. And behold, in thy childhood thou hast suffered afflictions and much sorrow, because of the rudeness of thy brethren.

2 Nevertheless, Jacob, my first-born in the wilderness, thou knowest the greatness of God; and he shall consecrate thine afflictions for thy gain.

3 Wherefore, thy soul shall be blessed, and thou shalt dwell safely with thy brother, Nephi; and thy days shall be spent in the service of thy God. Wherefore, I know that thou art redeemed, because of the righteousness of thy Redeemer; for thou hast beheld that in the fulness of time he cometh to bring salvation unto men.

4 And thou hast beheld in thy youth his glory; wherefore, thou art blessed even as they unto whom he shall minister in the flesh; for the Spirit is the same, yesterday, today, and forever. And the way is prepared from the fall of man, and salvation is free.

Lehi's comforting words to Jacob regarding his afflictions in the wilderness being turned to him for good (vv. 1–2) reminds us of the Lord's words to Joseph Smith concerning his sufferings in Missouri, "that all these things shall give thee experience, and shall be for thy good" (D&C 122:7). The same principle is applicable to everyone.

Lehi gives two personal blessings to Jacob: (1) he would dwell safely with Nephi, his brother; and (2) his days would be spent in the service of God (v. 3). The first is a temporal blessing, and the second a spiritual one. While the record does not state much directly about these two blessings, it gives enough to confirm them. Jacob leaves with Nephi as part of those who "believed in the warnings and the revelations of God" (2 Nephi 5:6), and he shares teaching and preaching responsibilities with Nephi (2 Nephi 6–10 chapters). Nephi also commands Jacob to keep the "small plates" and the "other plates . . . and hand them down unto my seed from generation to generation" (Jacob 1:1–4). He thus replaces Nephi as the spiritual leader of his people.

Lehi mentions two events of which we have no record on the small plates, and which he equates with Jacob being redeemed. Jacob had apparently been shown a vision of the Lord's coming in the fulness (meridian) of time to bring salvation to men (v. 3). The fulness of time is obviously a reference to the earthly ministry of Christ when he made the atonement for all mankind. Paul uses the same expression in reference to the time of Christ: "But when the fulness of the time was come, God sent forth his Son, made of a woman, made under the law"

(Galatians 4:4). Perhaps it is called the fullness of time (not times)[4] because it is the time of most importance of all the times of the earth.

The second unrecorded event is a personal visit of the Savior to Jacob. Nephi later states: "And my brother, Jacob, also has seen him as I have seen him" (2 Nephi 11:3). Lehi compares this visit with the blessings of those to whom Jesus will appear during his earthly ministry. The basis of Lehi's comparison is made on the principle of the eternal nature of the gospel, the Spirit being the same yesterday, today, and forever (v. 4). We are given no other information in the Book of Mormon about Jacob's two experiences. Lehi concluded that Jacob had been saved from the fall. Salvation is a free gift to those who will meet the conditions of redemption. Lehi's statement declared the mission of Jesus' earthly ministry, and confirmed the fallen nature of man. Lehi had earlier declared: "all mankind were in a lost and fallen state, and ever would be save they should rely on this Redeemer" (1 Nephi 10:6). The fall is a basic doctrine of the gospel of Jesus Christ.

Lehi leaves the enumeration of Jacob's blessing and launches into a great doctrinal treatise of the agency of man, the fall, and the atonement.

2 Nephi 2:5–9 • Redemption Through the Holy Messiah

> 5 And men are instructed sufficiently that they know good from evil. And the law is given unto men. And by the law no flesh is justified; or, by the law men are cut off. Yea, by the temporal law they were cut off; and also, by the spiritual law they perish from that which is good, and become miserable forever.

> 6 Wherefore, redemption cometh in and through the Holy Messiah; for he is full of grace and truth.

> 7 Behold, he offereth himself a sacrifice for sin, to answer the ends

---

[4] The fullness of "times" is the last dispensation when the Lord will "gather together in one all things in Christ, both which are in heaven, and which are on earth; even in him" (Ephesians 1:10). The priesthood was restored in the last dispensation "for the last days and for the last time" (D&C 112:30).

of the law, unto all those who have a broken heart and a contrite spirit; and unto none else can the ends of the law be answered.

8 Wherefore, how great the importance to make these things known unto the inhabitants of the earth, that they may know that there is no flesh that can dwell in the presence of God, save it be through the merits, and mercy, and grace of the Holy Messiah, who layeth down his life according to the flesh, and taketh it again by the power of the Spirit, that he may bring to pass the resurrection of the dead, being the first that should rise.

9 Wherefore, he is the firstfruits unto God, inasmuch as he shall make intercession for all the children of men; and they that believe in him shall be saved.

These verses are Lehi's explanation of salvation as a free gift. In their fallen state, men are given the law and are instructed sufficiently to know good from evil (v. 5). Law[5] is the basic condition of agency. Everyone is born with the Spirit of Christ innately within him, and it "is given to every man, that he may know good from evil" (Moroni 7:16).

The second condition of agency is that man must be able to understand the law. The Lord revealed to this dispensation that the children are not received into the Church "unless [they] have arrived unto the years of accountability before God, and (are) capable of repentance" (D&C 20:71). The Lord also revealed that parents were responsible to teach the basic principles to their children before they become "eight years old" when "their children shall be baptized" (D&C 68:25–26). Older people "that hath no understanding (handicapped mentally)" are in the same category (D&C 29:50).

"By the law no flesh is justified" (v. 5) is saying what Paul said to the Romans; "For all have sinned, and come short of the glory of God" (3:23). Lehi says that "by the temporal law they were cut off"

---

[5] Lehi is not referring to the law of Moses but to eternal law. As taught in modern revelation: "There is a law, irrevocably decreed in heaven before the foundations of this world, upon which all blessings are predicated—And when we obtain any blessing from God, it is by obedience to that law upon which it is predicated.

(v. 5). Alma later explained: "Now we see that Adam did fall by the partaking of the forbidden fruit, according to the word of God; and thus we see, that by his fall, all mankind became a lost and fallen people.... And we see that death comes upon mankind, yea, the death which has been spoken of by Amulek, which is the temporal death" (Alma 12:22, 24). Eating of the fruit violated a law. "But of the tree of the knowledge of good and evil, thou shalt not eat of it, nevertheless, thou mayest choose for thyself, for it is given unto thee; but, remember that I forbid it, for in the day thou eatest thereof thou shalt surely die" (Moses 3:17; see also Genesis 2:17). The fruit apparently caused a temporal change, making Adam and Eve mortals and subject to death. Lehi states further; "by the spiritual law they perish from that which is good, and become miserable forever" (v. 5). They were cast out of the garden of Eden, and spiritually alienated from God. Alma also explained: "Therefore, as the soul could never die, and the Fall had brought upon all mankind a spiritual death as well as a temporal, that is, they were cut off from the presence of the Lord, it was expedient that mankind should be reclaimed from this spiritual death" (Alma 42:9). Being reclaimed from spiritual (and temporal) death would negate their misery forever.

According to Lehi: "redemption cometh in and through the Holy Messiah; for he is full of grace and truth" (v. 6). Salvation was in Christ, not in keeping the law. "There [was] a law given, and a punishment affixed" for the law being broken "justice claimeth the creature" (Alma 42:22). Since all have sinned, or broken the law, Christ offered his soul as a sacrifice for sin (v. 7) in the garden of Gethsemane, "and satisfied the demands of justice (the law)" (Mosiah 15:9). Therefore by his grace came the redemption. "He that keepeth his commandments receiveth truth and light, until he is glorified in truth and knoweth all truth" (D&C 93:28). Christ is "the Spirit of truth . . . And no man receiveth a fullness (of truth) unless he keepeth his commandments" (D&C 93:26–27). We progress towards eternal life as we receive truth, therefore by his truth cometh redemption. However, there is a condition placed upon the ends of the law being answered (paid). Only those who have a broken heart, realize that they caused Christ to suffer for them and are sorrowful (repentant) for doing so. They have a contrite spirit, when they are willing to be taught the truth, to and accept the truth and will have the law answered for them by Christ (v. 7).

"How great the importance to make [the plan of salvation] known unto the inhabitants of the earth, . . . there is no flesh that can dwell in the presence of God, save it be through the merits, and mercy, and grace of the Holy Messiah" (v. 8). Christ laid down his life and took it up as the first to rise from the dead. Thus, he brought about the resurrection to overcome the temporal law that was broken, whereby man became fallen and mortal and thus would suffer physical death (v. 8). He made intercession for all mankind to overcome the effects of the Fall if they believed in him (v. 9).

2 Nephi 2:10–13 • Opposition in All Things

10 And because of the intercession for all, all men come unto God; wherefore, they stand in the presence of him, to be judged of him according to the truth and holiness which is in him. Wherefore, the ends of the law which the Holy One hath given, unto the inflicting of the punishment which is affixed, which punishment that is affixed is in opposition to that of the happiness which is affixed, to answer the ends of the atonement—

11 For it must needs be, that there is an opposition in all things. If not so, my first-born in the wilderness, righteousness could not be brought to pass, neither wickedness, neither holiness nor misery, neither good nor bad. Wherefore, all things must needs be a compound in one; wherefore, if it should be one body it must needs remain as dead, having no life neither death, nor corruption nor incorruption, happiness nor misery, neither sense nor insensibility.

12 Wherefore, it must needs have been created for a thing of naught; wherefore there would have been no purpose in the end of its creation. Wherefore, this thing must needs destroy the wisdom of God and his eternal purposes, and also the power, and the mercy, and the justice of God.

13 And if ye shall say there is no law, ye shall also say there is no sin. If ye shall say there is no sin, ye shall also say there is no righteousness. And if there be no righteousness there be no happiness.

And if there be no righteousness nor happiness there be no punishment nor misery. And if these things are not there is no God. And if there is no God we are not, neither the earth; for there could have been no creation of things, neither to act nor to be acted upon; wherefore, all things must have vanished away.

The Atonement is infinite. It covers all men unconditionally by bringing them back into his presence (v. 10). The condition of the atonement is whether or not they can remain in his presence. "No unclean thing can dwell with God" (1 Nephi 10:21). This doctrine is taught throughout the Book of Mormon. Alma taught that those who are unclean at the judgment bar shall suffer "even a second death, which is a spiritual death . . . he shall die as to things pertaining unto righteousness" (Alma 12:12–16), or not remain in God's presence. Samuel the Lamanite warned:

> 17 But behold, the resurrection of Christ redeemeth mankind, yea, even all mankind, and bringeth them back into the presence of the Lord.
>
> 18 Yea, and it bringeth to pass the condition of repentance, that whosoever repenteth the same is not hewn down and cast into the fire; but whosoever repenteth not is hewn down and cast into the fire; and there cometh upon them again a spiritual death, yea, a second death, for they are cut off again as to things pertaining to righteousness. [Helaman 14:17–18]

We add Moroni's testimony:

> 13 And because of the redemption of man, which came by Jesus Christ, they are brought back into the presence of the Lord; yea, this is wherein all men are redeemed, because the death of Christ bringeth to pass the resurrection, which bringeth to pass a redemption from an endless sleep, from which sleep all men shall be awakened by the power of God when the trump shall sound; and they shall come forth, both small and great, and all shall stand before his bar, being redeemed and loosed from this eternal band of death, which death is a temporal death.
>
> 14 And then cometh the judgment of the Holy One upon them; and then cometh the time that he that is filthy shall be filthy still; and

he that is righteous shall be righteous still; he that is happy shall be
happy still; and he that is unhappy shall be unhappy still. [Mormon
9:13–14]

When men come back into the presence of God, they will be judged
according to the truth and holiness of Christ and God (v. 10). Truth
alone is not the criteria for judgment, but the truth and the holiness or
sanctification the judgment brings is the criteria.

A third principle of agency is that there must be an opportunity
to choose. The wrong choices, or breaking the law, brings a punishment
which is affixed (absolute) to the law. The right choices, or keeping
the law, brings happiness which is affixed (absolute) to the atonement.
Lehi calls this final state the ends of the law, or the ends of the atonement (v. 10). If the atonement is accepted through repentance and
righteous living with eternal happiness. If the atonement is rejected
through unbelief or wrongful living there will be eternal misery. In
the pre-mortal council it was resolved:

25 And we will prove them herewith, to see if they will do all
things whatsoever the Lord their God shall command them;

26 And they who keep their first estate shall be added upon; and
they who keep not their first estate shall not have glory in the same
kingdom with those who keep their first estate; and they who keep
their second estate shall have glory added upon their heads for ever
and ever. [Abraham 3:25–26]

Having opposition in all things helps determine one's eternal nature.
One must choose righteousness or wickedness, holiness or misery,
good or bad. One cannot live eternally in both conditions. A person
becomes righteous, holy, and good or a person becomes wicked,
miserable, and bad. Thus he or she becomes "a compound in one" of
these conditions (v. 11). The purpose of the creation was to make us
happy eternal beings (v. 12). Lehi equates law with righteousness, happiness, and God. God is an eternal, righteous, happy being. Through
obeying the law his children become like him. Without the law there
would have been no God, and thus no creation, no earth and no children

(v. 13). Thus Lehi equates God with law, making them both eternal and co-equal.

2 Nephi 2:14–16 • Things to Act and Things to be Acted Upon

> 14 And now, my sons, I speak unto you these things for your profit and learning; for there is a God, and he hath created all things, both the heavens and the earth, and all things that in them are, both things to act and things to be acted upon.
>
> 15 And to bring about his eternal purposes in the end of man, after he had created our first parents, and the beasts of the field and the fowls of the air, and in fine, all things which are created, it must needs be that there was an opposition; even the forbidden fruit in opposition to the tree of life; the one being sweet and the other bitter.
>
> 16 Wherefore, the Lord God gave unto man that he should act for himself. Wherefore, man could not act for himself save it should be that he was enticed by the one or the other.

God created all things, but some things were created to act, and some things were created to be acted upon (v. 14). "In the end of man" refers to the purpose for which men were to be placed on earth. Men were placed upon the earth to act. Our first parents were Adam and Eve. They were to subdue the earth, "and have dominion over the fish of the sea, and over the fowls of the air, and over every living thing that moveth upon the earth" (Genesis 1:28). Therefore, all these things were to be acted upon. That dominion was to be a righteous dominion, but there was opposition, even the forbidden fruit in opposition to the tree of life (v. 15). As quoted above, when told of the forbidden fruit, Adam and Eve were told to "remember thou mayest choose for thyself, for it is given unto thee" (Moses 3:17). They would be accountable for how they used the earth, and how they exercised their dominion over all things upon the earth. They could not be accountable for their choices if they were not enticed by one choice or another (v. 16).

2 Nephi 2:17–19 • An Angel of God Falls from Heaven

17 And I, Lehi, according to the things which I have read, must needs suppose that an angel of God, according to that which is written, had fallen from heaven; wherefore, he became a devil, having sought that which was evil before God.

18 And because he had fallen from heaven, and had become miserable forever, he sought also the misery of all mankind. Wherefore, he said unto Eve, yea, even that old serpent, who is the devil, who is the father of all lies, wherefore he said: Partake of the forbidden fruit, and ye shall not die, but ye shall be as God, knowing good and evil.

19 And after Adam and Eve had partaken of the forbidden fruit they were driven out of the garden of Eden, to till the earth.

Lehi quotes or paraphrases from the plates of brass to show where the opposition to Adam and Eve had originated. An angel of God fell from heaven and became the devil (v. 17). He "rebelled against [God], and sought to destroy the agency of man, which I, the Lord God had given him" (Moses 4:3). As revealed to Joseph Smith:

36 And it came to pass that Adam, being tempted of the devil— for, behold, the devil was before Adam, for he rebelled against me, saying, Give me thine honor, which is my power; and also a third part of the hosts of heaven turned he away from me because of their agency;

37 And they were thrust down, and thus came the devil and his angels. [D&C 29:36–37]

Because the devil was eternally miserable, he sought the misery of all mankind (v. 18). Thus, the saying, "misery loves company." After Adam and Eve were driven out of the garden of Eden, the devil became the opposition to mankind's happiness. "And he became Satan, yea, even the devil, the father of all lies, to deceive and to blind men, and to lead them captive at his will, even as many as would not hearken unto my voice" (Moses 4:4). Lehi explains more about Adam and Eve.

2 Nephi 2:20–25 • Adam Fell that Men Might Be

20 And they have brought forth children; yea, even the family of all the earth.

21 And the days of the children of men were prolonged, according to the will of God, that they might repent while in the flesh; wherefore, their state became a state of probation, and their time was lengthened, according to the commandments which the Lord God gave unto the children of men. For he gave commandment that all men must repent; for he showed unto all men that they were lost, because of the transgression of their parents.

22 And now, behold, if Adam had not transgressed he would not have fallen, but he would have remained in the garden of Eden. And all things which were created must have remained in the same state in which they were after they were created; and they must have remained forever, and had no end.

23 And they would have had no children; wherefore they would have remained in a state of innocence, having no joy, for they knew no misery; doing no good, for they knew no sin.

24 But behold, all things have been done in the wisdom of him who knoweth all things.

25 Adam fell that men might be; and men are, that they might have joy.

In their fallen and mortal state, caused by their partaking of the fruit, Adam and Eve were able to have children, and thus became the first parents "of *all* the family of the earth" (v. 20; italics added). Wherefore, all the inhabitants of the earth are the descendants of Adam and Eve.

To fulfill the will or plan of God, Lehi explains that the children of Adam, or all the people of the earth, had their days prolonged to live upon the earth. This provided them a probationary time, or a time to be tested, and a time to be able to repent of their wrong choices while living upon the earth. This time was needed because all men were lost (fallen) because of the transgressions of their parents, Adam and Eve (v. 21). The Lord told Adam: "Inasmuch as thy children are conceived in (a world of)⁶ sin, even so when they begin to grow up, sin conceiveth in their hearts, and they taste the bitter, that they know to prize the good" (Moses 6:55).

Lehi expounded on the purpose of the fall. Had there been no fall things would have remained constant (v. 22). Therefore there would have been no death. This doctrine, and other doctrines taught by Lehi, is confirmed in the Book of Moses. Enoch taught: "Because that Adam fell, we are; and by his fall came death; and we are made partakers of misery and woe," and the Lord told Adam that the "fall bringeth death" (Moses 6:59).

Another factor of the Fall was the birth of children to Adam and Eve. Had there been no fall, "they would have had no children." Remaining "in a state of innocence" (v. 19) implies that the process of creating children was not known. However, as stated above, Alma 12:22 teaches that "Adam did fall by the partaking of the forbidden fruit," and Lehi records that children were born after they were driven out of the Garden of Eden (2:19–20). Although it says they "would" have had no children, the text supports they "could" have had no children, it being biologically impossible. Regardless, children were not born unto Adam and Eve until after the Fall. The Book of Moses does not say they could have had no children, but does sustain there being no children until after the Fall. After listening to Adam prophesying about the Fall, Eve said: "Were it not for our transgression we never should have had seed, and never should have known good and evil" (Moses 5:11).

The Fall was purposeful, and was "in the wisdom of him who knoweth all things. Adam fell that men might be; and men are, that

---

⁶ David wrote in the Psalm: "Behold I was shapen in iniquity; and in sin did my mother conceive me" (51:3). This has led to the doctrine of original sin in the Christian world, but that David was referring to a "world of sin," as interpreted above, is shown from the phrase that follows "when they begin to grow up." Also, this interpretation is sustained in a later Psalm of David's: "the wicked are estranged from the womb: they go astray as soon as they be born, speaking lies" (58:3). He does not say all children, but the wicked; and they go astray after they are born, not when they are born.

they might have joy" (vv. 24–25). The Fall was to bring mortality, and men were placed on earth "to bring to pass the immortality and eternal life of man" (Moses 1:39). Man must receive a fullness of truth by keeping the commandments of God, die, and be resurrected, or "be inseparably connected [to] receive a fulness of joy" (D&C 93:27–28, 33). Joseph Smith gave us a similar teaching: "We came to this earth that we might have a body and present it pure before God in the celestial kingdom. The great principle of happiness consists in having a body" (*TPJS*, 181). Without the Atonement, we cannot be pure before God. Lehi now teaches us this doctrine.

2 Nephi 2:26–29 • The Great Mediator of all Men

26 And the Messiah cometh in the fulness of time, that he may redeem the children of men from the fall. And because that they are redeemed from the fall they have become free forever, knowing good from evil; to act for themselves and not to be acted upon, save it be by the punishment of the law at the great and last day, according to the commandments which God hath given.

27 Wherefore, men are free according to the flesh; and all things are given them which are expedient unto man. And they are free to choose liberty and eternal life, through the great Mediator of all men, or to choose captivity and death, according to the captivity and power of the devil; for he seeketh that all men might be miserable like unto himself.

28 And now, my sons, I would that ye should look to the great Mediator, and hearken unto his great commandments; and be faithful unto his words, and choose eternal life, according to the will of his Holy Spirit;

29 And not choose eternal death, according to the will of the flesh and the evil which is therein, which giveth the spirit of the devil power to captivate, to bring you down to hell, that he may reign over you in his own kingdom.

Lehi again bears witness of the Messiah coming to redeem all men from the Fall (v. 26). Again, the fullness of time apparently refers to the earthly ministry of Christ as suggested in the comments on 2 Nephi

2:3. Because of the Atonement, men are free forever, meaning the atonement has been made for all men. However, if they are acted upon rather than act for themselves as directed by the light and truth of Christ, the law will act upon them at the last day (v. 26). The Atonement will not pay for their sins, and they will suffer spiritual death. Once more their agency is emphasized; "they are free to choose (agency) liberty and eternal life through the great mediator of all men, or to choose captivity and death according to the captivity and power of the devil" (v. 27). They may follow Christ or Satan.

Lehi desires his sons to "choose eternal life, according to the will of his Holy Spirit" (v. 28). In summary, the sons have the ability to choose. They have received the law and understand it. By making the right choices (acting by the Spirit) they will maintain their freedom and come back into his presence as the Lord had assured Lehi. He desires that the sons not follow the "will of the flesh, and the evil which is therein" (v. 29). This verse should not be interpreted to mean that the flesh itself is evil. The flesh is the avenue through which the devil tempts man, and gives him power to captivate individuals. The Fall was "the cause of all mankind becoming carnal, sensual, and devilish, knowing evil from good, subjecting themselves to the devil," and if he "persists in his own carnal nature, and goes on in the ways of sin and rebellion against God, remaineth in his fallen state and the devil hath all power over him" (Mosiah 16:3, 5). The Spirit must be our guiding light, not the temptations that come because of our flesh.

2 Nephi 2:30 • The Object, the Everlasting Welfare of your Souls

> 30 I have spoken these few words unto you all, my sons, in the last days of my probation; and I have chosen the good part, according to the words of the prophet. And I have none other object save it be the everlasting welfare of your souls. Amen.

Lehi extends his doctrinal treatise on agency, the Fall, and the Atonement to his son Jacob and to all his sons (vv. 28–30). His having "chosen the good part," suggests he has selected the most important and appropriate teachings, not saying everything that could be said about these subjects. The Prophet from whom he selected these words was Moses whose five books were "engraven on the plates of brass" (1 Nephi 5:10–11). His object was to make the welfare of children's souls the object of every righteous parent.

SACRED WRITING

Preaching which is Sacred:
2 Nephi 1:1–5, 12–27   Lehi concerning the promised land, and admonitions to his sons to awake.

Revelations which are Sacred:
2 Nephi 1:28–29   Lehi blesses Laman and Lemuel.

2 Nephi 1:30–32   Lehi blesses Zoram.

2 Nephi 2   Lehi blesses Jacob and extends the good part to all his sons.

Prophesying:
2 Nephi 1:6–12   Lehi concerning the promised land.

Doctrines Learned:

1 Nephi 1:5   The Americas are a promised land, choice above all other lands.

1 Nephi 1:6   None were brought to this land unless by the hand of the Lord.

1 Nephi 1:8   This land was kept from the knowledge of other nations lest it be overrun, and there be no place for an inheritance.

1 Nephi 1:20   If the commandments of God are kept, this land will prosper.

2 Nephi 2:4   The Spirit is the same yesterday, today, and forever.

2 Nephi 2:5–6   No man is justified by the law, redemption comes through the Holy Messiah.

2 Nephi 2:10	All men will be judged according to the truth and holiness in Christ.
2 Nephi 2:11	Opposition in all things is necessary to bring about God's eternal purposes.
2 Nephi 2:14	God created things to act and things to be acted upon.
2 Nephi 2:16	Man cannot act unless he is enticed by one source or another.
2 Nephi 2:17	The devil fell from heaven having sought evil before God.
2 Nephi 2:18–19	The devil enticed Eve. Adam and Eve were driven out of the garden.
2 Nephi 2:20	Adam and Eve brought forth all the family of the earth.
2 Nephi 2:21	This life is a probationary period for all to repent.
2 Nephi 2:22	There was no death before the Fall.
2 Nephi 2:23	There would have been no children without the Fall.
2 Nephi 2:26	The Messiah redeemed men from the Fall and makes them free.
2 Nephi 2:27	Men are free to choose eternal life or captivity and death.
2 Nephi 2:28	The flesh gives the devil power to captivate.

General Authority Quotes:

Elder Spencer W. Kimball • 2 Nephi 1:13

We have discussed elsewhere that other class of people who are basically unrepentant because they are not "doing the commandments." They are Church members who are steeped in lethargy. They neither drink nor commit the sexual sins. They do not gamble nor rob nor kill. They are good citizens and splendid neighbors, but spiritually speaking they seem to be in a long, deep sleep. They are doing nothing seriously wrong except in their failure to do the right things to earn their exaltation. To such people as this, the words of Lehi might well apply. [*Miracle of Forgiveness*, 211–12]

The Prophet Joseph Smith • 2 Nephi 2:4

The great plan of salvation is a theme that ought to occupy our strict attention, and be regarded as one of heaven's best gifts to mankind. No consideration whatever ought to deter us from showing ourselves approved in the sight of God, according to his divine requirement. Men not unfrequently forget that they are dependent upon heaven for every blessing which they are permitted to enjoy, and that for every opportunity granted them they are to give an account. [*TPJS*, 68]

First Presidency Origin of Man • 2 Nephi 2:15

"God created man in his own image, in the image of God created he him; male and female created he them."

In these plain and pointed words the inspired author of the book of Genesis made known to the world the truth concerning the origin of the human family. Moses, the prophet-historian, who was "learned" we are told, "in all the wisdom of the Egyptians," when making this important announcement, was not voicing a mere opinion. He was speaking as the mouthpiece of God, and his solemn declaration was for all time and for all people. No subsequent revelator of the truth has contradicted the great leader and law-giver of Israel. All who have since spoken by divine authority upon this theme have confirmed his simple and sublime proclamation. Nor could it be otherwise. Truth has but one source, and all revelations from heaven are harmonious one with the other.

Jesus Christ, the Son of God, is "the express image" of his Father's person (Hebrews 1:3). He walked the earth as a human being, as a perfect man, and said, in answer to a question put to him: "He that hath seen me hath seen the Father" (John 14:9). This alone ought to solve the problem to the satisfaction of every thoughtful, reverent mind. It was in this form that the Father and the Son, as two distinct personages, appeared to Joseph Smith, when, as a boy of fourteen years, he received his first vision.

The Father of Jesus Christ is our Father also. Jesus himself taught this truth, when he instructed his disciples how to pray: "Our Father which art in heaven," etc. Jesus, however, is the first born among all the sons of God—the first begotten in the spirit, and the only begotten in the flesh. He is our elder brother, and we, like him, are in the image of God. All men and women are in the similitude of the universal Father and Mother, and are literally sons and daughters of Deity.

Adam, our great progenitor, "the first man," was, like Christ, a pre-existent spirit, and, like Christ, he took upon him an appropriate body, the body of a man, and so became a "living soul." The doctrine of pre-existence pours wonderful flood of light upon the otherwise mysterious problem of man's origin. It shows that man, as a spirit, was begotten and born of heavenly parents, and reared to maturity in the eternal mansions of the Father, prior to coming upon the earth in a temporal body to undergo an experience in mortality.

The Church of Jesus Christ of Latter-day Saints, basing its belief on divine revelation, ancient and modern, proclaims man to be the direct and lineal offspring of Deity. By his Almighty power God organized the earth, and all that it contains, from spirit and element, which exist co-eternally with himself.

Man is the child of God, formed in the divine image and endowed with divine attributes, and even as the infant son of an earthly father and mother is capable in due time of becoming a man, so that undeveloped offspring of celestial parentage is capable, by experience through ages and aeons, of evolving into a God. [See *Messages of First Presidency*, 5:243–244]

Elder Delbert L. Stapley • 2 Nephi 2:15–16

The opposing forces in life are essential for our growth and development. It is required of us to recognize the powers that lead us away from the Spirit of the Lord, and to choose the path of righteousness, which will lead us back into the presence of God. As we succeed in this "tug-of-war" between the opposing forces of good and evil, we will bring joy into our lives here and earn rewards and exaltation in the life to come. [CR, April 1968, 29]

President David O. McKay • 2 Nephi 2:17–27

God is standing in the shadow of eternity, it seems to me, deploring now the inevitable results of the follies, the transgressions, and the sins of his wayward children, but we cannot blame him for these anymore than we can blame a father who might say to his son:

"There are two roads, my son, one leading to the right, one leading to the left. If you take the one to the left, it will bring success and happiness. If you take the one to the right, it will lead you to misery and unhappiness; and perhaps death, but you choose which you will. You must choose; I will not force you."

The young man starts out and, seeing the allurements and the attractiveness of the road to the right, and thinking it is a shortcut to his happiness, he concludes to take it. The father knows what will become of him. He knows that not far from that flowery path there is a mire-hole into which his boy will fall; he knows that after he struggles out of that mire-hole he will come to a slough into which he will flounder. He sees others who have chosen that path in that same slough, and he knows that in their struggle to get on dry land there will be fighting. He could see it long before the boy reached that condition, and he could, therefore, foretell it. The father loves the boy just the same and would still continue to warn him and plead for him to return to the right path.

God, too, has shown the world, through his prophets in ages gone by, that many of his people, individuals as well as nations, would choose the path that leads to misery and death, and he foretold it, but the responsibility is upon those who would not heed God's message, not upon God. But in his infinite wisdom, he will overrule these transgressors for the good of all his sons and daughters. His love for them is always manifest. [*Improvement Era*, Feb. 1964, 84–85]

Elder Howard W. Hunter • 2 Nephi 2:27

There has never been a time when man has been forced to do good or forced to obey the commandments of God. He has always been given his free choice—his free moral agency. If one looks back through the events of history, there come into view the results of the greatness of men who kept the commandments of the Lord and made the choice on his side. One also sees strewn along the wayside the ruins that stand as silent reminders of those who chose otherwise. Both had their free moral agency. [CR, April 1966, 47]

Elder Marion G. Romney • 2 Nephi 2:27

This doctrine that man is not morally responsible for his own acts, which is gaining wide acceptance in the world today, is the doctrine of the evil one. If you will read the Book of Mormon, you will be convinced of that, and you will have a defense against it if you will accept the Book of Mormon. [CR, April, 1949]

Challenges to Eternal Life:

1. Remain free from captivity by being united with the prophets in one mind and heart and by putting on the armor of righteousness (2 Nephi 2:21–23)
2. Analyze your activities for one day and see when you react and when you act. Make a commitment to seek the Spirit to help you act (2 Nephi 2:14)
3. Read your patriarchal blessing and see what doctrinal admonitions you are given, and be cognizant of where it fits into your life.
4. Choose a challenge or message from this reading, and incorporate it into your life.

Chapter Eleven

Great Covenants With Joseph

2 Nephi 3–5

*H*istorical Setting: Lehi blesses his son Joseph, the children of Laman, the children of Lemuel, and all the household of Ishmael after they arrive in the promised land (see the historical setting of chapter ten). Lehi dies and shortly the Lord warns Nephi, and all who believe in the revelations of God, to flee because his brothers seek to take his life. They travel "in the wilderness for the space of many days," and settle in a place they call Nephi and "call themselves the people of Nephi" (2 Nephi 5:6–9). Thirty years had passed away, and Lehi is commanded to make a second set of plates, the ones we are reading (2 Nephi 5:28–33). The next ten years, forty years after leaving Jerusalem, are summarized in one statement; "we had already had wars and contentions with our brethren" (2 Nephi 5:34). The history of the people was kept on the other plates.

Precepts of these Chapters:

2 Nephi 3:25 • "Hearken unto the words of . . . Nephi, and it shall be done unto thee even according to the words which I have spoken.

2 Nephi 4:34 • I will trust in thee forever, I will not put my trust in the arm of flesh; for I know that cursed is he that putteth his trust in the arm of flesh."

The words spoken unto Joseph by his father Lehi are also applicable to us because most of us also are descendants of Joseph who was sold into Egypt, either by our actual bloodline or by adoption. An outline of the words spoken by Lehi and Nephi are given in preparation for a deeper study.

OUTLINE • 2 NEPHI 3–5

➤ 3:1–3   Lehi spoke to Joseph, his last-born son, who was born in the wilderness during his greatest sorrow.

   a.   This most precious land was consecrated for him and his seed, and his brothers if they will keep the commandments (v. 2).

   b.   Joseph's seed shall not utterly be destroyed (v. 3).

➤ 3:4–6   Great covenants were made to Joseph who was sold into Egypt.

   a.   A righteous branch of his seed would be raised up, not the Messiah, but a branch to be broken off (v. 5).

   b.   The Messiah will be manifest to them in the latter days in the spirit of power (v. 5).

      1.   He will bring them out of hidden darkness unto light.

      2.   He will bring them out of captivity unto freedom.

➤ 3:7–15   A choice seer would be raised up to the fruit of Joseph's (of Egypt) seed.

   a.   He will be esteemed highly by the fruit of Joseph's loins, and do a great work to bring them to a knowledge of the covenants of the Father (v. 7).

   b.   He will be commanded to do none other work (v. 8).

   c.   He shall be great like unto Moses (v. 9).

   d.   Moses will deliver the Lord's people out of Egypt, but the seer will bring forth the Lord's word (vv. 10–12).

      1.   His word will convince them of the word already gone forth.

      2.   Those from the loins of Joseph shall write, and those from the loins of Judah shall write.

> 3. The writings shall grow together unto the confounding of false doctrines and laying down of contentions.

> 4. They will establish peace among the seed of Lehi, and bring them to a knowledge of their fathers and the Lord's covenants.

e. Out of weakness the seer will be made strong, unto the restoring of the house of Israel (v. 13).

f. Those who seek to destroy the seer shall be confounded (v. 14).

g. The seer's name shall be after his father and Joseph of Egypt, and shall bring salvation to his people as did Joseph of Egypt (v. 15).

➤ 3:16–17 Joseph was as sure concerning this seer as he was about Moses.

a. Moses to be given power in a rod (v. 17).

b. He will be given judgment in writing (v. 17).

c. He will not be mighty in speaking, but the Lord will write his law by the finger of his own hand (v. 17).

d. The Lord will make a spokesman for him (v. 17).

➤ 3:18–21 The Lord will raise up a spokesman for the seer.

a. The spokesman shall write the writings of Joseph's seed for Joseph's seed (v. 18).

b. The spokesman shall declare it (v. 18).

c. The words shall come forth as if from the dust and cry repentance (v. 19–20).

d. The words shall be made strong by the Lord (v. 21).

➤ 3:22–25 Lehi speaks to his son Joseph about the covenant to Joseph of old.

a. His son Joseph's seed shall not be destroyed because they will hearken to the words of the book (v. 23).

b. One among Joseph's (son of Lehi) seed, will rise up and

do much good both in word and deed to restore much to the house of Israel (v. 24).

   c.   Hearken to the words of Nephi and Lehi's words will be fulfilled (v. 25).

➤ 4:1–2   Nephi speaks concerning the prophecies of his father about Joseph of Egypt.

   a.   He truly prophesied concerning all his seed (v. 2).

   b.   There are not many greater prophecies (v. 2).

   c.   They are written upon the plates of brass (v. 2).

➤ 4:3–7   Lehi speaks to the sons and daughters of Laman.

   a.   The Lord promises that if you keep the commandments you will be blessed (v. 4).

   b.   Lehi knows that if you are brought up in the way you should go you will not depart from it (v. 5).

   c.   If you are cursed, the curse will be taken from you and answered upon your parents (v. 6).

   d.   The Lord will not suffer the sons and daughters to perish, but will be merciful to their seed (v. 7).

➤ 4:8–9   Lehi speaks to the sons and daughters of Lemuel.

   a.   He leaves the same blessing as upon the seed of Laman (v. 9).

   b.   They will not be destroyed but in the end they will be blessed (v. 9).

➤ 4:10   Lehi spoke to all the household of Ishmael (unrecorded).

➤ 4:11   Lehi speaks to Sam and his seed.

   a.   They shall inherit the land like Nephi.

   b.   They shall be numbered with Nephi's seed, be like them, and be blessed.

➤ 4:12   Lehi waxed old, died, and was buried.

➤ 4:13–14   Both Laman and Lemuel are angry with Nephi because of the admonitions of the Lord. Both Nephi and his father had spoken many things unto them that were written on the plates of brass.

➤ 4:15–35   Nephi writes the things of his soul, and many of the scriptures from the plates of brass.

a. He delights in the scriptures, ponders them, and writes for the profit of his children (v. 15).

b. His soul delights in things of the Lord, and he ponders on the things he has seen and heard (v. 16).

c. His heart sorrows because of his flesh, and he grieves over his iniquities (vv. 17–19).

1. He is encompassed about because of his temptations and sins.

2. He desires to rejoice, but his heart grieves over his sins.

d. He has had many great spiritual experiences (not enumerated here), but his heart weeps (vv. 20–29).

1. He slackens his strength because of his afflictions.

2. He angers because of his enemies.

e. He rejoices and asks that he may shake at the appearance of sin, that the gates of hell be shut before him, and he be encircled in the Lord's righteousness (vv. 30–33).

f. He will trust in the Lord forever, and not in the arm of flesh (v. 35).

➤ 5:1–4   Nephi cries unto the Lord because of his brethren's anger, but they seek to take his life.

a. They say they will not have him rule over them, which they feel he seeks to do (v. 3).

b. Being the ruler belongs to them because they are older (v. 3).

c. Nephi does not write all of their words (v. 4).

➤ 5:5–18   The Lord warns Nephi to take his family and depart into the wilderness.

a. Zoram, Sam, Jacob, Joseph, his sisters, and all who

believe in the revelations of God go with him (v. 6).

b. They travel many days and they settle in the place they call Nephi, and call themselves the people of Nephi (vv. 7–9).

c. They observe the commandments according to the law of Moses, and prosper exceedingly (vv. 10–11, 13).

d. Nephi brought the records and the ball or compass with them (v. 12).

e. He makes swords after the pattern of Laban's sword to defend themselves (v. 14).

f. He teaches his people to build with wood, metals, and precious ores which are in great abundance (v. 15).

g. He builds a temple after the manner of Solomon but with not as many precious things (v. 16).

h. He taught them to be industrious and labor with their own hands (v. 17).

i. They desire Nephi to be their king, but he says there should be no king (v. 18).

➤ 5:19–25   The word of the Lord was fulfilled.

a. Nephi should be their ruler and their teacher (v. 19).

b. Inasmuch as they do not hearken to the Lord's word, the people were cut off (v. 20).

c. The Lord caused a cursing and a skin of blackness to come upon the Lamanites that they might not be enticing to Nephi's people (v. 21).

d. Those who mixed with the cursed seed were also cursed (v. 22–23).

e. The Lamanites became an idle people, full of mischief, and were a scourge to stir up Nephi's people to remember the Lord (v. 24–25).

➤ 5:26–27   Nephi consecrated Jacob and Joseph to be priests and teachers. The Nephites lived in happiness.

➤ 5:28–33   Thirty years had passed away since they left Jerusalem, and Nephi kept the record on plates he had made.

a. He is commanded to make these plates (vv. 30–31).

b. He engraved that which was pleasing to God, and if his people (their seed) are pleased with the things of God, they will be pleased with these plates (v. 32).

c. The more particular history is on the other plates (v. 33).

➤ 5:34   Forty years had passed away, and the Nephites had had wars and contentions with their brethren the Lamanites.

NOTES AND COMMENTARY

Introduction: Lehi declared: "And great were the covenants of the Lord which he made unto Joseph [of Egypt]" (2 Nephi 3:4). Unfortunately, the accounts of these covenants (note they were plural) have been lost, "because of the many plain and precious things which have been taken out of the [Bible]" (1 Nephi 13:29). Fortunately, because Lehi had the plates of brass, the promise of the Lord made to Joseph of "a righteous branch of the house of Israel" being raised up in the latter days, and "A choice seer will I raise up out of the fruit of thy (Joseph of Egypt) loins" has been restored through the Book of Mormon (2 Nephi 3:5–7). We will consider what has been restored, and look forward to a further restoration of covenants, promises, and prophesies concerning Joseph of Egypt.

2 Nephi 3:1–4 • Promises to Joseph Son of Lehi

1 And now I speak unto you, Joseph, my last-born. Thou wast born in the wilderness of mine afflictions; yea, in the days of my greatest sorrow did thy mother bear thee.

2 And may the Lord consecrate also unto thee this land, which is a most precious land, for thine inheritance and the inheritance of thy seed with thy brethren, for thy security forever, if it so be that ye shall keep the commandments of the Holy One of Israel.

3 And now, Joseph, my last-born, whom I have brought out of the wilderness of mine afflictions, may the Lord bless thee forever, for thy seed shall not utterly be destroyed.

4 For behold, thou art the fruit of my loins; and I am a descendant

of Joseph who was carried captive into Egypt. And great were the covenants of the Lord which he made unto Joseph.

As with Jacob, Lehi's other son born in the wilderness, only a few verses are directly referring to Joseph, the last born in the wilderness. There are two major points directed to Joseph: (1) may the Lord consecrate the promised land unto him and his seed forever; and (2) the promise that his seed would not be destroyed. As cited earlier, "the knowledge of a Savior" was to come "to the Nephites, and the Jacobites, and the Josephites, and the Zoramites, through the testimony of their fathers (The Book of Mormon)" and to the Lamanites (D&C 3:16–17), confirming that many of Joseph's seed are today among the people we call the Lamanites.

Lehi spoke of himself and his son Joseph being descendants of Joseph who was carried captive into Egypt; and then, as mentioned above, declares that "great were the covenants of the Lord which he made unto Joseph" (v. 4). As shown to Nephi in vision, the covenants made to Joseph would be among the "many covenants of the Lord have they (that great and abominable church) taken away" (1 Nephi 13:26). The Prophet Joseph Smith restored much of what Lehi quotes, and more in his inspired translation of Genesis 50. These restorations will be cited as they pertain to the following verses. Thus there are two witnesses that established the validity of the promises made to Joseph of Egypt. The text from Lehi's blessing to his son Joseph gives the evidence that these covenants were to be fulfilled in the latter days.

2 Nephi 3:5–6 (JST, Genesis 50:24–26)
• Promises to Joseph of Egypt

5 Wherefore, Joseph truly saw our day. And he obtained a promise of the Lord, that out of the fruit of his loins the Lord God would raise up a righteous branch unto the house of Israel; not the Messiah, but a branch which was to be broken off, nevertheless, to be remembered in the covenants of the Lord that the Messiah should be made manifest unto

24 And Joseph said unto his brethren, I die, and go unto my fathers; and I go down to my grave with joy. The God of father Jacob be with you, to deliver you out of affliction in the days of your bondage; for the Lord hath visited me, and I have obtained a promise of the Lord, that out of the fruit of my loins, the Lord God will raise up a righteous branch out of my

them in the latter days, in the spirit of power, unto the bringing of them out of darkness unto light—yea, out of hidden darkness and out of captivity unto freedom.

6 For Joseph truly testified, saying: A seer shall the Lord my God raise up, who shall be a choice seer unto the fruit of my loins. [2 Nephi 3:5–6]

loins; and unto thee, whom my father Jacob hath named Israel, a prophet; [not the Messiah who is called Shilo] and this prophet shall deliver my people out of Egypt in the days of thy bondage.

25 And it shall come to pass that they shall be scattered again; and a branch shall be broken off, and shall be carried into a far country; nevertheless they shall be remembered in the covenants of the Lord, when the Messiah cometh; for he shall be made manifest unto them in the latter days, in the Spirit of power; and shall bring them out of darkness into light; out of hidden darkness, and out of captivity unto freedom.

26 A seer shall the Lord my God raise up, who shall be a choice seer unto the fruit of my loins. [JST, Genesis 50:24–26]

All that follows "And Joseph said unto his brethren, I die, and" in JST, Genesis 50:24–26 was restored by the Prophet Joseph. A comparison of Lehi's text and the JST text shows that Lehi was only quoting what was applicable to his people. The first part of the covenant made to Joseph of Egypt was that "the Lord God would raise up a righteous branch unto the house of Israel, not the Messiah, but a branch to be broken off" (v. 5). This righteous branch of the house of Israel was the same as the blessing upon Joseph of Egypt by his father Jacob quoted under the commentary of 1 Nephi 7:2–5. "Joseph is a fruitful bough, even a fruitful bough by a well; whose branches run over the wall" (Genesis 49:22). The Lord later confirmed to Jacob, son of Lehi, that the Nephites were the righteous branch promised to Joseph of Egypt. "Wherefore, thus saith the Lord, I have led this people forth out of the land of Jerusalem, by the power of mine arm, that I might raise up unto me a righteous branch from the fruit of the loins of Joseph" (Jacob 2:25). About five hundred years later Ammon, the son of King Mosiah, identified the Nephite people as "a branch of the tree of Israel, and has been lost from its body in a strange land" (Alma 26:36).

Two promises were given to this righteous branch of Israel. Through the Messiah being manifest to them in the latter days, they were to be brought "out of darkness unto light," and they were to be brought "out of captivity unto freedom" (v. 5). The JST, Genesis 50:25 contains the two promises. Being brought out of darkness unto light has come and will continue to come through the restoration of the fullness of the gospel among them. When the angel Moroni appeared to the boy Joseph Smith, the early morning of September 22, 1823; he "said that the fullness of the everlasting Gospel was contained in [The Book of Mormon], as delivered by the Savior to the ancient inhabitants [of America]" (JS—History, 1:34). In a revelation to Joseph Smith on the day of the organization of the Church, the Lord declared that he had given Joseph power "to translate the Book of Mormon," and that it contains "the fulness of the gospel of Jesus Christ to the Gentiles and to the Jews also" (D&C 20:8–9; see also 27:5; 42:12). Their being brought out of captivity unto freedom seems to be a political freedom and will be discussed later in the chapter.

The second part of the covenant to Joseph of Egypt stated that in the last days the Lord would raise up a choice seer from the loins of Joseph, a choice seer unto the fruit of Joseph's (of Egypt) loins (v. 6). The Lord said more about this seer than of the righteous branch. This is probably because the seer was to be the Lord's instrument in bringing about the spiritual delivery from darkness unto light. The spiritual delivery was to take place before the political delivery. As recorded in the Book of Mormon and the JST, Genesis 50 text, there are nine descriptions of the choice seer in Joseph's prophecy. All of the nine descriptions fit the Prophet Joseph Smith, thus verifying his being the seer spoken of by Joseph of Egypt. The nine will now be considered.

2 Nephi 3:7–8 (JST, Genesis 50:27–28)
• The Seer Esteemed Highly

7 Yea, Joseph truly said: Thus saith the Lord unto me: A choice seer will I raise up out of the fruit of thy loins; and he shall be esteemed highly among the fruit of thy loins.

27 Thus saith the Lord God of my fathers unto me, A choice seer will I raise up out of the fruit of thy loins, and he shall be esteemed highly among the fruit of thy loins; and unto

And unto him will I give commandment that he shall do a work for the fruit of thy loins, his brethren, which shall be of great worth unto them, even to the bringing of them to the knowledge of the covenants which I have made with thy fathers.

8 And I will give unto him a commandment that he shall do none other work, save the work which I shall command him. And I will make him great in mine eyes; for he shall do my work. [2 Nephi 3:7–8]

him will I give commandment that he shall do a work for the fruit of thy loins, his brethren.

28 And he shall bring them to the knowledge of the covenants which I have made with thy fathers; and he shall do whatsoever work I shall command him. [JST, Genesis 50:27–28]

The differences between the 2 Nephi text and the JST may be because Joseph Smith had not completed his work on the JST text, or perhaps Lehi was paraphrasing and adding emphasis on the fulfillment among his people. As noted above, Lehi did not always quote the complete text.

The fruit of Joseph's loins is divided into two major groups today. The first group is those who were scattered "among all nations, like as corn [wheat] is sifted in a sieve" (Amos 9:9), but have been gathered out as were the first generation of Church members, "the wheat from among the tares." Of these members the Lord said, "the priesthood hath continued through the lineage of your fathers—For ye are lawful heirs, according to the flesh" (D&C 86:7–9). The second group is those known to the members of the Church today as the Lamanites or the American Indians. Both of these groups have confirmed their reverence for Joseph Smith.

Typical of the esteem many early members of the Church held for Joseph Smith is the testimony of Brigham Young, Joseph's successor as president of the Church:

> I honor and revere the name of Joseph Smith. I delight to hear it; I love it. I love his doctrine. What I have received from the Lord, I have received by Joseph Smith; he was the instrument made use of. If I drop him, I must drop these principles; for they have not been revealed, declared, or explained by any other man since the days of the Apostles. If I lay down the Book of Mormon, I shall have to deny that Joseph is a Prophet; and if I lay down the doctrine and cease to

preach the gathering of Israel and the building up of Zion, I must lay down the Bible; and, consequently I might as well go home as undertake to preach without these three items.

I felt like shouting Hallelujah, all the time, when I think that I ever knew Joseph Smith, the Prophet whom the Lord raised up and ordained, and to whom he gave the keys and power to build up the kingdom of God on earth and sustain it.[7]

After Joseph's martyrdom, Elder John Taylor wrote: "Joseph Smith, the Prophet and seer of the Lord, has done more, save Jesus only, for the salvation of men in this world, than any other man that ever lived in it" (D&C 135:3). Such accolades as these, representative of thousands of others, have led some to accuse the Latter-day Saints of worshipping Joseph Smith. To that accusation the Church answers with an emphatic no—we do not worship him, but we reverence him as the people of Moses' time reverenced Moses, or the people of Abraham's time reverenced Abraham. The reverence given to Joseph certainly fulfills the prophetic words of the Lord to Joseph of Egypt: "He shall be esteemed highly among the fruit of thy loins" (v. 7).

The esteem of Joseph Smith among the Lamanites, the other major group of descendants of Joseph of Egypt, was not widespread early because Joseph did not have a lot of association with them. However, the following incident shows how the Lord was working with the Lamanites to acquaint them with him so he could instruct them.

The Indian chiefs remained at Nauvoo until the Prophet returned and had his trial. During their stay they had a talk with Hyrum Smith in the basement of the Nauvoo House. Wilford Woodruff and some of the others were present. They were not free to talk, and did not want to communicate their feelings until they could see the Prophet.

At length, on the 2nd day of July, 1843, President Smith and several of the Twelve met those chiefs in the courtroom, and about twenty of the elders. The following is a synopsis of the conversation which took place as given by the interpreter: The Indian orator arose and asked the Prophet if the men who were present were all his friends.

---

[7] *Discourses of Brigham Young*, sel. John A. Widtsoe [1941], 458.

Answer— "Yes."

He then said, "We as a people have long been distressed and oppressed. We have been driven from our lands many times. We have been wasted away by wars, until there are but few of us left. The white man has hated us and shed our blood, until it has appeared as though there would soon be no Indians left. We have talked to the Great Spirit, and the Great Spirit has talked to us. We have asked the Great Spirit to save us and let us live; and the Great Spirit has told us that he has raised up a great Prophet, chief, and friend, who would do us great good and tell us what to do; and the Great Spirit has told us that you are the man (pointing to the Prophet Joseph). We have now come a great way to see you, and hear your words, and to have you tell us what to do. Our horses have become poor traveling, and we are hungry. We will now wait and hear your word.

The Spirit of God rested upon the Lamanites, especially the orator. Joseph was much affected and shed tears. He arose and said unto them, "I have heard your words. They are true. The Great Spirit has told you the truth. I am your friend and brother, and I wish to do you good. Your fathers were once a great people. They worshipped the Great Spirit. The Great Spirit did them good. He was their friend; but they left the Great Spirit, and would not hear his words or keep them. The Great Spirit left them, and they began to kill one another, and they have been poor and afflicted until now.

The Great Spirit has given me a book, and told me that you will soon be blessed again. The Great Spirit will soon begin to talk with you and your children. This is the book which your fathers made. I wrote upon it (showing them the Book of Mormon). This tells what you will have to do. I now want you to begin to pray to the Great Spirit. I want you to make peace with one another, and do not kill any more Indians; it is not good. Do not kill white men; it is not good; but ask the Great Spirit for what you want, and it will not be long before the Great Spirit will bless you, and you will cultivate the earth and build good houses like white men. We will give you something to eat and to take home with you."

When the Prophet's words were interpreted to the chiefs, they all said it was good. The chief asked, "How many moons would it be before the Great Spirit would bless them?" He (Joseph) told them, not a great many.

At the close of the interview, Joseph had an ox killed for them, and they were furnished with some more horses, and they went home satisfied and contented.[8]

Joseph Smith certainly brought those of scattered Israel and the Lamanites, both of the seed of Joseph of Egypt, to a knowledge of the covenants the Lord had made with their fathers.

Joseph of Egypt prophesied that the seer would do no other work but what was commanded him (v. 8). Joseph Smith was commanded:

7 For thou shalt devote all thy service in Zion; and in this thou shalt have strength.

8 Be patient in afflictions, for thou shalt have many; but endure them, for, lo, I am with thee, even unto the end of thy days.

9 And in temporal labors thou shalt not have strength, for this is not thy calling. Attend to thy calling and thou shalt have wherewith to magnify thine office, and to expound all scriptures, and continue in laying on of the hands and confirming the churches. [D&C 24:7–9]

Joseph Smith fits the second characteristic foretold by Joseph of Egypt.

Joseph of Egypt also said the seer would be made great in the Lord's eyes (v. 8). Joseph Smith's greatness is shown by the revelations the Lord gave concerning him. The Church was to "give heed unto all his words and commandments which he shall give unto you as he receiveth them, walking in all holiness before me; For his word ye shall receive, as if from mine own mouth, in all patience and faith" (D&C 21:4–5). Oliver Cowdery was told: no one shall be appointed to receive commandments and revelations in this church excepting my servant Joseph Smith, Jun., for he receiveth them even as Moses. (D&C 28:2; see also 43:2–4). The Lord further promised Joseph Smith: "the keys of this kingdom shall never be taken from you, while thou art in the world, neither in the world to come; Nevertheless, through you shall

---

[8] *HC*, 5:479–81.

the oracles be given to another, yea, even unto the church" (D&C 90:3–4). In this promise, Joseph Smith is designated as the head of what Paul calls "the dispensation of the fulness of times" when God will "gather together in one all things in Christ, both which are in heaven, and which are on earth" (Ephesians 1:10). Joseph Smith is thus still doing the Lord's work behind the veil. As Brigham Young taught: "it is his mission to see that all the children of men in this last dispensation are saved, that can be, through the redemption. . . . He was foreordained in eternity to preside over this last dispensation" (*JD*, 7:289–90).

2 Nephi 3:9–10 (JST, Genesis 50:29)
• He Shall be Great Like Moses

9 And he shall be great like unto Moses, whom I have said I would raise up unto you, to deliver my people, O house of Israel.

10 And Moses will I raise up, to deliver thy people out of the land of Egypt. [2 Nephi 3:9–10]

29 And he shall be great like unto him whom I have said I would raise up unto you, to deliver my people, O house of Israel, out of the land of Egypt; for a seer will I raise up to deliver my people out of the land of Egypt; and he shall be called Moses. And by this name he shall know that he is of thy house; for he shall be nursed by the king's daughter, and shall be called her son. [JST, Genesis 50:29]

The covenants made to Joseph of Egypt also included the children of Israel being led out of Egypt by Moses. The fulfillment of this covenant is recorded in the present-day Bible in the book of Exodus. JST Genesis 50 gives more detail about Moses. Again it is obvious that Lehi is being selective in his quoting from the plates of brass, including only those things pertinent to the seer of the latter days. Joseph Smith was great like Moses as a few comparisons below will illustrate.

Joseph Smith "was called of God, and ordained an apostle of Jesus Christ, to be the first elder [head] of this [latter-day] church" (D&C 20:2). The Lord revealed that "no one shall be appointed to receive commandments and revelations in this church excepting my servant Joseph Smith, Jun., *for he receiveth them even as Moses*" (D&C 28:2;

italics added). He was "ordained President of the High Priesthood" (D&C 75 section heading). "The duty of the President of the office of the High Priesthood is to preside over the whole church, *and to be like unto Moses*—Behold, here is wisdom; yea, to be a seer, a revelator, a translator, and a prophet, having all the gifts of God which he bestows upon the head of the church" (D&C 107:91–92; italics added). Moses "saw God face to face, and he talked with him" (Moses 1:2). Joseph "saw two Personages, whose brightness and glory defy all description, . . . One of them spake unto me, calling me by name and said, pointing to the other—*This is My Beloved Son. Hear Him*! . . . I asked the Personages . . . I was answered [he talked with them]" (JS—H 1:17–18). Moses was told, "I have a work for thee, Moses, my son" (Moses 1:6). The angel Moroni told Joseph: "God had a work for me to do" (JS—H 1:33). Moses had a vision to prepare him to write Genesis, and at the end of the vision was told:

> 40 And now, Moses, my son, I will speak unto thee concerning this earth upon which thou standest; and thou shalt write the things which I shall speak.
>
> 41 And in a day when the children of men shall esteem my words as naught and take many of them from the book which thou shalt write, behold, I will raise up another like unto thee; and they shall be had again among the children of men—among as many as shall believe. (Moses 1:40–41)

After the vision, the Lord told Moses: "Behold, I reveal unto you concerning this heaven, and this earth; write the things which I speak" (Moses 2:1). Joseph Smith was the one raised up to give Moses' words "again to the children of men." Joseph was commanded to make an inspired translation of the Bible:

> 18 And I have given unto him [Joseph Smith] the keys of the mystery of those things which have been sealed, even things which were from the foundation of the world, and the things which shall come from this time until the time of my coming, if he abide in me, and if not, another will I plant in his stead.
>
> 19 Wherefore, watch over him that his faith fail not, and it shall be given by the Comforter, the Holy Ghost, that knoweth all things.

20 And a commandment I give unto thee—that thou shalt write for him; and the scriptures shall be given, even as they are in mine own bosom, to the salvation of mine own elect; [D&C 35:18–20]

The "Joseph Smith Translation" was the result of this commandment, part of which is the Book of Moses now published in the Pearl of Great Price.

Parallel	Moses	Joseph Smith
Receive revelation and commandments	Exodus 19:5–6	D&C 28:2
President of the high priesthood	Num. 12:6–8; Acts 7:38	D&C 107:91–92
Saw God face to face	Moses 1:22; Exod. 6:2–3	JS—H 1:17–18
God had a work for him to do	Moses 1:6	JS—H 1:31
Write the things God spoke	Moses 1:40–41	D&C 35:18–20
Deliver the Lord's people	Moses 1:26; Exod. 12	D&C 35:25
Given a spokesman	Exodus 4:14–16	D&C 100:9

Figure 7. Parallel between Moses and Joseph Smith

The list could go on, but the above comparisons are sufficient to establish the parallel between the two prophets, and sustain the third characteristic of the choice seer as fitting Joseph Smith. Joseph of Egypt lived a few hundred years before Moses, and thousands of years before Joseph Smith, but both had similar experiences.

2 Nephi 3:11–12 (JST, Genesis 50:30–31)
• Power to Bring Forth

11 But a seer will I raise up out of the fruit of thy loins; and unto him will I give power to bring forth my word unto the seed of thy loins—and not to the bringing forth my word only, saith the Lord, but to the convincing them of my word, which shall have already

30 And again, a seer will I raise up out of the fruit of thy loins, and unto him will I give power to bring forth my word unto the seed of thy loins; and not to the bringing forth of my word only, saith the Lord, but to the convincing them of my word, which shall have

gone forth among them.

12 Wherefore, the fruit of thy loins shall write; and the fruit of the loins of Judah shall write; and that which shall be written by the fruit of thy loins, and also that which shall be written by the fruit of the loins of Judah, shall grow together, unto the confounding of false doctrines and laying down of contentions, and establishing peace among the fruit of thy loins, and bringing them to the knowledge of their fathers in the latter days, and also to the knowledge of my covenants, saith the Lord. [2 Nephi 3:11–12]

already gone forth among them in the last days;

31 Wherefore the fruit of thy loins shall write, and the fruit of the loins of Judah shall write; and that which shall be written by the fruit of thy loins, and also that which shall be written by the fruit of the loins of Judah, shall grow together unto the confounding of false doctrines, and laying down of contentions, and establishing peace among the fruit of thy loins, and bringing them to a knowledge of their fathers in the latter days; and also to the knowledge of my covenants, saith the Lord. [JST, Genesis 50:30–31]

The JST Genesis 50 text begins with "And again" instead of the Second Nephi "But." Both in context are a comparison made to Moses, and these differences do not change the message. The word of the Lord that the seer was to bring forth to the seed of Joseph of Egypt (v. 11) was, of course, the Book of Mormon. That this record would also convince them of the word "which shall have already gone forth among them" (v. 11), being the Bible is sustained by revelation. The Lord revealed to the Prophet Joseph that one of the primary purposes of the Book of Mormon was to prove "to the world that the holy scriptures [the Bible] are true" (D&C 20:11). This also supports that the fourth description of the seer is the Prophet Joseph Smith.

Joseph of Egypt was further told that the writings of the fruit of [Joseph's] loins, and the writings of the fruit of the loins of Judah would grow together in four ways: (1) confounding of false doctrines and laying down of contentions; (2) establishing peace among the fruit of thy loins; (3) bringing them to the knowledge of their fathers in the latter days; and (4) bringing them to the knowledge of the Lord's covenants (v. 12). The converts to the Lord and his Church among the Gentiles or the Lamanites, especially those in Central and South America, exemplify the four ways the seed of Joseph and Judah growing together. As the Bible and the Book of Mormon are studied together, the false doctrines are corrected, and interpretations of scriptures are no longer argued. We become brothers and sisters in the gospel. We love and serve each other. We learn of their ancestors, and we learn from where they originated. Last of all we both learn that we are of the house of Israel and that we are the covenant people of the Lord. The Bible and the Book of Mormon compliment and supplement each other, and as Ezekiel prophesied, they "become one in [our] hand" (Ezekiel 37:17, 19).

The prophecy of Joseph of Egypt is similar to Ezekiel's well known "two sticks" prophecy partially quoted above. It is possible that Joseph's prophecy was lost among the Jews, which would explain why a similar prophecy was given to Ezekiel. Jeremiah, whose ministry was at this time, speaks of "the false pens of the scribes worketh for falsehoods" (Jeremiah 8:8).[9]

As time passes, this prophecy will be fulfilled more and more as the Bible and the Book of Mormon is studied together. The work of Joseph Smith started all of this.

2 Nephi 3:13–15 (JST, Genesis 50: 32–33)
• He Shall be Made Strong

13 And out of weakness he shall be made strong, in that day when my work shall commence among all my people, unto the restoring thee, O house of Israel, saith the Lord.

14 And thus prophesied Joseph, saying: Behold, that seer will the Lord bless; and they that seek to destroy him shall be confounded; for this promise, which I have obtained of the Lord, of the fruit of my loins, shall be fulfilled. Behold, I am sure of the fulfilling of this promise;

32 And out of weakness shall he be made strong, in that day when my work shall go forth among all my people, which shall restore them, who are of the house of Israel, in the last days.

33 And that seer will I bless, and they that seek to destroy him shall be confounded; for this promise I give unto you; for I will remember you from generation to generation; and his name shall be called Joseph, and it shall be

---

[9] The wording of Jeremiah quoted above is from the "marginal readings" or other possible translations of the traditional KJV Bible. Other translations of the Bible support the marginal reading. The Revised Standard Version renders it "the false pens of the scribes has made it into a lie." The New International Version states; "the lying pen of the scribes has handled it falsely."

15 And his name shall be called after me; and it shall be after the name of his father. And he shall be like unto me; for the thing, which the Lord shall bring forth by his hand, by the power of the Lord shall bring my people unto salvation. [2 Nephi 3:13–15]

after the name of his father; and he shall be like unto you; for the thing which the Lord shall bring forth by his hand shall bring my people unto salvation. [JST, Genesis 50:32–33]

Lehi quotes or paraphrases the end of verse thirteen: "unto the restoring thee, O house of Israel, saith the Lord." The JST account says: "Which shall restore them, who are of the house of Israel, in the last days" (v. 32). Lehi was speaking to the house of Israel, his people. Joseph Smith probably clarified the audience and the time because he was speaking primarily to the Gentiles and the House of Israel scattered among them in the latter days. Joseph was making the text more understandable, not necessarily correcting the text.

Joseph Smith III asked his mother, Emma Smith, if it was possible that his father had written the Book of Mormon and then dictated it to scribes. Emma said: "Joseph Smith could neither write nor dictate a coherent and well worded letter, let alone dictating a book like the Book of Mormon, and though I was an active participant in the scenes that transpired, and was present during the translation of the plates, and had cognizance of things as they transpired, it is a marvel to me, 'a marvel and a wonder,' as much so as to anyone else."[10]

While Emma describes the weakness Joseph had at the beginning of his ministry (v. 13), the growth and strength he gained through the blessings of the Lord are shown in the Doctrine and Covenants 121, 122, and 123. These three sections are excerpts from a letter he wrote in March 1839 while in Liberty Jail, Missouri, under extreme physical conditions. The full letter is recorded in the History of the Church 3:289–300, and both the sections in the Doctrine and Covenants and the full letter are too long to be quoted here, but they further exemplify

---

[10] The Saint's Advocate Oct. 1879, as quoted by Francis W. Kirkham, *A New Witness for Christ in America*, 2 vols. Independence, Mo., Press of Zion's Printing and Publishing Co. [1951] 1:195.

the strength Joseph attained. President Joseph Fielding Smith called this letter "one of the greatest letters that was ever penned by man."[11] It is really one of the great pieces of literature of this generation, especially when the conditions under which it was written are considered.

According to Oliver Cowdery, Joseph Smith's growth from weakness to spiritual strength also fulfills biblical prophecy. Oliver said that the angel Moroni told Joseph Smith that his work would fulfill the scripture: "God has chosen the foolish things of the world to confound the things which are mighty."[12] The wording of this scripture is a slight variation of 1 Corinthians 1:27. Joseph Smith certainly fulfilled this scripture as well as the fifth prophetic description of the seer given by Joseph of Egypt.

The promise of the seer's enemies being confounded (v. 14) was reiterated to Joseph Smith in a revelation to him in December 1831, following the publication of some newspaper articles by Ezra Booth, who had apostatized. The revelation read: "If any man lift his voice against you he shall be confounded in mine own due time" (D&C 71:10). The following example is just one of many of those times when Joseph's enemies were confounded.

> On July 8, 1838, Joseph Smith received a revelation calling the twelve on a mission to Great Britain. The revelation said: "Let them take leave of my saints in the city of Far West, on the twenty-sixth day of April next, on the building-spot of my house, saith the Lord." (D&C 118:5). Wilford Woodruff, one of the newly called members of the Twelve Apostles records: "On the morning of the 26th of April, 1839, notwithstanding the threats of our enemies that the revelation which was to be fulfilled this day should not be fulfilled; notwith-

---

[11] Joseph Fielding Smith, *Church History and Modern Revelation*, 2 vols. [1951], I:195.

[12] *Messenger and Advocate*, Feb. 1835, 79. Joseph recorded several scriptures that the angel Moroni told him were soon to be fulfilled, and then recorded: "He quoted many other passages of scripture, and offered many explanations which cannot be mentioned here" (JS—History 1:36–41). Oliver's article was written to inform the Church members of some of the other scriptures that were quoted by the angel.

standing ten thousand of the Saints had been driven out of the state by the edict of the governor; and notwithstanding the Prophet Joseph with his brother Hyrum, with other leading men, were in the hands of the enemies in chains and in prison, we moved on to the temple grounds in the city of Far West, held a council, and fulfilled the revelation and commandment given to us."[13]

As Joseph of Egypt prophesied, the sixth description of the seer, those that seek to destroy the choice seer would be destroyed (v. 14) fits Joseph Smith.

The seventh description of the choice seer also fits Joseph Jr., and his father Joseph Smith Sr. However, more important than the names coinciding is the similarity of the mission of Joseph of Egypt and Joseph Smith Jr. Just as Joseph of Egypt had preserved the house of Israel in Egypt so his family could later return to their promised land, Joseph Smith brought forth the Book of Mormon, which has been the means of gathering, or preserving, millions of Joseph of Egypt's descendants out of the Gentile nations to occupy the land given to "a remnant of the house of Joseph . . . the land of [their] inheritance" (3 Nephi 15:12–13). As declared in the Doctrine and Covenants, and confirmed by patriarchal blessings, those gathered in the latter days are of the house of Israel, and particularly of Ephraim and Manasseh, the sons of Joseph. The Lord revealed, in December 1832, that Church members had the priesthood "through the lineage of your fathers—For ye are lawful heirs, according to the flesh, and have been hid from the world with Christ in God" (D&C 86:8–9). In March 1838 Joseph Smith said regarding the rod spoken of in Isaiah 11:1:

> 4 Behold, thus saith the Lord: It is a servant in the hands of Christ, who is partly a descendant of Jesse as well as of Ephraim, or of the house of Joseph, on whom there is laid much power.
>
> 5 What is the root of Jesse spoken of in the 10th verse of the 11th chapter?

---

[13] Matthias F. Cowley, *Wilford Woodruff, History of His Life and Labors* [1970], 101.

> 6 Behold, thus saith the Lord, it is a descendant of Jesse, as well as of Joseph, unto whom rightly belongs the priesthood, and the keys of the kingdom, for an ensign, and for the gathering of my people in the last days. [D&C 113:4–6]

Although Joseph, in his modesty, did not identify himself as the rod or the root spoken of by Isaiah, he was that person. He was given "power from on high, by the means which were before prepared, to translate the Book of Mormon" (D&C 20:8), and "the keys of the kingdom [were] given unto [him]; which kingdom is coming forth for the last time (D&C 90:2). Joseph further interpreted: "Put on thy strength O Zion" (Isaiah 52:1) as "the authority of the priesthood, which she, Zion, has a right to by lineage" (D&C 113:8). The Lord further revealed that those [of the house of Israel] in the north countries " shall bring forth their rich treasures unto the children of Ephraim, my servants [Church members]."

> 31 And the boundaries of the everlasting hills shall tremble at their presence.
>
> 32 And there shall they fall down and be crowned with glory, even in Zion, by the hands of the servants of the Lord, even the children of Ephraim.
>
> 33 And they shall be filled with songs of everlasting joy.
>
> 34 Behold, this is the blessing of the everlasting God upon the tribes of Israel, and the richer blessing upon the head of Ephraim and his fellows. [D&C 133:30–34]

Jehovah made a promise to Abraham that the "right [of the priesthood] shall continue in thee, and in thy seed after thee (that is to say, the literal seed, or the seed of the body) shall all the families of the earth be blessed, even with the blessings of the gospel, which are the blessings of salvation, even of life eternal" (Abraham 2:11). "And as I (the Lord) said unto Abraham concerning the kindreds of the earth, even so I say unto my servant Joseph: In thee and in thy seed shall the kindred of the earth be blessed" (D&C 124:58). Joseph Smith and many

Church members were and are literal descendants of Abraham, Joseph of Egypt, and his son Ephraim.[14]

There is also a parallel between Jacob, the father of Joseph who was sold into Egypt, and Joseph Smith Sr., after whom Joseph the seer was named (v. 15). Both were patriarchs and gave blessings to their posterity. Jacob blessed Ephraim and Manasseh, sons of Joseph (Genesis 48), and his sons (Genesis 49). The seer Joseph Smith "conferred upon Joseph Smith, Sen., the Office and Priesthood of Patriarch of the Church" (*TPJS*, 38). Joseph the Seer taught: "Wherever the Church of Christ is established in the earth, there should be a Patriarch for the benefit of the posterity of the Saints, as it was with Jacob in giving his patriarchal blessing unto his sons" (*TPJS*, 151).

2 Nephi 3:16–18 (JST, Genesis 50:34–35)
• A Spokesman for Moses and the Seer

16 Yea, thus prophesied Joseph: I am sure of this thing, even as I am sure of the promise of Moses; for the Lord hath said unto me, I will preserve thy seed forever.

17 And the Lord hath said: I will raise up a Moses; and I will give power unto him in a rod; and I will give judgment unto him in writing. Yet I will not loose his tongue, that he shall speak much, for I will not make him mighty in speaking. But I will write unto him my law, by the finger of mine own hand; and I will make a spokesman for him.

18 And the Lord said unto me also: I will raise up unto the fruit of thy loins; and I will make for him a spokesman. And I, behold, I will give unto him that he shall write the writing of the fruit of thy loins, unto the fruit

34 And the Lord sware unto Joseph that he would preserve his seed for ever, saying, I will raise up Moses, and a rod shall be in his hand, and he shall gather together my people, and he shall lead them as a flock, and he shall smite the waters of the Red Sea with his rod.

35 And he shall have judgment, and shall write the word of the Lord. And he shall not speak many words, for I will write unto him my law by the finger of mine own hand. And I will make a spokesman for him, and his name shall be called Aaron.

[JST, Genesis 50:34–35]

---

[14] For a fuller treatise of Church members being of the literal seed of Ephraim and Manasseh see R. Wayne Shute, Monte S. Nyman, and Randy L. Bott, *Ephraim, Chosen of the Lord,* 1999.

of thy loins; and the spokesman of thy loins
shall declare it. [2 Nephi 3:16–18]

Again, Lehi is apparently paraphrasing the words of Joseph of
Egypt since the JST prophecy is more complete. The JST speaks of
Moses gathering and leading the Israelites, Moses smiting the Red Sea,
and it names Aaron as the spokesman for Moses. Lehi probably did
not include them because Nephi had testified of them before (1 Nephi
4:1–2; 17:23–26); and possibly he had also, since he spoke "many more
things which [Nephi did] not write in this book" (1 Nephi 10:15).

Joseph of Egypt lived several hundred years before Moses (about
1700 B.C. vs. 1400–1200 B.C.). Thus he foretold of two great leaders
who would deliver the house of Israel. What Moses did is now biblical
history, and is recorded in the book of Exodus. It is verified in the New
Testament and in the Book of Mormon. Joseph Smith was given many
blessings similar to Moses as discussed above, but two more of Moses'
blessings are mentioned here: having power in a rod and the Lord
writing unto him his law. Associated with both of these blessings, the
Lord made a spokesman for him (v. 17). The name of the spokesman
was Aaron (v. 34). Joseph Smith had these blessings as well.

The spokesman for Joseph Smith, the seer, was to "write the
writings of the fruit of [Joseph of Egypt's], unto the fruit of [Joseph
of Egypt's] loins; and the spokesman of [Joseph of Egypt's] loins shall
declare it" (v. 18). While there are other opinions, the spokesman here,
in the writer's opinion, was Oliver Cowdery. The Lord told Isaiah that
he would say to "the man that was not learned [Joseph Smith] . . . thou
shalt read the words which I shall give unto thee" (2 Nephi 27:19–20;
JST, Isaiah 29:20). In the translation process, Joseph read the words
given to him by revelation; and, as Oliver later testified, "I wrote with
my own pen the entire Book of Mormon [save a few pages], as it fell
from the lips of the Prophet Joseph Smith, as he translated by the gift
and power of God" (*HC*, 1:128).

Moses was to be given power in a rod, and Aaron was also granted
this power. As directed by the Lord, "Aaron cast down his rod before

Pharaoh, and his servants, and it became a serpent" (Exodus 7:10). Oliver was given "the spirit of revelation" (D&C 8:1–5), and also the gift of Aaron:

> 6 Now this is not all thy gift; for you have another gift, which is the gift of Aaron; behold, it has told you many things;
>
> 7 Behold, there is no other power, save the power of God, that can cause this gift of Aaron to be with you.
>
> 8 Therefore, doubt not, for it is the gift of God; and you shall hold it in your hands, and do marvelous works; and no power shall be able to take it away out of your hands, for it is the work of God (D&C 8:6–8).

The ability to hold the gift in his hands tells us it was an instrument of some kind. Although we do not know to what instrument the Lord alluded to here, the *Book of Commandments*, the first publication of some of Joseph's revelations, had a slightly different wording in the sixth verse; instead of "the gift of Aaron," it reads "the gift of working with the rod" (Chapter 7:3). Aaron's rod was a sacred instrument. After being cut from its mother tree, overnight it "brought forth buds, and bloomed blossoms, and yielded almonds" as a testimony to the rebellious of the house of Israel in the wilderness (Numbers 17:6–10). It was kept in "the ark of the covenant" with "the golden pot that had manna, . . . and the tables of the covenant" (Hebrews 9:4). Apparently Oliver was promised this sacred instrument, and although there is some secondary evidence of its being given, we do not know for sure if it was ever received.

Oliver was called "even as Aaron, to declare faithfully the commandments and the revelations, with power and authority unto the church" (D&C 28:3). As the Church grew and Oliver's duties increased, some of his duties were given to others. This has been a typical as the Church has grown. In October 1833, Sidney Rigdon was called and ordained "to be a spokesman unto my servant Joseph. And I will give unto him power to be mighty in testimony. And I will give unto thee power to be mighty in expounding all scriptures, that thou mayest be a spokesman unto him, and he shall be a revelator unto thee, that thou mayest know the certainty of all things pertaining to the things of my kingdom on the earth" (D&C 100:9–11).[15]

Moses wrote the law of the Lord (the law of Moses) for his people (v. 17). "This generation shall have [the Lord's] word [the Book of Mormon] through [Joseph Smith]" (D&C 5:10). The Book of Mormon is writing that comes from Joseph of Egypt's posterity (v. 18). Joseph Smith was also given "the law of the Church" for this generation (D&C 42 section heading). Although he was given a spokesman to declare the Lord's word (v. 18), he was mighty in speaking himself. Once more he meets the criteria for the eighth characteristic of the choice seer spoken of by Joseph of Egypt.

2 Nephi 3:19–21 • The Words that are Expedient shall Cry from the Dust

19 And the words which he shall write shall be the words which are expedient in my wisdom should go forth unto the fruit of thy loins. And it shall be as if the fruit of thy loins had cried unto them from the dust; for I know their faith.

20 And they shall cry from the dust; yea, even repentance unto their brethren, even after many generations have gone by them. And it shall come to pass that their cry shall go, even according to the simpleness of their words.

21 Because of their faith their words shall proceed forth out of my mouth unto their brethren who are the fruit of thy loins; and the weakness of their words will I make strong in their faith, unto the remembering of my covenant which I made unto thy fathers.

---

[15] Some have interpreted 2 Nephi 3:17 as referring to Joseph Smith not being "mighty in speaking," but the text is speaking of Moses. Also, Joseph being "mighty in testimony" as quoted above is a contradiction to that interpretation. Furthermore, the following is typical of his speaking ability. "This is an imperfect sketch of a very interesting discourse, which occupied more than two hours in delivery, and was listened to with marked attention, by the vast assembly present." (May 16, 1841.) *DHC* 4:358–60 (*TPJS*, 189).

Joseph Smith did not add any more words to JST, Genesis 50, that were quoted by Lehi.

The ninth characteristic of the choice seer could be considered an extension of both the fourth and the eighth one, since they both deal with the writing of the fruit of the loins of Joseph of Egypt. Because it deals more with the message of those writings, it will be considered as a separate characteristic.

"The words which are expedient in [the Lord's] wisdom [that] should go forth" (v. 19) were "the words of them which have slumbered [the Nephites]" (2 Nephi 27:6) who were destroyed. "The things which are sealed [the sealed part of the plates]" (2 Nephi 27:7–8) were not translated, but "shall be made known unto future generations" (D&C 5:9). The first words "shall cry from the dust; yea, even repentance unto their brethren, even after many generations" (v. 20). Their coming forth will fulfill Isaiah's words: "thou shalt be brought down, and shalt speak out of the ground" (Isaiah 29:4; see also 2 Nephi 27:16). Thus Joseph of Egypt and Isaiah are two witnesses of the coming forth of the Book of Mormon, and again designate Joseph as the choice seer of the latter days. The Lord promises to make the words of the Book of Mormon "strong in their faith, unto the remembering of their covenant" (v. 21). As Moroni promised: "he will manifest the truth of it unto you, by the power of the Holy Ghost" (Moroni 10:4).

There is no other person in these latter days to whom all nine of these characteristics could apply.

2 Nephi 3:22–25 • A Mighty Descendant of Joseph, Son of Lehi

22 And now, behold, my son Joseph, after this manner did my father of old prophesy.

23 Wherefore, because of this covenant thou art blessed; for thy seed shall not be destroyed, for they shall hearken unto the words of the book.

24 And there shall rise up one mighty among them, who shall do

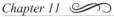

much good, both in word and in deed, being an instrument in the hands of God, with exceeding faith, to work mighty wonders, and do that thing which is great in the sight of God, unto the bringing to pass much restoration unto the house of Israel, and unto the seed of thy brethren.

25 And now, blessed art thou, Joseph. Behold, thou art little; wherefore hearken unto the words of thy brother, Nephi, and it shall be done unto thee even according to the words which I have spoken. Remember the words of thy dying father. Amen.

Lehi finishes quoting Joseph of Egypt at this point (v. 22), and returns to the blessing of his son, Joseph. This is important to know because Lehi is prophesying about his own son, not Joseph Smith. He prophesies that Joseph's posterity will not be destroyed, for they shall hearken to the Book of Mormon (v. 23). Since the Book of Mormon was not available until 1830, Lehi must have meant that they would be preserved. In his foreknowledge the Lord knew they would hearken when the Book of Mormon became available. He then prophesied that one among his son Joseph's seed would do much good and bring to pass much restoration to the house of Israel, and to the seed of his brethren (v. 24). Joseph Smith brought forth the Book of Mormon, and the one among them (Joseph's, son of Lehi, seed) was to hearken to the book brought forth. Therefore it is difficult to relate the prophecy to Joseph Smith. Joseph Smith's work was to bring Joseph of Egypt's seed "out of darkness unto light," and "the one mighty among them was to bring them "out of captivity unto freedom" (2 Nephi 3:5). The interpretation of there being two separate persons has been given by modern day apostles. President Joseph Fielding Smith taught that "father Lehi made one promise to his son Joseph and that was that from his seed would arise one who should" fulfill 2 Nephi 24, and then he added:

That the remnants of Joseph, found among the descendants of Lehi, will have part in this great work is certainly consistent, and the great work of the restoration the building of the temple and the city of Zion, or New Jerusalem, will fall to the lot of the descendants of Joseph, but it is Ephraim who will stand at the head and direct the work.[16]

Elder Spencer W. Kimball declared:

> The Lamanite must rise in majesty and power . . . And in the day
> when their prophet shall come, one shall rise . . . mighty among them
> . . . being an instrument in the hands of God, with exceeding faith,
> to work mighty wonders . . . (2 Nephi 3:24). When the time is right,
> the lord will raise him up. [CR, Oct. 1947, 22]

Lehi's final admonition to his youngest son Joseph is the last recorded words of the old patriarch who led the families of Joseph out of Jerusalem. His mission is now completed and he awaited his death.

2 Nephi 4:1–2 • No Prophecies Greater than Joseph of Egypt

> 1 And now, I, Nephi, speak concerning the prophecies of which my father hath spoken, concerning Joseph, who was carried into Egypt.
>
> 2 For behold, he truly prophesied concerning all his seed. And the prophecies which he wrote, there are not many greater. And he prophesied concerning us, and our future generations; and they are written upon the plates of brass.

Nephi adds his own testimony of the prophecies of Joseph who was sold into Egypt. He implies that there are other prophecies that were not mentioned. This should whet our appetite for the time when they "go forth unto all nations, kindreds, tongues, and people who were of [Joseph's] seed" (1 Nephi 5:18). In 1836 the Saints in Kirtland, Ohio, purchased some mummies and some that had scrolls containing the writings of Joseph of Egypt. Joseph Smith "commenced the translation of some of the characters or hieroglyphics, and much to our joy found one of the rolls contained the writings of Abraham, another the writings of Joseph of Egypt" (*HC,* 2:235–36). A small portion of the scroll of Abraham was translated, and is now published as the Book

---

[16] Joseph Fielding Smith, *Doctrines of Salvation*, comp. Bruce R. McConkie, 3 vols. [1955], 2:251.

of Abraham in The Pearl of Great Price. Some day we hope to have
the scroll of Joseph and its translation as well. Through these two
sources can learn more about the great prophecies of Joseph of Egypt
(v. 2).

2 Nephi 4:3–10 • Lehi Blesses the Children of Laman, Lemuel. and Ishmael

3 Wherefore, after my father had made an end of speaking
concerning the prophecies of Joseph, he called the children of Laman,
his sons, and his daughters, and said unto them: Behold, my sons, and
my daughters, who are the sons and the daughters of my first-born,
I would that ye should give ear unto my words.

4 For the Lord God hath said that: Inasmuch as ye shall keep my
commandments ye shall prosper in the land; and inasmuch as ye will
not keep my commandments ye shall be cut off from my presence.

5 But behold, my sons and my daughters, I cannot go down to my
grave save I should leave a blessing upon you; for behold, I know that
if ye are brought up in the way ye should go ye will not depart from
it.

6 Wherefore, if ye are cursed, behold, I leave my blessing upon
you, that the cursing may be taken from you and be answered upon
the heads of your parents.

7 Wherefore, because of my blessing the Lord God will not suffer
that ye shall perish; wherefore, he will be merciful unto you and unto
your seed forever.

8 And it came to pass that after my father had made an end of
speaking to the sons and daughters of Laman, he caused the sons and
daughters of Lemuel to be brought before him.

9 And he spake unto them, saying: Behold, my sons and my
daughters, who are the sons and the daughters of my second son;
behold I leave unto you the same blessing which I left unto the sons
and daughters of Laman; wherefore, thou shalt not utterly be destroyed; but in the end thy seed shall be blessed.

10 And it came to pass that when my father had made an end of
speaking unto them, behold, he spake unto the sons of Ishmael, yea,
and even all his household.

The time period of the first three and one-half chapters of Second Nephi is not given. They seem to have all happened at the same time and setting, as a farewell testimonial from Lehi to his people before his death. Although we have no record of Lehi blessing Nephi, he undoubtedly did. This failure to record his blessing reflects the humility of Nephi. It certainly must have been a great blessing as the Lord had told him "thou shalt be a ruler and a teacher over thy brethren" (1 Nephi 2:22), and his father had told the three older sons that "if ye will not hearken unto [Nephi], I take away my first blessing, yes, even my blessing, and it shall rest upon him" (2 Nephi 1:29). Someday the record of that blessing will be available to us among the other Nephite records yet to come forth. This will further validate the greatness of Nephi.

Lehi calls all the children of his people and pronounces a final blessing upon their heads collectively before his death. These blessings are self-explanatory and somewhat repetitive, but a few observations should be made. The great concern for his wayward sons and their posterity is again evident. Lehi tells Laman's children that the Lord will not hold the children accountable for their parent's sins. Lehi is probably paraphrasing from the plates of brass, "Train up a child in the way he should go: and when he is old, he will not depart from it" (Proverbs 22:6) when he speaks to his older sons' children (v. 5). Solomon, who "spake three thousand proverbs" (1 Kings 4:32), is dated about 1000 B.C. and could easily have been included on the brass plates. A final observation, the Book of Mormon was to bring a "knowledge of the Savior" unto "the Lamanites, and the Lemuelites, and the Ishmaelites" (D&C 3:16, 18). This showed that Lehi's blessing that their seed would never perish was fulfilled (vv. 7, 9).

2 Nephi 4:11–12 • Lehi Blesses Sam, Waxes Old, Dies, and is Buried

> 11 And after he had made an end of speaking unto them, he spake unto Sam, saying: Blessed art thou, and thy seed; for thou shalt inherit the land like unto thy brother Nephi. And thy seed shall be numbered

with his seed; and thou shalt be even like unto thy brother, and thy seed like unto his seed; and thou shalt be blessed in all thy days.

12 And it came to pass after my father, Lehi, had spoken unto all his household, according to the feelings of his heart and the Spirit of the Lord which was in him, he waxed old. And it came to pass that he died, and was buried.

From this point on, Sam's descendants are never reckoned as a tribe but are counted as part of Nephi's seed. In the Doctrine and Covenants there are four other groups named to whom a knowledge of the Savior was to come: "the Nephites, and the Jacobites, and the Josephites, and the Zoramites" (D&C 3:17). Sam is not mentioned, making a total of seven including the three previously named above (D&C 3:16, 18). Many of the early Spanish Chroniclers refer to the seven tribes that came to Mesoamerica.[17]

How long Lehi lived after these blessings is not stated, but it was probably just "a few more days and I go the way of all the earth" (2 Nephi 1:14), as he stated when he began giving his blessings to the people. First Nephi 1–9 are an abridgment of "the record of my father" (1 Nephi 1:17). Nephi made the abridgment before he began the record we are here considering. We should look forward to reading the unabridged record.

2 Nephi 4:14–15 • Anger with Nephi Because of the Admonitions of the Lord

14 For I, Nephi, was constrained to speak unto them, according to his word; for I had spoken many things unto them, and also my father, before his death; many of which sayings are written upon mine other plates; for a more history part are written upon mine other plates.

15 And upon these I write the things of my soul, and many of the scriptures which are engraven upon the plates of brass. For my soul delighteth in the scriptures, and my heart pondereth them, and writeth

---

[17] See Diane E. Wirth, *A Challenge to the Critics*, chap. 13, *The Seven Tribes*, Horizon Publishers, Bountiful, Utah, 1986. The Spanish Chroniclers refer to the records kept by early Spanish settlers.

them for the learning and the profit of my children.

Laman and Lemuel's hard hearts are again illustrated. Earlier, Nephi had associated their spiritual disbelief with their being "like unto the Jews who were at Jerusalem, who sought to take away the life of my father" (1 Nephi 2:13). With Lehi gone, they refused to "hearken unto the voice of Nephi" (2 Nephi 1:28). Although they had had many great spiritual experiences, they were still "like unto the Jews." Great spiritual experiences do not necessarily bring salvation. However, what Nephi and his father had taught them, as well as those things that were written on Nephi's other plates (v. 14), certainly left them without excuse for their salvation.

2 Nephi 4:15–25 • Nephi Writes the Things of His Soul

15 And upon these I write the things of my soul, and many of the scriptures which are engraven upon the plates of brass. For my soul delighteth in the scriptures, and my heart pondereth them, and writeth them for the learning and the profit of my children.

16 Behold, my soul delighteth in the things of the Lord; and my heart pondereth continually upon the things which I have seen and heard.

17 Nevertheless, notwithstanding the great goodness of the Lord, in showing me his great and marvelous works, my heart exclaimeth: O wretched man that I am! Yea, my heart sorroweth because of my flesh; my soul grieveth because of mine iniquities.

18 I am encompassed about, because of the temptations and the sins which do so easily beset me.

19 And when I desire to rejoice, my heart groaneth because of my sins; nevertheless, I know in whom I have trusted.

20 My God hath been my support; he hath led me through mine afflictions in the wilderness; and he hath preserved me upon the waters of the great deep.

21 He hath filled me with his love, even unto the consuming of my flesh.

22 He hath confounded mine enemies, unto the causing of them to quake before me.

23 Behold, he hath heard my cry by day, and he hath given me knowledge by visions in the nighttime.

24 And by day have I waxed bold in mighty prayer before him; yea, my voice have I sent up on high; and angels came down and ministered unto me.

25 And upon the wings of his Spirit hath my body been carried away upon exceedingly high mountains. And mine eyes have beheld great things, yea, even too great for man; therefore I was bidden that I should not write them.

The rest of chapter 4 has been called "Nephi's Psalm" or "Nephi's Soliloquy," and has been set to poetry or music by several people. His love for the scriptures, for his children, and for the Lord is obvious. The feelings from his heart is one of the best, if not the best, illustrations of a sanctified man found anywhere in the scriptures. A few observations from these verses will sustain the premise of his sanctification. A fuller analysis of this beautiful rendition is not needed. It should be read and reread by all who want to attain this state of sanctification, the requirements for those "who were made pure and entered into the rest of the Lord their God" (Alma 13:12), thus gaining eternal life.

Nephi's temptations and sins will be enumerated in the second part of our analysis. His being supported by God in the wilderness, his enemies being confounded, the knowledge given him by vision, angels, and the wings of the Spirit carrying him upon exceedingly high mountains have been told us in limited detail in the book of First Nephi. The things he was forbidden to write because they were "even too great for man" (v. 25) would include, but not be limited to, "concerning the end of the world" which he was shown. He wrote "but a small part of the things that [he] saw" (1 Nephi 14:22, 24, 28).

2 Nephi 4:26–30 • Nephi's Sensitivity to Sin

26 O then, if I have seen so great things, if the Lord in his conde-

scension unto the children of men hath visited men in so much mercy, why should my heart weep and my soul linger in the valley of sorrow, and my flesh waste away, and my strength slacken, because of mine afflictions?

27 And why should I yield to sin, because of my flesh? Yea, why should I give way to temptations, that the evil one have place in my heart to destroy my peace and afflict my soul? Why am I angry because of mine enemy?

28 Awake, my soul! No longer droop in sin. Rejoice, O my heart, and give place no more for the enemy of my soul.

29 Do not anger again because of mine enemies. Do not slacken my strength because of mine afflictions.

30 Rejoice, O my heart, and cry unto the Lord, and say: O Lord, I will praise thee forever; yea, my soul will rejoice in thee, my God, and the rock of my salvation.

Nephi is extremely sensitive to sin. "The Lord cannot look upon sin with the least degree of allowance" (D&C 1:31). The sanctified man cannot "look upon sin save it were with abhorrence" (Alma 13:12). What Nephi enumerates as sin is rarely considered as sin by mortal man: guilt feelings for our thoughts (v. 26); slackening of strength because of our physical afflictions; or, anger because of our enemies (v. 27). Many people excuse or rationalize away their sins as the normal way of life for which God does not hold us accountable. The sanctified man makes no excuses for sin, but turns to the Lord and praises him for his blessings (v. 30).

2 Nephi 4:31–35 • Nephi Will Trust in the Lord Forever

31 O Lord, wilt thou redeem my soul? Wilt thou deliver me out of the hands of mine enemies? Wilt thou make me that I may shake at the appearance of sin?

32 May the gates of hell be shut continually before me, because that my heart is broken and my spirit is contrite! O Lord, wilt thou not shut the gates of thy righteousness before me, that I may walk in the path of the low valley, that I may be strict in the plain road!

33 O Lord, wilt thou encircle me around in the robe of thy righteousness! O Lord, wilt thou make a way for mine escape before mine enemies! Wilt thou make my path straight before me! Wilt thou not place a stumbling block in my way—but that thou wouldst clear my way before me, and hedge not up my way, but the ways of mine enemy.

34 O Lord, I have trusted in thee, and I will trust in thee forever. I will not put my trust in the arm of flesh; for I know that cursed is he that putteth his trust in the arm of flesh. Yea, cursed is he that putteth his trust in man or maketh flesh his arm.

35 Yea, I know that God will give liberally to him that asketh. Yea, my God will give me, if I ask not amiss; therefore I will lift up my voice unto thee; yea, I will cry unto thee, my God, the rock of my righteousness. Behold, my voice shall forever ascend up unto thee, my rock and mine everlasting God. Amen.

Nephi makes several requests of the Lord and concludes with a personal commitment. He wants the Lord to make him shake at the appearance of sin (v. 31). The mortal man "will justify in committing a little sin" (2 Nephi 28:8). Nephi asks that the gates of hell be shut before him, but realizes it is his responsibility to get them shut through his heart being broken and his spirit contrite (v. 32). He further realizes his dependence on the Lord to attain and retain his righteousness (vv. 32–33).

Nephi commits himself to trust in the arm (power) of the Lord, and not in the arm of flesh (v. 34). This is another characteristic of sanctified man. In our materialistic world the bank account, the intellect, and athletic or physical prowess are a few of the arms of flesh in which we trust. Nephi depends upon prayer to learn what course God wants him to follow (v. 35). Would that we might all be as committed as Nephi.

2 Nephi 5:1–4 • The Brothers Seek Nephi's Life

1 Behold, it came to pass that I, Nephi, did cry much unto the Lord my God, because of the anger of my brethren.

2 But behold, their anger did increase against me, insomuch that

they did seek to take away my life.

3 Yea, they did murmur against me, saying: Our younger brother thinks to rule over us; and we have had much trial because of him; wherefore, now let us slay him, that we may not be afflicted more because of his words. For behold, we will not have him to be our ruler; for it belongs unto us, who are the elder brethren, to rule over this people.

4 Now I do not write upon these plates all the words which they murmured against me. But it sufficeth me to say, that they did seek to take away my life.

Again, the brothers seek the life of Nephi. As a parallel to the life of Joseph of Egypt, his brothers "conspired against him to slay him" (Genesis 37:18). As Zoram, Sam, Jacob, and Joseph stood by Nephi (2 Nephi 5:6; quoted below), so Reuben, the older brother of Joseph of Egypt "delivered him out of [the older brother's] hands" (Genesis 37:21). However, Joseph of Egypt recognized that it was God "that sent me hither" (Genesis 45:8). We will now see how God intervened in the life of Nephi.

2 Nephi 5:5–9 • Those Who Believed in the Warnings and Revelations of God

5 And it came to pass that the Lord did warn me, that I, Nephi, should depart from them and flee into the wilderness, and all those who would go with me.

6 Wherefore, it came to pass that I, Nephi, did take my family, and also Zoram and his family, and Sam, mine elder brother and his family, and Jacob and Joseph, my younger brethren, and also my sisters, and all those who would go with me. And all those who would go with me were those who believed in the warnings and the revelations of God; wherefore, they did hearken unto my words.

7 And we did take our tents and whatsoever things were possible for us, and did journey in the wilderness for the space of many days. And after we had journeyed for the space of many days we did pitch our tents.

8 And my people would that we should call the name of the place

Nephi; wherefore, we did call it Nephi.

9 And all those who were with me did take upon them to call themselves the people of Nephi.

The Lord warning Nephi, and leading "those who believed in the revelations of God" into the wilderness, is an example of the principle that Nephi recorded earlier. The Lord "leadeth away the righteous into precious lands, and the wicked he destroyeth, and curseth the land unto them for their sakes" (1 Nephi 17:38). Nephi had taught that the Lord would lead the house of Israel out of Egypt. It was also the principle of the Lehi and his people being led out of Jerusalem. There are other examples of this principle later in the Book of Mormon.

This is the first time that Nephi's sisters are mentioned in the Book of Mormon (v. 6). How many sisters he had and how many of them followed him is not mentioned. Some of them had married Ishmaels sons as commented on under 1 Nephi 7:4–5 and learned from the Book of Lehi. That they traveled in the wilderness "for the space of many days" (v. 7) does not help us much geographically, nor is that the purpose of the Lord in giving us the Book of Mormon. The people calling "the place Nephi," and calling "themselves the people of Nephi" (vv. 8–9) is the birth of the Nephite nation.

2 Nephi 5:10–18 • Why the Nephites Prospered

10 And we did observe to keep the judgments, and the statutes, and the commandments of the Lord in all things, according to the law of Moses.

11 And the Lord was with us; and we did prosper exceedingly; for we did sow seed, and we did reap again in abundance. And we began to raise flocks, and herds, and animals of every kind.

12 And I, Nephi, had also brought the records which were engraven upon the plates of brass; and also the ball, or compass, which was prepared for my father by the hand of the Lord, according to that which is written.

13 And it came to pass that we began to prosper exceedingly, and to multiply in the land.

14 And I, Nephi, did take the sword of Laban, and after the manner of it did make many swords, lest by any means the people who were now called Lamanites should come upon us and destroy us; for I knew their hatred towards me and my children and those who were called my people.

15 And I did teach my people to build buildings, and to work in all manner of wood, and of iron, and of copper, and of brass, and of steel, and of gold, and of silver, and of precious ores, which were in great abundance.

16 And I, Nephi, did build a temple; and I did construct it after the manner of the temple of Solomon save it were not built of so many precious things; for they were not to be found upon the land, wherefore, it could not be built like unto Solomon's temple. But the manner of the construction was like unto the temple of Solomon; and the workmanship thereof was exceedingly fine.

17 And it came to pass that I, Nephi, did cause my people to be industrious, and to labor with their hands.

18 And it came to pass that they would that I should be their king. But I, Nephi, was desirous that they should have no king; nevertheless, I did for them according to that which was in my power.

Those who followed Nephi were the righteous. This is substantiated by their keeping the commandments of the Lord according to the law of Moses (v. 10). Why they kept the law of Moses is explained in 2 Nephi 25:24–30 and will be commented upon when those verses are discussed in a later chapter. Their taking the plates of brass and other sacred items with them (v. 12) is also evidence that those who followed Nephi had a desire to be righteous. These sacred items were kept intact, and handed down "from generation to generation" as commanded by the Lord (Jacob 1:3).

The Nephites prosperity in making swords for their defense and building and working in various metals (vv. 14–15) can be attributed to Nephi's teaching them to be industrious (v. 17). In the law of the Church, revealed in our dispensation, the Lord expressed his desire for the people to follow the "work of their own hands" and "not be idle" (D&C 42:40, 42). When people follow the Lord's counsel, they will be blessed and prosper. In contrast, the Lamanites "did become an idle people, full of mischief and subtlety, and did seek in the wilderness for beasts of prey (v. 25 quoted below).

The Nephites built a temple at their earliest convenience. This is an indication of their spirituality. Although other temples were built this is the first mention of a temple in the Book of Mormon (v. 16). Nephi's desire that the Nephites have no king will be discussed in the next chapter. His character is again reflected in his willingness to do for them what was in his power (v. 18).

2 Nephi 5:19–25 • The Curse Upon the Lamanites

19 And behold, the words of the Lord had been fulfilled unto my brethren, which he spake concerning them, that I should be their ruler and their teacher. Wherefore, I had been their ruler and their teacher, according to the commandments of the Lord, until the time they sought to take away my life.

20 Wherefore, the word of the Lord was fulfilled which he spake unto me, saying that: Inasmuch as they will not hearken unto thy words they shall be cut off from the presence of the Lord. And behold, they were cut off from his presence.

21 And he had caused the cursing to come upon them, yea, even a sore cursing, because of their iniquity. For behold, they had hardened their hearts against him, that they had become like unto a flint; wherefore, as they were white, and exceedingly fair and delightsome, that they might not be enticing unto my people the Lord God did cause a skin of blackness to come upon them.

22 And thus saith the Lord God: I will cause that they shall be loathsome unto thy people, save they shall repent of their iniquities.

23 And cursed shall be the seed of him that mixeth with their seed; for they shall be cursed even with the same cursing. And the Lord spake it, and it was done.

24 And because of their cursing which was upon them they did become an idle people, full of mischief and subtlety, and did seek in the wilderness for beasts of prey.

25 And the Lord God said unto me: They shall be a scourge unto

thy seed, to stir them up in remembrance of me; and inasmuch as they will not remember me, and hearken unto my words, they shall scourge them even unto destruction.

The prophecy that Nephi would be their ruler and teacher (v. 19) had been given when the Lord appeared to Nephi in the valley of Lemuel about thirty years before. It was given probably a few weeks after they initially left Jerusalem and Nephi had filled that role since that time. Lehi had recognized Nephi's being "an instrument in the hands of God, in bringing us forth into the land of promise" (2 Nephi 1:24).

The Lamanites had also been cut off from the presence of the Lord as prophesied (v. 20). This was the real cursing of the Lord (v. 21). Without the guidance of the Lord their iniquities would abound. The withdrawal of the Spirit from them individually would now come upon them collectively. Of course the coming generation would be born with the light of Christ, but it would not help them unless they repented of the ways of their fathers. Thus as Alma says: "they brought upon themselves the curse; and even so doth every man that is cursed bring upon himself his own condemnation" (Alma 3:19).

The skin of blackness (v. 21) should be read as a comparison to the lighter skin of the Nephites and not taken literally. It was brought upon the people to make them loathsome to the people of Nephi. Alma later says it was a mark "that thereby the Lord God might preserve his people, that they might not mix and believe in incorrect traditions which would prove their destruction" (Alma 3:7–8). It is important to distinguish between the curse and the mark. While there are many variations of skin color in the world, they do not specify any degree of righteousness or unrighteousness. The darker skin of the Lamanites was a distinction between a people of the same origin, and the Lord used the mark to keep the righteous separated from the wicked. As one continues to read the Book of Mormon, it will be evident that the Lord continually endeavored to teach the gospel to the Lamanites and bring them out of their wickedness. At times the efforts were very successful. The Nephites who apostatized and joined the Lamanites were cursed and cut off from the presence of the Lord (v. 23), but nothing was said about their being marked. As long as the Lamanites remained in their wicked ways, they were a scourge to stir up the Nephites to remember the Lord (v. 25).

2 Nephi 5:26–27 • Jacob and Joseph Consecrated Priests and Teachers

26 And it came to pass that I, Nephi, did consecrate Jacob and Joseph, that they should be priests and teachers over the land of my people.

27 And it came to pass that we lived after the manner of happiness.

Jacob and Joseph becoming priests does not refer to our present Aaronic Priesthood offices. President Joseph Fielding Smith explains:

There were no Levites who accompanied Lehi to the Western Hemisphere. Under these conditions the Nephites officiated by virtue of the Melchizedek Priesthood from the days of Lehi to the days of the appearance of our Savior among them. It is true that Nephi "consecrated Jacob and Joseph" that they should be priests and teachers over the land of the Nephites, but the fact that plural terms *priests and teachers* were used indicates that this was not a reference to the definite office in the priesthood in either case, but it was a general assignment to teach, direct, and admonish the people. Otherwise the terms priest and teacher would have been given, in the singular.[18]

Living after the manner of happiness (v. 27) is probably Nephi's way of saying they were basically following the commandments of God. As quoted and discussed in Chapter Six of this work, the Prophet Joseph taught that happiness comes from following the path of "virtue, uprightness, faithfulness, holiness, and keeping all of the commandments of God" (*TPJS*, 255–256).

---

[18] Joseph Fielding Smith, *Answers to Gospel Questions,* 5 vols. [1957], 1:124.

2 Nephi 5:28–34 • Another Set of Plates

28 And thirty years had passed away from the time we left Jerusalem.

29 And I, Nephi, had kept the records upon my plates, which I had made, of my people thus far.

30 And it came to pass that the Lord God said unto me: Make other plates; and thou shalt engraven many things upon them which are good in my sight, for the profit of thy people.

31 Wherefore, I, Nephi, to be obedient to the commandments of the Lord, went and made these plates upon which I have engraven these things.

32 And I engraved that which is pleasing unto God. And if my people are pleased with the things of God they will be pleased with mine engravings which are upon these plates.

33 And if my people desire to know the more particular part of the history of my people they must search mine other plates.

34 And it sufficeth me to say that forty years had passed away, and we had already had wars and contentions with our brethren.

The record we are now studying, First and Second Nephi, is the translation of the account that Nephi began engraving upon another smaller set of plates thirty years after Lehi left Jerusalem. The record kept upon the first set of plates was translated and written on "one hundred and sixteen pages of manuscript on foolscap paper." Martin Harris was acting as Joseph's scribe during the translation, and persuaded Joseph to let him show the manuscript to a few select persons. "He bound himself as [Joseph] required of him, took the writings, and went his way. Notwithstanding, however, the great restrictions which he had been laid under, and the solemnity of the covenant which he had made with me, he did show them to others, and by stratagem they got them from him, and they have never been recovered unto this day" (*HC,* 1:20–21). We will leave a further discussion of the lost manuscript for another section of this book. Suffice it to say that the two records are known in the Church today as the large plates of Nephi, and the small plates of Nephi. Today we have the small plates of Nephi (1 Nephi through Words of Mormon) and an abridgment of the large plates.

SACRED WRITING

Preaching which is Sacred:

2 Nephi 4:3–11	Lehi's final admonitions (blessings) to his children.
2 Nephi 4:15–35	Nephi writes (preaches to the reader) the things of his soul.

Prophesying:

2 Nephi 3:1–4	Lehi to his son Joseph.
2 Nephi 3:5–21	Joseph of Egypt concerning his seed.
2 Nephi 3:23–25	Lehi to his son Joseph.
2 Nephi 3:21–25	Nephi concerning the Lamanites.

Doctrines learned:

2 Nephi 3:4–5	The Lord covenanted with Joseph of Egypt to raise up a righteous branch of the house of Israel unto whom the Messiah would be manifest in the latter days, and bring his seed (the Lamanites) out of darkness unto light, and out of captivity unto freedom.
2 Nephi 3:6–8	A choice seer would be raised up to bring Joseph of Egypt's seed to a knowledge of the covenants made to their fathers.
2 Nephi 3:10, 17	Moses will be raised up to deliver the house of Israel out of Egypt.
2 Nephi 3:11–12	The writings of Joseph of Egypt's seed and the writings of Judah would grow together in the latter days to bring a knowledge of their fathers and a knowledge of the Lord's covenants.

2 Nephi 3:16–17	A spokesman would be raised up for both Moses and the choice seer.
2 Nephi 3:24	One mighty among the seed of Joseph, son of Lehi would be raised up to do a great work among his seed and the seed of his brothers.
2 Nephi 4:4–9	The cursing upon Laman and Lemuel would be taken from their seed and answered upon the head of their parents.
2 Nephi 5:20–21	The Lamanites were cursed by the Lord cutting them off from his presence. A darker skin came upon them as a mark of the curse, so they would not mix.
2 Nephi 5:23	Those who mixed with the Lamanites would receive the same curse.

General Authority Quotes:

President Joseph Fielding Smith • 2 Nephi 3:5–21

These prophecies concerning the work of Moses and that of Joseph Smith were recorded on the brass plates obtained by the sons of Lehi. In fulfillment of the Lord's promise, these few sentences have been restored; and we hereby learn something of the greatness of the Prophet Joseph Smith. Among those who were called in the great council, he held a place of distinction and honor and a wonderful work for the salvation, not only of the house of Israel but also for all mankind on the face of the earth, was foreordained and assigned to him ages before he was born.

President John Taylor spoke truly when he said:

Joseph Smith the Prophet and Seer of the Lord, has done more, save Jesus only, for the salvation of men in this world, than any other man that ever lived in it.

It seems to me that even we, the Latter-day Saints, who have accepted him as a prophet of God, have to a great extent failed to recognize him and esteem him as fully as we should for the great work which, under the guidance of Jesus Christ, he performed for us and for the whole world. Yet, like so many of the prophets of old, and even the Savior himself, he has received the thanks of an unbelieving world by sacrifice and martyrdom.

Any who think that the Father and the Son are without knowledge of the history of this world from its beginning to its end, have reason to humble themselves and repent. The day will surely come, when the Lord will reveal all that was made known to Enoch, Moses, and the brother of Jared, which is now hidden from our knowledge because of the hardness of our hearts, for this cannot come only in a day of humility and righteousness. [*Answers to Gospel Questions,* 5:184–85, 1972]

President Joseph Fielding Smith • 2 Nephi 5:21

The dark skin was placed upon the Lamanites so that they could be distinguished from the Nephites and to keep the two people from mixing. The dark skin was the sign of the curse. The curse was the withdrawal of the Spirit of the Lord and the Lamanites becoming a "loathsome and filthy people, full of idleness and all manner of abominations." The Lord commanded the Nephites not to intermarry with them, for if they did they would partake of the curse.

At the time of the Savior's visit to the Nephites all of the people became united, and the curse and the dark skin which was its sign were removed. The two peoples became one and lived in full harmony and peace for about two hundred years (Quotes 4 Nephi 1:17).

After the people again forgot the Lord and dissensions arose, some of them took upon themselves the name Lamanites and the dark skin returned. . . .

The dark skin of those who have come into the Church is no longer to be considered the sign of the curse. [*Answers to Gospel Questions,* 3:122–23, 1960]

Challenges to Eternal Life:

1. Study the Book of Mormon and the Bible together and mentally note how their teachings grow together as your knowledge increases (2 Nephi 3:12).
2. Select one of the characteristics of Nephi, as a sanctified man, and commit to live by it (2 Nephi 4:6–35).
3. Read your patriarchal blessing and commit to live for the word of the

Lord being fulfilled in your life, which is stipulated upon your obedience.

4.   Choose a challenge or message of your own from this reading and apply it to your life.

Chapter Twelve

Jacob Quotes Isaiah

2 Nephi 6–8, 10

*H*istorical Setting: The dates of these chapters, 559–545 B.C., given in the lower right hand corner of the page in the Book of Mormon, are not given more specifically. The first date is drawn from 1 Nephi 5:34, "forty years had passed away." The second date is taken from the beginning of Jacob's record, "fifty and five years had passed away from the time that Lehi left Jerusalem" (Jacob 1:1). There are no other dates given in the rest of the Second Book of Nephi. During the last fifteen years of Nephi's life, he recorded the history of his people on the "other plates," and "the things of God" were written upon these plates (1 Nephi 6:3–6).

The next five chapters of 2 Nephi (6–10) are two speeches given during a two-day gathering by Jacob, the brother of Nephi, to "the people of Nephi" as they by then called themselves (2 Nephi 5:9). Perhaps they were delivered during the first meeting as a body of people after having separated themselves from their brethren (2 Nephi 5) as indicated by the statement "my brother Nephi, unto whom ye look as a king and protector" (2 Nephi 6:2). Another possibility is that they assembled in a church conference, comparable to today's stake conference or general conference. The separation seemed to have occurred ten years earlier, but the time of the speeches is not given. The first speech constitutes 2 Nephi 6–9. These chapters may be the complete text of the words he spoke on the first day, but Nephi says that "Jacob spake many more things to my people" that weren't recorded (2 Nephi 11:1). The second speech was recorded in 2 Nephi 10 and was given the day following the first speech. Since chapter ten is short in comparison to the previous four chapters, it is possible that the many other things Jacob spoke that were not recorded were given on the second day. If so, it was probably a third sermon since chapter ten picks up where the first sermon ends, as promised, and ends with an "Amen" as does chapter nine.

Precepts of these chapters:

> And there are many things which have been spoken by Isaiah which may be likened unto you, because ye are of the house of Israel. [2 Nephi 6:5]

> Wherefore, my beloved brethren, reconcile yourselves to the will of God, and not to the will of the devil and the flesh; and remember, after ye are reconciled unto God, that it is only in and through the grace of God that ye are saved. [2 Nephi 10:24]

Isaiah 50–52:2, quoted by Jacob, is a message of hope to the whole house of Israel, showing how the covenant of Abraham will be extended to them in the last days through two great gathering places, Zion and Jerusalem.

Isaiah 50:4–9 is designated by Bible scholars as another "servant song" to Christ. The servant in Isaiah 42:1–4 is identified as Christ. The servant in chapter 49 was definitely identified as latter-day Israel. The servant here is also latter-day Israel, but the passage has a dual meaning as it also describes the mission of the Savior among the Jews (and possibly the other tribes of Israel) in the meridian of time. There are also those who feel, with some justification, that the servant spoken of in these verses is Isaiah himself. The dual meaning of the servant as Israel and Christ fits into the context of the overall message. The chapters in Second Nephi to be discussed here are outlined below to prepare us for a deeper study.

OUTLINE • 2 NEPHI 6–8, 10

➤ 6:1   The words which Jacob spake unto the people of Nephi.

➤ 6:2–3   Jacob has been called of God, ordained and consecrated by Nephi and has spoken exceedingly about many things.

     a.   Jacob is and has been desirous for the welfare of the people's souls (v. 3).

     b.   He has taught the words of his father and things written from the creation of the world (v. 3).

➤ 6:4–7   Jacob speaks of things which are and which are to come. He reads the words of Isaiah as desired by Nephi. He speaks that they may learn and glorify God.

     a.   Isaiah spake concerning all the house of Israel and his words may be likened unto the Nephites (v. 5).

     b.   Jacob quotes the present Isaiah 49:22–23.

➤ 6:8–13   Jacob comments on Isaiah's words.

     a.   Those at Jerusalem have been slain and carried away captive (v. 8).

     b.   The Lord has shown him that the Jews shall return again. The Messiah shall manifest himself to them but they shall scourge and crucify him (v. 9).

     c.   The judgment day shall follow; the Jews shall be smitten and afflicted (v. 10).

     d.   After they are afflicted they will be scattered and hated but after they come to the knowledge of their Redeemer, they will be gathered again (v. 11).

     e.   The Gentiles (Isaiah 49:22–23) who do not unite with the great and abominable church will be saved as the Lord fulfills his covenant (v. 12).

     f.   They who fight against Zion and the covenant people of the Lord will lick up the dust of the Lord's people who wait for the coming of the Messiah (v. 13).

➤ 6:14–15   Jacob quotes part of the present Isaiah 11:11 and paraphrases or quotes some of the plain and precious parts lost from Isaiah (see 1 Nephi 22:15–17).

➤ 6:16–8:25   Jacob quotes the present Isaiah 49:24–52:2.

➤ 7:1–3   The Lord has not cast off Israel forever.
   a. Their mother's bill of divorcement does not apply now (v. 1).
   b. The Lord has no creditors, so Israel was not sold (v. 1).
   c. Those who are cast off sell themselves (v. 1).
   d. Their mother (ancient Israel) was cast off (v. 1).
   e. The Jews did not respond when Christ came and were driven out (v. 2).
   f. When Christ called again there was none to answer (v. 2).
   g. The Lord has power to redeem Israel anyway (vv. 2–3).

➤ 7:4–9   The Lord God has given his servant power to redeem Israel anyway.
   a. The servant can speak and confound the wise (v. 4).
   b. He listened and followed revelation in spite of persecution (vv. 5–6).
   c. He will smite the contenders with the message of the gospel (vv. 7–8).
   d. He will smite those who condemn him (v. 9).

➤ 7:10–11   Those who walk in the light of their own reasoning will lie down in sorrow.

➤ 8:1–8   The righteous are invited to look back to the covenant made with Abraham and Sarah.
   a. The Lord will comfort Zion physically and socially (v. 3).
   b. A law will proceed from the Lord to Israel in the isles of the sea (vv. 4–5).
   c. The heavens, the earth and its inhabitants will vanish, but the Lord's salvation is forever (vv. 6–8).

d. Those who have the Lord's law written in their hearts need not fear the reproach of men (vv. 7–8).

➤ 8:9–16   Zion will put on her strength as in ancient days.

     a. The redeemed will return with singing and everlasting joy (v. 11).

     b. The Lord will comfort them (vv. 12–15).

     c. The Lord has directed and hidden them in his hand to be his people (v. 16).

➤ 8:17–23   Jerusalem will be comforted by two sons.

     a. She has drunk the cup of the Lord's fury and has no sons to guide her (vv. 17–18).

     b. Two sons will come to her to strengthen her (vv. 19–20).

     c. The cup of fury will be put into the hands of those who afflict Jerusalem (vv. 21–23).

➤ 8:24–25   Zion to put on her strength, and Jerusalem put on her beautiful garments.

     a. Zion will loose herself from the bands of her neck (v. 2).

     b. Jerusalem will rise from the dust and become a holy city (v. 2).

➤ 10:1–2   Jacob speaks of the righteous branch of his seed in future generations.

     a. Jacob has been shown that many of his people will perish in the flesh because of unbelief (v. 2).

     b. God will be merciful and restore them to the true knowledge of their Redeemer (v. 2).

➤ 10:3–9   Jacob speaks of Christ coming among the Jews

     a. An angel told Jacob last night that the Redeemer's name would be Christ (v. 3).

     b. It was expedient for him to come among the Jews for none other nation on earth would crucify their God (v. 3).

    c.   Mighty miracles among other nations would bring repentance, but priestcrafts and iniquities would cause them to crucify him (vv. 4–5).

    d.   The Jews shall not be destroyed but will be scattered among all nations (v. 6).

    e.   When they believe in Christ, they will be restored to the lands of their inheritance (v. 7).

    f.   The nations of the Gentiles shall be great in the eyes of God in carrying the Jews to their lands of inheritance. Jacob quotes Isaiah 49:22 (vv. 8–9).

➤ **10:10–17**   The Gentiles shall be blessed upon the land of Jacob's inheritance (the Americas).

    a.   It will be a land of liberty unto the Gentiles and there will be no kings unto the Gentiles (v. 11).

    b.   The Lord will fortify the land against all other nations (v. 12).

    c.   He that fights against Zion or raises up a king against Christ shall perish. Christ shall be their king and a light to them forever who hear his words (vv. 13–14).

    d.   As covenanted, Christ will destroy the secret works of darkness, murders, and abominations. Those who are not for him are against him (vv. 15–17).

➤ **10:18–23**   The seed of Lehi's people will be afflicted by the Gentiles but they will also be like a father to them. The Gentiles will be blessed and numbered with Israel.

    a.   The land is consecrated to Lehi's seed and those numbered among them. All men who dwell there shall worship Christ (v. 19).

    b.   Lehi's seed has been led to a better land and are upon an isle of the sea (v. 20).

    c.   Great promises are made to those upon the Isles of the Sea. The Lord has led some of the house of Israel away from time to time and remembers them also (vv. 21–22).

➤ **10:23–25**   Remember you are free to act for yourselves, to choose the way of everlasting death or the way of eternal life.

    a.   Reconcile yourselves to the way of God and not to the will of the devil. It is only through the grace of God that you are saved (v. 24).

    b.   May God raise you from death by the power of the resurrection and from everlasting death by the power of the Atonement that you may be saved in the eternal kingdom of God (v. 25).

NOTES AND COMMENTARY

Introduction: Jacob tells his people he will speak "concerning things which are, and which are to come" (2 Nephi 6:4). This phrase is similar to the definition of truth given in D&C 93:24 quoted previously. Wherefore, Jacob quotes Isaiah to show his people the present and also the future. Josephus makes an interesting statement about the prophecies of Isaiah that correspond to the statements of Jacob: "He [Isaiah] was by the confession of all, a divine and wonderful man in speaking truth; and out of the assurance that he had never written what was false, he wrote down all his prophecies, and left them behind in books, that their accomplishments might be judged of from the events by posterity."[1] We hope these words about the writings of Isaiah may be an incentive for us to "search these things diligently; for great are the words of Isaiah" as Jesus commanded (3 Nephi 23:1).

2 Nephi 6:1–4 • The Words of Jacob

    1 The words of Jacob, the brother of Nephi, which he spake unto the people of Nephi:

    2 Behold, my beloved brethren, I, Jacob, having been called of God, and ordained after the manner of his holy order, and having been consecrated by my brother Nephi, unto whom ye look as a king or a protector, and on whom ye depend for safety, behold ye know that I have spoken unto you exceedingly many things.

---

[1] Flavious Josephus, *Josephus: Complete Works*, trans. William Whiston, Grand Rapids, Mich., Kregal Publications [1972], Antiquities of the Jews, 10. 2.2.

3 Nevertheless, I speak unto you again; for I am desirous for the welfare of your souls. Yea, mine anxiety is great for you; and ye yourselves know that it ever has been. For I have exhorted you with all diligence; and I have taught you the words of my father; and I have spoken unto you concerning all things which are written, from the creation of the world.

4 And now, behold, I would speak unto you concerning things which are, and which are to come; wherefore, I will read you the words of Isaiah. And they are the words which my brother has desired that I should speak unto you. And I speak unto you for your sakes, that ye may learn and glorify the name of your God.

Jacob begins by reminding his brethren of previous occasions when he had spoken to them. He also reminds them of this authority to speak having been called by God, and ordained by Nephi (v. 2). His authority corresponds with the Fifth Article of Faith: "a man must be called of God, by prophecy, and by the laying on of hands by those who are in authority, to preach the Gospel and administer in the ordinances thereof." Jacob was speaking to his people, for "the welfare of [their] souls" (v. 3). He spoke for the same reason in his earlier speeches. He used his father's words as well as written scriptures. The selection of Isaiah as his text was two fold: to exemplify truth and because of Nephi's desire that he do so. The truthfulness of Isaiah's words should lead them to learn and glorify the name of their God (v. 4). The Savior also equated Isaiah's words with the definition of truth: "And all things that he spake have been and shall be, even according to the words which he spake" (3 Nephi 23:3).

2 Nephi 6:5–7 • The Prophecies of Isaiah

5 And now, the words which I shall read are they which Isaiah spake concerning all the house of Israel; wherefore, they may be likened unto you, for ye are of the house of Israel. And there are many things which have been spoken by Isaiah which may be likened unto you, because ye are of the house of Israel.

6 And now, these are the words: Thus saith the Lord God: Behold, I will lift up mine hand to the

Gentiles, and set up my standard to the people; and they shall bring thy sons in their arms, and thy daughters shall be carried upon their shoulders.

7 And kings shall be thy nursing fathers, and their queens thy nursing mothers; they shall bow down to thee with their faces towards the earth, and lick up the dust of thy feet; and thou shalt know that I am the Lord; for they shall not be ashamed that wait for me.

The observations of Jacob that Isaiah spoke concerning all the house of Israel is later substantiated by the Savior when he visited the Nephites and explained "that when they shall be fulfilled then is the fulfilling of the covenant which the Father hath made unto his people, O house of Israel" (3 Nephi 20:11–12). The passage that Jacob quoted, Isaiah 49:22–23, had been quoted by Nephi earlier (1 Nephi 21:22–23).[2] Nephi likened the passage unto the house of Israel in this land (America). Jacob now likened the passage unto the Jews in Jerusalem (see comments below). Both Jacob and Nephi use the phrase "liken (or likened) unto" (1 Nephi 19:23). It may appear that Jacob and Nephi are applying the scriptures and not giving the literal interpretation. However, Jacob's reasoning "for ye are of the House of Israel" (v. 5) suggests otherwise. It is more likely that Isaiah's prophecies are dual, the same prophecies will happen to various branches of the house of Israel. Jacob declares that Isaiah spoke many such prophecies (v. 5). This is verified by Jesus when he quoted other verses of Isaiah and likened them unto the Lamanites (Isaiah 52:8–10; 3 Nephi 16:18–20), and unto the Jews (Isaiah 52:8–10; 3 Nephi 20:32, 35).

2 Nephi 6:8–13 • Jacob's Interpretation

8 And now I, Jacob, would speak somewhat concerning these words. For behold, the Lord has shown me that those who were at Jerusalem, from whence we came, have been slain and carried away captive.

9 Nevertheless, the Lord has shown unto me that they should return

---

[2] The text in 2 Nephi is the same as in the KJV except for some minor punctuation variations. Both texts will only be quoted when there are significant differences.

again. And he also has shown unto me that the Lord God, the Holy One of Israel, should manifest himself unto them in the flesh; and after he should manifest himself they should scourge him and crucify him, according to the words of the angel who spake it unto me.

10 And after they have hardened their hearts and stiffened their necks against the Holy One of Israel, behold, the judgments of the Holy One of Israel shall come upon them. And the day cometh that they shall be smitten and afflicted.

11 Wherefore, after they are driven to and fro, for thus saith the angel, many shall be afflicted in the flesh, and shall not be suffered to perish, because of the prayers of the faithful; they shall be scattered, and smitten, and hated; nevertheless, the Lord will be merciful unto them, that when they shall come to the knowledge of their Redeemer, they shall be gathered together again to the lands of their inheritance.

12 And blessed are the Gentiles, they of whom the prophet has written; for behold, if it so be that they shall repent and fight not against Zion, and do not unite themselves to that great and abominable church, they shall be saved; for the Lord God will fulfil his covenants which he has made unto his children; and for this cause the prophet has written these things.

13 Wherefore, they that fight against Zion and the covenant people of the Lord shall lick up the dust of their feet; and the people of the Lord shall not be ashamed. For the people of the Lord are they who wait for him; for they still wait for the coming of the Messiah.

The source of Jacob's interpretation of the above Isaiah prophecy is a vision and an explanation given by an angel (vv. 8–11). We have no account of this vision, but the angel apparently was a part of the vision. The prophecy, now mostly history, outlines the destiny of the nation of Judah. The Jews would be slain and carried captive into Babylon (v. 8). The traditional dating of this captivity is 607–538 B.C., fulfilling the prophecy of Jeremiah that this whole land would "serve the king of Babylon seventy years" (Jeremiah 25:11–12). After the seventy years, Cyrus king of Persia, the new world power, issued a proclamation for the Jews to return to Jerusalem as Jacob was shown (v. 9).

1 Now in the first year of Cyrus king of Persia, that the word of the Lord by the mouth of Jeremiah might be fulfilled, the Lord stirred up the spirit of Cyrus king of Persia, that he made a proclamation throughout all his kingdom, and put it also in writing, saying,

32 Thus saith Cyrus king of Persia, The Lord God of heaven hath given me all the kingdoms of the earth; and he hath charged me to build him a house at Jerusalem, which is in Judah.

33 Who is there among you of all his people? his God be with him, and let him go up to Jerusalem, which is Judah, and build the house of the Lord God of Israel, (he is the God,) which is in Jerusalem. [Ezra 1:1–3]

As also shown to Jacob, the Holy One of Israel did manifest himself unto the Jews in the flesh (v. 9). He was born, ministered to them, and was crucified (A.D. 1–34, Book of Mormon dating). The Judgments of the Holy One of Israel then came upon them (v. 10). The Roman Conquest came in A.D. 70, and the Jews were scattered, smitten, and hated (after A.D. 70). The angel told Jacob that when the Jews come to the knowledge of their Redeemer, they would be gathered again in the latter days (v. 11).

Jacob also comments concerning the Gentiles spoken of in the prophecy of Isaiah. Nephi spoke of those in America (1 Nephi 22). Jacob spoke of those of whom the Jews were among. He doesn't identify the locality, but it was apparently basically in Europe where the Jews were scattered. It would also include all the other areas of the diaspora. Jacob's main concern is for those who will be saved, indicating an opportunity to receive the gospel. Part of the covenant made to Abraham was to bless all nations (Gentiles) (1 Nephi 22:9). Those who wait for the Messiah, whether Jew or Gentile, will be saved (v. 12). Those who unite with the great and abominable church and fight against Zion will not (v. 13). This part of the prophecy is still in the future.

2 Nephi 6:14–15 • Isaiah Is Further Quoted

14 And behold, according to the words of the prophet, the Messiah

will set himself again the second time to recover them; wherefore, he will manifest himself unto them in power and great glory, unto the destruction of their enemies, when that day cometh when they shall believe in him; and none will he destroy that believe in him.

15 And they that believe not in him shall be destroyed, both by fire, and by tempest, and by earthquakes, and by bloodsheds, and by pestilence, and by famine. And they shall know that the Lord is God, the Holy One of Israel.

Jacob apparently finishes telling us what the angel had told him and turns to the written text of Isaiah (v. 14). These words seem to be a combination of several prophecies. The Messiah setting himself "again the second time to recover" his people is quoting Isaiah 11:1 (2 Nephi 21:11). The manifesting of himself in great power unto the destruction of their enemies (vv. 14–15) is apparently a paraphrase or partial quote of the same prophecy Nephi quoted earlier (1 Nephi 22:15–17). These verses regarding the Second Coming of Christ are some of the "many plain and precious things taken away from the book" through the great and abominable church (1 Nephi 13:26–28).

2 Nephi 6:16–18 • Isaiah 49:24–26 is Quoted

16 For shall the prey be taken from the mighty, or the lawful captive delivered?

17 But thus saith the Lord: Even the captives of the mighty shall be taken away, and the prey of the terrible shall be delivered; **for the Mighty God shall deliver his covenant people**. For **thus saith the Lord**: I will contend with them that contendeth with thee—

18 And I will feed them that oppress thee, with their own flesh; and they shall be drunken with their own blood as with sweet wine; and all flesh shall know that I the Lord am thy Savior and thy Redeemer, the Mighty One of Jacob.

These verses were also quoted by Nephi (1 Nephi 21:24–26) and are about the covenant people of the house of Israel being delivered from the Gentiles. The bolded text (v. 17) is a comment inserted by Jacob for emphasis. Nephi interpreted the message to be the Lamanites in America being delivered from the Gentiles. Jacob is speaking of the Jews being delivered from the Gentiles. His commentary comes later in 2 Nephi 10.

Jacob continues reading from the Isaiah text included on the plates of brass, what is now Isaiah 50–52:2 in the KJV. There are many significant retentions in the Book of Mormon which help us understand these passages. Modern revelation confirms their interpretation.

2 Nephi 7:1–3 (Isaiah 50:1–3) • The Lord has Not Cast Off Israel Forever

Isaiah 50:1–3	2 Nephi 7:1–3	D&C 133:66–69
1 Thus saith the LORD, Where *is* the bill of your mother's divorcement, whom I have put away? or which of my creditors *is it* to whom I have sold you? Behold, for your iniquities have ye sold yourselves, and for your transgressions is your mother put away.	1 Yea, for thus saith the Lord: Have I put thee away, or have I cast thee off forever? For thus saith the Lord: Where is the bill of your mother's divorcement? To whom have I put thee away, or to which of my creditors have I sold you? Yea, to whom have I sold you? Behold, for your iniquities have ye sold yourselves, and for your transgressions is your mother put away.	66 In that day when I came unto mine own, no man among you received me, and you were driven out.
2 Wherefore, when I came, *was there* no man? when I called, *was there* none to answer? Is my hand shortened at all, that it cannot redeem? or have I no power to deliver? behold, at my rebuke I dry up the sea, I make the rivers a wilderness: their fish stinketh, because *there is* no water, and dieth for thirst.	2 Wherefore, when I came, there was no man; when I called, yea, there was none to answer. O house of Israel, is my hand shortened at all that it cannot redeem, or have I no power to deliver? Behold, at my rebuke I dry up the sea, I make their rivers a wilderness and their fish to stink because the waters are dried up, and	67 When I called again there was none of you to answer; yet my arm was not shortened at all that I could not redeem, neither my power to deliver. 68 Behold, at my rebuke I dry up the sea. I make the rivers a wilderness; their fish stink, and die for thirst.

they die because of thirst.

3 I clothe the heavens with blackness, and I make sackcloth their covering.	3 I clothe the heavens with blackness, and I make sackcloth their covering.	69 I clothe the heavens with blackness, and make sackcloth their covering.

Isaiah 50–52:12 is a continuation of the theme of Isaiah 49. Isaiah 49 concluded with a declaration that the Lord would fight for his people, Israel, against those who contended with them or with Zion, and that the great and abominable church would be warring within itself. Continuing in the same vein, the Lord here states his reasons for fighting on Israel's behalf. First, because "backsliding Israel committed adultery [the Lord] had put her away, and given her a bill of divorce; yet her treacherous sister Judah feared not, but went and played the harlot also" (Jeremiah 3:8). For this reason Judah was put away (taken into Babylon, and later scattered). However, the bill of divorcement that he gave to their "mother" (former-day Israel) is not in effect for latter-day Israel. Secondly, the Lord has not sold Israel to his creditors, for he has none (v. 1).

The Lord is using the metaphor of the ancient law of divorce given by Moses, wherein a man who has "found some uncleanness in [his wife]; then let him write her a bill of divorcement." However, he "may not take her again to be his wife" (Deuteronomy 24:1–4). While the Lord had divorced ancient Israel because of their iniquities, latter-day Israel was not included in that bill of divorcement.

Regarding the second reason for the Lord fighting for Israel, some scholars interpret the ancient law to say that a man could "sell his daughter to be a maidservant" either directly or in marriage to pay his creditors (Exodus 21:7), but the Lord is in debt to no one, so this law, even if it were interpreted correctly, does not apply here either. Therefore, there is no reason why the Lord would not deliver Israel from the hands of her oppressors, and he certainly had the power to do so.

There will be those in modern Israel who are not delivered, because they will suffer from the consequences of their own iniquities, just as those in former-day Israel suffered because of their transgressions. The Doctrine and Covenants clarifies the Lord's teachings in this matter. The context is the day of the Lord's fighting for Israel—the day spoken of by Moses and Malachi, when those who hearken not to the voice of the Lord will be cut off, and the proud and the wicked will be burned, leaving them "neither root [ancestors] nor branch [posterity]." Thus, they are no longer a part of Israel; their patriarchal lines are severed.

> 63 And upon them that hearken not to the voice of the Lord shall be fulfilled that which was written by the prophet Moses, that they should be cut off from among the people.

> 64 And also that which was written by the prophet Malachi: For, behold, the day cometh that shall burn as an oven, and all the proud, yea, and all that do wickedly, shall be stubble; and the day that cometh shall burn them up, saith the Lord of hosts, that it shall leave them neither root nor branch. [D&C 133:63–64; see also Deuteronomy 18:15, 18:19; Acts 3:23; 1 Nephi 22:20–21; 3 Nephi 20:23, 21:11; Malachi 4:1]

Doctrine and Covenants 133:66–69 contains "the answer of the Lord unto [those of Israel who are cut off]" (D&C 133:65) with slight variations from the words of Isaiah. A comparison of the three texts should help us understand the Isaiah passage.

When Christ came to his own in the meridian of time, the Jews collectively rejected the gospel (2 Nephi 7: 2). When he calls again (D&C 133:67), it will he his second appearance to them. Although the Jews will still not be ready for revelation, the Lord will have power to redeem them. This idea is amplified in Isaiah 5 or 2 Nephi 8.

The following verses (Isaiah 50:4–9) probably have dual meaning, referring to the time of both appearances. As quoted in Doctrine and Covenants 133:66–70, Isaiah 50:2–3,11 addresses those who were cut off from Israel, while Isaiah 50:4–10 describes those who brought the message of salvation. We will analyze the verses separately.

2 Nephi 7:4 (Isaiah 50:4) • The Tongue of the Learned

4 The Lord God hath given me the tongue of the learned, that I should know how to speak a word in season unto thee, O house of Israel. When ye are weary he waketh morning by morning. He waketh mine ear to hear as the learned. [2 Nephi 7:4]

4 The Lord GOD hath given me the tongue of the learned, that I should know how to speak a word in season to *him that is* weary: he wakeneth morning by morning, he wakeneth mine ear to hear as the learned. [Isaiah 50:4]

The Book of Mormon reading clearly shows that the servant is addressing the house of Israel. This verse has been interpreted as a reference to the twelve-year-old Christ as he sat in the temple in the midst of the doctors, who were "astonished at his understanding and answers" (Luke 2:46–47). Others, citing 2 Chronicles 36:15–16, have said that the verse refers to prophets' being called to preach to Jerusalem. However, this passage of Chronicles does not refer to the time of Christ's ministry or the restoration in the latter days which D&C 133 sets as the time periods of Isaiah's dual prophecy. The verse does fit the calling and mission of Joseph Smith and the elders of restored Israel who were to speak to the house of Israel in the latter days to gather them. It would be consistent with chapter 49 to identify the servant "me" as Joseph Smith and the elders of restored Israel, since the context is the continuation of that message.

2 Nephi 7:5–7 (Isaiah 50:5–7) • The Lord God Has Appointed Me

5 The Lord God hath opened mine ear, and I was not rebellious, neither turned away back.

6 I gave my back to the smiter, and my cheeks to them that plucked off the hair. I hid not my face from shame and spitting.

7 For the Lord God will help me, therefore shall I not be confounded. Therefore have I set my face like a flint, and I know that I shall not be ashamed.

In the JST verse 5 reads, "The Lord God hath *appointed* mine ears" rather than "*opened* mine ear." Joseph Smith was not correcting the text, but was clarifying the meaning in the language of the day. The subject is still the servant of Israel. The persecution of the Latter-day Saints, particularly in the days of Joseph Smith, is very similar to the events in these verses. The passage may also describe the persecution of the Savior as he was condemned. According to tradition, Isaiah also faced persecutors, eventually being sawn asunder with a wooden saw.

2 Nephi 7:8–9 (Isaiah 50:8–9) • The Lord Justifies His Servant

8 And the Lord is near, and he justifieth me. Who will contend with me? Let us stand together. Who is mine adversary? Let him come near me, and I will smite him with the strength of my mouth.

9 For the Lord God will help me. And all they who shall condemn me, behold, all they shall wax old as a garment, and the moth shall eat them up. [2 Nephi 7:8–9]

8 *He is* near that justifieth me; who will contend with me? let us stand together: who *is* mine adversary? let him come near to me.

9 Behold, the Lord GOD will help me; who *is* he *that* shall condemn me? lo, they all shall wax old as a garment; the moth shall eat them up. [Isaiah 50:8–9]

The Book of Mormon identifies the pronoun "he" as the Lord and retains the clause "and I will smite him with the strength of my mouth" (v. 8). The "me" that is justified again designates the servant Israel with whom the Lord will be near. This further shows that the Lord is not the servant, but is someone he has called. "The strength of his mouth" must have reference to the message of the restoration that the servant is sent to deliver. The Lord helping "me" (v. 9) also distinguishes between the Lord and the servant. The Book of Mormon wording also reads more clearly in declaring the fate of those who condemn the servant.

2 Nephi 7:10–11 (Isaiah 50:10–11) • Fear the Lord and Obey His Servant

10 Who is among you that feareth the Lord, that obeyeth the voice of his servant, that walketh in darkness and hath no light? [2 Nephi 7:10]

10 Who *is* among you that feareth the LORD, that obeyeth the voice of his servant, that walketh *in* darkness, and hath no light? let him trust in the name of the LORD, and stay upon his God. [Isaiah 50:10]

The Book of Mormon reading does not contain the last line of verse 10. Without it, verse 11 becomes a warning in the context of Isaiah 50:2–3 as clarified by Doctrine and Covenants 133. Those who will not follow revelation or heed the voice of the Lord's servant but walk in their own light of reason, will be cut off from Israel and will lie down in sorrow.

11 Behold all ye that kindle fire, that compass yourselves about with sparks, walk in the light of your fire and in the sparks which ye have kindled. This shall ye have of mine hand—ye shall lie down in sorrow. [2 Nephi 7:11]	70 And this shall ye have of my hand—ye shall lie down in sorrow. [D&C 133:70]

There are no significant differences in the 2 Nephi and King James texts, therefore only the 2 Nephi text and the Doctrine and Covenants text are quoted. The Lord gives a further description of latter-day Israel's fate in the verses that follow:

71 Behold, and lo, there are none to deliver you; for ye obeyed not my voice when I called to you out of the heavens; ye believed not my servants, and when they were sent unto you ye received them not.

72 Wherefore, they sealed up the testimony and bound up the law, and ye were delivered over unto darkness.

73 These shall go away into outer darkness, where there is weeping, and wailing, and gnashing of teeth.

74 Behold the Lord your God hath spoken it. Amen. [D&C 133:71–74]

2 Nephi 8:1–2 (Isaiah 51:1–2) • The Rock of Abraham

1 Hearken unto me, ye that follow after righteousness. Look unto the rock from whence ye are hewn, and to the hole of the pit from whence ye are digged.	1 Hearken to me, ye that follow after righteousness, ye that seek the LORD: look unto the rock *whence* ye are hewn, and to the hole of the pit *whence* ye are digged.
2 Look unto Abraham, your father, and unto Sarah, she that bare you; for I called him alone, and blessed him. [2 Nephi 8:1–2]	2 Look unto Abraham your father, and unto Sarah *that* bare you: for I called him alone, and blessed him, and increased him. [Isaiah 51:1–2]

The phrase that has been added to each of the verses in the KJV, or the words retained in the Book of Mormon text are insignificant. The KJV phrases were probably added by the translators to enhance the verse. The words *whence* and *that* being italicized in the KJV indicate the translators were unsure of their word selection.

The Book of Mormon teaches that the covenant made with Abraham and Sarah will be fulfilled in the latter days. Nephi said it would be "fulfilled in the latter days" (1 Nephi 15:18). Mormon said it would be fulfilled after the Lamanites "have been driven and scattered by the Gentiles" (Mormon 5:20). The Doctrine and Covenants sustains the teaching of the Book of Mormon. The Lord revealed to Joseph Smith that he was "of Abraham" and was to "do the works of Abraham" (D&C 132:31–32). Moreover, he said "unto [his] servant Joseph: In thee and in thy seed shall all the kindred of the earth be blessed" (D&C 124:58). The covenant made to Abraham is now being fulfilled. Isaiah's invitation for the righteous to look to Abraham and Sarah pertains to this same time period.

2 Nephi 8:3 (Isaiah 51:3) • The Lord will Comfort Zion

> 3 For the Lord shall comfort Zion, he will comfort all her waste places; and he will make her wilderness like Eden, and her desert like the garden of the Lord. Joy and gladness shall be found therein, thanksgiving and the voice of melody. (no significant differences)

The Prophet Joseph Smith proclaimed, "The whole of America is Zion itself from north to south, and is described by the prophets" (*TPJS*, 362). The physical and social blessings mentioned by Isaiah are to come to all the gathering places of the Saints in the land of Zion. The blessings pronounced upon Zion's waste places, wilderness, and deserts are reminiscent of the physical blessings that the Lord has promised those who keep the Sabbath in the land of Zion. These things will be given "for the benefit and use of man both to please the eye and to gladden the heart," and will all come "according to the law and prophets" (D&C 59:16–19, 22).

2 Nephi 8:4–5 (Isaiah 51:4–5) • A Law to Proceed from the Lord

> 4 Hearken unto me, my people; and give ear unto me, O my nation; for a law shall proceed from me, and I will make my judgment to rest for a light for the people.

> 5 My righteousness is near; my salvation is gone forth, and mine arm shall judge the people. The isles shall wait upon me, and on mine arm shall they trust. (no significant differences)

The "law" which will come from the Lord may be the U.S. Constitution (see comments on 2 Nephi 12:2–3), the Book of Mormon, or both. The law is associated with judgment (vv. 4–5), and it will come forth from the "isles." Jacob considered the Americas an isle of the sea (2 Nephi 10:20–21, commented on later in this chapter). The law is to judge the nations as well as the people. Nephi later says "the nations who possess [the Book of Mormon records] shall be judged of them" (2 Nephi 25:21–22). The same is true regarding the U.S. Constitution (see D&C 98:4–8).

2 Nephi 8:6–8 (Isaiah 51:6–8) • Look to the Heavens and the Earth

> 6 Lift up your eyes to the heavens, and look upon the earth beneath; for the heavens shall vanish away like smoke, and the earth shall wax old like a garment; and they that dwell therein shall die in like manner. But my salvation shall be forever, and my righteousness shall not be abolished.

> 7 Hearken unto me, ye that know righteousness, the people in whose heart **I have written** *my law,* fear ye not the reproach of men, neither be ye afraid of their revilings.

> 8 For the moth shall eat them up like a garment, and the worm shall eat them like wool. But my righteousness shall be forever, and my salvation from generation to generation.

The text of the KJV is the same except for one phrase (v. 7). The Book of Mormon says "in whose heart **I have written** my law," and the KJV says "in whose heart is my law." In his second general epistle, the apostle Peter expressed teachings similar to the three Isaiah verses:

10 But the day of the Lord will come as a thief in the night; in the which the heavens shall pass away with a great noise, and the elements shall melt with fervent heat, the earth also and the works that are therein shall be burned up.

11 *Seeing* then *that* all these things shall be dissolved, what manner *of persons* ought ye to be in *all* holy conversation and godliness,

12 Looking for and hasting unto the coming of the day of God, wherein the heavens being on fire shall be dissolved, and the elements shall melt with fervent heat?

13 Nevertheless we, according to his promise, look for new heavens and a new earth, wherein dwelleth righteousness. [2 Peter 3:10–13]

The Book of Mormon retentions (see bold words in the text) calls to mind the promise given in Jeremiah that a new covenant will be established with Judah and Israel in the latter days, unlike the one when he brought them out of Egypt, but "I will put my law in their inward parts, and write it in their hearts; and will be their God, and they shall be my people" (Jeremiah 31:31–33). This further indicates that Isaiah is referring to the latter days.[3]

2 Nephi 8:9–10 (Isaiah 51:9–10) • Zion to put on Strength

9 Awake, awake! Put on strength, O arm of the Lord; awake as in the ancient days. Art thou not **he** that hath cut Rahab, and wounded the dragon?	9 Awake, awake, put on strength, O arm of the LORD; awake, as in the ancient days, **in the generations of old**. Art thou not **it** that hath cut Rahab, *and* wounded the dragon?
10 Art thou not **he** who hath dried the sea, the waters of the great deep; that hath made	10 *Art* thou not **it** which hath dried the sea, the waters of the great deep; that hath

---

[3] At the end of the prophecy in Jeremiah 30, Jeremiah says "in the latter days ye shall consider it." A footnote suggests "fully understand." At the beginning of chapter 31, from which the above prophecy is taken, he says it will come to pass "At the same time," or also in the latter days.

the depths of the sea a way for the ransomed to pass over? [2 Nephi 8:9–10]	made the depths of the sea a way for the ransomed to pass over? [Isaiah 51:9–10]

Isaiah 51:1–8 (2 Nephi 8:1–8) speaks of a general promise of the covenant of Abraham being fulfilled as discussed above. Isaiah now speaks of the two specific places where the covenant people will gather. He speaks first of Zion or America (vv. 9–16, and then of Jerusalem (vv. 17–23). The last two verses (vv. 24–25), Isaiah 52:1–2, are a summation of the Lord's challenges to both gathering places. The Book of Mormon retains the word "he" for the KJV "it" (vv. 9–10). The KJV adds "in the generations of old" following "as in ancient days" (v. 9). These differences are not significant. In these verses, Isaiah cites acts of strength that the Lord has accomplished in times past as evidence of the Lord's power to redeem his people in the latter days.

2 Nephi 8:11–14 (Isaiah 51:11–14) • The Redeemed of the Lord Shall Return to Zion

11 Therefore, the redeemed of the Lord shall return, and come with singing unto Zion; and everlasting joy **and holiness** shall be upon their heads; **and** they shall obtain gladness and joy; sorrow and mourning shall flee away.	11 Therefore the redeemed of the LORD shall return, and come with singing unto Zion; and everlasting joy *shall be* upon their head: they shall obtain gladness and joy; *and* sorrow and mourning shall flee away.
12 I am he; yea, I am he that comforteth you. **Behold**, who art thou, that thou shouldst be afraid of man, **who** shall die, and of the son of man, **who** shall be made like unto grass?	12 I, *even* I, *am* he that comforteth you: who *art* thou, that thou shouldest be afraid of a man *that* shall die, and of the son of man *which* shall be made *as* grass;
13 And forgettest the Lord thy maker, that hath stretched forth the heavens, and laid the foundations of the earth, and hast feared continually every day, because of the fury of the oppressor, as if he were ready to destroy? And where is the fury of the oppressor?	13 (no differences)
14 The captive exile hasteneth, that he may be loosed, and that he should not die in the pit, nor that his bread should fail.	14 (no differences)

The "redeemed of the Lord" who were to "return, and come with singing unto Zion" with "everlasting joy" (v. 11) are identified in the Doctrine and Covenants as "the righteous [who] shall be gathered out from among all nations, and shall come to Zion, singing with songs of everlasting joy" (D&C 45:71; see also 66:11; 101:18). Only the righteous coming to Zion is consistent with **and holiness** that is retained in the Book of Mormon text. Their joy will be because the Lord will comfort them, and they will no longer fear the natural man who has oppressed them, and kept them in bondage to the Gentile culture (vv. 12–14). The return has begun, but it will not be completed until the center place of Zion is built up "that the prophets might be fulfilled" (D&C 101:19).

2 Nephi 8:15–16 (Isaiah 51:16) • Covered in the Shadow of the Lord's Hand

15 But I am the Lord thy God, whose waves roared; the Lord of Hosts is **my** name.

16 And I have put my words in thy mouth, and have covered thee in the shadow of mine hand, that I may plant the heavens and lay the foundations of the earth, and say unto Zion: **Behold**, thou art my people. [2 Nephi 8:15–16]

15 But I *am* the LORD thy God, **that divided the sea**, whose waves roared: The LORD of hosts *is* **his** name.

16 And I have put my words in thy mouth, and **I** have covered thee in the shadow of mine hand, that I may plant the heavens, and lay the foundations of the earth, and say unto Zion, Thou *art* my people. [Isaiah 51:16]

The phrase "that divided the sea" in the KJV, but not in the Book of Mormon, was probably added by some scribe to clarify the phrase that follows "whose waves roared" (v. 15). However the Lord's control of the waters is not limited to Moses' dividing the Red Sea. Putting words in the servant's mouth and covering Israel in his hand (v. 16) is similar to 1 Nephi 21:2 (see note there). That Zion will be recognized as the Lord's people is also part of the promise of the "new covenant" spoken of in Jeremiah 31:31–33, and commented on above.

2 Nephi 8:17–18 (Isaiah 51:17) • Judah Has None to Guide Her

17 Awake, awake, stand up, O Jerusalem, which hast drunk at the hand of the Lord the cup of his fury—thou hast drunken the dregs of the cup of trembling wrung out—

17 Awake, awake, stand up, O Jerusalem, which hast drunk at the hand of the LORD the cup of his fury; thou hast drunken the dregs of the cup of trembling, *and* wrung *them* out.

18 And none to guide her among all the sons she hath brought forth; neither that taketh her by the hand, of all the sons she hath brought up.

18 *There is* none to guide her among all the sons *whom* she hath brought forth; neither *is there any* that taketh her by the hand of all the sons *that* she hath brought up.

The differences in the King James text of these two verses were apparently added to make it read better in English as the italicized words indicate.

Isaiah now speaks of the second gathering place of the covenant people, Jerusalem. The people are invited to awaken from their long sleep of apostasy. They have been through the pronounced "furnace of affliction" (see 1 Nephi 20:10).

Because Judah's sons are without the priesthood, there is no proper leadership. This is the same thought contained in Isaiah 50:2 as interpreted in Doctrine and Covenants 133:67. Both refer to Judah (see note on 2 Nephi 7:1–3).

2 Nephi 8:19–20 (Isaiah 51:19–20) • Two Sons Come to Judah

19 These *two* **sons** are come unto thee, who shall be sorry for **thee**—*thy* desolation and destruction, and the famine and the sword—and by whom shall I comfort thee?

19 These two *things* are come unto thee; who shall be sorry for thee? desolation, and destruction, and the famine, and the sword: by whom shall I comfort thee?

20 Thy sons have fainted, *save these two*; they lie at the head of all the streets; as a wild bull in a net, they are full of the fury of the Lord, the rebuke of thy God. [2 Nephi 8:19–20]

20 Thy sons have fainted, they lie at the head of all the streets, as a wild bull in a net: they are full of the fury of the LORD, the rebuke of thy God. [Isaiah 51:19–20]

The Book of Mormon (bold) identifies the two "things" in verse 19 (italicized in the KJV) as "sons." Because the people of Judah have no sons with the priesthood among them, two other sons (who have the priesthood) are to be sent to them. Because these "sons" are to bear the priesthood, they have to come from among the Latter-day Saints. They will be the "two witnesses" spoken of in Revelation.

> 3 And I will give *power* unto my two witnesses, and they shall prophesy a thousand two hundred *and* threescore days, clothed in sackcloth.
>
> 4 These are the two olive trees, and the two candlesticks standing before the God of the earth.
>
> 5 And if any man will hurt them, fire proceedeth out of their mouth, and devoureth their enemies: and if any man will hurt them, he must in this manner be killed.
>
> 6 These have power to shut heaven, that it rain not in the days of their prophecy: and have power over waters to turn them to blood, and to smite the earth with all plagues, as often as they will.
>
> 7 And when they shall have finished their testimony, the beast that ascendeth out of the bottomless pit shall make war against them, and shall overcome them, and kill them.
>
> 8 And their dead bodies *shall lie* in the street of the great city, which spiritually is called Sodom and Egypt, where also our Lord was crucified.
>
> 9 And they of the people and kindreds and tongues and nations shall see their dead bodies three days and an half, and shall not suffer their dead bodies to be put in graves.
>
> 10 And they that dwell upon the earth shall rejoice over them, and make merry, and shall send gifts one to another; because these two prophets tormented them that dwelt on the earth.
>
> 11 And after three days and an half the Spirit of life from God entered into them, and they stood upon their feet; and great fear fell upon them which saw them. [Revelation 11:2–11]

As the Prophet Joseph was translating the scriptures (JST), he was given a revelation identifying the two witnesses spoken of above.

15 Q. What is to be understood by the two witnesses, in the eleventh chapter of Revelation?

A. They are two prophets that are to be raised up to the Jewish nation in the last days, at the time of the restoration, and to prophesy to the Jews after they are gathered and have built the city of Jerusalem in the land of their fathers. [D&C 77:15]

Elder LeGrand Richards has written: "No doubt these prophets will be called and ordained and sent by the First Presidency of The Church of Jesus Christ of Latter-day Saints."[4] Elder Bruce R. McConkie has further stated, "No doubt they will be members of the Council of the Twelve or of the First Presidency of the Church."[5] These two prophets will use the power of God [the priesthood] to rebuke those gathered against Judah (v. 20). As Enoch of old, they may speak "the word of the Lord, and the earth trembled, and the mountains fled, even at his command; and the rivers were turned out of their course" (Moses 7:13). As a wild bull in a net cannot be fully contained (v. 20), the enemy will not control the two sons until they are killed, and then they will be resurrected according to the record of John the Beloved quoted above.

2 Nephi 8:21–23 (Isaiah 51:21–23)
• The Lord Pleads for His People

21 Therefore hear now this, thou afflicted, and drunken, and not with wine:

22 Thus saith thy Lord, the Lord and thy God pleadeth the cause of his people; behold, I have taken out of thine hand the cup of trembling, the dregs of the cup of my fury; thou shalt no more drink it again.

23 But I will put it into the hand of them that afflict thee; who have said to thy soul: Bow down, that we may go over—and thou hast laid thy body as the ground and as the street to them that went over.

---

[4] LeGrand Richards, *Israel Do You Know* [1954], 197.

[5] Bruce R. McConkie, *Doctrinal New Testament Commentary,* 3 vols. [1996-73], 3:509.

The differences in the King James text were made to make it easier to read in English and are not significant, therefore the text is not quoted.

These verses refer to those who come against Judah in the last days, the Gentile nations in the battle of Armageddon. The Lord will come to the aid of his people and plead their cause. The Prophet Amos foretold also in these words:

9 Proclaim ye this among the Gentiles; Prepare war, wake up the mighty men, let all the men of war draw near; let them come up:

10 Beat your plowshares into swords, and your pruninghooks into spears: let the weak say, I *am* strong.

11 Assemble yourselves, and come, all ye heathen, and gather yourselves together round about: thither cause thy mighty ones to come down, O LORD.

12 Let the heathen be wakened, and come up to the valley of Jehoshaphat: for there will I sit to judge all the heathen round about.

13 Put ye in the sickle, for the harvest is ripe: come, get you down; for the press is full, the fats overflow; for their wickedness *is* great.

14 Multitudes, multitudes in the valley of decision: for the day of the LORD *is* near in the valley of decision.

15 The sun and the moon shall be darkened, and the stars shall withdraw their shining.

16 The LORD also shall roar out of Zion, and utter his voice from Jerusalem; and the heavens and the earth shall shake: but the LORD *will be* the hope of his people, and the strength of the children of Israel.

17 So shall ye know that I *am* the LORD your God dwelling in Zion, my holy mountain: then shall Jerusalem be holy, and there shall no strangers pass through her any more. [Joel 3:9–17; see also Zechariah 12–14; D&C 45:42–53]

2 Nephi 8:24–25 (Isaiah 52:1–2) • Zion and Jerusalem to Awake

24 Awake, awake, put on thy strength, O Zion; put on thy beautiful

garments, O Jerusalem, the holy city; for henceforth there shall no more come into thee the uncircumcised and the unclean.

25 Shake thyself from the dust; arise, sit down, O Jerusalem; loose thyself from the bands of thy neck, O captive daughter of Zion.

The only difference in the King James text, other than punctuation, is the italicized "and" inserted before arise in the second clause of verse twenty-five. These two verses summarize what the Lord said about the two gathering places of Zion and Jerusalem. They are also quoted in two other places in the Book of Mormon. When the Savior visited the Nephites, he specified that these verses would be fulfilled when the Jews were gathered to Jerusalem in the last days. He also added one word to the text which was not quoted by Jacob: "Awake, awake *again*, and put on thy strength, O Zion" (3 Nephi 20:36–37). This was probably because Zion, or America, was "awakening at the time of the Savior's visit and "putting on her strength," but the Savior knew that within 400 years the Nephites would lose that strength and fall again into a spiritual sleep. The use of the word "again" indicated a dual interpretation of the Isaiah text in this instance, and supports the idea that there are other dual interpretations throughout Isaiah. Moroni, in his final admonition as he finished the record, paraphrased these verses and added "that thou mayest no more be confounded, that the covenants of the Eternal Father which he hath made unto thee, O house of Israel, may be fulfilled" (Moroni 10:31).

In March 1838, the Prophet Joseph Smith gave the following interpretation of these verses in answer to a question about what Isaiah meant by "Put on thy strength, O Zion":

He had reference to those whom God should call in the last days, who should hold the power of priesthood to bring again Zion, and the redemption of Israel; and to put on her strength is to put on the authority of the priesthood, which she, Zion, has a right to by lineage; also to return to that power which she had lost. [D&C 113:8]

He also gave the meaning of Zion loosing herself from the bands of her neck:

We are to understand that the scattered remnants are exhorted to return to the Lord from whence they have fallen; which if they do, the promise of the Lord is that he will speak to them, or give them revelation. See the 6th, 7th, and 8th verses. The bands of her neck are the curses of God upon her, or the remnants of Israel in their scattered condition among the Gentiles. [D&C 113:10]

Doctrine and Covenants 82:14 also declares that "Zion must arise and put on her beautiful garments." The putting on her beautiful garments probably has reference to the building of temples and being cleansed in the sight of the Lord. Jerusalem is to put on her beautiful garments and become a holy city. A temple will eventually be built in Jerusalem. The Prophet Joseph Smith said: "Judah must return, Jerusalem must be rebuilt, and the temple, and water come out from under the temple, and the waters of the Dead Sea be healed. It will take some time to rebuild the walls of the city and the temple, &c; and all these things must be done before the Son of Man will make His appearance" (*TPJS*, 286). Much of the Prophet's prophecy has already taken place but it will be fully fulfilled as the Millennium is ushered in.

Jerusalem's becoming a holy city refers to the city being rebuilt. The Jaredite prophet Ether foretold it:

5 And he spake also concerning the house of Israel, and the Jerusalem from whence Lehi should come—after it should be destroyed it should be built up again, a holy city unto the Lord; where-fore, it could not be a new Jerusalem for it had been in a time of old; but it should be built up again, and become a holy city of the Lord; and it should be built unto the house of Israel.

11 And then also cometh the Jerusalem of old; and the inhabitants thereof, blessed are they, for they have been washed in the blood of the Lamb; and they are they who were scattered and gathered in from the four quarters of the earth, and from the north countries, and are partakers of the fulfilling of the covenant which God made with their father, Abraham.

12 And when these things come, bringeth to pass the scripture which saith, there are they who were first, who shall be last; and there are they who were last, who shall be first. [Ether 13:5, 11–12]

Great blessings await Judah and Jerusalem as foretold by Isaiah and other prophets.

2 Nephi 10:1–2 • The Righteous Branch

1 And now I, Jacob, speak unto you again, my beloved brethren, concerning this righteous branch of which I have spoken.

2 For behold, the promises which we have obtained are promises unto us according to the flesh; wherefore, as it has been shown unto me that many of our children shall perish in the flesh because of unbelief, nevertheless, God will be merciful unto many; and our children shall be restored, that they may come to that which will give them the true knowledge of their Redeemer.

This chapter is a partial account of what Jacob spoke on the second day of an apparently great Nephite conference. He promised to speak more of the covenant made to the house of Israel to raise up a righteous branch in future generations. True to his promise, this is the subject of his speech. The source of his information once more comes from a vision. He previously mentioned that he had seen Jerusalem (2 Nephi 6:8), and now he mentions having seen his own people. He had apparently seen much of what Nephi had seen, that many of his people would perish in the flesh, but would later be restored to a true knowledge of their Redeemer.

2 Nephi 10:3–9 • The Scattering and Gathering of the Jews

3 Wherefore, as I said unto you, it must needs be expedient that Christ—for in the last night the angel spake unto me that this should be his name—should come among the Jews, among those who are the more wicked part of the world; and they shall crucify him—for thus it behooveth our God, and there is none other nation on earth that would crucify their God.

4 For should the mighty miracles be wrought among other nations they would repent, and know that he be their God.

5 But because of priestcrafts and iniquities, they at Jerusalem will stiffen their necks against him, that he be crucified.

6 Wherefore, because of their iniquities, destructions, famines, pestilences, and bloodshed shall come upon them; and they who shall not be destroyed shall be scattered among all nations.

7 But behold, thus saith the Lord God: When the day cometh that they shall believe in me, that I am Christ, then have I covenanted with their fathers that they shall be restored in the flesh, upon the earth, unto the lands of their inheritance.

8 And it shall come to pass that they shall be gathered in from their long dispersion, from the isles of the sea, and from the four parts of the earth; and the nations of the Gentiles shall be great in the eyes of me, saith God, in carrying them forth to the lands of their inheritance.

9 Yea, the kings of the Gentiles shall be nursing fathers unto them, and their queens shall become nursing mothers; wherefore, the promises of the Lord are great unto the Gentiles, for he hath spoken it, and who can dispute?

In addition to his prior vision, an angel had spoken unto him during the night between his two speeches. The angel declared the name of the Messiah that "should come among the Jews." The name was Christ. He was to be crucified among them because "there was none other nation on earth that would crucify their God" (v. 3). This should not be taken as an indictment of all the Jewish people. People do change through the generations. Joseph Smith said of his generation: "This generation is as corrupt as the generations of the Jews that crucified Christ; and if he were here today, and should preach the same doctrine he did then, they would put him to death" (*TPJS*, 328). Joseph's statement is verified by that generation putting him to death. Our generation, speaking collectively, is probably worse than the generation of Joseph Smith.

One of the causes of the wickedness of the Jews was priestcraft (v. 5). Priestcraft is defined in the Book of Mormon, "priestcrafts are that men preach and set themselves up for a light unto the world, that they may get gain and praise of the world; but they seek not the welfare of Zion" (2 Nephi 26:29). There is no mention of priestcrafts in the Bible, probably because it was removed with other "plain and precious things which have been taken out of the book" (1 Nephi 13:29). Satan, the founder of the great and abominable church, who was responsible for those things being taken out, would certainly like to keep the source of Christ being crucified anonymous.

The scattering and gathering of Judah is foretold by Jacob (vv. 6–8). The gathering will come when they believe in Christ, and it will be a literal gathering, "restored in the flesh" (v. 7), they will come from various parts of the earth, especially from among the Gentiles.

The forepart of Jacob's prophecy seems to be taken from other sections of Isaiah (chapter 52, see 3 Nephi 20), but the latter part is from Isaiah 49:22–23, part of which is quoted again by Jacob (v. 9). Nephi used these verses concerning the house of Israel in America. Jacob uses them in relationship to the Jews, another evidence of dual prophecy.

2 Nephi 10:10–19 • God Has Said the Gentiles Would be Blessed in America

10 But behold, this land, said God, shall be a land of thine inheritance, and the Gentiles shall be blessed upon the land.

11 And this land shall be a land of liberty unto the Gentiles, and there shall be no kings upon the land, who shall raise up unto the Gentiles.

12 And I will fortify this land against all other nations.

13 And he that fighteth against Zion shall perish, saith God.

14 For he that raiseth up a king against me shall perish, for I, the Lord, the king of heaven, will be their king, and I will be a light unto them forever, that hear my words.

15 Wherefore, for this cause, that my covenants may be fulfilled which I have made unto the children of men, that I will do unto them while they are in the flesh, I must needs destroy the secret works of darkness, and of murders, and of abominations.

16 Wherefore, he that fighteth against Zion, both Jew and Gentile,

both bond and free, both male and female, shall perish; for they are they who are the whore of all the earth; for they who are not for me are against me, saith our God.

17 For I will fulfil my promises which I have made unto the children of men, that I will do unto them while they are in the flesh—

18 Wherefore, my beloved brethren, thus saith our God: I will afflict thy seed by the hand of the Gentiles; nevertheless, I will soften the hearts of the Gentiles, that they shall be like unto a father to them; wherefore, the Gentiles shall be blessed and numbered among the house of Israel.

19 Wherefore, I will consecrate this land unto thy seed, and them who shall be numbered among thy seed, forever, for the land of their inheritance; for it is a choice land, saith God unto me, above all other lands, wherefore I will have all men that dwell thereon that they shall worship me, saith God.

Jacob shifts his subject to this land, the Americas. It appears that he is quoting but does not give his source. Perhaps the angel told him what God had said. Even if it is a paraphrase, it does not correlate with the Isaiah passages he had quoted the day before. God had said the Gentiles would be blessed in the Americas. America will be a land of liberty and there will be no kings in the land.

Continuing to quote God, Jacob said God will fortify this land against all nations, and whoso fights against Zion (America) shall perish (vv. 12–13). The Lord, the king of heaven, will be the king of this land so that his covenants may be fulfilled. To bring this about he must destroy the secret works of darkness and abomination (vv. 14–15).

Still quoting, we are given an important insight into the identification of the great and abominable church. It is not an organization per se, but those from whatever lineage, affiliation, or gender that fight Zion (v. 16). To bring about his purposes, the Lord will afflict the seed of the Nephites by the hand of the Gentiles, but will soften the hearts of the Gentiles that they will be like fathers to the Nephites (vv. 17–18). For this they shall be blessed. These concepts seem to be based again on Isaiah 49:22–23. Jacob concluded his quoting with the promise of

America being the choice land above all other lands (v. 19). It will be interesting to find the complete sources of these great promises.

2 Nephi 10:20–22 • The Isles of the Sea

20 And now, my beloved brethren, seeing that our merciful God has given us so great knowledge concerning these things, let us remember him, and lay aside our sins, and not hang down our heads, for we are not cast off; nevertheless, we have been driven out of the land of our inheritance; but we have been led to a better land, for the Lord has made the sea our path, and we are upon an isle of the sea.

21 But great are the promises of the Lord unto them who are upon the isles of the sea; wherefore as it says isles, there must needs be more than this, and they are inhabited also by our brethren.

22 For behold, the Lord God has led away from time to time from the house of Israel, according to his will and pleasure. And now behold, the Lord remembereth all them who have been broken off, wherefore he remembereth us also.

Although driven out from Jerusalem, Jacob knows they have been led to a far better land of promise. His acknowledgment of being on an isle of the sea confirms the ancient belief that every place away from the land they knew was considered to be an island. Some of the promises made to those on the isles of the sea are enumerated in 1 Nephi 21 (Isaiah 49) and commented on in 1 Nephi 22. Jacob knew his people were included in these promises.

2 Nephi 10:23–25 • The Power of the Atonement

23 Therefore, cheer up your hearts, and remember that ye are free to act for yourselves—to choose the way of everlasting death or the way of eternal life.

24 Wherefore, my beloved brethren, reconcile yourselves to the will of God, and not to the will of the devil and the flesh; and remember, after ye are reconciled unto God, that it is only in and through the grace of God that ye are saved.

25 Wherefore, may God raise you from death by the power of the resurrection, and also from everlasting death by the power of the

atonement, that ye may be received into the eternal kingdom of God, that ye may praise him through grace divine. Amen.

These three verses are apparently a summary of both days of instruction. However, more is on the first day's sermon. Verse twenty-three and twenty-four reflect Lehi's teachings in 2 Nephi 2. The last verse (25) is extremely important. It separates the two aspects of the Atonement, the power of the resurrection and the power to overcome spiritual or everlasting death. Collectively they are called the Atonement, but specifically the two are separated in their purposes and accomplishments.

SACRED WRITING

Preaching which is Sacred:

2 Nephi 6–10	Jacob's two sermons to his people

Revelation which is Great:

2 Nephi 6:8–13	An angel to Jacob
2 Nephi 6:14–8:52	Words of Isaiah quoted by Jacob
2 Nephi 10:3–19	An angel to Jacob

Doctrines Learned:

2 Nephi 6:4	Isaiah spoke of things which are and things which are to come (truth).
2 Nephi 6:5	Isaiah spoke concerning all the house of Israel.
2 Nephi 6:11	The Jews will be gathered to the lands of their inheritance when they come to the knowledge of their Redeemer.
2 Nephi 6:12	The Gentiles who repent and do not fight against Zion and unite with the great and abominable church will be saved.
2 Nephi 6:14	The Messiah will manifest himself in power and great glory and destroy the enemies of the covenant people of the Lord who believe not in him. He will

	destroy them by fire, tempest, earthquake, blood-shed, pestilence and famine, and they will know that he is the Holy One of Israel.
2 Nephi 7:1	Israel sold themselves for iniquity but will be gathered again.
2 Nephi 8:1–2	Israel is to look to Abraham and Sarah—the original covenant will be fulfilled.
2 Nephi 8:11	The redeemed of the Lord shall return and come singing unto Zion.
2 Nephi 8:19	Two sons shall come to Jerusalem and comfort her.
2 Nephi 10:3	Christ came among the Jews because none other nation would crucify their God (at that time).
2 Nephi 10:5	Priestcrafts and iniquities among the Jews were the cause of Jesus' crucifixion.
2 Nephi 10:6–7	The Jews who were not destroyed after Jesus' crucifixion were scattered among all nations and will be gathered when they believe in Christ.
2 Nephi 10:9	The kings and queens of the Gentiles will be nursing fathers and mothers to the Jews in their scattered condition.
2 Nephi 10:11–12	America shall be a land of liberty to the Gentiles; there shall be no kings upon the land, and the Lord will fortify the land against other lands.
2 Nephi 10:16	Those who fight against Zion, both Jew and Gentile, are the whore of all the earth, for those not for Christ are against him.
2 Nephi 10:18	The Gentiles shall afflict the seed of Lehi, but they will also nurse them, and the believing Gentiles shall be numbered with Israel.
2 Nephi 10:20–21	The Lord made great promises to the isles of the sea; the Americas were considered a part of those promises.

General Authority Quotations:

Elder Henry D. Moyle • 2 Nephi 7:11 (Isaiah 50:11)

If there is any one group of people in the Church for whom I feel the sorriest, it is those who brand themselves as intellectuals. I believe that that class of people can go to apostasy along a broader road and through a wider gate than any other group. . . . There is no man upon this earth, no matter how great an intellect he has or will develop, who can prove that there is no God. Any man who undertakes to develop the thesis of proving a negative just lacks the initial intelligence to know that you cannot disprove or prove a negative. From the time of Adam until this day there have been men who have known that God lives, and there is no intellectual who can disprove it to them or to the world.

And so this Church, which believed at the very outset that the glory of God is intelligence and has done more to encourage its membership to become intellectual than any other church upon the face of the earth, in any era, does not look upon intellect as its God. That is what these intellectual apostates do, and they are not sufficiently intelligent to know when they have apostatized. They live in darkness and, at the same time, they are under the impression that they live in an atmosphere available to you and to me who are not so "intellectual;" I am not willing to concede that they are any smarter than we are.

I want to tell you that I think the humblest elder in the Church who knows what he knows and has the courage and the conviction to testify to the world what he knows is just as intellectual as a man can be. Under the inspiration of the Spirit of the Lord, that man's mind will develop, it will reach its maximum capacity, and he will accomplish more in mortality than the man without the Holy Spirit who strives, along man-made lines, to accomplish a mortal goal . . . your work is first, foremost, and primarily spiritual in nature; and except as you develop within you a compatibility with the Spirit and enjoy the manifestations of the Spirit in your work, you are not succeeding. Any man who does not have the courage of his convictions, who is willing to the slightest degree to compromise with anyone, anywhere, and under any circumstances in this world is, to that extent, unworthy of the priesthood he holds. And, certainly, he is on the way to losing his appreciation of the existence of God which forms, of course, the very foundation for the gospel of Jesus Christ, for our belief, for our existence, and for our intelligence itself.

There is nothing more sacred to us than our intelligence and, unfortunately, the adversary is conscious of that fact. Therefore, he will utilize our intelligence to destroy us wherever he can get a foothold, or even a toehold. It is a sign, it is the evidence of a wise man—the truly great intellect—to know what to do with his power of mind when he is so blessed. When we utilize these faculties of ours, which are God-given and which are our inheritance, in the mortal interest of man farther than to assist in the building up of the kingdom of God here upon the earth, we will fail and we will lose our testimony. . . . [Address to Seminary and Institute Faculty, Brigham Young University, June 27, 1962]

Elder George Albert Smith • 2 Nephi 10:10–14

In the Book of Mormon, "The American volume of scripture," the Lord has given us information pertaining to this land upon which we dwell and called it a land favored above all other lands. I recommend that not only you Latter-day Saints read the Book of Mormon, but that our Father's other children read it. They will find it contains, in addition to what the Bible has said about the world, what the Lord has said about this Western Hemisphere—that this should be a land of liberty unto the Gentiles, and that no king should dwell upon this land, but that he, the God of heaven, would be our King and would fortify this land against all the nations, that this should be a land of peace and happiness, on condition that we would honor the God of this earth, the Father of us all. The factor controlling the promise is that we must keep the commandments of our Heavenly Father or it cannot be realized. [CR, April, 1937]

Challenges to Eternal Life:

1. Choose a teaching from Isaiah in this reading that you understand and liken it unto yourself that you may learn of and glorify God (2 Nephi 6:4).

2. Remember that Christ is your King, and a light to you forever. Therefore hear his words and follow them (2 Nephi 10:14).

3. Make a commitment to your Father in Heaven to recognize his grace and

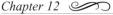

follow his will. (2 Nephi 10:24)

4. Choose a challenge of your own from this reading and apply it to your life.

Chapter Thirteen

The Atonement

2 Nephi 9

*H*istorical Setting: See the historical setting of Chapter Twelve. This chapter is the conclusion of Jacob's first day sermon.

Precepts of this chapter:

> 50 Come, my brethren, every one that thirsteth, come ye to the waters; and he that hath no money, come buy and eat; yea, come buy wine and milk without money and without price.

> 51 Wherefore, do not spend money for that which is of no worth, nor your labor for that which cannot satisfy. Hearken diligently unto me, and remember the words which I have spoken; and come unto the Holy One of Israel, and feast upon that which perisheth not, neither can be corrupted, and let your soul delight in fatness. [Nephi 9:50–51]

> 1 Ho, every one that thirsteth, come ye to the waters, and he that hath no money; come ye, buy, and eat; yea, come, buy wine and milk without money and without price.

> 2 Wherefore do ye spend money for *that which is* not bread? and your labour for *that which* satisfieth not? hearken diligently unto me, and eat ye *that which is* good, and let your soul delight itself in fatness. [Isaiah 55:1–2]

President Joseph Fielding Smith has said concerning this chapter:

> One of the most enlightening discourses ever delivered in regard

to the atonement is found in the ninth chapter of II Nephi in the Book of Mormon. It is the counsel given by Jacob, the brother of Nephi. It should be carefully read by every person seeking salvation. We have been taught that the greatest gift of God is eternal life, and eternal life comes through obedience to all the commandments and covenants to man by our Heavenly Father.

There is an overwhelming lack of understanding in the world in relation to these principles of salvation and exaltation given to prepare mankind for a place in the kingdom of God, and this lack causes many to stumble. There is no excuse on the part of members of the church for they have received the necessary revelation directly from the heavens in this Dispensation of the Fulness of Times. The great mission of the Son of God has been revealed in the Book of Mormon and the Doctrine and Covenants more clearly than any other place. Many passages that have been misunderstood, and therefore mistranslated in the Bible, are clarified in these sacred volumes. [1]

An outline of the chapter is included in for a deeper study.

OUTLINE • 2 NEPHI 9

➤ 9:1–3   Jacob had read Isaiah that his people might know of the Lord's covenants with all the house of Israel.

    a. The Lord has spoken to the Jews by his holy prophets from the beginning until they are restored to the true church, and gathered to their land of promise (v. 2).

    b. His people should rejoice because of the promised blessings (v. 3).

➤ 9:4–9   Because of their searching, many know of things to come.

    a. Their flesh must waste away and die, but in their bodies they shall see God (v. 4).

    b. The Creator shall show himself to those at Jerusalem, become subject to man in the flesh, and die for all men, that all men may become subject to him (v. 5).

---

[1] *Answers to Gospel Questions*, comp. Joseph Fielding Smith Jr., 5 vols. [1957–66], 4:57–58.

    c.   Death will come upon all men, therefore there must be a power of resurrection, or our flesh would arise no more (vv. 6–7).

    d.   The Fall came by transgression, men were cut off from the Lord, and without an infinite atonement, our spirits would become subject to the devil (vv. 6–9).

        1.   Our spirits would become like him and become angels to the devil.

        2.   The devil transforms himself nigh unto an angel of God and stirs up man to secret combinations of murder and works of darkness.

➤ 9:10–19   God prepares a way to escape from the death of the body and the death of the spirit.

    a.   The grave must deliver the body by the power of the resurrection (vv. 11–12).

    b.   Hell must deliver up the spirits and they will be restored to the body (vv. 11–12).

    c.   All men will become incorruptible and immortal (vv. 13–14).

        1.   We shall have a perfect knowledge of all our guilt, uncleanness, and nakedness.

        2.   The righteous shall have a perfect knowledge of their enjoyment and be clothed with righteousness.

    d.   When they become immortal they must appear before the judgment seat of the Holy One of Israel (vv. 15–18).

        1.   The righteous shall be righteous still.

        2.   The filthy shall be filthy and go into everlasting torment like as fire and brimstone.

        3.   The righteous shall inherit the kingdom of God.

    e.   The mercy of the Holy One of Israel delivers his saints from the devil and death and hell (v. 19).

➤ 9:20–22   God knows all things and comes to save all men.

    a.   He suffers the pain of all men, women, and children who belong to the family of Adam (v. 21).

       b. He suffers that all men might be resurrected and stand before him at the judgment bar (v. 22).

➤ 9:23–26   He commands all men to repent and be baptized, having perfect faith in the Holy One of Israel, or they cannot be saved in the kingdom of God.

       a. If they will not repent, they will be damned (v. 24).

       b. He has given a law, and where there is no law, there is no punishment and no condemnation (v. 25).

       c. The Atonement satisfies the demands of justice for all who have not the law (v. 26).

➤ 9:27–39   Wo unto those who have the law and commandments given and transgresseth them.

       a. The learned who think they are wise and hearken not to the counsel of God, but to be learned is good if they hearken to the counsels of God (vv. 28–29).

       b. The rich who despise the poor (v. 30).

       c. The deaf that will not hear (v. 31).

       d. The blind that will not see (v. 32).

       e. The uncircumcised of heart, the knowledge of their iniquities shall smite them (v. 33).

       f. The liar, for he shall be thrust down to hell (v. 34).

       g. The murderer who deliberately killeth (v. 35).

       h. Those who commit whoredoms, for they shall be thrust down (v. 36).

       i. Those who worship idols; the devil delights in them (v. 37).

       j. All those who die in their sins, for they shall return to God and behold his face and remain in their sins (v. 38).

➤ 9:40   Those who say Jacob has spoken hard things against them revile against the truth. The righteous love the truth.

➤ 9:41–43   Come unto the Lord, the path is narrow but in a straight course. The keeper of the gate, the Holy One of Israel, employs no servant and cannot be deceived.

   a.   He will not open to those whom he despises, unless they cast away their pride and consider themselves fools before God (v. 42).

   b.   The happiness of the saints shall be hid from them forever (v. 43).

➤ 9:44–48   Jacob shakes his garments, or shakes their iniquities from his soul.

   a.   Shake off the chains that bind you and come to the God of salvation (v. 45).

   b.   Prepare your souls for the day of judgment (v. 46).

   c.   It is expedient for Jacob to awaken them to the awful reality of sins (vv. 47–48).

      1.   If they were holy, he would speak of holiness.

      2.   He must teach them the consequences of sin.

➤ 9:49–52   Jacob abhors sin and delights in righteousness. He praises the Holy One of Israel.

   a.   He quotes Isaiah, giving an invitation to come unto Christ (v. 50–51).

   b.   The words of God say: pray continually by day, give thanks by night (v. 52).

➤ 9:53   How great are the covenants of the Lord and his condescensions to men.

   a.   The seed of Jacob's people will not be utterly destroyed (v. 53).

   b.   In future generations, they shall become a righteous branch of Israel (v. 53).

➤ 9:55   Jacob will declare the remainder of his words on the morrow.

NOTES AND COMMENTARY

Introduction: The Atonement is the most important doctrine of the gospel of Jesus Christ and yet the least understood. The Bible tells us that it happened, but the Book of Mormon tells us why and how it happened, and what must be done as an individual to get the full benefits of it.

2 Nephi 9:1–2 • Covenants with all the house of Israel

1 And now, my beloved brethren, I have read these things that ye might know concerning the covenants of the Lord that he has covenanted with all the house of Israel—

2 That he has spoken unto the Jews, by the mouth of his holy prophets, even from the beginning down, from generation to generation, until the time comes that they shall be restored to the true church and fold of God; when they shall be gathered home to the lands of their inheritance, and shall be established in all their lands of promise.

These two verses are a summation of the two plus chapters of Isaiah (49:24–52:1) that Jacob has just quoted. Once more Jacob affirms that Isaiah's prophecies are dual, referring to the several branches, or all of the house of Israel.

Jacob has emphasized in the previous chapters how the Lord's covenants will be fulfilled with the Jews. His summary does the same. The ultimate filling of the Jewish covenant will be when they are "restored to the true church of God" (v. 2). To have the church restored tells us they once had a church among them. This was true before the meridian of time as shown when Zoram, Laban's servant supposes that Nephi "spake of the brethren of the church" (1 Nephi 4:26). Stephen, the martyr, also taught in the New Testament, that Moses "was in the church in the wilderness" (Acts 7:38). However, the church will not be restored among the Jews until after or "when they shall be gathered home to the lands of their inheritance, and shall be established in all the lands of their inheritance" (v. 3). The plural usage of "lands" is interesting. It could refer to various areas within the land of Canaan, or it could refer to other lands away from Canaan. Nephi said later, "in the days that the prophecies of Isaiah shall be fulfilled men shall know of a surety, at the times when they shall come to pass" (2 Nephi

25:7). We will know about the "lands" question then, if not before.

There are six major points in Jacob's sermon on the Atonement. The first major point follows.

2 Nephi 9:3–9 • Why the Atonement was needed

3 Behold, my beloved brethren, I speak unto you these things that ye may rejoice, and lift up your heads forever, because of the blessings which the Lord God shall bestow upon your children.

4 For I know that ye have searched much, many of you, to know of things to come; wherefore I know that ye know that our flesh must waste away and die; nevertheless, in our bodies we shall see God.

5 Yea, I know that ye know that in the body he shall show himself unto those at Jerusalem, from whence we came; for it is expedient that it should be among them; for it behooveth the great Creator that he suffereth himself to become subject unto man in the flesh, and die for all men, that all men might become subject unto him.

6 For as death hath passed upon all men, to fulfil the merciful plan of the great Creator, there must needs be a power of resurrection, and the resurrection must needs come unto man by reason of the fall; and the fall came by reason of transgression; and because man became fallen they were cut off from the presence of the Lord.

7 Wherefore, it must needs be an infinite atonement—save it should be an infinite atonement this corruption could not put on incorruption. Wherefore, the first judgment which came upon man must needs have remained to an endless duration. And if so, this flesh must have laid down to rot and to crumble to its mother earth, to rise no more.

8 O the wisdom of God, his mercy and grace! For behold, if the flesh should rise no more our spirits must become subject to that angel who fell from before the presence of the Eternal God, and became the devil, to rise no more.

9 And our spirits must have become like unto him, and we become devils, angels to a devil, to be shut out from the presence of our God, and to remain with the father of lies, in misery, like unto himself; yea, to that being who beguiled our first parents, who transformeth himself nigh unto an angel of light, and stirreth up the children of men unto

secret combinations of murder and all manner of secret works of darkness.

Jacob bears testimony that even though "our flesh must waste away and die; nevertheless, in our bodies we shall see God" (v. 4). There is much controversy in the world concerning a physical resurrection. The Book of Mormon confirms a physical resurrection. Although the KJV records: "And though after my skin worms destroy this body, yet in my flesh shall I see God" (Job 19:26), other versions translate this verse "without my flesh shall I see God," exactly the opposite (the Revised Standard Version). The Pearl of Great Price adds a second witness of a physical resurrection. Adam testified: "and again in the flesh shall I see God" (Moses 5:10). The Book of Mormon gives more testimony later on (see Alma 11:43–48; 40:23). The Doctrine and Covenants adds another witness: "And the spirit and the body are the soul of man. And the resurrection from the dead is the redemption of the soul" (D&C 88:15–16).

Jesus Christ, the great creator, "for the world was made by him" (John 1:10), was to come and make an Atonement. This was necessary because of the fall. Therefore we are taught in the sequence of the Creation, the Fall, and the Atonement.

There were two reasons that an Atonement was necessary: because of the fall, "death hath passed upon all men; and man was cut off from the presence of the Lord" (v. 6). Jacob explains that the Atonement must be infinite, and all inclusive, or our flesh would rot and crumble to its mother earth, to rise no more and our spirits become subject to the devil (vv. 7–8). This death brought about the death of the body and the death of the spirit, and the Atonement was needed to overcome those deaths. Without the power of the resurrection, the corruptible blood of the body would not be replaced with an incorruptible substance. Without the Atonement, being subject to the devil and his angels would have eventually worn all men down, and they would have become like him (v. 9). We cannot associate with evil and not be affected. The Fall left us to become like Satan, but the Atonement allows us to attain salvation and become like God.

Satan has the power to transform himself "nigh unto an angel of light," but not into an angel of light. Those who have seen angels of light should not be deceived. Moses had seen God when God's glory came upon him, but after, when Satan appeared to Moses, he asked "where is thy glory" . . . I can look upon thee in the natural man" (Moses 1:13–14). Since most have not had this experience, the devil is able to deceive them. Through such deception, Satan induces man to form "secret combinations, or murder and all manner of secret works of darkness" (v. 9).

2 Nephi 9:10–19 • What the Atonement Did

10 O how great the goodness of our God, who prepareth a way for our escape from the grasp of this awful monster; yea, that monster, death and hell, which I call the death of the body, and also the death of the spirit.

11 And because of the way of deliverance of our God, the Holy One of Israel, this death, of which I have spoken, which is the temporal, shall deliver up its dead; which death is the grave.

12 And this death of which I have spoken, which is the spiritual death, shall deliver up its dead; which spiritual death is hell; wherefore, death and hell must deliver up their dead, and hell must deliver up its captive spirits, and the grave must deliver up its captive bodies, and the bodies and the spirits of men will be restored one to the other; and it is by the power of the resurrection of the Holy One of Israel.

13 O how great the plan of our God! For on the other hand, the paradise of God must deliver up the spirits of the righteous, and the grave deliver up the body of the righteous; and the spirit and the body is restored to itself again, and all men become incorruptible, and immortal, and they are living souls, having a perfect knowledge like unto us in the flesh, save it be that our knowledge shall be perfect.

14 Wherefore, we shall have a perfect knowledge of all our guilt, and our uncleanness, and our nakedness; and the righteous shall have a perfect knowledge of their enjoyment, and their righteousness, being clothed with purity, yea, even with the robe of righteousness.

15 And it shall come to pass that when all men shall have passed from this first death unto life, insomuch as they have become immor-

tal, they must appear before the judgment-seat of the Holy One of Israel; and then cometh the judgment, and then must they be judged according to the holy judgment of God.

16 And assuredly, as the Lord liveth, for the Lord God hath spoken it, and it is his eternal word, which cannot pass away, that they who are righteous shall be righteous still, and they who are filthy shall be filthy still; wherefore, they who are filthy are the devil and his angels; and they shall go away into everlasting fire, prepared for them; and their torment is as a lake of fire and brimstone, whose flame ascendeth up forever and ever and has no end.

17 O the greatness and the justice of our God! For he executeth all his words, and they have gone forth out of his mouth, and his law must be fulfilled.

18 But, behold, the righteous, the saints of the Holy One of Israel, they who have believed in the Holy One of Israel, they who have endured the crosses of the world, and despised the shame of it, they shall inherit the kingdom of God, which was prepared for them from the foundation of the world, and their joy shall be full forever.

19 O the greatness of the mercy of our God, the Holy One of Israel! For he delivereth his saints from that awful monster the devil, and death, and hell, and that lake of fire and brimstone, which is endless torment.

In addition to an Atonement being needed because man was fallen, the second major point of Jacob's great sermon is to show what the Atonement did. As stated above, the Atonement overcame the death of the body and the death of the spirit (v. 10). Jacob explains how the grave will deliver up its captive bodies, and hell and paradise must deliver up their spirits (vv. 11–12). This same doctrine is taught in the Book of Revelation:

12 And I saw the dead, small and great, stand before God; and the books were opened: and another book was opened, which is *the book* of life: and the dead were judged out of those things which were written in the books, according to their works.

13 And the sea gave up the dead which were in it; and death and hell delivered up the dead which were in them: and they were judged every man according to their works.

14 And death and hell were cast into the lake of fire. This is the second death.

15 And whosoever was not found written in the book of life was cast into the lake of fire. [Revelation 20:12–15]

Other places in the Book of Mormon teach this same doctrine (see Alma 12:12–18; Helaman 14:15–18).

Jacob adds a further dimension to the doctrine of the resurrection. When the spirit and the body of the righteous are restored (resurrected), their knowledge shall be perfect (v. 13). The wicked will have a perfect knowledge of all their guilt, uncleanness, and nakedness (v. 14). Everything we do is recorded in our brain and will be remembered at the time of the resurrection. President Joseph F. Smith said:

> In reality a man cannot forget anything. He may have a lapse of memory; he may not be able to recall at the moment a thing that he knows or words that he has spoken; he may not have the power at his will to call up these events and words; but let God Almighty touch the mainspring of the memory and awaken recollection, and you will find then that you have not forgotten a single idle word which you have spoken![2] [*Latter-day Prophets Speak*, 56]

"The righteous shall have a perfect knowledge of their enjoyment, and their righteousness" (v. 14). "Their enjoyment" must refer to the knowledge of the Atonement having cleansed them of the sins and transgressions for which they had repented. "All have sinned and come short of the glory of God" (Romans 3:23), so no one is exempt. The knowledge of "their righteousness" must refer to the many good works they have done. Jacob explains that this will take place after the resurrection when they appear before the judgment bar of God (v. 15). At the resurrection, the "righteous shall be righteous still, and they who are filthy shall be filthy still" (v. 16). The resurrection does not cleanse people, the Atonement does. They will be quickened (resurrected) by a portion of the glory that they have prepared themselves to receive

---

[2] Daniel H. Ludlow, *Latter-day Prophets Speak*, 56 .

(see D&C 88:15–32). If they have not made the Atonement efficacious to their lives, it will have no effect. The filthy will remain filthy. The justice of God is illustrated through the judgment (v. 17). The righteous saints, who have endured the crosses of the world, will inherit the kingdom of God (v. 18). The mercy of God is illustrated through the Atonement delivering the saints from death and hell (v. 19).

2 Nephi 9:20–22 • How the Atonement was made

20 O how great the holiness of our God! For he knoweth all things, and there is not anything save he knows it.

21 And he cometh into the world that he may save all men if they will hearken unto his voice; for behold, he suffereth the pains of all men, yea, the pains of every living creature, both men, women, and children, who belong to the family of Adam.

22 And he suffereth this that the resurrection might pass upon all men, that all might stand before him at the great and judgment day.

Jacob's third major point was to explain how the Atonement was made. Jesus was able to make the Atonement because of his complete foreknowledge or omniscience of the inhabitants of the earth. "He knoweth all things and there is not anything save he knows it" (v. 20). Without this knowledge he could not make an infinite or an all inclusive atonement. But he did make an infinite atonement; "he suffereth the pains of all men, yea, the pains of every living creature, both men, women, and children, who belong to the family of Adam" (v. 21). The family of Adam is "the family of all the earth" (2 Nephi 2:20). He "suffereth these things for all" (D&C 19:16), "that the resurrection might pass upon all men [overcome physical death], that all might stand before him at the great and judgment day" (2 Nephi 2:22).

2 Nephi 9:23–26 • How to Get the Benefit of the Atonement

23 And he commandeth all men that they must repent, and be baptized in his name, having perfect faith in the Holy One of Israel, or they cannot be saved in the kingdom of God.

24 And if they will not repent and believe in his name, and be baptized in his name, and endure to the end, they must be damned; for the Lord God, the Holy One of Israel, has spoken it.

25 Wherefore, he has given a law; and where there is no law given there is no punishment; and where there is no punishment there is no condemnation; and where there is no condemnation the mercies of the Holy One of Israel have claim upon them, because of the atonement; for they are delivered by the power of him.

26 For the atonement satisfieth the demands of his justice upon all those who have not the law given to them, that they are delivered from that awful monster, death and hell, and the devil, and the lake of fire and brimstone, which is endless torment; and they are restored to that God who gave them breath, which is the Holy One of Israel.

The fourth major point made by Jacob was how to get the benefit of the Atonement in our lives. There are two basic things required for the Atonement to be effective in our lives: (1) we must repent and be baptized (by a legal administrator), and (2) we must have perfect faith in the Holy One of Israel (v. 23). To have perfect faith is to accept that Christ does know all of our sins and did vicariously suffer for them. Without such faith, we have not fully accepted Jesus as our Redeemer and will be damned. To be damned is to have our progression stopped. We will not have place in the Celestial kingdom of God (v. 24), but will be given a degree of glory for which we are prepared.

Jacob gives another category of people upon whom the Atonement will have an effect, those who were given no law (v. 25). The Atonement satisfies the demands of justice upon those who lived without opportunity for the law of Christ (v. 26). Although Jacob does not qualify the people who receive no law, there are three groups within the no law category. Joseph Smith was shown that "all children who die before they arrive at the years of accountability are saved in the celestial kingdom of heaven" (D&C 137:10; see also 18:41; 20:71). This age is "eight years old" (D&C 68:25). The Lord made a covenant with Abraham: "And I will establish a covenant of circumcision with thee, and it shall be my covenant between me and thee, and thy seed after thee, in their generations; that thou mayest know for ever that children are not accountable before me until they are eight years old" (JST, Genesis 17:11). Mormon taught that "all little Children are alive in Christ" (Moroni 8:22). The same doctrine was taught to the Jerusalem disciples: "Then were there brought unto him little children, that he should put his hands on them and pray. And the disciples rebuked them, saying, There is no need, for Jesus hath said, Such shall be saved" (JST, Matthew 19:13).

Those who are mentally handicapped are also covered by the Atonement. Mormon also told his son Moroni that "all they that are without the law" are alive in Christ (Moroni 8:22). In a revelation to Joseph Smith, the Lord said:

> 46 But behold, I say unto you, that little children are redeemed from the foundation of the world through mine Only Begotten;
>
> 47 Wherefore, they cannot sin, for power is not given unto Satan to tempt little children, until they begin to become accountable before me;
>
> 48 For it is given unto them even as I will, according to mine own pleasure, that great things may be required at the hand of their fathers.
>
> 49 And, again, I say unto you, that whoso having knowledge, have I not commanded to repent?
>
> 50 And he that hath no understanding, it remaineth in me to do according as it is written. And now I declare no more unto you at this time. Amen. [D&C 29:46–50]

The third group is those who live in an environment where the gospel is not accessible, or "they who died without law" (D&C 76:72). Jacob's statement seems directed to this group. He says "they are restored to that God who gave them breath, which is the Holy One of Israel" (v. 26). That this group will have an opportunity to accept the gospel in the spirit world will not be discussed at this time.[3]

2 Nephi 9: 27–39 • What Prevents the Effects of the Atonement

27 But wo unto him that has the law given, yea, that has all the commandments of God, like unto us, and that transgresseth them, and that wasteth the days of his probation, for awful is his state!

28 O that cunning plan of the evil one! O the vainness, and the frailties, and the foolishness of men! When they are learned they think they are wise, and they hearken not unto the counsel of God, for they set it aside, supposing they know of themselves, wherefore, their wisdom is foolishness and it profiteth them not. And they shall perish.

29 But to be learned is good if they hearken unto the counsels of God.

30 But wo unto the rich, who are rich as to the things of the world. For because they are rich they despise the poor, and they persecute the meek, and their hearts are upon their treasures; wherefore, their treasure is their god. And behold, their treasure shall perish with them also.

31 And wo unto the deaf that will not hear; for they shall perish.

32 Wo unto the blind that will not see; for they shall perish also.

33 Wo unto the uncircumcised of heart, for a knowledge of their iniquities shall smite them at the last day.

34 Wo unto the liar, for he shall be thrust down to hell.

35 Wo unto the murderer who deliberately killeth, for he shall die.

36 Wo unto them who commit whoredoms, for they shall be thrust down to hell.

37 Yea, wo unto those that worship idols, for the devil of all devils delighteth in them.

---

[3] For an explanation of the Book of Mormon teachings on the subject, see Monte S. Nyman, The State of the Soul Between Death and the Resurrection, chap. 11 in *The Book of Mormon: ALMA, The Testimony of the Word*, Sixth Annual Book of Mormon Symposium, 1991, ed. Monte S. Nyman and Charles D. Tate, Jr. Brigham Young University, Provo, Utah 1992.

> 38 And, in fine, wo unto all those who die in their sins; for they shall return to God, and behold his face, and remain in their sins.

> 39 O, my beloved brethren, remember the awfulness in transgressing against that Holy God, and also the awfulness of yielding to the enticings of that cunning one. Remember, to be carnally-minded is death, and to be spiritually-minded is life eternal.

Jacob's fifth point is what prevents the effect of the Atonement from coming upon us. He warns those who have the law given unto them and transgress the commandments of God. Without listing all of the warnings, a few observations are made below.

Verse twenty-eight and twenty-nine should be read together to get the correct concept. Learning can be one's downfall or one's progression towards salvation. Verse thirty seems to condemn all who are rich, but a cross reference to Jacob 2:19 will give a deeper dimension of obtaining riches. Verses thirty-one and thirty-two address the spiritually deaf and blind, not those who are physically impaired. The uncircumcised of heart refers to an unclean person, or those who have evil desires in their hearts. The heart is the equivalent of the spirit of a person. Circumcision was a law for physical cleanliness and thus is symbolic of having a clean heart or spirit.

Elder Marvin J. Ashton defined a lie (v. 34) as "any communication given to another with intent to deceive" (CR, April, 1982, 10). This certainly broadens the concept. The qualification of "the murderer who deliberately killeth, for he shall die" (v. 35) is an important consideration in the death penalty. In verse thirty-six "them who commit whoredoms" are those who are sexually immoral, but should not be limited to just those sins. There are other kinds of whoredoms that the scriptures call abominations. Abominations refer to other character destroying actions. The worshipping of idols (v. 37) may take many forms other than graven images, i.e., money, position, power, and other material possessions.

Jacob gives a summary or catch all warning to cover all other sins that he has not enumerated. Those who die in their sins, he says "shall return to God, and behold his face, and remain in their sins" (v. 38). This seems to be equating the devil and his angels with sons of perdition, as he defined earlier (v. 16). Alma taught that at death we "are taken home to that God who gave [us] life" (Alma 40:11). After quoting this, President Joseph F. Smith added; "where there is a separation, a partial judgment," going to paradise or outer darkness,[4] various places in the spirit world. To actually see the face of God "and remain in their sins" seems to be speaking of the long range judgment of the sons of perdition.

Jacob concludes with this admonition: "Remember, to be carnally minded is death, and to be spiritually minded is life eternal" (v. 39). Paul gives the same warning in Romans 8:6. This admonition is an eternal doctrine or principle, and therefore, it is probable that both Jacob and Paul are quoting from an earlier source that was originally in their scriptures.

2 Nephi 9:40–49 • Why the Atonement Must Be Taught

40 O, my beloved brethren, give ear to my words. Remember the greatness of the Holy One of Israel. Do not say that I have spoken hard things against you; for if ye do, ye will revile against the truth; for I have spoken the words of your Maker. I know that the words of truth are hard against all uncleanness; but the righteous fear them not, for they love the truth and are not shaken.

41 O then, my beloved brethren, come unto the Lord, the Holy One. Remember that his paths are righteous. Behold, the way for man is narrow, but it lieth in a straight course before him, and the keeper of the gate is the Holy One of Israel; and he employeth no servant there; and there is none other way save it be by the gate; for he cannot be deceived, for the Lord God is his name.

42 And whoso knocketh, to him will he open; and the wise, and the learned, and they that are rich, who are puffed up because of their learning, and their wisdom, and their riches—yea, they are they whom

---

[4] Joseph F. Smith, *Gospel Doctrine*, 11th ed. [1959], 448.

he despiseth; and save they shall cast these things away, and consider themselves fools before God, and come down in the depths of humility, he will not open unto them.

43 But the things of the wise and the prudent shall be hid from them forever—yea, that happiness which is prepared for the saints.

44 O, my beloved brethren, remember my words. Behold, I take off my garments, and I shake them before you; I pray the God of my salvation that he view me with his all-searching eye; wherefore, ye shall know at the last day, when all men shall be judged of their works, that the God of Israel did witness that I shook your iniquities from my soul, and that I stand with brightness before him, and am rid of your blood.

45 O, my beloved brethren, turn away from your sins; shake off the chains of him that would bind you fast; come unto that God who is the rock of your salvation.

46 Prepare your souls for that glorious day when justice shall be administered unto the righteous, even the day of judgment, that ye may not shrink with awful fear; that ye may not remember your awful guilt in perfectness, and be constrained to exclaim: Holy, holy are thy judgments, O Lord God Almighty—but I know my guilt; I transgressed thy law, and my transgressions are mine; and the devil hath obtained me, that I am a prey to his awful misery.

47 But behold, my brethren, is it expedient that I should awake you to an awful reality of these things? Would I harrow up your souls if your minds were pure? Would I be plain unto you according to the plainness of the truth if ye were freed from sin?

48 Behold, if ye were holy I would speak unto you of holiness; but as ye are not holy, and ye look upon me as a teacher, it must needs be expedient that I teach you the consequences of sin.

49 Behold, my soul abhorreth sin, and my heart delighteth in righteousness; and I will praise the holy name of my God.

The last or sixth major point of Jacob's sermon deals with why the Atonement must be taught. The pleading of Jacob for his brethren to hearken to his words and not consider them as hard doctrine (v. 40), reminds us of Nephi's earlier response to Laman and Lemuel: he "had spoken hard things against the wicked, according to the truth; and the righteous have I justified" (1 Nephi 16:2). Jacob's declaration that "the keeper of the gate is the Holy One of Israel; and he employeth no servant there: and there is none other way save it be by the gate; for he cannot be deceived" (v. 41). This is an important and significant doctrine but needs some explanation. Earlier, Nephi had been told by an angel, as he was shown a vision of the future Nephites, that "the twelve apostles of the Lamb . . . shall judge the twelve tribes of Israel," and the "twelve ministers whom thou beholdest [the Nephite twelve] shall judge [Nephi's] seed" (1 Nephi 12:9–10). This may sound contradictory, but the quorums of twelve spoken of here are special witnesses of Christ and will stand as witnesses to these groups they are designated to work with. They will testify of Christ both in word and in writing. The people will be accountable for what these brethren testified, and will be held accountable for their teachings at the judgment bar. However, Christ is the one who actually makes the final decision at the gate of judgment. The Father "hath committed all judgment unto the Son" (John 5:22). The final destiny of all who come to that gate, which is all of us, is beautifully stated in verses forty-two and forty-three. Those upon whom he pronounced the wo's (vv. 27–38) will not obtain "the happiness which is prepared for the saints" (v. 43). We need to appreciate and understand that there will be a perfect balance between justice and mercy when we are judged.

The shaking of Jacob's garments is an illustration of his magnifying his calling that he later speaks of more succinctly in the temple. He was taking the responsibility, "answering the sins of the people upon our own heads if we did not teach them the word of God with all diligence" (Jacob 1:19). He had told his people the truth, he was rid of their blood, leaving them accountable for their sins (v. 44). The prophet Ezekiel taught the same concept:

> 17 Son of man, I have made thee a watchman unto the house of Israel: therefore hear the word at my mouth, and give them warning from me.
>
> 18 When I say unto the wicked, Thou shalt surely die; and thou givest him not warning, nor speakest to warn the wicked from his wicked way, to save his life; the same wicked *man* shall die in his

iniquity; but his blood will I require at thine hand.

19 Yet if thou warn the wicked, and he turn not from his wickedness, nor from his wicked way, he shall die in his iniquity; but thou hast delivered thy soul.

20 Again, When a righteous *man* doth turn from his righteousness, and commit iniquity, and I lay a stumblingblock before him, he shall die: because thou hast not given him warning, he shall die in his sin, and his righteousness which he hath done shall not be remembered; but his blood will I require at thine hand.

21 Nevertheless if thou warn the righteous *man*, that the righteous sin not, and he doth not sin, he shall surely live, because he is warned; also thou hast delivered thy soul. [Ezekiel 3:17–21]

Jacob pleads with his brethren to repent and come unto Christ, "the rock of [their] salvation" (v. 45). He urges them to come to the reality of the judgment bar and to prepare their souls for that time (vv. 46–47). As their teacher, he would like to teach them of holiness, but because of their sins it was "expedient to teach [them] the consequences of sin" (v. 48). Jacob is a good example to us of how we ought to function in our church callings and priesthood responsibilities. He showed concern for his people and magnified his priesthood.

2 Nephi 9:50–51 (Isaiah 55:1–2)
• The Atonement Is a Free Gift

50 Come, my brethren, every one that thirsteth, come ye to the waters; and he that hath no money, come buy and eat; yea, come buy wine and milk without money and without price.

51 Wherefore, do not spend money for that which is of no worth, nor your labor for that which cannot satisfy. Hearken diligently unto me, and remember the words which I have spoken; and come unto the Holy One of Israel, and feast upon that which perisheth not, neither can be corrupted, and let your soul delight in fatness. [2 Nephi 9:50–51]

1 Ho, every one that thirsteth, come ye to the waters, and he that hath no money; come ye, buy, and eat; yea, come, buy wine and milk without money and without price.

2 Wherefore do ye spend money for *that which is* not bread? and your labour for *that which* satisfieth not? hearken diligently unto me, and eat ye *that which is* good, and let your soul delight itself in fatness. [Isaiah 55:1–2]

In conclusion, Jacob quotes the invitation from the book of Isaiah for all to partake of the Atonement. In comparing the Book of Mormon text with the King James text the Book of Mormon is more complete, another evidence of "plain and precious things taken away from the [Bible]" (1 Nephi 13:29). Nephi later paraphrases the first verse of the above quotation, in the same context (2 Nephi 26:25). The Atonement is available to us without material cost, and will satisfy the hunger and thirst of our souls.

2 Nephi 9:52–54 • Remember the Words of God and Give Thanks

> 52 Behold, my beloved brethren, remember the words of your God; pray unto him continually by day, and give thanks unto his holy name by night. Let your hearts rejoice.
>
> 53 And behold how great the covenants of the Lord, and how great his condescensions unto the children of men; and because of his greatness, and his grace and mercy, he has promised unto us that our seed shall not utterly be destroyed, according to the flesh, but that he would preserve them; and in future generations they shall become a righteous branch unto the house of Israel.
>
> 54 And now, my brethren, I would speak unto you more; but on the morrow I will declare unto you the remainder of my words. Amen.

The words of God that Jacob invited them to remember (v. 52) are certainly more than the two verses of Isaiah that he quotes on the Atonement. He speaks of the great covenants of the Lord, his condescension to make the Atonement, and the future righteous branch of the house of Israel (v. 53). The covenants of the Lord, specifically to Jacob's people, were made with Joseph of Egypt (2 Nephi 3). The condescensions of God were shown to Nephi (1 Nephi 11). He spoke more of the righteous branch (2 Nephi 10) on the morrow as was discussed in the last chapter of this work. He desired his people to search all of their scriptures, and we should do the same.

SACRED WRITING

Preaching which is Sacred:

2 Nephi 9   Jacob's great sermon on the Atonement.

Doctrines Learned:

2 Nephi 9:2   The Jews shall be restored to the true church (restored
                     shows that they previously had a church).

2 Nephi 9:4   Although our flesh must die, in our bodies (resurrected)
                     we shall see God.

2 Nephi 9:5   The great Creator suffered himself to become subject
                     to man in the flesh and die for all men so that all men
                     might become subject unto him.

2 Nephi 9:6   The fall came by reason of transgression and by the fall
                     all men were cut off from the presence of the Lord.

2 Nephi 9:7   An infinite Atonement was required so that man's cor-
                     ruptible body could be made incorruptible.

2 Nephi 9:8–9   If there had been no resurrection, our spirits would have
                     eventually become subject to the devil, angels to the
                     devil.

2 Nephi 9:10–12   The Atonement also delivers man from the grasp of hell
                     or the death of the spirit.

2 Nephi 9:14   At the resurrection, the wicked shall have a perfect
                     knowledge of their guilt and uncleanness and the
                     righteous shall have a perfect knowledge of their enjoy-
                     ment and purity.

2 Nephi 9:15   All men must appear before the judgment seat of the
                     Holy One of Israel to be judged according to the holy
                     judgment of God.

2 Nephi 9:16–18   After the judgment, the righteous will remain righteous
                     and the filthy will remain filthy whose torment is as a
                     lake of fire and brimstone. The righteous shall inherit
                     the kingdom of God.

2 Nephi 9:20   The Holy One of Israel knoweth all things (concerning

the inhabitants of the earth) and there is nothing that he does not know.

2 Nephi 9:21 The Holy One of Israel suffered the pains of every man, woman, and child who belongs to the family of Adam (an infinite atonement) in order that the resurrection and judgment might come.

2 Nephi 9:23 All men must repent, be baptized, and have perfect faith in the Holy One of Israel or they cannot be saved in the kingdom of God.

2 Nephi 9:25–26 Where there is no law given, there is no punishment or condemnation, but the mercies of the Holy One of Israel have claim on them because of the Atonement satisfying the demands of justice.

2 Nephi 9:29 To be learned is good if one hearkens to the commandments of God.

2 Nephi 9:38 Those who die in their sins, return to God, behold his face, and die in their sins (probably speaking of long range).

2 Nephi 9:39 To be carnally minded is death, and to be spiritually minded is life eternal. (This statement was made long before Paul stated it.)

2 Nephi 9:41 The keeper of the gate (to eternal life) is the Holy One of Israel. He employeth no servant there and he cannot be deceived.

General Authority Quotations:

The Prophet Joseph Smith • 2 Nephi 9:20

The great Jehovah contemplated the whole of the events connected with the earth, pertaining to the plan of salvation, before it rolled into existence, or ever "the morning stars sang together" for joy; the past, the present, and the future were and are, with Him, one eternal "now;" He knew of the fall of Adam, the iniquities of the antediluvians, of the depth of iniquity that would be connected with the human family, their weakness and strength, their power and glory, apostasies, their crimes, their righteousness and iniquity; He comprehended the fall of man, and his redemption; He knew the plan of salvation and pointed it out; He was acquainted with the situation of all nations and with their destiny; He ordered all things according to the council of His own will; He knows the situation of both the living and the dead, and has made ample provision for their redemption, according to their several circumstances, and the laws of the kingdom of God, whether in this world, or the world to come. [*TPJS*, 220]

By a little reflection it will be seen that the idea of the existence of these attributes in the Deity is necessary to enable any rational being to exercise faith in him; for without the idea of the existence of these attributes in the Deity men could not exercise faith in him for life and salvation; seeing that without the knowledge of all things, God would not be able to save any portion of his creatures; for it is by reason of the knowledge which he has of all things, from the beginning to the end, that enables him to give the understanding to his creatures by which they are partakers of eternal life; and if it were not for the idea existing in the minds of men that God had all knowledge it would be impossible for them to exercise faith in him. [*Lectures on Faith*, 4:11]

Elder James E. Talmage • 2 Nephi 9:21

Christ's agony in the Garden (of Gethsemane) is unfathomable by the finite mind, both as to intensity and cause. The thought that he suffered through fear of death is untenable. Death to him was preliminary to resurrection and triumphal return to the Father from whom He had come, and to a state of glory even beyond what he had possessed before; and, moreover, it was within his power to lay down his life voluntarily. He struggled and groaned under a burden such as no other being who has lived on earth might even conceive as possible. It was not physical pain, nor mental anguish alone, that caused him to suffer such torture as to produce an extrusion of blood from every pore; but a spiritual agony of soul such as only God was capable of suffering. No other man, however great his powers of physical or mental endurance, could have suffered so; foe his human organism would have succumbed, and syncope would have produced unconsciousness and welcome oblivion. [*Jesus the Christ*, 1959, 613]

Elder Theodore M. Burton • 2 Nephi 9:28–29

A university education, I believe, would be desirable for every intelligent man and woman in the world, but I must speak the same warning that Paul spoke: "Beware lest any man spoil you through philosophy and vain deceit, after the tradition of men, after the rudiments of the world, and not after Christ."

Now, brothers and sisters, I would like to stress this word, "rudiments," because I think this is a key to this passage. A rudiment means the beginning of knowledge. A little knowledge is a dangerous thing, and too many men and women who have become experts in a tiny field of learning think that because they are trained in that field of learning, they are experts in all fields of learning. Many men who are well-trained in one limited field feel that this equally qualifies them to express learned opinions in the field of faith and religion, although many of them have never done any studying nor taken a class in these subjects. So, I say that the problem is not that they know too much, but that they know too much of what just isn't so. Actually, they know too little. They have closed their minds to anything except the philosophies of men.

Now, brothers and sisters, in our Church in this day and age, when education is becoming more and more popular and more and more necessary, there is grave danger of intellectual apostasy. The problem is that of a closed mind, as I see it. Jacob taught this beautifully, as we read it in the Book of Mormon. [quotes 2 Nephi 9:28–29]

That we should emphasize, "To be learned is good."

What causes intellectual apostasy? Why do some learned men and women turn from the faith? It is not learning, for there are hundreds of us, thousands of us, equally well-trained. It isn't being exposed to different ideas, for we too were exposed to these ideas in the finest universities of the land. Why, then, do they lose their testimony. Principally out of vanity and pride. They want to impress others with their learning. To put it indelicately, it is the problem of the swelled head, because that is exactly what the prophet said.

"Who so knocketh" Jacob said, "to him will he open; and the wise, and the learned, and they who are rich, who are puffed up" and that you see is exactly what he said—"who are puffed up because of their learning, and their wisdom, and their riches— yea, they are they whom he despiseth; and save they shall cast these things away, and consider themselves fools before God, and come down in the depths of humility, he will not open unto them" (2 Nephi 9:42). [CR, April, 1961, 128–29]

Challenges to Eternal Life:

1. Read 2 Nephi 9:28–39 and note your reaction. Do you feel they are harsh or do you feel shaken? If so, read verse 40 and then see which one of the previous admonitions you felt was harsh. This should give you something to work on. The way to work on them is given in verses 41–43.

2. Read 2 Nephi 9:48. Are we missing some opportunity of being taught of holiness because we have to be warned of the consequences of sin? Analyze the messages that were given at your last Stake Conference.

3. In light of 2 Nephi 9:51 analyze how you spend your time and means, and outline steps to gain those things that are of worth.

4. Choose a challenge or modern message of your own from the readings and incorporate it into your life.

Chapter Fourteen

Isaiah, a Third Witness of Christ

2 Nephi 11; 16; 25:1–8

*H*istorical Setting: See historical setting, chapter 12. Between the forty-first and fifty-fifth year after Lehi left Jerusalem, Nephi introduced and recorded thirteen consecutive chapters of Isaiah upon his small plates (2 Nephi 2–14 of the modern version). He comments on these Isaiah chapters in 2 Nephi 25–30. This chapter discusses the introduction, one chapter of Isaiah (his call to the ministry), and the first eight verses of Nephi's commentary (2 Nephi 25:1–8).

Precepts of these chapters:

> Whoso of my people shall see [Isaiah's] words may lift up their hearts and rejoice for all men. [2 Nephi 11:8]

> [The words of Isaiah] shall be of great worth unto [my people] in the last days; for in that day shall they understand them. [2 Nephi 25:8]

After quoting the present-day thirteen consecutive chapters of Isaiah, Nephi acknowledges that Isaiah was "hard for many of [his] people to understand" (2 Nephi 25:1). The reasons for this difficulty will be discussed later, but his introduction telling us why he delights in Isaiah's words will give us a basis for understanding the next several chapters of this work. An outline of the reading assignment for this chapter follows in preparation for a deeper study.

OUTLINE • 2 NEPHI 11; 16; 25:1–8

➤ 11:1   Jacob spake many more things at this time that were not written.

➤ 11:2–4 Nephi writes the words of Isaiah in which he delights.

     a. Isaiah saw the Redeemer as had Nephi (v. 2).

     b. Jacob also has seen him (v. 3).

     c. God establishes the truth of his word by the words of three or more witnesses (v. 3).

     c. The law of Moses was given, and all things to typify of Christ (v. 4).

➤ 11:5–7 Nephi delights also in the covenants of the Lord.

     a. He delights in the eternal plan of deliverance from death (vv. 5–6).

     b. If there is no Christ, there is no God or creation, but there is a God, who is Christ, who cometh in the fulness of times (v. 7).

➤ 11:8   Nephi writes some of Isaiah's words so that we may rejoice for all men.

➤ 16:1–8 Isaiah sees the Lord on his throne.

     a. The vision of the Lord is described (vv. 1–4).

       1. The seraphim are above the throne of the Lord (vv. 2–3).

       2. The posts of the door and the house are described (v. 4).

     b. Isaiah is cleansed and called of the Lord (vv. 5–8).

       1. Isaiah recognizes his need to be cleansed (v. 5).

       2. The seraphim pronounce him cleansed (vv. 6–7).

       3. The Lord calls and Isaiah responds (v. 8).

     c. Isaiah is called to the ministry (vv. 9–12).

       1. He is to proclaim truth to "this people." vv. 9–10).

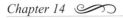

        2.   He is to go forth until the land is desolate (vv. 11–12).

    d.   Isaiah is told that a tenth will return (v. 13).

> 25:1–6   Nephi speaks concerning Isaiah for he is hard for many of his people to understand.

    a.   They know not concerning the manner of prophesying among the Jews (v. 2).

        1.   Nephi had not taught them the manner of the Jews.

        2.   The Jews works were of darkness and doings of abominations.

    b.   Nephi wants them to know of the judgments of God (v. 3).

    c.   Isaiah is plain to those who have the spirit of prophecy (v. 4).

    d.   Nephi shall prophesy in plainness to his people (v. 4).

    e.   The Jews understand the things spoken unto them by the prophets (v. 5).

    f.   Nephi had dwelt at Jerusalem, knows the regions round about, and the judgments of God that hath come to pass among the Jews (v. 6).

> 25:7–8   Nephi proceeds with his own prophecy.

    a.   In the days the prophecies of Isaiah are fulfilled men shall know of their surety (v. 7).

    b.   Isaiah's words shall be of great worth in the last days (v. 8).

NOTES AND COMMENTARY

Introduction: Flavius Josephus, the Jewish historian who wrote or abridged a record of the people of Israel at the time of the Roman conquest of Jerusalem A.D. 70, said of Isaiah:

> He was by the confession of all, a divine and wonderful man in speaking truth; and out of the assurance that he had never written what was false, he wrote down all his prophecies, and left them behind him

in books, that their accomplishment might be judged of from the events of posterity.[1]

The three reasons for Nephi's quoting Isaiah are summarized under the Notes and Commentary of 2 Nephi 11:2–5, cited immediately below. In this chapter we will discuss only the first reason, Isaiah as a witness of the Redeemer. He is the third person cited by Nephi to have seen the pre-mortal Christ, along with him and Jacob.

2 Nephi 11:1 • Jacob Spoke Many More Things

1 And now, Jacob spake many more things to my people at that time; nevertheless only these things have I caused to be written, for the things which I have written sufficeth me.

The fact that Jacob spake many more things that were not written was commented on in Chapter Twelve.

2 Nephi 11:2–5 • Why Nephi quoted Isaiah

2 And now I, Nephi, write more of the words of Isaiah, for my soul delighteth in his words. For I will liken his words unto my people, and I will send them forth unto all my children, for he verily saw my Redeemer, even as I have seen him.

3 And my brother, Jacob, also has seen him as I have seen him; wherefore, I will send their words forth unto my children to prove unto them that my words are true. Wherefore, by the words of three, God hath said, I will establish my word. Nevertheless, God sendeth more witnesses, and he proveth all his words.

4 Behold, my soul delighteth in proving unto my people the truth of the coming of Christ; for, for this end hath the law of Moses been given; and all things which have been given of God from the beginning of the world, unto man, are the typifying of him.

5 And also my soul delighteth in the covenants of the Lord which he hath made to our fathers; yea, my soul delighteth in his grace, and

---

[1] Josephus: Complete works, trans. William Whiston, Grand Rapids, Mich.: Kregel Publications [1972], Antiquities of the Jews, 10. 2. 2.

in his justice, and power, and mercy in the great and eternal plan of deliverance from death.

Here are given three reasons why Nephi recorded Isaiah's testimony. The first one is that Isaiah was a witness of the Redeemer, complying with the law of witnesses, "In the mouth of two or three witnesses shall every word be established" (Deuteronomy 19:15, see also Matthew 18:16). Isaiah serves as a third witness of Christ along with Nephi and Jacob. Nephi's vision of Christ was apparently given while his father was camped in the valley of Lemuel, a few weeks after the family left Jerusalem. Nephi recorded that "I did cry unto the Lord; and behold he did visit me" (1 Nephi 2:16). However, it does not say that he saw him, although it does state "that the Lord spake unto me" (2 Nephi 2:19). Therefore, there may have been another occasion that Nephi did not record since the account of Jacob's seeing him was not recorded either. Our knowledge of Jacob's vision comes from Lehi stating to Jacob: "And thou hast beheld in thy youth his glory" (2 Nephi 2:4). The vision of Isaiah seeing Christ is recorded in 2 Nephi 16 (Isaiah 6), discussed below.

A second reason for Nephi quoting Isaiah was to prove the coming of Christ which would fulfill the law of Moses. The birth of Immanuel, which means "God with us," through a virgin was prophesied by Isaiah (7:14, 2 Nephi 17:14). He further foretold of his various roles and titles (Isaiah 9:6–7; 2 Nephi 19:6–7). The Isaiah chapters concerning Isaiah's prophecies of Christ will be discussed in a subsequent chapter of this work.

Nephi's third reason for quoting Isaiah was because of "the covenants of the Lord which he had made to our fathers" (v. 5). Jacob had quoted Isaiah 49:24–52:1, in the speeches Nephi had just recorded, as proof of the covenants of the Lord (see 2 Nephi 6:16–8:25 discussed in the previous chapter).

Nephi now quotes other chapters for proof of the covenants of the Lord. The chapters quoted by Nephi do not identify the covenants as clearly as the aforementioned prophecies of Christ tell of his coming.

Nevertheless, they are there, the building of a temple in the top of the mountains (2 Nephi 12:2–3, Isaiah 2:2–3), the second gathering of Israel (2 Nephi 21:11, Isaiah 11:11), and the gathering to the lands of promises (2 Nephi 24:1–2). These will also be discussed in subsequent chapters.

2 Nephi 11:6–7 • Christ is a God

6 And my soul delighteth in proving unto my people that save Christ should come all men must perish.

7 For if there be no Christ there be no God; and if there be no God we are not, for there could have been no creation. But there is a God, and he is Christ, and he cometh in the fulness of his own time.

The Nephites understood that Christ was the God who led the children of Israel through the wilderness, or the Jehovah of the Old Testament. The New Testament taught the same doctrine (see 1 Corinthians 10:1–4), but is not generally recognized in the Christian world. The Book of Mormon clearly makes this significant contribution. Nephi also knew he would come "in the fulness of his own time." This was another way of acknowledging Christ's total control of the earth.

2 Nephi 11:8 • Isaiah Introduced

8 And now I write some of the words of Isaiah, that whoso of my people shall see these words may lift up their hearts and rejoice for all men. Now these are the words, and ye may liken them unto you and unto all men.

This verse was given as an introduction to Nephi recording the thirteen consecutive chapters of Isaiah (2–14). 2 Nephi 25–30 were Nephi's commentary on these thirteen chapters. Nephi anticipated the joy that could come from studying the words of Isaiah. He also suggested that the reader liken them unto themselves and unto all men. This verse serves as a major precept for this chapter.

2 Nephi 16 (Isaiah 6) • Isaiah's Vision of the Lord

This chapter is generally considered to be the first revelation given to Isaiah. This opinion is based on Isaiah's recounting, in this chapter, his call to the ministry through a personal vision of the Lord. The symbolic description of the Lord, Isaiah's calling and his mission, and a prophecy of the future were outlined above. The Book of Mormon has several differences from the KJV, but only two significant retentions.

2 Nephi 16:1–4 (Isaiah 6:1–4) • The Lord Sitting on His Throne

1 In the year that king Uzziah died, I saw also the Lord sitting upon a throne, high and lifted up, and his train filled the temple.

2 Above it stood the seraphim; each one had six wings; with twain he covered his face, and with twain he covered his feet, and with twain he did fly.

3 And one cried unto another, and said: Holy, holy, holy, is the Lord of Hosts; the whole earth is full of his glory.

4 And the posts of the door moved at the voice of him that cried, and the house was filled with smoke.

There is only one insignificant difference in the Book of Mormon and the King James texts (also some slight punctuation differences). Therefore, only the Book of Mormon text is quoted above. The word seraphim in the Book of Mormon is spelled seraphims in the KJV (v. 2). The suffix "im," as translated from the Hebrew, makes a word plural and masculine and thus the meaning of the two texts are the same.

John the Revelator, whose mission was similar to Isaiah's, described his vision of heaven in the same figurative terms.

2 And immediately I was in the spirit: and, behold, a throne was set in heaven, and *one* sat on the throne.

8 And the four beasts had each of them six wings about *him;* and

they were full of eyes within: and they rest not day and night, saying, Holy, holy, holy, Lord God Almighty, which was, and is, and is to come. [Revelation 4:2, 8]

In describing John's revelation, the Prophet Joseph Smith explained the symbolism of the eyes and wings.

4 Q. What are we to understand by the eyes and wings, which the beasts had?

A. Their eyes are a representation of light and knowledge, that is, they are full of knowledge; and their wings are a representation of power, to move, to act, etc. [D&C 77:4]

The Doctrine and Covenants speaks elsewhere of "all the seraphic hosts of heaven" (D&C 38:1); and of the "bright, shining seraphs around [the Lord's] throne, with acclamations of praise, singing Hosanna to God and the Lamb" (D&C 109:79). These two references, and thus Isaiah 6:2–3, undoubtedly refer to the angelic hosts of heaven praising their God. The angelic host acknowledging that the whole earth is "full of his glory" (v. 3) is confirmed in modern revelation.

12 Which light [glory] proceedeth forth from the presence of God to fill the immensity of space—

13 The light which is in all things, which giveth life to all things, which is the law by which all things are governed, even the power of God who sitteth upon his throne, who is in the bosom of eternity, who is in the midst of all things. [D&C 88:12–13]

The Book of Revelation also identifies the smoke that filled the house (v. 4) as being "from the glory of God, and from his power" (Revelation 15:8).

2 Nephi 16:5 (Isaiah 6:5) • Isaiah's Reaction to the Vision

5 Then said I: **Wo** is **unto** me! for I am undone; because I am a man of unclean lips; and I dwell in the midst of a people of unclean lips; for mine eyes have seen the King, the Lord of Hosts.

The only differences between the Book of Mormon and the King James texts in this verse, other than slight punctuation, are the bolded words "unto" which is not in the KJV and the word "wo" which is spelled "woe." Therefore, only the Book of Mormon text is quoted here.

Isaiah's awareness of his unworthiness to be in the presence of God is not a unique feeling. Even though the Lord was not attended by glory, "When Simon Peter saw [the miracle of the fish], he fell down at Jesus' knees, saying, Depart from me; for I am a sinful man, O Lord. For he was astonished, and all that were with him, at the draught of the fishes which they had taken" (Luke 5:8–9). Following Moses' vision of the earth and its inhabitants, he acknowledged "that man is nothing, which thing I never had supposed" (Moses 1:9–10). After King Benjamin had taught his subjects of the Savior's Atonement, they fell "to the earth, for the fear of the Lord had come upon them. And they had viewed themselves in their own carnal state, even less than the dust of the earth," and pleaded for the atoning blood of Christ to cleanse them from their carnal state (Mosiah 4:1–2).

2 Nephi 16:6–7 (Isaiah 6:6–7) • Isaiah's Sins Purged

6 Then flew one of the seraphim unto me, having a live coal in his hand, which he had taken with the tongs from off the altar;

7 And he laid it upon my mouth, and said: Lo, this has touched thy lips; and thine iniquity is taken away, and thy sin purged.

The word "seraphim" is again spelled "seraphims," and "has" is spelled "hath" in the KJV. These are the only differences, other than punctuation, and so only the Book of Mormon text is quoted here.

The live coal laid upon his mouth would be analogous to his being "wrought upon and cleansed by the power of the Holy Ghost" referred to by Moroni in the Book of Mormon (Moroni 6:4, see also 2 Nephi 31:17). Isaiah's sins were forgiven (v. 7).

2 Nephi 16:8 (Isaiah 6:8) • Isaiah's Mission

> 8 Also I heard the voice of the Lord, saying: Whom shall I send, and who will go for us? Then I said: Here am I; send me.

Other than punctuation, the only difference between the Book of Mormon and the KJV texts is the inversion of "I said" (Book of Mormon) and "said I" (KJV). Therefore, only the Book of Mormon text is quoted here.

Isaiah's volunteering exemplifies the great desire one feels to serve the Lord when under the influence of his Spirit. Peter was determined to follow Christ wherever he went, and told him "I will lay down my life for thy sake" (John 13:36–37). It is true that he later denied that he knew the Savior, as Christ had prophesied; but after the Holy Ghost came upon Peter, he did lay down his life for Christ as the Savior had foretold.[2]

> 18 Verily, verily, I say unto thee, When thou wast young, thou girdedst thyself, and walkedst whither thou wouldest: but when thou shalt be old, thou shalt stretch forth thy hands, and another shall gird thee, and carry *thee* whither thou wouldest not.
>
> 19 This spake he, signifying by what death he should glorify God. And when he had spoken this, he saith unto him, Follow me. [John 21:18–19]

2 Nephi 16:9–10 (Isaiah 6:9–10) • Make the Heart of this People Fat

The Book of Mormon clarifies these two difficult verses. It teaches that the people to whom Isaiah was sent would fail to understand his message of their own accord. The KJV implies that the Lord did not want them to understand (v. 9).

---

[2] According to tradition, both Paul and Peter were martyred in Rome at about the same time. Peter, at his own request, was crucified with his head down, for he felt unworthy to die in the same manner as his Lord. Our Prophets and Principles, published by the *Instructor*, Salt Lake City, Utah, 1956, 99.

9 And he said: Go and tell this people—Hear ye indeed, but they understood not; and see ye indeed, but they perceived not.

10 Make the heart of this people fat, and make their ears heavy, and shut their eyes—lest they see with their eyes, and hear with their ears, and be converted and be healed. [2 Nephi 16:9–10]

9 And he said, Go, and tell this people, Hear ye indeed, but understand not; and see ye indeed, but perceive not.

10 Make the heart of this people fat, and make their ears heavy, and shut their eyes; lest they see with their eyes, and hear with their ears, and understand with their heart, and convert, and be healed. [Isaiah 6:0–10]

The "making fat" of the hearts of the people (v. 10) seems to refer to Isaiah's being called to make the truth so plain that they would either have to accept it or harden their hearts against it. According to Brigham Young and Willard Richards this was how the Lord hardened Pharaoh's heart in Egypt:

> God has promised to bring the house of Israel up out of the land of Egypt at his own appointed time; and with a mighty hand and an outstretched arm and great terribleness (Deut. 26:8). He chose to do these things that His power might be known and his name declared throughout all the earth, so that all nations might have the God of heaven in remembrance, and reverence His holy name; and to accomplish this it was needful that He should meet with opposition to give Him an opportunity to manifest His power; therefore He raised up a man, even Pharaoh, who, He foreknew, would harden his heart against God of his own free will and choice, and would withstand the Almighty in His attempt to deliver His chosen people, and that to the utmost of his ability; and he proved himself worthy of his choice, for he left no means unimproved which his wicked heart could devise to vex the sons of Abraham, and defeat the purposes of the Most High, which gave the God of Abraham the opportunity to magnify his name in the ears of the nations, and in sight of this wicked king, by many mighty signs and wonders, sometimes even to the convincing of the wicked king of his wickedness, and of the power of God (Exodus 8:28, etc.), and yet he would continue to rebel and hold the Israelites in bondage; and this is what is meant by God's hardening Pharaoh's heart. He manifested Himself in so many glorious and mighty ways, that Pharaoh could not resist the truth without becoming harder; so that at last, in his madness, to stay the people of God, he rushed his

hosts into the Red Sea and they were covered with the floods. [*HC*, 4:263–264]

The last half of Isaiah 6:10 may be misread and lead to the conclusion that the Lord does not want the people to be converted and healed. The real meaning of the last part of the verse, as it is fully quoted in the New Testament, is a declaration that the people did not want to understand, lest they should be converted so that the Lord could heal them (see Matthew 13:14–15 and Acts 28:26–27).

In other words, these people did not want to know the truth. They enjoyed living in sin, and did not want to be converted and then have to change their life-styles.

Isaiah 6:11–12 • Until the Cities Be Without Inhabitant

11 Then said I: Lord, how long? And he **said**: Until the cities be wasted without inhabitant, and the houses without man, and the land be utterly desolate;

12 And the Lord have removed men far away, **for** there shall be a great forsaking in the midst of the land. [2 Nephi 16:11–12]

Other than punctuation, the only differences in the Book of Mormon and the King James texts are the bold "said" (v. 11) is translated as "answered" in the KJV; and the bolded "for" (v. 12) is translated as "and" in the KJV. Also, the word "Lord" (v. 12) is translated LORD in the KJV. The KJV LORD usually represents Jehovah who is the Old Testament Christ (see Exodus 6:2–3 and John 8:58–59). This representation fits the context of the message. Other differences are insignificant, and so the Book of Mormon text is the only one quoted.

The length of Isaiah's ministry is sometimes interpreted by scholars to be until mortal man is no more, suggesting he would continue his work in the Spirit World after his death. While this principle is true (see D&C 138:57), the historical context suggests that Isaiah's mission was to warn the Northern ten tribes of Israel until they were overrun and taken captive by the Assyrians (721 B.C.). This was the message of doom to Northern Israel. The message of hope that follows supports the historical context.

Isaiah 6:13 • A Tenth Shall Return

13 But yet **there** shall be a tenth, and **they** shall return, and shall be eaten, as a teil-tree, and as an oak whose substance is in them when they cast their leaves; so the holy seed shall be the substance thereof. [2 Nephi 16:13]

13 But yet in it *shall be* a tenth, and *it* shall return, and shall be eaten: as a teil tree, and as an oak, whose substance *is* in them, when they cast *their leaves: so* the holy seed *shall be* the substance thereof. [Isaiah 6:13]

The Book of Mormon retains the two bolded words that give a more complete understanding of this verse. This prophecy clearly shows that, although the cities of Israel will be destroyed and the inhabitants scattered, a remnant of that "holy seed" will return to inhabit the land. Northern Israel or the "lost tribes" were taken captive by Assyria in 721 B.C. Judah returned (538 B.C.) after they were taken captive by Babylon (607 B.C.), but the other lost tribes of Israel never returned. Therefore, their return, as prophesied in these verses was to be in the latter days. This gathering fits the context of Isaiah's words. A marginal reading in the KJV sheds further light on the phrase "shall be eaten." The KJV states, "when it is returned, and hath been broused." This has reference to a purging of those who are to be scattered. Isaiah's analogy of a tree losing its leaves indicates that the tenth to return will be from a new generation.

The tenth does not have to indicate a percentage, but may refer to one of the ten tribes that were taken by the Assyrians. That tribe would be Ephraim, "my [the Lord's] firstborn" or the birthright holder (see Jeremiah 31:9), who is being gathered or returning in these latter days. Other translations support the KJV marginal reading. The New International Version (NIV) reads: "But as the terebrinth and the oak leave stumps when they are cut down, so the holy seed will be the stump in the land." A study note at the bottom of the NIV page states, "stump out of which the nation will grow again." The Revised Standard Version (RSV) and the New King James Version have very similar wording. The trees mentioned are the deciduous trees that shed or cast their leaves. The leaves are then scattered (among the Gentiles), but one tribe of the ten will return.

The stump reminds us of the mother tree in the Zenos' allegory of the house of Israel into which the branches of Israel will be grafted back (see Jacob 5:51–56). The nation of Israel growing again has reference to the restoration in the latter days. The scattered leaves (the aftermath of the apostasy) will be gathered again. The birthright tribe of Ephraim will be the chosen one to restore that nation. That restoration is well underway, and the natural branches of the Lamanites, Jews, and lost tribes will be grafted back in that order.

> 63 Graft in the branches; begin at the last that they may be first, and that the first may be last, and dig about the trees, both old and young, the first and the last; and the last and the first, that all may be nourished once again for the last time. [Jacob 5:63]

The Lamanites were the last to be taken away (600 B.C.), and so will be the first one's restored to the mother trunk. That grafting has begun but the major restoration is yet to be restored. The Jews were gathered again as mentioned above, but were scattered again in A.D. 70 through the Roman conquest. They were to be the second one's grafted back. While the physical gathering has already begun the spiritual return or grafting back into the mother trunk has not yet taken place. Nephi included more of Isaiah's prophecies about the branches being grafted back in other chapters. These will be discussed in later chapters of this work. According to the allegory the ten tribes were to be the last ones to return. The prophecies of Isaiah and other Book of Mormon prophets also tell us of their return and will be considered later. The order of the grafting as given in the allegory will undoubtedly be restored as foretold.

2 Nephi 25:1–6 • Why Isaiah is not Understood

> 1 Now I, Nephi, do speak somewhat concerning the words which I have written, which have been spoken by the mouth of Isaiah. For behold, Isaiah spake many things which were hard for many of my people to understand; for they know not concerning the manner of

prophesying among the Jews.

2 For I, Nephi, have not taught them many things concerning the manner of the Jews; for their works were works of darkness, and their doings were doings of abominations.

3 Wherefore, I write unto my people, unto all those that shall receive hereafter these things which I write, that they may know the judgments of God, that they come upon all nations, according to the word which he hath spoken.

4 Wherefore, hearken, O my people, which are of the house of Israel, and give ear unto my words; for because the words of Isaiah are not plain unto you, nevertheless they are plain unto all those that are filled with the spirit of prophecy. But I give unto you a prophecy, according to the spirit which is in me; wherefore I shall prophesy according to the plainness which hath been with me from the time that I came out from Jerusalem with my father; for behold, my soul delighteth in plainness unto my people, that they may learn.

5 Yea, and my soul delighteth in the words of Isaiah, for I came out from Jerusalem, and mine eyes hath beheld the things of the Jews, and I know that the Jews do understand the things of the prophets, and there is none other people that understand the things which were spoken unto the Jews like unto them, save it be that they are taught after the manner of the things of the Jews.

6 But behold, I, Nephi, have not taught my children after the manner of the Jews; but behold, I, of myself, have dwelt at Jerusalem, wherefore I know concerning the regions round about; and I have made mention unto my children concerning the judgments of God, which hath come to pass among the Jews, unto my children, according to all that which Isaiah hath spoken, and I do not write them.

Nephi recognized that even though they had left Jerusalem only one hundred years or so after Isaiah concluded his writings, Isaiah was a difficult book for his people to understand (v. 1). Nearly twenty-six hundred more years have passed since that time. If it was hard for Nephi's people who came from the same geographical area and time period to understand Isaiah, his words would in turn be even more difficult for us to understand today. The passage of time is not the only thing that makes Isaiah hard to understand. To come to an understanding requires that we diligently study Isaiah's words as the Savior commanded (3 Nephi 23:1). To search is to carefully and thoroughly examine in an effort to discover the message. To search is also to inspect or explore possible places of concealment. Nephi tells us how to do this.

Nephi gives three ways to understand Isaiah. The first is to understand the manner of prophesying among the Jews (v. 1). However, Nephi had not taught his "children after the manner of the Jews" because of the works of darkness and abominations that had been among the Jews (v. 2). Jeremiah, who was a prophet in Jerusalem at the time of Lehi, confirmed the existence of these dark conditions in Jerusalem. He had warned: "A conspiracy is found among the men of Judah, and among the inhabitants of Jerusalem" (Jeremiah 11:9). Similar to Nephi, Alma also commanded his son Helaman not to teach the people of the secret abominations of the Jaredites "lest peradventure they should fall into darkness also and be destroyed" (Alma 37:25–32). His reluctance to teach concerning this manner among the Jews was probably a preventive measure to avoid introducing similar works among his people. Nevertheless, Nephi understood Isaiah's words, and the Jews to whom these words were addressed also knew their meaning (vv. 5–6). Preventing the introduction of abominations and works of darkness among the people of today is still desirable. Through the Book of Mormon we can learn the message of Isaiah without such knowledge.

Nephi knew about the regions round about Jerusalem,[3] and had taught his children about the judgments of God which had come upon the Jews because of their abominations (v. 6).[4] This helped interpret the words of Isaiah. He wanted those who received his record to know that the judgments of God would come upon all nations according to

---

[3] For the geography of the land see the maps of the various time periods in the appendix of the LDS publication of the Bible. Many other Bibles also have a map section included.

[4] See the overview at the end of the chapter.

the words God had spoken (v. 3). We will have a better understanding of Isaiah if we also know of the geography of the lands given to Abraham and his posterity, the judgments of God that had already come upon them (their history), and what will happen to the nations in the future (the prophecies). Knowledge of the geography and history of the land can be obtained from the scholars of the world, but these scholars do not always recognize the judgments of God within the histories they write. Nephi and others from the Book of Mormon who quote and give interpretive commentary upon Isaiah's writings recognize the hand of God in the history of the Jews.

Some have supposed that learning the Hebrew language would teach us the manner of prophesying among the Jews. While that would be beneficial in other ways, it is not the key to understanding Isaiah. The Hebrew text has also lost plain and precious parts from its text. However, there are a few things we learn from both the Hebrew and the English text. We learn that the Jewish prophets almost always followed a pattern of warning with a message of doom (destruction) followed by a message of hope (the restoration in the future days). They also used dual prophecy, both in time and in places. Jacob spoke of the same prophecy of Isaiah being fulfilled by the Jews (2 Nephi 6, Isaiah 49:22–26), that Nephi had said would be fulfilled in the Isles of the Sea (1 Nephi 21–22). Jesus quoted Isaiah 52:8–10 as a prophecy to the Lamanites (3 Nephi 16:16–20), and later quoted it as being fulfilled among the Jews (3 Nephi 20:30–35). These patterns can be seen in both the English and the Hebrew texts. The key to understanding Isaiah is in the text and commentary of Isaiah found in the Book of Mormon and in the Doctrine and Covenants.

The second way given by Nephi to understand Isaiah was to be "filled with the spirit of prophecy" (v. 4). The spirit of prophecy and of revelation comes through "much prayer and fasting" (Alma 17:3). Nephi told us what he had learned from Isaiah by the Spirit. His comments after quoting Isaiah should be a primary source for obtaining and understanding of Isaiah. The Spirit will also teach us things written or not written by Isaiah. As we live worthy to receive the Spirit, the

Spirit will bear record of the correct interpretation of Isaiah and its application to our lives (see 2 Nephi 32:2–5).

2 Nephi 25:7–8 • Known in the Day that They are Fulfilled

> 7 But behold, I proceed with mine own prophecy, according to my plainness; in the which I know that no man can err; nevertheless, in the days that the prophecies of Isaiah shall be fulfilled men shall know of a surety, at the times when they shall come to pass.

> 8 Wherefore, they are of worth unto the children of men, and he that supposeth that they are not, unto them will I speak particularly, and confine the words unto mine own people; for I know that they shall be of great worth unto them in the last days; for in that day shall they understand them; wherefore, for their good have I written them.

The third way for us to understand Isaiah is an important one, and one that is often overlooked when Nephi's admonition is read. According to Nephi, it is to live "in the days that the prophecies of Isaiah shall be fulfilled" (v. 7). This fulfillment will come in the last days (v. 8). The experience of Martin Harris taking the characters copied from the golden plates along with their translation to the learned Charles Anthon is a good example of Nephi's third key. This will be discussed in a later chapter, but today neither Jews nor Christians understand Isaiah's prophecy that coincides with this event. Neither would we if it had not already happened. There are other prophecies recorded by Isaiah that we do not understand because they have not yet come to pass.

The words of Isaiah are hard to be understood, but one can come to an understanding of his words by knowing the manner of prophesying among the Jews, by being filled with the spirit of prophecy, and by living in the day when the prophecies of Isaiah are fulfilled. Any one of these ways, or a combination of them, may bring an understanding of Isaiah, although it will probably come "line upon line, precept upon precept, here a little and there a little" (2 Nephi 28:30; Isaiah 28:10). However the understanding comes, it will bring the modern reader to proclaim with the Savior, "Great are the words of Isaiah" (3 Nephi 23:1).

THE JUDGMENTS OF GOD UPON THE JEWS

2000 B.C.	Abraham is given the land "from the river of Egypt unto the great Euphrates (Genesis 15:18). The land inheritance was passed on to his posterity, Isaac and Jacob. Jacob has twelve sons, his name is changed to Israel and they become the twelve tribes of Israel.
Around 1700 B.C.	Joseph is sold into Egypt (Genesis 37), and the family of Jacob comes down into Egypt because of the famine in the land of Canaan, an indication of wickedness. After Joseph's death the Egyptians place Israel into bondage.[5]
Between 1400–1200 B.C.	Moses delivers Israel out of their bondage to Egypt. They spend 40 years in the wilderness. Moses is translated and Joshua leads them into the promised land. After Joshua dies, the period of the Judges is one of great wickedness.
Around 1100 B.C.	Saul is appointed king over Israel in spite of the Lord's warning about Kings.
Around 1050 B.C.	David becomes king of Israel
Around 1000 B.C.	Solomon reigns as king.
About 975 B.C.	The ten tribes revolt and the kingdom of Israel is divided into the Northern ten tribes and the kingdom of Judah in the South.

---

[5] Because of the uncertainty and controversy over the Old Testament dating, the above dates are very general, rounded off, and approximate. The intent is to merely give an overview. The teacher can fill in the details as desired.

About 722 B.C.	The Northern ten tribes are taken captive into Assyria. They become known as the "lost tribes."
About 607 B.C.	Judah is captured by Nebuchadnezzar and taken in bondage to the Babylonians. Many Jews are taken captive into Babylon for 70 years as Jeremiah had prophesied (Jeremiah 25:12).
600 B.C.	Lehi and his party leave Jerusalem.
589 B.C.	Jerusalem is destroyed by Babylon and the Jews are scattered again.
538 B.C.	Cyrus decrees that the Jews can return and rebuild their temple. Many return.
A.D. 70	The Romans destroy Jerusalem and the Jews scatter throughout the world (known as the diaspora).
October 24, 1841	Elder Orson Hyde dedicates the land for the return of the Jews.
May 15, 1948	The nation of modern Israel is born.

SACRED WRITING

Preaching Which is Sacred:

| 2 Nephi 11 | Nephi preaches to the reader about Isaiah through his writing. |
| 2 Nephi 25:1–8 | Nephi teaches us how to understand Isaiah. |

Revelation Which is Great:

| 2 Nephi 16 | Isaiah's call to the ministry |

Prophesying:

| 2 Nephi 25:7 | Nephi prophesies that when the prophecies of Isaiah |

	are fulfilled, men shall know of a surety of their fulfillment.
2 Nephi 25:8	Nephi prophesies that in the last days men shall understand the prophecies of Isaiah.

Doctrines Learned:

2 Nephi 11:2–3	Christ appeared personally to mortals in Old Testament times.
2 Nephi 11:4	The law of Moses and all things from the beginning typify Christ.

General Authority Quotations:

Bruce R. McConkie • 2 Nephi 11

If our eternal salvation depends upon our ability to understand the writings of Isaiah as fully and truly as Nephi understood them—and who shall say such is not the case! —how shall we fare in that great day when with Nephi we shall stand before the pleasing bar of Him who said: 'Great are the words of Isaiah'? (3 Nephi 23:1). . . .

The Book of Mormon is the world's greatest commentary on the book of Isaiah.

And I may be so bold as to affirm that no one, absolutely, no one, in this age and dispensation has or does or can understand the writings of Isaiah until he first learns and believes what God has revealed by the mouths of his Nephite witnesses as these truths are found in that volume of holy writ of which he himself swore this oath: " . . . as your Lord and your God liveth it is true" (D&C 17:6). [*Ensign*, Oct. 1973, 81]

Challenges to Eternal Life:

1. Pray for the Spirit as you study these chapters of Isaiah. Rejoice in the things you learn (2 Nephi 25:4).

2. Study the geography of the land of ancient Israel and the history and prophecies in the Bible of those people so that you may better understand Isaiah and progress towards eternal life (2 Nephi 25:6).

3. As you study Isaiah, recognize the prophecies of Isaiah that have already

come to pass. Rejoice and thank the Lord for being a part of their fulfillment (2 Nephi 11:8).

4. Choose a challenge from your reading that you have seen fulfilled and apply it to your life.

Chapter Fifteen

The Covenants of the Lord

2 Nephi 12–14

*H*istorical Setting: Isaiah prophesied about 740 B.C. to 697 B.C.
Nephi writes his prophecies upon the small plates sometime
between 559 and 545 B.C.

Precepts of this Reading:

> And there shall be a tabernacle for a shadow in the daytime from
> the heat, and for a place of refuge, and a covert from storm and from
> rain. [2 Nephi 14:6]

OUTLINE • 2 NEPHI 12–14

12:2–5   The Lord will judge among nations and bring peace.

      a.   The mountain of the Lord's house will be established
in the tops of the mountains, and all nations will flow
unto it (v. 2).

      b.   Many people will go to the house of the God of Jacob
to be taught (v. 3).

      c.   Out of Zion will go forth the law (v. 3).

      d.   The word of the Lord will go forth from Jerusalem
(v. 3).

      e.   All nations will cease making weapons of war and will
be at peace (v. 4).

      f.   The house of Jacob is invited to come and walk in the light of the Lord (v. 5).

➤ 12:6–22   The Lord has forsaken his people, the house of Jacob, and they will be brought down.

      a.   They seek after the philosophies and learning of men (v. 6).

      b.   Their hearts have turned to material things (v. 7).

      c.   They worship idols, the works of their own hands (v. 8).

      d.   They are lifted up in pride (v. 9).

      e.   The wicked hide because of their fear of the Lord (vv. 10–11).

      f.   The day of the Lord will come upon all people everywhere and cause them to forsake their idols (vv. 12–18).

      g.   The wicked will flee to the caves and the mountains because of fear (vv. 19–21).

      h.   The people are admonished to stop following after man (v. 22).

➤ 13:1–15   Jerusalem will fall because its inhabitants have rebelled against God.

      a.   The Lord will take away their economic prosperity (v. 1).

      b.   He will take away their great leadership (vv. 2–3).

      c.   Children, babes, and women will rule over Judah and oppress them (vv. 3–4, 12).

      d.   Judah will resort to family leadership, but men will refrain from leading (vv. 6–7).

      e.   Immorality even as Sodom will cause their destruction, but the righteous will be saved (vv. 9–11).

      f.   Because their leaders will cause them to err, the Lord will bring judgment upon their leaders (vv. 12–15).

➤ 13:16–14:1 Zion will also be smitten.

      a.   Social conditions will bring the Lord's judgments (vv. 16–17).

    b.   Religious conditions will bring the Lord's judgments (vv. 18–24).

    c.   A great war will kill off the men, leaving seven women to one man (13:25–14:1).

➤ 14:2–6   The branch of the Lord will be beautiful and glorious in that day.

    a.   The Lord will cleanse Zion and Jerusalem (vv. 2–4).

    b.   He will protect every dwelling place and assembly of Zion (vv. 5–6).

NOTES AND COMMENTARY

Introduction: Many people suggest skipping the Isaiah chapters on the first reading of the Book of Mormon and even on subsequent readings. Elder Boyd K. Packer gave this timely advice against that suggestion:

> You, too, may be tempted to stop there, but do not do it! Do not stop reading! Move forward through those difficult-to-understand chapters of Old Testament prophecy, even if you understand very little of it. Move on, if all you do is skim and merely glean an impression here and there. Move on, if all you do is look at the words. [CR, April 1986, 74. See a longer excerpt from this excellent address under "Quotations of General Authorities"]

The second and third verses of 2 Nephi 12 (Isaiah 2) are quite familiar to many members of the Church. Read these two verses and mentally note their meaning, then study the notes and commentary to enlarge your understanding.

2 Nephi 12–14 • (Isaiah 2–4)

It is unusual that Nephi would quote thirteen consecutive chapters of Isaiah (2–14) and begin with chapter 2 instead of chapter 1. However, this is understandable. Scholars consider the first chapter an introduction to the compilation of the prophecies of Isaiah and other later writings. It is quite obvious that the book of Isaiah is a compilation of various prophecies given at different times. However, chapter 1 seems to be much more than an introduction; it is apparently a *preface* given by revelation specifically for that purpose. Thus it is closely akin to section 1 of the Doctrine and Covenants.[6]

Three chapters of Isaiah are required to present Isaiah's vision of Judah and Jerusalem. Parts of chapters 2 and 3 paint quite a dismal picture, but chapter 4 describes the final glorious condition of "the branch [or church] of the Lord." This is an example of the doom or destruction message followed by the hope or future restoration pattern of "the manner of prophesying of the Jews" (2 Nephi 25:1) discussed in the previous chapter. If the reader is going to teach this material, two hours or class periods should be scheduled to adequately discuss the contents. As a suggestion, 2 Nephi 12 should be the content of the first hour, and 2 Nephi 3–4 should be the content of the second hour. Otherwise important parts will have to be skipped.

2 Nephi 12:1 (Isaiah 2:1) • Concerning Judah and Jerusalem

> 1 The word that Isaiah, the son of Amoz, saw concerning Judah and Jerusalem:

Except for punctuation, the Book of Mormon and the King James texts are identical, therefore, only the Book of Mormon text is quoted.

Although Isaiah notes that he saw things concerning Judah and Jerusalem (Isaiah 2:1), his vision includes references to three different peoples and two different lands. He speaks of Judah in the land of Jerusalem, of the "daughters of Zion," and of the "branch of the Lord" in the land of Zion. The prophet Joseph Smith declared, "The prophets have spoken and written upon it [Zion]; but I will make a proclamation that will cover a broader ground. *The whole of America is Zion itself from north to south, and is described by the Prophets, who declare that it is the Zion where the mountain of the Lord should be, and that*

---

[6] For a fuller explanation and comparison of the two prefaces see Monte S. Nyman, *Great are the Words of Isaiah* [1980], chap. 3.

it should be in the center of the land. When elders shall take up and examine the old prophecies in the Bible, they will see it" (*TPJS*, 362). Thus, the "daughters of Zion" refer to those who inhabit the Americas.

The "branch of the Lord" spoken of by Isaiah consists of those who are "escaped of Israel" (those of Israel who will have escaped the judgments which are to come upon the world in the last days). He speaks of these as being from the daughters of Zion and from Jerusalem. Therefore, the three peoples include the inhabitants of Jerusalem in general, the inhabitants of Zion in general, and the specific group from Zion and Jerusalem who constitute the beautiful and glorious branch (Church) of the Lord. The two lands include the land of Jerusalem and the land of the Americas.

The Savior justified Isaiah's inclusion of the Gentiles: "For surely he spake as touching all things concerning my people which are of the house of Israel; therefore it must needs be that he must speak also to the Gentiles" (3 Nephi 23:2). It was necessary to speak to or about the Gentiles to show all things concerning the house of Israel. It was also necessary to speak to or about Zion to show the ultimate destiny of Judah. An understanding of that ultimate destiny of both branches of Israel will cause all of Israel to "lift up their hearts and rejoice for all men." This validates Nephi's purpose for including Isaiah's words in his writings (2 Nephi 11:8).

Isaiah's vision centers around the restoration of the gospel, the Second Coming of Christ, and the ushering in of his Millennial reign. It also includes prophecies concerning Judah in Isaiah's own day. Since it is a vision of Judah and Jerusalem, this would be expected.

2 Nephi 12:2–3 (Isaiah 2:2–3) • Mountain of the Lord's House

2 And it shall come to pass in the last days, when the mountain of the Lord's house shall be established in the top of the mountains, and shall be exalted above the hills, and all nations shall flow unto it.	2 And it shall come to pass in the last days, *that* the mountain of the LORD's house shall be established in the top of the mountains, and shall be exalted above the hills; and all nations shall flow unto it.

3 And many people shall go and say, Come ye, and let us go up to the mountain of the Lord, to the house of the God of Jacob; and he will teach us of his ways, and we will walk in his paths; for out of Zion shall go forth the law, and the word of the Lord from Jerusalem. [2 Nephi 12:2–3]

3 And many people shall go and say, Come ye, and let us go up to the mountain of the LORD, to the house of the God of Jacob; and he will teach us of his ways, and we will walk in his paths: for out of Zion shall go forth the law, and the word of the LORD from Jerusalem. [Isaiah 2:2–3]

Nephi's quotes from the plates of brass have preserved several significant details. The King James scholars italicized "that" because they were unsure of the correct translation. The Book of Mormon and the JST have rendered "that" to "when." This is a very significant retention from the plates of brass. It specifies the time when the Lord would begin to establish the two nations of Israel in Zion and Jerusalem. Their establishment will lead to the ushering in of the Millennium.

While many Latter-day Saints believe that the establishment of "the mountain of the Lord's house" in the tops of the mountains represents the Salt Lake Temple (v. 2), it has a broader application. Some Old Testament prophets label Zion, the whole of America, (*TPJS*, 362 quoted above) as the "everlasting hills" of the "ancient mountains." Part of Jacob's blessing to Joseph, found in Genesis 49:26, reads: "The blessings of thy father have prevailed above the blessings of my progenitors unto the utmost bound of the everlasting hills: they shall be on the head of Joseph, and on the crown of the head of him that was separate from his brethren." Moses blessed Joseph "for the chief things of the ancient mountains, and for the precious things of the lasting hills" (Deuteronomy 33:15). This would suggest that Isaiah's prophecy relates to the whole continent, not just Salt Lake City. Wherefore, the first temple built in the "everlasting hills" of the Americas in this dispensation was the Kirtland Temple in 1836, and the Lord appeared to the Prophet Joseph Smith and Oliver Cowdery in that temple on 3 April 1836 (see D&C 110).

President Charles Penrose taught that the Savior's second coming will occur in three phases: (1) his appearances in the temples of Zion, unbeknown to the rest of mankind; (2) his appearance to the distressed and nearly vanquished sons of Judah; and (3) his appearance in glory to the world.[7] Actually, there have already been several appearances of the Lord in his temples, since a temple is his holy house. Elder Harold B. Lee once stated: "I know that this is the Lord's work, I know that Jesus Christ lives, and that he's closer to this Church and appears more often in holy places than any of us realize excepting sometimes to those to whom he makes his personal appearance. I know it and the time is hastening when he shall come again to reign as Lord of Lords and King of Kings."[8]

Further, in answer to the Prophet Joseph Smith's yearning prayer—"When will Zion be built up in her glory, and where will thy Temple stand, unto which all nations shall come in the last days?" (Section heading of D&C 57)—the Lord designated the land of Missouri as the place of the city of Zion, and "Independence is the center place; and a spot for the temple" unto which all nations should come (D&C 57:1–3). When the Savior visited the Nephites (A.D. 34), he gave them a sign for when "I shall gather in, from their long dispersion, my people, O house of Israel, and shall establish again among them my Zion" (3 Nephi 21:1). The sign was the coming forth of the Book of Mormon (see vv. 2–7). He warned the Gentiles of that day: "And I will execute vengeance and fury upon them, even as upon the heathen, such as they have not heard." He then promised:

> 22 But if they will repent and hearken unto my words, and harden not their hearts, I will establish my church among them, and they shall come in unto the covenant and be numbered among this the remnant of Jacob [or Joseph see 3 Nephi 15:12–13], unto whom I have given this land for their inheritance;
>
> 23 And they shall assist my people, the remnant of Jacob, and also

---

[7] *Millennial Star*, September 1859, reprinted in *The Improvement Era*, May, 1957, 326–327.

[8] Talk delivered at MIA June Conference, 29 June 1969, as printed in Living Prophets for a Living Church (Salt Lake City: The Church of Jesus Christ of Latter-day Saints, 1973), 119.

as many of the house of Israel as shall come, that they may build a city, which shall be called the New Jerusalem.

24 And then shall they assist my people that they may be gathered in, who are scattered upon all the face of the land, in unto the New Jerusalem. [3 Nephi 21:21–24]

The building of the New Jerusalem is to mark the gathering of all the tribes of Israel, and the work of the Father in gathering his people from all the nations of the earth (see 3 Nephi 21:24–29). The building of the temple in Jackson County, Missouri, seems to be the final fulfillment of the prophecy of Isaiah that the mountain of the Lord's house would be established in the tops of the mountains. Thus Isaiah's prophecy commences with the building of the Kirtland Temple and extends to the future building of the temple in Independence, Jackson County, Missouri.

In a broader sense, the establishment of the kingdom of God occurred earlier, on 6 April 1830, and was the commencement of the fulfillment of the prophecy of Isaiah 2:2–3. The temple could not be built until the kingdom was established. According to Oliver Cowdery, the angel Moroni quoted Isaiah 2:1–4 to Joseph Smith in September 1823 as one of the prophecies which was about to be fulfilled.[9] The Kirtland Temple was completed in 1836. At the dedication of that temple, Joseph Smith, by revelation, declared:

62 We therefore ask thee to have mercy upon the children of Jacob, that Jerusalem, from this hour, may begin to be redeemed;

63 And the yoke of bondage may begin to be broken off from the house of David;

64 And the children of Judah may begin to return to the lands which thou didst give to Abraham, their father. [D&C 109:62–64]

Following the dedicatory prayer, Joseph sent Elder Orson Hyde to Jerusalem to dedicate the land for the return of Judah as the revelation had decreed.

---

[9] *Messenger and Advocate*, April 1835, 110.

However, the temple in Salt Lake City is the major forerunner of the temple in Independence, Missouri. It is the ensign lifted unto the nations until the time the temple in Missouri is built. According to President Harold B. Lee, Elder Orson Pratt, who was one of the members of the twelve at the time, declared that the coming of the pioneers to the tops of the mountains was the beginning of the fulfillment of that prophecy. He "delivered an oration on that occasion, in which he declared that this was the beginning of the fulfillment of that prophecy that out of Zion should go forth the law and the word of the Lord from Jerusalem" (*Ensign*, Nov. 1971, 15).

Isaiah's prophecy clearly designates two headquarters for the righteous children of Israel in the latter days. President Joseph Fielding Smith declared: "there shall be two headquarters: Zion and Jerusalem, and out of these cities shall go forth the word of the Lord, and his commandments, not only to those who are members of the Church, but unto the nations of the earth, when his kingdom is fully established."[10] While the establishment of the Church in 1830 began the fulfillment of this prophecy, building the Salt Lake Temple was also a sign that the Jerusalem headquarters would soon be established. The gathering of the Jews was to be a slow process, but its commencement closely paralleled the movement of the Mormon pioneers to the West. The Salt Lake Temple was completed in 1893, after forty years of labor with periodic interruptions. "In 1878 an organization of the Jews was formed called the lovers of Zion, the purpose being to establish the Jews in Palestine.[11] The Zionist Federation, was commenced in 1896, and the first conference of this organization was held in Basel,

---

[10] Joseph Fielding Smith, *Doctrines of Salvation*, comp. Bruce R. McConkie, 3 vols. [1954], 1:176.

[11] It should be noted that the first Latter-day Saint temple in the west was built and dedicated on April 6, 1877, the St. George temple. This temple was another parallel of "when" the mountain of the Lord's house was established, the work of the Lord would commence among Judah and Jerusalem.

Switzerland, in 1897."[12] Just as the temple took many years to build, so had the movement of the Jews took many years.

One of the early beginnings was the journey of Elder Orson Hyde, under the direction of the Prophet Joseph Smith, to dedicate Palestine for the return of the Jews. It is of interest to note that Elder Hyde was sent a short time after the Kirtland Temple was completed. The dedication took place on the Mount of Olives on 24 October 1841 (see *HC*, 4:454–59). With the establishment of both headquarters, the Church members were to gather to Zion and the Jews to Jerusalem: "Let them, therefore, who are among the Gentiles flee unto Zion. And let them who be of Judah flee unto Jerusalem, unto the mountain of the Lord's house" (D&C 133:12–13). In the early days of the Church, however, Jews who were converted to the gospel were to gather in Zion rather than Jerusalem (*TPJS*, 180).

While verses 2 and 3 are usually treated as one prophecy, there are some unique aspects of verse 3 which may relate to a later time than the establishment of the temple. Of course, the settlement of the Saints in the valley of the Rocky Mountains brought people from many nations, but subsequent converts to the Church brought thousands more to those valleys from all over the world. Elder Mark E. Petersen wrote of the influx of immigrants to the Rocky Mountains as a fulfillment of this prophecy. He also referred to the tourists who visit Salt Lake Temple Square and the Church General Conferences as further fulfillment of Isaiah's prophecy that many people would say, "Let us go up to the mountain of the Lord."

In verse 2, Isaiah says that "the Lord's house shall . . . be exalted above the hills." Elder Petersen pointed out that all of the various translations of the Bible emphasize the "temple hill," and that most temples are built on eminent sites. He also identified the general conferences of the Church as a fulfillment of Isaiah's prophecy that "out of Zion shall go forth the law." This is especially true as these

---

[12] Joseph Fielding Smith, *Signs of the Times* [1970], 67.

conferences are broadcast to the world by radio and television.[13] However, President George Albert Smith taught a broader concept as he dedicated the Idaho Falls Temple. He taught that the "going forth" of the "law" is the establishment in the world of governments similar to "our constitutional form of government." In referring to this dedicatory prayer, President Harold B. Lee later said:

> I have often wondered what that expression meant, that out of Zion shall go forth the law. Years ago I went with the brethren to the Idaho Falls Temple, and I heard in that inspired prayer of the First Presidency a definition of the meaning of that term "out of Zion shall go forth the law." Note what they said: "We thank thee that thou hast revealed to us that those who gave us our constitutional form of government were men wise in thy sight and that thou didst raise them up for the very purpose of putting forth that sacred document [as revealed in Doctrine and Covenants section 101] . . .

> We pray that kings and rulers and the peoples of all nations under heaven may be persuaded of the blessings enjoyed by the people of this land by reason of their freedom and under thy guidance and be constrained to adopt similar governmental systems, thus to fulfill the ancient prophecy of Isaiah and Micah that " . . . out of Zion shall go forth the law and the word of the Lord from Jerusalem." [*IE*, Oct. 1945, 564; *Ensign*, Nov. 1971, 15]

The Prophet Joseph Smith also equated the "law" with the theocracy of God that will rule during the Millennium, as described in verse 4 (*TPJS*, 248–52). Elder Orson Pratt interpreted Isaiah's reference to "the law" as follows: "Out of Zion shall go forth the law says the prophet. What law? A law to regulate the nations, a law teaching them how to be saved, a law informing the kings and emperors and the nobles of the earth how they can save themselves, and how they can save their dead" (*JD*, 14:350). These interpretations combine the political and spiritual aspects of the law.

While Zion's camp was on Fishing River, Missouri, June 22, 1834, the Lord gave a revelation to Joseph Smith saying that the redemption

---

[13] Mark E. Petersen, *Why the Religious Life* [1966], 200–201, 305–307.

of Zion must wait for a little season:

> 10 That they themselves may be prepared, and that my people may be taught more perfectly, and have experience, and know more perfectly concerning their duty, and the things which I require at their hands.
>
> 11 And this cannot be brought to pass until mine elders are endowed with power from on high.
>
> 12 For behold, I have prepared a great endowment and blessing to be poured out upon them, inasmuch as they are faithful and continue in humility before me. [D&C 105:10–12]

The endowment of power comes in the Temple. The people are prepared there by being taught more perfectly. They know more perfectly what the Lord requires as they make covenants to live as they have been instructed. Therefore, as Isaiah said: the Lord "will teach us [perfectly] of his ways, and we will [covenant to] walk in his paths" (2 Nephi 2:3).

2 Nephi 12:4 (Isaiah 2:4) • Beat Their Swords into Plowshares

> 4 And he shall judge among the nations, and shall rebuke many people: and they shall beat their swords into plow-shares, and their spears into pruning-hooks—nation shall not lift up sword against nation, neither shall they learn war any more.

The verses in the Book of Mormon and the KJV are identical, except for punctuation; therefore only the Book of Mormon text is quoted.

The Lord judging among the nations is accomplished through the Book of Mormon. The angel "having the everlasting gospel [The Book of Mormon] to preach unto every nation, kindred, tongue, and people" also announced that "the hour of [God's] judgment is come" (Revelation 14:6–7). Nephi said: "the nations that possessed [the Book of Mormon] shall be judged by [the Book of Mormon]" (2 Nephi 25:22). These judgments of God will usher in the millennial reign. Note that

Isaiah speaks of the time from the building of the house of the Lord in Zion (1836) to the millennium (already nearly 170 years) in just 3 verses (Isaiah 2:2–4). Isaiah seems to speak of movements rather than events.

2 Nephi 12:5–9 (Isaiah 2:5–9) • Walk in the Light of the Lord

5 O house of Jacob, come ye and let us walk in the light of the Lord; yea, come, for ye have all gone astray, every one to his wicked ways.

6 Therefore, O Lord, thou hast forsaken thy people, the house of Jacob, because they be replenished from the east, and hearken unto soothsayers like the Philistines, and they please themselves in the children of strangers.

7 Their land also is full of silver and gold, neither is there any end of their treasures; their land is also full of horses, neither is there any end of their chariots.

8 Their land is also full of idols; they worship the work of their own hands, that which their own fingers have made.

9 And the mean man boweth not down, and the great man humbleth himself not, therefore, forgive him not. [2 Nephi 12:5–9]

5 O house of Jacob, come ye, and let us walk in the light of the LORD.

6 Therefore thou hast forsaken thy people the house of Jacob, because they be replenished from the east, and *are* soothsayers like the Philistines, and they please themselves in the children of strangers.

7 Their land also is full of silver and gold, neither *is there any* end of their treasures; their land is also full of horses, neither *is there any* end of their chariots:

8 Their land also is full of idols; they worship the work of their own hands, that which their own fingers have made:

9 And the mean man boweth down, and the great man humbleth himself: therefore forgive them not. [Isaiah 2:5–9]

The Book of Mormon supplies the second half of the original verse, which has been lost from the Bible translations (v. 5). The Book of Mormon shows that there would be a complete apostasy upon the earth before the time of the establishment of the mountain of the Lord's house. The characteristics of the apostasy are given in terms of Isaiah's day (vv. 6–8).[14] Therefore, the people of Jacob are invited to walk in the light of the Lord that would be taught in his holy house.

The Book of Mormon retention of the word "not" in two different places in verse nine makes it read sensibly. The word "mean" is a synonym for average in archaic English. Therefore, the "average" man or the great man does not rely on the Lord. The great man probably refers to the more educated, gifted, or prosperous man. The loss of the "not" leaves no reason for either one not to be forgiven. There are some interesting apologies offered by various commentators in the Christian world, trying to justify the present-day Bible readings.

2 Nephi 12:10–11 (Isaiah 2:10–11) • The Wicked Shall Hide for the Fear of the Lord

10 O ye wicked ones, enter into the rock, and hide thee in the dust, for the fear of the Lord and the glory of his majesty shall smite thee.

11 And it shall come to pass that the lofty looks of man shall be humbled, and the haughtiness of men shall be bowed down, and the Lord alone shall be exalted in that day. [2 Nephi 12:10–11]

10 Enter into the rock, and hide thee in the dust, for fear of the LORD, and for the glory of his majesty.

11 The lofty looks of man shall be humbled, and the haughtiness of men shall be bowed down, and the LORD alone shall be exalted in that day. [Isaiah 2:10–11]

The Book of Mormon phrase "O ye wicked ones" (v. 10) clearly identifies those who will be seeking to hide in the rocks and the dust for fear of the Lord and his glory. They will be compelled to be humble, not because of poverty but for their sins (compare Alma 32:13–14). The Lord will be exalted at this Second Coming because he will bring immortality and eternal life to the righteous (see Moses 1:39).

---

[14] They could be listed today as following the philosophies of men, materialistic goals, expansive transportation systems (cars, trains, airplanes, etc.), and the worship of designer clothes, art, music, homes, cars, etc.

2 Nephi 12:12–18 (Isaiah 2:12–18) • The Day of the Lord of Hosts Soon Cometh

12 For the day of the Lord of Hosts soon cometh upon all nations, yea, upon every one; yea, upon the proud and lofty, and upon every one who is lifted up, and he shall be brought low.

13 Yea, and the day of the Lord shall come upon all the cedars of Lebanon, for they are high and lifted up; and upon all the oaks of Bashan;

14 And upon all the high mountains, and upon all the hills, and upon all the nations which are lifted up, and upon every people;

15 And upon every high tower, and upon every fenced wall;

16 And upon all the ships of the sea, and upon all the ships of Tarshish, and upon all pleasant pictures.

17 And the loftiness of man shall be bowed down, and the haughtiness of men shall be made low; and the Lord alone shall be exalted in that day.

18 And the idols he shall utterly abolish. [2 Nephi 12:12–18]

12 For the day of the Lord of hosts *shall be* upon every *one that is* proud and lofty, and upon every *one that is* lifted up; and he shall be brought low:

13 And upon all the cedars of Lebanon, *that are* high and lifted up, and upon all the oaks of Bashan,

14 And upon all the high mountains, and upon all the hills *that are* lifted up,

15 And upon every high tower, and upon every fenced wall,

16 And upon all the ships of Tarshish, and upon all pleasant pictures.

17 And the loftiness of man shall be bowed down, and the haughtiness of men shall be made low: and the Lord alone shall be exalted in that day.

18 And the idols he shall utterly abolish. [Isaiah 2:12–18]

In the Book of Mormon, retention of the phrase "soon cometh upon all nations, yea" (v. 12) replaces the italicized "shall be" in the KJV. This phrase establishes the time when this prophecy will be fulfilled—the day the Lord will appear in glory to the entire world. The Book of Mormon retention of the phrase "Yea, and the day of the Lord shall come" (v. 13) replaces the introductory "and" in the KJV, further verifying the time period.

The 2 Nephi reading retains two phrases, "upon all nations" and "upon every people" (v. 14). It clearly shows the universal nature of the Lord coming in glory, the overall message of the above verses.

Again, Isaiah foretells the humbling of man and the exalting of the Lord alone at his Second Coming (vv. 17–18).

The late Dr. Sidney B. Sperry, who has helped members of the Church understand Isaiah, made the following comment about verse sixteen:

> In 2 Nephi 12:16 (cf. Isaiah 2:16) the Book of Mormon has a reading of remarkable interest. It prefixes a phrase of eight words not found in the Hebrew or King James versions. Since the ancient Septuagint (Greek) Version concurs with the added phrase in the Book of Mormon, let us exhibit the readings of the Book of Mormon (B.M.), the King James Version (KJ), and the Septuagint (LXX) as follows:
>
> > B.M. And upon all the ships of the sea,
> > K.J. --
> > LXX And upon every ship of the sea,
> >
> > B.M. and upon all the ships of Tarshish
> > K.J. And upon all the ships of Tarshish
> > LXX --
> >
> > B.M. and upon all pleasant pictures
> > K.J. and upon all pleasant pictures.
> > LXX and upon every display of fine ships.
>
> The Book of Mormon suggests that the original text of this verse contained three phrases, all of which commenced with the same opening words, "and upon all." By a common accident, the original Hebrew (and hence the King James) text lost the first phrase, which was, however, preserved by the Septuagint. The latter lost the second phrase and seems to have corrupted the third phrase. The Book of Mormon preserved all three phrases. Scholars may suggest that Joseph Smith took the first phrase from the Septuagint. The prophet did not know Greek, and there is no evidence that he had access to a copy of the Septuagint in 1829–1830 when he translated the Book of Mor-

mon.[15] [The Voice of Israel's Prophets, 1965, 90–91]

2 Nephi 12:19–22 (Isaiah 2:19–22) • The Glory of the Lord Shall Smite Them

19 And they shall go into the holes of the rocks, and into the caves of the earth, for the fear of the Lord shall come upon them and the glory of his majesty shall smite them, when he ariseth to shake terribly the earth.	19 And they shall go into the holes of the rocks, and into the caves of the earth, for fear of the LORD, and for the glory of his majesty, when he ariseth to shake terribly the earth.
20 In that day a man shall cast his idols of silver, and his idols of gold, which he hath made for himself to worship, to the moles and to the bats;	20 In that day a man shall cast his idols of silver, and his idols of gold, which they made *each one* for himself to worship, to the moles and to the bats;
21 To go into the clefts of the rocks, and into the tops of the ragged rocks, for the fear of the Lord shall come upon them and the majesty of his glory shall smite them, when he ariseth to shake terribly the earth.	21 To go into the clefts of the rocks, and into the tops of the ragged rocks, for fear of the LORD, and for the glory of his majesty, when he ariseth to shake terribly the earth.
22 Cease ye from man, whose breath is in his nostrils; for wherein is he to be accounted of? [2 Nephi 12:19–22]	22 Cease ye from man, whose breath *is* in his nostrils: for wherein is he to be accounted of? [Isaiah 2:19–22]

The Book of Mormon retains two phrases, "shall come upon them" and "shall smite them," in verses nineteen and twenty-one. The first retention seems insignificant, but the last shows that all attempts to hide will be fruitless. The reversal of majesty and glory seems insignificant. The previous commentary on Isaiah 2:10 is also applicable here, since the phrase "for the fear of the Lord and the glory of his majesty" is used in all three verses. The last verse (v. 22) is Isaiah's way of saying; do not trust in man (the arm of flesh), for man is nothing.

---

[15] *The Voice of Israel's Prophets* [1965], 90–91.

2 Nephi 13:1–3 (Isaiah 3:1–3) • Loss of Prosperity and Leadership

1 For behold, the Lord, the Lord of Hosts, doth take away from Jerusalem, and from Judah, the stay and the staff, the whole staff of bread, and the whole stay of water—

2 The mighty man, and the man of war, the judge, and the prophet, and the prudent, and the ancient;

3 The captain of fifty, and the honorable man, and the counselor, and the cunning artificer, and the eloquent orator.

Judah was prosperous during the time of Northern Israel's downfall (721 B.C.). Isaiah is speaking of what will happen in the future. The taking away of the staff of bread (the staff of life—the KJV says stay of bread), and the stay of water (v. 2) seems to describe her economic prosperity. It may be describing her fall in 589 B.C. (Book of Mormon dating), or it may be speaking of the time period following Christ's ministry among them in the flesh (A.D. 31–33). Perhaps it is a dual prophecy; it certainly fits both time periods.

Judah's blessing among the tribes of Israel was to be the political leader. "The sceptre shall not depart from Judah, nor a lawgiver from between his feet, until Shiloh come; and unto him *shall* the gathering of the people be" (Genesis 49:10). This blessing was also to be lost and was lost in both of the above time periods. The various leadership roles are mentioned in verses two and three. The loss will extend to their spiritual leaders as well, the prophet and the ancient (patriarch) (see 2 Nephi 9:15–16).

2 Nephi 13:4 (Isaiah 3:4) • Children and Babes Rule

4 And I will give children **unto them** to be their princes, and babes shall rule over them.

The bolded "unto them" has been lost from the King James text, the only difference in the two texts. A possible identification of the "children" who were to rule over the house of Judah is drawn from the Prophet Joseph Smith's explanation of John the Baptist's scathing pronouncement to the Pharisees and Sadducees that "God is able of these stones to raise up children unto Abraham" (Matthew 3:9). Joseph Smith identified the "stones" as the Gentiles (see *TPJS*, 319). Perhaps the same designation could be applied here; historically, the Jews have been scattered among the Gentiles, who have ruled over them.

With regard to the "babes" who would rule over them, as stated above, Jacob had blessed Judah with political leadership of all the house of Israel until the birth of Christ (Genesis 49:10, quoted above). This leadership, of course, should have been exercised through the priesthood, as shown by the Prophet Joseph Smith in commenting upon the dominion given to Adam (see *TPJS*, 57). For "babes" (or "children," if the word does not refer to the Gentiles) to rule over Judah, they would rule without the priesthood. The fulfillment of this prophecy can be seen in the following tabulation of the reign of the seven kings who rule from the death of Isaiah to the destruction of Jerusalem by Babylon in 589 B.C. (Book of Mormon dating).

King	Age When Appointed	Years of Reign	Biblical Label of Character
Manasseh	12	55	Evil (2 Kgs. 21:1–2)
Amon	22	2	Evil (2 Kgs. 21:19–20)
Josiah	8	31	Righteous (2 Kgs. 22:1–2)
Jehoahaz	23	3 mos.	Evil (2 Kgs. 23:31–32)
Jehoiakim	25	11 (3 years as puppet king in Babylon)	Evil (2 Kgs. 23:36–37)
Jehoiachin	18 (2 Chr. 36:9 says 8 yrs)	3 mos. (under Babylon)	Evil (2 Kgs. 24:8–9)
Zedekiah	21	11	Evil (2 Kgs. 24:17–19)

Figure 8. Book of Mormon dating

Note that these kings were appointed between the ages of eight and twenty-five, and all but one were labeled "evil" in the Bible. The priesthood was not conferred until age thirty (see Numbers 4:3);

Numbers 8:24 lists the age as twenty-five, but this may have referred to a preparatory five-year period.[16] Numbers 3:1–13 says the priesthood was reserved for the Levites, but Joseph Smith taught that King David held it (*TPJS*, 339).

2 Nephi 13:5–7 (Isaiah 3:5–7) • The People Shall be Oppressed

5 And the people shall be oppressed, every one by another, and every one by his neighbor; the child shall behave himself proudly against the ancient, and the base against the honorable.

6 When a man shall take hold of his brother of the house of his father, and shall say: Thou hast clothing, be thou our ruler, and let **not** this ruin come under thy hand—

7 In that day shall he swear, saying: I will not be a healer; for in my house there is neither bread nor clothing; make me not a ruler of the people. [2 Nephi 13:5–7, bold added]

5 And the people shall be oppressed, every one by another, and every one by his neighbour: the child shall behave himself proudly against the ancient, and the base against the honourable.

6 When a man shall take hold of his brother of the house of his father, *saying*, Thou hast clothing, be thou our ruler, and *let* this ruin *be* under thy hand:

7 In that day shall he swear, saying, I will not be an healer; for in my house *is* neither bread nor clothing: make me not a ruler of the people. [Isaiah 3:5–7]

The only retention of significance in the Book of Mormon is in verse 6, the last phrase of which states "and let **not** this ruin come under thy hand." The KJV has lost the word "not," which points to a desire to escape the coming ruin. This is apparently similar to the situation which came upon the wicked Nephites four years before the Savior visited them. "The people were divided one against another; and they did separate one from another into tribes, every man according to his family and his kindred and friends; and thus they did destroy the government of the land" (3 Nephi 7:2). The separation was not a righteous patriarchal division, but an attempt for survival.

---

[16] Josiah was the good king and worked daily with Jeremiah. He would probably have been given the priesthood when he became of age.

2 Nephi 13:8–9 (Isaiah 3:8–9) • The Show of Their Countenance

> 8 For Jerusalem is ruined, and Judah is fallen, because their tongues and their doings **have been** against the Lord, to provoke the eyes of his glory.
>
> 9 The show of their countenance doth witness against them, and doth declare their sin to be even as Sodom, and they cannot hide it. Wo unto their souls, for they have rewarded evil unto themselves!

The only difference in the Book of Mormon text is the bolded "have been," instead of the italicized *are* in the King James text. Therefore, only the Book of Mormon text is quoted.

The countenances of people reflects what they are. The people of Judah could not hide their immorality, which were even as the sins of Sodom, homosexuality. People also reflect their positive spiritual conditions. Alma described the born-again person as one who has "received [Christ's] image in your countenances" (Alma 5:14).

2 Nephi 13:10–12 • (Isaiah 3:10–12)

> 10 Say unto the righteous that it **is** well with them; for they shall eat the fruit of their doings.
>
> 11 Wo unto the wicked, **for they shall perish**; for the reward of their hands shall be upon them!
>
> 12 **And** my people, children are their oppressors, and women rule over them. O my people, they **who** lead thee cause thee to err and destroy the way of thy paths.

The Book of Mormon retains the phrase "for they shall perish" in place of "it shall be ill with him," much of which was italicized by the King James translators. The sterner punishment is more consistent with other scriptures regarding the Second Coming and the destruction of the wicked. For example, in modern revelation the Lord said: "And every corruptible thing, both of man, or of the beasts of the field, or of the fowls of the heavens, or of the fish of the sea, that dwells upon all the face of the earth, shall be consumed" (D&C 101:24). Other bold words in the Book of Mormon text, in the above quote and in the following ones, are insignificant differences.

Verse twelve refers to women ruling over Judah. Note that nothing derogatory is said about leadership by women per se, but obviously they would not be ruling with the priesthood. During Judah's dispersion among the Gentiles, there were undoubtedly many women who ruled over them, and in modern times Golda Meir has served as Israel's prime minister.

2 Nephi 13:13–15 (Isaiah 3:13–15) • The Lord Standeth to Judge the People

> 13 The Lord standeth up to plead, and standeth to judge the people.
>
> 14 The Lord will enter into judgment with the ancients of his people and the princes thereof; for ye have eaten up the vineyard **and** the spoil of the poor in your houses.
>
> 15 What mean ye? Ye beat my people to pieces, and grind the faces of the poor, saith the Lord God of Hosts.

The conditions of the Jewish people, described in the verses above, will remain, to one degree or another, until the Second Coming of Christ, when he comes to judge them (v. 13). His entering "into judgment with the ancients of his people and the princes thereof" (v. 14), is probably referring to the prophets and patriarchs who will stand as special witnesses, along with the apostles of Jesus' day, of the things they had taught the people. The people are accountable for those teachings. Mormon wrote:

> 18 Yea, behold, I write unto all the ends of the earth; yea, unto you, twelve tribes of Israel, who shall be judged according to your works by the twelve whom Jesus chose to be his disciples in the land of Jerusalem.
>
> 19 And I write also unto the remnant of this people, who shall also be judged by the twelve whom Jesus chose in this land; and they shall be judged by the other twelve whom Jesus chose in the land of Jerusalem. [Mormon 3:18–19]

Jesus told his apostles in Jerusalem that "when the Son of man shall sit in the throne of his glory, ye also shall sit upon twelve thrones, judging the twelve tribes of Israel" (Matthew 19:28; see also D&C 29:12).

2 Nephi 13:16–24 (Isaiah 3:16–24)
• The Daughters of Zion Smitten

16 Moreover, the Lord saith: Because the daughters of Zion are haughty, and walk with stretched-forth necks and wanton eyes, walking and mincing as they go, and making a tinkling with their feet—

17 Therefore the Lord will smite with a scab the crown of the head of the daughters of Zion, and the Lord will discover their secret parts.

18 In that day the Lord will take away the bravery of their tinkling ornaments, and cauls, and round tires like the moon;

19 The chains and the bracelets, and the mufflers;

20 The bonnets, and the ornaments of the legs, and the headbands, and the tablets, and the ear-rings;

21 The rings, and nose jewels;

22 The changeable suits of apparel, and the mantles, and the wimples, and the crisping-pins;

23 The glasses, and the fine linen, and hoods, and the veils.

24 And it shall come to pass, instead of sweet smell there shall be stink; and instead of a girdle, a rent; and instead of well set hair, baldness; and instead of a stomacher, a girding of sackcloth; burning instead of beauty.

Several insignificant words that are italicized in the King James text do not appear in the Book of Mormon text (vv. 18, 23, 24). The words were apparently placed there to make the text read more smoothly in English.

The term "daughter of Zion" probably has more than one meaning, and must be interpreted in context each time it occurs in the scriptures. Nephi's commentary on these Isaiah chapters that he wrote on the plates, seem to identify them as the inhabitants of America (see 2 Nephi 26:19–30), and will be discussed more fully later. The dictionary definitions of "haughty," "wanton," and "mincing," also suggest that Isaiah could easily have been referring to the inhabitants of the Americas, the Zion spoken of by the Old Testament prophets. The haughty are defined as those who are proud of self and scornful of others. Wanton is defined as undisciplined, unmanageable, lewd. Mincing is defined as short, feminine steps, or as plain speech. These definitions could apply to the attitudes and practices of many inhabitants in the Americas.

Many of the words in verses 18 through 23 may refer to religious garb of modern-day sectarians. These verses were designated in the chapter outline as a description of the religious conditions of Zion, and verses 16 and 17 as a description of the social conditions. These conclusions are based on the uses of those words according to modern dictionaries. A caul is a little cap. A chain is anything that binds or restrains. A mantle is a loose cloak without sleeves. A wimple is a cloth for the head arranged in folds about the head, cheek, chin, worn by nuns and formerly by other women.

2 Nephi 13:25–4:1 (Isaiah 3:25– 4:1)
• **Seven Women to One Man**

> 25 Thy men shall fall by the sword and thy mighty in the war.
>
> 26 And her gates shall lament and mourn; and she **shall be** desolate, **and** shall sit upon the ground.
>
> 1 And in that day, seven women shall take hold of one man, saying: We will eat our own bread, and wear our own apparel; only let us be called by thy name to take away our reproach.

The bold words are insignificant differences in the Book of Mormon and the King James texts.

The JST and the Hebrew Bible place this verse in the previous chapter, where it fits the context much better. The surplus number of women will result from the war described in Isaiah 3:25–26. While this verse has been interpreted by some as a prophecy of plural marriage in the Church, a close examination will show that it refers to the world, not the Church. The offer of marriage as described by Isaiah is not in keeping with the law of plural marriage as revealed in the Doctrine and Covenants. The proposal to marry (or merely live together) is made here by the women. Under the Lord's law of plural marriage, the man would initiate the marriage through revelation, after "the first [wife] had given her consent" (D&C 132:58–61).

The women described by Isaiah volunteer to remain economically independent rather than make the man responsible for their care "for they are given unto him to multiply and replenish the earth, according to my commandment" under the Lord's law (D&C 132:63, see also Jacob 2:30). The innate desire of the woman to be a wife and mother is noted in the phrase "to take away our reproach." To be childless was considered a reproach in ancient Israel. When Rachel, wife of Jacob, conceived and gave birth to her first son Joseph she said: "God hath taken away my reproach" (Genesis 30:23). When Elizabeth, the mother of John the Baptist, conceived she said: the Lord has taken "away my reproach" (Luke 1:25).

2 Nephi 14:2–4 (Isaiah 4:2–4) • The Branch of the Lord be Beautiful and Glorious

> 2 In that day shall the branch of the Lord be beautiful and glorious; the fruit of the earth excellent and comely to them that are escaped of Israel.
>
> 3 And it shall come to pass, they that are left in Zion and remain in Jerusalem shall be called holy, every one that is written among the living in Jerusalem—
>
> 4 When the Lord shall have washed away the filth of the daughters of Zion, and shall have purged the blood of Jerusalem from the midst thereof by the spirit of judgment and by the spirit of burning.

Again, in the King James text, there are several insignificant words that do not appear, or words that are italicized.

The beautiful and glorious "branch of the Lord" is the Church of Jesus Christ. It will not become beautiful and glorious until after it is cleansed (v. 4). The Church will be in both Zion and Jerusalem, but will be smaller because of the cleansing (v. 3). The Lord revealed that "upon my house shall [the cleansing] begin, and from my house it go forth" (D&C 112:25). General Moroni also taught "that God had said that the inward vessel shall be cleansed first, and then shall the outer vessel be cleansed also" (Alma 60:23). The spirit of judgment and the spirit of burning may refer to the destruction of the wicked as the time of the Second Coming approaches. Mormon declared: "it is by the wicked that the wicked are punished" (Mormon 4:5). The battle of Armageddon in Jerusalem (see Joel 3; Revelation 16:16), and the polarization of the righteous and the wicked in Zion will bring about the destruction. The latter is described below.

2 Nephi 14:5–6 (Isaiah 4:5–6) • The Glory of Zion—a Defense

5 And the Lord will create upon every dwelling-place of mount Zion, and upon her assemblies, a cloud and smoke by day and the shining of a flaming fire by night; for upon all the glory **of Zion** shall be a defence.

6 And there shall be a tabernacle for a shadow in the daytime from the heat, and for a place of refuge, and a covert from storm and from rain.

The Book of Mormon retains the words "of Zion" (v. 5). This is consistent with the beginning of the verse, and it suggests the protection of Zion and her stakes in a day when the world is in turmoil. For a fuller description of this time see Doctrine and Covenants 45:63–75 and 84:2–5. The latter of these passages identifies the cloud as "the glory of the Lord." The cloud "upon her assemblies" (v. 5) shows there is more than one place for the gathering of the Saints. This is consistent with the Lord's admonition to "stand ye in holy places, and be not moved, until the day of the Lord come; for behold, it cometh quickly"

(D&C 87:8). It is also consistent with the following prophecy given by Joseph Smith:

> The time is soon coming, when no man will have any peace but in Zion and her stakes. I saw men hunting the lives of their own sons, and brother murdering brother, women killing their own daughters, and daughters seeking the lives of their mothers. I saw armies arrayed against armies. I saw blood, desolation, fires. The Son of Man has said that the mother shall be against the daughter, and the daughter against the mother. These things are at our doors. They will follow the Saints of God from city to city. Satan will rage, and the spirit of the devil is now enraged. I know not how soon these things will take place; but with a view of them, shall I cry peace? No; I will lift up my voice and testify of them. How long you will have good crops, and the famine be kept off, I do not know; when the fig tree leaves, know then that the summer is nigh at hand. [*TPJS*, 161]

According to Oliver Cowdery, when the angel Moroni appeared to the Prophet Joseph Smith in September 1823, he quoted Isaiah 4:5–6 as one of the prophecies which was soon to be fulfilled.[17]

Elder Orson Pratt taught that the cloud which Isaiah said would protect Zion and her stakes will be literal and will be even as the cloud which watched over Moses and the children of Israel (see his quotation under "General Authority Quotations") .

The Lord uses the words of these verses from Isaiah in describing the latter-day Church.

> 4 For thus shall my church be called in the last days, even The Church of Jesus Christ of Latter-day Saints.
>
> 5 Verily I say unto you all: Arise and shine forth, that thy light may be a standard for the nations;
>
> 6 And that the gathering together upon the land of *Zion*, and upon her *stakes*, may be for a defense, and for a refuge from the storm, and from wrath when it shall be poured out without mixture upon the

---

[17] *Messenger and Advocate*, April 1835, 110.

whole earth. [D&C 115:4–6; see also 124:36 and 45:63–75 cited above; italics added]

When Jesus visited the Nephites he commanded that the words of Isaiah be searched (3 Nephi 23:1–2). He said:

11 Ye remember that I spake unto you, and said that when the words of Isaiah should be fulfilled—behold they are written, ye have them before you, therefore search them—

12 And verily, verily, I say unto you, that when they shall be fulfilled then is the fulfilling of the covenant which the Father hath made unto his people, O house of Israel.

13 And then shall the remnants, which shall be scattered abroad upon the face of the earth, be gathered in from the east and from the west, and from the south and from the north; and they shall be brought to the knowledge of the Lord their God, who hath redeemed them. [3 Nephi 20:11–13]

There are many other prophecies of Isaiah that are applicable to the covenants of the Lord to Israel, but the chapters written by Nephi that we have just discussed are certainly a part of "the covenants of the Lord which he made to our fathers" (Isaiah 11:5).

SACRED WRITING

Revelation Which is Great:

2 Nephi 12–14 (Isaiah 2–4)	Nephi quotes what Isaiah saw concerning Judah and Jerusalem. Many prophecies are included in his vision.

Doctrines Learned:

2 Nephi 12:3	Out of Zion shall go forth the law and the word of the Lord from Jerusalem.
2 Nephi 12:2	The mountain of the Lord's house (temple) shall be established in the top of the mountains; all nations shall flow unto it.
2 Nephi 14:2	The branch of the Lord (church) shall be beautiful and glorious to those escaped of Israel.

2 Nephi 14:3   The Lord will protect Zion and her stakes with a cloud and smoke by day and a flaming fire by night.

General Authority Quotations:

Elder Boyd K. Packer • The Words of Isaiah

The Book of Mormon is a book of scripture. It is another testament of Jesus Christ. It is written in biblical language, the language of the prophets.

For the most part, it is in easy-flowing New Testament language, with such words as spake for spoke, unto for to, with and it came to pass, with thus and thou and thine.

You will not read many pages into it until you catch the cadence of that language and the narrative will be easy to understand. As a matter of fact, most teenagers readily understand the narrative of the Book of Mormon.

Then, just as you settle in to a move comfortably along, you will meet a barrier. The style of the language changes to Old Testament prophecy style. For, interspersed in the narrative, are chapters reciting the prophecies of the Old Testament prophet Isaiah. They loom as a barrier, like a roadblock or a checkpoint beyond which the casual reader, one with idle curiosity, generally will not go.

You, too, may be tempted to stop there, but do not do it! Do not stop readings! Move forward through those difficult-to-understand chapters of Old Testament prophecy, even if you understand very little of it. Move one, if all you do is skim and merely glean an impression here and there. Move on, if all you do is look at the words.

Soon you will emerge from those difficult chapters to the easier New Testament style which is characteristic of the rest of the Book of Mormon.

Because you are forewarned about that barrier, you will be able to surmount it and finish reading the book.

You will follow the prophecies of the coming of the Messiah through the generations of Nephite people to that day when those prophecies are fulfilled and the Lord appears to them. [CR April, 1986, 74–75]

President Brigham Young • 2 Nephi 12:12

Jesus has been upon the earth a great many more times than you are aware of. When Jesus makes his next appearance upon the earth, but few of this Church and kingdom will be prepared to receive him and see him face to face and converse with him; but he will come to his temple. Will he remain and dwell upon the earth a thousand years, without returning? He will come here, and return to his mansion where he dwells with his Father, and come again to the earth, and return again to his Father, according to my understanding. Then angels will come and begin to resurrect the dead, and the Savior will also raise the dead, and they will receive the keys of the resurrection, and will begin to assist in that work. Will the wicked know of it? They will know just as much about that as they now know about "Mormonism," and no more. [*JD*, 7:142]

Elder Orson Pratt • 2 Nephi 14:4–6

I believe this building is called a Tabernacle, and it will accommodate from twelve thousand to fifteen thousand persons, and it is a tolerably cool place for the people in the heat of summer, especially to be a shade in the day time from the heat, and for a place of refuge and a covert from storms or tempests would affect a congregation that might be assembled in the Lord's Tabernacle; but I wish particularly to call your attention to the preceding verse—"The Lord shall create upon every dwelling-place of Mount Zion, and upon all her assemblies, a cloud and smoke by day, and the shining flame or pillar of fire by night."

I do not see any cloud covering this house, or the congregation that is before me. What is the reason? The time has not yet come. The time is to come when God will meet with all the congregation of his Saints, and to show his approval, and that he does love them, he will work a miracle by covering them in the cloud of his glory. I do not mean something that is invisible, but I mean that same order of things which once existed on the earth so far as the tabernacle of Moses was concerned, which was carried in the midst of the children of Israel as they journeyed in the wilderness.

Did God manifest himself in that tabernacle that was built according to the pattern which he gave unto his servant Moses? He did. In what way? In the day time a cloud filled that tabernacle. The Lord intended his people to be covered with the cloud continually, and he intended to reveal himself unto them, and to show forth his glory more fully amongst them; but they sinned so much in his sight that he declared—"My presence shall not go up with this people, lest I should break forth upon them in my fury and consume them in a moment." Because of their wickedness he withdrew his presence, and his glory in a great measure was taken from them; but still Moses was permitted to enter the tabernacle, and to behold the glory of God, and it is said that he talked with the Lord face to face—a blessings which God did intend to bestow upon all Israel had they kept his law and had not hardened their hearts against him.

But in the latter days there will be a people so pure in Mount Zion, with a house established upon the tops of the mountains, that God will manifest himself, not only in their Temple and upon all their assemblies, with a visible cloud during the day, but when the night shall come, if they shall be assembled for worship, God will meet with them by his pillar of fire; and when they retire to their habitations, behold each habitation will be lighted up by the glory of God—a pillar of flaming fire by night.

Did you ever hear of any city that was thus favored and blessed since the day that Isaiah delivered this prophecy? No, it is a latter-day work, one that God must consummate in the latter time when he begins to reveal himself, and show forth his power among the nations. [*JD*, 16:82]

Elder Orson Pratt • 2 Nephi 12:2–3

In obedience to the command of the Almighty, this people left their native countries and the graves of their ancestors, and came forth by thousands each succeeding year, and peopled this high and elevated region of our country. We came here because modern Prophets opened their mouths by the spirit of revelation and declared these mountains to be the abiding place of the latter-day Zion. We came to fulfill modern prophecies as well as the predictions of ancient Prophets. Have you not read, Latter-day Saints and strangers, in this good old book, a prediction, uttered some twenty-five hundred years ago, by the mouth of Isaiah, concerning the house of the Lord that was to be built in the latter days in the tops of the mountains? I presume that you have read it many a time; indeed I have heard Christian denominations of almost every sect, in their psalms and anthems, refer to this prophecy. They have spoken of the mountain of the house of the Lord, that should be established in the latter days upon the mountains.

It seems, then, that the people who would build this house of God in the latter days in the mountains, are called Zion, and from them should go forth the law. What law? Does this mean the civil law of the country, to govern all people? No. The people of this American republic, by their representatives in Congress, have enacted civil laws and formed a great and free government upon the face of this continent, by which the people in a civil capacity are governed. This, therefore, must have reference to the law of the Gospel, that God would reveal in the latter days unto Zion. From Zion shall go forth the law, says the Prophet, and then, to show more fully the nature of this great latter-day work, he exclaims in the next verse—"And he shall judge the nations, and shall rebuke many people, and they shall beat their swords into plowshares and their spears into pruning hooks; nation shall not lift up sword against nation, neither shall they learn war any more."

It is very evident from this last prediction which I have read, that a very great and important work should be done in the last days upon the mountains. The Lord has to prepare or build a house in the mountains. Will this not be a marvelous work and a wonder for the Lord to have a house in the latter days upon the earth? I think it will, especially when we remember that the earth has been without a house of God for a great many generations. If there had always been a house of God on the earth, the Prophet would never have uttered this prophecy; but for the last 1,600 years we might have gone from east to west, into the islands of the sea, seeking for a house of God, and we could not have found one. What I mean by a house of God, is one which God himself commanded to be built. I know that there are many houses built in all the great cities of this Republic, as well as in Europe, by the different religious sects, many of them superb buildings, and you will find written upon them generally, "The house of the Lord," "The house of God," "The church of Jesus," the house of God called "St. Paul's church," the house of God called "St. Peter's church," or "St. John's church." We can find plenty of them in New York, and in all the great cities and towns of our nation, also in Great Britain, and all the Christian nations of Europe, very grand, superb edifices, which have cost an immense amount of money. Did God command the building of any of these houses? If he did not, then they are not his houses, and they are nicknamed houses of the Lord by the builders or proprietors, while he, really, has nothing to do with them. Did he ever send an angel into any of these houses? No. When did he ever appear in his glory in these houses? Never. Did he ever say to the people, "You have built them according to the pattern which I gave unto you, and I now accept them." No such declaration was ever heard among all these Christian nations. The Lord has had no house on the earth for a great many centuries, and for that very reason the Prophet Isaiah was wrought upon by the Spirit of revelation to declare that such a great event as the Lord having a house on the earth in the latter days should be accomplished, and its location should be in the mountains. From this we may draw the conclusion that it must be in a very elevated region, when compared with the general level or surface of the country whereon it will be built.

There is one thing that will characterize Zion of the latter days: its people will not only be commanded to get up into the high mountain, but they will also be commanded to build unto the Lord a house in the mountains, the pattern of that house being given by inspiration, everything pertaining to it being dictated by the power of prophecy by the servants of the Most High God; and when the house is built, if no unclean thing is suffered to enter therein to defile it, God will come into his tabernacle; but if there be any unclean thing come into that house and defile it, he will not enter, for he dwells not in unholy temples, and he will not accept such a house as an offering at the hands of his Saints. But we read in the latter days God will accept the house that shall be built, and not only the house erected to his name, but also the dwelling-houses of his people, showing that they must be a very pure people, or he would not accept of their private dwellings.

When the Lord shall fulfill the words that the Prophet has spoken, by causing a house to be built to his name in the tops of the mountains, he says, "Many people shall go and say, 'Come ye, let us go up into the mountains of the Lord, to the house of the God of Jacob, that he may teach us of his ways, and we will walk in his paths!" What causes this great excitement among the nations of the earth of that day? They will hear of the glory and power of God, as manifested among his Saints in Zion. The Lord for a score or two of years has been working in order to establish among men, facilities for conveying knowledge to the uttermost corners of the earth. Within the memory of many now living, the discovery of the electric telegraph has been made, by means of which news of the doing of men in any country can be sent round the earth in less than 24 hours, and, if there was no intervention the electric fluid would carry news from any one point to the most distant nations in one second of time, and now, the earth is almost covered with a great network of wire to facilitate expeditious communication among the various nations. What is all this for? Is it simply to satisfy the greed of men in their commercial affairs? No, the Lord had a grander object in view. Men use the telegraph for the purpose I have named, and in many respects it is used to a good advantage, and it has been the means of bringing the nations into much closer relationship than formerly, and of extending among them a knowledge of the arts and sciences; but the great object which the Lord had in view when this great invention or discovery was brought forth, was to enable the knowledge to be sent from the mountain tops from the midst of his people in the latter days. The inquiry, will then be, among the distant nations, "What news from Zion;" "What is the Lord doing among that people?" Do you suppose they will hear with unconcern about a city which, with every dwelling-place it contains, will be lighted up with a supernatural light? No; this is one of the things which will make the people afar off, and their kings, say, "Let us go up to Zion," "let us go up to the mountain of the Lord, to the house of the God of Jacob." What for? "That he may teach us of his ways, and that we may walk in his paths." They will begin to discern the difference then between God's house and houses made by men, between that which God is doing in the earth and that which will be done by the wisdom of men.

Some people have supposed that the manifestation of the glory of God in the latter-days would not take place until Jesus comes in the clouds of heaven; but that is a mistake, it will take place before that time. Before the second advent of the Redeemer, the people of Zion will be acknowledged by God, as the great latter-day Church, that will be prepared for his coming, and they will hold the keys of power to teach mankind in the ways of the Lord. [*JD*, 16:80–81, 83–84]

Challenges to Eternal Life:

1. Make a commitment to prepare yourself to go to the temple or, if already endowed, to attend as regularly as possible and learn of his ways and covenant to live as he requires (2 Nephi 12:2–3).

2. Recognize the law out of Zion as at least partly the U.S. Constitution and support and sustain it in your political activities (2 Nephi 12:3).

3. Rely upon the Lord through looking to the Church and sustaining the officers of the ward and stake where you live as a refuge and defense against the storm and rain of the ways of the world (2 Nephi 14:6).

4. Choose a challenge from this reading and apply it to your life.

Chapter Sixteen

The Coming of Christ

2 Nephi 17:1–19:7

*H*istorical Setting: See Historical Setting Chapter 12. Nephi continues to write the words of Isaiah.

Precepts of this Reading:

6 And my soul delighteth in proving unto my people that save Christ should come all men must perish.

7 For if there be no Christ there be no God; and if there be no God we are not, for there could have been no creation. But there is a God, and he is Christ, and he cometh in the fulness of his own time. [2 Nephi 11:6–7]

Probably the most widely known prophecy of Isaiah is found in chapter 7, but very few people understand its historical setting or anything about the rest of the chapter. From the viewpoint of biblical criticism, this lack of understanding has resulted in several problems associated with the prophecy of a virgin conceiving and giving birth to Immanuel. An outline of the chapters in this reading will help us appreciate this prophecy and prepare us for a deeper study.

OUTLINE • 2 NEPHI 17:1–19:7

➤ 17:1–2   Syria and Ephraim threaten to war against Judah.

    a.   The enemy has not prevailed against Judah (v. 1).

b.   The king and the people are greatly concerned (v. 2).

➤ 17:3–9   The Lord sends Isaiah to Ahaz with a message not to fear.

a.   The threatened conquest will not come to pass (vv. 3–7).

b.   Ephraim shall not be a people within sixty-five years (v. 8).

➤ 17:10–17   The Lord gives Ahaz a sign.

a.   Ahaz rejects the offer of a sign (vv. 10–12).

b.   The Lord gives him a sign anyway (vv. 13–15).

c.   The lands of Ephraim and Syria will both be forsaken of their kings before eight years pass (v. 16).

➤ 17:17–25   The kings of Assyria and Egypt will punish Ahaz and Judah.

a.   A simpler life will replace the agricultural emphasis (vv. 21–23).

b.   The land will become briars and thorns; hunters will roam and animals will graze where there once was cultivated land (vv. 24–25).

➤ 18:1–4   Syria and Ephraim will be conquered by Assyria.

a.   The conquest will be written on a great scroll (v. 1).

b.   There are two witnesses of the written prophecy (v. 2).

c.   Isaiah's son is a sign of the time period (vv. 3–4).

➤ 18:5–8   The people of Judah will also be punished by Assyria.

a.   They refuse Shiloah and yet rejoice in the defeat of Syria and Ephraim (v. 6).

b.   The Lord will bring up Assyria like a mighty river overflowing all the land (vv. 7–8).

➤ 18:9–10   Those countries which have come against Israel shall also be punished.

➤ 18:11–22   Isaiah is commanded not to preach to Israel but to stand as a witness.

a.   Isaiah is to trust in the Lord (v. 13).

b. Both houses of Israel will stumble over Christ (vv. 14–15).

c. Isaiah is to seal up the law among the disciples (v. 16).

d. Isaiah has spoken and will wait upon the Lord (vv. 17–18).

e. The various sources of spiritualism must be measured against the law and the prophets (vv. 19–20).

f. The eventual result will be darkness and anguish (apostasy) (vv. 21–22).

➤ 19:1–7   The darkness will not last forever.

a. A light will come forth in various lands of Israel (vv. 1–2).

b. Joy will come as the yoke of the oppressor is broken (vv. 3–5).

c. The Son of God will come to the throne of David (vv. 6–7).

Notes and Commentary

Introduction: There are four prophecies in 2 Nephi 17 (Isaiah 7). As stated above, the Immanuel prophecy (about Christ's birth) is well known, but little is known about the other three. Each one has been fulfilled and is significant, but perhaps not in the way that some interpret them. First, let us consider the historical setting of the prophecies which will help us understand all four prophecies. The Book of Mormon text will be the only one quoted unless there are significant differences in the King James text. Bold words in the Book of Mormon text note differences, but if the differences are insignificant they will not be commented on.

2 Nephi 17:1–2 (Isaiah 7:1–2) • The Syria-Ephraim War

1 And it came to pass in the days of Ahaz the son of Jotham, the son of Uzziah, king of Judah, that Rezin, king of Syria, and Pekah the son of Remaliah, king of Israel, went up toward Jerusalem to war

against it, but could not prevail against it.

2 And it was told the house of David, saying: Syria is confederate with Ephraim. And his heart was moved, and the heart of his people, as the trees of the wood are moved with the wind.

The kings of Syria and of Northern Israel were invading Jerusalem because Judah would not join them in resisting the aggressions of Assyria (v. 1). Ahaz, king of Judah, sent messengers to the king of Assyria with a present to seek his help (see 2 Kings 16:5–18). Ahaz, along with his people, were afraid of the threatened conquest (v. 2).

2 Nephi 17:3–4 (Isaiah 7:3–4) • Isaiah and His Son to Meet Ahaz

3 Then said the Lord unto Isaiah: Go forth now to meet Ahaz, thou and Shearjashub thy son, at the end of the conduit of the upper pool in the highway of the fuller's field;

4 And say unto him: Take heed, and be quiet; fear not, neither be faint-hearted for the two tails of these smoking firebrands, for the fierce anger of Rezin with Syria, and of the son of Remaliah.

The Lord's commandment for Isaiah to take his son Shearjashub with him to meet Ahaz is apparently purposeful. A marginal note in the KJV shows the meaning of the son's name to be "The remnant shall return." This meaning comes from the prophecy given by the Lord to Isaiah at the time of his call "yet there shall be a tenth, and they shall return" (2 Nephi 16:13). The son's presence may have been to remind Ahaz of the prophecy that Judah would not be utterly destroyed, or it may have been to prepare Ahaz for the prophecy which Isaiah was to deliver.

Their meeting at the "upper pool" may have not been coincidental either. Many biblical scholars have suggested that Ahaz was there to inspect the water supply (just outside the city) and deciding how to protect it from the two invading forces. If this were the case, Ahaz thinking on these matters would also prepare him to receive the prophecy that Isaiah had been sent to deliver.

The designation of the two kings as "the two tails of these smoking firebrands" (v. 4) also carries meaning. A firebrand was a torch. The description of these two kings as tails that are smoking indicates that their strength had been spent, as a torch smokes only when it is burned out.

2 Nephi 17:5–9 (Isaiah 7:5–9) • Ephraim Will Not Be a People

> 5 Because Syria, Ephraim, and the son of Remaliah, have taken evil counsel against thee, saying:
>
> 6 Let us go up against Judah and vex it, and let us make a breach therein for us, and set a king in the midst of it, yea, the son of Tabeal.
>
> 7 Thus saith the Lord God: It shall not stand, neither shall it come to pass.
>
> 8 For the head of Syria is Damascus, and the head of Damascus, Rezin; and within three score and five years shall Ephraim be broken that it be not a people.
>
> 9 And the head of Ephraim is Samaria, and the head of Samaria is Remaliah's son. If ye will not believe surely ye shall not be established.

The evil counsel or conspiracy of the two kings of Syria and Ephraim (Northern Israel) will not come to pass (v. 7). Isaiah then utters the first prophecy. While Syria is to continue as a country with Damascus as its capital and King Rezin as its ruler, Judah's other enemy, Ephraim (the northern ten tribes of Israel), will not even be a people within sixty-five years (v. 8). Naming the two kings as the head may be a declaration of their following their own reasoning, not the Lord's will. Judah is also warned, if they do not believe what Isaiah says, they will be defeated, and "not be established" as a strong nation.

This prophecy of Ephraim not being a people was fulfilled, but exactly when is not certain. Several cities of the Northern Kingdom were captured by Tiglathpilesar shortly following this prophecy, "and carried [the inhabitants] captive to Assyria" (2 Kings 15:29). "In the seventeenth year of Pekah son of Remaliah, Ahaz the son of Jotham king of Judah began to reign" (2 Kings 16:1). Since Pekah's reign over Israel was only twenty years long, Israel's conquest would have occurred shortly after Isaiah's prophecy. Hoshea succeeded Pekah as king of Israel, and in the sixth year of his reign, Shalmaneser, king of Assyria, captured Samaria, the capital of Israel. Three years later he "carried Israel away into Assyria" (2 Kings 17:1–6). This happened following the death of Ahaz, but at least within twelve years after Isaiah gave his prophecy. After "the Lord removed Israel out of his sight, as he had said by all his servants the prophets . . . the king of Assyria [Shalmaneser] brought men from Babylon and [other countries] and placed them in the city of Samaria, and dwelt in the cities thereof" (2 Kings 17:24).

This marks the end of the occupancy of Samaria by the northern tribes of Israel. But did they exist longer as "a people"? Some writers refer to still another conquest by Assyria wherein King Manasseh was captured by the king of Assyria and carried captive into Babylon (see 2 Chronicles 33:11). This last conquest is very close to the precise sixty-five-year prophecy. However, the capture of King Manasseh has to do with Judah, not northern Israel, and consequently does not apply to the prophecy. Other writers acknowledge this and explain that Isaiah was just using a broad number of years to pronounce the end of the northern kingdom of Israel. There is yet another consideration. The ten northern tribes remained in Assyria for an undetermined number of years and then were led farther into the north (see 2 Esdras 13:39–48, an apocryphal writing; and compare D&C 133:26–34). These people have since been known as the lost tribes of Israel and are still not identified. The time of their being led into the north may also figure into the sixty-five-year time period spoken of by Isaiah. While the chronology may be uncertain, there is no uncertainty that the prophecy was fulfilled.

2 Nephi 17:10–12 (Isaiah 7:10–12) • Ask for a Sign of the Lord thy God

10 Moreover, the Lord spake again unto Ahaz, saying:

11 Ask thee a sign of the Lord thy God; ask it either in the depths, or in the heights above.

12 But Ahaz said: I will not ask, neither will I tempt the Lord.

Obviously Ahaz was not a believer, because he "sent messengers to Tiglath-pileser the king of Assyria" for help (2 Kings 16:7). Ahaz's disbelief is indicated when the Lord said to him: "If ye will not believe, surely ye shall not be established" (v. 9). There is further evidence in his reluctance to follow the admonition of the Lord. The Lord challenges him to ask for a sign "either in the depth, or in the height above." The RSV renders this phrase "let it be deep as Sheol or high as heaven." In other words, let it be from the spirit world or from God in heaven. Ahaz gives an interesting rationalization for his refusal, apparently quoting Deuteronomy 6:16, "neither will I tempt the Lord," to justify his actions. The irony of quoting scripture in refusing to follow the prophet of the Lord further exemplifies his disbelief.

2 Nephi 17:13–16 (Isaiah 7:13–16) • A Virgin Shall Bear a Son, Immanuel

13 And he said: Hear ye now, O house of David; is it a small thing for you to weary men, but will ye weary my God also?

14 Therefore, the Lord himself shall give you a sign—Behold, a virgin shall conceive, and shall bear a son, and shall call his name Immanuel.

15 Butter and honey shall he eat, that he may know to refuse the evil and **to** choose the good.

16 For before the child shall know to refuse the evil and choose the good, the land that thou abhorrest shall be forsaken of both her kings.

Bible critics have questioned, explained away, and apologized for the Immanuel prophecy. Many even argue that this is not a messianic prophecy. They claim that it relates to an event at the time of Isaiah: a young woman (these scholars reject the translation "virgin") was to give birth to a child, and while the child was still young the kings of

Syria and Ephraim would be taken away. They suggest further that Matthew was overzealous in using Old Testament prophecies to convince the Jews of the Messiah, and should not have used this passage. Others argue that this is a dual prophecy; there was a young woman in Isaiah's day who was to give birth to a child, but the passage was also applicable to the birth of the Son of God. There are still others who have carefully defended the prophecy as a messianic one.[1]

As Latter-day Saints, we have other sources besides the work of the scholars. Nephi also quoted Isaiah. This parallels Matthew's use of Old Testament prophecies. However, not only is this passage quoted in the Book of Mormon, but we also have the record of Nephi's vision of "a virgin most beautiful and fair" who "was carried away in the Spirit" and who was returned "bearing a child in her arms. And the angel said unto [Nephi]: Behold the Lamb of God, yea, even the Son of the Eternal Father" (1 Nephi 11:13, 19–21). We also have the prophecy of Alma that "he shall be born of Mary, at Jerusalem which is the land of our forefathers, she being a virgin . . . and bring forth a son, even the Son of God" (Alma 7:10). In spite of the advantage of modern revelation, however, we still need to understand and explain the famous Immanuel prophecy of Isaiah.

Only one verse of the prophecy is usually cited—verse 14—and it is usually cited out of context. When this prophecy is quoted in context and in its entirety it is easily interpreted as Messianic. Ahaz had refused to listen to Isaiah, and had refused a sign from the Lord. Therefore, the prophecy uttered by Isaiah was directed, not only to Ahaz, but to all the house of David. It is immaterial if others were present at the time.

Ahaz, as the king of Judah, had rejected the prophecy, and in so doing had "wearied" Isaiah, a man. He also had wearied God (v. 13), who had promised David that "thy kingdom shall be established forever" (2 Samuel 7:16). The King of kings was to come through

---

[1] See, Edward J. Young, *The New International Commentary on the Old Testament. The Book of Isaiah*, Grand Rapids, MI: William B. Erdmans [1965], 277–95.

Judah and David's lineage (see Genesis 49:10), so any appointed king who would believe and live righteously would be supported and sustained by the Lord himself.

The second prophecy uttered by Isaiah in this chapter, then, is both a reminder of this promise to Judah and David and a declaration of how the Lord would bring about its fulfillment in spite of a wicked king or a wicked generation. The Lord would bring this about through the miraculous conception of a God (Immanuel means "God with us") and the birth of that God unto a virgin. The coming of Christ was a well-known prophecy. All of the ancient prophets (in both the Old Testament and the Book of Mormon) knew and foretold of Christ's coming. Jacob, son of Lehi, testified "that none of the prophets have written, nor prophesied, save they have spoken concerning this Christ" (Jacob 7:11). Meeting in Jerusalem with the eleven apostles after his resurrection, Jesus taught them from the scriptures:

> These *are* the words which I spake unto you, while I was yet with you, that all things must be fulfilled, which were written in the law of Moses, and *in* the prophets, and *in* the psalms, concerning me. [Luke 24:44]

The law of Moses, the Prophets, and the Psalms (Writings) were the three divisions of the Hebrew Bible (Old Testament). It is possible that Isaiah was quoting a prophecy that had already been given. The point was, that even though Ahaz rejected the counsel and advice of Jehovah given through his prophet, and even if Ahaz led his people into captivity, the Lord Immanuel would still come as had been prophesied.

Isaiah then gives a further prophecy that may be considered a continuation of the second one. "For behold the child shall know to refuse the evil, and choose the good, the land that thou abhorrest shall be forsaken of both her kings" (v. 16). While this has been the problem verse to many critics in relating the Immanuel prophecy to the life of Christ, the problem is resolved in the context of the historical situation. Isaiah had given a prophecy to all of Judah concerning the house of

David. He now comes back to the situation at hand, the problem of Syria and Ephraim. Most critics have assumed that the child spoken of in verse 16 is the same child spoken of in verses 14 and 15. Could not the child in verse 16 be another child? Why was Isaiah told to take Shearjashub with him? Could the child not be Isaiah's son who was with him? A child is accountable "when eight years old" in the eyes of the Lord (D&C 68:25). In his first eight years he is to learn to distinguish between good and evil. Therefore, Isaiah could have been prophesying that the kings of Syria and Ephraim were both going to be forsaken of their kings in less than eight years. This would be before Shearjashub was eight years old which would make it less than eight years. This prophecy was also fulfilled: Pekah was killed by the conspiracy of Hoshea about three years after Ahaz was appointed king (see 2 Kings 15:30). The king of Assyria "slew Rezin," king of Syria, in response to Ahaz's plea for help as they went up and took Damascus (2 Kings 16:9). Thus within three years both of the kings Ahaz feared were removed, and the third prophecy of Isaiah was fulfilled. The age of Shearjashub is not given but considering that Isaiah's children were given him "for sign and for wonders in Israel from the Lord of Hosts" (Isaiah 8:18). It is feasible that his son's age fits this theory.

2 Nephi 17:17–25 (Isaiah 7:17–25) • The Lord Shall Shave with a Hired Razor

17 The Lord shall bring upon thee, and upon thy people, and upon thy father's house, days that have not come from the day that Ephraim departed from Judah, the king of Assyria.

18 And it shall come to pass in that day that the Lord shall hiss for the fly that is in the uttermost part of Egypt, and for the bee that is in the land of Assyria.

19 And they shall come, and shall rest all of them in the desolate valleys, and in the holes of the rocks, and upon all thorns, and upon all bushes.

20 In the same day shall the Lord shave with a razor that is hired, by them beyond the river, by the king of Assyria, the head, and the hair of the feet; and it shall also consume the beard.

21 And it shall come to pass in that day, a man shall nourish a young cow and two sheep;

22 And it shall come to pass, for the abundance of milk they shall give he shall eat butter; for butter and honey shall every one eat that is left in the land.

23 And it shall come to pass in that day, every place shall be, where there were a thousand vines at a thousand silverlings, **which** shall be for briers and thorns.

24 With arrows and with bows shall men come thither, because all the land shall become briers and thorns.

25 And all hills that shall be digged with the mattock, there shall not come thither the fear of briers and thorns; but it shall be for the sending forth of oxen, and the treading of lesser cattle.

All but verses 19 and 24 have insignificant words added by the King James translators, most of which are italicized.

The prophet Isaiah then uttered a fourth prophecy. King Ahaz wanted to ask the king of Assyria to come and help him, as mentioned earlier. Isaiah prophesied that the Lord was going to bring the king of Assyria upon Ahaz and all of Ephraim (northern Israel). This proved to be the worst devastation they had experienced since the twelve tribes had divided into the two nations of Ephraim and Judah (approximately 975 b.c.) (v. 17). The prophecy stated that the land that had been cultivated for agricultural purposes would be left uncultivated following the Assyrian conquest. The fly and the bee which would come upon Ephraim as a swarm (v. 18) are usually interpreted to be the armies of Egypt and Assyria. However, the invasion by Egypt is historically questionable. The prophecy therefore seems to refer to literal swarms of flies and bees inhabiting the land. The fly was and still is notorious in Egypt. The honeybee was apparently notorious in Assyria. After the land remained uncultivated the Lord would bring the insects from the lands of Egypt and Assyria. These insects would find a permanent home in the desolate valleys of Israel (v. 19). The Lord's "shaving with a razor that is hired" (v. 20) symbolized the comfort of having someone else perform a tedious or unpleasant task, such as shaving every morning. The Lord used the king of Assyria to do the unpleasant task of punishing Ephraim's wickedness. This punishment was be very thorough, as the whole body (land of northern Israel) was shaved. Following the devastating "shaving" of the agricultural land, it was used to graze a few animals (v. 21). The cow will produce milk, which will be used for making butter, and the honey gathered from bees will supplement the diet (v. 22). The main diet for the few nomadic people who remain upon the land will be milk or butter, and honey. Thus the land will become a land of milk and honey. The vineyards will be left uncared for and will quickly turn into briers and thorns. The silver glaze from the sun reflecting on the grape vines will no longer be seen (v. 23). Much of the land will be uninhabited and only the hunters shall go thither (there) seeking wild animals for food (v. 24). Small areas will be digged with the mattock (the hoe) for a few vegetables, but the formerly cultivated land will become primarily a grazing land for a few cattle (v. 25). When Assyria came and conquered northern Israel, she also came upon the regions round about, and thus Judah was also affected by this prophecy. Later prophecies of Isaiah foretell Judah also be conquered during Assyrias conquest of Israel (Isaiah 8:8).

2 Nephi 18–19 • (Isaiah 8–9)

The historical setting for chapter 18 is the same as in chapter 17. Chapter 17 was given to Ahaz and those few who were with him, and chapter 18 appears to say the same thing to a broader audience—all of Judah. It also concerns the fate of the kings of Syria and Israel and the coming onslaught of the king of Assyria upon them and Judah. Thus the Lord has given two witnesses. Chapter 19 continues from the Assyrian conquest prophesied in chapter 18 to the time of Christ's personal ministry.

2 Nephi 18:1–4 (Isaiah 8:1–4) • The Prophetess Conceives a Second Son

> 1 Moreover, **the word of** the Lord said unto me: Take thee a great roll, and write in it with a man's pen, concerning Maher-shalal-hash-baz.

> 2 And I took unto me faithful witnesses to record, Uriah the priest, and Zechariah the son of Jeberechiah.
>
> 3 And I went unto the prophetess; and she conceived and bare a son. Then said the Lord to me: Call his name, Maher-shalal-hash-baz.
>
> 4 For behold, the child shall **not** have knowledge to cry, My father, and my mother, **before** the riches of Damascus and the spoil of Samaria shall be taken away before the king of Assyria.

The differences in the two texts are insignificant. Both say the same thing with different wording. The King James text says "for before the child shall have knowledge" (v. 4).

A foot note in the LDS Bible gives the Hebrew meaning of Maher-shalal-hash-baz as "To speed to the spoil he hasteneth the prey." This name, which Isaiah was to write upon a great roll, was a witness of the speed with which Assyria was to take Syria and Ephraim.

The Lord says that before the infant can cry "mother" or "father," the prophecy will be fulfilled (v. 4). That would be two or three years at the most. Assyria's conquest of Israel took place within three years of the beginning of the reign of Ahaz (see note on Isaiah 7:14), so this prophecy was literally fulfilled. The time period of two or three years confirmed the interpretation of Isaiah 7:16 being Shearjashub. This interpretation would make him less than five years old since both the king of Syria and Ephraim were taken away "before the king of Assyria" in that three year period.

2 Nephi 18:5–8 (Isaiah 8:5–8) • The People of Judah Reject Christ

> 5 The Lord spake also unto me again, saying:
>
> 6 Forasmuch as this people refuseth the waters of Shiloah that go softly, and rejoice in Rezin and Remaliah's son;
>
> 7 Now therefore, behold, the Lord bringeth up upon them the waters of the river, strong and many, even the king of Assyria and all his glory; and he shall come up over all his channels, and go over all his banks.

> 8 And he shall pass through Judah; he shall overflow and go over, he shall reach even to the neck; and the stretching out of his wings shall fill the breadth of thy land, O Immanuel.

Having foretold the future of Israel, the kingdom to the north, the Lord now prophesied Judah's future. Isaiah used the metaphor of a calm pool or spring, the waters of Shiloh, to symbolize Christ (v. 6), and a strong overflowing river symbolized the king of Assyria (v. 7). Since Judah has rejected the still, small voice of the Spirit of Shiloh, the force of Assyria would overflow against them also. In the Assyrian conquest of northern Israel, some of the exterior territories of Judah were also affected. He spoke in the name of Immanuel, the child of the virgin (Isaiah 7:14), designating that he was Jehovah, the God of the Old Testament, who will come to earth and be "God with us."

2 Nephi 18:9–10 • (Isaiah 8:9–10)

> 9 Associate yourselves, O ye people, and ye shall be broken in pieces; and give ear all ye of far countries; gird yourselves, and ye shall be broken in pieces; gird yourselves, and ye shall be broken in pieces.
>
> 10 Take counsel together, and it shall come to naught; speak the word, and it shall not stand; for God is with us.

These two verses are acknowledged to be difficult. They seem to be a declaration against the countries coming upon Judah ("all ye of far countries") that they also will be broken in pieces because God (Immanuel) is with Judah and will eventually deliver her from all her enemies. This seems acceptable, as God holds "the destinies of all the armies of the nations of the earth" (D&C 117:6). The last line of verse 9 is apparently repeated for emphasis.

2 Nephi 18:11–18 (Isaiah 8:11–18) • Seal the Law Among My Disciples

> 11 For the Lord spake thus to me with a strong hand, and instructed me that I should not walk in the way of this people, saying:

12 Say ye not, A confederacy, to all to whom this people shall say, A confederacy; neither fear ye their fear, nor be afraid.

13 Sanctify the Lord of Hosts himself, and let him be your fear, and let him be your dread.

14 And he shall be for a sanctuary; but for a stone of stumbling, and for a rock of offense to both the houses of Israel, for a gin and a snare to the inhabitants of Jerusalem.

15 And many among them shall stumble and fall, and be broken, and be snared, and be taken.

16 Bind up the testimony, seal the law among my disciples.

17 And I will wait upon the Lord, that hideth his face from the house of Jacob, and I will look for him.

18 Behold, I and the children whom the Lord hath given me are for signs and for wonders in Israel from the Lord of Hosts, which dwelleth in Mount Zion.

The King James translators added two insignificant words to the text (vv. 12–14). These are also difficult verses, however, the Book of Mormon helps. Apparently the Lord had forbidden Isaiah to preach unto Israel and Judah (v. 11) as Mormon was forbidden to preach to the Nephites:

16 And I did endeavor to preach unto this people, but my mouth was shut, and I was forbidden that I should preach unto them; for behold they had wilfully rebelled against their God; and the beloved disciples were taken away out of the land, because of their iniquity. [Mormon 1:16]

However, Mormon was to "stand as an idle witness to manifest unto the world the things which [he] saw and heard, according to the manifestations of the Spirit which had testified of things to come" (Mormon 3:16). Isaiah's situation was similar. The Lord had left Israel and Judah without excuse by giving her two or three witnesses. The first was the sign given to Ahaz (Isaiah 7:14). The second sign was the great roll that Isaiah wrote upon. Two faithful witnesses also attested to the writing on the roll, Uriah and Zechariah (vv. 1–2). The third witness was the name of the son of Isaiah, Maher-shalal-hash-baz (destruction is imminent) (v. 3). Isaiah was to sanctify the Lord of Hosts and to fear him (v. 13); the Lord would then be his sanctuary. However, the Lord would be a stumbling block to both the unbelieving houses of Israel (v. 14).

To those disciples who would hearken, Isaiah was to "bind up the testimony" and "seal the law" (v. 16). Prophets both ancient and modern are given power to bind and seal something on earth and have it sealed in heaven. Peter was given "the keys of the kingdom: and whatsoever thou shalt bind on earth shall be bound in heaven: and whatsoever thou shalt loose on earth shall be loosed in heaven" (Matt. 16:19; see also 18:18). Modern-day servants had "power given [to them] to seal both on earth and in heaven" (D&C 1:8; see also 68:12). While the sealing may be a sealing unto heaven or a sealing against heaven, as shown in the various references cited, Isaiah was charged to seal up the disciples to heaven. Isaiah attested that he would follow the Lord's directions, and wait for further instructions (v. 17). He further acknowledged that he and his children (through their names) were witnesses of the Lord to Israel (v. 18).

2 Nephi 18:19–22 (Isaiah 8:19–22)
• To the Law and to the Testimony

> 19 And when they shall say unto you: Seek unto them that have familiar spirits, and unto wizards that peep and mutter—should not a people seek unto their God for the living to hear from the dead?
>
> 20 To the law and to the testimony; **and** if they speak not according to this word, it is because there is no light in them.
>
> 21 And they shall pass through it hardly bestead and hungry; and it shall come to pass that when they shall be hungry, they shall fret themselves, and curse their king and their God, and look upward.
>
> 22 And they shall look unto the earth and behold trouble, and darkness, dimness of anguish, and shall be driven to darkness.

While again there are two insignificant words added by the King James translators (vv. 19, 22), the punctuation difference between the

Book of Mormon and the King James texts (v. 19) needs to be commented upon. As punctuated, the King James text asks two questions at the end of verse 19. The second question is not a complete sentence. It is the same question asked in the Book of Mormon text. The question was an answer given by those who were told not to seek revelation from sources of witchcraft. Their answer was an attempt to justify their actions.

When people request and receive revelation from sources not of God, these sources are to be tested according to the law (of Moses) and the testimony (of the prophets). The Prophet Joseph Smith used the same phrase, "to the law and to the testimony" (v. 20) in reference to testing the principles he was teaching. Joseph said, "these principles are poured out all over the scriptures" (*TPJS*, 373–374).

Isaiah saw into the future of both houses of Israel. He saw that both houses would fall into captivity and darkness (apostasy) (vv. 21–22). The following verses are the basis of this interpretation.

2 Nephi 19:1–2 (Isaiah 9:1–2) • A Great Light in Galilee

1 Nevertheless, the dimness shall not be such as was in her vexation, when at first he lightly afflicted the land of Zebulun, and the land of Naphtali, and afterwards did more grievously afflict by the way of the **Red Sea** beyond Jordan in Galilee of the nations.

2 The people that walked in darkness have seen a great light; they that dwell in the land of the shadow of death, upon them hath the light shined.

The Gospel of Matthew quotes these verses as an introduction to the great Galilean period of the Savior's ministry. This period was the first and possibly the most successful of the various parts of the Savior's ministry (as usually designated in New Testament studies). When the land of Canaan was divided among the twelve tribes of Israel, the tribes of Zebulun and Naphtali lay to the west of the Sea of Galilee and formed the northern border of Israel next to the gentile nations of Galilee. The phrase "way of the sea" has puzzled many scholars, but the Book of Mormon has retained the identity of this body of water as the Red Sea. The king of Assyria took "all the land of Naphtali and carried them captive into Assyria" during Isaiah's lifetime (2 Kings 15:29). The phrase "afterwards did more grievously afflict by the way of the Red Sea beyond Jordan in Galilee of the nations," probably has reference to a later invasion by Assyria. Matthew noted that although Israel had lost blessings due to wickedness and subsequent subjection to Assyria, the blessings would come again through the "light" of Christ as he ministered unto Judah in Galilee.

2 Nephi 19:3–5 (Isaiah 9:3–5) • Increase the Joy, Break the Yoke of Captivity

> 3 Thou hast multiplied the nation, and increased the joy—they joy before thee according to the joy in harvest, and as men rejoice when they divide the spoil.
>
> 4 For thou hast broken the yoke of his burden, and the staff of his shoulder, the rod of his oppressor.
>
> 5 For every battle of the warrior is with confused noise, and garments rolled in blood; but this shall be with burning and fuel of fire.

These verses precede the foretelling of the birth of Christ, but announce the effect of his mission. He will bring them the joy of the gospel, break the darkness of their apostasy, and deliver them from their captivity to sin.

The King James text has added the word "not" preceding "increased the joy" (v. 3). Other versions (RSV; NIV) are translated the same as the Book of Mormon. However, the New Catholic Edition is the same as the KJV. The Hebrew text is not clear, but the Book of Mormon text and the other similar versions fit the context of the other verses. The Book of Mormon does not have the phrase "as in the day of Midian" at the end of verse four. This could have been an intentional omission by Nephi because this phrase did not apply to his people.

2 Nephi 19:6–7 (Isaiah 9:6–7) • Unto Us a Child is Born

> 6 For unto us a child is born, unto us a son is given; and the government shall be upon his shoulder; and his name shall be called, Wonderful, Counselor, The Mighty God, The Everlasting Father, The Prince of Peace.
>
> 7 Of the increase of government and peace there is no end, upon the throne of David, and upon his kingdom to order it, and to establish it with judgment and with justice from henceforth, even forever. The zeal of the Lord of Hosts will perform this.

The angel who appeared to Mary identified the Son who was to be born to her:

> 31 And, behold, thou shalt conceive in thy womb, and bring forth a son, and shalt call his name JESUS.
>
> 32 He shall be great, and shall be called the Son of the Highest: and the Lord God shall give unto him the throne of his father David. [Luke 1:32]

The angel who spoke to the shepherds on the night of Christ's birth paraphrased Isaiah:

> 10 And the angel said unto them, Fear not: for, behold, I bring you good tidings of great joy, which shall be to all people.
>
> 11 For unto you is born this day in the city of David a Saviour, which is Christ the Lord. [Luke 2:10–11]

The only difference in the Book of Mormon and the King James texts is the capitalization of the words "Mighty and Everlasting." Since the capitalization further designate the greatness and the Fatherhood of Christ, it is significant.

Just as Nephi delighted "in proving unto my people the truth of the coming of Christ" (2 Nephi 11:4), the Church periodically proclaims to the world the fulfillment of these prophetic words of Isaiah. For example, as part of one of their Christmas messages the First

Presidency wrote: "we do know, that our Redeemer lives, and that the prophetic utterance of Isaiah is fulfilled," and then they quoted part of Isaiah 9:1–7.[2] We also echo another of Nephi's declarations; "save Christ should come all men must perish" (2 Nephi 11:6). As the Second Coming of Christ looms on the horizon, the words of Isaiah and Christ will be further fulfilled.

SACRED WRITING

Revelation Which is Great:

2 Nephi 17:1–19:7	Nephi quotes Isaiah concerning Israel and Christ.

Prophesying:

2 Nephi 17:4–9	Isaiah prophesies that Ephraim will no longer be a people.
2 Nephi 17:10–14	Isaiah prophesies of a virgin bearing a son, Immanuel.
2 Nephi 17:15	Isaiah prophesies the death of the two kings of Syria and Ephraim.
2 Nephi 17:16–25	Isaiah prophesies of the land of Israel being shaved with a razor that is hired.
2 Nephi 18:3–4	Before Isaiah's second son can cry mother and father, the king of Assyria shall take Syria and Ephraim.

Doctrines Learned:

2 Nephi 17:14	Christ was to be born of a virgin.
2 Nephi 18:18	Isaiah's children were for signs and wonders in Israel.
2 Nephi 18:21–19:2	Great darkness (apostasy) came upon both houses of Israel until a light (Christ) came.
2 Nephi 19:7	Christ was to be the final king of David forever.

---

[2] *Messages of the First Presidency*, comp. James R. Clark [1970], 4:171–72.

General Authority Quotations

Elder Mark E. Petersen • 2 Nephi 7:14

And did it not come to pass just as the prophet said?

Was not the virgin birth heralded among the shepherds who watched their flocks that night and by the angelic hosts who sang their hosannahs? Did not even the wise men, far away in the East, recognize it? And was not Herod so frightened by it that he killed the little children in an effort to destroy the newborn king?

The scripture was so detailed in describing the coming of the Lord that it predicted the flight into Egypt to escape Herod's wrath, as it also foretold the King's destruction of the little babes in Bethlehem. [CR, Oct.,1965, 60]

President Howard W. Hunter • 2 Nephi 19:6–7

I bear solemn and grateful witness that Jesus is the Christ, the Savior of the world. Certainly he is the center of our worship and the key to our happiness. Let us follow the Son of God in all ways and in all walks of life. Let us make him our exemplar and our guide.

We are at a time in the history of the world and the growth of the Church when we must think more of holy things and act more like the Savior would expect his disciples to act. We should at every opportunity ask ourselves, "What would Jesus do?" and then act more courageously upon the answer. We must be about his work as he was about his Father's. We should make every effort to become like Christ, the one perfect and sinless example the world has ever seen. [CR, Oct., 1994, 118]

Only Christ can be our ideal, our "bright and morning star" (Revelation 22:16). Only he can say without *any* reservation: "Follow me; learn of me; do the things you have seen me do. Drink of my water and eat of my bread. I am the way, the truth, and the life. I am the law and the light. Look unto me and ye shall live. Love one another as I have loved you" (see Matthew 11:29; 16:24; John 4:13–14; 6:35, 51; 7:37; 13:34; 14:6; 3 Nephi 15:9; 27:21). [CR, April, 1994, 83]

Challenges to Eternal Life:

1. Place your life in the hands of Christ and follow him that you do not perish (2 Nephi 11:6).

2. Review the signs of the Second Coming (JS—Matthew 1:22–33) and make a resolution to watch for them as his Second Coming approaches (2 Nephi 18:18).

3. Go to the law and to the testimony (the scriptures) and if what you read and hear is not according to the standard works know there is no light in it (2 Nephi 18:20).

4. Choose a challenge of your own from this reading and apply it to your life.

Chapter Seventeen

The Message to Judah

2 Nephi 25:9–20; 15; 30:7

*H*istorical Setting: After Nephi speaks of the difficulty of under-standing Isaiah's word's, he says; "I proceed with mine own prophecy, according to my plainness" (2 Nephi 25:7). The first part of this reading (2 Nephi 25:9–20) includes Nephi's prophecies or commentary on the future of Judah. His prophecies are based on the writings of Isaiah. The second part (2 Nephi 15; Isaiah 5) is a song or parable addressed to "the inhabitants of Jerusalem, and the men of Judah" (2 Nephi 15:3). The last part (2 Nephi 30:7) is a summary of the Book of Mormon message to Judah.

Precepts of this Reading:

> As the Lord God liveth, there is no other name given under heaven save it be this Jesus Christ, of which I have spoken, whereby man can be saved. [2 Nephi 25:20]

These chapters in the Book of Mormon speak of three different time periods of the nation and people of Judah. These periods are the time of their destruction and captivity by Babylon (around 600 B.C.), the meridian of time (when Christ came among them), and the last days. The first two are now history. The third is now beginning. Our discussion will follow the sequence of the text mentioned above, so there will be an overlapping of the three time periods. An outline of these three parts in preparation for a deeper study follows.

OUTLINE • 2 NEPHI 25:9–20; 15; 30:7

➤ 25:9–20   Nephi prophesies concerning the Jews.

     a.   The Jews were destroyed because of iniquity (v. 9).

        1.   They have been destroyed in previous generations because of iniquity.

        2.   None have been destroyed save it was foretold by the prophets.

     b.   The Jews were destroyed after Lehi left except those carried captive to Babylon (v. 10).

     c.   They shall return again to the land of Jerusalem (vv. 11–13).

        1.   They will have wars and rumors of wars.

        2.   The Only Begotten of the Father shall manifest himself in the flesh and they will reject him.

        3.   They will crucify him and after his is laid in a sepulchre three days he will rise with healing in his wings to save those who believe in the kingdom of God.

     d.   After the Messiah has risen, Jerusalem shall be destroyed again and the Jews shall be scattered among all nations (vv. 14–15).

     e.   After the Jews have been scattered and scourged for many generations they shall believe in Christ and look not for another Messiah (v. 16).

     f.   The Lord will set his hand the second time to recover his people (vv. 17–19).

        1.   He will proceed to do a marvelous work and a wonder.

        2.   He will bring forth his words which will judge them and convince them of the true Messiah.

        3.   There is only one Messiah, he who was rejected by the Jews.

4. The Messiah cometh in six hundred years after Lehi left Jerusalem.

5. His name shall be Jesus Christ, the Son of God.

g. Nephi has spoken plainly that you cannot err (v. 20).

1. These things will happen as surely as Moses brought Israel out of Egypt.

2. There is none other name save Jesus Christ whereby man can be saved.

➤ 15:1–7   The parable and interpretation are given.

a. The parable likens Israel to a vineyard (vv. 1–6).

b. The interpretation is explained (v. 7).

➤ 15:8–23   Six warnings are given.

a. A warning is given against socialism (vv. 8–10).

b. A warning is given against alcoholism (vv. 11–17).

c. Israel is warned against gross dishonesty and a distorted value system (vv. 18–19).

d. She is warned against a perverted moral code (v. 20).

e. There is a warning against pseudo-intellectualism (v. 21).

f. A warning is given against false and misleading advertising (vv. 22–23).

➤ 15:24–25   The Lord's hand is stretched out in judgment upon his people.

➤ 15:26–30   The ensign (Book of Mormon) is lifted to the nations.

a. The messengers will come with speed (vv. 26–28).

b. The prey will be carried away safely (v. 29).

c. Darkness will remain upon the land deserted by the righteous of Israel (v. 30).

➤ 30:7   Nephi speaks to his brethren concerning the Jews which are scattered. They shall begin to believe in Jesus Christ and shall begin to gather in upon all the face of the land, and become a delightsome people.

NOTES AND COMMENTARY

Introduction: On August 6, 1833, the Lord revealed to Joseph Smith that the Saints were to "renounce war and proclaim peace" and to "turn the hearts of the Jews unto the prophets, and the prophets unto the Jews" (D&C 98:16–17). When the time comes to teach the gospel to the Jews,[1] the prophecies of Isaiah and other Old Testament prophets, along with the Book of Mormon should be the approach used to "turn the hearts of the Jews unto the prophets." As these prophets are likened "unto the Jews," the Spirit will testify of their truth. The materials that follow should prepare us for that day.

2 Nephi 25:9–11 • Destruction Foretold by the Prophets

> 9 And as one generation hath been destroyed among the Jews because of iniquity, even so have they been destroyed from generation to generation according to their iniquities; and never hath any of them been destroyed save it were foretold them by the prophets of the Lord.
>
> 10 Wherefore, it hath been told them concerning the destruction which should come upon them, immediately after my father left Jerusalem; nevertheless, they hardened their hearts; and according to my prophecy they have been destroyed, save it be those which are carried away captive into Babylon.
>
> 11 And now this I speak because of the spirit which is in me. And notwithstanding they have been carried away they shall return again, and possess the land of Jerusalem; wherefore, they shall be restored again to the land of their inheritance.

Nephi begins his prophecies against Judah with an eternal principle, the Lord always warns a people by the prophets before they are destroyed. Nephi, in abridging his father's record, stated:

---

[1] At the time of this writing, the Church is not proselyting among the Jews. However, there are many prophecies in addition to those discussed in this chapter that foretell their being taught i.e. Isaiah chapters 18; 26; 52, and the Savior's commentary on Isaiah 52 (3 Nephi 20:29–42).

4 For it came to pass in the commencement of the first year of the reign of Zedekiah, king of Judah, (my father, Lehi, having dwelt at Jerusalem in all his days); and in that same year there came many prophets, prophesying unto the people that they must repent, or the great city Jerusalem must be destroyed. [1 Nephi 1:4]

The biblical record confirms Nephi's statement.

14 Moreover all the chief of the priests, and the people, transgressed very much after all the abominations of the heathen; and polluted the house of the LORD which he had hallowed in Jerusalem.

15 And the LORD God of their fathers sent to them by his messengers, rising up betimes, and sending; because he had compassion on his people, and on his dwelling place:

16 But they mocked the messengers of God, and despised his words, and misused his prophets, until the wrath of the LORD arose against his people, till *there was* no remedy. [2 Chronicles 36:14–16]

Jeremiah, Habakkuk, Zephaniah, and Lehi were some of the prophets who warned Judah before they were destroyed. There were others, but we do not have their records (see 1 Nephi 19:10).

Nephi left Jerusalem with his father Lehi about 600 B.C. The Babylonians came in 607 B.C. (traditional dating) and took many of the Jewish people into captivity. In 588–586 B.C. the Babylonians came into the land of Judah and destroyed them as a nation. Many who were not destroyed then went into Egypt (see Jeremiah 43). Jeremiah prophesied the length of time they would remain in Babylon:

11 And this whole land shall be a desolation, *and* an astonishment; and these nations shall serve the king of Babylon seventy years. [Jeremiah 25:11]

After seventy years (538 B.C.), as Jeremiah had prophesied, Cyrus, king of Persia, issued a decree that the Jews could return to their promised land (v. 11).

1 Now in the first year of Cyrus king of Persia, that the word of the LORD by the mouth of Jeremiah might be fulfilled, the LORD stirred up the spirit of Cyrus king of Persia, that he made a proclama-

tion throughout all his kingdom, and *put it* also in writing, saying,

2 Thus saith Cyrus king of Persia, The LORD God of heaven hath given me all the kingdoms of the earth; and he hath charged me to build him an house at Jerusalem, which *is* in Judah.

3 Who *is there* among you of all his people? his God be with him, and let him go up to Jerusalem, which *is* in Judah, and build the house of the LORD God of Israel, (he *is* the God,) which *is* in Jerusalem.

4 And whosoever remaineth in any place where he sojourneth, let the men of his place help him with silver, and with gold, and with goods, and with beasts, beside the freewill offering for the house of God that *is* in Jerusalem. [Ezra 1:1–4]

2 Nephi 25:12–13 • The Only Begotten Manifest in the Flesh

12 But, behold, they shall have wars, and rumors of wars; and when the day cometh that the Only Begotten of the Father, yea, even the Father of heaven and of earth, shall manifest himself unto them in the flesh, behold, they will reject him, because of their iniquities, and the hardness of their hearts, and the stiffness of their necks.

13 Behold, they will crucify him; and after he is laid in a sepulchre for the space of three days he shall rise from the dead, with healing in his wings; and all those who shall believe on his name shall be saved in the kingdom of God. Wherefore, my soul delighteth to prophesy concerning him, for I have seen his day, and my heart doth magnify his holy name.

After their return from Babylon they experienced wars and rumors of wars until the time of Christ, the Only Begotten of the Father, was born among them. Nephi acknowledged that Christ was the Father (Creator) of heaven and earth and foretold that the Jews would reject him (v. 12). He prophesied of his being crucified and being resurrected after being in the sepulchre for three days (v. 13). It is significant for New Testament study to note that it was three days and not part of three days.

Nephi's prophecy that Christ will rise "with healing in his wings" is recorded in Malachi in the Old Testament. However, Malachi had not been born so it is evident that another prophet had prophesied of this earlier. Nephi's testimony that he had seen Christ's day probably refers to his vision of Jerusalem as recorded in 1 Nephi 11.

2 Nephi 25:14–20 • There is Only One Messiah

14 And behold it shall come to pass that after the Messiah hath risen from the dead, and hath manifested himself unto his people, unto as many as will believe on his name, behold, Jerusalem shall be destroyed again; for wo unto them that fight against God and the people of his church.

15 Wherefore, the Jews shall be scattered among all nations; yea, and also Babylon shall be destroyed; wherefore, the Jews shall be scattered by other nations.

16 And after they have been scattered, and the Lord God hath scourged them by other nations for the space of many generations, yea, even down from generation to generation until they shall be persuaded to believe in Christ, the Son of God, and the atonement, which is infinite for all mankind—and when that day shall come that they shall believe in Christ, and worship the Father in his name, with pure hearts and clean hands, and look not forward any more for another Messiah, then, at that time, the day will come that it must needs be expedient that they should believe these things.

17 And the Lord will set his hand again the second time to restore his people from their lost and fallen state. Wherefore, he will proceed to do a marvelous work and a wonder among the children of men.

18 Wherefore, he shall bring forth his words unto them, which words shall judge them at the last day, for they shall be given them for the purpose of convincing them of the true Messiah, who was rejected by them; and unto the convincing of them that they need not look forward any more for a Messiah to come, for there should not any come, save it should be a false Messiah which should deceive the people; for there is save one Messiah spoken of by the prophets, and that Messiah is he who should be rejected of the Jews.

19 For according to the words of the prophets, the Messiah cometh in six hundred years from the time that my father left Jerusalem; and according to the words of the prophets, and also the word of the angel of God, his name shall be Jesus Christ, the Son of God.

20 And now, my brethren, I have spoken plainly that ye cannot err. And as the Lord God liveth that brought Israel up out of the land of Egypt, and gave unto Moses power that he should heal the nations after they had been bitten by the poisonous serpents, if they would cast their eyes unto the serpent which he did raise up before them, and also gave him power that he should smite the rock and the water should come forth; yea, behold I say unto you, that as these things are true, and as the Lord God liveth, there is none other name given under heaven save it be this Jesus Christ, of which I have spoken, whereby man can be saved.

The Romans destroyed the Jews as a nation in A.D. 70 (v. 14). Those who survived were scattered among all the nations (v. 15). This scattering is known today as the diaspora. The scourging of the Jews for many generations (v. 16) was prophesied earlier by Zenos (see 1 Nephi 19:13). This persecution of the Jews is known today as anti-semitism. The Lord setting his hand the second time to restore his people (v. 17) is a quotation from Isaiah 11:11 (2 Nephi 21:11). Nephi's words that follow are his commentary on that verse.

Since Isaiah spoke concerning all the house of Israel, as stated earlier (2 Nephi 6:5), this prophecy should not be limited to the Jews. Moroni quoted the entire chapter to Joseph Smith in September 1823 and said it would soon to be fulfilled (JS—History 1:40). The marvelous work and a wonder foretold by Nephi (v. 17) is the bringing forth of the Book of Mormon (see 2 Nephi 29:1–2). His words that shall judge them also refer to the Book of Mormon (compare D&C 5:5–10). The rest of the eighteenth verse gives the message of the Book of Mormon to the Jewish people to convince them. This message is that there is only one Messiah, the one who was crucified among them, the one spoken of by the prophets. Nephi concludes his prophecy by stating the time period of the Messiah's birth, 600 years from the time Lehi left Jerusalem and by giving the name of the Messiah—Jesus Christ (v. 19).

Christ's name was known by the prophets although it is currently not in the Old Testament. The angel who spoke his name is probably the one who appeared to Jacob (see 2 Nephi 10:3). Nephi emphasized that he had spoken plainly that his words could not err, and as the Lord liveth that did great miracles in Egypt, he will do such things in the future. Once more he declares that there is no other name given under heaven whereby man can be saved (v. 20). Peter made this same declaration: "Neither is there salvation in any other: for there is none other name under heaven given among men, whereby we must be saved" (Acts 4:12). This message is repeated throughout the Book of Mormon (see 2 Nephi 31:21; Mosiah 3:17; 5:8). Perhaps Peter and Nephi are quoting from a common source, an Old Testament prophecy that was also upon the plates of brass.

2 Nephi 15 • (Isaiah 5)

This chapter is one of the few parables in the Old Testament, and uses imagery similar to that which Jesus used in several parables during his ministry among the Jews. The interpretation of the parable, also given by Isaiah, definitely identifies the vineyard as the house of Israel and the pleasant plant as the men of Judah. Such parables as the laborers in the vineyard (Matthew 20:1–16), the two sons (Matthew 21:28–32), the wicked husbandman (Matthew 21:33–44; Mark 12:1–11; Luke 20:9–18), the barren fig tree (Luke 13:6–9), and the true vine (John 15:1–8) all use the same imagery.

There is also a resemblance to the allegory of Zenos, which is recorded in the Book of Mormon (Jacob 5) and was once in the Old Testament record. Jacob recorded it from the plates of brass (see Jacob 5:1). Paul seemed to be quoting from it when he wrote to the church in Rome (see Romans 11:17–24). Both concern the whole house of Israel.

The Book of Mormon has retained several aspects of the Isaiah 5 text, only a few of which are significant.

2 Nephi 15:1–2 (Isaiah 5:1–2) • The Choicest Vine of the Vineyard

> 1 And then will I sing to my well-beloved a song of my beloved, touching his vineyard. My well-beloved hath a vineyard in a very fruitful hill.
>
> 2 And he fenced it, and gathered out the stones thereof, and planted it with the choicest vine, and built a tower in the midst of it, and also made a wine-press therein; and he looked that it should bring forth grapes, and it brought forth wild grapes.

The Book of Mormon introduces the parable with the words "and then" in place of the KJV "now." This modification identifies the time period of chapter 5 as the same period spoken of in chapters 2 and 4, the last days. However, the parable is a general description of the house of Israel and the house of Judah, the causes of their captivity, and why the Lord is angry with them. What the Lord will do to correct their situation will happen in the last days.

The tower built in the midst of the vineyard could have been the temple built by Solomon. This inference is drawn from the latter-day parable concerning another tower (temple) that is to be built upon a "very choice piece of land" (Jackson County, Missouri), but has not yet been built (see D&C 101:43–62).

2 Nephi 15:3–7 (Isaiah 5:3–7) • The Vineyard Will be Laid Waste

> 3 And now, O inhabitants of Jerusalem, and men of Judah, judge, I pray you, betwixt me and my vineyard.
>
> 4 What could have been done more to my vineyard that I have not done in it? Wherefore, when I looked that it should bring forth grapes it brought forth wild grapes.
>
> 5 And now go to; I will tell you what I will do to my vineyard—I will take away the hedge thereof, and it shall be eaten up; and **I will** break down the wall thereof, and it shall be trodden down;
>
> 6 And I will lay it waste; it shall not be pruned nor digged; but

there shall come up briers and thorns; I will also command the clouds
that they rain no rain upon it.

7 For the vineyard of the Lord of Hosts is the house of Israel, and
the men of Judah his pleasant plant; and he looked for judgment, and
behold, oppression; for righteousness, but behold, a cry.

The declaration "what could have been done more to my vineyard"
is the same phrase used by the master of the vineyard in the allegory
of Zenos (see Jacob 5:47). Although Zenos refers to the whole vineyard, and not just the "pleasant plant" of Judah as designated by Isaiah,
both conditions show that the Lord gives full opportunity within the
framework of man's agency wherein man must choose and do his part.

What the Lord will do to his vineyard is repeated in 2 Nephi
17:17–25 (Isaiah 7:17–25), and was discussed in the previous chapter.
Assyria is the Lord's hired razor (2 Nephi 17:20) to do his damaging
work (v. 5), except for the Lord withholding the rain (v. 6). His doing
so is another evidence of the Lord using the weather to accomplish
his purposes. Amos quotes the Lord saying: "And I also have with-
holden the rain from you, when there were yet three months to the
harvest" (Amos 4:7 see also Amos 4:6–10; Helaman 12:7–17; D&C
43:25). Following Assyria's conquest, the land will become briars and
thorns as foretold in both chapters (2 Nephi 5:6; 17:23).

2 Nephi 15:8–10 (Isaiah 5:8–10)
• A Warning against Socialism

8 Wo unto them that join house to house, till there **can** be no place,
that they may be placed alone in the midst of the earth!

9 In mine ears, said the Lord of Hosts, of a truth many houses shall
be desolate, and great and fair cities without inhabitant.

10 Yea, ten acres of vineyard shall yield one bath, and the seed
of a homer shall yield an ephah.

This is the first of six warnings that apparently caused the downfall
of northern Israel, and were given as a caution to Judah. Identifying
this warning as socialism needs some explanation. Most commentators

identify these verses as a warning against the land grabbers of Isaiah's day. However, joining house to house results in "there **can** be no place" to be alone in the midst of the earth (v. 8). For some unknown reason the Book of Mormon leaves out the King James phrase "that lay field to field." One of the basic principles of government is to provide "the right and control of property" (D&C 134:2), which is essential for the establishment of the law of consecration, one of the ultimate goals of the Church. This law requires the individual initiative and private ownership of property (see D&C 42:30–32; 51:1–5; 78:14). It appears that Israel had been forfeiting her individual freedoms to a central government that was controlling the property. Judah was warned against doing the same thing. The result was Israel being scattered instead of being gathered (see Helaman 7:17–19). Thus, many great and fair cities were left desolate without inhabitants (v. 9). The agricultural production almost ceased. Ten acres of vineyard would produce only one bath (eight and one-fourth gallons), or an ephah (the dry-measure equivalent of a bath). The land of America was preserved for the establishment of a free people:

> 4 For it is wisdom in the Father that they should be established in this land, and be set up as a free people by the power of the Father, that these things might come forth from them unto a remnant of your seed, that the covenant of the Father may be fulfilled which he hath covenanted with his people, O house of Israel. [3 Nephi 21:4]

The covenant made with Jacob, the father of the twelve tribes of Israel, was:

> 22 And behold, this people will I establish in this land, unto the fulfilling of the covenant which I made with your father Jacob; and it shall be a New Jerusalem. And the powers of heaven shall be in the midst of this people; yea, even I will be in the midst of you. [3 Nephi 20:22]

The New Jerusalem cannot be established in a socialistic society where individual initiative and private ownership required for the law of consecration is denied.

2 Nephi 15:11–21 (Isaiah 5:11–21)
• Four Other Warnings

11 Wo unto them that rise up early in the morning, that they may follow strong drink, that continue until night, and wine inflame them!

12 And the harp, and the viol, the tabret, and pipe, and wine are in their feasts; but they regard not the work of the Lord, neither consider the operation of his hands.

13 Therefore, my people are gone into captivity, because they have no knowledge; and their honorable men are famished, and their multitude dried up with thirst.

14 Therefore, hell hath enlarged herself, and opened her mouth without measure; and their glory, and their multitude, and their pomp, and he that rejoiceth, shall descend into it.

15 And the mean man shall be brought down, and the mighty man shall be humbled, and the eyes of the lofty shall be humbled.

16 But the Lord of Hosts shall be exalted in judgment, and God that is holy shall be sanctified in righteousness.

17 Then shall the lambs feed after their manner, and the waste places of the fat ones shall strangers eat.

18 Wo unto them that draw iniquity with cords of vanity, and sin as it were with a cart rope;

19 That say: Let him make speed, hasten his work, that we may see it; and let the counsel of the Holy One of Israel draw nigh and come, that we may know it.

20 Wo unto them that call evil good, and good evil, that put darkness for light, and light for darkness, that put bitter for sweet, and sweet for bitter!

21 Wo unto the wise in their own eyes and prudent in their own sight!

The differences in the Book of Mormon and King James texts are insignificant. These four warnings seem self-explanatory, therefore we will give only a general statement about each. The first is alcoholism (vv. 11–17). The alcoholic is identified as one who begins drinking in the morning, and this drinking is usually associated with music that does not invite the Spirit of the Lord. It affects all walks of life.

The second warning represents gross dishonesty and a distorted value system, whose advocates justify their actions by questioning the validity of God's commandments (vv. 18–19).

The third warning is against the so called "new morality" of our day where chastity and fidelity are labeled as outdated. It extends beyond the moral values of sex (v. 20).

The fourth warning is against pseudo-intellectualism, the reliance upon one's own wisdom rather than the revelations of the Lord (v. 21).

2 Nephi 15:22–25 (Isaiah 5:22–25)
• A Sixth Warning and Conclusion

> 22 Wo unto the mighty to drink wine, and men of strength to mingle strong drink;

> 23 Who justify the wicked for reward, and take away the righteousness of the righteous from him!

> 24 Therefore, as the fire devoureth the stubble, and the flame consumeth the chaff, their root shall be rottenness, and their blossoms shall go up as dust; because they have cast away the law of the Lord of Hosts, and despised the word of the Holy One of Israel.

> 25 Therefore, is the anger of the Lord kindled against his people, and he hath stretched forth his hand against them, and hath smitten them; and the hills did tremble, and their carcasses were torn in the midst of the streets. For all this his anger is not turned away, but his hand is stretched out still.

The last warning of this chapter is, alcohol related but it also seems to fit the false and misleading advertising of our day. Famous athletes, movie stars, and other celebrities are paid to endorse products that are harmful and lead people into sin (vv. 22–23). When Assyria came, those who despised the word (warnings) of the Holy One of Israel were destroyed as if by fire (v. 24–25). However, the warnings are also extended to the latter days, "his anger is not turned away, but his hand is stretched out still" (v. 25). All of these sins threaten our societies today. Before the Second Coming, the Lord will gather the righteous from the wicked unto Zion and Jerusalem, and there will be another destruction of the wicked.

We will leave an extensive analysis of these six warnings for a more thorough study of Isaiah.[2]

2 Nephi 15:26–28 (Isaiah 5:26–28)
• Lift Up an Ensign to the Nations

26 And he will lift up an ensign to the nations from far, and will hiss unto them from the end of the earth; and behold, they shall come with speed swiftly; none shall be weary nor stumble among them.

27 None shall slumber nor sleep; neither shall the girdle of their loins be loosed, nor the latchet of their shoes be broken;

28 Whose arrows **shall be** sharp, and all their bows bent, **and** their horses' hoofs shall be counted like flint, and their wheels like a whirlwind, their roaring like a lion.

The six warnings that caused the downfall of the house of Israel anciently, and threaten us today, may be corrected by giving heed to the ensign lifted up in the last days. An ensign is a standard or pennant to be seen by others. The ensign and the time period of it being raised up is identified in the Book of Mormon.

1 But behold, there shall be many—at that day when I shall proceed to do a marvelous work among them, that I may remember my covenants which I have made unto the children of men, that I may set my hand again the second time to recover my people, which are of the house of Israel;

2 And also, that I may remember the promises which I have made unto thee, Nephi, and also unto thy father, that I would remember your seed; and that the words of your seed should proceed forth out of my mouth unto your seed; and my words (the Book of Mormon) shall hiss forth unto the ends of the earth, for a standard unto my people,

---

[2] See Monte S. Nyman, *Great Are the Words of Isaiah*, 43–45.

which are of the house of Israel. [2 Nephi 29:1–2]

The word "hiss" has a different connotation than the present-day meaning of disapproval. As translated from the Hebrew, it means to quietly proclaim. In Isaiah it is used to identify the going forth of the gospel to the ends of the earth. The ensign is further identified in the Doctrine and Covenants:

> 9 And even so I have sent mine everlasting covenant into the world, to be a light to the world, and to be a standard for my people, and for the Gentiles to seek to it, and to be a messenger before my face to prepare the way before me. [D&C 45:9]

The Book of Mormon is the Ensign used by the Lord to bring his people to the everlasting covenants of the gospel. As they enter into these covenants, they are gathered into the Church, and it becomes an ensign also.

> 4 For thus shall my church be called in the last days, even The Church of Jesus Christ of Latter-day Saints.
>
> 5 Verily I say unto you all: Arise and shine forth, that thy light may be a standard for the nations. [D&C 115:4–5]

The combination of these ensigns, which are really one ensign, will eliminate the six sins that the Lord warned of earlier in the chapter.

Elder LeGrand Richards has identified verses 27 and 28 as a description of the modern means of transportation that would carry the Lord's messengers to every nation.

> Since there were no such things as trains and airplanes in that day, Isaiah could hardly have mentioned them by name, but he seems to have described them in unmistakable words. How better could "their horses' hooves be counted like flint, and their wheels like a whirl-wind" than in the modern train? How better could "Their roaring . . . be like a lion" than in the roar of the airplane." Trains and airplanes do not stop for night. Therefore, Isaiah was justified in saying: "none shall slumber nor sleep; neither shall the girdle of their loins be loosed, nor the latchet of their shoes be broken?" With this manner of transportation the Lord can really "hiss unto them from the end of the

earth," that "they shall come with speed swiftly." [*Marvelous Work and a Wonder* (1967), 236]

Elder Orson Pratt referred to the immigrants' coming to Salt Lake by railroad in two or three days, instead of ninety or one hundred days it took before the railroad, as an example of Isaiah's prophecy being fulfilled (see *JD*, 16:84, under General Authorities Quotes, end of chapter).

2 Nephi 15:29–30 (Isaiah 5:29–30)
• The Prey Carried Way Safely

> 29 They shall roar like young lions; yea, they shall roar, and lay hold of the prey, and shall carry away safe, and none shall deliver.

> 30 And in that day they shall roar against them like the roaring of the sea; and if **they** look unto the land, behold, darkness and sorrow, and the light is darkened in the heavens thereof.

While verses 26 through 28 seem to describe the messengers sent to the nations, verses 29 and 30 describe the "prey" leaving these lands. The prey are those of Israel, missionaries or members, who, because of the persecution and tribulation which come against them and the turmoil in the land, will be fleeing to Zion for safety. This seems to be describing the fulfilling of the times of the Gentiles, when the gentile nations will completely reject the gospel. When the Savior visited the Nephites, he described this time:

> 10 And thus commandeth the Father that I should say unto you: At that day when the Gentiles shall sin against my gospel, and shall reject the fulness of my gospel, and shall be lifted up in the pride of their hearts above all nations, and above all the people of the whole earth, and shall be filled with all manner of lyings, and of deceits, and of mischiefs, and all manner of hypocrisy, and murders, and priest-crafts, and whoredoms, and of secret abominations; and if they shall do all those things, and shall reject the fulness of my gospel, behold, saith the Father, I will bring the fulness of my gospel from among them. [3 Nephi 16:10]

The gospel may be taken from these nations on an individual basis rather than from all of them at once.

2 Nephi 30:7 • Shall Begin to Believe—
Shall Begin to Gather

> 7 And it shall come to pass that the Jews which are scattered also shall begin to believe in Christ; and they shall begin to gather in upon the face of the land; and as many as shall believe in Christ shall also become a delightsome people.

Nephi summarizes the Book of Mormon message to the Jews as when they "shall begin to believe in Christ . . . they shall begin to gather in upon the face of the land." The key word in Nephi's message is "begin." The Doctrine and Covenants teaches the same time pattern. In the dedicatory prayer of the Kirtland temple, given by revelation (see Section Heading), it was asked:

> 62 We therefore ask thee to have mercy upon the children of Jacob, that Jerusalem, from this hour, may begin to be redeemed;
>
> 63 And the yoke of bondage may *begin* to be broken off from the house of David;
>
> 64 And the children of Judah may *begin* to return to the lands which thou didst give to Abraham, their father. [D&C 109:62–64; italics added]

The building of that temple was the beginning of the gathering (see chapter 15). The attitude of Jewish people toward Jesus Christ has certainly mellowed in the past century. While he was not even mentioned in their homes and synagogues before, he is now spoken of more openly and many think of him as a great teacher, philosopher, or even a prophet. At the same time, there are now around five million or so of the Jewish people who have gathered to the modern nation of Israel. Nephi's prophecy is also beginning to be fulfilled.

Sacred Writing

Revelation Which is Great:

2 Nephi 15	Nephi writes the revelation of Isaiah concerning Judah, the choicest vine.

Prophesying:

2 Nephi 25:9–20	Nephi interprets Isaiah and prophecies of the last days.
2 Nephi 30:7	Nephi prophesies of the gathering of the Jews as they begin to believe in Christ.

Doctrines Learned:

2 Nephi 25:9	No nations are destroyed before they are warned by the prophets.
2 Nephi 25:17–18	When the Lord restores his people the second time, he will do a marvelous work (the Book of Mormon) to convince the Jews there is only one Messiah, who was rejected by them.
2 Nephi 25:19–20	The prophets and an angel foretold the name of Jesus, the only name whereby man can be saved.
2 Nephi 30:7	As the Jews gather and begin to believe in Christ, they shall become a delightsome people.

General Authority Quotations

President David O. McKay • 2 Nephi 15:26

On Bedloe Island, at the entrance of New York harbor, there stands a Statue of Liberty, a light to the nations. What it has meant to thousands and hundreds of thousands of the downtrodden of Europe has been most graphically expressed by Israel Zangwill in that impressive production *The Melting Pot*, from which I quote (David the immigrant Jew is speaking).

"When I look at our Statue of Liberty, I just seem to hear the voice of America: 'Come unto me all ye who are weary and heavy-laden, and I will give you rest'."

What that Statue of Liberty has symbolized to the oppressed and downtrodden of Europe, the gospel of Jesus Christ is to the world.

The restored gospel, the Church, has reared an ensign to the nations, and with words as comprehensive as those I have read in the revelation (D&C 45:9), invites the world to peace, to rest, to contentment. [CR, April 1963, 96–7]

Elder Orson Pratt • 2 Nephi 15:26

Sure enough we come with great speed, as Isaiah has said in the fifth chapter—the Lord should hiss unto thee from the ends of the earth, he should lift up an ensign for the nations, and they should come with speed swiftly; just as you emigrants do when you get on board of these railroads, when, instead of being ninety or a hundred days coming to this elevated region, as was the case for several years, you come in two or three days. "They shall come with speed swiftly, and he shall lift up an ensign from afar." Not in Palestine, where the Prophet was delivering his prediction, that would have been near by. Not an ensign that was to be raised up in Jerusalem, or any-where in that land; but God was to begin the great latter-day work afar off from Jerusalem. [*JD*, 16:84]

President Joseph Fielding Smith • 2 Nephi 30:7

Not many of the Jews, I take it from my reading of the scriptures, will believe in Christ before he comes. The Book of Mormon tells us that they shall *begin* to believe in him. They are now *beginning* to believe in him. The Jews today look upon Christ as a great Rabbi. They have accepted him as one of their great teachers; they have said that, "He is a Jew, the greatest Rabbi of them all," as one stated it. When the gospel was restored in 1830, if a Jew had mentioned the name of Christ in one of the synagogues, he would have been rebuked. Had a rabbi referred to him, the congregation would have arisen and left the building. And so we see the sentiment has changed. Now I state this on Jewish authority that they are beginning to believe in Christ, and some of them are accepting the gospel.

But the main of them will gather to Jerusalem in their unbelief; the gospel will be preached to them; some of them will believe. Not all of the Gentiles have believed when the gospel has been proclaimed to them, but the great body of the Jews who are there assembled will not receive Christ as their

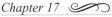
Redeemer until he comes himself and makes himself manifest unto them. [*Doctrines of Salvation*, 3:9]

President Wilford Woodruff • 2 Nephi 30:7

I wish in this testimony to say that the time is not far distant when the rich men among the Jews will be called upon to use their abundant wealth to gather the dispersed of Judah, and purchase the ancient dwelling places of their fathers in and about Jerusalem, and rebuild the holy city and temple. [Matthias F. Cowley, *Wilford Woodruff—history of his life and labors* (1964), 509]

Challenges to Eternal Life:

1. Recognize that Christ is the only name whereby man can be saved, and follow him in your everyday walk of life. Ask yourself, "What would Christ do?" as you make choices (2 Nephi 25:20).

2. Lift up the Book of Mormon as an ensign to those with whom you associate, in and out of the Church (2 Nephi 15:26).

3. As the Jews are beginning to believe, be an example to them and to all others that you are blessed by taking his name upon you (2 Nephi 30:7).

4. Choose a challenge of your own from this reading and apply it to your life.

Chapter Eighteen

The Message to the Lamanites

2 Nephi 25:21–26:11; 19:8–20:34; 30:4–6

Historical Setting: Again, there are three parts to our reading: Nephi's commentary addressed to his seed (2 Nephi 25: 21–26:11), Isaiah's prophecies and warnings to the remnant that shall return (2 Nephi 19:7–20:34; Isaiah 9:8–10:34), and Nephi's summary statement concerning his seed (2 Nephi 30:4–6).

Precepts of This Reading:

> And now behold, I say unto you that the right way is to believe in Christ, and deny him not; and Christ is the Holy One of Israel; wherefore ye must bow down before him, and worship him with all your might, mind, and strength, and your whole soul; and if ye do this ye shall in nowise be cast out. [2 Nephi 25:29]

Part of Isaiah 9 (2 Nephi 19:1–7) was discussed in Chapter 16, "The Coming of Christ." The rest of Isaiah 9 and the first part of Isaiah 10 predicts the rejection of Christ by the house of Israel (2 Nephi 19:8–20:4). Isaiah 10:5–19 (2 Nephi 20:5–19) predicts the punishment of the Assyrians because they do not recognize the hand of the Lord to them. This is 2 Nephi 19:8–20:19 is therefore Isaiah's message of doom to Israel and the Gentiles. Isaiah follows his message of doom with a message of hope, a remnant shall return to the mighty God (2 Nephi 20:20–34). Nephi's commentary is directed to his seed. However, it should not be limited to them, because it is applicable to all the house of Israel. The future of the Lamanites, summarized in 2 Nephi 30:4–6, is also included. An outline of his words follows as a preparation for a deeper study.

OUTLINE • 2 NEPHI 25:21–26:11; 19:8–20:34; 30:4–6

➤ 25:21–30   Nephi speaks concerning his seed.

    a.   The writings of Nephi shall be preserved and handed down from generation to generation (vv. 21–22).

        1.   Joseph's (Lehi's son's) seed shall never perish.

        2.   The writings shall go forth according to the will and pleasure of God.

        3.   The nations who possess these writings shall be judged of them.

    b.   Nephi and others labor diligently to write to persuade his people to believe in Christ for it is by grace we are saved after all we can do (v. 23).

    c.   We believe in Christ but we keep the law of Moses until that law be fulfilled (vv. 24–25).

        1.   The law of Moses was given to bring us to Christ.

        2.   The law is dead unto us but we keep it because of the commandments.

    d.   We talk, rejoice, preach, prophesy, and write of Christ that our children may know the source of a remission of their sins (vv. 26–27).

        1.   We speak of the law that our children may know its deadness.

        2.   After the law is fulfilled, they need not harden their hearts against Christ.

    e.   The words written by Nephi shall stand as a testimony against his people (v. 28).

        1.   They are sufficient to teach any man the right way, to believe in Christ and deny him not.

        2.   By denying Christ ye deny the prophets and the law.

    f.   You must bow down before him and worship him with

all your might, mind, strength, and your whole soul (v. 29).

g. You must keep the performances and ordinances of God until the law of Moses is fulfilled (v. 30).

26:1–11   Nephi speaks of Christ's visit to America.

a. The words Christ speaks shall be the law you should follow (v. 1).

b. Many generations shall pass away and there shall be wars and contentions (v. 2).

c. Signs of the Messiah's birth, death and resurrection shall be given (v. 3).

d. The death and resurrection day shall be great and terrible for the wicked (vv. 3–6).

    1. They perish because they cast out the prophets and the saints.

    2. The day that cometh shall burn the proud and the wicked.

    3. Those that kill the prophets and the saints shall be swallowed up, covered, carried away, crushed and ground to powder.

    4. They will be visited with thunders, lightnings, earthquakes, and all manner of destructions.

e. Nephi is nearly consumed by what he saw, but he must cry unto God, thy ways are just (v. 7).

f. The righteous that hearken to the prophets and look forward to Christ shall not perish (vv. 8–9).

    1. The Son of Righteousness shall appear to them and heal them.

    2. They shall have peace for three generations and many of the fourth.

g. A speedy destruction follows these peaceful generations (vv. 10–11).

    1. They sell themselves for pride and foolishness.

2. They yield to the devil and choose works of darkness.

3. The Spirit of the Lord withdraws and then cometh speedy destruction.

➤ 19:8–20:4   Israel is warned of the evils that brought God's destroying judgments upon Ephraim.

a. The Lord warns against pride and stoutness of heart (19:9–12).

b. Judah's leaders cause the people to err (19:13–17).

c. Wickedness encompasses as a fire (19:18–21).

d. The poor and the needy are neglected (20:1–4).

➤ 20:5–19   The Lord will accomplish his purposes through the Gentiles.

a. He will send Assyria against Israel (vv. 5–6).

b. The king of Assyria will not recognize the Lord but will boast in his own accomplishments (vv. 7–11).

c. The Lord will punish the Assyrians following his judgments upon Israel and Judah (vv. 12–19).

➤ 20:20–34   In the times of the Gentiles, the Lord will return a remnant of Israel.

a. The Lord's people who dwell in Zion will not be afraid of the Assyrians (the Gentiles) (vv. 24–26).

b. The burden of the Gentiles will be broken off (vv. 27–34).

➤ 30:4–6   Nephi speaks to his brethren concerning the remnant of their seed.

a. When the book is carried to them (v. 3), they shall know that they came out of Jerusalem and are descendants of the Jews.

b. The gospel of Jesus Christ shall be declared to them (the Lamanites) and they shall be restored to the knowledge of their fathers and also Jesus Christ (v. 5).

c. The scales of darkness shall begin to fall from their

eyes, and many generations shall not pass away until they become a pure and delightsome people (v. 6).

Notes and Commentary

Introduction: Enos, son of Jacob, asked the Lord to preserve a record of the Nephites, to be brought forth at some future day that the Lamanites might be brought to salvation. The Lord responded positively to Enos' request and said, "Thy *fathers* have also required of me this thing" (Enos 1:12–18; italics added). "Fathers," being plural, tells us that Jacob and Lehi had also asked that a record be preserved. We will now examine how the Lord fulfilled his promise through Nephi. The Lord acknowledges this promise and fulfillment in modern revelation.

46 And, behold, all the remainder of this work does contain all those parts of my gospel which my holy prophets, yea, and also my disciples, desired in their prayers should come forth unto this people.

47 And I said unto them, that it should be granted unto them according to their faith in their prayers;

48 Yea, and this was their faith—that my gospel, which I gave unto them that they might preach in their days, might come unto their brethren the Lamanites, and also all that had become Lamanites because of their dissensions.

49 Now, this is not all—their faith in their prayers was that this gospel should be made known also, if it were possible that other nations should possess this land;

50 And thus they did leave a blessing upon this land in their prayers, that whosoever should believe in this gospel in this land might have eternal life;

51 Yea, that it might be free unto all of whatsoever nation, kindred, tongue, or people they may be.

52 And now, behold, according to their faith in their prayers will I bring this part of my gospel to the knowledge of my people. Behold, I do not bring it to destroy that which they have received, but to build it up. [D&C 10:46–52]

Note that the Lamanites include all that had become Lamanites (v. 48).

2 Nephi 25:21–22 • Why Nephi Wrote

21 Wherefore, for this cause hath the Lord God promised unto me that these things which I write shall be kept and preserved, and handed down unto my seed, from generation to generation, that the promise may be fulfilled unto Joseph, that his seed should never perish as long as the earth should stand.

22 Wherefore, these things shall go from generation to generation as long as the earth shall stand; and they shall go according to the will and pleasure of God; and the nations who shall possess them shall be judged of them according to the words which are written.

Nephi stated two reasons for keeping the records. The first one was because the Lord had promised Joseph of Egypt that his seed would never be destroyed (v. 21). As a descendant of Joseph, Nephi kept the record so that it could save the posterity of Joseph when the records were brought forth in the latter days. The second reason was that his record might also give the other nations an opportunity for salvation. Nephi prophesied that his record would go to other nations according to the will and pleasure of God. Those nations who possess it will be judged by it (v. 22). Elder Marion G. Romney declared: "For me there could be no more impelling reason for reading the Book of Mormon than this statement of the Lord that we shall be judged by what is written in it" (CR, April 1960,110). All nations will be judged by it. As John the revelator prophesied, the angel "having the everlasting gospel to preach unto them that dwell on the earth [was to go] unto every nation, and kindred, and tongue and people" (Revelation 14:6). To be judged by the record means they will have the opportunity to accept it or reject it. As stated in the Doctrine and Covenants:

13 Therefore, having so great witnesses, by them shall the world be judged, even as many as shall hereafter come to a knowledge of this work.

14 And those who receive it in faith, and work righteousness, shall receive a crown of eternal life;

15 But those who harden their hearts in unbelief, and reject it, it shall turn to their own condemnation—[D&C 20:13–15]

Going to all nations will also fulfill the covenant to Abraham: "In thy seed shall the kindreds of the earth be blessed" (1 Nephi 22:9).

2 Nephi 25:23–27 • Saved by Grace After All We Can Do

23 For we labor diligently to write, to persuade our children, and also our brethren, to believe in Christ, and to be reconciled to God; for we know that it is by grace that we are saved, after all we can do.

24 And, notwithstanding we believe in Christ, we keep the law of Moses, and look forward with steadfastness unto Christ, until the law shall be fulfilled.

25 For, for this end was the law given; wherefore the law hath become dead unto us, and we are made alive in Christ because of our faith; yet we keep the law because of the commandments.

26 And we talk of Christ, we rejoice in Christ, we preach of Christ, we prophesy of Christ, and we write according to our prophecies, that our children may know to what source they may look for a remission of their sins.

27 Wherefore, we speak concerning the law that our children may know the deadness of the law; and they, by knowing the deadness of the law, may look forward unto that life which is in Christ, and know for what end the law was given. And after the law is fulfilled in Christ, that they need not harden their hearts against him when the law ought to be done away.

The act of engraving the Book of Mormon was laborious, but the writers had a common purpose for keeping the records. It is to persuade their children and their brethren to believe in Christ and through him to be reconciled to God. Besides believing that through the grace of Christ they could be saved. The writers knew that salvation also depended on their works (v. 23). This is one of Nephi's great theological teachings. Many in the Christian world believe in salvation only through the grace of Christ and place no emphasis on works. They quote Ephesians to justify their position.

> For by grace are ye saved through faith; and that not of yourselves: it is the gift of God: Not of works, lest any man should boast. [Ephesians 2:8–9]

Others propose that it is our works that will save us and quote Paul's admonition to "work out your own salvation with fear and trembling" (Philippians 2:12). They use other references from Paul to support their beliefs, (i.e. Romans 2:6–13; 2 Corinthians 5:10). Some even refer to James 2:14–26, "faith without works is dead" as a contradictory theology to Paul's teachings. If fully read and understood there are no contradictions between Paul's and James' teachings, or even between Paul's theology. Nor does Nephi's statement contradict the New Testament teachings. Nephi's declarations on gaining salvation are succinct and definitive: "it is by grace that we are saved after all we can do" (2 Nephi 25:23). Lehi taught the same theology: "there is no flesh that can dwell in the presence of God, save it be through the merits, and mercy, and grace of the Holy Messiah" (2 Nephi 2:8). Also Jacob, son of Lehi, testified: "remember, after ye are reconciled unto God, that it is only in and through the grace of God that ye are saved" (2 Nephi 10:24).

In spite of their full understanding of salvation through Christ, Nephi explains why they were still observing the law of Moses. The law was given to bring people to an understanding and acceptance of Jesus Christ. Paul called it a "schoolmaster to bring us unto Christ" (Galatians 3:24). Since the Nephites had accomplished the purpose of the law by attaining a great knowledge of Christ and faith in him, the law was now dead unto them (vv. 24–25). However, they still observed "those outward performances until the time that he should be revealed to them"(Alma 25:15) because it was a commandment (v. 25). The law was to be observed until Christ came and said "the law in me is fulfilled, for I have come to fulfil the law; therefore it hath an end" (3 Nephi 15:5). Both Moroni and Paul refer to Christ as "the author and finisher of our faith" (Moroni 6:4; Hebrews 12:2). The law of Moses was not finished until Christ was sacrificed as the Lamb of God and said "It is finished [all prophecies fulfilled]" (John 19:30).

The extent to which the Nephites kept the law is not given except that they kept the "outward performances" (Alma 25:15 more fully quoted above). It is assumed that they had outgrown what the author of Hebrews says "consisted only in meats and drinks, and divers washings, and carnal ordinances, imposed on them until the time of reformation" (JST, Hebrews 9:10), or what may be referred to as the minutia of the law. It is further assumed that they offered "both gifts and sacrifices" that were symbolic of Christ (Hebrews 9:9). There is no mention of specific calendar sacrifices being observed although some have drawn parallels between the calendar sacrifices and certain Nephite events. Elder Bruce R. McConkie observed: "There is, at least, no intimation in the Book of Mormon that the Nephites offered the daily sacrifices required by the law or that they held the various feasts that were part of the religious life of their Old World kinsmen."[1]

Certainly Christ was the center of the Nephite worship and the center of what they taught of their children. They also wanted their children to know of the deadness of the law (vv. 26–27). The Nephites did not pray unto Christ, but addressed their prayers to the Father through the name of Christ (see 2 Nephi 32:9; Jacob 4:5; 3 Nephi 18:19).

2 Nephi 25:28–30 • Spoken Sufficient to Teach Any Man the Right Way

28 And now behold, my people, ye are a stiffnecked people; wherefore, I have spoken plainly unto you, that ye cannot misunderstand. And the words which I have spoken shall stand as a testimony against you; for they are sufficient to teach any man the right way; for the right way is to believe in Christ and deny him not; for by denying him ye also deny the prophets and the law.

29 And now behold, I say unto you that the right way is to believe

---

[1] *The Promised Messiah* [1978], 427.

in Christ, and deny him not; and Christ is the Holy One of Israel; wherefore ye must bow down before him, and worship him with all your might, mind, and strength, and your whole soul; and if ye do this ye shall in nowise be cast out.

30 And, inasmuch as it shall be expedient, ye must keep the performances and ordinances of God until the law shall be fulfilled which was given unto Moses.

Nephi concludes his remarks on the law of Moses with a stern warning to his people that they have been plainly taught and will be accountable for his words (v. 28). His teachings, "sufficient to teach any man the right way . . . to believe in Christ, and deny him not" is also sufficient to teach the reader in the latter day that "Christ is the Holy One of Israel; wherefore ye must bow down before him, and worship him with all your might, mind, strength, and your whole soul" (vv. 28–29). We worship Christ through words, song, and actions, but we worship the Father in prayer through Christ.

The Nephites, in the meantime, were still admonished to keep the law of Moses until it was fulfilled (v. 30).

2 Nephi 26:1–7 • The Destruction of the Wicked at the Time of Christ

1 And after Christ shall have risen from the dead he shall show himself unto you, my children, and my beloved brethren; and the words which he shall speak unto you shall be the law which ye shall do.

2 For behold, I say unto you that I have beheld that many generations shall pass away, and there shall be great wars and contentions among my people.

3 And after the Messiah shall come there shall be signs given unto my people of his birth, and also of his death and resurrection; and great and terrible shall that day be unto the wicked, for they shall perish; and they perish because they cast out the prophets, and the saints, and stone them, and slay them; wherefore the cry of the blood of the saints shall ascend up to God from the ground against them.

4 Wherefore, all those who are proud, and that do wickedly, the

day that cometh shall burn them up, saith the Lord of Hosts, for they shall be as stubble.

5 And they that kill the prophets, and the saints, the depths of the earth shall swallow them up, saith the Lord of Hosts; and mountains shall cover them, and whirlwinds shall carry them away, and buildings shall fall upon them and crush them to pieces and grind them to powder.

6 And they shall be visited with thunderings, and lightnings, and earthquakes, and all manner of destructions, for the fire of the anger of the Lord shall be kindled against them, and they shall be as stubble, and the day that cometh shall consume them, saith the Lord of Hosts.

7 O the pain, and the anguish of my soul for the loss of the slain of my people! For I, Nephi, have seen it, and it well nigh consumeth me before the presence of the Lord; but I must cry unto my God: Thy ways are just.

These seven verses are still addressing the children of Nephi and his brethren. However, the time frame is the meridian of time rather than their own generation. It should be remembered that Nephi is foretelling what will happen to his people. Those already familiar with the Book of Mormon will recognize that it did happen precisely as he said. The wicked perished because they cast out and killed the prophets and the saints. The blood of the saints ascends unto God and the consequences that follow are a representation of the justice of God that will eventually and assuredly come (vv. 3–6). Verse four is quoted in Malachi 4:1 in the King James Bible, but the book of Malachi had not been written at the time of Nephi's writing (between 559 and 545 B.C.).

Nephi and Malachi are obviously quoting from an earlier source that was upon the plates of brass and preserved among the records available to Malachi. There are other evidences of the writings attributed to Malachi being present before 600 B.C. Malachi 4:1 is quoted in 1 Nephi 22:15; and Malachi 4:2 is quoted in 1 Nephi 22:24. 1 Nephi 22:15 suggest that it may have originally been from Isaiah.

Nephi laments the destruction of his people, but recognizes that the ways of God are just (v. 7).

2 Nephi 26:8–11 • The Destruction In the Fourth Generation From Christ

8 But behold, the righteous that hearken unto the words of the prophets, and destroy them not, but look forward unto Christ with steadfastness for the signs which are given, notwithstanding all persecution—behold, they are they which shall not perish.

9 But the Son of righteousness shall appear unto them; and he shall heal them, and they shall have peace with him, until three generations shall have passed away, and many of the fourth generation shall have passed away in righteousness.

10 And when these things have passed away a speedy destruction cometh unto my people; for, notwithstanding the pains of my soul, I have seen it; wherefore, I know that it shall come to pass; and they sell themselves for naught; for, for the reward of their pride and their foolishness they shall reap destruction; for because they yield unto the devil and choose works of darkness rather than light, therefore they must go down to hell.

11 For the Spirit of the Lord will not always strive with man. And when the Spirit ceaseth to strive with man then cometh speedy destruction, and this grieveth my soul.

Nephi does not dwell long on the righteous who will be saved (v. 8), for he sees another destruction coming. He recognizes the healing power of Christ, and the peace that will be among them for three generations and part of the fourth (vv. 8–9), but he laments the "speedy destruction" that will follow this peaceful period (v. 10). This destruction will be the end of the Nephites as a nation. Nephi gives two reasons for the Nephite destruction: (1) their pride and foolishness; and (2) their following the devil and choosing works of darkness (v. 10). The works of darkness were secret combinations that formed among them (cp v. 22). These two problems resulted in the withdrawal of the Spirit of the Lord and the speedy destruction of his people. This causes Nephi to grieve more (v. 11). These examples serve as a warning to the inhabitants of the earth today. Those who do not heed this warning will "go down to hell" like the wicked Nephites.

We now return to the prophecies of Isaiah that Nephi had recorded earlier.

2 Nephi 19:8–12 (Isaiah 9:8–12)
• Pride and Stoutness of Heart

> 8 The Lord sent **his** word unto Jacob and it hath lighted upon Israel.
>
> 9 And all the people shall know, even Ephraim and the inhabitants of Samaria, that say in the pride and stoutness of heart:
>
> 10 The bricks are fallen down, but we will build with hewn stones; the sycamores are cut down, but we will change them into cedars.
>
> 11 Therefore the Lord shall set up the adversaries of Rezin against him, and join his enemies together;
>
> 12 The Syrians before and the Philistines behind; and they shall devour Israel with open mouth. For all this his anger is not turned away, but his hand is stretched out still.

The Book of Mormon retains the identifying "his word" rather than "a word" in the KJV (v. 8). This retention broadens the meaning to include the gospel rather than just a single prophecy. This specifically fits the context of the sins or reasons for which the Lord's judgments are to come upon northern Israel or Ephraim. Perhaps Nephi saw it as a dual prophecy of the Nephites being destroyed, because Jacob said "Isaiah spake concerning all the house of Israel" (2 Nephi 6:5).

Although Isaiah's above prophecy follows the prophecy of the birth of Christ discussed in the last chapter (Isaiah 9:6–7), he now returns to the reasons for which Israel is going to be smitten by the Assyrians (about 722 B.C.).

The first evil that will bring the judgments of God upon Ephraim is the pride of their hearts. This was also a cause of the Nephite destruction (2 Nephi 26:10). They had failed to recognize the judgments that had already come upon them and had rationalized that if their dwellings were destroyed they would rebuild with better materials. Their reliance upon the material things and their own abilities was evidence of their pride which caused their downfall. The description of this evil, and the other three that follow, all end with the same pronouncement: "for all this his anger is not turned away, but his hand is stretched out still" (v. 12). God's judgment is imminent.

2 Nephi 19:13–17 (Isaiah 9:13–17)
• Leaders Cause Them to Err

13 For the people turneth not unto him that smiteth them, neither do they seek the Lord of Hosts.

14 Therefore will the Lord cut off from Israel head and tail, branch and rush in one day.

15 The ancient, he is the head; and the prophet that teacheth lies, he is the tail.

16 For the leaders of this people cause them to err; and they that are led of them are destroyed.

17 Therefore the Lord shall have no joy in their young men, neither shall have mercy on their fatherless and widows; for every one of them is a hypocrite and an evildoer, and every mouth speaketh folly. For all this his anger is not turned away, but his hand is stretched out still.

The second evil to bring the destructive judgments of God upon Israel is her wicked leaders, both the political and the religious leaders. The "head" refers to the government, and the "tail" refers to the false prophets (v. 15). The branch and the rush (v. 14) is Hebrew parallelism, repeating the same thing. The rush includes the leaves, stems, or needles extending from the branch of a tree or plant. The words are arranged differently and read better in the Book of Mormon than the King James text (vv. 14–15), but the message is the same.

2 Nephi 19:18–21 (Isaiah 9:18–21)
• Wickedness Burneth as a Fire

18 For wickedness burneth as the fire; it shall devour the briers and thorns, and shall kindle in the thickets of the forests, and they shall mount up like the lifting up of smoke.

19 Through the wrath of the Lord of Hosts is the land darkened,

and the people shall be as the fuel of the fire; no man shall spare his brother.

20 And he shall snatch on the right hand and be hungry; and he shall eat on the left hand and they shall not be satisfied; they shall eat every man the flesh of his own arm—

21 Manasseh, Ephraim; and Ephraim, Manasseh; they together shall be against Judah. For all this his anger is not turned away, but his hand is stretched out still.

The third evil to visit Israel is the wickedness that is likened to a forest fire. The fire of wickedness will sweep on, using the people for fuel. All will be consumed in wickedness. This wickedness is so severe that brothers will "consume" brothers, members of their own families, and even themselves—and will still not be satisfied.

2 Nephi 20:1–4 (Isaiah 10:1–4) • Turn Away the Needy and the Poor

1 Wo unto them that decree unrighteous decrees, and that write grievousness which they have prescribed;

2 To turn **away** the needy from judgment, and to take away the right from the poor of my people, that widows may be their prey, and that they may rob the fatherless!

3 And what will ye do in the day of visitation, and in the desolation which shall come from far? to whom will ye flee for help? and where will ye leave your glory?

4 Without me they shall bow down under the prisoners, and they shall fall under the slain. For all this his anger is not turned away, but his hand is stretched out still.

The fourth and final evil pronounced by Isaiah is the neglect of the poor and the needy. How we care for the poor and needy is a high priority to the Lord. To neglect them brings his judgment upon us. The following was revealed to the Prophet Joseph:

17 For the earth is full, and there is enough and to spare; yea, I prepared all things, and have given unto the children of men to be agents unto themselves.

18 Therefore, if any man shall take of the abundance which I have made, and impart not his portion, according to the law of my gospel, unto the poor and the needy, he shall, with the wicked, lift up his eyes in hell, being in torment. [D&C 104:17–18]

The law of the Lord's gospel is the fast offering program. The Lord expects us to contribute to it generously and not limit ourselves to contributing only to that program if our circumstances warrant otherwise.

The four sins or conditions which Isaiah listed as reasons for the Lord to stretch forth his hand in judgment upon ancient Israel are very applicable to our own day. As commented earlier, these are:

1. *Pride and stoutness of heart • 2 Nephi 19:9*

President Spencer W. Kimball recognized similar problems in this day as he dedicated the Washington D.C. Temple. "Our Father, in blessing thy people with prosperity, we pray that they may not be surfeited with flocks and herds and acres and barns and wealth which could bring them to worship these false Gods."[2]

2. *The leaders of this people caused them to err • 2 Nephi 19:16*

Note that both political and spiritual leaders of Isaiah's day were leading the people astray. We ought to appreciate and follow the leadership of a true prophet in this dispensation who is concerned over similar problems. In this same dedication President Kimball also said: "Father, we are concerned with the political world of today and that nations seem to need only the lighting of a match to bring war and desolation and destruction. Bless, we pray Thee, the leaders of nations, that they may rule wisely and righteously and give Thy people freedom to worship Thee in truth and righteousness. Stay the powers, our Father, that would bring us to the brink of annihilation."[2]

3. *Wickedness burneth as a fire (or runs rampant and unchecked) • 2 Nephi 19:18*

---

[2] Dedication of the Washington D.C. Temple, *Church News*, November 23, 1974, 4–5. The following two quotes are also from the dedicatory prayer.

President Kimball likewise expressed concern for the great wickedness of this era: "We are greatly concerned, our Father, with the widespread wickedness in this world, the blasphemy, the corruption, the pollution, the immorality, and we are reminded of days long past when the cities of the plains were destroyed, when cities were sacked, and buildings razed and people taken prisoner, to become slaves of enemy nations. We remember the devastation of a flood which was to cleanse the earth from pollution of men and now we see all the sins of the past being portrayed before our eyes again, when people worship the permissiveness of so called freedoms, walking blindly into the traps which must terminate in destructive calamities. Bless them, Father, that they may return to Thee in total righteousness."[2]

4. *The needy, the poor, the widows, and the fatherless are neglected*
    • *2 Nephi 20:1–2.*

These same conditions exist in our day and must not be allowed in our lives if we want to escape the judgments of God. The Lord has given the formula for the care of the poor and the needy. In clarifying D&C 104:16, referred to above, President Marion G. Romney has said: "We talked about how the rich are made low. They are made humble and submissive and obedient to the commandments of the Lord by giving of their means liberally—by giving to the bishop for the care of the poor. How do you exalt the poor as they receive? Well, there is only one way to do that and that is to make them self-sustaining. No man has self-respect when he is the recipient of a dole. If there is anything that he can do, he wants to do it. This program was set up not merely to feed and house and clothe people, it was set up to build people into self-respecting Latter-day Saints" [CR, April 1974, 179].

2 Nephi 20:5–11 (Isaiah 10:5–11) • Assyria, the Rod of the Lord's Anger

> 5 O Assyrian, the rod of mine anger, and the staff in their hand is **their** indignation.
>
> 6 I will send him against **a** hypocritical nation, and against the people of my wrath will I give him a charge to take the spoil, and to

take the prey, and to tread them down like the mire of the streets.

7 Howbeit he meaneth not so, neither doth his heart think so; but in his heart it is to destroy and cut off nations not a few.

8 For he saith: Are not my princes altogether kings?

9 Is not Calno as Carchemish? Is not Hamath as Arpad? Is not Samaria as Damascus?

10 As my hand hath found**ed** the kingdoms of the idols, and whose graven images did excel them of Jerusalem and of Samaria;

11 Shall I not, as I have done unto Samaria and her idols, so do to Jerusalem and to her idols?

In Mormon 4:5 we read, "But, behold, the judgments of God will overtake the wicked, and it is by the wicked that the wicked are punished." Assyria is an example of this principle. As Assyria punished the wicked nations of Syria and Ephraim in her own wicked indignation, so will God use or allow the wicked nations of today to punish other wicked nations.

2 Nephi 20:12–19 (Isaiah 10:12–19) • Punish the Stout Heart of the Gentile

12 Wherefore it shall come to pass that when the Lord hath performed his whole work upon Mount Zion and upon Jerusalem, I will punish the fruit of the stout heart of the king of Assyria, and the glory of his high looks.

13 For he saith: By the strength of my hand and by my wisdom I have done these things; for I am prudent; and I have moved the borders of the people, and have robbed their treasures, and I have put down the inhabitants like a valiant man;

14 And my hand hath found as a nest the riches of the people; and as one gathereth eggs that are left have I gathered all the earth; and there was none that moved the wing, or opened the mouth, or peeped.

15 Shall the ax boast itself against him that heweth therewith? Shall the saw magnify itself against him that shaketh it? As if the rod should shake itself against them that lift it up, or as if the staff should lift up itself as if it were no wood!

16 Therefore shall the Lord, the Lord of Hosts, send among his fat ones, leanness; and under his glory he shall kindle a burning like the burning of a fire.

17 And the light of Israel shall be for a fire, and his Holy One for a flame, and shall burn and **shall** devour his thorns and his briers in one day;

18 And shall consume the glory of his forest, and of his fruitful field, both soul and body; and they shall be as when a standard-bearer fainteth.

19 And the rest of the trees of his forest shall be few, that a child may write them.

The differences in the two texts are insignificant. The message is that Assyria was the Lord's instrument used to punish the house of Israel. In the Doctrine and Covenants the Lord says, "And in nothing doth man offend God, or against none is his wrath kindled, save those who confess not his hand in all things, and obey not his command-ments" (D&C 59:21). Assyria is also an example of this principle revealed to the Prophet Joseph Smith.

Although there is nothing said about Assyria's being given the opportunity to keep the commandments of God in these verses, when the full history is known it will undoubtedly show that Assyria did have that opportunity. This conclusion is drawn from the allegory of the house of Israel in Jacob 5, which outlined the future of the house of Israel. The wild olive branches are the Gentiles, who are to be grafted into the tree of Israel and given the opportunity to bear fruit. That some did bear fruit from this graft is shown by the Savior's declaration to his disciples to "look on the fields [of the Samaritans]; for they are white already to harvest" (John 4:31–38). The Samaritans were, in part, a product of the Assyrian conquest, as the Assyrians brought Babylo-nians and others "and placed them in the cities of Samaria instead of the children of Israel." They intermarried (were grafted) with the Israelites who were left behind when "Israel [was] carried away out of their own land to Assyria" (2 Kings 17:23–24). "The Jews [had] no dealings with the Samaritans" (John 4:9) because they felt they had polluted their birthright (see John 8:48 and the Bible Dictionary in the LDS Bible).

2 Nephi 20:20–23 (Isaiah 10:20–23)
• A Remnant Shall Return

> 20 And it shall come to pass in that day, that the remnant of Israel, and such as are escaped of the house of Jacob, shall no more again stay upon him that smote them, but shall stay upon the Lord, the Holy One of Israel, in truth.
>
> 21 The remnant shall return, yea, even the remnant of Jacob, unto the mighty God.
>
> 22 For though thy people Israel be as the sand of the sea, yet a remnant of them shall return; the consumption decreed shall overflow with righteousness.
>
> 23 For the Lord God of Hosts shall make a consumption, even determined **in** all the land.

Having prophesied the fate of Assyria, Isaiah now comes back to the promise of a remnant of Israel (message of hope). Although she will be scattered among the Gentiles, and will be dependent upon them, Israel will once again rely on the Holy One of Israel in truth and will return. Paul quotes Isaiah 10:22 (with other prophecies) to show the Romans, who were Gentiles, that the righteous of Israel will be saved as well as the Gentiles who "have attained to righteousness" (Romans 9:27–30). The expression "consumption decreed" (v. 22) is translated "destruction" (NIV) or "full end" (RSV) suggesting that Israel will be no longer a people, but will "overflow with righteousness." This seems to refer back to the idea that the remnant that will return will have returned to Christ and his gospel. The King James text has the clause in "the midst of" all the land (v. 23) that is not in the Book of Mormon. This clause may have meant that Zion was to be established in the midst, or "center place" of the land (D&C 57:3) as was revealed to the Prophet Joseph Smith. Zion's establishment was certainly understood by the ancient prophets, and the translators somehow knew this and included it in the translation. If this assumption is correct, the verse is still speaking of the remnant that will return.

2 Nephi 20:24–26 (Isaiah 10:24–26)
• Be Not Afraid of the Gentiles

> 24 Therefore, thus saith the Lord God of Hosts: O my people that dwellest in Zion, be not afraid of the Assyrian; he shall smite thee with a rod, and shall lift up his staff against thee, after the manner of Egypt.
>
> 25 For yet a very little while, and the indignation shall cease, and mine anger in their destruction.
>
> 26 And the Lord of Hosts shall stir up a scourge for him according to the slaughter of Midian at the rock of Oreb; and as his rod was upon the sea so shall he lift it up after the manner of Egypt.

These verses are a promise of eventual deliverance to the people who will dwell in Zion in the day that the remnant will return. Therefore it is directed to the members of the church, whether Lamanites or other descendants of Joseph, who have gathered. The "Assyrians" (v. 24) would thus symbolize the Gentiles who were inhabiting that land, and were ruling over the blood of Israel scattered among them or living under their rule. The plea is for the Israelites to rely upon the Lord. While they may have trials and tribulations, these will be short-lived, and the promised blessings of Israel will be restored (vv. 25–26).

2 Nephi 20:27–34 (Isaiah 10:27–34)
• The Burden and the Yoke Removed

> 27 And it shall come to pass in that day that his burden shall be taken away from off thy shoulder, and his yoke from off thy neck, and the yoke shall be destroyed because of the anointing.
>
> 28 He is come to Aiath, he is passed to Migron; at Michmash he hath laid up his carriages.
>
> 29 They are gone over the passage; they have taken up their lodging at Geba; Ramath is afraid; Gibeah of Saul is fled.
>
> 30 Lift up the voice, O daughter of Gallim; cause it to be heard unto Laish, O poor Anathoth.

31 Madmenah is removed; the inhabitants of Gebim gather themselves to flee.

32 As yet shall he remain at Nob that day; he shall shake his hand against the mount of the daughter of Zion, the hill of Jerusalem.

33 Behold, the Lord, the Lord of Hosts shall lop the bough with terror; and the high ones of stature shall be hewn down; and the haughty shall be humbled.

34 And he shall cut down the thickets of the forests with iron, and Lebanon shall fall by a mighty one.

Identifying the antecedents of the pronouns in verse 27 will give us a clearer understanding of Isaiah's intent. "His" burden (or yoke) has reference to the Gentile burden of oppression. "Thy" shoulder refers to the shoulder of Israel under that oppression. "Because of the anointing" seems to be a reference to the covenant of Abraham, a promise of blessings to the remnant. They are his descendants and thus chosen or anointed to receive the covenant blessings. Mormon said the covenant would be fulfilled in the last days.

19 And behold, the Lord hath reserved their blessings, which they might have received in the land, for the Gentiles who shall possess the land.

20 But behold, it shall come to pass that they shall be driven and scattered by the Gentiles; and after they have been driven and scattered by the Gentiles, behold, then will the Lord remember the covenant which he made unto Abraham and unto all the house of Israel. (Mormon 5:19–20)

The time frame given by Mormon fits the interpretation of the verses given above

The places mentioned in verses 28–34 are cities of Judah remaining after the conquest of Assyria (see 2 Kings 18:10–13).

2 Nephi 30:4–6 • The Future of the Lamanites

> 4 And then shall the remnant of our seed know concerning us, how that we came out from Jerusalem, and that they are descendants of the Jews.
>
> 5 And the gospel of Jesus Christ shall be declared among them; wherefore, they shall be restored unto the knowledge of their fathers, and also to the knowledge of Jesus Christ, which was had among their fathers.
>
> 6 And then shall they rejoice; for they shall know that it is a blessing unto them from the hand of God; and their scales of darkness shall begin to fall from their eyes; and many generations shall not pass away among them, save they shall be a pure and a delightsome people.

By their receiving the Book of Mormon through the Gentiles, the seed of Nephi (today's Lamanites) are to learn that they are descendants of the Jews. Nephi later qualifies the Jew as "them from whence I came" (2 Nephi 33:8). Nephi was a blood descendant of Manasseh (Alma 10:3), but had lived among the Jews therefore he is a cultural Jew. The Latter-day Saints who bring the Book of Mormon to the Lamanites are also cultural Gentiles. Although the Church members "are lawful heirs, according to the flesh, and have been hid from the world [scattered among the Gentiles] with Christ in God" (D&C 86:9), they are Israel who are "identified with the Gentiles" (109:60).

The Book of Mormon will be the means of teaching the Lamanites the gospel and restoring them to the knowledge of their fathers and of Jesus Christ (v. 5). The gospel will give spiritual and social blessings to them that will culminate in their becoming "a pure and delightsome people." The original edition of the Book of Mormon wording was "a white and delightsome people." Joseph Smith changed the word "white" to "pure" in the 1840 third edition of the Book of Mormon, probably because it gave a much broader description of the blessings that would be poured out. Subsequent editions of the Book of Mormon, printed after the Prophet's death, reverted back to the original word "white" for an unknown reason. The 1980 editions changed the word again to "pure" with the approval of the First Presidency and the Quorum of the Twelve.

SACRED WRITING

Revelation Which is Great:

2 Nephi 19:8–20:34	The revelation of Isaiah concerning the remnant of Israel returning.

Prophesying:

2 Nephi 25:20–26:11	Nephi interprets Isaiah and prophesies of the destruction of Israel, but includes the promise of their return.
2 Nephi 30:4–5	Nephi prophesies of the return of Joseph's seed to the covenants of the Lord.
2 Nephi 30:6	The remnant of Israel will become a pure and delightsome people.

Doctrines Learned:

2 Nephi 20:20–22	A remnant of Israel will be gathered in the latter-days.
2 Nephi 25:23	Man is saved by grace after all he can do.
2 Nephi 25:24–25	The law of Moses brought the Nephites to Christ but they still observed the outward ordinances until it was fulfilled.
2 Nephi 26:3	The martyred blood of the saints cries for justice.
2 Nephi 26:10–11	The Nephites were destroyed because of the pride and secret combinations, causing the Spirit to withdraw.

General Authority Quotations:

President Joseph Fielding Smith • 2 Nephi 30:4–6

It is true that Lehi and his family were descendants of Joseph through the lineage of Manasseh (Alma 10:3), and Ishmael was a descendant of Ephraim, according to the statement of the Prophet Joseph Smith. . . . The

Nephites were of the Jews, not so much by descent as by citizenship. . . .

Not only in the Book of Mormon are the descendants of Lehi called Jews, but also in the Doctrine and Covenants. In Section 19, verse 27, this is found: "Which is my word to the Gentile, that soon it may go to the Jew, of whom the Lamanites are a remnant, that they may believe the Gospel, and not look for a Messiah to come who has already come." Again, in giving instructions to the elders who had journeyed from Kirtland to Missouri, the Lord revealed the place for the building of the temple and gave instructions for the purchase of land "lying westward, even unto the line running directly between Jew and Gentile." This line westward was the dividing line between the whites and Indians. [*Answers to Gospel Questions* (1957), 1:142–43]

Elder Spencer W. Kimball • 2 Nephi 30:4–6

I should like to address my remarks to you, our kinsman of the isles of the sea and the Americas. Millions of you have blood relatively unmixed with gentile nations. Columbus called you "Indians," thinking he had reached the East Indies. Millions of you are descendants of Spaniards and Indians, and are termed *mestizos*, and you are called after your countries, for instance: Mexicans in Mexico; Guatemalans in Guatemala; Chilianos in Chile.

You Polynesians of the Pacific are called Samoan or Maori, Tahitian or Hawaiian, according to your Islands. There are probably sixty million of you on the two continents and on the Pacific Islands, all related by blood ties.

The Lord called you *Lamanites*, a name which has a pleasant ring, for many of the grandest people ever to live upon the earth were so called. In a limited sense, the name signifies the descendants of Laman and Lemuel, sons of your first American parent, Lehi; but you undoubtedly possess the blood of the other sons, Sam, Nephi, and Jacob. And you likely have some Jewish blood from Mulek, the son of Zedekiah, king of Judah. The name Lamanite distinguishes you from other peoples. It is not a name of derision or embarrassment, but of which to be very proud. [*The Teachings of Spencer W. Kimball* (1982), 596–597]

President Gordon B. Hinckley • 2 Nephi 30:4–6

We were recently with the Navajo Nation at Window Rock in Arizona. It was the first time that a President of the Church had met with and spoken to them in their capital. It was difficult to hold back the tears as we mingled with these sons and daughters of Father Lehi. In my imagination I have seen him weeping for his progeny who for so long have walked in poverty and pain.

But the shackles of darkness are falling. Some of them now are men and women of achievement. They have partaken of the fruits of education. They have come to know and love the gospel. They have become pure and delightsome.

But there is so much more to do among them. Alcohol and drugs literally destroy many of them. We must do more to help. As I look to the future, I envision the Spirit of the Lord being poured out upon these people. Education will unlock the door of opportunity, and the gospel will bring new light and understanding into their lives. . . .

We have now been in all the nations of South America and Central America, and we have seen miracles, with great gatherings of 30,000, 40,000, and 50,000 in football stadiums. These are all Latter-day Saints. In each case as we left there was a great waving of handkerchiefs, with tears in their eyes and in ours. . . .

These are strong and wonderful Latter-day Saints in whose hearts beat the same testimonies of Jesus and this work as beat in yours. [CR, Oct. 1997, 91]

Challenges to Eternal Life:

1. As you attend your church meetings this week, think of Christ as you sing, pray, and teach or listen; try to put your might, mind, and strength, and your whole soul towards Christ (2 Nephi 25:29).

2. Pray daily for the Spirit to be with you that you may be guided in the paths of righteousness (2 Nephi 26:11).

3. Review the reasons that caused Northern Israel's downfall and avoid those evils in your life (2 Nephi 9:8–10:4).

4. Choose a challenge of your own from this reading and apply it to your life.

Chapter Nineteen

The Message to the Gentiles

2 Nephi 26:12–27:35; 30:1–3

Historical Setting: Nephi prophesies about the Gentiles in the last days. He quotes extensively from another chapter of Isaiah (Isaiah 29, but he does not identify it) that he had not quoted previously. He does give a summary of the Gentiles future just as he had of the Jews and the Lamanites (2 Nephi 30:1–3). These chapters were written sometime between 560 and 545 B.C.

Precepts of this Reading:

> The Lord "inviteth them all to come unto him and partake of his goodness; and he denieth none that come unto him, black and white, bond and free, male and female; and he remembereth the heathen; and all are alike unto God, both Jew and Gentile." [2 Nephi 26:33]

Having prophesied of the Jews and the Lamanites, Nephi adds the third group of prominence in the latter days, the Gentiles. We should relate to Nephi's comments because we are the people of whom he speaks. An outline of these chapters is given to prepare us for a deeper study.

OUTLINE • 2 NEPHI 26:12–27:35; 30:1–3

➤ 26:12–13   Nephi speaks of the Gentiles.

a. They must be convinced that Jesus is the Christ, the Eternal God (v. 12).

b. Jesus manifests himself by the power of the Holy Ghost, working miracles, signs, and wonders, according to their faith (v. 13).

➤ 26:14–19   Nephi prophesies concerning the last days when the Lord shall bring forth his writings unto the children of men.

a. They will come after the Nephites have dwindled in unbelief and been smitten by the Gentiles (vv. 15–16).

1. Nephi paraphrases Isaiah 29:3, the Nephites brought down to the dust.

2. The words of the righteous shall be written, the prayers of the faithful heard.

3. Nephi paraphrases Isaiah 29:4. After they are destroyed, they will speak out of the ground by the power of God.

b. The Lord says they shall write the things done among them and they shall be sealed up in a book and not be destroyed (v. 17).

c. Nephi paraphrases Isaiah 29:5, those destroyed shall be so at an instant suddenly.

d. Those who dwindle in unbelief shall be smitten by the Gentiles (v. 19).

➤ 26:20–33   Nephi describes the Gentiles of the last days.

a. They are lifted up in pride and have stumbled (vv. 20–21).

1. They have built up many churches who put down the power and miracles of God and teach their own wisdom and learning.

2. The many churches cause envyings, strife, and malice.

b. There are also secret combinations as in times of old (v. 22).

1. The devil is the founder of all these things.

      2. He leadeth them with a flaxen cord until he binds them.

  c. The Lord worketh not in darkness (v. 24).

      1. He doeth not anything save for the benefit of the world.

      2. He lays down his life to draw all men to him.

  d. He invites all to partake of his salvation (vv. 24–28

      1. Nephi paraphrases Isaiah 55:1. Come unto me all ye ends of the earth.

      2. None are commanded to depart from their synagogues or houses of worship.

      3. Salvation is free and all men are privileged to partake.

  e. He commandeth there shall be no priestcrafts (v. 29).

      1. Men preach and set themselves up as a light to the world.

      2. They seek the gain and praise of the world.

      3. They seek not the welfare of Zion.

  f. The Lord commands that all men should have charity (vv. 30–31).

      1. Charity is love and without it man is nothing.

      2. Charity would not allow the laborer in Zion to perish.

      3. If the laborer in Zion labors for money he shall perish.

  g. The Lord has commanded there shall be no murder, lying, stealing, etc., and whoso doeth them shall perish (v. 32).

  h. All are invited to come to the Lord: black and white, bond and free, male and female. Heathen, Jew, and Gentile are alike unto God (v. 33).

➤ 27:1–5   In the days of the Gentiles, all the nations of the Gentiles and also the Jews will be drunken with iniquity and all manner of abominations.

      a.   Nephi quotes the present Isaiah 29:6–10 as evidence (vv. 2–5).

      b.   There are many significant retentions in the Book of Mormon text, especially (vv. 3–4) (Isaiah 29:9–10).

➤ 27:6–14   Nephi quotes these verses from Isaiah that have been lost from the original text (see JST, Isaiah 29:11–19). They tell what the Lord will do to counter the iniquity and abominations.

      a.   The Lord God will bring forth the words of (the Nephites) who have slumbered (v. 6).

      b.   The book shall be sealed which contains a revelation from God from the beginning of the world to the end thereof (v. 7).

      c.   The things that are sealed shall not be delivered in the day of the wickedness and abominations of the people (v. 8).

      d.   A man shall deliver the words of those who slumbered to another man (v. 9).

      e.   The sealed part shall be kept until the due time of the Lord (vv. 10–11).

          1.   They reveal all things from the foundation of the world to the end thereof.

          2.   At that day they will be read from the housetops by the power of Christ.

      f.   When the book is delivered to the man spoken of, it shall be hid from the world (vv. 12–14).

          1.   The man and three witnesses shall behold it by the power of God. They shall testify of its truth.

          2.   A few others will view it according to the will of God to bear testimony of his word.

          3.   In the mouth of as many witnesses as seemeth good to God will he establish his word.

➤ 27:15–19   The Lord shall say to whom he shall deliver the book.

      a.   Take these words that are not sealed to another that he may show them to the learned (v. 15).

    b.   To get the glory of the world and get gain, the learned shall say "Bring hither the book and I shall read it" (vv. 16–18).

        1.   The man shall say, "I cannot bring the book for it is sealed."

        2.   The learned shall say, "I cannot read it."

    c.   The Lord God will again deliver the book and the words to him who is not learned (v. 19).

➤ 27:20–23   Then shall the Lord God say unto the unlearned:

    a.   The learned shall not read them for they have rejected them (v. 20).

    b.   I am able to do mine own work, read the words I shall give thee (v. 20).

    c.   Touch not the things that are sealed, I will bring them forth in mine own due time (v. 21).

    d.   After you have read the words I commanded and obtained the witnesses I promised, seal up the book again and hide it until I reveal all things (v. 22).

    e.   I will show unto the world that I am a God of miracles, the same yesterday, today, and forever (v. 23).

➤ 27:24–35   Again the Lord shall say to him that shall read the words that shall be delivered him.

    a.   Verses 25–26 are basically the present Isaiah 29:13–14 concerning the coming forth of a marvelous work and a wonder.

    b.   Verse 27 is basically the present Isaiah 29:15–16 warning those who seek to hide their counsel from the Lord.

    c.   Verse 28 is basically the present Isaiah 29:17 showing Lebanon's becoming a fruitful field as a sign to follow the coming forth of the book.

    d.   Verses 29–35 are basically the present Isaiah 29:18–24

telling what effect the coming forth of the book shall have.

➤ 30:1–3   Nephi speaks to his brethren concerning the Gentiles.

    a.   Do not suppose you are more righteous than the Gentiles shall be, for except ye keep the commandments of God ye shall all likewise perish (v. 1).

    b.   Do not suppose that the Gentiles are utterly destroyed (v. 1).

    c.   As many of the Gentiles as will repent are the covenant people of the Lord, and as many of the Jews who will not repent will be cast off (v. 2).

    d.   Many of the Gentiles shall believe in the words of the book and shall carry them to the remnant of Nephi's seed (v. 3).

NOTES AND COMMENTARY

Introduction: The term Gentile has many different definitions. The Savior defined them when he visited the Nephites: "Blessed are the Gentiles because of their belief in me, in and of the Holy Ghost, which witnesses unto them of me and of the Father" (3 Nephi 16:6). The Gentiles, by this definition, are the Christian nations who believe in the Father, the Son, and the Holy Ghost. During his Jerusalem ministry, the Savior declared that he was "not sent but unto the lost sheep of the house of Israel" (Matthew 15:24). He also instructed the apostles to "Go not into the way of the Gentiles" (Matthew 10:5).

During his ministry, Jesus did not personally teach the Gentiles, but after he was resurrected he instructed his apostles: "Go ye therefore and teach all nations" (Matthew 28:19). Later, Peter received the revelation to take the gospel to the Gentiles (see Acts 10). Therefore, by this definition, the Gentiles are those nations that accepted the gospel through the teaching of the apostles. Paul identified himself as "a teacher of the Gentiles" (1 Timothy 2:7; 2 Timothy 1:11). Today, the Christian nations of the world would include the European nations, the United States, and Canada. Nephi's prophecies are consistent with this definition and have a significant message for us.

2 Nephi 26:12–13 • The Message to the Gentiles

> 12 And as I spake concerning the convincing of the Jews, that Jesus is the very Christ, it must needs be that the Gentiles be convinced also that Jesus is the Christ, the Eternal God;

> 13 And that he manifesteth himself unto all those who believe in him, by the power of the Holy Ghost; yea, unto every nation, kindred, tongue, and people, working mighty miracles, signs, and wonders, among the children of men according to their faith.

The message to the Gentiles is the same as the one given on the title page of the Book of Mormon; to convince them that Jesus is the Christ the Eternal God (v. 12). The difference in the two statements is that the title page capitalizes all of the letters, ETERNAL GOD, rather than just the first letter. The capitalization was probably for emphasis, but written either way, the title "Eternal God" is significant. It recognizes Jesus Christ as the God of this world before mortality, during mortality, and after mortality. It also acknowledges his eternal nature as the Son of God. Although not stated in this passage, he was Jehovah, the God of the Old Testament. Nephi wrote: "there is a God, and he is Christ, and he cometh in the fullness of his own time" (2 Nephi 11:7). He also called him "the God of Abraham, and of Isaac, and the God of Jacob" and quoted prophesies of his earthly ministry (1 Nephi 19:10).

A second message to the Gentiles is the manner by which he manifests himself to those who believe; by the power of the Holy Ghost. Through this power mighty miracles, signs, and wonders are wrought (v. 13). These manifestations are also unique to the true believers in the latter days. As will be noted later, a common belief is that such manifestations ceased with the apostles of Christ's day (see 2 Nephi 28:5–6).

2 Nephi 26:14–19 • Nephi Prophesies of the Book of Mormon

14 But behold, I prophesy unto you concerning the last days; concerning the days when the Lord God shall bring these things forth unto the children of men.

15 After my seed and the seed of my brethren shall have dwindled in unbelief, and shall have been smitten by the Gentiles; yea, after the Lord God shall have camped against them round about, and shall have laid siege against them with a mount, and raised forts against them; and after they shall have been brought down low in the dust, even that they are not, yet the words of the righteous shall be written, and the prayers of the faithful shall be heard, and all those who have dwindled in unbelief shall not be forgotten.

16 For those who shall be destroyed shall speak unto them out of the ground, and their speech shall be low out of the dust, and their voice shall be as one that hath a familiar spirit; for the Lord God will give unto him power, that he may whisper concerning them, even as it were out of the ground; and their speech shall whisper out of the dust.

17 For thus saith the Lord God: They shall write the things which shall be done among them, and they shall be written and sealed up in a book, and those who have dwindled in unbelief shall not have them, for they seek to destroy the things of God.

18 Wherefore, as those who have been destroyed have been destroyed speedily; and the multitude of their terrible ones shall be as chaff that passeth away—yea, thus saith the Lord God: It shall be at an instant, suddenly—

19 And it shall come to pass, that those who have dwindled in unbelief shall be smitten by the hand of the Gentiles.

Nephi equates the last days with the days when the Lord God would bring forth the records of his people (the Book of Mormon) unto the inhabitants of the earth (v. 14). The last days are those days after the remaining people of their seed (the Lamanites) had dwindled in unbelief and had been smitten by the Gentiles. His prophecies are an explanation of what Isaiah had said about the destruction of his people and the Book of Mormon coming forth.

Nephi paraphrases and comments on the present-day text of Isaiah 29:3–4 (vv. 15–16). Although the Nephite nation will have been destroyed, the righteous among them will have left a record hidden in the ground. This record will come forth as if those people were speaking from the ground. The reference to the "familiar spirit" out of the ground does not mean that the message is comparable to that in the Bible, as is often claimed, which refers to the ancient custom of witchcraft where people who were supposedly familiar with the dead, were able to call them up to speak to the present generation. However, the Nephite message will be written and proclaimed through the power of God and is as a familiar spirit, not witchcraft. The pronoun "him," to whom will be given "power, that he may whisper concerning them" (v. 16), may be a reference to Joseph Smith.

Writing the things that would be done among them (v. 17) seems to be a direct quotation, but, based upon 2 Nephi 27, Nephi is more likely quoting the original text of the present Isaiah 29,[3] it appears that Nephi is paraphrasing and commenting on what is now 2 Nephi 27:6. He also paraphrases the present Isaiah 29:5 (v. 18), foretelling the sudden destruction of the Nephites. Nephi then prophesies of those who dwindled in unbelief (those we know as Lamanites) being smitten by the Gentiles (v. 19).

2 Nephi 26:20–33 • The Gentiles in the Day the Book of Mormon Comes Forth

These verses are a commentary on Isaiah 3:15–23, and help us interpret who the daughters of Zion are, to whom these verses are addressed. The daughters of Zion are the inhabitants of the land of Zion. "The whole of America is Zion itself from north to south" (*TPJS*, 362). Jesus Christ covenanted to establish the Nephite people in the Americas "unto the fulfilling the covenant which I made with your father Jacob [father of the twelve tribes of Israel]; and it shall be a New

---

[3] The JST follows basically 2 Nephi 27 as the restored text of Isaiah 29.

Jerusalem" (3 Nephi 20:22). As a symbolic husband and wife making a marriage covenant, the Lord represents the husband and the covenant people represent the wife. Those who keep the covenants would be the offspring of the land. The Lord "reserved [the Nephites] blessings, which they might have received in the land, for the Gentiles who shall possess the land" because the Nephites had become wicked (Mormon 5:19). This fits the context of Nephi's commentary. The designation of daughters may be because the Israelites, the holders of the priesthood, had forfeited the right and the Gentiles, without the priesthood, were now upon the land. Nonetheless, Nephi addresses the Gentiles who are living in the Americas. We will quote the Isaiah passage and then give Nephi's commentary.

15 What mean ye? Ye beat my people to pieces, and grind the faces of the poor, saith the Lord God of Hosts. [2 Nephi 13:15; Isaiah 3:15]

20 And the Gentiles are lifted up in the pride of their eyes, and have stumbled, because of the greatness of their stumbling block, that they have built up many churches; nevertheless, they put down the power and miracles of God, and preach up unto themselves their own wisdom and their own learning, that they may get gain and grind upon the face of the poor. [2 Nephi 26:20]

"Because of the many plain and precious things which have been taken out of the [Bible] . . . an exceedingly great many [Gentiles] do stumble" (1 Nephi 13:29, see also v. 34), and the Book of Mormon "shall make known the plain and precious things which have been taken away from them" (1 Nephi 13:39). The stumbling of the Gentiles have led to their teaching with their own wisdom and learning in order to get gain and take advantage of the poor (v. 20).

16 Moreover, the Lord saith: Because the daughters of Zion are haughty, and walk with stretched-forth necks and wanton eyes, walking and mincing as they go, and making a tinkling with their feet— [2 Nephi 13:16; Isaiah 3:16]

21 And there are many churches built up which cause envyings, and strifes, and malice. [2 Nephi 26:21]

To be haughty is to be scornful and thus envious. Wanton suggests being unmanageable and thus causing strife. Mincing is to be effeminate or dainty and suggests that it may result in malice. While we must be careful in making parallels, the connection of the words in the Book of Mormon with those in the Isaiah passage are interesting and applicable to the Gentile society in which we live.

17 Therefore the Lord will smite with a scab the crown of the head of the daughters of Zion, and the Lord will discover their secret parts. [2 Nephi 13:17; Isaiah 3:17]

22 And there are also secret combinations, even as in times of old, according to the combinations of the devil, for he is the founder of all these things; yea, the founder of murder, and works of darkness; yea, and he leadeth them by the neck with a flaxen cord, until he bindeth them with his strong cords forever. [2 Nephi 26:22]

The times of old takes us back to Cain who entered into a secret oath with Satan (see Moses 5:29–31). This was the origin of secret combinations, and they have continued periodically from that day forward.

2 Nephi 26:23–28 • Nephi Comments On Secret Combinations

23 For behold, my beloved brethren, I say unto you that the Lord God worketh not in darkness.

24 He doeth not anything save it be for the benefit of the world; for he loveth the world, even that he layeth down his own life that he may draw all men unto him. Wherefore, he commandeth none that they shall not partake of his salvation.

25 Behold, doth he cry unto any, saying: Depart from me? Behold, I say unto you, Nay; but he saith: Come unto me all ye ends of the earth, buy milk and honey, without money and without price.

26 Behold, hath he commanded any that they should depart out of the synagogues, or out of the houses of worship? Behold, I say unto you, Nay.

27 Hath he commanded any that they should not partake of his salvation? Behold I say unto you, Nay; but he hath given it free for

all men; and he hath commanded his people that they should persuade all men to repentance.

28 Behold, hath the Lord commanded any that they should not partake of his goodness? Behold I say unto you, Nay; but all men are privileged the one like unto the other, and none are forbidden.

Nephi contrasts the works of God with that of Satan. Satan's work is in darkness with the intent to bind all men (v. 22). God's (Christ's) work is in the light to benefit all men (v. 23). Satan seeks to end life physically through murder and spiritually through sin (v. 22). When Nephi says Christ "loved the world, even that he layeth down his own life" for the salvation of all, (v. 24): he is paraphrasing Isaiah "Yet it pleased the Lord to bruise him" (Isaiah 53:10; Mosiah 14:10). Jesus confirmed Isaiah's prophecy to Nicodemus when he ministered on earth: "For God so loved the world, that he gave his only begotten Son, that whosoever believeth in him should not perish, but have everlasting life" (John 3:16). He also revealed to Orson Pratt through Joseph the Prophet that he "so loved the world that he gave his own life, that as many as would believe might become the sons of God. Wherefore you are my son" (D&C 34:3).

To show that all are invited to Christ, Nephi paraphrases Isaiah 55:1 (v. 25).[4] Nephi then asks three questions regarding the atonement being universal and answers each question in the negative. None are excluded from the houses of worship; none are excluded from the opportunity for salvation; and none are excluded from partaking of the goodness of the Lord (vv. 26–28).

Nephi seems to continue his commentary on Isaiah's writing.

18 In that day the Lord will take away the bravery of their tinkling ornaments, and cauls, and round tires like the moon;

29 He commandeth that there shall be no priestcrafts; for, behold, priestcrafts are that men preach and set themselves up for a light

---

[4] Jacob had previously quoted Isaiah 55:1–2 (2 Nephi 9:50–51). Nephi's quote is slightly different in wording, probably because he is applying it to the whole world while Jacob was applying it to his brethren.

19 The chains and the bracelets, and the mufflers;

20 The bonnets, and the ornaments of the legs, and the headbands, and the tablets, and the ear-rings;

21 The rings, and nose jewels;

22 The changeable suits of apparel, and the mantles, and the wimples, and the crisping-pins;

23 The glasses, and the fine linen, and hoods, and the veils. [2 Nephi 13:18–23; Isaiah 3:18–23]

unto the world, that they may get gain and praise of the world; but they seek not the welfare of Zion. [2 Nephi 26:29]

Nephi's definition of priestcraft will be used later to understand its practice among the Nephites. The association of Isaiah's words and the warning against priestcraft is strengthened by the dictionary definitions, especially the archaic or alternate meanings of several words used by Isaiah. For example: a muffler is a covering or veil or scarf worn as a protection or disguise. A bonnet is a women's head covering tied under the chin worn chiefly by children, or as a part of a uniform or habit. An ornament is an accessory article or object used in a church service. A mantle is a loose sleeveless cloth worn over other clothes, an enveloping robe or cloak. A wimple is a soft covering for the neck and sides of the face worn by nuns. A hood is a covering of an ecclesiastical garment (a monk's cowl). A veil is the outer covering of a nun's headdress.

Again Nephi gives the Lord's counterpart of the problem. He commands all to have charity and not suffer the laborers in Zion to perish. He warns of the eternal effects of laboring for money (vv. 30–31). He warns of many other iniquities, and concludes his prophecy with an invitation for all to come to Christ: black and white, bond and free, male and female, the heathen (non-Christian), Jew, Gentile (Christian)—because all are alike unto God[5] (v. 33).

It should be remembered that Nephi is prophesying concerning the conditions that would be prevalent in the day the Book of Mormon would come among the children of men (2 Nephi 26:14). Priestcraft is the fourth condition, the first three were: (1) the many churches stumbling because of the loss of the plain and precious parts from the Bible; (2) many churches would cause envyings, strife, and malice; and (3) secret combinations. All of these conditions were self-evident in the 1830s and still continue to one degree or another in our day.

2 Nephi 27:1 • The Days of the Gentiles

> 1 But, behold, in the last days, or in the days of the Gentiles—yea, behold all the nations of the Gentiles and also the Jews, both those who shall come upon this land and those who shall be upon other lands, yea, even upon all the lands of the earth, behold, they will be drunken with iniquity and all manner of abominations—

After various commentary on several passages of Isaiah, Nephi equates the last days with the days of the Gentiles and also the Jews coming upon the land of America and other lands, even upon all the lands of the earth. These nations "will be drunken with iniquity and all manner of abominations." His comments seem to be a preface to his quoting the rest of Isaiah 29.

2 Nephi 27:2–3 (Isaiah 29:7–8) • The Nations that Fight Against Zion

> 2 And when that day shall come they shall be visited of the Lord of Hosts, with thunder and with earthquake, and with a great noise, and with storm, and with tempest, and with the flame of devouring fire.

> 7 And the multitude of all the nations that fight against **Ariel**, even all that fight against her and her munition, and that distress her, shall be as a dream of a night vision.

---

[5] The definitions of the heathen being non-Christian and the Gentiles Christian are based on 3 Nephi 16:6, the Gentiles being those who believe in Christ and heathens being those who are taught the gospel after the Gentiles and the Jews have been given the opportunity (D&C 90:9–10).

3 And all the nations that fight against **Zion**, and that distress her, shall be as a dream of a night vision; yea, it shall be unto them, even as unto a hungry man which dreameth, and behold he eateth but he awaketh and his soul is empty; or like unto a thirsty man which dreameth, and behold he drinketh but he awaketh and behold he is faint, and his soul hath appetite; yea, even so shall the multitude of all the nations be that fight against Mount Zion. [2 Nephi 27:2–3]

8 It shall even be as when an hungry *man* dreameth, and, behold, he eateth; but he awaketh, and his soul is empty: or as when a thirsty man dreameth, and, behold, he drinketh; but he awaketh, and, behold, *he is* faint, and his soul hath appetite: so shall the multitude of all the nations be, that fight against mount Zion. [Isaiah 29:7–8]

The spiritual famine of the latter days, described in these verses, were also described by Amos.

11 Behold, the days come, saith the Lord GOD, that I will send a famine in the land, not a famine of bread, nor a thirst for water, but of hearing the words of the LORD:

12 And they shall wander from sea to sea, and from the north even to the east, they shall run to and fro to seek the word of the LORD, and shall not find *it*.

13 In that day shall the fair virgins and young men faint for thirst. [Amos 8:11–13]

Nephi's quoting of Isaiah has several variations from the King James text, but the most significant is the Book of Mormon's usage of "Zion" in place of the KJV "Ariel." In the JST, the Prophet Joseph Smith also made some slight changes in verse 8, but none in verse 7. This may indicate either that he did not complete the revision of this section in the JST or that the word "Ariel" may have a broader application than previously supposed. Note that the KJV verse 8 concludes with "mount Zion" and not "Ariel."

2 Nephi 27:4–5 (Isaiah 29:9–10) • Ye Have Rejected the Prophets

4 **For behold, all ye that doeth iniquity**, stay yourselves and wonder, for ye shall cry out, and cry; yea, ye shall be drunken but not

9 Stay yourselves, and wonder; cry ye out, and cry: they are drunken, but not with wine; they stagger, but not with strong drink.

with wine, ye shall stagger but not with strong drink.

5 For behold, the Lord hath poured out upon you the spirit of deep sleep. For behold, ye have closed your eyes, and ye have rejected the prophets; and your rulers, and the seers hath he covered because of your iniquity. [2 Nephi 27:4–5]

10 For the LORD hath poured out upon you the spirit of deep sleep, and hath closed your eyes: the prophets and your rulers, the seers hath he covered. [Isaiah 29:9–10]

The Book of Mormon retains an introduction to the KJV verse 9—"For behold, all ye that doeth iniquity"—designating that it was the iniquitous people who would "cry out." The 2 Nephi rendition of the next verse shows that these iniquitous people had closed their own eyes and rejected the prophets, and that the Lord had covered their rulers and seers because of their iniquity. The KJV reads as though the Lord were responsible for these problems, but the Book of Mormon shows that it was the people's choices that had brought upon them their conditions.

2 Nephi 27:6–14 • The Book Shall be Sealed

6 And it shall come to pass that the Lord God shall bring forth unto you the words of a book, and they shall be the words of them which have slumbered.

7 And behold the book shall be sealed; and in the book shall be a revelation from God, from the beginning of the world to the ending thereof.

8 Wherefore, because of the things which are sealed up, the things which are sealed shall not be delivered in the day of the wickedness and abominations of the people. Wherefore the book shall be kept from them.

9 But the book shall be delivered unto a man, and he shall deliver the words of the book, which are the words of those who have slumbered in the dust, and he shall deliver these words unto another;

10 But the words which are sealed he shall not deliver, neither shall he deliver the book. For the book shall be sealed by the power of God, and the revelation which was sealed shall be kept in the book until

the own due time of the Lord, that they may come forth; for behold, they reveal all things from the foundation of the world unto the end thereof.

11 And the day cometh that the words of the book which were sealed shall be read upon the house tops; and they shall be read by the power of Christ; and all things shall be revealed unto the children of men which ever have been among the children of men, and which ever will be even unto the end of the earth.

12 Wherefore, at that day when the book shall be delivered unto the man of whom I have spoken, the book shall be hid from the eyes of the world, that the eyes of none shall behold it save it be that three witnesses shall behold it, by the power of God, besides him to whom the book shall be delivered; and they shall testify to the truth of the book and the things therein.

13 And there is none other which shall view it, save it be a few according to the will of God, to bear testimony of his word unto the children of men; for the Lord God hath said that the words of the faithful should speak as if it were from the dead.

14 Wherefore, the Lord God will proceed to bring forth the words of the book; and in the mouth of as many witnesses as seemeth him good will he establish his word; and wo be unto him that rejecteth the word of God!

All of these verses were once a part of the original text of Isaiah but were lost (see JST, Isaiah 29:11–19). They contain many great truths, and should be studied as part of the text of Isaiah 29. The opening phase in verse 11 of the KJV—"And the vision of all"—is an authentication of the contents of the sealed portion of the record, "a revelation from God, from the beginning of the world to the ending thereof" (v. 7). Moroni gives us more information about its contents further verifying "the vision of all." He said it contained the vision shown unto the brother of Jared of "all the inhabitants of the earth which had been, and also all that would be; and he withheld them not from his sight, even unto the ends of the earth" (Ether 3:25).

The things that were sealed were not to be delivered in the day of the wickedness of the people (v. 8). The things sealed were to come forth in "the due time of the Lord" (v. 10). The Lord commanded the brother of Jared to "Write these things and seal them up; and I will show them in mine own due time unto the children of men" (Ether 3:27). The Lord further qualified the due time of the Lord to Moroni:

> 6 For the Lord said unto me: They shall not go forth unto the Gentiles until the day that they shall repent of their iniquity, and become clean before the Lord.
>
> 7 And in that day that they shall exercise faith in me, saith the Lord, even as the brother of Jared did, that they may become sanctified in me, then will I manifest unto them the things which the brother of Jared saw, even to the unfolding unto them all my revelations, saith Jesus Christ, the Son of God, the Father of the heavens and of the earth, and all things that in them are. [Ether 4:6–7]

In abridging the Jaredite record, Moroni addressed the future translator about "the things which have been sealed up; therefore touch them not in order that you may translate" (Ether 5:1). Joseph did not translate the sealed part, but "the day cometh that the words of the book that were sealed shall be read upon the housetops; and they shall be read by the power of Christ; and all things shall be revealed" (v. 11). How these things shall be read from the housetops is not specified, but with today's miracles of radio, television, satellite, and the internet, it is easy to see how it might happen (compare D&C 88:5–13).

Isaiah also foresaw the three witnesses to the Book of Mormon; Oliver Cowdery, David Whitmer, and Martin Harris (v.12). Their testimony is in the front of every copy of the Book of Mormon. The few others who were to bear testimony of his word (v. 13) include the eight witnesses whose testimony is also in the front of the Book of Mormon.[6]

---

[6] For further significance of their testimonies see B. H. Roberts comments under General Authority Quotes at the end of this Chapter.

2 Nephi 27:15–20 (Isaiah 29:11–12) • Show These Words to the Learned

15 But behold, it shall come to pass that the Lord God shall say unto him to whom he shall deliver the book: Take these words which are not sealed and deliver them to another, that he may show them unto the learned, saying: Read this, I pray thee. And the learned shall say: Bring hither the book, and I will read them.

16 And now, because of the glory of the world and to get gain will they say this, and not for the glory of God.

17 And the man shall say: I cannot bring the book, for it is sealed.

18 Then shall the learned say: I cannot read it.

19 Wherefore it shall come to pass, that the Lord God will deliver again the book and the words thereof to him that is not learned; and the man that is not learned shall say: I am not learned.

20 Then shall the Lord God say unto him: The learned shall not read them, for they have rejected them, and I am able to do mine own work; wherefore thou shalt read the words which I shall give unto thee. [2 Nephi 27:15–20]

11 And the vision of all is become unto you as the words of a book that is sealed, which *men* deliver to one that is learned, saying, Read this, I pray thee: and he saith, I cannot; for it *is* sealed:

12 And the book is delivered to him that is not learned, saying, Read this, I pray thee: and he saith, I am not learned. [Isaiah 29:11–12]

The Book of Mormon retains a much more detailed account of this prophecy than the King James text of Isaiah, which was literally fulfilled when Martin Harris took a copy of some of the translated characters from the plates to the learned linguist Professor Charles Anthon. Words from the unsealed part of the record to be given to "another" (Martin Harris) by the man to whom the book was delivered (Joseph Smith) (v. 9). The intentions of the learned were also foretold in Isaiah. The arguments regarding the authenticity of Martin Harris' visit will not be treated here; suffice it to say his story has been authenticated. He told one story and maintained it over the years, while Anthon told several contradictory stories.[7] The brief account given by Martin Harris (as recorded by Joseph Smith) shows the literal fulfillment of this prophecy (see JS—History 1:63–65).

Joseph Smith wrote that the angel Moroni quoted the prophecies of "the Old Testament" that were soon to be fulfilled (JS—History 1:36–41). He then wrote that "He [Moroni] quoted many other passages of scripture" to him that he did not record (JS—History 1:41). Oliver Cowdery, in relating some of those scriptures, cited Isaiah 29:11–14 as having been quoted by Moroni.[8] Moroni probably referred to the whole chapter.

The Book of Mormon text of Isaiah shows the detail of the prophecy when it records that the Lord God would "deliver *again* the book . . . to him that is not learned" (v. 19; italics added). The plates were taken from Joseph after the first 116 pages of translated manuscript were lost. The plates were later returned to him (*HC,* 1:21–23). The Book of Mormon text further shows that the Lord was giving an opportunity for the learned to reject these words before he showed the world that he was not dependent upon the learned for the accomplishment of his purposes (v. 20).

2 Nephi 27:21–23 • The Coming of the Sealed Part

21 Touch not the things which are sealed, for I will bring them forth in mine own due time; for I will show unto the children of men that I am able to do mine own work.

22 Wherefore, when thou hast read the words which I have commanded thee, and obtained the witnesses which I have promised unto thee, then shalt thou seal up the book again, and hide it up unto me, that I may preserve the words which thou hast not read, until I shall see fit in mine own wisdom to reveal all things unto the children of men.

---

[7] See General Authority Quotes, B. H. Roberts, 2 Nephi 27:15–20.

[8] *Messenger and Advocate*, Feb. 1835, 80.

23 For behold, I am God; and I am a God of miracles; and I will show unto the world that I am the same yesterday, today, and forever; and I work not among the children of men save it be according to their faith.

Joseph Smith also placed these verses, which concern the sealed section of the book (plates), in the JST Isaiah text. The Lord is able to do his own work (v. 21), he does not have to rely on the scholars of the world or any man, but will work his miracles as men exercise their faith.

2 Nephi 27:24–26 (Isaiah 29:13–14) • A Marvelous Work and a Wonder

24 And again it shall come to pass that the Lord shall say unto him that shall read the words that shall be delivered him:

25 Forasmuch as this people draw near unto me with their mouth, and with their lips do honor me, but have removed their hearts far from me, and their fear towards me is taught by the precepts of men—

26 Therefore, I will proceed to do a marvelous work among this people, yea, a marvelous work and a wonder, for the wisdom of their wise and learned shall perish, and the understanding of their prudent shall be hid. [2 Nephi 27:24–26]

13 Wherefore the Lord said, Forasmuch as this people draw near *me* with their mouth, and with their lips do honour me, but have removed their heart far from me, and their fear toward me is taught by the precept of men:

14 Therefore, behold, I will proceed to do a marvellous work among this people, *even* a marvellous work and a wonder: for the wisdom of their wise *men* shall perish, and the understanding of their prudent *men* shall be hid. [Isaiah 29:13–14]

The "marvellous work and a wonder" (v. 26; Isaiah 29:14) is associated with the Lord's setting "his hand again the second time to recover the remnant of his people" (2 Nephi 21:11; Isaiah 11:11, see 2 Nephi 25:17 and 29:1). This marvelous work would be accomplished through the bringing forth of the Lord's words, specified as the words of Nephi's seed (the Book of Mormon) in 2 Nephi 29:2. This is also confirmed by the Savior's words to the Nephites after his resurrection (see 3 Nephi 21:1–9).

Joseph Smith recorded that in the spring of 1820 two divine Personages appeared to him and told him that he should join no church because "they draw near to me with their lips, but their hearts are far from me, they teach for doctrines the commandments of men, having a form of godliness, but they deny the power thereof" (JS—H 1:17–19). Thus Isaiah's prophecy was fulfilled.

The Savior called the scribes and Pharisees "hypocrites," saying that Isaiah had prophesied of them and then quoted Isaiah 29:13 (see Matthew 15:7–9; Mark 7:6–7). This might lead some to believe that the prophecy was limited to the time of the Savior, and that it was fulfilled. But the fact that he quoted only verse 13, and not verse 14 with it, indicates that the Savior was saying that the Pharisees were the *kind* of people Isaiah prophesied of—not that they were the fulfillment of his prophecy.

Before the Book of Mormon was translated, the Lord repeatedly revealed through the Prophet Joseph that "a marvelous work and a wonder is about to come forth among the children of men" (D&C 4:1; 6:1; 11:1; 12:1; 14:1). This work was to correct the situation described in the previous verse in Isaiah (Isaiah 29:13; 2 Nephi 27:25).

2 Nephi 27:27–28 (Isaiah 29:15–17) • Seek to Hide Their Counsel From the Lord

27 **And** wo unto them that seek deep to hide their counsel from the Lord! And their works are in the dark; and they say: Who seeth us, and who knoweth us? **And they also say**: Surely, your turning of things upside down shall be esteemed as the potter's clay. **But behold, I will show unto them, saith the Lord of Hosts, that I know all their works. For shall the work** say of him that made it, he made me not? Or shall the thing framed say of him that framed it, he had no understanding?

28 **But behold, saith the Lord of Hosts: I will show unto the children of men that** it is yet a very little while and Lebanon shall be turned into a fruitful field; and the fruitful field shall be esteemed as a forest.

The bolded words show the Book of Mormon retentions. The King James text is identical to that not bolded except the last sentence is made a statement instead of a question by reversing "Is it." The word "and" introducing verse 27, indicates that it refers back to what has been said. The warning is to those who refuse the message of the "marvelous work and a wonder"—the Book of Mormon—which would come forth to correct the precepts of men. These men even try to work against it in secret. The Book of Mormon also retains the declaration that the Lord "will show unto them" that "I know all their works" (v. 27). This is at least partly a reference to those who would take the 116 pages of manuscript with the intent to change them and frustrate the works of God. In his foreknowledge, God had prepared the way to frustrate their work, the (small) plates of Nephi covering the same time period (see D&C 3 and 10).

The Book of Mormon retains the introductory "But behold, saith the Lord of Hosts; I will show unto the children of men that" (v. 28). This helps to confirm the time when this marvelous work was to come forth. A little while after the marvelous work and a wonder (the Book of Mormon) has come forth, "Lebanon shall be turned into a fruitful field, and the fruitful field shall be esteemed as a forest" (v. 28; Isaiah 29:17). Lebanon in this verse has been interpreted to be synonymous with Palestine, and the land would become fruitful temporally or agriculturally.[9] Elder Orson Pratt gave a spiritual interpretation of this verse:

> The book, therefore, that Isaiah prophesies of, is to come forth just before the great day of the restoration of Israel to their own lands; at which time Lebanon and all the land of Canaan is again to be blessed, while the fruitful field occupied by the nations of the Gentiles, "will be esteemed as a forest;" the multitude of the nations of the Gentiles are to perish, and their lands which are now like a fruitful field, are to be left desolate of inhabitants and become as Lebanon has been for many generations past; while Lebanon shall again be occupied

---

[9] See Joseph Fielding Smith, *Doctrines of Salvation*, comp. Bruce R. McConkie, 3 vols. [1954-56], 3:261–62.

by Israel, and be turned into a fruitful field. These great events could not take place until the Lord should first bring forth a book out of the ground.[10] [*Works*, 276–77]

2 Nephi 27:29–30 (Isaiah 29:18–19) • The Deaf Shall Hear the Words of the Book

29 And in that day shall the deaf hear the words of the book, and the eyes of the blind shall see out of obscurity and out of darkness.

30 And the meek also shall increase, **and** their joy **shall be** in the Lord, and the poor among men shall rejoice in the Holy One of Israel.

The "deaf" and the "blind" are those who have been deafened or blinded by the precepts of men. The Lord had described the same condition in existence at the time of Isaiah's call (see Isaiah 6:9). The effects of the book's coming forth are then described by Isaiah: the deaf shall hear, the blind shall see, and the meek and the poor shall rejoice in the Lord. The spiritually blind and deaf will be healed and see the kingdom of God, and hear the gospel. Elder Orson Pratt saw a literal fulfillment of Isaiah's prophecy in the physically deaf being restored to hearing: "Those who were so deaf that they could not hear the loudest sound, have had their ears opened to hear the glorious and most precious words of the Book of Mormon, and it has been done by the power of God and not of man."

2 Nephi 27:31–32 (Isaiah 29:20–21) • They Make a Man an Offender for a Word

31 For **assuredly as the Lord liveth they shall see that** the terrible one is brought to naught, and the scorner is consumed, and all that watch for iniquity are cut off;

32 **And they** that make a man an offender for a word, and lay a snare for him that reproveth in the gate, and turn aside the just for a thing of naught.

---

[10] *Orson Pratts Works*, Deseret News Press, Salt Lake City, Utah [1945], 276–77.

The Book of Mormon retains an opening phrase (bolded v. 31) that attributes to the Lord the action referred to in these verses, and also retains a more definite identification (bolded v. 32). The King James text is the same as that not bolded.

Joseph Smith, in writing of the persecution he and other Saints had suffered in Missouri, said: "We refer you to Isaiah, who considers those who make a man an offender for a word, and lay a snare for him that reproveth in the gate (v. 32, or 21). We believe that the old Prophet verily told the truth, and we have no retraction to make" (*TPJS*, 124).

2 Nephi 27:33–34 (Isaiah 29:22–23) • Jacob Shall Not be Ashamed

> 33 Therefore, thus saith the Lord, who redeemed Abraham, concerning the house of Jacob: Jacob shall not now be ashamed, neither shall his face now wax pale.
>
> 34 But when he seeth his children, the work of my hands, in the midst of him, they shall sanctify my name, and sanctify the Holy One of Jacob, and shall fear the God of Israel.
>
> (The Book of Mormon and the King James texts are the same, therefore only one is quoted.)

Abraham was promised that in his seed (the literal seed, or the seed of the body) shall all the families of the earth be blessed, even with the blessings of the gospel" (Abraham 2:11). The gathering of the house of Jacob mentioned here by Isaiah will be in preparation for the fulfillment of the covenant made to Abraham.

Elder Orson Pratt says that this restoration of the house of Jacob will come through the Book of Mormon:

> The house of Jacob has been made ashamed, and his face has waxed pale, ever since he was driven away from Lebanon or Canaan, but the Lord has now brought forth out of the ground a book which shall, accompanied by his power, restore the tribes of Jacob from the four quarters of the globe, and establish them in the land of Palestine and Lebanon forever; and His holy name they shall no more profane,

but shall be a righteous people throughout all their generations, while the earth shall stand, and they shall possess their promised land again in eternity, never more to pass away; therefore, they shall never again be made ashamed. It is in vain for the Gentiles to seek the conversion of Jacob, and to bring about their great redemption, only in the way that the Lord God of Israel hath predicted and appointed: they may call meetings and conventions to convert the Jews, but let them know assuredly that the book spoken of by Isaiah is to accomplish the salvation of the house of Jacob, and bring about the restoration of all Israel, while the Gentiles who will not receive it and be numbered and identified with the house of Jacob, must surely perish, yea, and they shall be utterly wasted with storm and tempest, with earthquakes and famine, with the flame of devouring fire, and their fruitful lands shall be esteemed as a forest, while Jacob shall dwell in safety forever. [*Works*, 278; see also 2 Nephi 25:17–18; 29:1–2]

2 Nephi 27:35 (Isaiah 29:24) • They Shall Learn Doctrine

35 They also that erred in spirit shall come to understanding, and they that murmured shall learn doctrine.

(The Book of Mormon and the King James texts are the same, therefore only one text is quoted).

One of the major purposes of the Book of Mormon specifically, and of the gospel in general, is to learn doctrine. The above verse is quoted in the Introduction of this work in support of this purpose. Before the Book of Mormon had been published, Hyrum Smith was told: "Wait a little longer, until you shall have my word, my rock, my church, and my gospel, that you may know of a surety my doctrine" (D&C 11:16).

At the end of each chapter of this work the doctrines learned in that section of the Book of Mormon are listed. The main doctrines of the restored gospel learned from the Book of Mormon are outlined in a revelation given on the day the Church was organized (see D&C 20:17–36). Along with the apostles and prophets, the Book of Mormon prevents us from being "tossed to and fro, and carried about with every wind of doctrine" (Ephesians 4:11, 14).

2 Nephi 30:1–3 • Gentiles Who Repent are Covenant People

1 And now behold, my beloved brethren, I would speak unto you; for I, Nephi, would not suffer that ye should suppose that ye are more righteous than the Gentiles shall be. For behold, except ye shall keep the commandments of God ye shall all likewise perish; and because of the words which have been spoken ye need not suppose that the Gentiles are utterly destroyed.

2 For behold, I say unto you that as many of the Gentiles as will repent are the covenant people of the Lord; and as many of the Jews as will not repent shall be cast off; for the Lord covenanteth with none save it be with them that repent and believe in his Son, who is the Holy One of Israel.

3 And now, I would prophesy somewhat more concerning the Jews and the Gentiles. For after the book of which I have spoken shall come forth, and be written unto the Gentiles, and sealed up again unto the Lord, there shall be many which shall believe the words which are written; and they shall carry them forth unto the remnant of our seed.

The Gentiles are also given the opportunity to become the covenant people of the Lord, as many as will repent will be adopted into the house of Israel (v. 2). "As many as receive this Gospel shall be called after [Abraham's] name, and shall be accounted [Abraham's] seed" (Abraham 2:10). The Gentiles—the cultural Gentiles will carry the Book of Mormon to the remnant of Nephi's seed (v. 3). Again, the "cultural Gentiles" are the Latter-day Saints, the house of Israel who were scattered among the Gentiles but have been gathered out or adopted from among them, but "who are identified with the Gentiles" (D&C 109:60).

SACRED WRITING

Revelation Which is Great:

2 Nephi 26:15–17, 25; 27:2–35   Nephi quotes all but the first two verses of Isaiah 29 and Isaiah 55:1 concerning the Gentiles.

Prophesying:

2 Nephi 26:12–33   Nephi prophesies concerning the future of the Gentiles.

2 Nephi 30:1–3   Nephi prophesies concerning the future of the Gentiles.

Doctrines Learned:

2 Nephi 26:12–13   The Book of Mormon will convince the Gentiles that Jesus is the Eternal God.

2 Nephi 26:22–24   God does not work in darkness and secret.

2 Nephi 26:29   Priestcraft is when men set themselves up as a light to the world to get the gain and praise of the world, and they seek not the welfare of Zion.

2 Nephi 26:33   All are invited to come to Christ; black and white, bond and free, male and female, heathen, Jew, and Gentile. All are alike unto God.

2 Nephi 27:7–10   The sealed portion of the Nephite plates contain a revelation from the beginning of the world to the end thereof. God is omniscient.

2 Nephi 27:12–14   The Book of Mormon will be established in the world by the mouth of as many witnesses as seemeth good to God.

2 Nephi 27:20   God is able to do his own work. He does not need the learned of the world to do it.

2 Nephi 27:23   God is a God of miracles and will show the

	world that he is the same yesterday, today, and forever.
2 Nephi 27:35	The Book of Mormon will bring men to understand and learn doctrine.

General Authority Quotations:

Elder B. H. Roberts • 2 Nephi 27:15–20 (Isaiah 29:11–12)

Martin Harris gave one account and stuck to it. Charles Anthon, however, contradicted himself in his accounts of the incident. To E.D. Howe on February 17, 1834, he wrote: "He requested an opinion from me in writing which, of course, I decline to give." To Dr. T. W. Coit on April 3, 1841, he wrote: "but as no one until the present time has even requested from me a statement in writing." Also, "he requested me to give him my opinion in writing about the paper which he has shown me. I did so without hesitation, partly for the man's sake. . . . The import of what I wrote was, as far as I can now recollect, simply this, that the marks in the paper appeared to be merely an imitation of various alphabetical characters, and had, in my opinion, no meaning at all in connection with them. . . ." [*A Comprehensive History of the Church*, 1:103, 104, 106]

Elder B. H. Roberts • 2 Nephi 27:12–14

But the testimony of the three and eight witnesses, respectively, stands or falls together. If the pure fabrication theory is adopted to explain away the testimony of the eight witnesses, there is no reason why it should not be adopted to explain away the testimony of the three. But every circumstance connected with the testimony of all these witnesses, as we have seen, cried out against the theory of "pure fabrication." It is in recognition of the evident honesty of the three witnesses that the theory of mental hallucination is invented to account for their testimony; and it is also the evident honesty of the eight witnesses that leads to the admission by many anti-"Mormon" writers that Joseph Smith must have had some kind of plates which he exhibited to the eight witnesses, though he may not have obtained them through supernatural means.

The theory of pure fabrication of the testimony of the witnesses is absolutely overwhelmed by the evidence of their honesty. But what have the "pure fabrication" theory to account for the testimony of eight witnesses, and the "mental hallucination" theory to account for the testimony of the three? If the testimony of the eight is pure fabrication is not the testimony of the three pure fabrication also? Or, at least, is it not most likely to be so? For if conscious fraud, and pure fabrication lurk anywhere in Joseph Smith's and the eleven witnesses' account of the coming forth of the Book of Mormon, would it not exist throughout the whole proceeding?

The hallucination theory breaks down under the force of the matter-of-fact testimony of the eight witnesses, from which all possible elements of hallucination are absent.

The manifestation of divine power, through which the three witnesses received their testimony, destroys the theory of deception alleged to have been practiced by the Prophet on the credulity of the eight witnesses by exhibiting plates either manufactured by himself or some ancient plates accidentally discovered.

Such, then, is the force of this direct testimony of the eleven witnesses to the truth of the Book of Mormon—the testimony of the three and the eight when considered together. It is so palpably true that it cannot be resolved into illusion or mistake. It is so evidently honest that it cannot be resolved into pure fabrication. It is of such a nature that it would not possibly have been the result of deception wrought by the cunning of Joseph Smith. There remains after these but one other theory. "The witnesses were honest." They saw and heard and handled what they say, and heard, and handled. [*A Comprehensive History of the Church*, 1:153–155]

David O. McKay • 2 Nephi 26:33

. . . To proclaim the truth that each individual is a child of God and important in his sight; that he is entitled to freedom of thought, freedom of speech, freedom of assembly; that he has the right to worship God according to the dictates of his conscience. In this positive declaration, we imply that organizations or churches which deprive the individual of these inherent rights are not in harmony with God's will nor with his revealed word. . . . [CR, Apr. 1954, "Civil Rights"]

Elder Hugh B. Brown • 2 Nephi 26:33

During recent months, both in Salt Lake City and across the nation, considerable interest has been expressed in the position of The Church of Jesus Christ of Latter-day Saints on the matter of civil rights. We would like it to be known that there is in this Church no doctrine, belief, or practice that is intended to deny the enjoyment of full civil rights by any person regardless of race, color, or creed.

We say again, as we have said many times before, that we believe that all men are the children of the same God, and that it is a moral evil for any person or group of persons to deny any human being the right to gainful employment, or full educational opportunity, and to every privilege of citizenship, just as it is a moral evil to deny him the right to worship according to the dictates of his own conscience.

We have consistently and persistently upheld the Constitution of the United States, and as far as we are concerned this means upholding the constitutional rights of every citizen of the United States.

We call upon all men, everywhere, both within and outside the Church, to commit themselves to the establishment of full civil equality for all of God's children. Anything less than this defeats our high ideal of the brotherhood of man. . . . [CR, Oct. 1963; or *Improvement Era*, Dec. 1963, 1058]

Challenges to Eternal Life:

1. Be cognizant of the mighty miracles, signs, and wonders that are being manifest among the Lord's people today. Acknowledge the power of the Holy Ghost that is among us (2 Nephi 26:13).

2. Make a conscious effort to seek the welfare of Zion in your everyday life in Zion not just on Sunday (2 Nephi 26:29–30).

3. Consider the many doctrines that are taught in this section of the Book of Mormon and commit to live by those doctrines.

4. Choose a challenge of your own from the reading and apply it to your life.

Chapter Twenty

The Fall of Satan

2 Nephi 28–29; 23–24

*H*istorical Setting: Sometime between 559 and 545 B.C. Nephi continued his prophecies of the day when the Book of Mormon would come forth to the Gentiles.

Precepts of this Reading:

> For behold, thus saith the Lord God: I will give unto the children of men line upon line, precept upon precept, here a little and there a little; and blessed are those who hearken unto my precepts, and lend an ear unto my counsel, for they shall learn wisdom; for unto him that receiveth I will give more; and from them that shall say, We have enough, from them shall be taken away even that which they have. [2 Nephi 28:30]

The four Book of Mormon chapters included in this reading are Nephi's prophecies of the last days (2 Nephi 28–29), and two chapters of Isaiah he had previously written on the plates (2 Nephi 23–24; Isaiah 13–14). Although Nephi's prophecies are not specifically a commentary on these chapters of Isaiah, they are definitely related. An outline of the chapters from 2 Nephi will show this relationship, and prepare us for a deeper study.

OUTLINE • 2 NEPHI 28–29; 23–24

➤ 28:1   Nephi spoke by the Spirit and his words shall come to pass.

➤ 28:2   The book will be of great worth to the children of men, especially to his seed.

➤ 28:3–18   Nephi expounded upon the churches (among the Gentiles) which were not built unto the Lord.

a. Each shall say I am the Lord's church (vv. 3–4).

   1. They shall contend one with another.

   2. Their priests shall contend one with another.

   3. They shall teach their own learning and deny the Holy Ghost.

b. They deny the power of the Holy One of Israel and say: (vv. 5–6).

   1. There is no God, he has done his work and given his power to men.

   2. Believe not miracles. This day he is not a God of miracles.

c. Many shall say eat, drink, and be merry, tomorrow we die and it shall be well with us (v. 7).

d. Many shall say eat, drink, and be merry but fear God—he will justify in committing a little sin. Tomorrow we die and will be beaten with a few stripes and at last be saved (vv. 8–9).

   1. Teach false and vain and foolish doctrines.

   2. Seek deep to hide their counsels from the Lord, work in darkness.

e. The blood of the saints shall cry from the ground against them (v. 10).

f. They have all gone astray and become corrupted (vv. 11–14).

   1. Because of pride, false teachers, and false doctrines.

> 2. They rob the poor because of their fine sanctuaries and clothing.
>
> 3. They persecute the meek and the poor in heart.
>
> 4. They wear stiff necks and high heads.
>
> 5. There are a few humble followers of Christ, but in some instances they err because they are taught by the precepts of men.

g. The Lord warns all of those who pervert the right way of the Lord. They shall be thrust down (vv. 15–17).

> 1. Wo to those who revile against that which is good.
>
> 2. When they are fully ripe in iniquity they shall perish.
>
> 3. Those who repent will not be destroyed.

h. The great and abominable church shall tumble to the earth and great shall be its fall (v. 18).

➤ 28:19–22   The kingdom of the devil must shake and those who belong to it must repent or the devil will grasp them.

a. He shall stir them up to anger against that which is good (v. 20).

b. He will pacify and lull them into carnal security and say all is well in Zion (v. 21).

c. He will flatter and say there is no hell and no devil (v. 22).

d. They are grasped by death and hell and will be judged by their works (vv. 23–28).

> 1. Wo to those at ease in Zion.
>
> 2. Wo to those who cry all is well.
>
> 3. Wo to those who hearken to the precepts of men and deny the power of God and the gift of the Holy Ghost.
>
> 4. Wo to those who say we have received and need no more.
>
> 5. Wo to all who are angry because of the truth of God.

        e.   Wo to those who say they have received the word of God and need no more (vv. 29–31).

            1.   Nephi quotes Isaiah 28:13 outlining how the Lord gives revelation and explains what happens when it is received or rejected.

            2.   Cursed is the man who hearkens to the precepts of men unless the precepts are given by the power of the Holy Ghost. (This verse may originally have been a part of Isaiah.)

        f.   Wo to the Gentiles saith the Lord God of Hosts (v. 32).

            1.   Although the Lord will lengthen out his arm to them, they will deny him.

            2.   He will be merciful if they will repent and come unto him.

➤ 29:1–3   There will be many Gentiles who will say "A Bible, a Bible! We have a Bible and there cannot be any more Bible."

        a.   The Lord will remember his covenants and set his hand the second time to recover his people, the house of Israel (v. 1).

        b.   He will remember his promise to Nephi and his father that Nephi's words would go to the ends of the earth for a standard to the house of Israel (v. 2).

➤ 29:4–14   The Lord answers the Gentiles who say they have a Bible and need no more Bible.

        a.   Fools, the Bible shall proceed from the Jews, what thank ye the Jews for it (v. 4).

        b.   Ye Gentiles have cursed them and hated them and not sought to recover them. These things will return on your own heads (v. 5).

        c.   There are more nations than one. I created all men and remember those on the isles of the sea and will bring forth my word unto all the nations (vv. 6–7).

        d.   The testimony of two nations is a witness that I am God (vv. 8–9).

1. I remember one nation like unto another and speak the same words to each.
2. When the two nations run together, the testimony of the two nations run together also.
3. I prove unto many that I am the same God yesterday, today, and forever.

e. Because ye have a Bible do not suppose you have all my words, neither need ye suppose that I have not caused more to be written (vv. 10–12).

1. I command all men in the east, west, north, and south and isles of the sea to write.
2. I will judge every man according to that which is written.
3. I speak to the Jews, the Nephites, the other tribes, and they shall write it.
4. I also speak to all the nations of the earth, and they shall write it.

f. The Jews shall have the words of the Nephites, the Nephites shall have the words of the Jews, and the Nephites and the Jews shall have the words of the lost tribes, and the lost tribes shall have the words of the Jews and the Nephites (v. 13).

g. The house of Israel shall be gathered unto the lands of their possession and the Lord's word shall be gathered in one (v. 14).

h. The Lord will show unto all who fight against his word and his people that he covenanted with Abraham that he would remember his seed (v. 14).

➤ 23:1 The burden of Babylon that Isaiah saw. The superstructure.

➤ 23:2–5 The ensign is to be lifted upon a high mountain.

a. Those who respond to this call are invited into the gates of the nobles (v. 2).

b. The whole land of Babylon will be destroyed (v. 5).

➤ 23:6–18   Destruction will come at the day of the Lord (the Second Coming).

   a.   Fear, pain, and amazement will come upon men (vv. 7–8).

   b.   The land will be laid desolate and sinners destroyed (v. 9).

   c.   Wonders will appear in the heavens (v. 10).

   d.   The destruction of the wicked will leave but a few men (vv. 11–12).

   e.   The earth will remove from her place (v. 13).

   f.   Men will be chased, children killed, goods spoiled, wives ravished (vv. 14–18).

➤ 23:19–22   Ancient Babylon will be overthrown as was Sodom and Gomorrah.

   a.   Babylon will never be inhabited by man (v. 20).

   b.   Wild beasts will have the land (vv. 21–22).

➤ 24:1–3   The house of Israel will be established in its own land.

   a.   Strangers (Gentiles) will be joined with them (v. 1).

   b.   Israel will rule over the Gentiles (v. 2).

   c.   Israel will rest from her sorrow and bondage (v. 3).

➤ 24:4–14   A proverb will be taken up against the king of Babylon in the day of Israel's restoration.

   a.   Satan will be cast from the earth (v. 4–8).

   b.   He will be received in hell, where he is cast (vv. 9–11).

   c.   Though he fell from heaven, he aspires to be God (vv. 12–14).

   d.   He will fall into hell (spirit prison) and be scorned (vv. 15–17).

   e.   He will eventually be cast out of hell into outer darkness (vv. 18–21).

➤ 24:22–27   As the Lord has said, so it will happen.

a. The Lord will rise up against Babylon (vv. 22–23).

b. He will tread down the king of Assyria (the Gentiles) (v. 25).

c. His hand will be upon all nations (vv. 26–27).

➤ 24:28 This revelation was given in the year King Ahaz died.

➤ 24:29–32 The Lord will establish Zion.

a. Palestine will not rejoice over Assyria's fall (vv. 29–30).

b. Another devastation will come from the north to make Palestine cry (v. 31.).

c. A reason to rejoice is given: Zion will be established and the poor of the Lord will trust in Zion (v. 32).

NOTES AND COMMENTARY

Introduction: On March 8, 1831, the Lord warned the people of his church of "the doctrines of devils, or the commandments of men; for some are of men, and others of devils" (D&C 46:7; see also 3 Nephi 27:10–12). Nephi gives a similar but more detailed warning. He also gives some guidelines for recognizing revelations that come from God.

2 Nephi 28:1–2 • Of Great Worth to the Children of Men

1 And now, behold, my brethren, I have spoken unto you, according as the Spirit hath constrained me; wherefore, I know that they must surely come to pass.

2 And the things which shall be written out of the book shall be of great worth unto the children of men, and especially unto our seed, which is a remnant of the house of Israel.

Nephi bears his testimony regarding what he has spoken, and of the value of the Book of Mormon in bringing about the blessings promised by Isaiah.

2 Nephi 28:3–8 • The Churches and Revelations of Men

3 For it shall come to pass in that day that the churches which are built up, and not unto the Lord, when the one shall say unto the other: Behold, I, I am the Lord's; and the others shall say: I, I am the Lord's; and thus shall every one say that hath built up churches, and not unto the Lord—

4 And they shall contend one with another; and their priests shall contend one with another, and they shall teach with their learning, and deny the Holy Ghost, which giveth utterance.

5 And they deny the power of God, the Holy One of Israel; and they say unto the people: Hearken unto us, and hear ye our precept; for behold there is no God today, for the Lord and the Redeemer hath done his work, and he hath given his power unto men;

6 Behold, hearken ye unto my precept; if they shall say there is a miracle wrought by the hand of the Lord, believe it not; for this day he is not a God of miracles; he hath done his work.

7 Yea, and there shall be many which shall say: Eat, drink, and be merry, for tomorrow we die; and it shall be well with us.

8 And there shall also be many which shall say: Eat, drink, and be merry; nevertheless, fear God—he will justify in committing a little sin; yea, lie a little, take the advantage of one because of his words, dig a pit for thy neighbor; there is no harm in this; and do all these things, for tomorrow we die; and if it so be that we are guilty, God will beat us with a few stripes, and at last we shall be saved in the kingdom of God.

The day of which Nephi speaks is the day spoken of by Isaiah, when the Book of Mormon comes forth (2 Nephi 27; Isaiah 29). These verses describe the teachings of the various churches in Joseph Smith's day. All claim to be the Lord's church (v. 3) and contend with one another over which one is right (v. 4). Nephi's description fits perfectly the situation in Joseph Smith's teen years that led him to ask, "which of all the sects was right?" (JS—History 1:18).

5 Some time in the second year after our removal to Manchester,

there was in the place where we lived an unusual excitement on the subject of religion. It commenced with the Methodists, but soon became general among all the sects in that region of country. Indeed, the whole district of country seemed affected by it, and great multitudes united themselves to the different religious parties, which created no small stir and division amongst the people, some crying, "Lo, here!" and others, "Lo, there!" Some were contending for the Methodist faith, some for the Presbyterian, and some for the Baptist. [JS—History 1:5]

Because of the religious fervor that spread throughout the country, historians refer to the time as the "burned over district," one religious revival after another.

The mission of the Holy Ghost is to "teach you in all things and bring all things to your remembrance" (John 14:26). Without the Holy Ghost, which Nephi sees the priests are denying, they are left to their own reasoning and learning (v. 4). It was the same condition that Paul warned against: "Ever learning, and never able to come to the knowledge of the truth" (1 Timothy 3:7).

Denying revelation or the power of God by saying God does not work with men today, that his work was completed in Jesus' day (v. 5) infers that God is unfair and a respecter of persons. As Nephi said earlier "all are alike unto God" (2 Nephi 26:33). Jesus reveals the answer to this false supposition in the following chapter (2 Nephi 29) so we will leave further response until then. Those who deny miracles, again saying God has done his work, that miracles ended with the apostles of old (v. 6), are without faith. In Mormon's word; "if these things [miracles] have ceased, then has faith ceased also; and awful is the state of man, for they are as though there had been no redemption made" (Moroni 7:38).

The churches teaching that all will be saved eventually, that this life is just to experience mortality (v. 7), is a slight variation of Satan's alternate plan to the Father's—the idea that was rejected in the beginning in which Satan said "I will be thy son, and I will redeem all mankind that one soul shall not be lost, and surely I will do it; wherefore give me thine honor," thus he "sought to destroy the agency of man" (Moses 4: 1, 3). Agency is the gift of God that allows men "to act for themselves and not be acted upon" (2 Nephi 2:26) as was discussed in Chapter 2 of this work.

Those who say God "will justify in committing a little sin . . . there is no harm in this . . . and at last we shall be saved in the kingdom of God" (v. 8) are saying in the language of our day that God loves all his children unconditionally, no one is perfect, he doesn't expect perfection. Jesus taught: "I would that ye should be perfect even as I, or your Father who is in heaven is perfect" (3 Nephi 12:48; see also Matthew 5:48). God's love is perfect (1 John 4:18), but there are conditions placed upon his blessing his children. As Nephi said, "the Lord esteemeth all flesh in one; he that is righteous is favored of God" (1 Nephi 17:35). In a modern revelation, the Lord said: "If you keep not my commandments, the love of the Father shall not continue with you, therefore you shall walk in darkness" (D&C 95:12). Nephi is warning us against this reasoning.

2 Nephi 28:9–14 • All Have Become Corrupted

9 Yea, and there shall be many which shall teach after this manner, false and vain and foolish doctrines, and shall be puffed up in their hearts, and shall seek deep to hide their counsels from the Lord; and their works shall be in the dark.

10 And the blood of the saints shall cry from the ground against them.

11 Yea, they have all gone out of the way; they have become corrupted.

12 Because of pride, and because of false teachers, and false doctrine, their churches have become corrupted, and their churches are lifted up; because of pride they are puffed up.

13 They rob the poor because of their fine sanctuaries; they rob the poor because of their fine clothing; and they persecute the meek and the poor in heart, because in their pride they are puffed up.

14 They wear stiff necks and high heads; yea, and because of pride, and wickedness, and abominations, and whoredoms, they have all

gone astray save it be a few, who are the humble followers of Christ; nevertheless, they are led, that in many instances they do err because they are taught by the precepts of men.

Nephi describes the functioning and conditions of all the churches, or "the Apostasy" as known in Church literature. Although the Apostasy began shortly after Christ organized the Church in the meridian of time, Nephi describes the churches in the day when the Book of Mormon came forth. All of the churches had become corrupt, but various churches had different teachings and practices, as noted by Nephi's periodic "there shall be many which say" (vv. 7, 9). He mentioned several of the false doctrines, but "after this manner" (v. 9) tells us that there are other doctrines that he did not mention. Isaiah 29:15 (2 Nephi 27:27) says that the churches of this time sought to hide their counsels from the Lord (v. 9). This suggests that the leadership of the churches knew they were doing something wrong, and formed a bureaucracy that worked in darkness rather than in the light of Christ.

The blood of the Saints (v. 10) is a declaration of many members of the true church that were killed because of the apostasy that took place when other churches began to form. The blood crying from the ground is a demand that justice take its course. Mercy cannot rob justice (see Alma 42:24–25), and because those who brought about the apostasy knew what they were doing, they will be accountable for those murders. The Lord declared unto Cain "thy brothers blood [Abel's] crieth unto me from the ground" (Genesis 4:10). Jehu, the newly anointed king over Israel was told: "Thus saith the LORD God of Israel, I have anointed thee king over the people of the LORD, *even* over Israel. And thou shalt smite the house of Ahab thy master, that I may avenge the blood of my servants the prophets, and the blood of all the servants of the LORD, at the hand of Jezebel" (2 Kings 9:6–7). Thus, Nephi is saying that all of the Saints that were killed following the time of Christ would also require justice to take its course. It would require justice to come upon those wicked people who opposed the restoration of the gospel when the Book of Mormon came forth. The martyrs would include Joseph and Hyrum Smith and others of whom the Lord said:

> 34 Thy brethren have rejected you and your testimony, even the nation that has driven you out;
>
> 35 And now cometh the day of their calamity, even the days of sorrow, like a woman that is taken in travail; and their sorrow shall be great unless they speedily repent, yea, very speedily.
>
> 36 For they killed the prophets, and them that were sent unto them; and they have shed innocent blood, which crieth from the ground against them. [D&C 136:34–36]

Nephi pronounces the complete apostasy that would occur. All of the churches were included and a chief factor, along with the false teachers and false doctrines, was that of pride (vv. 11–12). Fine sanctuaries, fine clothing, persecution, wickedness, abominations, and whoredoms all came about because of pride (v. 13).

Although there has been a complete apostasy, Nephi recognizes the few humble followers of Christ who are nevertheless led astray by the precepts or teachings of men. The prophet Joseph Smith gave this description of these people: "For there are many yet on the earth among all sects, parties, and denominations, who are blinded by the subtle craftiness of men, whereby they lie in wait to deceive, and who are only kept from the truth because they know not where to find it" (D&C 123:12).

2 Nephi 28:15–17 • Wo to All who Pervert the Right Way of the Lord

> 15 O the wise, and the learned, and the rich, that are puffed up in the pride of their hearts, and all those who preach false doctrines, and all those who commit whoredoms, and pervert the right way of the Lord, wo, wo, wo be unto them, saith the Lord God Almighty, for they shall be thrust down to hell!
>
> 16 Wo unto them that turn aside the just for a thing of naught and revile against that which is good, and say that it is of no worth! For the day shall come that the Lord God will speedily visit the inhabitants

of the earth; and in that day that they are fully ripe in iniquity they shall perish.

17 But behold, if the inhabitants of the earth shall repent of their wickedness and abominations they shall not be destroyed, saith the Lord of Hosts.

Nephi is quoting the Lord in all three of these verses, but he does not give the source. It is both a warning (vv. 15–16) and a plea for the sinners to repent (v. 17). When a people are "fully ripe in iniquity" (v. 16), then comes "the fullness of the wrath of God," and he "destroyeth the nations of the wicked" (1 Nephi 17:35, 37).

2 Nephi 28:18–19 • The Fall of the Great and Abominable Church

18 But behold, that great and abominable church, the whore of all the earth, must tumble to the earth, and great must be the fall thereof.

19 For the kingdom of the devil must shake, and they which belong to it must needs be stirred up unto repentance, or the devil will grasp them with his everlasting chains, and they be stirred up to anger, and perish;

20 For behold, at that day shall he rage in the hearts of the children of men, and stir them up to anger against that which is good.

The fall of the great and abominable church, she who brought about the apostasy and "slayeth the saints of God, yea, and tortureth them and bindeth them down. . . , and bringeth them down into captivity" (1 Nephi 13:5), is foretold by Nephi. This would include all the churches he had just described. He had previously given this description of the same churches:

23 For the time speedily shall come that all churches which are built up to get gain, and all those who are built up to get power over the flesh, and those who are built up to become popular in the eyes of the world, and those who seek the lusts of the flesh and the things of the world, and to do all manner of iniquity; yea, in fine, all those who belong to the kingdom of the devil are they who need fear, and

tremble, and quake; they are those who must be brought low in the dust; they are those who must be consumed as stubble; and this is according to the words of the prophet. [1 Nephi 22:23]

Nephi's prophecy may have been based upon Isaiah (see 2 Nephi 24:4–24; Isaiah 14:4–24). John the Revelator saw and foretold the fall of Babylon, which he uses to represent the great and abominable church.

8 And there followed another angel, saying, Babylon is fallen, is fallen, that great city, because she made all nations drink of the wine of the wrath of her fornication.

9 And the third angel followed them, saying with a loud voice, If any man worship the beast and his image, and receive *his* mark in his forehead, or in his hand,

10 The same shall drink of the wine of the wrath of God, which is poured out without mixture into the cup of his indignation; and he shall be tormented with fire and brimstone in the presence of the holy angels, and in the presence of the Lamb:

11 And the smoke of their torment ascendeth up for ever and ever: and they have no rest day nor night, who worship the beast and his image, and whosoever receiveth the mark of his name. [Revelation 14:8–11; see also chapters 17 and 18]

2 Nephi 28:20–23 • The Doctrines of the Devils

20 For behold, at that day shall he rage in the hearts of the children of men, and stir them up to anger against that which is good.

21 And others will he pacify, and lull them away into carnal security, that they will say: All is well in Zion; yea, Zion prospereth, all is well—and thus the devil cheateth their souls, and leadeth them away carefully down to hell.

22 And behold, others he flattereth away, and telleth them there is no hell; and he saith unto them: I am no devil, for there is none— and thus he whispereth in their ears, until he grasps them with his awful chains, from whence there is no deliverance.

23 Yea, they are grasped with death, and hell; and death, and hell, and the devil, and all that have been seized therewith must stand

before the throne of God, and be judged according to their works, from whence they must go into the place prepared for them, even a lake of fire and brimstone, which is endless torment.

Nephi outlines three ways in which Satan brings his people into his captivity. They are: (1) He stirs them up to anger against that which is good; (2) He pacifies them by saying all is well in Zion and leads them carefully down to hell; and (3) flatters them into believing that there is no hell and no devil. Those who follow any or all of Satan's methods will end up in endless torment (v. 23). Endless punishment is often misunderstood. In a revelation to the Prophet Joseph the Lord explained:

> 6 Nevertheless, it is not written that there shall be no end to this torment, but it is written *endless torment.*
>
> 7 Again, it is written *eternal damnation;* wherefore it is more express than other scriptures, that it might work upon the hearts of the children of men, altogether for my name's glory.
>
> 8 Wherefore, I will explain unto you this mystery, for it is meet unto you to know even as mine apostles.
>
> 9 I speak unto you that are chosen in this thing, even as one, that you may enter into my rest.
>
> 10 For, behold, the mystery of godliness, how great is it! For, behold, I am endless, and the punishment which is given from my hand is endless punishment, for Endless is my name. Wherefore—
>
> 11 Eternal punishment is God's punishment.
>
> 12 Endless punishment is God's punishment. [D&C 19:6–12]

An analysis of Satan's methods of captivating people shows that he has a program for all people. Although there is an overlapping, the stirring up to anger usually works with people who lack understanding, or are not educated about the things of God. Those who are apathetic, or middle of the roaders, are usually content to not be involved and do nothing about the environment of sin and corruption. This is often referred to as the middle class. Flattery seems to work best with those who think they are a little more learned than others, the pseudo-intellectuals (see 2 Nephi 9:28). They rationalize or reason their way out of believing in a Satan or a hell, and thus feel they are of a higher class or status. Satan will use whatever program will work, and if one doesn't work he will try another (see also D&C 10:20–27).

2 Nephi 28:24–29 • A Series of Warnings

24 Therefore, wo be unto him that is at ease in Zion!

25 Wo be unto him that crieth: All is well!

26 Yea, wo be unto him that hearkeneth unto the precepts of men, and denieth the power of God, and the gift of the Holy Ghost!

27 Yea, wo be unto him that saith: We have received, and we need no more!

28 And in fine, wo unto all those who tremble, and are angry because of the truth of God! For behold, he that is built upon the rock receiveth it with gladness; and he that is built upon a sandy foundation trembleth lest he shall fall.

29 Wo be unto him that shall say: We have received the word of God, and we need no more of the word of God, for we have enough!

The chapter concludes with a series of wo's based upon the teachings and functions of the evil churches and of the devil. The following chart associates the wo with the teaching or function.

Wo		**Teaching**	
v. 24–25	At ease in Zion	v. 21	Zion prospereth
v. 26	Precepts of men, deny the power of God	v. 4–5, 31	Teach their own learning
		v. 20	That which is good
v. 28	Angry with the truth of God	v. 5–6	The Redeemer has done his work
v. 27–29	We have received enough		

2 Nephi 28:30–32 • Revelation Comes Line upon Line

30 For behold, thus saith the Lord God: I will give unto the children of men line upon line, precept upon precept, here a little and there a little; and blessed are those who hear-

13 But the word of the LORD was unto them precept upon precept, precept upon precept; line upon line, line upon line; here a little, *and* there a little; that they might go, and

ken unto my precepts, and lend an ear unto my counsel, for they shall learn wisdom; for unto him that receiveth I will give more; and from them that shall say, We have enough, from them shall be taken away even that which they have. [2 Nephi 28:30]

fall backward, and be broken, and snared, and taken. [Isaiah 28:13]

> 31 Cursed is he that putteth his trust in man, or maketh flesh his arm, or shall hearken unto the precepts of men, save their precepts shall be given by the power of the Holy Ghost.
>
> 32 Wo be unto the Gentiles, saith the Lord God of Hosts! For notwithstanding I shall lengthen out mine arm unto them from day to day, they will deny me; nevertheless, I will be merciful unto them, saith the Lord God, if they will repent and come unto me; for mine arm is lengthened out all the day long, saith the Lord God of Hosts.

Nephi quotes Isaiah (2 Nephi 28:30; Isaiah 28:13), as a wo or warning to those who say we need no more of the word of God. The King James text does not make sense, sounding as if God will punish those who receive revelation line upon line. The Book of Mormon text, quoting the Lord but not attributing it to Isaiah, is obviously the original text of Isaiah before plain and precious parts were lost. Those who accept revelation will receive more, line upon line. Those who say they have enough will lose even that which they had received. The fulfillment of Isaiah's words is exemplified in all ages of the world when apostasy sets in, and in our own day when people fall away from the church. Verse 31 may also have once been a part of the Isaiah text, but it is not in present-day Bibles.

The last verse (32) is also quoting the Lord, but the source is not identified. It is probably addressed to the Gentiles because they are the people among whom the Book of Mormon came. The warning is given in preparation for what Nephi says in 2 Nephi 29.

2 Nephi 29:1–3 • Nephi's Writings, A Standard to the People

1 But behold, there shall be many—at that day when I shall proceed to do a marvelous work among them, that I may remember my covenants which I have made unto the children of men, that I may set my hand again the second time to recover my people, which are of the house of Israel;

2 And also, that I may remember the promises which I have made unto thee, Nephi, and also unto thy father, that I would remember your seed; and that the words of your seed should proceed forth out of my mouth unto your seed; and my words shall hiss forth unto the ends of the earth, for a standard unto my people, which are of the house of Israel;

3 And because my words shall hiss forth—many of the Gentiles shall say: A Bible! A Bible! We have got a Bible, and there cannot be any more Bible.

Having warned against rejecting more of the word of God (28:29–30), Nephi identifies the time when there shall come forth more of the word of God. It will be when the Lord sets his "hand again the second time to recover [his] people . . . the house of Israel," as he had covenanted to do (v. 1). In speaking of this second gathering, Nephi is quoting from Isaiah 11:11, a chapter that the angel Moroni told Joseph Smith, in September 1823, "was about to be fulfilled" (JS—History 1:40). Moroni had also stated, when he was abridging the Jaredite records, that "when ye shall receive this record [the Book of Mormon] ye may know that the work of the Father [the gathering of Israel] has commenced upon all the face of the land" (Ether 4:17).

The Lord reminds Nephi of the promise made to him and his father that the words of their seed, the Book of Mormon, would be brought forth unto their seed (v. 2). We have no specific account of the Lord's promise to Nephi and Lehi, but we do have the same promise given to Enos, son of Jacob, grandson of Lehi.

16 And I had faith, and I did cry unto God that he would preserve the records; and he covenanted with me that he would bring them forth

unto the Lamanites in his own due time.

17 And I, Enos, knew it would be according to the covenant which he had made; wherefore my soul did rest.

18 And the Lord said unto me: Thy fathers have also required of me this thing; and it shall be done unto them according to their faith; for their faith was like unto thine. [Enos 1:16–18]

"Thy fathers" (v. 18) may be a general reference to Nephi and Lehi, or perhaps Enos' father Jacob was also given this promise.

Another promise of the Lord was that the words of Nephi's seed, the Lord's word (the Book of Mormon) would "hiss forth unto the ends of the earth for a standard unto . . . the house of Israel." This interprets more of the words of Isaiah. The phrase "for a standard unto my people" is a paraphrase of Isaiah 49:22 (1 Nephi 21:22) which speaks of the Gentiles being nursed through this standard. Therefore, we can identify the standard spoken of by Isaiah as the Book of Mormon. To "hiss forth unto the ends of the earth" is a paraphrase of Isaiah 5:26 (2 Nephi 15:26), and interprets the ensign used in that same verse as the Book of Mormon. The lifting up of a banner spoken of in Isaiah 13:2 (2 Nephi 23:2) also refers to the Book of Mormon.

The same Hebrew word may be translated as "standard," "ensign," or "banner." Thus from 2 Nephi 29:2 we learn that all of these words in the Book of Isaiah are references to the Book of Mormon. Nephi also equates the Book of Mormon with the "marvelous work" of the latter days (v. 1). When Jesus visited the Nephites, in referring to the Book of Mormon, he spoke of "a marvelous work" that his servant would "bring forth unto the Gentiles" (Nephi 21:9–11).

Coming back to the concept with which Nephi began this chapter, the reaction of the Book of Mormon coming forth, he identifies "the many" of whom he speaks as being the Gentiles among whom the Book of Mormon would be brought forth. Their reaction of "A Bible! A Bible! We have got a Bible, and there cannot be any more Bible" (v. 3), is the reaction that Nephi had warned against earlier; "we need no more of the word of God, for we have enough" (28:29).

2 Nephi 29:4–6 • What Thank They the Jews for the Bible?

4 But thus saith the Lord God: O fools, they shall have a Bible; and it shall proceed forth from the Jews, mine ancient covenant people. And what thank they the Jews for the Bible which they receive from them? Yea, what do the Gentiles mean? Do they remember the travails, and the labors, and the pains of the Jews, and their diligence unto me, in bringing forth salvation unto the Gentiles?

5 O ye Gentiles, have ye remembered the Jews, mine ancient covenant people? Nay; but ye have cursed them, and have hated them, and have not sought to recover them. But behold, I will return all these things upon your own heads; for I the Lord have not forgotten my people.

6 Thou fool, that shall say: A Bible, we have got a Bible, and we need no more Bible. Have ye obtained a Bible save it were by the Jews?

The response of the Lord to the Gentile's reactions to the Book of Mormon is well known among the Latter-day Saints and needs no commentary. However, the same might be said concerning the travails and labors of many through the dark ages in copying and preserving the biblical record through those perilous times.

2 Nephi 29:7–12 • The Testimony of Two Nations

7 Know ye not that there are more nations than one? Know ye not that I, the Lord your God, have created all men, and that I remember those who are upon the isles of the sea; and that I rule in the heavens above and in the earth beneath; and I bring forth my word unto the children of men, yea, even upon all the nations of the earth?

8 Wherefore murmur ye, because that ye shall receive more of my word? Know ye not that the testimony of two nations is a witness unto you that I am God, that I remember one nation like unto another? Wherefore, I speak the same words unto one nation like unto another. And when the two nations shall run together the testimony of the two nations shall run together also.

9 And I do this that I may prove unto many that I am the same

yesterday, today, and forever; and that I speak forth my words according to mine own pleasure. And because that I have spoken one word ye need not suppose that I cannot speak another; for my work is not yet finished; neither shall it be until the end of man, neither from that time henceforth and forever.

10 Wherefore, because that ye have a Bible ye need not suppose that it contains all my words; neither need ye suppose that I have not caused more to be written.

11 For I command all men, both in the east and in the west, and in the north, and in the south, and in the islands of the sea, that they shall write the words which I speak unto them; for out of the books which shall be written I will judge the world, every man according to their works, according to that which is written.

12 For behold, I shall speak unto the Jews and they shall write it; and I shall also speak unto the Nephites and they shall write it; and I shall also speak unto the other tribes of the house of Israel, which I have led away, and they shall write it; and I shall also speak unto all nations of the earth and they shall write it.

These verses show the Lord's law of witnesses as he commands his words to be written among all the peoples of the earth. Four records are identified (v. 12).

1. The record of the Jews = the Bible
2. The record of the Nephites = the Book of Mormon
3. The record of the lost tribes = yet to come forth
4. The record to all the nations of the earth = the Doctrine and Covenants, "the voice of the Lord unto all men" (D&C 1:1–4)

The Lord remembers all men. He speaks to one nation like unto another. Men need not suppose that the Bible contains all his words. These statements are the answers to the precepts of men that there is no God today for he has done his work as spoken of in 2 Nephi 28:5–6.

2 Nephi 29:13–14 • All to Have the Record When Gathered

13 And it shall come to pass that the Jews shall have the words of the Nephites, and the Nephites shall have the words of the Jews; and the Nephites and the Jews shall have the words of the lost tribes of Israel; and the lost tribes of Israel shall have the words of the Nephites and the Jews.

14 And it shall come to pass that my people, which are of the house of Israel, shall be gathered home unto the lands of their possessions; and my word also shall be gathered in one. And I will show unto them that fight against my word and against my people, who are of the house of Israel, that I am God, and that I covenanted with Abraham that I would remember his seed forever.

All three of these records will eventually be had by each of the other three groups of the house of Israel. In doing so the Lord will establish his word in the mouth of two or more witnesses. These tribes will also be gathered to their promised lands of inheritance, and that part of the covenant of Abraham will then be fulfilled.

2 Nephi 23–24 • (Isaiah 13–14)

There is undoubtedly a dual message within these two chapters. The basic message is against the old Babylon, which existed before Isaiah's time and became a world power under King Nebuchadnezzar after Assyria's downfall, and after the ministry of Isaiah. Babylon became the epitome of wickedness in the ancient world, and was used by the Lord as the symbol of the wicked world when he commanded: "Go ye out from among the nations, even from Babylon, from the midst of wickedness, which is spiritual Babylon" (D&C 133:14).

The same symbolism is used in the Book of Revelation (14:8–11; chapters 17–18). Thus a greater message is given to modern-day Babylon, the wickedness of our world. It is often difficult to know which Babylon the text is referring to, and it may be that sometimes if refers to both at the same time. Because Nephi included these two chapters in the Book of Mormon record, it would appear that the majority of the text refers to the latter days.

Chapter 24 (Isaiah 14) contains an interesting proverb against the king of Babylon. Babylon represents the wicked world, and the king of that wickedness is none other than Satan himself. The graphic description of Satan's fall is most interesting.

There are several significant retentions in the Book of Mormon text that aid in understanding the message.

2 Nephi 23:1–2 (Isaiah 13:1–2) • A Banner Upon the High Mountain

> 1 The burden of Babylon, which Isaiah the son of Amoz did see.
>
> 2 Lift ye up **a** banner upon the high mountain, exalt the voice unto them, shake the hand, that they may go into the gates of the nobles.

The burden of Babylon (v. 1) is the message of doom or the inevitable downfall of Babylon. That the Babylon spoken of here includes more than ancient Babylon is obvious from the rest of the chapter that clearly speaks of the time of the Second Coming of Christ. "Spiritual Babylon," identified above (D&C 133:14), will fall at the time of the Second Coming. Various other sections in the Doctrine and Covenants use Babylon in this context (see D&C 1:16; 35:11; 64:24; 86:3). The book of Revelation, also cited above, speaks of the same time period. Jeremiah chapters 50 and 51 contain the words of the Lord against Babylon. His prophecies are more detailed than Isaiah's and seem to be directed toward ancient Babylon.

The word "banner" (v. 2) may be better translated "ensign," as in Isaiah 5:26. The King James translators rendered the same Hebrew word in three different ways: ensign (Isaiah 11:10), banner (Isaiah 13:2), and standard (Isaiah 62:10). The Book of Mormon uses the word "banner," but the Joseph Smith Translation reads "my banner," which clarifies that it was the Lord's banner that was to be raised. The banner or ensign being lifted up upon the high mountain may also be the establishment of the kingdom of God, as in Isaiah 2:2. The exalted voice in 2 Nephi 23:2 could be the "voice of the Lord" crying, "Go ye out of Babylon" (D&C 133:4–8; Isaiah 52:11). "That they may go into the gates of the noble" is an invitation for all who accept the restored gospel "who are among the Gentiles [to] flee to Zion. And let them who be of Judah flee unto Jerusalem" (D&C 133:12–13; compare Revelation 18:4).

2 Nephi 23:3–5 (Isaiah 13:3–5) • I Have Commanded my Sanctified Ones

3 I have commanded my sanctified ones, I have also called my mighty ones, for mine anger **is not upon** them that rejoice in my highness.

4 The noise of the multitude in **the** mountains like as of a great people, a tumultuous noise of the kingdoms of nations gathered together, the Lord of Hosts mustereth the hosts of the battle.

5 They come from a far country, from the end of heaven, **yea**, the Lord, and the weapons of his indignation, to destroy the whole land.

The King James text says "*even* them" instead of the bolded "is not upon them" (v. 14). The italics in the King James text is showing the word was placed there by the translators to make it read better. The other differences bolded (vv. 4–5) are insignificant. These verses, along with verse 2, have the same basic message as the parable of the wheat and the tares.

24 The kingdom of heaven is likened unto a man which sowed good seed in his field:

25 But while men slept, his enemy came and sowed tares among the wheat, and went his way.

26 But when the blade was sprung up, and brought forth fruit, then appeared the tares also. [Matthew 24:24–26]

29 Let both grow together until the harvest, and in the time of harvest, I will say to the reapers, Gather ye together first the wheat into my barn; and the tares are bound in bundles to be burned. (JST, Matthew 13:29; see also D&C 86:1–7]

The messengers who are gathered (2 Nephi 23:3) are to be sent to warn of the coming destruction of Babylon (the tares), and to invite the righteous (the wheat) to gather out. The Book of Mormon retention (v. 3) fits the context of the entire passage better. This gathering includes the forces of heaven (the destroying angels) who will follow the first messengers and will literally destroy the nation of wickedness, spiritual Babylon.

2 Nephi 23:6–8 (Isaiah 13:6–8) • The Day of the Lord is at Hand

> 6 Howl ye, for the day of the Lord is at hand; it shall come as a destruction from the Almighty.

> 7 Therefore shall all hands be faint, every man's heart shall melt;

> 8 And they shall be afraid; pangs and sorrows shall take hold of them; they shall be amazed one at another; their faces shall be as flames.

The day of the Lord is the Second Coming. Following "take hold of them," (v. 8) the KJV has a phrase "they shall be in pain as a woman that travaileth" that is not in the Book of Mormon, but this deletion does not alter the meaning or the context of the verse.

2 Nephi 23:9–10 (Isaiah 13:9–10) • He Shall Destroy the Sinner

> 9 Behold, the day of the Lord cometh, cruel both with wrath and fierce anger, to lay the land desolate; and he shall destroy the sinners thereof out of it.

> 10 For the stars of heaven and the constellations thereof shall not give their light; the sun shall be darkened in his going forth, and the moon shall not cause her light to shine.

After the elect (wheat) is gathered, the sinners (tares) will be destroyed (v. 9). "The destruction of the wicked, which is the end of the [telestial] world" (JS—History 1:4), will be accompanied by changes in the heavens (v. 10). Several scriptures refer to changes in the stars, the sun, and the moon at the time of the Second Coming (see

Joel 2:32; D&C 29:14; 34:9; 45:42; 88:87; 133:49; JS—History 1:33).
2 Nephi 23:11–12 (Isaiah 13:11–12) A Man More Precious than Fine
Gold

> 11 And I will punish the world for evil, and the wicked for their
> iniquity; I will cause the arrogancy of the proud to cease, and will lay
> down the haughtiness of the terrible.

> 12 I will make a man more precious than fine gold; even a man
> than the golden wedge of Ophir.

In the April 1974 general conference, President Spencer W. Kimball stated that it seemed hard for many members of the Church to live
in the world and yet not be of the world. He then quoted verse 11 as
a warning to those who were following worldly ways (see CR, Apr.
1974, 6). The honest or righteous men will be few in comparison to
the wicked and thus more precious than fine gold (v. 12).

2 Nephi 23:13–16 (Isaiah 13:13–16) • The Earth Shall Remove Out of her Place

> 13 Therefore, I will shake the heavens, and the earth shall remove
> out of her place, in the wrath of the Lord of Hosts, and in the day of
> his fierce anger.

> 14 And it shall be as the chased roe, and as a sheep that no man
> taketh up; **and** they shall every man turn to his own people, and flee
> every one into his own land.

> 15 Every one that is **proud** shall be thrust through; yea, and every
> one that is joined **to the wicked** shall fall by the sword.

> 16 Their children also shall be dashed to pieces before their eyes;
> their houses shall be spoiled and their wives ravished.

The cosmological changes that will affect the earth at the time of
Christ's Second Coming (v. 13) is partially quoted or paraphrased in
modern revelation. The Lord says he will "cause the heavens to shake
for your good" (D&C 21:6 and 35:24). Therefore, this movement of
the earth is apparently for the benefit of the righteous and to the
detriment of the wicked. There will be more than the house of Israel

gathering, for every man will flee to his own land (v. 14). The patriarchal orders established after the flood (see Genesis 10) will perhaps
be part of the restoration of this dispensation.

> 10 That in the dispensation of the fulness of times he might gather
> together in one all things in Christ, both which are in heaven, and
> which are on earth; *even* in him: [Ephesians 1:10]

The addition of the bolded "and" (v. 14) is insignificant. However,
the Book of Mormon translation of verse 15 contains some significant
retentions. The King James text states, "every one that is found shall
be thrust through" instead of the bolded "proud." The King James text
would leave no survivors, while the Book of Mormon limits it to the
proud. Also, the King James text says "every one that is joined *unto
them,*" rather than joined "to the wicked." The italics are in the King
James text shows that the words were placed there by the translators
to make it read better. The Book of Mormon retentions point to a
Second Coming prophecy. However, beginning with verse 14, Isaiah
seems to describe the literal conquest of Babylon by the Medes. Thus,
it appears to be a dual prophecy including spiritual Babylon.

2 Nephi 23:17–22 (Isaiah 13:17–22) • Babylon Shall Never be Inhabited Again

> 17 Behold, I will stir up the Medes against them, which shall not
> regard silver and gold, **nor** shall they delight in it.
>
> 18 Their bows shall also dash the young men to pieces; and they
> shall have no pity on the fruit of the womb; their eyes shall not spare
> children.
>
> 19 And Babylon, the glory of kingdoms, the beauty of the
> Chaldees' excellency, shall be as when God overthrew Sodom and
> Gomorrah.
>
> 20 It shall never be inhabited, neither shall it be dwelt in from
> generation to generation: neither shall the Arabian pitch tent there;
> neither shall the shepherds make their fold there.
>
> 21 But wild beasts of the desert shall lie there; and their houses

shall be full of doleful creatures; and owls shall dwell there, and satyrs shall dance there.

22 And the wild beasts of the islands shall cry in their desolate houses, and dragons in their pleasant palaces; and her time is near to come, and her day shall not be prolonged. **For I will destroy her speedily; yea, for I will be merciful unto my people, but the wicked shall perish**.

This prophecy is definitely about ancient Babylon and has been fulfilled. There are about 800 acres of ruins there that have never been inhabited since the destruction. Remains of the destruction can still be seen.

There are some insignificant differences in the King James text (v. 17). The Book of Mormon retains a complete sentence at the end of the chapter (v. 22) regarding the destruction of the wicked and the Lord's mercy to his people—those who will accept him as their God. This ending is a good transition into the next chapter. In commenting on Isaiah's words, Nephi declared that ancient Babylon would be destroyed and that the Jews would therefore be "scattered by other nations" (2 Nephi 25:15).

2 Nephi 24:1–3 (Isaiah 14:1–3) • Israel to Return to Their Lands

1 For the Lord will have mercy on Jacob, and will yet choose Israel, and set them in their own land; and the strangers shall be joined with them, and they shall cleave to the house of Jacob.

2 And the people shall take them and bring them to their place; **yea, from far unto the ends of the earth; and they shall return to their lands of promise**. And the house of Israel shall possess them, **and** the land of the Lord **shall be** for servants and handmaids; and they shall take them captives **unto whom** they were captives; and they shall rule over their oppressors.

3 And it shall come to pass in **that** day that the Lord shall give thee rest, from thy sorrow, and from thy fear, and from the hard bondage wherein thou wast made to serve.

These three verses are an extension of the final thought in the Book of Mormon rendition of Isaiah 13:22. The Lord's mercy will be shown when he gathers his people back to their own land. The strangers who will be joined with them (v. 1) are most probably the Gentiles who will have accepted the gospel while the house of Israel is being gathered. The Book of Mormon retains the bolded eighteen-word retention that emphasizes the extent of the gathering of Israel—"from far unto the ends of the earth"—and establishes that there will be "lands of promise" (more than one) for the gathering (v. 2). The other bolded segments clarify the text and shows a reversal of the ruling class. Whereas Israel had been captive and in bondage to the Gentiles, the Israelites will now rule over their former oppressors (in righteousness). The wording "that day" instead of the KJV "the day," clearly designates the time when Israel will be gathered and free from bondage.

2 Nephi 24:4–8 (Isaiah 14:4–8) • A Proverb Against the King of Babylon

4 **And it shall come to pass in that day**, that thou shalt take up this proverb against the king of Babylon, and say: How hath the oppressor ceased, the golden city ceased!

5 The Lord hath broken the staff of the wicked, the scepters of the rulers.

6 He who smote the people in wrath with a continual stroke, he that ruled the nations in anger, is persecuted, and none hindereth.

7 The whole earth is at rest, and is quiet; they break forth into singing.

8 Yea, the fir-trees rejoice at thee, and **also** the cedars of Lebanon, saying: Since thou art laid down no feller is come up against us.

The Book of Mormon underlining (v. 4) again retains a designation of the time spoken of: "in that day" referring to the gathering of the last days (vv. 1–3).

Verses 4 through 21 are generally considered to be a poem, which Dr. Sidney B. Sperry called "one of the finest examples of Hebrew poetry in the Bible."[1] While the poem contains a description of Satan as the ruler of spiritual Babylon, the message is a dual one. Satan, of course, is described under the guise of the ancient king of Babylon, Nebuchadnezzar.

This section of the poem describes the beginning of the Millennium, when Satan will be bound and the earth will rest. The reference is to rulers who have come under the influence of Satan, and not solely to Nebuchadnezzar or one of his successors. The binding of Satan at the beginning of the thousand years is also prophesied in the New Testament. An angel laid hold of Satan "and bound him a thousand years" (Revelation 20:1–3; see also D&C 88:110; 101:28). The Book of Mormon says that "because of the righteousness of his [the Lord's] people, Satan has no power; wherefore, he cannot be loosed for the space of many years; for he hath no power over the hearts of the people, for they dwell in righteousness, and the Holy One of Israel reigneth" (1 Nephi 22:26). Therefore, three different volumes of scripture testify of his being bound, and Nephi quotes "the prophet," probably Isaiah since he had previously been quoting him, saying "the time cometh speedily that Satan shall have no more power over the hearts of the children of men" (1 Nephi 22:15).

The fir trees rejoicing because no feller (woodsman cutting down the trees) is come up against them (v. 8) is symbolic of the millennium when Satan is bound and "shall not have power to tempt any man" (D&C 101:28).

2 Nephi 24:9–11 (Isaiah 14:9–11)
• The Reception in Hell

> 9 Hell from beneath is moved for thee to meet thee at thy coming; it stirreth up the dead for thee, even all the chief ones of the earth; it hath raised up from their thrones all the kings of the nations.

> 10 All they shall speak and say unto thee: Art thou also become weak as we? Art thou become like unto us?

---

[1] *The Voice of Israel's Prophets* [1965], 44.

11 Thy pomp is brought down to the grave; the noise of thy viols **is not heard**; the worm is spread under thee, and the worms cover thee.

This section of the poem foretells Satan's restriction to the spirit world of hell during the millennial years of peace on earth and describes the reaction of hell's inhabitants when it is announced that he is assigned there. The bolded retention (v. 11, not in the KJV) clarifies the text.

That Satan will have influence in the spirit world is shown by the Prophet Joseph Smith's statement that "when we have power to put all enemies under our feet in this world, and a knowledge to triumph over evil spirits in the world to come, then we are saved" (*TPJS*, 297). Amulek also warned of the devils power there:

34 Ye cannot say, when ye are brought to that awful crisis, that I will repent, that I will return to my God. Nay, ye cannot say this; for that same spirit which doth possess your bodies at the time that ye go out of this life, that same spirit will have power to possess your body in that eternal world.

35 For behold, if ye have procrastinated the day of your repentance even until death, behold, ye have become subjected to the spirit of the devil, and he doth seal you his; therefore, the Spirit of the Lord hath withdrawn from you, and hath no place in you, and the devil hath all power over you; and this is the final state of the wicked. (Alma 34:34–35)

When Satan is bound in the spirit world, "the chief ones of the earth"—those leaders who were influential in the devil's kingdom while they lived upon the earth—will assemble to greet him. When they see him, they will be amazed at his having lost his power (v. 10).

2 Nephi 24:12–14 (Isaiah 14:12–14)
• The Aspirations of Satan

12 How art thou fallen from heaven, O Lucifer, son of the morning! Art thou cut down to the ground, which did weaken the nations!

13 For thou hast said in thy heart: I will ascend into heaven, I will

exalt my throne above the stars of God; I will sit also upon the mount of the congregation, in the sides of the north;

14 I will ascend above the heights of the clouds; I will be like the Most High.

The King James text says; "*how* art thou cut down," and the italicized *how* shows it was placed there by the translators. The punctuation is the same in both texts. The deletions from the Book of Mormon makes the text more sensible.

Isaiah here described Lucifer's fall from heaven in the pre-mortal existence. John the Revelator described the same event:

7 And there was war in heaven: Michael and his angels fought against the dragon; and the dragon fought and his angels,

8 And prevailed not; neither was their place found any more in heaven.

9 And the great dragon was cast out, that old serpent, called the Devil, and Satan, which deceiveth the whole world: he was cast out into the earth, and his angels were cast out with him. [Revelation 12:7–9]

Moses was told why Satan was cast out:

3 Wherefore, because that Satan rebelled against me, and sought to destroy the agency of man, which I, the Lord God, had given him, and also, that I should give unto him mine own power; by the power of mine Only Begotten, I caused that he should be cast down;

4 And he became Satan, yea, even the devil, the father of all lies, to deceive and to blind men, and to lead them captive at his will, even as many as would not hearken unto my voice. [Moses 4:3–4; see also Abraham 3:27–28]

Isaiah's reference to Satan as a "son of the morning" (v. 12) is usually interpreted to mean that he was one of the early spirits born of our Father in Heaven. A vision of his fall, given to Joseph Smith and Sidney Rigdon, enlarges upon his objectives.

25 And this we saw also, and bear record, that an angel of God

who was in authority in the presence of God, who rebelled against the Only Begotten Son whom the Father loved and who was in the bosom of the Father, was thrust down from the presence of God and the Son,

26 And was called Perdition, for the heavens wept over him—he was Lucifer, a son of the morning.

27 And we beheld, and lo, he is fallen! is fallen, even a son of the morning!

28 And while we were yet in the Spirit, the Lord commanded us that we should write the vision; for we beheld Satan, that old serpent, even the devil, who rebelled against God, and sought to take the kingdom of our God and his Christ—

29 Wherefore, he maketh war with the saints of God, and encompasseth them round about. [D&C 76:25–29]

The Saints are the members of the Church and his war with them is to oppose their following the plan of God. His objective—to become God (v. 13)—is echoed by his followers, who are collectively described as "that which . . . seeketh to become a law unto himself" (D&C 88:35). Lehi, getting his information from what he had read, apparently from the plates of brass, further describes Satan's objective:

17 And I, Lehi, according to the things which I have read, must needs suppose that an angel of God, according to that which is written, had fallen from heaven; wherefore, he became a devil, having sought that which was evil before God.

18 And because he had fallen from heaven, and had become miserable forever, he sought also the misery of all mankind. [2 Nephi 2:17–18]

The common slogan "misery loves company" was probably drawn from Satan's objective, to make us miserable because he is miserable.

2 Nephi 24:15–17 (Isaiah 14:15–17)
• Satan's Arrival in Hell

15 Yet thou shalt be brought down to hell, to the sides of the pit.

16 They that see thee shall narrowly look upon thee, and **shall** consider thee, **and shall say**: Is this the man that made the earth to tremble, that did shake kingdoms?

17 **And** made the world as a wilderness, and destroyed the cities thereof, **and** opened not the house of his prisoners?

(The bolded differences in the two texts are insignificant)

Isaiah now prophesies the devil's fall from earth to the spirit prison as the millennium is ushered in (v. 15), and notes that those who inhabit the spirit prison will be astonished (v. 16). Satan, who had such a great influence upon the kingdoms of the earth, is now powerless and unable to do anything for those who are prisoners. As Mormon abridged the records of the Nephites, he warned "those who perverteth the ways of the Lord . . . that the devil will not support his children at the last day, but doth speedily drag them down to hell" (Alma 30:60). The house of the prisoners will not be opened (v. 17) until "the thousand years are expired" (Revelation 20:7).

2 Nephi 24:18–21 (Isaiah 14:18–21)
• Satan Cast Out of Hell

18 All the kings of the nations, **yea**, all of them, lie in glory, every one **of them** in his own house.

19 But thou art cast out of thy grave like an abominable branch, and the **remnant** of those that are slain, thrust through with a sword, that go down to the stones of the pit; as a carcass trodden under feet.

20 Thou shalt not be joined with them in burial, because thou hast destroyed thy land and slain thy people; the seed of evil-doers shall never be renowned.

21 Prepare slaughter for his children for the iniqui**ties** of their fathers, that they do not rise, nor possess the land, nor fill the face of the world with cities.

The King James text says "raiment"(clothing) instead of the bolded "remnant." The Book of Mormon better fits the context of the verse.

The concluding section of the poem describes a further fall of

Satan. "All the kings of the nations, even all of them" will be given some degree of glory in the houses or mansions that they have prepared themselves to receive (v. 18). Satan will not receive any glory, however (v. 19), but will be cast "into outer darkness, where there is weeping, and wailing, and gnashing of teeth" (D&C 133:73).

2 Nephi 24:22–28 (Isaiah 14:22–28)
• The Lord Will Rise on Babylon

> 22 For I will rise up against them, saith the Lord of Hosts, and cut off from Babylon the name, and remnant, and son, and nephew, saith the Lord.
>
> 23 I will also make it a possession for the bittern, and pools of water; and I will sweep it with the besom of destruction, saith the Lord of Hosts.
>
> 24 The Lord of Hosts hath sworn, saying: Surely as I have thought, so shall it come to pass; and as I have purposed, so shall it stand—
>
> 25 That I will **bring** the Assyrian in my land, and upon my mountains tread him under foot; then shall his yoke depart from off them, and his burden depart from off their shoulders.
>
> 26 This is the purpose that is purposed upon the whole earth; and this is the hand that is stretched out upon all nations.
>
> 27 For the Lord of Hosts hath purposed, and who shall disannul? And his hand is stretched out, and who shall turn it back?
>
> 28 In the year that king Ahaz died was this burden.

These verses appear to be directed to ancient Babylon. The word "besom" (v. 13) means the same as our modern word "broom." The context is the same as for those who live in the promised land (the Americas) who "shall serve God, or they shall be swept off when the fullness of his wrath shall come upon them" (Ether 2:9–10).

The King James text says; "I will break the Assyrian in my land" instead of the bolded "bring" the Assyrian,"(v. 25). The message is the same with either word. There is another insignificant deletion in the King James text (v. 26). The Assyrian represents the Gentiles, and the purpose of the Lord is to give all the gentile nations an opportunity to be numbered with Israel (see 3 Nephi 30:1–2). The judgments of God will be poured out upon those who reject this opportunity. Mormon made a similar prophecy concerning the Gentiles after they have an opportunity to accept the gospel.

22 And then, O ye Gentiles, how can ye stand before the power of God, except ye shall repent and turn from your evil ways?

23 Know ye not that ye are in the hands of God? Know ye not that he hath all power, and at his great command the earth shall be rolled together as a scroll?

24 Therefore, repent ye, and humble yourselves before him, lest he shall come out in justice against you—lest a remnant of the seed of Jacob shall go forth among you as a lion, and tear you in pieces, and there is none to deliver. [Mormon 5:22–24]

Isaiah's prophecy of Babylon was given in the year that king Ahaz died (v. 28), but it was not fulfilled at that time. Whether the whole prophecy concerning Babylon was given at that time or the verses that follow is unclear, but it does not really matter, since both have reference to a future and not an immediate time.

2 Nephi 24:29–32 (Isaiah 14:29–32)
• The Lord Hath Founded Zion

29 Rejoice not thou, whole Palestina, because the rod of him that smote thee is broken; for out of the serpent's root shall come forth a cockatrice, and his fruit shall be a fiery flying serpent.

30 And the first-born of the poor shall feed, and the needy shall lie down in safety; and I will kill thy root with famine, and he shall slay thy remnant.

31 Howl, O gate; cry, O city; thou, whole Palestina, art dissolved; for there shall come from the north a smoke, and none shall be alone in his appointed times.

32 What shall then answer the messengers of the nations? That the Lord hath founded Zion, and the poor of his people shall trust in it.

The messengers of the nations (v. 32) are the Lord's servants in the latter days. The message of hope, pronouncing the Lord's work of seeking "to bring forth and establish the cause of Zion" (D&C 6:6) is now well underway and will continue until it is completed.

SACRED WRITING

Revelation Which is Great:

2 Nephi 23:1–24:3	(Isaiah 13:1–14:3) Isaiah sees the future of ancient Babylon and spiritual Babylon, the wickedness of the world.
2 Nephi 24:4–32	(Isaiah 14:4–32) Isaiah's proverb against the king of Babylon (Satan).

Prophesying:

2 Nephi 28	Nephi describes the churches in the day the Book of Mormon will come forth, and the fall of the great and abominable church and the kingdom of the devil.
2 Nephi 29	Nephi tells the reaction of the Gentiles to the Book of Mormon, the Lord's answer to them, and of other records of the Lord to come forth.

Doctrines to be Learned:

2 Nephi 28:18	The great and abominable church must fall.
2 Nephi 28:19	The kingdom of the devil will be shaken, and those who belong to it will perish.
2 Nephi 28:30	Those who accept revelation will be given more, and those who reject it will lose even what they have.
2 Nephi 29:1	Israel will be gathered a second time.
2 Nephi 29:2	The Book of Mormon is a standard for the house of Israel.
2 Nephi 29:4	The Bible comes from the Jews.
2 Nephi 29:8	When two nations come together the testimony of

	God to those nations comes together.
2 Nephi 29:10–13	The Lord speaks to all nations and each nation shall receive the others records.
2 Nephi 29:14	God covenanted to Abraham to remember his seed forever.
2 Nephi 24:13–14	(Isaiah 14:13–14) Satan's objective is to overthrow God and become God himself.
2 Nephi 24:19–20	(Isaiah 14:19–20) Satan will be cast out into a place of no glory.
2 Nephi 24:1–2	(Isaiah 14:1–2) The Lord will return the house of Israel to their promised lands in the last days.

General Authority Quotations

Elder George Albert Smith • 2 Nephi 28:21

"And thus the devil cheateth their souls and leadeth them away carefully down to hell." And that is the way he does it, that's exactly the way [Satan] does it. He does not come and grab you bodily and take you into his territory, but he whispers, 'Do this little evil,' and when he succeeds in that, another little evil and another, and, to use the expression quoted, 'He cheateth their souls.' That's what he does. He makes you believe that you are gaining something when you are losing. So it is every time we fail to observe a law of God or keep a commandment, we are being cheated, because there is no gain in this world or in the world to come but by obedience to the law of our Heavenly Father. Then again, that peculiar suggestion, "And he leadeth them *carefully* away down to hell" is significant, that is his method. Men and woman in the world today are subject to that influence, and they are being drawn here and there, and that whispering is going on and they do not understand what the Lord desires them to do, but they continue in the territory of the evil one, subject to his power where the Spirit of the Lord will not go. [CR, April 1918, 18]

Elder Ezra Taft Benson • 2 Nephi 28:21

I would like to raise this warning, my brothers and sisters. In this period of apparent goodwill—good feelings toward the Church—when it seems as if we have no great obstacle any more as we once had, there should be deep concern. In my judgment, in the hour of our success is our greatest danger. And apparently this is an hour of great success. No more persecution—persecution which once tended to drive us together, and make us united! Now we seem to be accepted by the world. Will it mean disunity? Will it mean that we will rest on our laurels and sit back, as it were, and think that all is well in Zion? I think there is real danger in this period, this period of praise and commendation. I am happy for it, provided we be careful, that we be on our guard. The praise of the world will not save us. It will not exalt us in the celestial kingdom. Only the living of the principles of the gospel will bring us salvation and exaltation. And so I hope that our performance in living the gospel will be equal to the commendation and the praise we are receiving, that our performance will at least equal our reputation, and we have a good reputation. God grant that we may merit all the good things that have been said about us, and that more good things might be accurately said about us in the future.

I realize that the devil is alert. He is the enemy of this work. He is the enemy of all righteousness, and I know that he is clever, that he never takes a holiday. He works overtime. He is ingenious. I am confident he will devise new ways to fight this work. We may not know just what form those schemes will take, but we must be vigilant. . . .

I think it was Nephi who said that the time would come when there would be a tendency for people to become pacified; they would be lulled away into a false security; there would be those who would be at ease in Zion, saying, "Zion prospers, all is well;" and that the devil would cheat their souls and lead them carefully down to hell (see 2 Nephi 28:21).

I think we need to be on the alert today to see that that does not happen in the Church. I had occasion many times on this last tour through Europe, as I have had before, to thank the Lord for the Word of Wisdom. Many were the conversations we had regarding the Church, and particularly those my good wife had, as we sat at dinners, luncheons, etc., and it came to their attention that we did not drink liquor, smoke, etc. Immediately they wanted to know more about the Church, and always there was commendation for our standards. Never once was there any embarrassment. Always there was a feeling of gratitude and thanksgiving on our part at the end of the day or evening because of the standards which the God of heaven has provided in this Church.

This was the same no matter how high the station of the officials with whom we sat. And I say to you, it always will be true of men of goodwill, men of character. As Latter-day Saints we cannot afford to let down our standards, to refuse to live the gospel completely and fully. [CR, Oct. 1955, 109–10]

Elder Spencer W. Kimball • 2 Nephi 28:22

Yes, the devil is decidedly a person. He is also clever and trained. With thousands of years of experience behind him he has become superbly efficient and increasingly determined. Young people often feel and say, when governing hands are outstretched to them, "I can take care of myself." In fact even more experienced adults cannot afford to be sure of their resistance to Satan. Teenage girls or boys certainly need to be properly fortified and protected if they are to cope with the efficient, highly-trained, superior powers which are ever alert to opportunities for temptation.

It is a smart, young or old, who will accept advice and counsel from experienced people who know the pitfalls, the crumbling walls, and the cracking dams which bring on destruction. [*The Miracle of Forgiveness* (1969), 21–22]

The Prophet Joseph Smith • 2 Nephi 24:12 (Isaiah 14:12)

Salvation is nothing more nor less than to triumph over all our enemies and put them under our feet. And when we have power to put all enemies under our feet in this world, and a knowledge to triumph over all evil spirits in the world to come, then we are saved, as in the case of Jesus, who was to reign until He had put all enemies under His feet, and the last enemy was death.

Perhaps there are principles here that few men have thought of. No person can have this salvation except through a tabernacle.

Now, in this world, mankind are naturally selfish, ambitious and striving to excel one above another; yet some are willing to build up others as well as themselves. So in the other world there are a variety of spirits. Some seek to excel. And this was the case with Lucifer when he fell. He sought for things which were unlawful. Hence he was sent down, and it is said he drew many away with him; and the greatness of his punishment is that he shall not have a tabernacle. This is his punishment. So the devil, thinking to thwart the decree of God, by going up and down in the earth, seeking whom he may destroy—any person that he can find that will yield to him, he will bind him, and take possession of the body and reign there, glorying in it mightily, not caring that he had got merely a stolen body; and by and by someone having authority will come along and cast him out and restore the tabernacle to the rightful owner. The devil steals a tabernacle because he has not one of his own: but if he steals one, he is always liable to be turned out of doors. [*TPJS*, 297–98]

Challenges to Eternal Life:

1. Have you ever used any of the following tricks of self-deceit?

    Just this once; everyone else does it; John made me do it; I would have been a poor sport to have refused; It isn't doing wrong; It's because I am cold; It is Christmas Day, etc.; This is the last time; I hate people who are perfect. [2 Nephi 28:8]

    Be cognizant of your use of these and correct your activity rather than accuse yourself.

2. Do you become angry over the programs of the Church because they take up your time or deny you some worldly pleasure? Analyze yourself in this light (2 Nephi 28:20).

3. Do you have an attitude of, or are you in a state of apathy toward the Gospel of Jesus Christ? Analyze your activities as well as your attitude in this light (2 Nephi 28:21)

4. "Flattereth that there is no hell and no devil." This is the pseudo-intellectual. Do you accept that you will be judged by your works? (2 Nephi 28:22–23). Analyze yourself in this light.

5. Select a challenge or modern-day message from this reading and incorporate it into your life.

Chapter Twenty-One

About to be Fulfilled—
the Millennium

2 Nephi 30:8–19; 21–22

After Nephi summarized the message to the Jews, the Lamanites, and the Gentiles (2 Nephi 30:1–7 as discussed in chapters 17, 18, and 19), he quoted and commented on Isaiah 11:4–9 (2 Nephi 30:9–15). He had written earlier the entire eleventh chapter on the plates of brass without comment (2 Nephi 21). The verses quoted in 2 Nephi 30 (Isaiah 11:4–9) describe Christ's millennial reign. The preceding verses, Isaiah 11:1–3, speak of the Lord's servant who will bring forth the Book of Mormon and establish the Church prior to the millennium. The verses of Isaiah 11 that follow those quoted in 2 Nephi 30 refer again to the second great gathering of Israel. The second gathering will begin prior to the millennium, but will probably extend into it. We will discuss the text in the sequence of Isaiah's eleventh chapter (2 Nephi 21) and insert Nephi's comments of 2 Nephi 30 between the appropriate verses of Isaiah 11. Isaiah 12 (2 Nephi 22) is a song of praise to Jehovah. An outline of the three chapters follows as a preparation for a deeper study.

OUTLINE • 2 NEPHI 30:8–19; 21–22

➤ 21:1–4; 30:8–10   A rod will come out of the stem of Jesse, and a branch shall grow out of his roots.

    a.   The Spirit of the Lord will rest upon the rod, the servant of the Lord (2 Nephi 21:1–3).

    b.   The Lord God will commence his work of restoration among all nations, kindreds, tongues, and people (2 Nephi 30:8).

    c.   The earth will be smitten with the word of his mouth (2 Nephi 21:4; 30:4).

    d.   A great division will soon come among the people and the wicked will be destroyed (2 Nephi 30:10).

➤ 21:5–9; 30:11–18   Righteousness and faithfulness will be the pattern of the millennium.

    a.   The animosity between animals and between man and animals will cease (vv. 5–9).

    b.   The earth will be full of the knowledge of the Lord (v. 9; 30:15–17).

        1.   The things of all nations will be made known to men.

        2.   All things will be revealed; no secrets, no darkness, and nothing sealed.

    c.   Satan will have no power over men for a long time (30:18).

➤ 21:10–16   A root of Jesse will stand as an ensign.

    a.   The Gentiles will seek this ensign (v. 10).

    b.   The Lord will set his hand a second time to recover the remnant of his people (v. 11).

    c.   He will assemble the outcasts of Israel and the dispersed of Judah (v. 12).

    d.   The envy between Judah and Ephraim will cease, and they will occupy the land promised to Ephraim (vv. 13–14).

    e.   He will smite the tongue of the Egyptian sea, and men shall go over dry shod (v. 15).

    f.   The remnant that left from Assyria will return (v. 16).

➤ 22:1–6   A song of praise will be sung to Jehovah.

    a.   Jehovah is Israel's strength and salvation (v. 2).

    b.   Israel shall draw water from the well of salvation (v. 3).

    c.   Israel will praise his name among all the people of the earth (vv. 4–6).

NOTES AND COMMENTARY

Introduction: Isaiah 11 should be of special significance to Latter-day Saints because the angel Moroni quoted it to Joseph Smith in September 1823 and said "that it was about to be fulfilled" (JS—History 1:40). We also have some of the verses interpreted in the Doctrine and Covenants. A diagram of the sentence along with the Doctrine and Covenants comments is a good beginning.

2 Nephi 21:1 (Isaiah 11:1) • A Rod out of the Stem of Jesse

> 1 And there shall come forth a rod out of the stem of Jesse, and a branch shall grow out of his roots.

The basic diagram of the sentence is enlightening (see diagram on following page).

The subject of the first half of the compound sentence is the rod. The rod is to come from the root of Jesse. The interpretation of the passage has been given by Joseph Smith in Doctrine and Covenants 113:1–4.

1.   Who is the Stem of Jesse spoken of in the 1st, 2d, 3d, 4th, and 5th verses of the 11th chapter of Isaiah?

2.   Verily thus saith the Lord: It is Christ.

3.   What is the rod spoken of in the first verse of the 11th chapter of Isaiah, that should come of the Stem of Jesse?

4.   Behold, thus saith the Lord: It is a servant in the hands of Christ, who is partly a descendant of Jesse as well as of Ephraim, or of the house of Joseph, on whom there is laid much power.

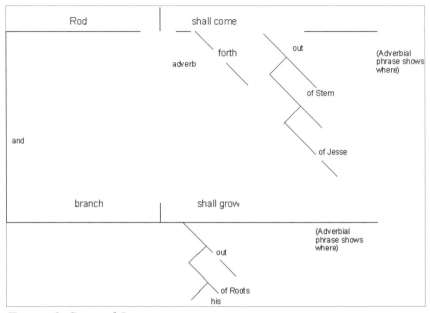

Figure 9. Stem of Jesse

The stem of Jesse is Christ. Jesse was the father of king David. The book of Revelation identifies Jesus in a similar manner. "I Jesus have sent mine angel to testify unto you these things in the churches. I am the root and the offspring of David, *and* the bright and morning star" (Revelation 22:1–6; see also 5:5). That the servant is Joseph Smith himself seems evident. President Brigham Young taught that Joseph was a "pure Ephraimite," and this was confirmed by President Joseph Fielding Smith.[2]

His being a pure Ephraimite does not necessarily mean he had only the blood of Ephraim in his veins, but may mean that he has the literal blood of Ephraim. This is also evidenced by the fact that his father, Joseph Smith Sr. was the Patriarch to the Church, which office belongs to "the oldest man of the blood of Joseph or of the seed of Abraham"

---

[2] See *Doctrines of Salvation*, comp. Bruce R. McConkie, 3 vols. [1956], 3:253–54 for both statements.

(*TPJS*, 151). Joseph Smith would likely have had the blood of other tribes in his veins as well, since Israel lived among the Gentiles for hundreds of years. Certainly Joseph Smith had "much power" laid upon him, as D&C 113:4 states. He was given power to "translate the Book of Mormon" (D&C 20:8). Therefore Joseph Smith was the servant in the hands of Christ. All this fits well with the angel Moroni's declaration to Joseph Smith that the eleventh chapter of Isaiah was about to be fulfilled

The branch is the subject of the second half of the compound sentence. It was to grow out of the roots. To grow out of the roots suggests that it was to follow the work of the servant. The work of the servant was to bring forth the Book of Mormon. Joseph Smith was given "a gift to translate" and was commanded to "pretend to no other gift until my purpose is fulfilled in this; for I will grant unto you no other gift until [the Book of Mormon] is finished" (D&C 5:4). The Church was not organized until the Book of Mormon translation was completed. Therefore, it was the Church that was to grow out of the roots of Christ. "Branch" is capitalized in the KJV leading some to interpret it to refer to Christ, but it is not capitalized in the Book of Mormon. The roots seem to be the roots of the stem of Jesse [Christ], and a branch would grow from him, and would be his Church, but thus would not be him personally. Zenos mentioned that the branches of Israel would be grafted into the mother tree and would grow as mentioned in the allegory of Zenos (see Jacob 5:54–60).

2 Nephi 21:2–4 (Isaiah 11:2–4) • The Spirit of the Lord Upon the Servant

2 And the Spirit of the Lord shall rest upon him, the spirit of wisdom and understanding, the spirit of counsel and might, the spirit of knowledge and of the fear of the Lord;

3 And shall make him of quick understanding in the fear of the Lord; and he shall not judge after the sight of his eyes, neither reprove after the hearing of his ears.

4 But with righteousness shall he judge the poor, and reprove with equity for the meek of the earth; and he shall smite the earth with the

rod of his mouth, and with the breath of his lips shall he slay the wicked.

The traditional interpretation of these verses is that they describe Christ. This is supported by passages in the book of Revelation:

> 15 And out of his mouth goeth a sharp sword, that with it he should smite the nations: and he shall rule them with a rod of iron: and he treadeth the winepress of the fierceness and wrath of Almighty God.
>
> 16 And he hath on *his* vesture and on his thigh a name written, KING OF KINGS, AND LORD OF LORDS. [Revelation 19:15–16; see also 2:16]

However, Isaiah 11:2–4 must be understood within the context established in verse 1, including the "rod" (servant) mentioned there, and verse 2 through 4 especially may refer to Joseph Smith. "The Spirit of the Lord shall rest upon him [the servant]" (v. 2). The Lord revealed: "this generation shall have my word through [Joseph Smith]" (D&C 5:10). After summarizing his message to the Gentiles, the Lamanites, and the Jews (2 Nephi 30:1–7), all to be fulfilled in the latter days, Nephi says: " the Lord God shall commence his work among all nations . . . to bring about the restoration of his people upon the earth" (2 Nephi 30:8). Joseph Smith headed the latter-day work among all nations to restore God's people. He was given the keys of the kingdom, "which kingdom is coming forth for the last time," and promised that "the keys of this kingdom shall never be taken from you, while thou art in the world, neither in the world to come" (D&C 90:2–3).

Nephi quoted Isaiah 11:4–9 after his prophesy of the restoration of God's people and added his comments (2 Nephi 30:9–15). In 2 Nephi 30:9 (Isaiah 11:4), Nephi uses "the Lord God" instead of the pronoun "*he* will judge the people." After all, the servant was to be an instrument in the hands of Christ to "commence his work" (v. 8). Since the Book of Mormon was brought forth by Joseph Smith to begin the Lord's work, and Jesus Christ will cleanse the earth and slay the wicked (v. 2) to conclude his work and bring about the millennium, Nephi's change seems appropriate. As the Spirit of the Lord came upon

Joseph Smith, he did attain wisdom, understanding, and knowledge as he began the work (2 Nephi 21:2). Furthermore, Joseph did also judge in righteousness through the Spirit of the Lord (2 Nephi 21:3).

2 Nephi 30:8 • Commence His Work Among All Nations

> 8 And it shall come to pass that the Lord God shall commence his work among all nations, kindreds, tongues, and people, to bring about the restoration of his people upon the earth.

All nations who possess the Book of Mormon "shall be judged of them according to the words which are written" (2 Nephi 25:21–22). That will eventually be all nations, for the everlasting gospel as contained in the Book of Mormon, shall go to all nations.

> 6 And I saw another angel fly in the midst of heaven, having the everlasting gospel to preach unto them that dwell on the earth, and to every nation, and kindred, and tongue, and people,
>
> 7 Saying with a loud voice, Fear God, and give glory to him; for the hour of his judgment is come: and worship him that made heaven, and earth, and the sea, and the fountains of waters. [Revelation 14:6–7]

The hour of the Lord's judgment began with the coming forth of the Book of Mormon. Joseph Smith did begin to smite the earth with the Book of Mormon—the rod of his mouth. Of course, the judgment spoken of is positive as well as negative.

> 13 Therefore, having so great witnesses, by them shall the world be judged, even as many as shall hereafter come to a knowledge of this work.
>
> 14 And those who receive it in faith, and work righteousness, shall receive a crown of eternal life;
>
> 15 But those who harden their hearts in unbelief, and reject it, it shall turn to their own condemnation—
>
> 16 For the Lord God has spoken it; and we, the elders of the church, have heard and bear witness to the words of the glorious

Majesty on high, to whom be glory forever and ever. Amen. [D&C 20:13–16]

In Isaiah's words, "the rod of his mouth" is the word of God. Nephi saw "that the rod of iron . . . was the word of God" (1 Nephi 11:25; see also JST, Revelation 2:26–27; 12:5; 19:15). Through the word of God will come "equity for the meek of the earth" (a crown of eternal life), and "slay the wicked" (condemnation and not receive eternal life).

2 Nephi 30:10 • A Great Division Among the People

10 For the time speedily cometh that the Lord God shall cause a great division among the people, and the wicked will he destroy; and he will spare his people, yea, even if it so be that he must destroy the wicked by fire.

Nephi's comment inserted after quoting Isaiah 11:4 (2 Nephi 30:9) is explaining what will lead up to the slaying of the wicked. The great division among the people began with the organization of the Church in April of 1830. Those who will accept the gospel and remain faithful will be led to the establishment of a Zion society. The early saints were repeatedly admonished to "keep my commandments, and seek to bring forth and establish the cause of Zion" (D&C 6:7; 11:6; 12:6; 14:6). The Prophet Joseph said: "We ought to have the building up of Zion as our greatest object" (*TPJS*, 160).

Satan does not sit idly by. He is well aware of the coming of Zion and does everything in his power to stop it or at least slow it down. The Prophet Joseph observed: "In relation to the kingdom of God, the devil always sets up his kingdom at the very same time in opposition to God" (*TPJS*, 365). As the time of Christ's visit among the Nephites approached, the devil's pattern was shown in the establishment an growth of secret combinations among the Nephites.

27 And it came to pass that the ninety and third year did also pass away in peace, save it were for the Gadianton robbers, who dwelt upon the mountains, who did infest the land; for so strong were their holds and their secret places that the people could not overpower them;

therefore they did commit many murders, and did do much slaughter among the people.

28 And it came to pass that in the ninety and fourth year they began to increase in a great degree, because there were many dissenters of the Nephites who did flee unto them, which did cause much sorrow unto those Nephites who did remain in the land.

29 And there was also a cause of much sorrow among the Lamanites; for behold, they had many children who did grow up and began to wax strong in years, that they became for themselves, and were led away by some who were Zoramites, by their lyings and their flattering words, to join those Gadianton robbers.

30 And thus were the Lamanites afflicted also, and began to decrease as to their faith and righteousness, because of the wickedness of the rising generation. [3 Nephi 1:27–30]

Note that the increase came from the dissenters of the faith and the rising generation, the same pattern can be described in the Church in the latter-days. The Lord foretold two movements that would precede his Second Coming:

34 And again, verily I say unto you, O inhabitants of the earth: I the Lord am willing to make these things known unto all flesh;

35 For I am no respecter of persons, and will that all men shall know that the day speedily cometh; the hour is not yet, but is nigh at hand, when peace shall be taken from the earth, and the devil shall have power over his own dominion.

36 And also the Lord shall have power over his saints, and shall reign in their midst, and shall come down in judgment upon Idumea, or the world. [D&C 1:34–36]

Now, over one hundred and seventy years later, the fulfillment of the Lord's declaration is obvious, the Saints have grown both temporally and spiritually towards becoming a Zion society, and the world's wickedness has escalated. Joseph Smith saw the day when peace would be taken from the earth:

The time is soon coming, when no man will have any peace but in Zion and her stakes. I saw men hunting the lives of their own sons, and brother murdering brother, women killing their own daughters, and daughters seeking the lives of their mothers. I saw armies arrayed against armies. I saw blood, desolation, fires. The Son of Man has said that the mother shall be against the daughter, and the daughter against the mother. These things are at our doors. They will follow the Saints of God from city to city. Satan will rage, and the spirit of the devil is now enraged. I know not how soon these things will take place; but with a view of them shall I cry peace? No; I will lift up my voice and testify of them. How long you will have good crops, and the famine be kept off, I do not know; but when the fig tree leaves, know that the summer is nigh at hand. [*TPJS*, 161]

As we see Joseph's prophecy being fulfilled, we must work to be a part of the Zion society.

2 Nephi 21:5 (Isaiah 11:5; 2 Nephi 30:11)
• The Millennium Comes

> 5 And righteousness shall be the girdle of his loins, and faithfulness the girdle of his reins.

This verse describes the Millennium after the wicked are destroyed by fire (2 Nephi 30:10), or the glory that attends his coming (see D&C 101:23–25). The pronoun "*his*" represents Christ. The "girdle" is his clothing, symbolic of his character. He is clothed with righteous actions. His "reins" represent his feelings of pure love or perfect love (see Moroni 7:48 and 1 John 4:16–19).

2 Nephi 21:6–8 (Isaiah 11:6–8; 2 Nephi 30:12–14)
• Enmity of All Flesh Shall Cease

> 6 The wolf also shall dwell with the lamb, and the leopard shall lie down with the kid, and the calf and the young lion and fatling together; and a little child shall lead them.

> 7 And the cow and the bear shall feed; their young ones shall lie down together; and the lion shall eat straw like the ox.

> 8 And the sucking child shall play on the hole of the asp, and the weaned child shall put his hand on the cockatrice's den.

These verses further describe the millennial reign of Christ for which his servants are preparing. Nephi, in quoting these verses, added "And then" (2 Nephi 30:12). The enmity between animals and between man and animals is verified in modern revelation. "And in that day the enmity of man, and the enmity of beasts, yea, the enmity of all flesh, shall cease from before my face" (D&C 101:26). In this section, the Lord enlarges upon the millennial conditions (101:27–34), but they will not be discussed here.

2 Nephi 21:9 (Isaiah 11:9; 2 Nephi 30:15)
• The Earth Full of Knowledge

> 9 They shall not hurt nor destroy in all my holy mountain, for the earth shall be full of the knowledge of the Lord, as the waters cover the sea.

The end of the destruction foretold in the first part of this verse seems to be a summary of the previous three verses. The rest of the verse gives the reason for this happy state.

Joseph Smith gave a different rendering of the last part of verse nine—"the earth will be filled with sacred knowledge, as the waters cover the great deep" (*TPJS*, 93)—and indicated that this prophecy would be fulfilled after Israel is gathered. President Joseph Fielding Smith has stated, "If the knowledge of the Lord covers the earth as the waters do the sea, then it must be universally received."[3] Elder Orson Pratt taught that this great knowledge which was to cover the earth (v. 9) was to include a restoration of all the records which had been kept in former dispensations, and he enumerated many of these records (see *JD*, 16:47ff.; see also D&C 5:9; Helaman 3:13–15; 3 Nephi 26:8–12; Ether 3:25; 4:7).

Elder Pratt also taught that:

> The earth will be made new, and great knowledge will be imparted to the inhabitants thereof, as predicted in the 11th chapter of the

---

[3] *Doctrines of Salvation*, 3:65.

prophecy of Isaiah. The knowledge of God will then cover the earth as the waters cover the mighty deep. There will be no place of ignorance, no place of darkness, no place for those that will not serve God. Why? Because Jesus, the Great Creator, and also the Great Redeemer, will be himself on the earth, and his holy angels will be on the earth, and all the resurrected Saints that have died in former dispensations will all come forth, and they will be on the earth. What a happy earth this creation will be, when this purifying process shall come, and the earth be filled with the knowledge of God as the waters cover the great deep! [*JD*, 21:324–35]

2 Nephi 30:16–18 • All Things Shall be Revealed

16 Wherefore, the things of all nations shall be made known; yea, all things shall be made known unto the children of men.

17 There is nothing which is secret save it shall be revealed; there is no work of darkness save it shall be made manifest in the light; and there is nothing which is sealed upon the earth save it shall be loosed.

18 Wherefore, all things which have been revealed unto the children of men shall at that day be revealed; and Satan shall have power over the hearts of the children of men no more, for a long time. And now, my beloved brethren, I make an end of my sayings.

Nephi's comments are consistent with the comments and scriptures quoted above, and add a few insights. "The things of all nations" being known (v. 16) ties back to his foretelling of all the house of Israel being gathered and his "word also shall be gathered in one" (2 Nephi 29:12–14).

All secrets and works of darkness being revealed (v. 17) was enlarged upon in a revelation to Joseph Smith in December 1832. Six angels shall each sound their trump and "reveal the secret acts of men, and the mighty works of God" in each of the six thousand years that preceded the millennium (D&C 88:108–110). The "sealed upon the earth" that are loosed (v. 17) probably refer to those who are in bondage to something or someone.

Satan having no more power over the hearts of men (v. 18) is worded slightly different in the Doctrine and Covenants; he "shall not

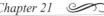

have power to tempt any man" (101:28). As Nephi said previously, Satan has no power because "they dwell in righteousness, and the Holy One of Israel reigneth" (1 Nephi 22:26). In another revelation to Joseph Smith in February 1831, the Lord said, "Satan shall be bound, and when he is loosed again he shall only reign for a little season, and then cometh the end of the earth" (D&C 43:31). The "little season" will be at the end of the millennium. The "end of the earth" is the end of its mortal period before it is "sanctified from all unrighteousness, that it may be prepared for the celestial glory" (D&C 88:17–20).

"The end of [Nephi's] sayings" (v. 18) was the end of his prophecies based upon the text of Isaiah. He does add a few words "concerning the doctrine of Christ" (see 2 Nephi 31:1–2 and the discussion in the next chapter).

2 Nephi 21:10 (Isaiah 11:10) • The Root of Jesse, An Ensign

> 10 And in that day there shall be a root of Jesse, which shall stand for an ensign of the people; to it shall the Gentiles seek; and his rest shall be glorious.

After prophesying of the millennium, Isaiah prophesies of a second great gathering of Israel, the first one being the exodus from Egypt (see also Jeremiah 16:14–16). This gathering commences before the Second Coming, but probably continues into the millennium.

The root of Jesse is identified in Doctrine and Covenants 113:5–6 as "a descendant of Jesse, as well as of Joseph, unto whom rightly belongs the priesthood, and the keys of the kingdom, for an ensign, and for the gathering of my people in the last days." The fact that these keys of the kingdom were given to Joseph Smith for time and eternity (D&C 90:2–4 partially quoted above) helps us identify him as the servant. Joseph being spoken of twice in the same chapter has led some to feel it must be a different person spoken of in the second reference. However, Joseph is spoken of in a different mission than the first. His second mission was to fulfill the covenant made to Abraham. In 1841 the Lord revealed to Joseph:

> 58 And as I said unto Abraham concerning the kindreds of the earth, even so I say unto my servant Joseph: In thee and in thy seed shall the kindred of the earth be blessed. [D&C 124:58]

Just as Isaiah prophesied of another mission for Joseph after telling of his first, the Lord waited until the first mission was completed before informing Joseph of the second mission (he knew before 1841 as shown below). The blessing of all the kindred of the earth included taking the gospel to the Gentiles. Paul quoted the Isaiah passage (Isaiah 11:10), with slightly different wording, as evidence that the Gentiles were to receive the gospel.

This wording also helps to identify the servant as Joseph Smith; "And again, Esaias saith, There shall be a root of Jesse, and he that shall rise to reign over the Gentiles; in him shall the Gentiles trust" (Romans 15:12). Joseph Smith was designated to reign over the Gentiles as shown below.

2 Nephi 21:11–12 (Isaiah 11:11–12)
• The Second Great Gathering

> 11 And it shall come to pass in that day that the Lord shall set his hand again the second time to recover the remnant of his people which shall be left, from Assyria, and from Egypt, and from Pathros, and from Cush, and from Elam, and from Shinar, and from Hamath, and from the islands of the sea.
>
> 12 And he shall set up an ensign for the nations, and shall assemble the outcasts of Israel, and gather together the dispersed of Judah from the four corners of the earth.

The Prophet Joseph Smith, in a letter dated January 4, 1833, provided this enlightening comment on verse 11:

> The time has at last arrived when the God of Abraham, of Isaac, and of Jacob, has set his hand again the second time to recover the remnants of his people, which have been left from Assyria, and from

Egypt, and from Pathron, and from Cush, and from Elam, and from Shinar, and from Hamath, and from the islands of the sea, and with them to bring in the fulness of the Gentiles, and establish that covenant with them, which was promised when their sins should be taken away. See Isaiah xi; Romans xi: 25, 26 and 27, and also Jeremiah xxxi: 31, 32, and 33. This covenant has never been established with the house of Israel, nor with the house of Judah, for it requires two parties to make a covenant, and those two parties must be agreed, or no covenant can be made.

Christ, in the days of His flesh, proposed to make a covenant with them, but they rejected Him and His proposals, and in consequence thereof, they were broken off, and no covenant was made with them at that time. But their unbelief has not rendered the promise of God of none effect: no, for there was another day limited in David, which was the day of His power; and then His people, Israel, should be a willing people;—and He would write His law in their hearts, and print it in their thoughts; their sins and their iniquities He would remember no more. [*TPJS*, 14–15]

The Lord setting his hand the second time to recover his people is associated with the "marvelous work and a wonder" prophesied in Isaiah 29:14 and in 2 Nephi 25:17 and 29:1. The standard or "ensign" spoken of in Isaiah 11:12 is identified in 2 Nephi 29:2 as the words of Nephi's seed (the Book of Mormon). This has also been more broadly interpreted by the General Authorities as The Church of Jesus Christ of Latter-day Saints. This certainly fits the concept of an ensign. Jacob, the Book of Mormon prophet, said that the day the Lord set his hand the second time to recover his people would be the day the Lord would send his servants to prune his vineyard for "the last time," as foretold in the allegory of Zenos (see Jacob 6:2).

2 Nephi 21:13–14 (Isaiah 11:13–14)
• Ephraim and Judah Reunited

13 The envy of Ephraim also shall depart, and the adversaries of Judah shall be cut off; Ephraim shall not envy Judah, and Judah shall not vex Ephraim.

14 But they shall fly upon the shoulders of the Philistines towards

the west; they shall spoil them of the east together; they shall lay their hand upon Edom and Moab; and the children of Ammon shall obey them.

These verses describe a return to a united kingdom of Israel as it was before the division following the reign of Solomon. The northern tribes were called Ephraim and Judah and half of Benjamin consisted of the southern kingdom. Ephraim will at the time of this reuniting occupy the promised land of Joseph—the Americas. "The Father hath given it unto [the remnant of Joseph]" (3 Nephi 15:12–13). Isaiah's prophecy speaks of more than a geographical uniting; it is a spiritual and political reuniting. Abraham was promised the land "from the river of Egypt unto the great river, the river Euphrates" (Genesis 15:18), which has never as yet been completely occupied by Abraham's children under one head. In Isaiah's time the Philistines occupied the area of the present-day Gaza Strip on the Mediterranean coast, which falls within the geography of Abraham's promised land. Edom, the descendants of Esau, occupied the area of Mt. Seir to the south and the east. Moab, the descendants of Lot and his eldest daughter, occupied the territory directly to the north of Edom on the east side of the Jordan River. Together, the Edomites and the Moabites represented the expansion of the land of Abraham on the east. The children of Ammon, the descendants of Lot and his younger daughter, occupied the land directly north of Moab on the east side of the Jordan. Today these all constitute the modern nation of Jordan.

That this prophecy is yet to be fulfilled is shown by the declaration that the children of Ammon will obey the house of Israel. None of this land east of the Jordan is under the rule of the house of Israel, nor has the envy yet fully departed from between Ephraim and Judah to bring about a united rule.

2 Nephi 21:15 (Isaiah 11:15) • The Tongue of the Egyptian Sea

15 And the Lord shall utterly destroy the tongue of the Egyptian sea; and with his mighty wind he shall shake his hand over the river,

and shall smite it in the seven streams, and make men go over dry
shod.

Nephi said that "in the days that the prophecies of Isaiah shall be
fulfilled men shall know of a surety, at the times when they shall come
to pass" (2 Nephi 25:7). This prophecy in verse 15 is one of those
which will probably not be understood until it comes to pass, but when
it does there will be no doubt that it is fulfilled. The identification of
"the tongue of the Egyptian sea" and "the river," which today is
uncertain in the minds of biblical scholars, will become certain when
the Lord delivers his people. According to Oliver Cowdery, the events
in this verse and those in verse 16 would need to occur so that the
gatherings could be fully accomplished.[4] Elder Orson Pratt referred
to this prophecy as a "literal transaction."

> The same thing, not a spiritual, but a literal transaction, as the Lord
> smote the tongue of the Egyptian sea in ancient days, and caused his
> people to go through on a highway in the midst of those mighty waters
> which stood like walls on each side of the assembly of Israel. So in
> the latter days he will not only cut off the tongue of the Egyptian sea,
> but the river in its seven streams will also be divided and men will
> go through dryshod. This is the testimony of the prophets concerning
> the events that are to take place when the times of the Gentiles are
> fulfilled. [*JD*, 14:66]

2 Nephi 21:16 (Isaiah 11:16) • A Highway for the Remnant

> 16 And there shall be a highway for the remnant of his people
> which shall be left, from Assyria, like as it was to Israel in the day
> that he came up out of the land of Egypt.

The remnant that left from Assyria is, of course, the ten tribes who
were taken into the north. The apocryphal book of 2 Esdras tells of
miracles which will attend their return like those that attended their
departure: "Then they dwelt there until the last time: and now, when

---

[4] *Messenger and Advocate*, April 1835, 111.

they are about to come again, the Most High will stop the channels of the river again, so that they may be able to pass over. Therefore you saw the multitude gathered together in peace" (2 Esdras 13:46–47). The Doctrine and Covenants gives an even more sure prophecy of the event spoken of in Isaiah:

> 26 And they who are in the north countries shall come in remembrance before the Lord; and their prophets shall hear his voice, and shall no longer stay themselves; and they shall smite the rocks, and the ice shall flow down at their presence.
>
> 27 And an highway shall be cast up in the midst of the great deep.
>
> 28 Their enemies shall become a prey unto them,
>
> 29 And in the barren deserts there shall come forth pools of living water; and the parched ground shall no longer be a thirsty land.
>
> 30 And they shall bring forth their rich treasures unto the children of Ephraim, my servants.
>
> 31 And the boundaries of the everlasting hills shall tremble at their presence.
>
> 32 And there shall they fall down and be crowned with glory, even in Zion, by the hands of the servants of the Lord, even the children of Ephraim.
>
> 33 And they shall be filled with songs of everlasting joy. [D&C 133:26–33]

The rich treasures brought to Ephraim are probably the records kept among them. The Lord promised that the Jews, the Nephites, and the lost tribes would all have each others records (2 Nephi 29:13).

Moses prophesied that the seed of Joseph would be gathered "for the chief things of the ancient mountains, and for the precious things of the lasting hills." The gathering would "push the people together to the ends of the earth: and they are the ten thousands of Ephraim, and they are the thousands of Manasseh" (Deuteronomy 33:15–17; compare Genesis 49:22–26). A revelation to Joseph Smith, in August 1831, endorses this prophecy as speaking of our day by stating that the elders of my church "shall push the people together from the ends of the earth" (D&C 58:44–45).

The revelation quoted above (D&C 133:26–33) also helps to identify the Americas as the place of gathering since Ephraim is now gathered in America. Many of these people returning from the north shall also return to the Holy Land where they have been given an inheritance.

Ether, the Jaredite prophet prophesied that those "from the north countries, and are partakers of the fulfilling of the covenant which God made with their father, Abraham" would be gathered to Jerusalem (Ether 13:11; see also Ezekiel 47–48). The details and sequence of this gathering are yet to be revealed.

The crown of glory, given by the hands of Ephraim, the Lord's servants, is undoubtedly the temple endowment. Enoch was guided to Mount Simeon where he "was clothed upon with glory" (Moses 7:2–3). Isaiah prophesied that a residue (remnant) of Ephraim would, in that day (upon returning) receive "a crown of glory" from the Lord (Isaiah 28:5). The first presidency of Peter, James, and John were endowed on the mount of transfiguration according to President Joseph Fielding Smith.[5] With all of these occasions pointing to the temple ordinances, the rich treasures brought to the Lord's servants Ephraim (D&C 133:30) could also include genealogical records. Modern Ephraim is building temples rapidly where these blessings can be administered.

2 Nephi 22:1–6 (Isaiah 12:1–6)
• A Song of Praise to Jehovah

1 And in that day thou shalt say: O Lord, I will praise thee; though thou wast angry with me thine anger is turned away, and thou comfortedest me.

2 Behold, God is my salvation; I will trust, and not be afraid; for

---

[5] *Doctrines of Salvation*, 2:165.

the Lord JEHOVAH is my strength and my song; he also has become my salvation.

3 Therefore, with joy shall ye draw water out of the wells of salvation.

4 And in that day shall ye say: Praise the Lord, call upon his name, declare his doings among the people, make mention that his name is exalted.

5 Sing unto the Lord; for he hath done excellent things; this is known in all the earth.

6 Cry out and shout, thou inhabitant of Zion; for great is the Holy One of Israel in the midst of thee.

This song of praise will be sung in the day of Israel's great restoration. The water that is drawn "out of the wells of salvation" is also promised by John the Revelator: "I will give unto him that is athirst of the fountain of the water of life freely" (Revelation 21:6). During his ministry Jesus told the woman of Samaria of living water: "But whosoever drinketh of the water that I shall give him shall never thirst; but the water that I shall give him shall be in him a well of water springing up into everlasting life (John 4:10, 14). Later, at the feast of tabernacles, he identified the water:

37 In the last day, that great *day* of the feast, Jesus stood and cried, saying, If any man thirst, let him come unto me, and drink.

38 He that believeth on me, as the scripture hath said, out of his belly shall flow rivers of living water.

39 (But this spake he of the Spirit, which they that believe on him should receive: for the Holy Ghost was not yet *given;* because that Jesus was not yet glorified.) [John 7:37–39]

The Holy Ghost will "testify of [Christ]" (John 15:26), and will "teach you all things" (John 14:26). Those who drink freely will be led to eternal life.

SACRED WRITING

Revelation which is Great:

2 Nephi 21:1–4	Isaiah foretells of the Lord's servant restoring the Church and the word of God.
2 Nephi 21:5–9	Isaiah describes the conditions of the millennium.
2 Nephi 21:10–16	Isaiah foretells the second great gathering of Israel in the latter days.

Prophesying which is Sacred:

2 Nephi 30:8	Nephi prophesies of a great division among the people and the wicked being destroyed.
2 Nephi 30:16–18	Nephi prophesies of all things being revealed in the millennium.

Doctrines Learned:

2 Nephi 30:10	The people will be separated into the righteous and the wicked before Christ comes.
2 Nephi 21:9	The earth shall be full of the knowledge of the Lord in the millennium.
2 Nephi 30:18	Satan will have no power during the millennium.

General Authority Quotations:

President Joseph Fielding Smith • 2 Nephi 21:9

. . . the day spoken of by Isaiah, when peace and righteousness shall rule the earth. [quotes Isaiah 11:9]

Can we not hasten that day by manifesting a little more faith, a little more desire to seek for knowledge and a little more obedience to the commandments, "to give diligent heed to the words of eternal life?" [*Answers to Gospel Questions* (1957), 1:xvii]

Elder George Albert Smith • 2 Nephi 30:8

The Lord shall commence his work among all nations: Has he fulfilled that promise? If there is anybody in this house past seventy-five years of age who will take the time to think of what has occurred since the Book of Mormon was first published, he will discover that almost every implement, almost every convenience now enjoyed by mankind, has come since the Book of Mormon issued from the press in the year 1830. We are witnesses this day that in a hundred years this world has made progress along most lines greater than in all the previous centuries since the earth was created and our first parents came upon it. The Lord has said he would commence his work among all nations. Man had had his trial; men for thousands of years had worked at it. But when the Lord set his hand and when he began to quicken the minds of men by the inspiration of his holy power men began to work out wonderful inventions that have changed the entire conditions of this world. I say unto you that after a hundred years we are living in a new world. But the work of the Lord has only just begun. [CR. April 1930, 67–68]

The Prophet Joseph Smith • 2 Nephi 30:10

And now I am prepared to say by the authority of Jesus Christ, that not many years shall pass away before the United States shall present such a scene of *bloodshed* as has not a parallel in the history of our nation: pestilence, hail, famine, and earthquake will sweep the wicked of this generation from off the face of the land, to open and prepare the way for the return of the lost tribes of Israel from the north country. [*TPJS, 17*]

Challenges to Eternal Life:

1. The servant in the Lord's hand today is the President of the Church. Read his conference addresses, *Ensign* editorials, and reports of his teachings in the Church News and resolve to heed his counsel (2 Nephi 21:1–4).
2. Commit to staying with the Church and its leaders no matter what trials and persecutions come or divisions that may take place (2 Nephi 30:10).
3. As all things will be revealed in the millennium, resolve now to learn what has been revealed in preparation for what is to come (2 Nephi 30:16–18).
4. Choose a challenge from the reading and apply it to yourself.

Chapter Twenty-Two

The Doctrine of Christ

2 Nephi 31–33

Historical setting: Fifty-five years after Lehi's group left Jerusalem, Nephi gave Jacob, his younger brother, "a commandment to write upon these plates" (Jacob 1:1). Shortly after that "Nephi died" (Jacob 1:12). Since these are the last words that Nephi recorded upon the plates, we assume they were written just before he died, around 544 B.C. There are no historical facts given in his writings after 2 Nephi 5:34, about fifteen years earlier.

Precepts of these chapters:

> 19 And now, my beloved brethren, after ye have gotten into this strait and narrow path, I would ask if all is done? Behold, I say unto you, Nay; for ye have not come thus far save it were by the word of Christ with unshaken faith in him, relying wholly upon the merits of him who is mighty to save.

> 20 Wherefore, ye must press forward with a steadfastness in Christ, having a perfect brightness of hope, and a love of God and of all men. Wherefore, if ye shall press forward, feasting upon the word of Christ, and endure to the end, behold, thus saith the Father: Ye shall have eternal life. [2 Nephi 31:19–20]

The last three chapters written by Nephi upon the small plates of Nephi are some of the most important ones in the entire Book of Mormon. They outline the path that leads to eternal life—or the plan

of salvation. An outline of the chapters follows in preparation for a
deeper study.

Outline • Nephi 31–33

➤ 31:1–4   Nephi writes but a few things which he knows must surely
come to pass, and a few of the words of Jacob.

    a. He must write a few words concerning the doctrine of
Christ (vv. 2–3).

        1. He shall speak plainly for his soul delights in plain-
ness.

        2. The Lord works in plainness among the children
of men.

        3. The Lord speaks to man according to their language
and understanding.

    b. Nephi reminds the reader that he has spoken concerning
that prophet who should baptize the Lamb of God (v. 4).

➤ 31:5–14   If the Lamb of God, being holy, hath need to be baptized
to fulfill all righteousness, how much more need have we,
being unholy, to be baptized by water.

    a. Nephi asks how the Lamb of God fulfills all righteous-
ness (vv. 6–11).

        1. He witnessed unto the Father that he would be
obedient in keeping his commandments.

        2. After his baptism, the Holy Ghost descended in the
form of a dove.

        3. He set the example for the children of men to follow
the strait path, and the narrow gate they should
enter.

        4. We cannot follow Christ unless we are willing to
keep the commandments of the Father.

        5. The Father said to repent and be baptized in the
name of My Beloved Son.

    b. The voice of the Son came to Nephi saying; He that is
baptized in my name, will the Father give the Holy

Ghost like unto me, therefore follow me (vv. 12–14).

1. Follow the Son with full purpose of heart, no hypocrisy or deception before God, but with real intent, repenting of your sins, witnessing to the Father you are taking the name of Christ by baptism, then shall ye receive the Holy Ghost.

2. Then cometh the baptism of fire and the Holy Ghost.

3. Then can ye speak with the tongue of angels and shout praises to the Holy One of Israel.

4. After being baptized and receiving the baptism by fire and the Holy Ghost, it would have been better had ye not known me than to deny me.

➤ 31:15–21 Nephi heard the voice of the Father say: the words of my Beloved Son are true and faithful. He that endures to the end shall be saved.

a. Nephi knows this is true, wherefore he said to do the things I have seen your Lord and Redeemer do (vv. 16–17).

1. They were shown to Nephi that ye might know the gate we should enter.

2. The gate is repentance and baptism and then comes a remission of sins by fire and the Holy Ghost.

b. Then ye are in the strait and narrow path that leads to eternal life (vv. 18–20).

1. Ye have entered in by the gate.

2. Ye have done according to the commandments of the Father and the Son.

3. Ye have received the Holy Ghost, which witnesses of the Father and the Son that if ye have entered in by the way ye shall receive it.

c. After ye are in this strait and narrow path ye must continue to follow the word of Christ with unshaken faith and rely on him (v. 19–20).

1. Press forward with steadfastness in Christ, having

a perfect brightness of hope and a love of God and of all men.

    2.   Feast upon the words of Christ, endure to the end, and obtain eternal life.

d. This is the only way or name whereby one can be saved in the kingdom of God (v. 21).

    1.   This is the doctrine of Christ.

    2.   This is the only true doctrine of the Father, the Son, and the Holy Ghost which is one God without end.

➤ 32:1–6   Nephi supposed that his brethren pondered in their hearts what they should do after they had entered into the way.

a. Receive the Holy Ghost and ye can speak with the tongue of angels (vv. 2–3).

    1.   Angels speak by the power of the Holy Ghost, and speak the words of Christ.

    2.   Feast upon the words of Christ for they will tell you all things to do.

b. If you cannot understand Nephi's words it is because you ask not, neither do you knock (vv. 4–5).

    1.   You are not brought into his light.

    2.   The Holy Ghost will show you all things what you should do.

c. This is the doctrine of Christ (v. 6).

    1.   You will be given no more doctrine until after he comes in the flesh.

    2.   Then you shall do the things he says unto you.

➤ 32:7–9   The Holy Ghost stopped Nephi's utterance.

a. He is left to mourn because of unbelief, wickedness, ignorance, and the stiffneckedness of men. They will not search knowledge nor understand great knowledge when he gives it to them in plainness (v. 7).

b. If you hearken unto the Spirit, the Spirit teaches you to pray (vv. 8–9).

    1.   The evil spirit teaches you not to pray.

2. You must pray always and not faint.

3. Do not perform anything until you pray unto the Father in the name of Christ that he will consecrate it unto the welfare of your soul.

➣ 33:1–5 Nephi cannot write all the things which were taught, neither is he mighty in writing like unto speaking.

    a. When a man speaks by the power of the Holy Ghost, the Holy Ghost carries it unto the hearts of men (v. 1).

    b. Many people harden their hearts against the Holy Spirit that it has no place in them. They cast away things that are written and esteem them as not (v. 2).

    c. What Nephi has written is of great worth, especially to his people (v. 3).

        1. He prays continually for them.

        2. He knows God will hear his cry.

    d. The Lord will consecrate his prayers for the good of his people (vv. 4–5).

        1. The words he has written in weakness will become strong unto them.

        2. They persuade them to do good and make known to them of their fathers.

        3. They speak of Jesus and persuade to believe in him and endure to the end.

        4. They speak harshly against sin according to the plainness of the truth.

        5. If they are angry with Nephi's words, they have the spirit of the devil.

➣ 33:6–9 Nephi glories in plainness, in truth, and in Jesus for he had redeemed his soul from hell.

    a. He has charity for his people and great faith in Christ that he shall meet many souls spotless at his judgment seat (v. 7).

    b. He has charity for the Jews from which people he came (v. 8).

    c. He has charity for the Gentiles also (v. 9).

    d. He has hope for none of these except they are reconciled to Christ (v. 9).

        1. Enter the narrow gate.

        2. Walk in the strait path that leads to eternal life and continue to the end.

➤ 33:10–12   Nephi admonishes his brethren, the Jews, and all the ends of the earth to believe in Christ.

    a. If you believe not in these words, believe in Christ (v. 10).

    b. If you believe in Christ you will believe in these words for they are the words of Christ (v. 10).

    c. They teach all men that they should do good (v. 10).

    d. Judge whether they are the words of Christ (v. 11).

        1. Christ will show at the last day with power and great glory that they are his words.

        2. You and Nephi will stand face to face before his bar and you will know he was commanded to write them.

    e. Nephi prays to the Father in the name of Christ that many of us, if not all, will be saved in his kingdom at that great and last day.

➤ 33:13–15   Nephi speaks farewell until that great day shall come to all the ends of the earth as the voice of one crying from the dust.

    a. He speaks an everlasting farewell to those who will not partake of the goodness of God and respect the words which shall proceed from the mouth of the Lamb of God (v. 14).

        1. The words of the Jews, the Nephites, and those which shall come.

        2. These words shall condemn us at the last day.

    b. What Nephi seals on earth shall be brought against you at the judgment bar, for the Lord has commanded Nephi, and he must obey (v. 15).

NOTES AND COMMENTARY

Introduction: A popular topic and title for speakers a few years ago was "The Last Lecture." The idea was for the speaker to tell the audience what he would tell them if he knew he was about to die, and his message was the most important advice he could give his listeners to follow for the rest of their lives. This was Nephi's approach for he knew his last words recorded upon these plates would be the last ones translated for our latter-day generation to read. What he recorded was the most important information for every reader of the Book of Mormon.

2 Nephi 31:1–3 • The Doctrine of Christ

> 1 And now I, Nephi, make an end of my prophesying unto you, my beloved brethren. And I cannot write but a few things, which I know must surely come to pass; neither can I write but a few of the words of my brother Jacob.

> 2 Wherefore, the things which I have written sufficeth me, save it be a few words which I must speak concerning the doctrine of Christ; wherefore, I shall speak unto you plainly, according to the plainness of my prophesying.

> 3 For my soul delighteth in plainness; for after this manner doth the Lord God work among the children of men. For the Lord God giveth light unto the understanding; for he speaketh unto men according to their language, unto their understanding.

Nephi apparently knows he is coming to the end of his life. He ends his commentary and prophesying, mainly based upon the prophecies of Isaiah, to record a few things concerning the "doctrine of Christ." He acknowledges that his record has been but a few words compared to what he has been shown and what has been revealed to him. He has included a few of his brother Jacob's speeches as well (2 Nephi 6–10), but these have also been few in comparison to what Jacob said.

Nephi's comment about speaking unto men "according to their language, unto their understanding" (v. 3) was reaffirmed in a revelation to the prophet Joseph Smith concerning the compilation of the Book of Commandments that later became the Doctrine and Covenants:

> Behold, I am God and have spoken it; these commandments are of me, and were given unto my servants in their weakness, after the manner of their language, that they might come to understanding. [D&C 1:24]

The phrase in the revelation "that they might come to understanding" reflects Nephi's words a little more clearly.

Nephi's desire to speak of the doctrine of Christ so that his people might come to an understanding, shows the same pattern Isaiah used regarding the coming forth of the Book of Mormon: "They also that erred in spirit shall come to understanding, and they that murmured shall learn doctrine" (2 Nephi 27:35; Isaiah 29:24).

2 Nephi 31:4–14 • The Baptism of the Lamb of God

> 4 Wherefore, I would that ye should remember that I have spoken unto you concerning that prophet which the Lord showed unto me, that should baptize the Lamb of God, which should take away the sins of the world.
>
> 5 And now, if the Lamb of God, he being holy, should have need to be baptized by water, to fulfil all righteousness, O then, how much more need have we, being unholy, to be baptized, yea, even by water!
>
> 6 And now, I would ask of you, my beloved brethren, wherein the Lamb of God did fulfil all righteousness in being baptized by water?
>
> 7 Know ye not that he was holy? But notwithstanding he being holy, he showeth unto the children of men that, according to the flesh he humbleth himself before the Father, and witnesseth unto the Father that he would be obedient unto him in keeping his commandments.
>
> 8 Wherefore, after he was baptized with water the Holy Ghost descended upon him in the form of a dove.
>
> 9 And again, it showeth unto the children of men the straitness of the path, and the narrowness of the gate, by which they should enter, he having set the example before them.
>
> 10 And he said unto the children of men: Follow thou me. Where-

fore, my beloved brethren, can we follow Jesus save we shall be willing to keep the commandments of the Father?

11 And the Father said: Repent ye, repent ye, and be baptized in the name of my Beloved Son.

12 And also, the voice of the Son came unto me, saying: He that is baptized in my name, to him will the Father give the Holy Ghost, like unto me; wherefore, follow me, and do the things which ye have seen me do.

13 Wherefore, my beloved brethren, I know that if ye shall follow the Son, with full purpose of heart, acting no hypocrisy and no deception before God, but with real intent, repenting of your sins, witnessing unto the Father that ye are willing to take upon you the name of Christ, by baptism—yea, by following your Lord and your Savior down into the water, according to his word, behold, then shall ye receive the Holy Ghost; yea, then cometh the baptism of fire and of the Holy Ghost; and then can ye speak with the tongue of angels, and shout praises unto the Holy One of Israel.

14 But, behold, my beloved brethren, thus came the voice of the Son unto me, saying: After ye have repented of your sins, and witnessed unto the Father that ye are willing to keep my commandments, by the baptism of water, and have received the baptism of fire and of the Holy Ghost, and can speak with a new tongue, yea, even with the tongue of angels, and after this should deny me, it would have been better for you that ye had not known me.

The prophet of whom Nephi has spoken was John the Baptist. He had seen him in a vision baptizing the Lamb of God (1 Nephi 11:27). Lehi had also prophesied of John (1 Nephi 10:7–10). Nephi's reference to John at this time is to set the stage for explaining the purpose or doctrine of Christ's baptism. The reference to the Lamb of God who should take away the sins of the world is speaking of Jesus as a person, not of his baptism.

Nephi gives three reasons for the Lamb of God being baptized. The first was to fulfill all righteousness (v. 5). The plan presented in the pre-mortal council for God's spirit children to come to earth was to "prove them herewith, to see if they will do all things whatsoever the

Lord their God shall command them" (Abraham 3:25). As "the Firstborn" spirit Son of God (D&C 93:21) he was to keep the commandments of the Father. Thus he was baptized as a witness to the Father, or a covenant, that he would be obedient to his commandments or follow the righteous plan of salvation (v. 7). Baptism is a covenant between God and man.

The second reason for Jesus being baptized was for a witness of the Holy Ghost. Baptism was a commandment, or a prerequisite, for receiving the Holy Ghost. The Holy Ghost descended upon Jesus after he was baptized (v. 8). The form of a dove should be translated as "the sign of the dove" according to the Prophet Joseph Smith. "The sign of the dove was instituted before the creation of the world, a witness for the Holy Ghost, and the devil cannot come in the sign of the dove." The sign was given to John to signify the truth of the deed" (*TPJS*, 276 and Facsimile No. 2, Figure 7 in the Book of Abraham in the Pearl of Great Price). Although the Holy Ghost itself may have been seen by some (see Luke 3:22), it seems that an actual dove was also present as a witness to those who were not spiritually ready to see the Holy Ghost, but were capable of recognizing the significance of the sign of the dove.

The third reason for Jesus being baptized was for an example to the children of men (v. 9). Baptism is the gate to the path to eternal life as will be shown later. Jesus demonstrated the strictness of the path and the narrowness of the gate by which one enters the path. Strait means narrow and restricted. The straitness of the path shows the restrictions that are placed on a person to get to the gate. The narrowness of the gate shows the inflexible or limited entrances to the path. The gate is baptism (v. 17) and the strait path to baptism is repentance. Therefore the example set by Christ to be baptized shows it is important to repent of the violations of the commandments required to be baptized and to accept the proper mode of baptism. These actions help one to enter into the path that leads to eternal life. That path on earth is the Church of Jesus Christ. Therefore we take upon us the name of Christ by baptism.

In light of these three reasons for Christ's baptism. Nephi gives three reasons for us to be baptized. The first reason is because we are unholy and need to be baptized for a remission of our sins (v. 5). The second reason is to witness to the Father that we are willing to keep his commandments (v. 10). Nephi also adds that we witness to the Father that we are willing to take upon us the name of Christ at this time. Our taking his name could be counted as another reason, but Nephi seems to make it a part of our witness to keep the commandments (v. 13). The Book of Mormon later explains that we "have entered into a covenant with [God]" through this witness (Mosiah 18:10, 13). The third reason comes from the voice of the Son declaring that the Father will give the Holy Ghost to those that are baptized (v. 12). Nephi then summarizes and emphasizes that we must enter into this covenant of baptism with full purpose of heart, without hypocrisy or deceit (v. 13). He implores the children of men to follow the Savior and receive the baptism of fire and of the Holy Ghost as the Father had commanded in the righteous plan of salvation. Those who receive the baptism of fire and the Holy Ghost will be able to speak with the tongue of angels and shout praises to the Holy One of Israel (v. 13). The voice of the Son came again unto him saying that after entering into the covenant of baptism and receiving the baptism of fire and the Holy Ghost, if the covenant was not kept, it would be better to not have known him. It is a serious and sacred experience.

2 Nephi 31:15 • Endure to the End to be Saved

15 And I heard a voice from the Father, saying: Yea, the words of my Beloved are true and faithful. He that endureth to the end, the same shall be saved.

The final step of the plan of salvation is to endure to the end (v. 15). However, there is another consideration. JST, John 1:19 says: "And no man has seen God at any time, except he hath borne record of the Son; for except it is through him no man can be saved." When Nephi heard the voice of the Father is not certain. It may have been as he was writing this record, or it may have been during the vision of Jerusalem when he saw the prophet baptizing the Lamb of God.

This is the only account in the present-day scriptures where the Father does more than introduce the Son, particularly if the voice of the Father was actually heard by Nephi. Nephi said he heard "a voice *from* the Father" (emphasis added). Therefore, it could be something the Father said but was quoted by the Son. This happened when Jesus visited the Nephites (see 3 Nephi 15:16; 16:7–8, 10, 14). The voice of the Son and the Father was heard together twice (vv. 11–12 and 14–15). The last time, "Yea, the words of my Beloved are true and faithful," confirms what the Son had just said. Regardless, all of the statements in 2 Nephi 31 that are attributed to the Father bear record of the Son and what he taught in the plan of salvation.

This whole chapter is based on Nephi's experience of being shown the birth and ministry of Christ many years earlier (1 Nephi 11).

2 Nephi 31:16–21 • The Strait and Narrow Path to Eternal Life

16 And now, my beloved brethren, I know by this that unless a man shall endure to the end, in following the example of the Son of the living God, he cannot be saved.

17 Wherefore, do the things which I have told you I have seen that your Lord and your Redeemer should do; for, for this cause have they been shown unto me, that ye might know the gate by which ye should enter. For the gate by which ye should enter is repentance and baptism by water; and then cometh a remission of your sins by fire and by the Holy Ghost.

18 And then are ye in this strait and narrow path which leads to eternal life; yea, ye have entered in by the gate; ye have done according to the commandments of the Father and the Son; and ye have received the Holy Ghost, which witnesses of the Father and the Son, unto the fulfilling of the promise which he hath made, that if ye entered in by the way ye should receive.

19 And now, my beloved brethren, after ye have gotten into this strait and narrow path, I would ask if all is done? Behold, I say unto you, Nay; for ye have not come thus far save it were by the word of

Christ with unshaken faith in him, relying wholly upon the merits of him who is mighty to save.

20 Wherefore, ye must press forward with a steadfastness in Christ, having a perfect brightness of hope, and a love of God and of all men. Wherefore, if ye shall press forward, feasting upon the word of Christ, and endure to the end, behold, thus saith the Father: Ye shall have eternal life.

21 And now, behold, my beloved brethren, this is the way; and there is none other way nor name given under heaven whereby man can be saved in the kingdom of God. And now, behold, this is the doctrine of Christ, and the only and true doctrine of the Father, and of the Son, and of the Holy Ghost, which is one God, without end. Amen.

Nephi's explanation of how to endure to the end is again attributed to the Father. He summarizes what has already been said, but also states that a remission of sins comes by fire and by the Holy Ghost (vv. 16–17). This baptism implies a two step process. The first step is to be "wrought upon and cleansed by the Holy Ghost" (Moroni 6:4). The second step is a filling or spiritual renewing:

25 And the first fruits of repentance is baptism; and baptism cometh by faith unto the fulfilling the commandments; and the fulfilling the commandments bringeth remission of sins;

26 And the remission of sins bringeth meekness, and lowliness of heart; and because of meekness and lowliness of heart cometh the visitation of the Holy Ghost, which Comforter filleth with hope and perfect love, which love endureth by diligence unto prayer, until the end shall come, when all the saints shall dwell with God. [Moroni 8:25–26]

Fulfilling the commandments "with full purpose of heart" (v. 13) is apparently the prerequisite to being cleansed by the Holy Ghost. Enduring by "diligence unto prayer" is the prerequisite to being guided along the path to eternal life (v. 18). After they are on the path to eternal life, or after they have been baptized, they must press forward with "a steadfastness in Christ" (v. 20). "Faith on the Son of God" brings "the power of the Holy Ghost" (1 Nephi 10:17). They must also have "a perfect brightness of hope, and a love of God and of all men" (v. 20). The "Comforter filleth with hope and perfect love" (Moroni 8:26). While pressing forward on the path they must feast "upon the words of Christ and endure to the end" to obtain eternal life (v. 20). The function of the Holy Ghost in this capacity is explained in 2 Nephi 32.

Nephi then stresses to his brethren that this is the only way or name (Christ) whereby salvation in the kingdom of God comes (v. 21). The oneness of the Godhead is declared. The singular verb speaking of the three members of the Godhead is used because Nephi is speaking of there being only one doctrine for all three: the Father, the Son, and the Holy Ghost. The doctrine of Christ that Nephi said he "must speak concerning" (2 Nephi 31:2) is also the doctrine of the Father and the Holy Ghost.

2 Nephi 32:1–6 • Speak with the Tongues of Angels

1 And now, behold, my beloved brethren, I suppose that ye ponder somewhat in your hearts concerning that which ye should do after ye have entered in by the way. But, behold, why do ye ponder these things in your hearts?

2 Do ye not remember that I said unto you that after ye had received the Holy Ghost ye could speak with the tongue of angels? And now, how could ye speak with the tongue of angels save it were by the Holy Ghost?

3 Angels speak by the power of the Holy Ghost; wherefore, they speak the words of Christ. Wherefore, I said unto you, feast upon the words of Christ; for behold, the words of Christ will tell you all things what ye should do.

4 Wherefore, now after I have spoken these words, if ye cannot understand them it will be because ye ask not, neither do ye knock; wherefore, ye are not brought into the light, but must perish in the dark.

5 For behold, again I say unto you that if ye will enter in by the way, and receive the Holy Ghost, it will show unto you all things what ye should do.

6 Behold, this is the doctrine of Christ, and there will be no more doctrine given until after he shall manifest himself unto you in the flesh. And when he shall manifest himself unto you in the flesh, the things which he shall say unto you shall ye observe to do.

Nephi anticipated that many of his readers would not understand the meaning of speaking with the tongue of angels (v. 2), so he further explained what it means. Since Christ and the Holy Ghost are one in doctrine, and angels speak by the power of the Holy Ghost, they teach the words that Christ would speak (v. 3). Therefore, the formula given by Nephi to speak these same words is to feast upon Christ's words. A feast, especially in the Jewish culture from where Nephi came, is when you eat for hours partaking of all of the delicious foods that are before you. The symbolism of feasting on Christ's words is to study widely, for long hours that you may understand the doctrine of Christ. Through studying the words of Christ it will tell you, by study, how you should live.

Nephi adds a disclaimer to his formula. If we do not ask (prayer) and knock (try to live as the words of Christ tell you), we will not come into the light of what we must do, but will perish in the darkness of the world (v. 4). He then adds the comment that the Holy Ghost will show us what we should do. There is a difference in the Holy Ghost showing us, and the words of Christ telling us what to do. As stated above, study will give us spiritual knowledge. The Holy Ghost will bring us personal revelation. This is learning by faith. We need both sources in our lives to follow the path to eternal life. The Lord has instructed us to "seek learning, even by study and also by faith" (D&C 88:118).

Those who followed Nephi's formula had sufficient to lead them on the path to eternal life until the time of Christ's coming in the flesh. After Christ had fulfilled the law of Moses, further instructions would be given (v. 6).

2 Nephi 32:7–9 • The Spirit Teaches a Man to Pray

7 And now I, Nephi, cannot say more; the Spirit stoppeth mine utterance, and I am left to mourn because of the unbelief, and the wickedness, and the ignorance, and the stiffneckedness of men; for they will not search knowledge, nor understand great knowledge, when it is given unto them in plainness, even as plain as word can be.

8 And now, my beloved brethren, I perceive that ye ponder still in your hearts; and it grieveth me that I must speak concerning this thing. For if ye would hearken unto the Spirit which teacheth a man to pray ye would know that ye must pray; for the evil spirit teacheth not a man to pray, but teacheth him that he must not pray.

9 But behold, I say unto you that ye must pray always, and not faint; that ye must not perform any thing unto the Lord save in the first place ye shall pray unto the Father in the name of Christ, that he will consecrate thy performance unto thee, that thy performance may be for the welfare of thy soul.

The formula for obtaining eternal life, as given above (vv. 3–5), and in the higher law of Christ, is to: "Ask, and it shall be given unto you; seek, and ye shall find; knock, and it shall be opened unto you" (3 Nephi 14:7; Matthew 7:7). If we ask (pray), seek (study), and knock (live the principles), the way is opened unto us.

The devil has a counter program to obstruct the attainment of eternal life. Instead of studying, men are prone to not believe and remain in ignorance, not being willing to search for knowledge. Instead of trying to live the gospel, men fall into the wickedness of the world, and because of their pride (stiffneckedness), they will not pray or ask God for his Spirit (v. 7). The evil spirit teaches a man not to pray (v. 8) while the Holy Ghost will guide our prayers and teach us the things for which we should pray. "Likewise the Spirit also helpeth our infirmities: for we know not what we should pray for as we ought: but the Spirit itself maketh intercession for us with groanings [striving] which cannot be uttered [expressed]"[1] (Romans 8:26; see also Ephesians 6:18; and Jude 1:20; 3 Nephi 19:24).

The pattern for prayer in our life, to "not perform anything unto the Lord save in the first place ye shall pray unto the Father in the name of Christ" (v. 9) is confirmed in modern revelation: "And in nothing doth man offend God, or against none is his wrath kindled, save those who confess not his hand in all things, and obey not his commandments" (D&C 59:21).

2 Nephi 33:1–2 • The Holy Ghost Carries the Words to our Heart

1 And now I, Nephi, cannot write all the things which were taught among my people; neither am I mighty in writing, like unto speaking; for when a man speaketh by the power of the Holy Ghost the power of the Holy Ghost carrieth it unto the hearts of the children of men.

2 But behold, there are many that harden their hearts against the Holy Spirit, that it hath no place in them; wherefore, they cast many things away which are written and esteem them as things of naught.

The brother of Jared was "mighty in writing" (Ether 12:24) while Nephi was mighty in speaking. Nephi was not aware of the writings of the brother of Jared at this time so he was not making a comparison as Moroni did in the verse cited above.

The Holy Ghost, as a teacher, carries the message of the speaker unto the listener's heart, or testifies to him. The Spirit may also testify to the speaker that the listener knows the message he is hearing is true "by the manifestation of the Spirit"(Alma 7:17).

2 Nephi 33:3–5 • Persuades to do Good and to Believe in Jesus

3 But I, Nephi, have written what I have written, and I esteem it

---

[1] It would be better thus: "The Spirit maketh intercession for us with *striving* which cannot be *expressed*" (*TPJS*, 278; italics added).

as of great worth, and especially unto my people. For I pray continually for them by day, and mine eyes water my pillow by night, because of them; and I cry unto my God in faith, and I know that he will hear my cry.

4 And I know that the Lord God will consecrate my prayers for the gain of my people. And the words which I have written in weakness will be made strong unto them; for it persuadeth them to do good; it maketh known unto them of their fathers; and it speaketh of Jesus, and persuadeth them to believe in him, and to endure to the end, which is life eternal.

5 And it speaketh harshly against sin, according to the plainness of the truth; wherefore, no man will be angry at the words which I have written save he shall be of the spirit of the devil.

Nephi's words will be made strong by the Holy Ghost as explained above. His words may have five effects upon the reader (v. 4). First, they will persuade them to do good (v. 4). Moroni concluded the Book of Mormon with a similar evaluation: "And whatsoever thing is good is just and true; wherefore, nothing that is good denieth the Christ, but acknowledgeth that he is" (Moroni 10:6). President Joseph F. Smith taught that true religion "makes good men better men, and it takes even bad men and makes good ones of them."[2] Secondly, Nephi's words help his people know more about their fathers (v. 4). Earlier, Nephi said they would know "they are of the house of Israel, and that they are of the covenant people of the Lord" (1 Nephi 15:14). Thirdly, his words "speaketh of Jesus, and persuadeth them to believe in him" (v. 4). The gospel of John was written for the same reason: "But these are written, that ye might believe that Jesus is the Christ, the Son of God; and that believing ye might have life through his name" (John 20:31). Jesus said: "This is the work of God, that ye believe on him [me] whom he hath sent" (John 6:29).

The fourth effect was for Nephi's words to become strong because they spoke "harshly against sin, according to the plainness of the truth"

---

[2] *Gospel Doctrine*, 11th ed. [1959], 75.

(v. 5). His words are consistent with New Testament teachings. After teaching the unbelieving Pharisees, Jesus warned: "If ye were blind, ye should have no sin: but now ye say, We see; therefore your sin remaineth" (John 9:41). One of the missions of the Comforter was to "reprove [convince][3] the world of sin . . . because they believe not on me" (John 16:8–9). Paul admonished the saints to "Abstain from all appearance of evil" (1 Thessalonians 5:22). To sin is to "transgress the law of God contrary to [one's] own knowledge" (Mosiah 2:33). The fifth effect was to become angry with the words of Nephi. Those who are angry are of the spirit of the devil (v. 5). He has stirred "them up to anger against that which is good," and they "are angry because of the truth of God" (2 Nephi 28:20, 28).

2 Nephi 33:6–9 • Jesus Redeemed the Soul of Nephi

6 I glory in plainness; I glory in truth; I glory in my Jesus, for he hath redeemed my soul from hell.

7 I have charity for my people, and great faith in Christ that I shall meet many souls spotless at his judgment-seat.

8 I have charity for the Jew—I say Jew, because I mean them from whence I came.

9 I also have charity for the Gentiles. But behold, for none of these can I hope except they shall be reconciled unto Christ, and enter into the narrow gate, and walk in the strait path which leads to life, and continue in the path until the end of the day of probation.

Nephi implies that his calling and election has been made sure (v. 6). If only this verse were read it may seem to be just a general statement about the Atonement of Christ, but his comments in verse 7 about charity extends the general meaning to one about Nephi specifically. Charity is the requirement for becoming like Christ and attaining the Celestial Kingdom.

46 Wherefore, my beloved brethren, if ye have not charity, ye are nothing, for charity never faileth. Wherefore, cleave unto charity,

---

[3] The KJV gives "convince" as an alternate reading for reprove.

which is the greatest of all, for all things must fail—

47 But charity is the pure love of Christ, and it endureth forever; and whoso is found possessed of it at the last day, it shall be well with him. [Moroni 7:46–47]

Nephi has charity for three groups of people to whom he knows his words will go: the Lamanites, the Jews, and the Gentiles (see comments, 2 Nephi 30:4 concerning Nephi being a Jew, v. 8). All three of those groups must be reconciled to Christ. This is why the Book of Mormon was written. Every person in any of these three groups must follow the plan of salvation that Nephi explained in 2 Nephi 31. He again summarizes them here: (1) Enter the narrow gate (have faith and repent and be baptized); (2) walk in the straight path that leads to eternal life (join the Church and follow its teachings as guided by the Holy Ghost); and, (3) endure to the end of their mortal probation (be faithful unto the end) (v. 9).

Nephi does not address the lost tribes whom he had previously said would receive the words of his seed (the Book of Mormon). He probably didn't because he knew or felt their receiving Nephi's record would not be until the millennial reign or just before (see 3 Nephi 21:23–26). The Lamanites, Gentiles, and at least many of the Jews would receive it before the millennium.

2 Nephi 33:10–12 • Believe in the Words of Christ

10 And now, my beloved brethren, and also Jew, and all ye ends of the earth, hearken unto these words and believe in Christ; and if ye believe not in these words believe in Christ. And if ye shall believe in Christ ye will believe in these words, for they are the words of Christ, and he hath given them unto me; and they teach all men that they should do good.

11 And if they are not the words of Christ, judge ye—for Christ will show unto you, with power and great glory, that they are his words, at the last day; and you and I shall stand face to face before his bar; and ye shall know that I have been commanded of him to write these things, notwithstanding my weakness.

> 12 And I pray the Father in the name of Christ that many of us,
> if not all, may be saved in his kingdom at that great and last day.

Again Nephi addresses the three groups of people and equates their believing in Christ and his words with doing good (v. 9). The two go hand in hand. Mormon makes a similar equation as he ends his record nearly a thousand years later.

> 9 For behold, this is written for the intent that ye may believe that;
> and if ye believe that ye will believe this also; and if ye believe this
> ye will know concerning your fathers, and also the marvelous works
> which were wrought by the power of God among them (Mormon 7:9).

If they believe in Christ they will believe in Nephi's (and his seed's) words. They must believe in Nephi's words because Christ is really their author (v. 10). That they are his words will be confirmed at the last day or the Second Coming, and when the words of Nephi will go to the lost tribes.

Once more Nephi exemplifies charity as he prays that many if not all will be saved in the kingdom of God.

2 Nephi 33:13–15 • The Judgment Bar of Christ

> 13 And now, my beloved brethren, all those who are of the house
> of Israel, and all ye ends of the earth, I speak unto you as the voice
> of one crying from the dust: Farewell until that great day shall come.
>
> 14 And you that will not partake of the goodness of God, and
> respect the words of the Jews, and also my words, and the words
> which shall proceed forth out of the mouth of the Lamb of God,
> behold, I bid you an everlasting farewell, for these words shall
> condemn you at the last day.
>
> 15 For what I seal on earth, shall be brought against you at the
> judgment bar; for thus hath the Lord commanded me, and I must obey.
> Amen.

Nephi again extends his final words to all the house of Israel and all the people of the earth; to every nation, kindred, tongue, and people who will eventually receive his record (see Rev. 14:6–7). He speaks as Isaiah prophesied, "as the voice of one crying from the dust," indirectly through his record, but bids them farewell until the judgment day (v. 13). To those who reject his words he bids an everlasting farewell for they will be condemned (v. 14). Nephi will be at the judgment bar and all will know that his words are true.[4] The words of the Book of Mormon will either save them or condemn them when they come to the judgment day.

13 Therefore, having so great witnesses, by them shall the world be judged, even as many as shall hereafter come to a knowledge of this work.

14 And those who receive it in faith, and work righteousness, shall receive a crown of eternal life;

15 But those who harden their hearts in unbelief, and reject it, it shall turn to their own condemnation— [D&C 20:13–15]

SACRED WRITING

Preaching which is Sacred:

2 Nephi 31–33	Nephi speaks (in writing) concerning the doctrine of Christ.

Doctrines Learned:

2 Nephi 31:3	God speaks unto man according to his language and understanding.
2 Nephi 31:5, 9	The Lamb of God was baptized to fulfill all righteousness (the plan of salvation).
2 Nephi 31:7	Baptism is a witness unto the Father that we will be obedient in keeping his commandments.
2 Nephi 31:8	The Holy Ghost descended upon Christ after his baptism in the form (sign) of a dove.

---

[4] Nephi is probably one of the four angels mentioned in D&C 77:8 interpreting Rev. 7:1 as a cross reference to Rev. 14:6–7 would illustrate. The other three would be Jacob, Mormon, and Moroni, the three principle engravers upon the plates from which the Book of Mormon was translated and which contains the everlasting gospel to go to every nation, kindred, tongue, and people.

The Doctrine of Christ—2 Nephi 31–33

Fallen Man	GATE Repentance and Baptism	Path to Eternal Life—Strait and Narrow	Scriptures	GATE Calling & Election Made Sure	Eternal Life
Light of Christ Judge Good & Evil (John 1:9 & Moroni 7:16) Giveth Light (2 Nephi 31:3) Christ baptized—take away the sins of the world 1. fulfill all righteousness 31:15, plan of salvation 2. witness to Father 31:7, keep His commandments 3. Holy Ghost descended dove 31:8, 12; Father gave the Holy Ghost 31:12 4. Example to man 31:9	1. Remission of sins—unholy 31:5 2. Covenant to keep commandments 31:10 3. Enter path to eternal life 31:9 4. Receive the Holy Ghost 31:12-13	**Holy Ghost—1st Comforter** 1. Baptism of fire and Holy Ghost 31:13, 17 2. Speak with tongues of angels 31:13, 17; Speak words of Christ 32:3; Carry it into hearts of men 33:1 3. Witness of the Father & Son 31:18 4. Show you all things to do 31:5	**Scriptures** 1. Feast on words of Christ. Tell you what to do 31:3; Brightness of Hope a. Ask=pray—spirit teaches 32:8–9; press forward—steadfastness in Christ b. Knock=live, love God and all men 31:20 2. Persuades men to do good 3. Persuades men to believe in Christ 4. Speaks harshly against sin, 33:10, challenge.		**Jesus Christ—2nd Comforter** 1. Endure to end 2. Personal Visit T. 150, Lehi; 2 Nephi 11:3, 33:6, 1:15 3. Revelation 13:5–6, more sure word of prophecy

Figure 10. The Doctrine of Christ

2 Nephi 31:12	Baptism is the prerequisite to receiving the Holy Ghost.
2 Nephi 31:13	The Baptism of fire enables a person to speak with the tongue of angels.
2 Nephi 31:14	To Christ after being baptized by fire and the Holy Ghost, it would be better if they had not known him.
2 Nephi 31:15–16	Those who endure to the end shall be saved.
2 Nephi 31:17–18	The gate by which one enters the path to eternal life is repentance and baptism by water.
2 Nephi 31:17	A remission of sins comes by baptism of fire and the Holy Ghost.
2 Nephi 31:20	After entering the path to eternal life, one must press forward with a steadfastness in Christ, having a perfect brightness of hope, a love of God and of all men, and endure to the end.
2 Nephi 31:21	There is no other way [baptism] or name [Christ] under heaven whereby man can be saved.
2 Nephi 31:21	The doctrine of Christ is the doctrine of the Father and of the Son and of the Holy Ghost which is one God.
2 Nephi 32:3, 5	The words of Christ tell you what to do and the Holy Ghost shows you what to do.
2 Nephi 32:8	The Spirit teaches us to pray; the devil teaches us not to pray.
2 Nephi 33:1	The Holy Ghost carries the message to the heart.

| 2 Nephi 33:5 | Anger against the Book of Mormon is because of the spirit of the devil. |
| 2 Nephi 33:6 | Nephi's calling and election is made sure. |

General Authority Quotations

Joseph Smith the Prophet • 2 Nephi 31:12

Circumcision is not baptism, neither was baptism instituted in the place of circumcision. . . .

You might as well baptize a bag of sand as a man, if not done in view of the remission of sins and getting of the Holy Ghost. Baptism by water is but half a baptism, and is good for nothing without the other half—that is, the baptism of the Holy Ghost.

The Savior says, "Except a man be born of water and of the Spirit, he cannot enter into the kingdom of God." [*TPJS*, 314]

Elder George Q. Cannon • 2 Nephi 31:12

Now can you conceive of a oneness more close, more complete than the oneness that exists between the Father and the Son? It is impossible for the human mind to get the faintest idea of any difference of opinion or expression or action between the Father and Son. We worship them as one God—not three Gods, not two Gods but as one God. The Father and the Son are the two personages of Deity, with the Holy Ghost as their ministering Spirit or agent. We worship them as one. We do not separate them in our thoughts and in our feelings. . . .

While they are two personages, they are but one—one in feeling, one in thought, one in mind, one in everything, in fact, in every direction in which their power is or can be exercised. And in all the records that have come down to us from the Son of God there is one thing that stands out clearly and prominently throughout all the teachings and acts of our Lord and Savior Jesus Christ and that is His entire devotion to the Father, His complete submission to the will of the Father and His oft-expressed desire to know and to do that will. It is wonderful the submission that the Savior manifested in his life, when we think of His great dignity and the position that He occupied. . . . [*Gospel Truth*, ed. Jerred L. Newquist (1974) 1:205]

President Joseph Fielding Smith • 2 Nephi 33:2

Now I am going to say something that maybe I could not prove, but I believe is true, that we have a great many members of this Church who have never reached a manifestation through the Holy Ghost. Why? Because they have not made their lives conform to the truth. And the Holy Ghost will not dwell in unclean tabernacles where perhaps the light of Christ remains. But the Holy Ghost will not dwell in unclean tabernacles or disobedient tabernacles. The Holy Ghost will not dwell with that person who is unwilling to obey and keep the commandments of God or who violates those commandments willfully. In such a soul the spirit of the Holy Ghost cannot enter.

That great gift comes to us only through humility and faith and obedience. Therefore, a great many members of the Church do not have that guidance. Then some cunning, crafty individual will come along teaching that which is not true, and without the guidance which is promised to us through our faithfulness, people are unable to discern and are led astray. It depends on our faithfulness and our obedience to the commandments of the Lord if we have the teachings, the enlightening instruction, that comes from the Holy Ghost.

When we are disobedient, when our minds are set upon the things of this world rather than on the things for the kingdom of God, we cannot have the manifestations of the Holy Ghost. Did you ever stop to think what a great privilege it is for us to have the companionship of one of the members of the Godhead? Have you thought of it that way? That is our privilege, if we keep the commandments the Lord has given us. [Address to BYU student body, Oct. 25, 1961, or *Church News*, Nov. 4, 1961, 14]

Elder Marion G. Romney • 2 Nephi 32:2–5

Now, it is very important, my brethren, that we each live so that we can have this spirit of the Lord. Its importance did not cease with the death of the Prophet Joseph Smith. In 1879 two years after the Prophet Brigham Young had died, President Wilford Woodruff was down in the mountains of Arizona traveling with Lot Smith. On one occasion, he had a vision or a dream in which he saw Brigham Young and Orson Hyde, and he asked Brigham Young if he would not come with him to Arizona and speak to the people. Brigham Young answered that he had done his talking in the flesh and that work was now left for Elder Woodruff and others to do. In his diary, President Woodruff quotes President Young as saying: "Tell the people to get the spirit of the Lord and keep it with them."

Brigham Young had a similar experience in his lifetime. In February, 1847, he had a dream in which the Prophet Joseph Smith appeared to him. It was a glorious dream. You will find it in the history of the Church written by Brother Cannon. Brigham Young expressed his sorrow that he was separated from the companionship of President Smith, the Prophet, and asked why he could not come with him. The Prophet told him he would have to wait awhile.

Then Brigham Young asked him if he had a message for them, and the Prophet stepped toward him, looking very earnestly, yet patiently, and said (I quote from the words of the Prophet in that dream of Brigham Young's):

"Tell the brethren to be humble and faithful and be sure to keep the Spirit of the Lord, that it will lead them aright. Be careful and not turn away the still, small voice; it will teach them what to do and where to go; it will yield the fruits of the kingdom. Tell the brethren to keep their hearts open to the conviction, so that when the Holy Ghost comes to them, their hearts will be ready to receive it."

That is one way, brethren, to get the spirit of the Lord, and it is one absolute requirement to keep our hearts open to conviction, so that we can hear the word of God and receive the Holy Ghost's promptings when they come. It is a terrible calamity for men or nations to become laws unto themselves. You know, the Lord said: "That which seeketh to become a law unto itself . . . cannot be sanctified by law, neither by mercy, justice, nor judgment, therefore they must remain filthy still."

The Prophet in this statement to Brigham Young continues:

"They can tell the Spirit of the Lord from all other spirits—it will whisper peace and joy to their souls; it will take malice, hatred, strife and all evil from their hearts, and their whole desire will be to do good, bring forth righteousness, and build up the kingdom of God."

The Prophet Joseph continued:

"Tell the brethren if they will follow the Spirit of the Lord, they will go right. Be sure to tell the brethren to keep the Spirit of the Lord; and if they will, they will find themselves just as they were organized by our Father in Heaven before they came into the world. Our Father in Heaven organized the human family, but they are all disorganized and in great confusion."

Joseph again said to him, "Tell the people to be sure to keep the Spirit of the Lord and follow it and it will lead them just right." [CR, April 1944, 140–41]

Elder Marion G. Romney • 2 Nephi 33:1

I urge you to get acquainted with this great book. Read it to your children: they are not too young to understand it. I remember reading it with one of my lads when he was very young. On one occasion I lay in the lower bunk and he in the upper bunk. We were each reading aloud alternate paragraphs of those last three marvelous chapters of Second Nephi. I heard his voice breaking as though he had a cold, but we went on to the end of the three chapters. As we finished he said to me, "Daddy, do you ever cry when you read the Book of Mormon?"

"Yes, son," I answered, "sometimes the Spirit of the Lord so witnesses to my soul that the Book of Mormon is true that I do cry."

"Well," he said, "that is what happened to me tonight."

I know not all of them will respond like that, but I know that some of them will, and I tell you this book was given to us of God to read and to live by, and it will hold us as close to the Spirit of the Lord as anything I know. Won't you please read it? [CR, April 1949, 49]

Elder Boyd K. Packer • 2 Nephi 33:1, 6

I said there was a question that could not be taken lightly nor answered at all without the prompting of the Spirit ("Have you seen him?"). I have not asked that question of others, but I have heard them answer it—but not when they were asked. They have answered it under the promptings of the Spirit, on sacred occasions, when the "Spirit beareth record" (D&C 1:39).

I have heard one of my brethren declare: "I know from experiences, too sacred to relate, that Jesus is the Christ."

I have heard another testify: "I know that God lives; I know that the Lord lives. And more than that, I know the Lord."

It was not their words that held the meaning or the power. It was the Spirit

"... for when a man speaketh by the power of the Holy Ghost the power of the Holy Ghost carrieth it into the hearts of the children of men" (2 Nephi 33:1).

I speak upon this subject in humility, with the constant feeling that I am the least in every way of those who are called to this holy office. [CR, April, 1971, 124]

President J. Reuben Clark • 2 Nephi 33:1–2

The very words of the revelation (D&C 63:4) recognize that the Brethren may speak when they are **not** "moved upon by the Holy Ghost," yet only when they do so speak, as so "moved upon" is what they say Scripture. No exceptions are given to this rule or principle. It is universal in its application.

The question is, how shall we know when the things they have spoken were said as they were "moved upon by the Holy Ghost?"

I have given some thought to this question, and the answer thereto so far as I can determine is: We can tell when the speakers are "moved upon by the Holy Ghost" only when we, ourselves, are "moved upon by the Holy Ghost."

In a way, this completely shifts the responsibility from them to us to determine when they so speak.

We might here profitably repeat what Brother Brigham preached:

"I am more afraid that this people have so much confidence in their leaders that they will not inquire for themselves whether they are led by Him. I am fearful they settle down in a state of blind self-security, trusting their eternal destiny in the hands of their leaders with a reckless confidence that in itself would thwart the purposes of God in their salvation." [J. Reuben Clark, Selected Papers, ed. David H. Yarn Jr., Brigham Young University Press, Provo, Utah 1984, 95–96]

Elder Marion G. Romney • 2 Nephi 33:5, 10

It is about the Book of Mormon I want to talk today. I do so with just one objective in mind: to get you to read it.

I have read it a little, I believe in it, and I love it. I recommend that every person within the sound of my voice read the Book of Mormon. I can testify, as did Nephi, that the things written therein persuadeth all men to do good.

It will enrich the life of every person who will read it, unless he is in rebellion against the truth; and in that event it will advise him of his awful fate unless he changes his ways. [CR, April 1949, 36]

President Joseph Fielding Smith • 2 Nephi 30:4, 33:8

The Nephites were of the Jews, not so much by descent as by citizenship, although in the long descent from Jacob, it could be possible of some mixing of the tribes by intermarriage . . .

Not only in the Book of Mormon are the descendants of Lehi called Jews, but also in the Doctrine and Covenants. In Section 19, verse 27, this is found: "Which is my word to the Gentile, that soon it may go to the Jew, of whom the Lamanites are a remnant, that they may believe the gospel, and look for a Messiah to come who has already come." . . . gave instruction for the purchase of land "lying westward, even unto the line running directly between Jew and Gentile." This line westward was the dividing line between the whites and Indians. [*Answers to Gospel Questions* (1957), 1:142–43]

Challenges to Eternal Life:

1. Do you think you will ever see Nephi (2 Nephi 33:11)? Would you like to? Would you like to remain in the presence of Jesus with Nephi having eternal life? *A formula is presented—start today!*

   a. Study: Don't just read; search for ways to improve, to understand great knowledge (2 Nephi 32:7).

   b. Pray: Ask for understanding, for guidance in your prayers, and strength to carry out the answers received (2 Nephi 32:9).

   c. Live: Do the things the Spirit directs you to follow after (2 Nephi 32:9).

2. As you partake of the sacrament this week consider the significance of baptism as Nephi has written (2 Nephi 31). Rededicate you life to take upon you the name of Christ.

3. As you read the Book of Mormon, note the number of times it persuades you to be good. Follow those persuasions as you associate with your family and friends (2 Nephi 33:4).

4. Choose a challenge or a modern-day message from the reading and incorporate it into your life.

Scripture Index

OLD TESTAMENT

New Testament

JOSEPH SMITH TRANSLATION

Genesis	PAGE
17:11	500
50	408, 413, 416, 426
50:24–26	407, 408
50:25	408
50:29	413
50:27–28	408, 409
50:30–31	415, 416
50:32–33	417, 418
50:34–35	422

Isaiah	
11	657
29:11–19	644, 657
29:20	423
42:19–20	326
49:25	343

Matthew	PAGE
3:12, 19	97
3:13, 19	47
13:29	698
19:13	500
24	179

John	
1:19	748

Hebrews	
9:10	623

Revelation	
2:26–27	723
12:5	723
19:15	723

BOOK OF MORMON

1 Nephi	PAGE
1	9, 10, 22
1:1	30, 32, 34, 51
1:1–7:22	9
1:1–3	11, 18
1:4	30, 94, 127, 206, 261, 597
1:4–6	20
1:4–15	11

1 Nephi (cont.)	PAGE
1:4–20	20
1:5	393
1:6	30, 393
1:6–8	368, 369
1:6–14	30
1:7	30
1:7–8	97
1:7–11	23

DOCTRINE AND COVENANTS

PEARL OF GREAT PRICE

Topical Index

—S—